- **Improved Windows NT Diagnostics Tool.** Windows NT Server 4 includes an improved Windows NT diagnostics program for examining the system.
- **DCOM (Distributed Component Object Model).** The Component Object Model (COM) allows software developers to create component applications. Windows NT Server and Windows NT Workstation 4 include Distributed COM (DCOM), which extends COM to allow components to communicate across networks.
- **DNS Server.** Windows NT 4 has a completely new version of the DNS (domain naming system) service. Features include a graphical administration utility and integration with WINS services for dynamic updates of host names and addresses.

The Professional Reference Section

Besides updates to the newest version of Windows NT, *Robert Cowart's Windows NT 4 Unleashed, Professional Reference Edition,* has also added a robust reference section. When you need information about the Registry, boot process, NT applications, or differences between NT Server, NT Workstation, and Windows 95, you'll find this new section (located at the back of the book) invaluable. The following is a list of appendixes included in the Reference Section:

A	New Features in Windows NT Server 4
B	Windows NT Workstation 4 Versus Windows NT Server 4
C	New Features in NT Workstation 4
D	An NT Command-Prompt Reference
E	What's on the CD-ROM?
F	The Windows NT Boot Process
G	Mouseless Survival Guide: Keyboard Commands
H	Keyboard Shortcuts
I	The Windows NT Registry
J	Windows NT Technical Information Sources
K	Glossary

Robert Cowart's Windows NT 4™

Professional Reference Edition

Robert Cowart

SAMS
PUBLISHING

201 West 103rd Street
Indianapolis, IN 46290

UNLEASHED

—To Kathy, for her ever-inventive support.

Copyright ©1997 by Sams Publishing

PROFESSIONAL REFERENCE EDITION

International Standard Book Number: 0-672-31001-5

Library of Congress Catalog Card Number: 96-70402

2000   99   98   97   4   3   2   1

Interpretation of the printing code: the rightmost double-digit number is the year of the book's printing; the rightmost single-digit, the number of the book's printing. For example, a printing code of 97-1 shows that the first printing of the book occurred in 1997.

Composed in AGaramond and MCPdigital by Macmillan Computer Publishing

Printed in the United States of America

Trademarks

Publisher and President	*Richard K. Swadley*
Acquisitions Manager	*Greg Wiegand*
Development Manager	*Dean Miller*
Managing Editor	*Cindy Morrow*
Marketing Manager	*Gregg Bushyeager*
Assistant Marketing Manager	*Michele Milner*

Acquisitions Editor
Kim Spilker

Development Editor
Dean Miller

Software Development Specialist
Patty Brooks

Production Editor
Lisa M. Lord

Copy Editors
Fran Blauw
Chuck Hutchinson
Heather Stith

Technical Reviewer
Jeff Perkins

Resource Manager
Deborah Frisby

Indexer
Christine Nelsen

Editorial Coordinator
Bill Whitmer

Technical Edit Coordinator
Lynette Quinn

Formatter
Frank Sinclair

Editorial Assistant
Sharon Cox

Cover Designer
Tim Amrhein

Book Designer
Gary Adair

Production Team Supervisors
Brad Chinn
Charlotte Clapp

Production
Jenaffer Brandt
Mona Brown
Cynthia Davis
Ayanna Lacey

Contents

Part III Networking Windows NT

12 An Overview of Windows NT Networking 375

13 Designing and Installing Your Windows NT Network 391

Acknowledgments

A book of this size and technical substance takes considerable effort. A number of people have helped over the almost nine months involved in completing this Herculean task. Developing a book that isn't just another user's guide took a great deal of thought and interaction among people scattered across the country. In the first edition, I thought a book on NT could be pretty much a simple adaptation of my existing books on Windows 3.*x* and Windows 95. As talks progressed, it seemed that this approach would be less and less the case. NT was an entirely new animal that required special treatment, with an emphasis on network administration, installation, maintenance, and troubleshooting. More people were brought to the table, and, thanks to CompuServe and the Internet, the physical proximity of the writers wasn't an issue. Daily e-mail and file transmission over the wires sufficed. Perhaps one day the writers and editors will meet in real, not virtual, space.

I would like to thank the powers-that-be at Sams Publishing for offering the opportunity to work on such a timely project as this. I believe NT to be a pivotal product in a field that has captured my attention and been the focus of my professional activity for more than a decade. I'm pleased to have been given the chance to head up the project. Thanks certainly go to my agent, Bill Gladstone, for putting me in touch with Sams. Thanks to Gregg Bushyeager for initially refining this book's proposed contents. To Mark Taber, who originally developed this book, great thanks on several counts, not the least of which is patience. Several glitches along the way were unnerving to us all, and Mark held steady in the storm, keeping me on track and applying just the right amount and right kind of pressure—the kind but firm whip-cracking that every writer knows he or she needs! For this fourth edition, thanks to Kim Spilker for her patience, and for her help in locating a writer knowledgeable in Internet Web setups using NT. And last, but not least, thanks to my friends and family who regularly have to put up with my seemingly eternal disappearance.

And, of course, considerable thanks goes to the entire Sams team, including Dean Miller, Lisa Lord, and all others from editorial and production to sales and marketing—the often invisible and underappreciated people who make the book business happen.

Thanks to Eric Braun for all his help on the reference section.

About the Authors

Robert Cowart is a best-selling author on the subject of Windows NT and Windows 95. He has worked in the computer industry for more than 16 years as an engineer, technical support specialist, writer, and teacher. He has written for *PC Week*, *PC Technical Journal*, *Microsoft Systems Journal*, *PC World*, and *PC Magazine*. He has written 18 books, 11 of them about Windows.

Tim Parker is a consultant and technical writer based in Ottawa, Canada. He is a technical editor for *SCO World Magazine* and a contributing editor for *UNIX Review*, *Advanced Systems Magazine*, and *Canadian Computer Reseller*. He has written more than 800 feature articles and two dozen books. When not writing, Tim is a private pilot, scuba diver, white-water kayaker, and general adrenaline junkie.

Tell Us What You Think!

As a reader, you are the most important critic and commentator of our books. We value your opinion and want to know what we're doing right, what we could do better, what areas you'd like to see us publish in, and any other words of wisdom you're willing to pass our way. You can help us make strong books that meet your needs and give you the computer guidance you require.

Do you have access to CompuServe or the World Wide Web? Check out our CompuServe forum by typing GO SAMS at any prompt. If you prefer the World Wide Web, check out our site at http://www.mcp.com.

> **NOTE**
>
> If you have a technical question about this book, call the technical support line at 317-581-3833.

As the publishing manager of the group that created this book, I welcome your comments. You can fax, e-mail, or write me directly to let me know what you did or didn't like about this book—as well as what we can do to make our books stronger. Here's the information:

FAX: 317-581-4669

E-mail: opsys_mgr@sams.samspublishing.com

Mail: Dean Miller
         Sams Publishing
         201 W. 103rd Street
         Indianapolis, IN 46290

Introduction

Windows NT is a pivotal software product. In an industry where few can even be sure what type of computer they'll be using tomorrow, much less what software will be running on it, Windows NT (which stands for *New Technology*) brings to the table a whole new set of questions—and capabilities.

The first real "industrial strength" operating system intended for the enormous installed base of IBM-compatible computers, Windows NT offers what PC tinkerers of a decade ago could only have classified as a mainframe operating system. Not merely an upgrade of Windows 3.*x* (although it looks much like it), NT is a serious operating system intended to meet the computing needs of power users, government agencies, and large industry. And rather than being a bandage approach to meeting a need, Windows NT was ported "down" to PCs from its mainframe UNIX predecessors, rather than ported "up" from a single-user system, with some spit and bailing wire to hold it together.

Fearing NT's strengths, computer monoliths such as IBM, Sun, and Novell have mounted major marketing campaigns and product development efforts to derail a potential industry-wide shift to the Microsoft NT camp. After all, these competitors (most notably Novell) have for years enjoyed the lion's share of success in PC-based local networking. NT disinformation—or at least obfuscation—abounds, especially in the press, which is constantly at odds with itself over NT's rewards versus its shortcomings.

Debates about hefty hardware requirements, questionable DOS and Windows 3.*x* performance, and where Windows 95 fits into the 32-bit landscape keep us all entertained. But make no mistake about it—the chemistry is very, very good. A 32-bit multitasking, multithreading, fault-tolerant, networkable, and highly secure operating system, combined with the many thousands of Windows applications available today, along with the visionary software company Microsoft, makes Windows NT the hands-down winner in the battle for a mission-critical operating system in the corporate enterprise setting.

Although these paragraphs might have the ring of press hype, this wasn't necessarily the attitude of this book's authors before their year of experimentation with NT while researching and writing the first edition of *Windows NT Unleashed*. Based solely on our collective experience with computer operating systems, with corporate clients dependent on real-world applications and networking, and with market trend analysis, we forged our opinions.

This book tries to explain what makes NT such a strong product, why the industry is leaning in its direction, and how to get the most out of it.

What You Should Know Before Reading This Book

Windows NT 4 Unleashed explains both basic and advanced material on the topic of Windows NT. It doesn't assume you know anything about Windows NT. However, it does assume you have knowledge about Microsoft Windows 3.*x* and possibly about Windows 95, and that you're fairly familiar with their use. This book also assumes you have been around IBM PCs and are familiar with their operation, such as how MS-DOS works, how printers and modems work, and to some degree how local area networks (LANs) operate. Furthermore, this book assumes you're probably using NT because you're either in a work environment where Windows NT is running on your workstation or that you're managing such a network or workgroup in one way or another. Beyond that, this book doesn't make assumptions. Technobabble computer terms often are explained the first time they appear. Complex concepts also are explained when they first appear. In addition, a glossary is included. So, whether you're an NT novice or a hard-core computer junkie, you're likely to learn quite a bit. You're neither "snowed" by geek-speak nor condescended to.

Audience

Writing a book about a software product as ambitious as Windows NT hasn't been easy. Finding writers who know enough about such a new and feature-rich product was difficult enough, but figuring out just who will be using NT and what they will want to know posed another serious challenge.

Clearly, just doing a port of an existing Windows 3.*x* book wasn't enough. Windows NT is a much richer product aimed at a more sophisticated audience with different needs. In developing a strategy for determining this book's coverage, we had to carefully consider just who will be using NT and to what ends. "Will single users really want it?" "What about developers?" "Will it be installed primarily in corporate settings?" "Will NT servers be used primarily for application servers, or as workstations?" "How much coverage of NT Advanced Server should we include?" "Should integration of existing systems, such as LAN Manager and Novell, with Windows NT be a key topic?" "Should we discuss NT multimedia, software development on the NT platform, Remote Access Services?" You get the idea. The strategy time and again came down to including as much as possible for all users.

Standalone NT Workstation Users

There are times when a person might want to use Windows NT on a single, non-networked workstation. Typically, this would be in instances where system stability, the ability to have separate user accounts on a single workstation, multioperating system capability, or development of NT applications would be high-priority needs.

If you're such a user, *Robert Cowart's Windows NT 4 Unleashed* gives you all you need to know about installing NT, upgrading from Windows 3.x or Windows NT Workstation 3.51, partitioning your hard disk, booting alternative operating systems such as DOS and OS/2, and even running with hard disks formatted with other file systems, such as FAT and HPFS.

Of course, all the basics of NT are covered, and they apply to single users, too: giving up the Program Manager and File Manager in favor of the new Windows 95–like Desktop and GUI, all the Control Panel applets (which are extensive in NT), Disk Administrator, and User Manager. You'll also find more-than-ample coverage of multimedia hardware and driver installation, installing on RISC machines, such as the DEC Alpha and MIPS 4000, and system maintenance guidelines for topics like adding and removing hard drives, upgrading your hardware (memory, video, processor), running automated backups, recovering lost data from stripe sets, and so forth.

NOTE

In the previous edition, we included coverage of Schedule+ (for organizing your daily appointments and arranging group scheduling), but it's been dropped from the NT 4.0 package. However, it's included in Windows for Workgroups and Windows NT 3.x. It's also available separately for Windows NT, either alone or bundled with Microsoft Office and Exchange Server.

NT Users on a Network

Should you already be on, or if you upgrade to, a networking installation of Windows NT, you're in for a treat. All the basics are covered here—and in English. Networking is a complex world in and of itself. Hundreds of buzzwords, not to mention many types of network cards, cabling, interrupt settings, topologies, and protocols, make networking one of computing's black arts. The author of Part III, "Networking Windows NT," has (figuratively speaking) a black belt in networking with Windows, Novell, and UNIX. Both WAN and LAN operations are covered, as is remote access into NT systems by modem. If you haven't yet installed the physical network, this book offers ample help in the decision-making process. Text and illustrations explain clearly issues on networking theory, topologies, cabling types, optimum workstation organization, NT's "domain-based" architecture, and many other advanced topics. The chapters were written by people who design, install, maintain, teach, and write about PC-based networks.

Systems Administrators

If you're a systems administrator or an MIS professional, managing PCs can be a nightmare. Windows NT can make your job much easier if you know what you're doing. *Robert Cowart's Windows NT 4 Unleashed, Professional Reference Edition*, takes the attitude that most readers will be administrators—either of their own system or of an extended network of NT or non-NT workstations. This book emphasizes not just what a particular command or utility does to the NT system, Registry, network, or domain, but when and why an administrator would want to use it.

Under one cover are not only all the basic instructions for running NT's supplied systems-administrator applications—User Manager, Disk Administrator, Event Viewer, and Performance Monitor—but also detailed instructions on topics such as the following:

- Installing NT to new workstations over the network
- Maintaining security and passwords for users and workstations you supervise
- Running network OLE so that your users can share their ClipBook data
- Setting up, using, and managing printer servers
- Preparing for power outages by using NT's UPS service
- Maximizing mass storage and guarding against data loss by using volume sets, stripe sets, and stripe sets with parity
- Managing and automating local and remote tape backups
- Remote systems administration
- Setting up the Replicator service to synchronize directories across the network
- Understanding and using trusted domains
- Optimizing the NT system, with coverage ranging from the Control Panel to CONFIG.NT and AUTOEXEC.NT, SCSI drives, CD-ROMs, RAM upgrade tips, and NT Setup migration of Windows 3.*x* .INI settings
- Using and optimizing alternative operating environments—DOS, Windows 3.*x*, POSIX, and OS/2
- A wide variety of troubleshooting tips and tricks

Web Developers

Because NT is well on its way to becoming the most popular PC-based operating system for Internet Web servers, budding Webmasters will benefit from reading this book. Part IV of the book, "Setting Up a World Wide Web Site Using NT Workstation," covers all the ins and outs of piecing together a complete NT-based Web server. Sanjaya Hettihewa, well-established as a Web expert, covers such topics as copyright legalities, secure transactions on the Web, and how to design your own Web pages.

This Book's Conventions

In this book, the term *NT* often replaces the term *Windows NT*. Likewise, *DOS* is often used interchangeably with *MS-DOS*.

Windows commands are often double-barreled because you must open a menu and then choose a command. In this book, such an action is written with the menu name and command name separated by a vertical bar. For example, the command "Choose File|Save" means "Open the File menu and choose Save."

Code lines, error messages, and other terms appear in `monospace`. Placeholders appear in *`italic monospace`*, and material you actually type is shown in **`bold monospace`**.

Problem avoidance is 90 percent of success in network and systems management, so helpful notes, tips, cautions, and warnings are presented along the way in hopes of avoiding calamity. Dialog-box options are often included in a table, with discussions and notes about complex choices. In addition, many numbered lists are included that guide you through a process step by step.

IN THIS PART

An Introduction to Windows NT

I

PART

What Is Windows NT?

CHAPTER 1

IN THIS CHAPTER

Windows NT is Microsoft's top-of-the-line, corporate-oriented operating system. Targeting the needs and demands of corporate MIS departments and hoping to woo corporate buyers sniffing out OS/2 or UNIX alternatives to DOS, Windows 3.*x*, and Windows 95, Microsoft spent at least four years developing a robust and feature-rich operating system intended to meet the rigorous demands of enterprise-wide corporate settings. Windows NT has now been through several versions, growing more powerful and useful for both servers and workstations as the software has matured and CPUs have become more powerful. With Windows NT 4, Microsoft offers an operating system that outclasses any other desktop operating system (including the Windows family and OS/2) and rivals UNIX workstation power in many cases.

If you've kept up with press reviews and articles about Windows NT, you might already know a bit, if not a lot, about NT.

> **NOTE**
>
> Most NT users (or those considering a switch to NT) are highly computer-literate, so I will dispense with detailed explanations of fundamental computer terminology. Appendix K, "Glossary," has definitions of some of those terms.

Windows NT is a multithreaded, preemptive multitasking operating system with full 32-bit memory addressing. It supports DOS, Windows, Win32 GUI and character-based applications, POSIX-compliant and character-based OS/2 1.*x* applications, and it includes integrated networking, security, and administration tools. It can run on single or multiple CPUs without modification, and it supports Intel processors as well as DEC Alpha, MIPS, and Power PC chips.

A key feature of Windows NT is that it was designed as *the* future operating system from Microsoft. Windows 95 is a short-term bridge to the more reliable and robust NT platform. Two other important features are NT's internal *client/server* model, in which the internals of the operating system are divided into these two categories (client and server), and dynamic disk-caching, which uses disk space across multiple drives as available, noticeably enhancing performance.

Preemptive Multitasking

In systems that can run multiple programs at once (not just switchers like Software Carousel, which suspends one application while resuming another), some means of keeping all the tasks running is needed—much as a traffic cop, standing in the middle of a major intersection and blowing a whistle, conducts traffic.

Suppose you have a spreadsheet recalculation going, a COM port is receiving a fax, and you're typing a letter at the keyboard. As you know, all these activities can occur simultaneously in a typical Windows 3.1 or a Windows 95 session (although not always smoothly).

> **NOTE**
>
> When I use the term *Windows 3.1*, it also includes Windows 3.11 and Windows for Workgroups 3.11.

In Windows 3.1, simultaneous application execution might not behave as you'd expect because of the way Windows 3.1's "traffic cop" works. Windows 3.*x* doesn't really have an intelligent scheduler. Applications are supposed to be written so that they relinquish CPU time at regular (very short) intervals, allowing other tasks to be performed. Not all applications do this religiously, however, and Windows itself can't enforce adherence to the standard. A poorly written Windows 3.1 application can actually hog the CPU for enough time to effectively kill some time-dependent applications, such as data-acquisition programs. Try formatting a disk with File Manager (not in a DOS window) while trying to run a communications session (or anything else), and you'll see what I mean.

Windows 3.1's method of multitasking was called *cooperative multitasking*. By contrast, Windows NT's preemptive multitasking scheduler actually helps the traffic cop direct traffic as it sees fit. That is, NT can preempt one program in favor of another, democratically allotting CPU cycles or even stealing them when necessary.

Windows 95 gives you a bit of each of these worlds. Under Windows 95, 16-bit applications don't and can't run any "smarter" than they did under Windows 3.1—they can still tie up the operating system. Even 32-bit programs must wait for 16-bit applications to yield before they can continue. On the other hand, if you're running 32-bit applications under Windows 95, you can expect smoother performance because preemptive multitasking is in effect. By contrast, NT runs 16-bit applications in a separate "virtual machine" that's treated as a separate 32-bit program and smoothly multitasked. The result is that 16-bit applications can't tie up an NT system.

One result of preemptive multitasking is that the user no longer needs to consider the resources a certain task will consume, nor does he have to allow one task to finish processing before starting another. Process mixes that previously might have caused problems in Windows 3.1 shouldn't cause even a hiccup in NT. Background communications sessions, for example, shouldn't drop data while other CPU-intensive tasks are running.

> **NOTE**
>
> The number of programs that can load and execute in an NT system is limited by the amount of virtual memory available, as set by the paging file size. When this amount is exceeded, NT will lag.

In NT, a single task is much less likely to hold up the system for longer than a blink of an eye. What's more, pressing tasks can be given a higher priority than others. For example, keyboard input, mouse movement, or data coming in through a port could be given special attention by NT's scheduler.

Multithreading

There has been enough talk about NT's (and Windows 95's) ability to run *threads* and about its *multithreading* capabilities to make you wonder whether you're in a sewing class. Before I continue, here's a quick rundown of the significance of threading, in case you don't know. (I cover this topic more in Chapter 2, "The Architectural and Operational Design of Windows NT.")

All tasks performed by NT can be classified as *processes*. During any given period, NT is executing a wide variety of processes. These might include checking a user's password, keeping track of the system's clock, accessing data from a disk, doing a memory fetch from RAM, or doing a mathematical calculation.

In NT, processes can be broken down even further into *threads*. In fact, scheduling events in NT is actually based on the thread unit, not the process. Most processes contain only a single thread, but they can consist of multiple threads if the programmer chooses.

The important point is that programs devised to take advantage of NT's ability to service threads can be run very smoothly—more smoothly than under Windows 3.1. For example, one complaint about multimedia programs in Windows 3.1 is that live video sometimes doesn't execute smoothly if a sound file is being played simultaneously. Although this problem can be due to a slow processor, it probably happens because the CPU's cycles aren't being evenly distributed between processes, even with a lightning-fast CPU. Under NT, this is much less likely to happen. In addition, as explained later in this chapter and in Chapter 2, NT's architecture allows threads in a single application (as well as in separate applications or NT services) to be offloaded to secondary CPUs in multiprocessor systems, further smoothing thread execution.

Is NT Really New Technology?

Although NT stands for *new technology,* what it offers the user isn't really all that new. Most of NT's features existed before its release and were available in other forms. NT 4 looks and behaves much like Windows 95, it has networking not unlike the best Novell has to offer, and internally it's much like UNIX.

Windows NT and the Windows family of operating systems provide a common interface—encapsulating many common tasks into one package. The days of the cryptic character-based operating systems are slowly dying. Further, Windows NT is cheaper at $389 (for the Workstation version) than many competitors. NT lets you leave the arenas of expensive proprietary operating systems and equipment such as the WANG, with the freedom of greater connectivity.

NT wraps it all up nicely and neatly in one package—a package that works right out of the box. With just a little work, you can have NT up and running on a single station or on hundreds of machines. Installation from a CD-ROM is almost automatic, and installation across a network is even easier.

Your networked mix can incorporate any collection of DOS, Windows, Windows for Workgroups, Windows 95, OS/2, UNIX, Novell NetWare, and NT machines. Support for IPX/SPX, TCP/IP, and remote access services by modem also extend NT's interoperability outside the normal PC domain into the mainframe and WAN territories.

OS Features Aren't Everything

If the demand was only for a serious operating system with most or even all of these features, NT might not have been worth waiting for. Corporations heavily invested in PC-based information systems could have adopted UNIX or OS/2 en masse by now. Both of these systems offer much of what NT has, but the success of an operating system, particularly in business settings, has more to do with application availability than with any other variable.

Apple was aware of this basic OS truth when it dispersed its Apple evangelists to entice application developers into writing programs for their new brainchild, the Macintosh. Without application availability, the Mac would never have taken off. Its predecessor, the Lisa, went over like a lead balloon for just that reason. The demise of the NeXT "cube" is another good case in point. It was a terrific machine, but due to a scarcity of applications, loyal users of PCs and Macs just couldn't be wooed away. (Of course, its high price didn't help any, either.)

The operating system market isn't only application-driven, however. It's also driven by cost practicalities. As the PC market has matured, users have become less prone to overnight conversions from one type of machine—or even application—to another. The learning curve and data commitments involved in today's systems and applications are much greater than they were back in the days of the Apple II or the CP/M. It behooves MIS professionals to seriously consider the long-term investment cost of conversions to new applications, hardware, and training when they're shopping for operating systems. Over the past 10 years, compatibility and interoperability have become more of an issue when people are making critical hardware and software choices.

Perspective

As of this writing, the personal computer world can be divided into three primary operating system camps: Mac, DOS, and Windows. A fourth, UNIX, is also showing up in greater numbers and various forms on the desktop. The interoperability of PCs has become an issue only since MIS departments and corporations in general have finally come to terms with the irrefutable fact that PCs are here to stay, and that the bulk of applications these days—even games—are being designed for the Windows environment. This happened in the late 1980s after a significant installed base of IBM PCs came into existence, many of them networked.

Since the advent of the Apple II and VisiCalc, MIS directors have slowly lost a desperate battle to hold onto and wield absolute control over corporate data processing through their mainframes. Independent single users in the corporate setting experienced a new freedom over their computing chores as soon as they learned to perform many simple tasks by themselves, such as running a spreadsheet for data analysis. Suddenly, the days of waiting for a batch job to be done or a letter to be typed became a thing of the past.

Aside from interdepartmental power struggles that resulted from this democratization of CPU time in the workplace, some very real issues concerning data integrity were born. In a sense, personal computing was great, because it took a portion of the workload away from the MIS departments. However, concerns over data validity and security—problems that MIS people thought had been addressed by their software years ago—now lurked around the corner again. In so-called *mission-critical* or *line-of-business* applications, large and often valuable corporate databases can't realistically be put in the hands of everyday users without jeopardizing the health of a company's data-processing backbone.

Many advances over the past 10 years have tried to address this problem and serve the needs of MIS professionals, power users, and others with high-end computing requirements. Novell (among others) has made great strides in providing networking extensions to MS-DOS. With products such as Novell's "fault-tolerant" system, DOS has become a fairly reliable networking platform, offering at least a fair amount of security for sensitive, valuable data. Likewise, the downward price spiral of minicomputer workstations running UNIX or UNIX-like operating systems has brought multitasking, mainframe-like power to many smaller corporations.

Where Do NT Workstation and NT Server Fit In?

Windows NT addresses many of these issues, and then some. Becuase of the impact NT will have on the huge installed base of Windows users, it's likely to usher in a new era of high-end computing on the desktop for the following reasons:

- It runs on 486 and higher PCs (with some probable hardware upgrades), although a Pentium is recommended.

- It runs most well-behaved DOS and Windows applications that don't try to access the machine's hardware directly. Therefore, programs were instantly available for NT the moment it was released. This is a central NT feature.

- It offers security and robust kernel solidity—features that many corporations and government institutions require for their mission-critical applications.

These additional key features make Windows NT an attractive operating system for the power user or corporate computing MIS professional:

- NT is written from the ground up as an operating system; it's not just a GUI laid on top of DOS.

■ NT has the look and behavior of Windows 95, so Windows 95 users don't have to be retrained to use NT.

■ Scalable architecture means that NT can run on different types of computers—from single CPUs (both Intel x86 and RISC chips) to multiple processor-based systems (sometimes called *symmetric* multiprocessor systems).

■ NT offers high reliability. Unlike DOS and DOS/Windows, NT incorporates a robust *microkernel* design that prevents a single misbehaving application from pulling down the whole system. The microkernel is based on both the well-accepted and time-tested UNIX derivative called the *Mach microkernel* and the VMS operating system.

NOTE

Dave Cutler, the designer of the VMS operating system, was hired by Microsoft to create Windows NT. He and his team combined aspects of the Mach microkernel design and VMS to produce a composite design that led to the final Windows NT.

■ Application compatibility means that NT can run a mix of any of these classes of applications: DOS, Windows 3.*x*, POSIX-compliant, MS OS/2 1.*x* character-based programs, and new 32-bit NT applications. A command prompt similar to the DOS prompt in Windows 3.1 supports execution of DOS, 16-bit Windows, POSIX, OS/2, or 32-bit NT applications from the command line. (POSIX is a UNIX implementation that ensures source-code compatibility of UNIX applications that comply with the standard. NT complies with character-based POSIX application requirements.)

■ Complete support for Windows Object Linking and Embedding (OLE) is supported for data sharing between applications—even over the network.

■ Because of file system compatibility, Windows NT can work with four types of file systems: FAT, HPFS, NTFS, and Windows 95's VFAT. FAT (DOS's file scheme) is widely used, HPFS is used by OS/2, and NTFS is the proprietary Windows NT file system. Because NT supports an installable file system, future file systems are easy to add and support. Because one of the key selling features of Windows 95 is support for long filenames through its VFAT system, NT's compatibility with it is key. You can actually dual-boot a single system in either NT or Windows 95 and have access to VFAT drives complete with long filenames.

■ NT also gives you file system enhancements. Aside from being able to convert FAT and HPFS partitions to NTFS, NT's file system offers advanced security features, supports long filenames (up to 256 characters), and provides automatic error correction if a bad sector is detected. Advanced features allow creation of *stripe sets*, in which multiple disks are used simultaneously to speed disk I/O, and *mirrored disks*, which are used to increase data safety through storage redundancy.

> **NOTE**
>
> Although Windows NT supports long filenames on FAT and FAT-32 partitions, only NTFS partitions support the advanced security features.

- NT has a built-in networking solution. The basics of LAN Manager and Windows for Workgroups are built into NT for simple peer-to-peer or client/server networking, with no need for add-on software modules. NT supports industry-standard network protocols, with built-in drivers for NetBEUI, IPX/SPX, TCP/IP, and other transports. NT is compatible with popular existing networks, such as Novell NetWare, Banyan VINES, and Microsoft LAN Manager. For larger networks and remote access capabilities, the NT Server product (available at an extra cost) supplies additional features, such as Macintosh and mainframe connectivity.

- As for security, NT provides U.S. government C2-level security features. For most purposes, NT has essentially bulletproof security that can prevent an unauthorized user from entering the system or otherwise gaining access to files on the hard disk. NTFS partitions can't be reached without a proper password, so files are protected. Tools for assigning permission levels for different tasks are supplied, giving you great flexibility in security arrangements.

- Multiple users can have accounts on the same NT machine. A user account on a machine includes a username and password and a series of user privileges assigned by the administrator. Users can hide directories or files from other users and choose settings. Logging onto the system automatically activates all saved settings from the user's previous sessions. If users have been assigned high enough privileges, they can share or stop sharing system resources on the network (such as printers and files), or they can alter the rights other net users have when accessing them.

- NT is part of the Microsoft product line. Microsoft has been fairly good (although not perfect, by any means) at designing products that mesh. As of NT's release, this is still fairly true. NT was designed to fit smoothly into the existing product line of operating systems and GUIs. As a result, if you're using MS-DOS, Windows 3.*x*, Windows for Workgroups, or Windows 95, migration to NT is relatively easy. Most of your existing applications will work fine. Although there have been reports that some 16-bit applications run slower under NT, many will actually run faster because of NT's incorporation of 32-bit disk, screen, and printer drivers. Just as with upgrading from Windows 3.*x* to Windows 95, an upgrade to NT can be done so that your Windows 95 or Windows 3.*x* settings are imported into NT. After installation, your NT Program Manager and Control Panel settings will be automatically preconfigured to previously existing settings.

NOTE

In all fairness, although this isn't typically mentioned in magazine reviews of NT, some 16-bit Windows applications—especially disk-intensive applications—run much faster under NT than in Windows 3.*x* or Windows 95 because of NT's dynamic disk cache, mentioned earlier. However, to gain this benefit, you must add additional RAM, typically well above the 12M or 16M minimum suggested for NT systems. A 32M NT Server platform, for example, runs such disk-intensive applications very efficiently.

NT Versus DOS and Windows 3.*x*

Although some NT users will be making a lateral (some would say downward) move from UNIX or OS/2, most newcomers to NT will be migrating upward from the DOS/Windows 3.*x* platform or the Windows 95 platform. Because these are the most likely scenarios, they invite comparison for most readers.

Because you've read the press announcements and reviews, or possibly because you've read other books on the subject, you might have already decided to switch to Windows NT for specific reasons.

Because the DOS/Windows 3.*x* marriage has been with us for so long and is still highly prevalent despite the explosion of Windows 95 in the market, take a look at how NT compares to that operating environment. Next, I'll compare NT to Windows 95 and other operating systems, such as OS/2 and UNIX.

The Role of DOS

Despite the enormous popularity of Windows 3.0 and 3.1 (some estimates put the user base as high as 60 million), these GUIs are really only shells placed on top of DOS. This is also true of other PC-based GUIs, such as Digital Research's GEM, the now-defunct TopView from IBM, and VisiCorp's VisiOn.

The real culprit in this scenario is DOS—not that DOS is any slouch, of course. After all, it's been estimated that more than 100 million copies of DOS are in existence, and that more than 10,000 applications are available for it. As a result, no responsible MIS professional or computer user would want to discount the importance of DOS compatibility when making an operating system choice. All too often, programs—whether major applications or minor utilities—are available only in a DOS version.

But as strong a workhorse as it is, DOS was never designed to be a multitasking operating system, much less to have a graphical user interface tacked on top. In other words, Windows has been a "kludge job"—something held together with spit and baling wire. As any veteran Windows user knows, strange and frustrating anomalies often crop up in Windows as a result of this unlikely marriage.

For example, when one Windows program (or DOS program running under Windows) crashes, it might very well bring the whole system and any other running applications to their knees. This is particularly a problem with Windows 3.0. Windows 3.1 is more forgiving about runaway programs, but limitations in the DOS architecture still prevented building a crashproof shell.

On the up side, many DOS lovers converted to Windows simply because it offered a pretty good means of task switching and multitasking. They could run multiple DOS applications and switch between them—much as Software Carousel, Multiple Choice, and DesqView do—but with the added convenience of also running Windows applications and of windowing DOS applications into small boxes that could be jumped to simply by clicking on them.

NT's DOS

How does NT's DOS work, and how does NT do DOS without the limitations of DOS? For starters, when NT boots, DOS does not. You can opt to install NT so that you have an option of booting DOS *or* NT, but you never load both. NT does have a kernel operating system, one responsible for much of what DOS does under Windows 3.*x*—for example, keyboard and screen I/O, managing loadable device drivers, and handling disk I/O requests. Then, on top of that, NT contains modules called *environment subsystems* that emulate the DOS environment. (There are also modules for POSIX, OS/2, 16-bit Windows, and 32-bit Windows environments.) The DOS environment subsystem supplies all the system services that DOS normally does. However, these functions are integrated seamlessly into NT; they don't sit below it.

The DOS box isn't a DOS session per se, as it is in Windows 3.1. There, Windows actually spawns a session of DOS, running COMMAND.COM. In NT, the system architects decided to offer DOS's functionality while avoiding DOS's limitations and using the benefits of NT CPU scheduling, system security, and crash protection. This is done through DOS emulation with a 32-bit application called CMD.EXE, which is a superset of MS-DOS that not only provides MS-DOS compatibility but also lets you run Windows, OS/2, and POSIX applications from the command line.

NOTE

The DOS session created when you run a DOS application from the command window (CMD.EXE) is quite flexible because it's configurable. Just as DOS that boots on a PC can be configured from AUTOEXEC.BAT and CONFIG.SYS, the DOS session that gets created within NT can be configured with loadable device drivers, TSRs, and so forth. Chapter 8, "Using the Control Panel to Configure Windows NT," covers this in detail.

The NT DOS emulator supports all the usual DOS commands, and then some. When you launch a DOS program under NT, NT creates a *VDM (virtual DOS machine)* that tricks the DOS program into thinking it's running on its own PC. NT sets up one VDM for each DOS application you run. Each VDM has all the hooks needed to handle both 16-bit and 32-bit DOS calls, in compliance with DOS 6. A full 16M of standard DOS (segmented) application and data memory space is supplied to the VDM. In addition, the documentation states that the popular memory managers are supported. Figure 1.1 illustrates how virtual DOS machines run independently of one another on top of NT.

FIGURE 1.1.
Several DOS sessions running on top of NT in virtual DOS machines (VDMs).

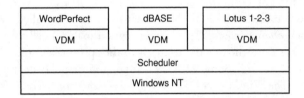

There are certain limitations to the DOS support, which you might expect. For NT to ensure data security and system stability, its DOS emulator intercepts all I/O processes, routing data to their destinations. This is handled by I/O interceptors, which in turn hand data to the kernel for dispatching.

Any traditionally designed DOS programs that perform their I/O using standard DOS system calls will run under NT as expected. Those that write directly to hardware for which device drivers prevent direct access—for example, the hard-disk drivers—will be thwarted by NT, leading to an error message and termination of the program. Disk caching and communications applications are typical programs that do this. Overall, this approach gives you a high level of system security. The result should be fewer virus problems with DOS programs under NT, because most viral programs try to write directly to the hard disk boot tracks or directories, and NT won't allow this.

Another limitation of NT's DOS emulator concerns device drivers. If your DOS application requires a loadable device driver to operate, you might have trouble running it in NT because the driver won't be loaded. If NT allowed loading of device drivers, it would probably mean circumventing the NT Executive's security features because many device drivers attempt to access hardware directly. In time, modified versions of DOS applications will become available for NT, but in the meantime you might have to run the application under real DOS running outside NT.

Windows on Win32 (WOW)

As with DOS applications, 16-bit Windows programs run in an emulation VDM created on-the-fly by NT—but there's a catch. Here's how it works: You launch a 16-bit Windows application in NT by using the Windows 95–like interface with the Start button, then selecting the application group, then choosing the application name itself from pop-up menus.

> **NOTE**
>
> You also can type the program's .EXE filename at the DOS prompt (called the *command prompt* in NT) or enter the program's name in the Task List box.

From information in the file header, NT then recognizes the 16-bit Windows program and launches a VDM, just as it does when you run a DOS program. The VDM includes DOS and an emulation of Windows called *Windows on Win32* (*WOW*). As with DOS emulation, the Windows emulation fakes all the standard system calls (called *APIs* in Windows, for *application programming interfaces*). When a program makes a call to a standard Windows 3.*x* API, WOW intercepts the call and routes it to the appropriate source—usually the NT Executive or a Win32 API call. Some APIs are mapped to internal code integrated into the WOW environment. The Windows NT 32-bit *graphical display interface* (*GDI*) manages the application's display onscreen for such things as image and text display, window locations, and so forth.

The interesting thing about 16-bit Windows applications is that, unlike DOS sessions, after the first application is run, launching additional Windows 3.1 applications doesn't create another VDM and WOW session. It's no more necessary than running multiple copies of normal Windows 3.1 when you want to run Terminal and Notepad at the same time. This arrangement is needed to allow maximum Windows 3.1 compatibility, as well as DDE and OLE communication between applications.

> **NOTE**
>
> To offer extra robustness, NT gives you the ability to execute 16-bit Windows in separate VDMs. Although this requires more system resources, such as paging file space, it offers the advantage that if the application crashes, WOW won't come down with it.

After a WOW VDM environment is launched the first time, additional Windows 3.1 applications are just dumped into it as separate program threads, as shown in Figure 1.2.

FIGURE 1.2.

Multiple 16-bit Windows applications run in the same VDM.

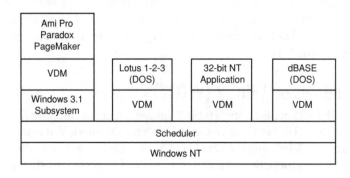

The good news is that this means less software overhead to NT and, because the NT thread manager is preemptive, no unruly application is allowed to hog the CPU's attention and slow down your other applications. The bad news is that because all 16-bit Windows applications are running in the same VDM, an errant application can pull down the whole VDM like a house of cards, as shown in Figure 1.3. This won't crash NT, but it might crash any running 16-bit Windows applications.

FIGURE 1.3.
One crashed 16-bit Windows program can pull down the WOW VDM, but not the whole system.

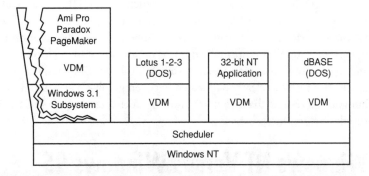

TIP

Although the WOW VDM might crash due to a misbehaving Windows application, you don't have to restart NT to launch the WOW environment again. Simply running another 16-bit Windows application is enough.

As with DOS applications, only well-behaved Windows applications are likely to run successfully under NT. So beware: Some Windows 3.*x* programs write directly to the Windows GDI (usually to speed up display performance) instead of making calls to the API. Under NT, the GDI isn't going to be where the application expects it, so these unruly programs may not execute properly. (See Chapter 11, "Maintenance and Troubleshooting," under the topic "Running DOS and Windows 3.*x* Applications.")

Speed Issues: DOS and Windows 3.*x* Applications in NT

As I mentioned earlier, the big plus to running DOS and Windows 3.*x* applications on NT is the additional security the system offers. The applications will still run (in fact, Microsoft believes that more than 90 percent of them will run without a hitch), and you can rest peacefully in the knowledge that your hard disk *FATs* (*file allocation tables*), files, or boot tracks aren't going to be creamed by runaway programs, and that no unauthorized personnel will have access to your files. Also, because all I/O calls are intercepted and mapped by NT, you can have multiple applications vying for I/O ports (for example, serial and parallel ports), and NT will run interference to prevent data collisions.

That's the good news. The bad news is that emulation, particularly with the kind of security that's built into NT, takes big-time computing power. The end result is that your DOS and 16-bit Windows applications run slower under NT than in their native environments. On average, 16-bit Windows applications run between 10 and 50 percent slower under NT, depending on the type of computation being performed. As mentioned earlier, some disk-intensive applications on hardware with enough RAM installed might improve in performance.

As a rule, graphically intensive applications such as CorelDRAW! and full-blown graphical word processors, such as WordPerfect for Windows, take the greatest hit. Programs primarily doing calculations (for example, spreadsheets) show less speed degradation because the CPU is just doing calculations as it normally does, as opposed to moving lots of graphics around onscreen and internally converting several 16-bit API calls to 32-bit calls. Speed degradation on DOS applications isn't as clearly delineated between graphical and nongraphics-oriented programs, but you can assume that programs running in character-mode DOS perform faster than those running in graphics mode.

Windows NT Versus Windows 95

Because virtually all popular applications have been or are now being converted for Windows 95, 16-bit Windows programs will soon be a thing of the past. In fact, to garner the Windows 95–compatible logo from Microsoft, Windows 95–compatible applications must be written to the Win32 API and be capable of running on NT. There's a strong incentive for software makers to convert their applications so that they perform nicely on NT. The upshot is that NT is a natural next step for Windows 95 users, without any performance penalty or application incompatibility whatsoever. With that perspective in mind, take a closer look at how Windows 95 compares with NT.

Well aware of the kludge of the DOS/Windows 3.*x* marriage, Microsoft set out to create a real operating system. Six million lines of code and $150 million later, NT was born. Ideally, Microsoft wants to support only a single operating system, but because many PCs still can't run NT (there are a lot of 386s out there, as well as machines with less than 12M of RAM), this isn't possible now. Eventually though, if Microsoft has its way (and it probably will, if history is any indicator), everyone will be running NT in one form or another.

For the time being, Microsoft has provided a bridge from Windows 3.*x* to NT. That bridge— with a relatively short life of about three to five years—is Windows 95. Windows 95 runs most 32-bit NT programs, as well as DOS and Windows 3.*x* programs, because it uses essentially (with slight modifications) the same API as NT. It also runs on "legacy" 386-based machines having as little as 4M of RAM.

To get developers to port their applications to 32-bits, Microsoft has made the public hungry for features built into the Win32 API and Windows 95 operating system, such as long filenames, preemptive multitasking, and memory protection. Another plus is that 32-bit versions of popular programs run faster than their 16-bit counterparts do when compared on the same Windows 95 system. The industry at large has recognized the importance of Win32 API, so that now even competitors are adopting it. For example, both DEC and IBM now offer developer's extension APIs for VMS and OS/2 that allow easy porting of applications to the Win32 API.

Despite the hoopla and technical advances—such as Plug-and-Play, an attractive interface, additional memory protection, and a 32-bit file system—much of Windows 95 borrows from Windows 3.*x*. Why did Microsoft cut corners when it already had an impressive blueprint for a true 32-bit operating system it could borrow from? Because scaling down NT into something like "NT Lite" wasn't possible, much less desirable, from Microsoft's point of view.

Here's why Microsoft didn't scale down NT: NT's design fits a different category altogether. It's oriented toward client/server at its core level, and turning it into a small-workstation operating system would be like trying to get an elephant through your front door. Instead, a few NT architectural concepts were cut and pasted into Windows 95, a few completely new ones like Plug-and-Play were added, and a flashy interface was pasted on. As a result, you can still see vestiges of the DOS/Windows kludge job in Windows 95, so you still have an operating system that acts unstable, runs multiple programs jerkily at times, and crashes for unknown reasons.

To commend it, Windows 95 does sport well-integrated communications and the ability to run more programs simultaneously than Windows 3.*x* does. Plug-and-Play is useful, too; plug in a new card (especially in a notebook), plug in a Plug-and-Play printer, or insert your portable into its docking station, and Windows 95 reconfigures itself accordingly. Network support is strong, too, with all the popular protocols included. Windows 95 is highly compatible with a plethora of existing hardware (more so than NT is), runs almost every existing 16-bit and DOS application, is great for playing games, and earns high marks in the appearance category.

Does it have serious problems for use in the large-scale enterprise computing installations? Yes. For example, one faulty 16-bit or 32-bit application can pull down the whole operating system, not just the 16-bit VDM, as in NT. This is because critical portions of the operating system core code are left bare as unprotected 16-bit code. (This was done intentionally for backward compatibility reasons.) House-cleaning after a crashed application is better than it was in Windows 3.*x*, but it's still not perfect; therefore, even if an application crashes and the system continues to run, it might become "unstable" and crash later. To increase support for 16-bit and DOS applications, Windows 95 allows programs to access central operating system code and directly manipulate system interrupts. Either of these can potentially crash the system.

Should you need to compare features of the members of the Microsoft Windows family, Table 1.1 should prove helpful; it compares the most salient operating system features.

Table 1.1. A comparison of Windows NT and the rest of the Windows family.

Feature	16-bit Windows 3.1	Windows 3.1 with Win32s	Windows for Workgroups	Windows 95	Windows NT
Virtual memory	Yes	Yes	Yes	Yes	Yes
Multitasking	Cooperative	Cooperative	Cooperative	Preemptive	Preemptive
Preemptive multi-tasking for 16-bit applications	No	No	No	No	Yes
Preemptive multi-tasking for 32-bit applications	No	No	No	Yes	Yes
Multithreading	No	No	No	Yes	Yes
Symmetric multiprocessing	No	No	No	No	Yes
Portability	No	No	No	No	Yes
Access security	No	No	No	No	Yes
Runs 16-bit real-mode Windows applications	Yes	Yes	Yes	Yes	No
Runs 16-bit standard-mode Windows applications	Yes	Yes	Yes	Yes	Most
Runs 16-bit enhanced-mode Windows applications	Yes	Yes	Yes	Yes	Yes
Runs 32-bit Windows applications	No	Yes	No	Yes	Yes
Runs OS/2 applications character mode only	No	No	No	No	1.x
Supports POSIX	No	No	No	No	Yes
Supports DOS FAT	Yes	Yes	Yes	Yes	Yes

Feature	16-bit Windows 3.1	Windows 3.1 with Win32s	Windows for Workgroups	Windows 95	Windows NT
Supports OS/2 HPFS	No	No	No	No	Yes
Supports NTFS	No	No	No	No	Yes
Built-in networking	No	No	Yes	Yes	Yes
Built-in e-mail	No	No	Yes	Yes	Yes
386 or higher CPU required	No	Yes	Yes	Yes	Yes
Supports RISC chips	No	No	No	No	Yes
Fault tolerance	No	No	No	No	Yes

NT Versus OS/2

Windows NT and IBM's OS/2 have similar roots. Both were born at Microsoft, but OS/2 came first, originally a joint development effort of Microsoft and IBM. When a falling-out between the two companies happened in 1990, IBM took over OS/2 and Microsoft began work on NT. Subsequently, the companies have developed these two 32-bit operating systems independently. Their common ancestry and similar design philosophies, however, give OS/2 and NT many similar features.

In general, OS/2 offers slightly speedier performance than NT, has less demanding system requirements, and is more compatible with DOS applications, and NT offers somewhat better crash protection and security and decidedly superior device support.

OS/2 (I include Warp and Warp Connect when using this generic term) systems are multithreaded, preemptive multitasking operating systems with a graphical user interface similar to Windows. The difference between Warp and Warp Connect is that Connect includes extra network protocols. Otherwise, the packages are much the same. On the other hand, NT Workstation and NT Server are significantly different packages; Server sports an impressive set of advanced features above those of Workstation.

As opposed to NT, OS/2 runs only on Intel-based processors. OS/2 can run 16-bit and 32-bit OS/2 applications, as well as 16-bit DOS and Windows applications (the latter by using Windows 3.1, which is included with or accessed by Warp). On the other hand, OS/2 Warp doesn't run Win32 or NT 32-bit applications.

Multitasking performance is comparable between NT and OS/2. However, OS/2's multitasking works somewhat differently from NT's in queuing I/O requests from applications. OS/2's design can result in I/O bottlenecks that can slow system responsiveness, as perceived by the user, but NT isn't likely to suffer in this way.

Both NT and OS/2 support large amounts of memory; the addressable memory area for both is 4G. OS/2 applications are allotted 4GB (NT applications only 2G), but OS/2 limits space for the application code to 512M, allowing the applications private access to the remaining portion of its own 4G address space for data. Not that this is really a big deal—at least not yet. Even with the explosive growth of application size (so-called *bloatware*), the biggest programs I've seen are in the range of 2M to 4M. Besides, your applications can really see no more memory than what is free (including virtual hard disk memory set aside by a paging file).

OS/2 doesn't use TrueType fonts, except when you're running Windows applications. Otherwise, it uses Adobe's ATM. Although ATM is available for Windows 3.1 and Windows for Workgroups, most Windows users prefer TrueType fonts because they're built into Windows and they're cheap and readily available. Some even come packaged with all versions of Windows.

HPFS Versus NTFS

OS/2 Warp supports an advanced file system called High Performance Files System (HPFS), similar to NT's NTFS. HPFS supports filenames up to 254 characters long, as well as "extended attributes" above and beyond the normal DOS (FAT) attribute settings (date, time, system, hidden, archive, and read/write). With extended attributes, programs can store notes about a file, such as key phrases, the file's editing history, the author of the file, and so on, as part of the directory entry. NT offers similar features in NTFS, but also includes support for access control security, which allows an administrator to assign individual and group permission rights to every file and directory. Also, NT's disk fault-tolerance features, such as RAID 5 and mirror disk sets, exceed those of OS/2.

OS/2 Networking

The networking version of OS/2 called Warp Connect offers built-in peer networking services (including a NetWare client, TCP/IP support, and a full set of Internet software tools). Warp Connect includes support for the following clients and protocols: IBM Peer for OS/2, IBM OS/2 LAN Requester 4.0, Novell NetWare Client Version 2.11 for OS/2, LAN Distance Remote 1.11, Gopher, FTP, telnet, and TCP/IP for OS/2 version 3.0.

Because of its IBM background, SNA (systems network architecture) is well supported. This is an important feature in the many settings that historically have been connected to IBM mainframes. In addition, many other popular protocols, such as TCP/IP, APPC, NetBIOS, and LU 6.2, are supported, so OS/2 machines can be connected as workstations (clients) on most popular LANs. One particularly strong point is that an OS/2 machine can perform as a Novell NetWare server, but an NT machine can't, as of this writing, because Novell seems uninterested in sharing its server code with Microsoft. No doubt this is an issue that Microsoft will address quickly in hopes of capturing more of the Netware server market.

Stability and Crash Protection

At the time of NT's initial release, OS/2 was more successful at running DOS and Windows 3.*x* applications without error—partly because OS/2 has been around longer and bugs have been resolved, but mostly because NT's security prevents programs not in strict compliance with API rules from wreaking havoc on the system. It's a trade-off between compatibility and robustness at this point, with robustness taking the upper hand. For those concerned with security, the trade-off is an acceptable one.

Final Analysis

In the final analysis, NT has a leg up on OS/2 Warp and OS/2 Connect in several ways:

- NTFS is more capable than HPFS because of its security and fault-tolerance features.
- NT's internal security is more advanced and pervasive than OS/2's, extending not only to disk operations but to all system events (application threads, system calls, memory accesses, and so on).
- NT is portable to RISC and multiprocessor systems.
- NT is directly compatible with Windows for Workgroups, Windows 95, and LAN Manager. Simply install the necessary network cards, cable the machines together, boot up, and you have a functioning LAN.
- NT has built-in networking, and extensive, secure networking is available with NT Server.
- NT is fully 32-bit; however, parts of OS/2 left over from earlier versions are written in 16-bit. In addition, NT can easily be modified to support other operating systems by simply adding operating system emulator modules (environment subsystems, discussed in Chapter 2). This will probably ensure a longer life span and faster upgrading for NT than for OS/2.

Table 1.2 compares Windows NT and OS/2 features. In particular, notice the C2-level security, 32-bit application support, and NTFS differences.

Table 1.2. Feature comparisons of Windows NT and OS/2.

Feature	OS/2 Warp	Windows NT
Portability	Planned	Yes
Symmetric multiprocessing	No	Yes
Virtual memory	Yes	Yes
Object-oriented user interface	Yes	No

continues

Table 1.2. continued

Feature	OS/2 Warp	Windows NT
Internationalization	Codepage	Unicode
C2-level security	No	Yes
DOS FAT file system	Yes	Yes
High-performance file system (HPFS)	Yes	Yes
NT file system (NTFS)	No	Yes
Runs DOS applications	Yes	Yes
Runs 16-bit Windows applications	Yes	Yes
Runs OS/2 16-bit applications	Yes	Text-only
Runs OS/2 32-bit applications	Yes	No
Runs 32-bit Windows applications	No	Yes
Application protection	Yes	Yes
Multitasking	Yes	Yes
Multithreading	Yes	Yes
Multiple message queues to prevent data bottlenecks	No	Yes

NT Versus UNIX

Contrary to popular opinion, UNIX is no longer the inscrutable operating system that only engineers and computer geeks can use. Its popularity among nonacademics is on the rise as a graphical operating system. In fact, much of Windows NT has its origins in a variation of UNIX called Mach, developed at Carnegie-Mellon University. In the past several years, UNIX has become standardized among its many vendors, giving it an even stronger foothold in the marketplace. With its recent acquisition of the portion of AT&T that invented UNIX (AT&T's UNIX Systems Laboratory), Novell might indeed give Microsoft a run for its money with its own UnixWare product. Other major players in the UNIX market are SCO, IBM, DEC, SunSoft, and NeXT, with their products SCO UNIX, AIX, ULTRIX, Solaris, and NeXTSTEP, respectively.

NT and UNIX have much in common, which is good news. The multiprocessing, multitasking, and networking capabilities of NT's Object Manager and Process Manager owe much to UNIX's own time-tested architecture (as well as to VMS design concepts, as mentioned earlier).

In addition to multitasking, UNIX and NT have another feature in common—the most important feature of NT, according to some analysts. It's called *RPC* (remote procedure call) *support*. Windows NT Server provides RPC support services so that programs written to take advantage of them do so. In the future, this might result in very efficient execution of complex programs, in effect turning a network into a huge multiprocessor computer that can be dynamically assigned to any number of tasks that network users are running.

> **NOTE**
>
> See Chapter 2 for more details on the internal architecture of NT and for descriptions of the Object and Process Managers.

Devices

A major similarity between NT and UNIX is in how they interact with devices attached to the computer. To design an operating system that's as flexible as possible, UNIX and NT both connect to the world through device drivers that appear as files. When either UNIX or NT wants to send data to or fetch data from a screen, keyboard, I/O port, memory, or disk file, the same internal approach is used: They simply route the process to a device that appears to the operating system as a sequential file. Regardless of the device's physical nature (such as a pressed key, a memory location, or a COM port), all these objects are treated in the same manner.

Memory Allocation

NT and UNIX use memory in similar ways, too. Both can access a large, "flat" memory space of many megabytes. NT and UNIX programmers don't have to deal with any of the problems inherent in a 16-bit PC application's need for segmented addressing schemes. NT typically offers a memory space of 4G per application. (This is virtual memory, of course, because you'll probably have only 16M of real RAM.) Actually, only 2G of that space is available for the application; the rest is for NT's use. Many UNIX systems offer about the same amount. Both systems prevent applications from stepping on each other's toes, because memory blocks allotted to one process or application can be protected from access by another process. A key difference between UNIX systems on PCs and NT is that, however annoying it is that NT requires 12M to 16M of RAM, UNIX systems tend to require more.

GUI Treatment

Over the years, UNIX has had several graphical interfaces, and there has been little standardization among these GUIs. One of the key advantages of NT over UNIX is simply that it adopted the Windows GUI, an interface that has more or less been set in stone through mass popularity. In the UNIX world, contending GUIs such as OPEN LOOK and Motif present problems for users and applications developers alike. Users can be confused when jumping between systems with different GUIs, and developers have to decide which GUI or GUIs they'll tune their application for.

Software Compatibility: Market Considerations

The point about software applications driving the operating system market is worth reiterating here. Although UNIX and its variations, such as Solaris and NeXTSTEP, offer advantages (NeXTSTEP is a great development environment for programmers because of its true object-oriented approach), few of them offer significant support for DOS or Windows applications. For establishments that are moving up in processing power and already well ensconced in a DOS/Windows applications mix, UNIX won't make the cut. However, for those who have previously invested in UNIX applications, systems, terminals, networking, and so forth, one of the PC-based UNIX contenders could make good sense as an affordable alternative when you take into account adding fully loaded workstations.

It's true that UNIX has some advanced features, such as distributed file services and parallel processing, that NT does not, and, almost like religious believers, its followers are loyal and ubiquitous. A huge pool of UNIX experts worldwide has been developing utilities, applications, and extensions to the operating system for many years. Microsoft is in only the infant stages of developing support for NT. On the downside, however, UNIX is a behemoth, and it's not fully standardized. A full-blown version V of UNIX takes up a huge amount of disk space (almost 100M) and comes on close to 100 disks. It also requires a lot of upkeep.

In the long run, the phenomenal popularity of DOS and Windows applications in the horizontal market (nonspecific applications, such as spreadsheets, databases, and word processors) will ensure NT's success (or that of other Windows derivatives), and it makes NT the better choice for most power-user business needs—whether on the network or on the standalone desktop. Although NT is much like UNIX in terms of features, it's more elegant and efficient. NT also incorporates advances inspired by Dave Cutler and his VMS development team. It offers much of UNIX's functionality without the ever-growing plethora of nonstandard functions and add-ons that UNIX has accumulated over the years.

Based on the Carnegie-Mellon Mach microkernel and VMS model, NT was designed to be the real Windows that PC people were waiting for, or the manageable operating system that UNIX hackers dreamed of taking home with them. As future versions of 32-bit-compatible Windows programs become readily available (Win32s and NT applications from many vendors are available now, and more are on the way), UNIX's hope of widespread popularity on the desktop is likely to be dashed.

NT's Advanced Features

So much for a brief look at NT's basic features and the main contenders against NT. Before I move on to discuss the detailed architecture of NT in the next chapter, this section gives you an overview of the NT services and features that distinguish it from Windows 3.*x* and Windows 95:

- Networking
- Fault tolerance

- Multiprocessor support
- NTFS file services
- Hardware support
- System administration tools

Networking

Windows NT comes in two versions—Windows NT Workstation and Windows NT Server—that differ primarily in networking and security. With the standard NT desktop operating system, you get peer-to-peer networking, server networking, remote access services, and all the administration tools typically needed to maintain a network server. (See "Other Advantages of NT Server," later in this chapter.)

Both systems are built around the same basic core NT kernel and interface, and both have C2-level government security features. NT Workstation is meant to connect smaller workgroups, typically within a single site on a departmental level. However, with the Server package, you get a greater degree of fault tolerance and larger network capabilities and connectivity options. You also get remote access administration capabilities, meaning that you can perform administrative duties from a remote station (even over the phone) instead of having to perform them at the server station. You even get additional support for AppleTalk, allowing Apple Macintosh users to coexist happily on your NT network.

Both systems are built around the Network Device Interface Specification (NDIS) version 3.0. This means that you can connect to other Microsoft products (and other brands), such as LAN Manager for OS/2. TCP/IP support in both NT and NT Server means connectivity to UNIX systems. Other support packages can provide IBM and VAX connectivity, which might be even more important, especially in the corporate environment.

Windows for Workgroups Support and Windows 95 Support

In the forthcoming battle of the high-end operating systems, the likely focal point will be the LAN, so Windows NT was made compatible with as many existing network types as possible. The good news is that, unlike many networking solutions (including the many capable but complex UNIX PC systems), networking with NT is simple and fairly painless right out of the box—this alone might win the hearts of many MIS managers.

Both NT and NT Server allow you to connect hardware systems running NetWare, Banyan VINES, and Microsoft LAN Manager networks, as well as Windows for Workgroups (WFW) and Windows 95. The first three are more common in the field than Windows for Workgroups (despite Microsoft's efforts to push that product). However, if you're running WFW or Windows 95, getting up and running is a no-brainer. NT really is plug-and-play compatible with WFW and Windows 95 as well as with Microsoft's DOS networking analogue, Workgroup Connection. Just hook up an existing WFW or Windows 95 network to a standard NT Server, share some directories and printers from the server, and you're in business. What you've got is a peer-to-peer network with the NT station also acting as a server.

> **NOTE**
>
> Because of the similarities of network interaction and presence between WFW and Windows 95 peer-to-peer networks or standalone stations, WFW is often used to represent both types of systems. When you see *WFW* in reference to connections, shares, or other management issues, Windows 95 workstations are also implied.

The advantage over what you had on a standard WFW peer-to-peer network is that your server can be locked up tight as a drum with serious password protection, assignable user privileges, and fault-tolerant hard disk functions. Not only can WFW stations access FAT partitions on the server, they can also take advantage of the advanced features of the NTFS file system (such as security and media fault-detection and repair).

> **NOTE**
>
> Long filenames aren't available to DOS or DOS/Windows 3.x machines attached to NTFS partitions over the network. NT truncates filenames for use by non-NT workstations, as explained later in this chapter in "NTFS File Services." However, Windows 95 users can see long filenames.

> **NOTE**
>
> Windows for Workgroups 3.11 is an extension of WFW with a few features that allow it to interface more neatly with NT. For example, 3.11 adds domain support for NT Server networks, which supplies user authentication functions, much as the NT client machines do. Windows 95 has similar features.

Network administrators also have sophisticated control over file and directory accessibility and user rights on a network, even with WFW clients. For example, rights to a host of activities—such as read/write privileges, programmer privileges, forcing obligatory password changes or uniqueness, backing up files, forcing a system shutdown, and changing the system time—can be individually assigned on a user-by-user basis. Administrators can also opt to build an audit trail by using an automatic event logger, recording who logs on and off the system, which files and directories were accessed, and other details.

Sharing network resources in NT uses the same method as Windows 95. This makes it probably one of the simplest to manage. To share a directory, highlight the directory's file folder in

My Computer and right-click to bring up the pop-up menu and select Sharing. Fill in a few details on the Sharing page of the properties window that appears, and the task is done.

> **NOTE**
>
> An important distinction between NT and WFW/Windows 95's sharing models is that security is set at the share level when you share a resource such as a directory or a printer in WFW. That is, you have the option of declaring some properties about the share, such as whether the directory is read-only or read/write. Specific network users who will have access to the resource aren't declared. You can declare a password in some cases, but this restricts access only for people who don't know the password. With NT, shares can easily be restricted to individual users or to preset groups of users. When a user tries to access a resource, the resource server (the workstation containing the shared resource) checks the identity of the potential client and either grants or refuses access to the resource based on the user's identity (username and password).

Other Network Support

Most networked PCs run Novell products, such as NetWare or NetWare Lite, because Novell has cooperated with Microsoft by offering to share its client-side software. Assuming that hardware requirements aren't a big issue, one of the key advantages of NT is how easily you can get Windows onto a Novell network. Connecting to a NetWare network with Windows 3.1 requires three levels (four modules) of software, but connecting with NT needs just one level. You also gain NT's inherent's security and connectivity advantages.

Novell and Microsoft have, through their collaborations, made sure that clients running Windows 3.1, Windows for Workgroups, Windows NT, and Windows NT Server can connect to Novell servers just as easily as they can to other servers, such as LAN Manager.

For obvious reasons, Novell isn't interested in sharing its code for the server side of the equation. After all, NT Server hopes to capture some of the networking market share that Microsoft has failed to gain with LAN Manager and Windows for Workgroups. Microsoft has been forced to write its own server code, but it looks as though NT Server is a fairly successful challenge to Novell's servers. It matches much of Novell's functionality, such as file and print serving, and has important extra features, such as RPC support, extensive fault-tolerance and security, Remote Access Services, environment subsystems, disk striping and volume sets, and excellent user administration tools.

Some analysts suggest that Microsoft intends NT Server servers to perform as 32-bit NT application servers on established Novell networks. Therefore, instead of converting your Novell servers to NT, just add some NT Server units to your network mix and allow users to run high-performance 32-bit NT applications from them.

Fault Tolerance

NT Server gives you a couple of fault-tolerance options worth noting (and well known by Novell aficionados). They are generically known as *disk mirroring* and *disk striping*; specifically, they're known as *RAID 1* and *RAID 5*. (*RAID* stands for *redundant array of inexpensive drives*.)

With RAID 1, you can set up each hard disk in the server with a mirror disk containing a carbon copy of the disk's data. Whenever a write occurs on the primary drive, an identical change is made to the mirror disk. Although this procedure requires two hard disks for every one you want in action, the advantages can be well worth it. If the operating system detects an error, such as a lost file or sector, the second drive is accessed to retrieve it. In a worst-case scenario, when the primary drive crashes or fails, the backup takes over without a hiccup.

> **NOTE**
>
> To fully implement hard-disk fault tolerance, you should install multiple disk controllers as well as disks, which Windows NT allows you to do. The mirror disk is then on a second controller, so that if the first controller card fails, the second one takes over immediately.

RAID 5 is a different story—it wasn't designed for avoiding downtime and data loss. A RAID 5 array looks like a single volume (for example, drive E:) to the system. When the system tries to write a file to disk, the information is spread (striped) across several disks instead of written on a single one, resulting in a significant throughput increase. What's odd is that the data is broken up among drives, so it doesn't exist on any single drive. However, if striping is used with the parity option, enough data is stored on the set to allow operation of the system (and access to the files), even if one disk in the array becomes crippled.

Finally, a third fault-tolerance option allows uninterruptible power supply (UPS) operation of NT clients and servers. Through a serial port connection between the UPS and NT machines, NT is warned of a power outage or a brownout. All users connected to the server are notified, and after a specified period that depends on the UPS's capacity, NT begins to shut down.

Remote Access Services (RAS)

Remote access services let users dial into the network from a remote computer (such as a laptop) over phone lines. Operationally, interaction works just as though the users were in the office. As soon as users are logged on and recognized as valid, they have access to any service they're authorized for, even if that service attaches them to another domain, a mainframe, or another type of LAN. You could call from home, log in, send a print job to a laser printer, use some data on a mainframe, run applications, leave e-mail for other users, interact with company scheduling programs, and so on.

Remote access is included in the standard NT product, too, but only one user can call it at a time. On the NT Server version, multiple callers can log on simultaneously. (The maximum is 256, but this number is limited by how many COM ports you have available.)

NT's built-in RAS isn't the same as commonly used products, such as PC-Anywhere, Close-Up, and Carbon Copy. These DOS products let you log on and run Windows or DOS programs from remote locations, but they actually control the host machine, which is different than logging onto a network or workstation as a user and being validated with a password. With those DOS products, applications still run on the host machine while the remote access software simply shunts keyboard and screen I/O to the remote machine. With NT's RAS, you tie into the network just as any workstation does. Additional security is supplied by an optional "dial-back" setting that forces the workstation to dial up the remote computer at a predetermined location (phone number) to further prevent unauthorized users from gaining access. All this extra security is built into NT. In addition, an administrator can easily enable or disable dial-up authority for each user.

Other Advantages of NT Server

Windows NT is designed to be the local workgroup solution when you need more control than what's offered by a peer-to-peer network (such as Windows for Workgroups, LANtastic, or Novell Lite). But what about large corporations or agencies with many departments and possibly even different physical sites around the country?

For the complex requirements of sophisticated interdepartmental networking communications or for interplatform networking, you might want to consider the more sophisticated NT Server. NT Server shares the core design and desktop appearance of the standard $300 NT. The price is higher, however, and extensions to NT are added, supplying support for the following:

- The "domain" model for establishing very large networks, meaning enterprise-wide connectivity and interconnectivity with other networking platforms and the necessary tools for administering such domains
- Wide area networking capabilities
- Connectivity services for mainframes and minicomputers
- Macintosh connectivity

Although it's not truly complete in its first release, NT Server is a long-range project for Microsoft. It clearly is the direction Microsoft intends to take for serious corporate users. Microsoft has promised the following features in the works for NT Server:

- SNA support for IBM and compatible mainframes and support of AS/400 environments via 5250 emulation
- An enterprise-wide messaging system called EMS (Enterprise Message System)
- An enterprise-wide network management system called SMS (System Management Server)

In the domain model, each NT Server typically serves a departmental workgroup, then you network the Server machines to create a domain. Any collection of network servers and clients that shares the same security access database is considered the domain; therefore, the design is flexible. However, the topography is normally laid out as shown in Figure 1.4.

FIGURE 1.4.

Two domains of five workstations each are attached to create a single, larger network. Each domain has at least one NT server.

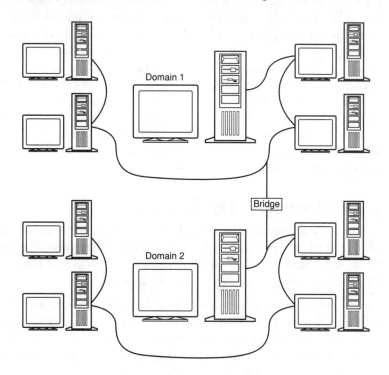

Windows NT Server comes with administrative tools beyond those supplied with standard NT: management tools for administering domains, a Server Manager for both local and remote management of a particular server, and a Profile Editor to tweak the specifics of each user's rights and account details.

NT Server domain cooperation is based on an interserver relationship called *trust*, which is used as a hedge against the inevitable network slowdown caused by the level of security that NT incorporates. Without trust, each time a user tried to use a file or other service from a server on the network, a complex series of authentication procedures would take place just to make sure the user was legitimate. To prevent this security-checking replication, servers have *trust relationships* with one another.

Multiprocessor Support

Both versions of NT support multiple processors running in the same machine. Although the standard NT version supports only one or two CPUs, NT Server allows up to four.

Adding CPUs is the perfect solution to sluggish performance as networks get larger, the application mix grows heavier, high throughput becomes a must, or custom applications grow too extensive. Of course, the traditional fix of adding RAM helps, too, and throwing CPUs at an NT machine running applications not written with multiprocessor execution in mind won't give you a leg up, to say the least. Although the NT Executive automatically dispatches threads to detected CPUs, effectively splitting up the workload across them, the application must be written to take advantage of NT's multithreading to do so. (NT itself handles dispatching threads to the detected CPUs.) Microsoft's SQL Server supports NT multiple threads on SMP systems, and other developers are following suit.

NT's CPU detection and performance upgrading is automatic. For example, a multi-CPU machine called the AcerFrame 3000 MP50 allows you to add additional 486 DX-50s at will. To get NT to recognize and use additional CPUs, simply plug in the new CPU cards and reboot NT. The NT kernel detects the additional computing power, and the thread dispatcher begins giving it tasks as soon as you run multithreaded applications.

NTFS File Services

Chief among NT's strong points is the NT File System (NTFS). Based largely on Microsoft's experience with OS/2, NTFS ups the ante over OS/2's High Performance File System (HPFS) by adding a few additional features.

As mentioned, NT can read and work with DOS (FAT) and HPFS disks in their native formats and convert them to the file system optimized for use with NT. Windows NT can also recognize and work with VFAT partitions created under Windows 95. Hard disk volumes can also be partitioned into a mix of all three. NT recognizes and works with directories and files from any host partition, meaning that you can share NTFS, FAT, and HPFS on a network. Other NT clients (actually running NT on their machines) will have access to any of the three file formats. Windows for Workgroups or other DOS-based systems can have access to shared FAT and NTFS partitions; however, NTFS long filenames will be truncated.

> **TIP**
>
> If you intend to share NTFS directories with non-NT workstations, you might want files in those directories to comply with standard "8.3" DOS-style filenames so that those workstations won't have to deal with truncated filenames.

Long Filenames

As Mac, OS/2, and now Windows 95 users (among others) will certainly agree, DOS's 8.3 filename restriction (eight characters, a period, and a three-letter extension) is a perennial frustration. Most PC people have grown used to it, but Microsoft seems to have finally gotten the message. NT allows names with up to 256 characters, including spaces and periods, and it differentiates between uppercase and lowercase letters.

> **NOTE**
>
> The uppercase/lowercase distinction applies only to the onscreen display of filenames, not to NT's recognition of filenames for access or execution. It's merely a visual convenience.

In File Manager, a typical file listing might look like this:

```
History of Asian Music
```

However, you can't create long filenames with any DOS or Windows 3.1 application; you get an error message stating that such a filename isn't valid. Only programs designed for NT allow the actual use of long filenames, so relief from DOS's naming limitation isn't going to be instantaneous. (Of course, you can rename files in NT's File Manager.)

The key question is, "What does NT do with filenames so that DOS and Windows 3.1 applications running under NT can use them?" When running under NT, these programs can access the NTFS directory, but normally they couldn't read the longer filenames.

Here's the trick: When you save a file with an NT application, it automatically generates a shorter, 11-character name that DOS and Windows 3.1 can read. That name is stored on disk along with the long filename, and Windows 95 users, when networked to the NTFS directory on the NT machine, can see the whole name. Figure 1.5 shows what happens to filenames when they're saved and reloaded with different operating systems and file formats.

FIGURE 1.5.

How NTFS serves long filenames to other operating systems.

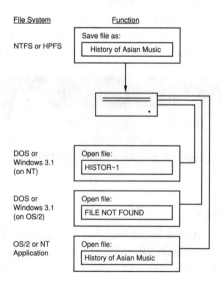

Summary

This chapter discusses the specific features that clearly make Windows NT one of the most powerful operating systems available for PCs. It compares NT to competing PC-based and mainframe-based operating systems on several points. Clearly, NT is much more powerful, flexible, and configurable than its predecessor, Windows 3.1, although they're almost identical in appearance. Windows 95 represents an important way station toward a full 32-bit model, but it too has limitations that are vestiges of DOS and Windows 3.*x*. More like UNIX or VMS in internal design, NT is much more portable, extensible, and practical because of the number of compatible applications it can run. In a nutshell, Windows NT offers the following:

- mature multitasking
- fault tolerance
- extensive networking abilities
- RPC support
- extensibility
- easy connectivity with Windows for Workgroups, Windows 95, LAN Manager, TCP/IP, and RAS
- backward compatibility with DOS, 16-bit Windows applications, some OS/2 packages, and character-based POSIX applications

Add to this NT's C2-level security compliance, and the package is complete. Despite the additional hardware requirements NT demands (particularly in the RAM and CPU departments), it's clearly an operating system with a bright future. Forthcoming Microsoft operating system products will definitely be based on the NT model, further ensuring NT's success. Windows NT should figure strongly in any far-sighted corporate or government projections for operating system and networking system allocations for this reason alone. It will eventually be on every laptop and desktop computer if Bill Gates and Microsoft get their way—and there's little to suggest they won't.

CHAPTER 2

The Architectural and Operational Design of Windows NT

IN THIS CHAPTER

Windows NT is a complex and capable operating system—certainly a far cry from its DOS/ Windows 3.1-combination predecessor. It's a full-blown multiuser operating system that borrows from sophisticated mainframe operating systems' design principles, such as preemptive multitasking and multithreading. You've also seen how NT compares to other PC and mainframe-based operating system alternatives like OS/2 and UNIX.

This chapter delves into the inner workings of NT, discussing its architectural design and some specific differences between 16-bit Windows and NT. NT 4 has introduced a few changes to the architecture of the operating system over the earlier 3.5*x* versions of NT. First, though, take a look at how NT fits into the overall Microsoft Windows strategy.

NT's Market Position

NT's appearance is deceiving. The first time I saw NT running, it was at a Microsoft-sponsored expo in San Francisco about a year before NT's release. Having written several books about Windows, I was quite interested in how NT's changes in user interface and overall functionality would affect rewrites of my existing books. I was surprised to find that, for the most part, it looked and acted just like Windows 95, with a few added applications (primarily administrative management tools for networks) thrown in.

Clearly, Microsoft has achieved what it set out to do: make potential NT users feel at home with a product that looks just like the Windows they know but is actually a very different animal. In fact, this is the design philosophy behind all Microsoft Windows products, from Modular Windows to Mobile Windows, Windows 3.1, Windows for Workgroups, Windows 95, and, finally, Windows NT. Other new Windows categories will be coming down the pike, such as Windows for interactive television. (The details for this medium are being hotly debated, but Microsoft is currently a big player in the discussions.)

Microsoft's bet is that once people are familiar with the Windows user interface, any version of it can be easily learned. Table 2.1 shows Microsoft's multiplatform market strategy for its Windows products.

Table 2.1. Microsoft's multilevel Windows products.

Product	Platform	Audience
Windows NT	High-end CISC and RISC machines, including those with up to 16 multiprocessors	Power users and corporations needing enterprise-wide network services and mainframe connectivity. Good platform for developing mainframe applications.

Product	Platform	Audience
Windows for Workgroups and Windows 95	IBM PCs and compatibles with Intel-compatible CPUs 386 and higher	Small businesses needing peer-to-peer networking or interconnectivity with NT. Many users say that even on a standalone system like a laptop, these are the versions of Windows to consider if you're not running Windows NT. The feature set of both is rich, and NT compatibility is high.
Windows 3.1/DOS or Windows 95	IBM PCs and compatibles with Intel-compatible CPUs	Most desktop PC application users who have no need for networking.
Modular Windows	Home interactive multimedia systems/pocket PDAs (personal data assistants) with various CPU types	Games and other services on home appliances; users who want small electronic organizers for different functions.

Windows NT sits at the top of the current heap, at least for the time being. Other high-end products are sure to appear, both to augment NT and to update other existing products (for example, Windows 95, BackOffice, and Internet server software packages). In any case, Microsoft emphasizes the painless transition as you move up the Windows ladder, in the hope of cornering the market on graphical user interfaces. The basics of Microsoft Windows's design are likely to endure for some time.

Some analysts believe that one of NT's main strengths is that it offers an excellent downsizing platform for corporate developers and, eventually, the perfect upsizing target for workstation users. For example, corporate folks can use the Microsoft C/C++, COBOL, and FORTRAN compilers on NT machines to develop applications for larger machines (where they usually need only recompiling if the programming code is written to be portable).

An Overview of NT's Design

Now that you've seen NT compared to other Microsoft operating systems, take a look at NT's inner workings. Composed of several million lines of code and costing 150 million dollars, it couldn't be undertaken without a great deal of forethought. Coding began only after a thorough architectural design and line of attack were agreed on by the main programmers and system architects. Much of the design, coding, and planning behind NT were the work of Dave

Cutler, who also developed an operating system for the DEC PDP-11 (called RSX-11M) and the VMS operating system that runs on the DEC VAX system.

The NT design model included several higher-order goals distinct from applications, tools, or utilities—that is, the inner functionality that's mostly invisible to the user. Fulfilling these goals is what makes Windows NT superior to its predecessor. Although other design issues exist, the main architectural premises were to give NT the following features:

- Compatibility with existing code
- Ability to be easily extensible
- Scalability
- Portability
- Networking ability, with distributed processing
- Security

The next sections briefly examine what each of these design goals means and how NT carries them out. Next, you'll take a look at NT's architectural model and components.

The NT System Model

To delve into NT's design, you first need an understanding of the basic model NT is based on. An operating system's functioning is very complex, requiring code built in many layers. Without a basic theoretical model to build on, an operating system's writers could easily become mired in the details of their own code. Decisions at critical points are harder to make without the model's guidance. Over the years, operating systems engineers have developed some basic theories (and resulting models) used when they design a new operating system; here are the three most common models:

- Monolithic
- Layered
- Client/server

User and Kernel Modes

All three models have one thing in common: They each divide operating system tasks into at least two categories—*user mode* and *kernel mode*. The kernel is the innermost (core) part of the operating system. Code that runs in kernel mode has access to system hardware and system data. To protect the operating system and stored data (such as files), only certain code is allowed to run in kernel mode. All other code, such as that for applications, runs in user mode.

In most operating systems, for example, applications run in user mode, so they don't have direct access to system resources, such as the hard disk. The user-mode application must ask the kernel to access the hard disk. The application isn't permitted to write directly to the disk, because a mistake in the writing process could scramble other unrelated data files—including the operating system itself.

> **NOTE**
>
> Some mainframe operating systems are actually divided into more than two modes (sometimes called *rings*) of the CPU to provide additional protection layers. The VAX, for instance, might use ring 0 for the kernel, but also use ring 1 for other kernel services (such as a database engine) and ring 2 for additional services while using ring 3 for the user portion of the operating system. An operating system can provide these extra extensions to offer more security and robustness. Microsoft could have implemented additional rings in NT but decided not to because of the software overhead needed for ring transitions; this decision resulted in faster performance and a more robust system model.

> **NOTE**
>
> Virus programs are an example of breaching this "containment field" approach. A virus program that writes to the boot tracks of a hard disk circumnavigates the user/kernel privilege agreement by using its own code to write to the hard disk, rather than asking the operating system (which would normally prevent the system-track modifications).

This distinction between the nonprivileged user mode and privileged kernel mode is important in understanding the differences between the three operating system models.

The Monolithic Model

In typical monolithic operating systems, many functions (or procedures) are built into the system. Each procedure can call another procedure, with messages passing between them. In other words, there's no central traffic cop ensuring the integrity of the messages or controlling the flow in a specific direction, so faulty programs can cause system failures. (See Figure 2.1.) It's also difficult to extend the system's functionality because monolithic systems usually aren't modular enough to allow one procedure to be updated without causing problems with other procedures.

The Layered Model

Layered systems are somewhat better at directing traffic flow because data can't be passed between procedures at random. Instead, it must be sent through a hierarchy of layers, much like a chain of military command. As in military communications, commands are passed downward only to lower layers, not upward. (See Figure 2.2.) This approach adds more structure to the way operations are performed; it also prevents lower layers from wreaking havoc on the whole system and helps with debugging. The layered system's more modular design makes replacing subsystems easier, so updating the operating system is simpler. In general, layered operating systems supply a much more resilient, stable backbone for computing systems than nonlayered models do.

FIGURE 2.1.

A flow diagram of a monolithic operating system.

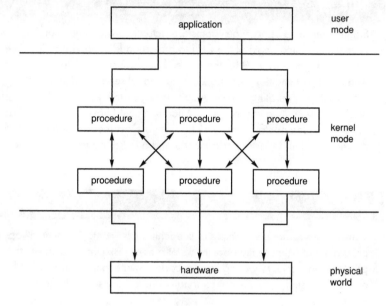

FIGURE 2.2.

A flow diagram of a layered operating system.

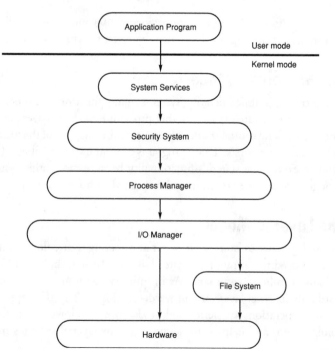

The Client/Server Model

NT's design draws heavily from the client/server model, treating applications as clients because they ask for services, such as having the operating system put a window on the screen or having data sent to the printer or written to a disk. These requests are made through the *NT Executive*, which manages the requests by queuing them up and passing them on to the appropriate servers, which supply canned functions built into the operating system. Because servers can supply their services to any number of clients (applications), the operating system's size is kept down.

> **NOTE**
>
> There's a distinction between client/server applied to networking models and client/server applied to an operating system's inner workings. In network discussions, client/server usually means client workstations and server workstations and sharing resources like printers and directories. In operating system models, client/server refers to sharing internal services.
>
> The same term is used in both cases because each has a client entity and a server entity and shares resources of one type or another. In NT, these models have more in common with one another than they do with some other operating system. An NT programmer can, for example, simply replace any RPC call in a program with an LPC call, and NT will request the service of the local computer (or vice versa). As a result, it's possible to distribute the operating system itself among multiple machines.

The NT Executive isn't limited to calling only local servers. NT's client/server model is extensive enough to support servers on other machines or other processors. NT can provide this support seamlessly, without the application caring about any network interactions that may be involved. (See Figure 2.3.)

FIGURE 2.3.

A flow diagram of a client/server operating system.

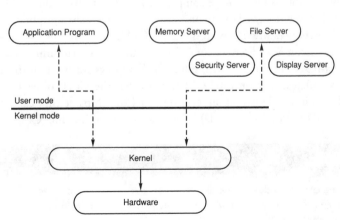

Compatibility

Any new operating system hoping to compete must offer high compatibility with existing software. For NT to stand a chance in the market, it had to offer new features *and* support existing features that users were familiar with. This meant NT had to be compatible not only with Microsoft products, but also with others. The design team finally decided that NT should be compatible with popular existing file systems, applications, and networks.

As discussed in Chapter 1, the final outcome was a compatibility mix not offered by other current operating system products (although OS/2 comes the closest). By using tricks like software emulation and making key software components modular, NT's compatibility with other products ended up as follows:

- Existing file system compatibility: FAT and Windows 95's VFAT.
- Existing application compatibility: DOS, Windows, Windows 95, OS/2 version 1.*x* character-based (except on MIPS and DEC Alpha, where OS/2 compatibility isn't available), LAN Manager, and POSIX-compliant applications.
- Existing networks: NetWare, Banyan VINES, LAN Manager, Windows for Workgroups; connectivity for TCP/IP, SNMP, SNA, NetBEUI, and data link control (DLC); remote access services to support Point-to-Point Protocol (PPP), Serial Line Internet Protocol (SLIP), and X.25 protocols.

Types of Compatibility

Compatibility is a difficult goal, requiring much patience and testing with existing applications. Sometimes, *reverse engineering* (analyzing an operating system by dissecting its components) is needed when operating system specifications aren't available.

Compatibility is made more complicated by variations in the CPUs of target computers. Because NT was designed to run on a variety of CPUs, existing applications that run on NT might not be *binary-compatible* with the target CPUs, meaning they might not work. Suppose a user wants to run WordPerfect for Windows under NT running on a MIPS R4000 or a DEC Alpha-based machine. WordPerfect for Windows was written to run under DOS/Windows 3.1—which means on Intel CPUs. However, the CPUs of MIPS and DEC machines have different internal instruction sets from Intel x86 chips, so they can't directly execute the binary code (.EXE files, for example) of programs written for Intel CPUs.

> **NOTE**
>
> The almost exclusive use of Intel processors in PCs means that PC users have been protected from most binary-compatibility issues. Intel's design philosophy (partly coordinated with Microsoft) has been to build in backward compatibility, allowing more recent chips, such as the 486 and the Pentium, to directly execute programs written even 10 years ago for 8086 and 8088 16-bit processors.

One way around this problem is to build *source-code compatibility* into the operating system instead of *binary compatibility,* requiring each application to be recompiled into new binary code for each CPU. Users would have to purchase new versions of each application they wanted to run on a different CPU, just as they do now when faced with the incompatibility of Macintosh and PC programs. For this reason, source-code compatibility was an unacceptable solution.

Environment Subsystems

To solve this binary-compatibility problem, NT uses *environment subsystems,* which intercept binary code requests from a CPU or operating system and translate them into instructions NT can successfully execute.

An environment subsystem is really just a program, called a *virtual machine,* that makes an application act as though it's running on its own machine (or at least is in the environment it was written for). When a DOS program runs in the DOS subsystem, for example, it behaves as though it were the only program running on a PC. When it asks DOS to print to the printer, write to the screen, read the keyboard, or read a sector from the hard disk, it seems to be interacting with DOS, even though it isn't. The DOS environment subsystem is programmed to respond to the application so that its system calls are responded to properly.

When you try to run any type of program in NT, here's what happens:

1. NT tries to determine what type of environment the program is designed for. If the program type isn't recognized, an error message is generated, and nothing happens.

2. If NT does recognize the program type, it calls up the necessary environment subsystem.

3. NT loads the program into the environment and executes it.

As the program is running, the environment subsystem is busy translating different program types, including actual CPU instructions. However, because many applications that run on NT are actually written for and can execute on Intel-compatible processors, most of the translations are for API calls.

> **NOTE**
>
> APIs, or *application programming interfaces,* are tools built into operating systems used to help perform a task in a program. For example, an API might put a window or dialog box onscreen at a certain location or store a file on the hard disk.

For an environment subsystem to successfully run programs written for the environment it's emulating, it has to recognize calls to the source operating system's API and translate (map) them to NT APIs that effectively perform the same functions.

Suppose an OS/2 application running under NT asks to write a file to the disk because the user wants to save some work. The OS/2 application calls the appropriate OS/2 API for writing to the disk. The application doesn't recognize that it's running in a simulated OS/2 environment under NT, but that doesn't matter. NT's OS/2 environment subsystem intercepts the disk call and maps it to an NT (Win32) call. This call is then passed to the NT Executive, which carries out the task—writing the file to the disk.

Running programs under NT gives you the advantages of more security and functionality (such as multiprocessor support and disk fault-tolerance). For example, NT prevents programs of different types from "stepping on each other," which can cause system crashes. It does this by giving each subsystem its own memory space that can't be touched by other subsystems or programs. For this reason, the environment subsystems are called *protected subsystems*. Working with the NT Executive and I/O functions also lets you write data to the disk in many formats, as discussed earlier. Using the environment subsystem also allows applications to run faster, using more advanced CPU arrangements, such as multiple processors or superfast processors like DEC Alpha 150s.

Because NT's environment subsystems are written as standalone server modules (remember the client/server operating system model), they can easily be replaced or upgraded. You can also add modified environments if you discover program bugs or want extensions to NT.

Environment Subsystem Details

NT 4 has several environment subsystems; each supplies a specific environment and API to programs:

- Win32
- DOS
- Windows 3.*x*
- OS/2
- POSIX

NT treats the environment subsystems as servers, so they can have many clients, meaning each can serve several applications at once. If, for example, you're running two Windows 3.1 applications, both are managed by the same copy of the Windows 3.1 environment subsystem. This subsystem's API server can be called by both applications to perform the same functions, and the subsystem decides which one to serve first. Because only one copy of the code provides the service, the effects of maintaining duplicate resources are minimized.

Also note that each subsystem operates in user mode, rather than in kernel mode. This helps protect the operating system's kernel from faulty subsystems or applications.

The Win32 Subsystem

Of the four environment subsystems, the Win32 subsystem is the most central to NT's functioning. It controls the NT interface—the screen, keyboard, input, and mouse activities for whatever you're doing in NT, even if you're running an OS/2 or another type of program. The other subsystems—OS/2, DOS/Windows, and POSIX—all send their translated API calls to the Win32 subsystem for execution. Because it's also used to run 32-bit programs written for NT or Windows 95, this subsystem does double duty. Figure 2.4 illustrates the relationship between the other subsystems and the Win32 subsystem.

FIGURE 2.4.

The relationship of the environment subsystems.

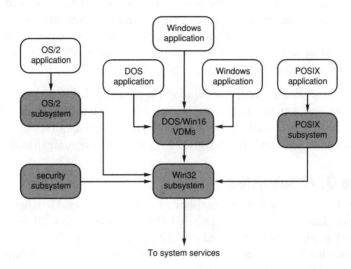

To system services

2

ARCHITECTURAL
AND OPERATIONAL
DESIGN

The DOS Subsystem

Because DOS isn't a multitasking operating system, its subsystem differs from the others. When you try to run a DOS program, NT launches the DOS protected subsystem, which creates a *Virtual DOS Machine* (*VDM*). A VDM is an emulator that creates a simulated or virtual PC with its own 16M of segmented memory space, required device drivers, support for most memory managers, and I/O system call support. For DOS applications, each one you launch gets its own VDM and separate "DOS window," just as it does in Windows 3.*x*.

The DOS VDM window under NT is compatible with all the DOS 5.0 specifications, and it operates properly as long as the DOS application uses the DOS system calls for all input and output and doesn't try to access hardware directly. When an I/O request is trapped (detected) by the subsystem, it's passed on to the NT Executive (or, in some cases, the Win32 API) and processed. An application that tries to write directly to hardware is terminated, and you'll see an onscreen message to that effect.

There are two interesting additions to the NT DOS window in NT 4. First, you can launch Windows NT applications from it by entering the .EXE filename at the command prompt. Second, you can change the window's foreground and background colors—something that should have been included in Windows 3.1!

The 16-Bit Windows Subsystem

The 16-bit Windows environment subsystem is actually based on the DOS VDM. When you launch a 16-bit Windows application, NT creates a new VDM. This VDM is a simulated PC with DOS running and with 16M of virtual memory assigned.

After the VDM is created, the Windows emulator (WOW, discussed in Chapter 1) is loaded, giving you a multitasking simulation (cooperative rather than preemptive, however) of Windows 3.1. Although it supplies all the APIs of 16-bit Windows, its internal structure is different. System calls made by an application are mapped to Win32 calls and executed by the Win32 subsystem or the NT Executive.

As with DOS programs, any Windows application that tries direct hardware access fails; the call is trapped by NT and the application is terminated. However, multiple Windows applications don't need additional VDMs, as multiple DOS applications do. Each 16-bit Windows application launched after the first one is set up as a separate thread within the same WOW.

The OS/2 Subsystem

The OS/2 subsystem is less complicated, at least in theory. First, because the base NT configuration supports only character-based OS/2 programs, no GUI support is required. Second, OS/2 applications are designed with 32-bit multiuser capabilities, so the protected-mode subsystem has less mapping to do. A VDM isn't necessary—just a subsystem that correctly maps the OS/2 calls to the related NT services.

NOTE

NT won't run OS/2 2.x or OS/2 Warp applications—only character-mode applications that run under OS/2 1.x.

The POSIX Subsystem

As discussed in Chapter 1, different interface standards exist for UNIX applications and systems. UNIX is so ubiquitous, and used by so many institutions that have tried to modify it, that there are few standards—especially when it comes to user interfaces.

POSIX, a response to this problem, is an attempt to standardize UNIX application code so it can be more easily ported to other systems. NT's POSIX subsystem currently supports only character-based applications, so once again, the subsystem isn't as complex as one that, for example, emulates a Motif GUI. No VDM is created—just a protected space to run the application and a call interceptor that remaps calls to the Win32 environment subsystem and NT Executive. As with the other systems, illegal hardware calls are trapped by the NT Executive.

Extensibility

Making NT flexible and extensible was a high priority for NT designers. *Extensibility* in applications and operating system software allows a programmer to quickly and cost-efficiently upgrade or extend the software's functionality. Rapidly changing requirements for computer hardware and application hardware mean that an operating system's extensibility is important to its continued success. For this reason, NT was written to allow modifications for future upgrades and porting to other computer classes with relatively few complications.

As you've seen, NT's design is modular, which makes extensibility easy. For example, the environment subsystems, although closely woven into NT's while running, are actually standalone modules that can be rewritten separately and plugged into NT, if needed. They aren't even loaded into memory unless they're needed.

Similarly, NT's other major components are written and function as modules: the security subsystem, the hardware abstraction layer (HAL), and the NT Executive (kernel, I/O Manager, Object Manager, security reference monitor, process monitor, local procedure call (LPC) facility, and Virtual Memory Manager).

How does extensibility work? If you've experimented with the Windows 3.1 Control Panel or File Manager, you've probably noticed that they're both modular and extensible (though they're much simpler programs, of course, than NT). They can easily be upgraded to supply new services to the user, without requiring any changes to the core application. You just need to alter the initialization file listing for File Manager (WINFILE.INI) or add .CPL files to the system directory for the Control Panel.

NT can grow to match the needs of its users by replacing an old module with a new one. Modularity is such a strong feature in NT that many system services can be started by using the Control Panel's Services applet after NT is running. Future upgrades of NT (unlike DOS) will probably consist of a disk with a few add-on modules that can support a new class of applications, fix a bug, or offer new services, such as extra security or network protocol support.

If Microsoft is responsive to user requests for extensibility, availability might not be a problem. At the worst, Microsoft might at least share enough code with other software vendors so that extensions to NT become available through other channels. Time will tell how generous Microsoft intends to be in sharing its operating system code. No doubt deals with vendors will be limited to those that pose no threat to Microsoft's future marketing of its own NT extensions.

Symmetric Multiprocessing

As mentioned in Chapter 1, NT uses symmetric multiprocessing as its model for scalability. Figures 2.5 and 2.6 illustrate the differences between symmetric and asymmetric multiprocessing.

FIGURE 2.5.

In symmetric multiprocessing, all processing (including the operating system and applications) is spread among available CPUs.

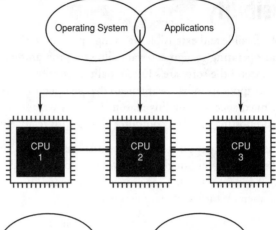

FIGURE 2.6.

In asymmetric multiprocessing, the operating system code is run by one CPU; the other CPUs run applications.

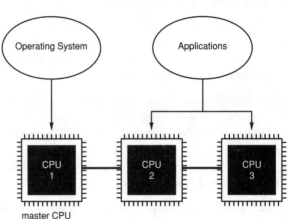

Using symmetric methodology means that the operating system is less likely to come to a standstill if the master CPUs stop functioning for some reason. Also, because operating system tasks can be handed off to other processors, the system runs more smoothly and efficiently.

Asymmetric operating systems are easier to design and build and can even be monolithic. Using symmetric processing efficiently, on the other hand, is more difficult and requires that the operating system itself be threaded or broken down into separate processes. The benefits, however, are great. For example, operating system subtasks can be routed to different processors, increasing system efficiency and avoiding underuse of CPUs. I/O processing could be handled by one CPU while the security subsystem, for example, is handled by another.

Scalability

Scalability refers to an operating system's ability to take advantage of additional resources—particularly CPU resources that might be added to a computer's hardware arsenal. When installed on a uniprocessor machine, NT's Thread Manager sends all processes to the only CPU in the system. When there's only one processor, however, system performance can be slowed by bottlenecks in the single-thread queue.

Because of its internal design, NT isn't necessarily bound by single-CPU constraints. NT's built-in CPU detection lets it automatically redirect threads and processes to available CPUs (from 1 to 16), increasing system operational throughput. To support multiple CPUs in an Intel-based machine, the system must have been designed for multiprocessors from the start. You can't just add another CPU to an existing single-CPU system. On the other hand, most RISC and CISC systems support easy installation of extra CPUs.

> **NOTE**
>
> Only Windows NT programs are designed to take advantage of the multithreading benefits of scalability. Even if a developer writes a program using the Win32 API, that doesn't mean the program can use multiprocessors; it has to use the multithreading hooks in the API.
>
> Also, the Win32s subset of the Win32 API doesn't support multithreading, so although it can create programs that will run under both Windows 3.x and Windows NT, these programs won't benefit from multiple processors. That doesn't mean that overall system throughput won't improve with multiple processors, just that an application might not work as quickly or smoothly as it could. You might have to wait for a word processor to quit printing (or at least spooling to the Print Manager) before you can get back to writing, or for a spreadsheet to recalculate before entering more numbers. Win32 programs also don't benefit from NT's application-level security features.
>
> You can work around this problem, however, if there are enough CPUs to provide one CPU per application. Even if the application isn't written to take advantage of symmetric multi-processing, NT can route the application to an idle CPU, which might execute the application more quickly than if its threads were split between multiple CPUs tied up with other tasks.

Portability

One of UNIX's best features is that it has been ported to many other platforms. UNIX or UNIX work-alikes run on CPUs ranging from 8-bit Zilog Z-80s running in tandem (using a UNIX spin-off called Micronix) to 32-bit and larger CPUs from Texas Instruments, AMD, and Motorola. UNIX is available for many different workstations—DEC, Sun, IBM, Silicon Graphics, and Hewlett-Packard, to name a few. Obviously, UNIX's calling card is flexibility. The result? Users can upgrade their hardware without having to throw away their operating systems and applications.

DOS users have also enjoyed a certain degree of flexibility. Upward mobility from 8088s all the way to Pentiums has been a great boon to Microsoft (which has strongly promoted DOS) and DOS users. With little effort except the expense, most users have brought their favorite

DOS and Windows applications up through the ranks of CPUs to super-fast 32-bit processors that were unaffordable only a few years ago. The vast number of PC clones in the workplace has forced hardware prices down to rock-bottom levels, making powerful systems available even to students on shoestring budgets.

Still, DOS and Windows have required Intel or Intel-compatible (because of legal judgments that allow other chip manufacturers to compete with Intel) CPUs to run. UNIX, on the other hand, has more platform independence.

With NT, Microsoft wants to make dependence on Intel a thing of the past. With modular design and code portability in mind, NT can already be run on CISC and RISC chips in different formations. The Intel 80x86, MIPS R4000, and DEC Alpha currently are supported, too. Other CPUs can be accommodated in the future by recompiling NT's modules (using software compilers).

However, although Microsoft claims that 32-bit NT applications are fully portable, requiring only a "simple recompile," that claim doesn't represent the whole picture. Applications still have to go through trouble-shooting, and software developers must decide whether they have enough support resources before jumping onto a new hardware platform. You'll probably see many 32-bit applications on Intel-based NT before seeing much for MIPS or Alpha. Software manufacturers are already cautious enough about jumping on the NT bandwagon without having to decide whether they should fine-tune their programs for other CPUs.

Another downside concerning portability is that DOS and Windows 3.1 applications are written for Intel chips, so if you're upgrading your NT system with a MIPS or Alpha and you want to run DOS and Windows programs, you might be disappointed in performance. You'll get great performance (especially with the 150 MHz Alpha) with 32-bit programs written for the host machine, but DOS and Windows 3.*x* programs will be run through emulators that might slow down the applications' performance. Depending on how the application is written (the ratio of native CPU code to the number of API calls), it might run faster, but testing is probably needed to determine that. Before you switch to another NT platform, you should do some research or perform some real-life experiments.

On the bright side, NT's portability could spark a lively competition between CPU makers, meaning users would benefit from a CPU speed and price war. You can expect to see serious NT-compatible workstations go through an evolution similar to that of DOS workstations.

Networking with Distributed Processing

As you know, Windows NT has networking built in. NT's base version and NT Server support peer-to-peer and client/server networking topologies. An NT network can be constructed "out of the box" with just network cards and cables, or it can be added to an existing network, such as a Novell or LAN Manager client/server system. This type of plug-and-play functionality has been well implemented in NT. Whether you want to give up your investment in your current network operating system is another question. There will probably be some bugs to fix if you switch immediately to NT or NT Server, and (as mentioned in Chapter 1) NT Server isn't exactly inexpensive, so for large enterprise-wide networks, you need to consider the per-server price tag.

> **NOTE**
>
> When you're pricing network server software (and even application software), make sure you factor in licensing fees. The upfront cost of NT Server might be higher, but the overall cost could be lower. Licensing fees aren't issued based on the number of client connections per server, but rather on a per-service basis. Server and client licenses have been separated. A single server license is required for each physical server on the network, but a single client license can connect to an unlimited number of servers.

Another feature that might tip the scales in NT's favor is network-related, too—distributed processing. NT implements something called *remote procedure calls*, or *RPCs*. Similar to the *local procedure calls* that operating systems like NT sometimes use to send messages between applications, RPCs are calls that a computer running an application can send to another computer for CPU help. NT's multithreading is designed to support RPCs to distant computers spread across a network. In an ideal arrangement, if an NT server finds itself bogged down in a large queue of threads, it can dispatch or offload some threads to other processors on the network, thus lightening its own burden. This spreads the CPU's chores out to idle networked CPUs in much the same way that multiple processors coexisting on the local machine cooperate.

Security

Besides the environment subsystems, there's another type of subsystem: an *integral subsystem*. NT has several integral subsystems, but the main one is the *security subsystem*. This subsystem is a user-mode client, just like the environment subsystems; however, its sole purpose is to provide security for the NT system.

For example, a user who hasn't been granted rights might try to access the system. The security subsystem prevents this by requiring a password for each user. If the password is entered incorrectly, the user is denied access to the system. Also, each user can have a set of specific privileges controlling his or her level of access to the system resources—files, directories, drives, networks, modems, ports, and so on. The system administrator assigns these privileges to the user.

Virtually all aspects (inner and outer) of NT are overseen by security management services that make NT quite secure. Windows NT meets U.S. government requirements for C2-level security. This isn't the highest level of security for an operating system, but it's high enough for the bulk of work run on computers.

> **NOTE**
>
> NT can be upgraded to B2-level security in future custom versions.

The NT Executive

In this chapter, I've referred to the NT Executive several times. The Executive is the heart of NT's architecture, and it includes everything except the protected-mode subsystems and the actual hardware.

Recall that the operating system code can run in two modes—user (unprivileged) mode and kernel (privileged) mode—and that all the subsystems (such as the DOS, POSIX, and OS/2 environment subsystems) run in user mode. By contrast, the NT Executive runs in kernel mode, which means it has access to all of NT's critical internal data structures and procedures. Figure 2.7 shows where the Executive fits into the picture.

FIGURE 2.7.

The NT Executive forms the heart of Windows NT.

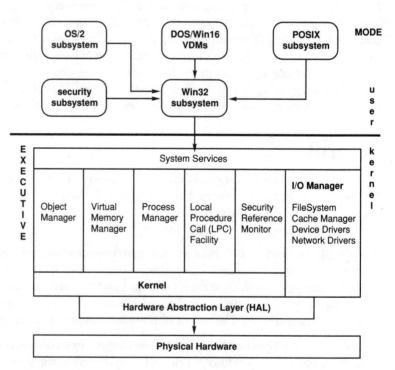

Note in Figure 2.7 that the NT Executive is composed of all the components pictured below the dark line, except for the hardware. It supplies all the *native services* the client environment subsystems can't—virtual memory management, I/O, thread scheduling, and so forth. When a subsystem needs a service performed, it sends the call to the appropriate NT Executive manager. NT runs in the restricted kernel mode for a moment to protect itself from foreign intervention, then performs the requested action. When the task is done, control returns to the calling party (typically a subsystem).

The System Services Module

Actually, when a subsystem asks to have a service performed (such as getting memory allocated for a program you just launched), it must ask the System Services module to handle it. The System Services module then sends the message to the Virtual Memory Manager (VMM). The same procedure would take place in other services. When a program is launched, for example, NT must supply at least one thread for it. The subsystem would request a thread from System Services, which in turn asks the appropriate manager for the thread. Control returns to the subsystem only after the thread is created.

When System Services is used as the buffer between the subsystems and the Executive services and managers, critical components of NT can be more easily updated. Take your local telephone system, for example. If a central switching office didn't connect your phone to other phone lines, making changes to numbers or services could mean major rewiring. The phone company might have to run new wires across town or even across the country. By using central offices, the phone company can easily change and update equipment, change phone numbers, and change services. The System Services portion of the Executive works in much the same way.

The Other Modules

These eight modules make up the remainder of the Executive:

- Object Manager
- Virtual Memory Manager
- Process Manager
- Local Procedure Call Facility
- Security Reference Monitor
- I/O Manager
- System Kernel
- Hardware Abstraction Layer

Each of these modules performs a specific type of task necessary for NT's internal operation. Because this book isn't intended for programmers or computer scientists, but for professionals managing NT-based systems, I won't go into much depth on each of them.

The Object Manager

Although it's not truly an object-oriented operating system, NT does use so-called "objects" as the basic operating element for interactions between user mode and kernel mode—for example, when a subsystem needs access to shared resources.

An *object* is a data structure that represents a service that can be shared by more than one process. For example, a physical device, such as a port, could be shared by several applications. When port access is requested, the source subsystem calls the Service Manager and asks for it. The Service Manager then calls the Object Manager, which creates a new object representing the request. Even invisible processes like threads can be objects, so they're a little hard to visualize.

By creating objects, NT (and programmers) can more easily keep track of system resources, such as shared memory, ports, processes, and files. In a sense, it democratizes important events and resources in an NT session by giving them a *handle*. After getting a handle, all these types of objects—whether a physical resource, a process, or an event—can be dealt with uniformly by the Object Manager and other NT modules. For example, the Security Reference Monitor can examine an object for validation or prevent its unauthorized use.

The Object Manager makes sure that objects don't gobble up too much memory and that there aren't too many objects of a specific type (which might overrun system resources). It also gets rid of objects that seem to have been abandoned by their source ("garbage collection"), which can happen when an application terminates improperly.

The Virtual Memory Manager

Virtual memory is simulated RAM memory. When RAM memory is low, NT uses hard-disk space to simulate what looks like RAM space to applications, but is actually the result of temporarily "swapping" data in RAM to the hard disk to free up RAM for the requested activity. The result looks and acts like a computer system with more RAM memory than what's physically there. Later, the data is read back into RAM. The advantage of virtual memory is cost; hard-disk space is much cheaper than physical RAM. The disadvantage is reduced speed because hard-disk reading and writing are much slower than RAM-based data transfer.

The Virtual Memory Manager manages the virtual memory for each process that might request it. This task means preventing processes from overwriting other virtual memory "pages" on disk and managing other options, such as preventing swapping to disk in cases when an application requests faster performance.

The Process Manager

The Process Manager's job is to create and terminate processes and threads when calling applications need them. If an application wants to create a new process, for example, the request is sent through the active server environment subsystem to the System Services module. It's then sent to the Process Manager, which creates a formal process request to send to the Object Manager, which creates an identity for it. The process is then started.

When the process is finished (for example, the file is fully written to disk), the Process Manager terminates the thread.

The Local Procedure Call (LPC) Facility

The LPC Facility's job is to supply a communication link between two threads that belong to separate processes. (Remember that processes are composed of threads—at least one thread per process.) For example, the printing and editing functions of a word processor could be coded into the application as two separate threads.

Sometimes separate threads need to exchange data. A spellchecker written as a separate thread might want to pass a correctly spelled word to the editor for placement in a document. Normally, there's no easy avenue for this data passage because threads are executed by the CPU as separate entities. In this case, when one thread needs to send data to another thread belonging to a separate process, the LPC Facility steps in. Message passing is done by requisitioning a temporary memory pool from which the data is handed off to the second thread. After the handoff, the memory is freed up for other use.

The Security Reference Monitor

As mentioned, the Object Manager often works with the Security Reference Monitor to make sure objects aren't accessed (accidentally or intentionally) by unauthorized users. A user can be an actual person (someone trying to access a file or a port, for instance), or it can be a process, thread, or some kind of event. In any case, preventing illegal attempts to access objects is called *object access control*, and this is what the Security Reference Monitor does.

All processes in NT are given an *access token*, which lists the permissions (rights) granted to the user who started the process. Typically, these rights are assigned by the system administrator to a specific user. Say the user is Joe, who starts a process (a word processor, for example) that tries to access an object, such as a file. Each object has a list of access rights (called an *access control list*, or *ACL*), so when Joe's process tries to access the file, the file's ACL and Joe's access token are compared by the Security Manager. It checks whether Joe has permission to use the file. If the ACL and access token compare favorably, the object is made available to Joe's process, the file opens, and Joe can start editing the document. Otherwise, access is denied and a dialog box onscreen warns the user of an illegal attempt. In some cases, NT just doesn't display certain objects—directories, printers, menu items, and so forth—that are out-of-bounds for a certain category of user.

NT's Security Reference Monitor is intelligent in the way it does its security checks. Rather than checking the lists against each other every time Joe wants access to the file (for example, each time the file is saved during a working session), NT checks only the first time. This prevents the system from slowing to a crawl when many processes and users log onto the system and begin working.

The I/O Manager

Input/output systems are one of the more complex issues in computer science and operating systems design. Interfacing with the outside world often takes a little spit and baling wire, so getting printers, modems, data-acquisition devices, video displays, SCSI devices, keyboards, mice, and other objects to work correctly and efficiently is often a nightmare. Programmers often have to work *around* an operating system (DOS or a combination of DOS and Windows, for example) just to get an application or peripheral to work well enough to keep users happy.

NT's I/O Manager tries to make life easier for both users and programmers. First, one of its features allows most I/O software drivers to be loaded on-the-fly without restarting Windows NT. So while NT is running, you can power up a tape drive unit, a network card, a new printer, an external CD-ROM drive, or whatever, then load the driver in NT and you're up and running. This feature is especially important in large networks, where taking down the server just to load a new driver would be a nuisance. Second, NT's I/O system is designed so that removing and installing new drivers of any sort (including file system drivers, like those for FAT, HPFS, and NTFS) can be done as a module replacement.

NOTE

Unfortunately, not all NT drivers can be loaded and unloaded without a reboot. Loading a new video or tape backup driver, for example, requires a reboot.

The I/O Manager's job is to process applications' I/O requests. Here's how the I/O Manager handles an I/O request: When an application asks for an I/O service, such as sending data to a printer, the message first goes through the environment subsystem running the application. It's then passed through System Services to the I/O Manager. The I/O Manager determines which driver should be used and sends the data to it in the form of an I/O request packet, or IRP. The driver then processes the data accordingly for the physical device, which often requires some sort of translation—for example, into PostScript code for one type of printer or into HPCL code for an HP printer. After the data is successfully sent to the device (through The Hardware Abstraction Layer explained later in this chapter), the driver returns the IRP to the I/O Manager, which deletes the packet. Figure 2.8 illustrates this process.

The System Kernel

The kernel is the Grand Central Station of NT. Almost everything that happens in NT passes through the kernel in one way or another. NT's kernel is of the "microkernel" variety, a scaled-down version of larger kernels used in big systems like UNIX and Digital Equipment Corporation's VMS operating system. Some of this scaling down was done by offloading traditional kernel chores to the Executive modules discussed in the previous sections.

FIGURE 2.8.

A flow diagram of the I/O process.

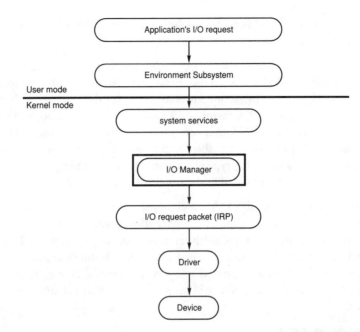

Still, the kernel plays a key role in NT's operation. Its main job is to schedule and dispatch threads and processes, so it continually queues up data, sends it to the CPU(s), and routes it after processing. The kernel also handles interrupts from sources such as the keyboard or other physical devices and is responsible for managing *exceptions*—error conditions resulting from system violations such as divide-by-zero errors or attempts to write over protected memory areas.

The kernel also synchronizes multiple CPUs by carefully managing how data threads are divided up between them and prepares and restarts the system in case of a power failure.

The Hardware Abstraction Layer

Ideally, NT's design is so modular that running it on different computers requires replacing just the Hardware Abstraction Layer and some of the I/O drivers. This might turn out to be true someday. Based on its experience with installable device drivers in DOS, and then with even greater system independence in Windows, Microsoft has realized that keeping hardware as far out of the operating system as possible is the way to ensure success in the operating system market.

One of Windows' strongest selling points, for example, has been that it's easy to write software drivers for many different types of screens, printers, mouses, SCSI devices, sound cards, video cards, and other hardware items. This isolates Windows and DOS from their supporting hardware on any given system. As a result, application developers know that if their programs run on one Windows machine, they're likely to run on another—regardless of whether that system's screen has VGA, SVGA, or other resolution, and regardless of what printer, network, keyboard, or mouse is attached.

NT takes this hardware isolation approach a step further by using not only device drivers, but also a whole replaceable layer of the operating system responsible for interacting with the hardware: the Hardware Abstraction Layer, or HAL. It's the final barrier between the system hardware (including the CPU, memory, I/O ports, keyboard, video, and so forth) and the rest of NT. The only parts of NT that communicate directly with the HAL are the kernel and the I/O drivers. Applications, the other Executive modules, and the environment subsystems don't know anything about what type of computer they're running on, what type or number of processors are involved, or whether the system is on a network.

Ideally, using a replaceable HAL module will allow NT to be ported to any number of system types with minimal recoding of the Executive modules and the system kernel. This may be overly hopeful, because there are differences in the way dissimilar CPUs and support hardware (such as caches and hardware memory managers) schedule and process data. Such management is a part of the HAL, so some rewriting seems inevitable. However, abstracting a system's hardware layer as much as possible will keep rewrite time to a minimum.

Summary

This chapter has discussed the architecture and operational design of Windows NT, covered the features of the modules and subsystems that make up NT, and showed the importance of these elements in a modern, extensible operating system. You have also learned about the overall design philosophy that the Microsoft and NT design team applied while developing the system.

You should now have a pretty good handle on what NT is, how it compares to competitive operating systems and GUIs, and where it fits into the Microsoft marketing strategy. You should also have a good understanding of NT's modular structure and overall operational design.

> **NOTE**
>
> Administrative tools, such as the User Manager, Registry Editor, and Event Viewer, are covered in Part II, "Windows NT System Administration."

Working with Windows NT

IN THIS CHAPTER

CHAPTER 3

This chapter covers the basics of working with Windows NT. The primary focus is on running applications under NT, and working with user-oriented Control Panel settings (as opposed to administrator-related settings). For these discussions, I assume that you're familiar with Windows 95's use of these programs, so the emphasis is on differences between Windows 95 and Windows NT. However, I have included some review material in case you're a little rusty on your Windows techniques, or if you're a user on an NT network or workstation who isn't a Windows "jock."

One of the first differences you might notice with NT is that you're asked to log onto the system before you gain access to anything. The logon information (username and password) lies at the heart of the NT security system. After the username and password are correctly entered, all resource privileges assigned to a user by the administrator, such as access to drives, directories, applications, printers, and backup devices, go into effect.

Although pressing Ctrl+Alt+Delete causes a DOS machine to reboot, it doesn't have the same effect on NT. This key combination is used to thwart potential "Trojan horse" viruses or programs that attempt to bypass NT's security system by luring users into typing their passwords into phony dialog boxes. When you press Ctrl+Alt+Delete, NT tries to flush out any such insidious programs, and it brings up the NT Logon dialog box.

When starting a Windows NT session, you have to log in with a valid username and (usually) a password. The system administrator assigns the username when making a new account for a user, and the name must be unique.

NOTE

You set up accounts with the User Manager program, explained in Chapter 10, "Optimizing Windows NT: Performance Determinants."

On a single-person system, only one user account and one administrator account are likely to be in use. In fact, if during installation you opt to skip setting up a user account, only the administrator account is set up. (The administrator always has at least one account.)

The user always selects the password, and the system administrator can enforce the user to change it regularly. To change the password, the user can press Ctrl+Alt+Delete after logging onto NT. (Changing the password is covered in Chapters 10 and 12, "An Overview of Windows NT Networking.")

After you click OK in the password dialog box, NT checks the password database. If the fields in the database don't match, you see an error message. Press Enter and try typing the password again. If the account policy for this user account has the Account lockout option enabled, the account is locked after the maximum number of attempts have been made within the selected time frame. This feature prevents would-be intruders from breaking in by trying a series of incremental entries. You can turn on the account by clearing the Account Locked checkbox for the user account in User Manager.

If you were using files on another workstation's drives the last time you ran NT, NT tries to restore those connections, as they're called, when you log on.

If the remote computer to which your NT system is trying to reconnect isn't online, or its directories aren't shared for network use, you see an error message.

Clicking Yes in response to this message isn't like a "Retry" in DOS; rather, it causes NT to abandon the attempt to make the current connection (the one listed in the dialog box) and move to the next one. Clicking No abandons the process for any and all connections that were made and saved from the previous session.

Typically, failure to connect is the result of other workstations not being online or having failed to republish (share) the directories to which you were previously connected. This situation often occurs at the start of a new workday, because not everyone powers up at the same time. In this case, NT adds the appropriate drive icons to either Network Neighborhood or My Computer, just as though the connection had been made, but doesn't actually make the connection. Clicking the drive icon or performing some other action that calls on the remote drive initiates an attempt to reconnect. If the workstation is then online, the process works as expected. Typically, all you have to do is click Yes for each dialog box that appears. If a reconnection can't be made, an error dialog box explaining the problem appears.

Organizing Applications

The NT Program Manager used in Windows NT 3.5 and Windows 3.1 has been replaced with the Windows 95 GUI, using a Start box to display all program groups, as shown in Figure 3.1. If you're used to Windows 95, the interface is similar.

FIGURE 3.1.

The Windows NT interface is like that of Windows 95.

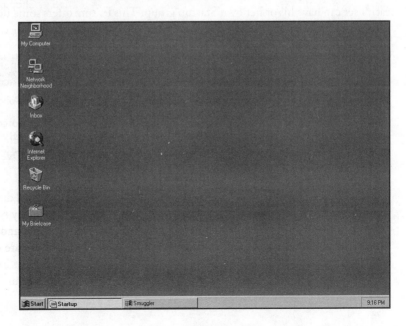

Notice the familiar layout of the Start button's options. If you chose to migrate settings from an existing Windows 95 installation when you ran NT Setup, you might have a few additional groups yet retain most of your Windows 95 interface.

Unlike the single group icon type in Windows 3.1, NT has two types: personal and common. When you create a new program group (as explained later in this chapter), you can declare which type it is. Personal icons appear only during a session in which the user who created them has logged onto the system. Common icons appear to all users, regardless of who has logged on.

By using the common icon, administrators can more easily give all the users on a machine access to a suite of applications or documents. For example, if the computer is in the Finance department, you might want all users to have access to Quicken, Excel, and 1-2-3. Just create a common group with these icons in it, and all users will then see that group in their Startup menus.

NOTE

The downside to this arrangement is that any user on the workstation can alter common groups. If one user modifies the group by adding or deleting icons, rearranging them, or altering their properties, this change affects all workstation users.

Startup Group

The Startup group has the same function in NT as in Windows 95. The only difference is that each user can have his or her own Startup group. This feature offers some flexibility for system administrators because it allows for fine-tuning the NT environment for each user.

TIP

You might want to create several NT setups for yourself, with specific applications groups, applications, documents, startup applications, and desktop arrangements. To do so, you have to create multiple user identities for yourself with User Manager (explained in Chapter 10) and then set up the Startup menu to your liking and save the configuration.

Adding New Folders

With Windows NT, as with Windows 95, you can create, move, copy, and delete folders and icons. In the following sections, I provide reminders in case your skills are rusty.

Adding Icons

To add a new folder or shortcut, follow these steps:

1. Right-click anywhere on the screen where no window or existing icon appears. From the pop-up menu, choose New.

2. Choose the type of item you want to create, such as a folder or shortcut. A new folder appears on the desktop with the name underneath, waiting for you to enter a name. (See Figure 3.2.)

FIGURE 3.2.

When a new folder is created, you can enter any name you want.

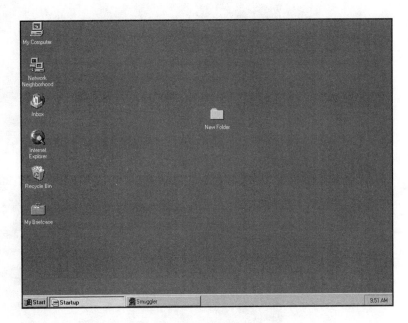

3. Finish entering the name of the folder. After you name the folder, you can set the characteristics of the folder or shortcut. Right-click the folder, and from the pop-up menu that appears, choose Properties. The Properties sheet then appears, as shown in Figure 3.3.

At the bottom of the General page, you can set permissions for this new folder. Click the parameters you want to set.

On the Sharing page, shown in Figure 3.4, you can decide whether the folder is to be shared. If you don't want to share the folder, leave the default at Not Shared. Otherwise, set the sharing as you need it.

FIGURE 3.3.

Using the Properties sheet for a newly created folder, you can set its characteristics.

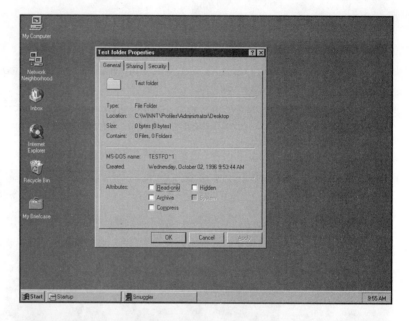

FIGURE 3.4.

On this page, you can set the sharing characteristics of the new folder.

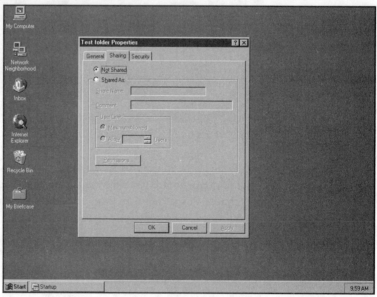

On the Security page, you can set different aspects of the folder or shortcut's access rights. As shown in Figure 3.5, this page has three sections to it. The Permissions box lets you set directory access permissions. On the Permissions dialog box shown in Figure 3.6, you can select the groups that have access.

FIGURE 3.5.

Use the Security page to set file permissions and ownership, as well as auditing processes.

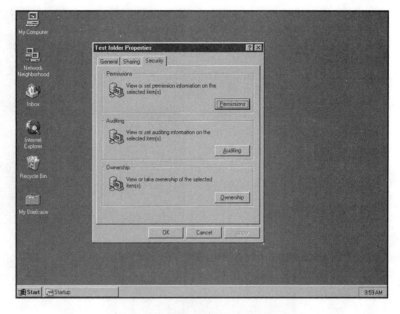

FIGURE 3.6.

Set group access permissions to the folder with this dialog box.

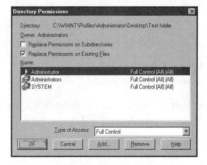

The Owner dialog box, shown in Figure 3.7, appears when you click the Ownership button on the Security page. In this dialog box, you can assign the folder's ownership.

FIGURE 3.7.

Use this dialog box to take ownership of the folder, or leave the ownership as is.

Auditing a file or directory allows you to track who opens it and for what reason. You control auditing through the Auditing window, which you activate by clicking Auditing on the Security page. On the resulting window, shown in Figure 3.8, you can set several levels of auditing.

Figure 3.8.

*Use this window to
enable auditing to track
access to the file or
folder.*

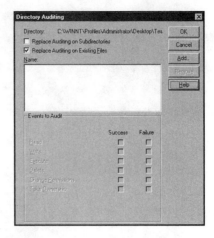

Copying, Moving, and Deleting Folders

You can easily copy, move, and delete folders in Windows NT, just as in Windows 95. To copy a program icon, follow these steps:

1. Select the icon.
2. Open the pop-up menu by right-clicking, and then choose Copy.
3. Move elsewhere on the desktop, and right-click to open another pop-up menu.
4. Choose Paste. The copy of the folder then appears on the desktop. You can change the name to whatever you want.

To move a folder, you follow the same procedure, except use the Cut option on the pop-up menu instead of the Copy option. To delete a folder, follow these steps:

1. Select the folder.
2. Press Delete, then click Yes when prompted in the confirmation dialog box.

Aligning Icons and Windows

To line up all the icons neatly in a window, choose Window | Align Icons. When it tries to align icons, Windows NT arranges them to fit the window as best it can. If there isn't enough room to display all the icons in the window as it's currently sized, scroll bars appear. If you enlarge or reduce the window's size, the icons remain in the same layout until you align them again (unless Auto Arrange is on).

If you want icons in a group window to rearrange themselves automatically to fit the window when you change its dimensions, choose Options | Auto Arrange.

Ways to Run Programs in Windows NT

You can run programs several ways in Windows NT. These methods include a couple of choices not available in Windows 3.1:

- Icons
- Run command
- My Computer
- Command line
- Batch files
- Task Manager

Executing Programs from Icons

The easiest way to run programs is via the Start menu. NT generates an appropriate window for the application type and launches the application in the window. If the program is of the DOS variety, for example, a DOS window is spawned, and the DOS application runs in it, using the color and font settings last saved. (Details of these settings are described in Chapter 5, "Sharing Data Between Applications by Using Clipboard, ClipBook, DDE, and OLE.")

As mentioned earlier, NT offers a Startup group too, just like Windows 95 uses for automating program execution. Simply adding some icons to the Startup group causes these applications (or documents) to run when you log onto NT.

> **TIP**
>
> Applications in the Startup group aren't necessarily executed in the order in which the icons appear in the Startup group window. They're executed in the order they were added to the group. If you want to change the order of execution, you must move the icons to another group, save the settings, and add them to the Startup group in the desired order.
>
> Windows applications execute before non-Windows applications, regardless of the order in which applications are added to the Startup group.

Using the Run Command

The Start menu has a Run command as one option toward the bottom of the menu list. Choosing the Run command opens the dialog box shown in Figure 3.9. Just enter a program name and click OK.

3

WORKING WITH
WINDOWS NT

FIGURE 3.9.
The Run command
dialog box.

If you don't know where the program you want to execute is, or you're not sure about the name, click the Browse button to display the dialog box shown in Figure 3.10. Here you can find the program and select it.

FIGURE 3.10.
In the Browse window,
you can find the
program you want to
execute.

Executing Programs from My Computer

For experienced users, the My Computer dialog box is a good alternative to the Startup menu for running programs. To launch a program, double-click the name of any executable file or any file with an associated application. NT does the rest.

Obviously, you can launch only executable and document files with associations. If you double-click the names of other types of files, such as DLLs, the window shown in Figure 3.11 appears. In this window, you can choose which application to use to open the file you selected.

FIGURE 3.11.
When NT can't decide
which application a file
belongs to, it lets you
select the application by
using this window.

> **NOTE**
>
> An *association* is a declared link between files with a specific three-letter extension and an application that can work with that file. Clicking the name of a .WRI file, for example, runs Write and loads the .WRI file because an association exists between the two.

Running Programs from the Command Line

The NT command-line interpreter (DOS prompt equivalent) is more versatile than its DOS counterpart. Although the NT command line appears to be functionally equivalent to DOS 5 (and much of DOS 6), recall from Chapters 1, "What Is Windows NT?" and 2, "The Architectural and Operational Design of Windows NT," that it really is a DOS emulator, not a true DOS session as in Windows 3.1. Some DOS applications run more slowly under the emulator than under real DOS. This isn't necessarily the case, however. The speed penalty depends on the application design. A program that is disk-intensive or that makes many API calls typically runs faster under NT than in its native DOS because of the emulator's use of NT's disk caching and 32-bit API mapping. By contrast, applications running significant amounts of native 16-bit DOS code are slowed down by the translation from 16-bit to 32-bit machine language (a process called *thunking*).

The NT command prompt isn't called the DOS prompt because it isn't DOS, and also because it's not restricted to running DOS programs. In Windows 3.1, typing a Windows program name at the DOS prompt (for example, **pbrush**) and pressing Enter results only in the error message This program requires Microsoft Windows.

With NT, no such error message exists. The program runs, regardless of whether it's a DOS, OS/2, 16-bit Windows, Win32s, or Windows NT application. NT simply spawns the appropriate application window, loads the application into it, and gets you up and running.

So if you're a command-prompt keyboard type, bring up a command-prompt box and start running your programs from it, if you like. Commonly used commands such as DIR, FORMAT, and CHKDSK are supported, too. See Appendix D, "An NT Command-Prompt Reference," for a complete listing of the DOS prompt commands and syntax, and see the following section for more information.

> **NOTE**
>
> In Windows NT, you can configure the MS-DOS environment based on settings in your AUTOEXEC.BAT files and two other files, AUTOEXEC.NT and CONFIG.NT. Using these files, you can load TSRs and device drivers, or you can set up memory managers before
>
> *continues*

3

WORKING WITH WINDOWS NT

continued

running DOS applications. In addition to these files, you also can create PIFs similar to the ones in Windows 3.1 for declaring specifics about how NT services the DOS session. See Chapter 5 for information about configuring the DOS environment.

When you start an application by simply entering its name at the command prompt, the current window is taken over by the new application.

Running Programs from Batch Files

In addition to having a more intelligent command prompt than Windows 3.1, NT supports batch files for programs other than DOS programs. This inefficient command prompt was a major drawback of Windows 3.1, and a number of third-party programs attempted to address it. Specifically, the problem was that there was no way to run Windows programs from batch files. Because the NT command prompt is intelligent enough to identify program types, you can run batch files even with a mixture of program types. For example, you can run this file at the command prompt:

```
cls
echo Here comes Microsoft Word for 16-bit Windows
pause
c:\winword\winword
cls
echo Here comes a DOS DIR command
pause
dir c:\winword\*.doc
echo Here comes an OS/2 application
word
echo All Done!
```

NOTE

Just as with DOS batch files, you can write the files using any nonformatting ASCII/ANSI text editor, such as Notepad, or you can use this command:

```
copy con: filename.bat
```

Then enter the lines for the batch file. On the last line (that is, a new blank line), end the file by pressing Ctrl+Z and pressing Enter.

You can assign the batch file to an icon in on the desktop or in the Startup menu, or execute it from the command prompt. When the batch file executes, each program is run in order from the top down, just as in a normal batch file. For instance, in the previous example, WinWord runs first, in a new window. The batch file then moves to the background but stays open. When you quit WinWord, its window closes and the command-prompt window comes to the foreground, presenting a DIR listing. After that, the OS/2 program runs.

As you might imagine, running programs from batch files can be a boon for anyone wanting to automate procedures in Windows. Perhaps you regularly perform a series of tasks in the same order. For example, you might go about acquiring some data through a communications program or data acquisition board, then run a spreadsheet or statistical analysis package to work with the data, and then catalog the data somewhere or send it across the network or to another user by modem. Using batch files that mix and match programs running on a variety of platforms could be great.

> **TIP**
>
> In addition to standard DOS batch file commands, you can also use Windows 3.1 Recorder to automate tasks while a 16-bit Windows program is running. However, no 32-bit version of Recorder is supplied with NT, probably because the Recorder program "bombs" easily—particularly when you try to record and replay mouse movements. In my experience, using Windows 3.1 Recorder macros with 32-bit NT applications causes error messages from NT when the macros are executed. Using Recorder macros with 3.1 applications running under NT tends to work better, probably because all Windows 3.1 applications are running in the same session, so they can share resources such as those offered by Recorder. Keep your eyes peeled for third-party NT macro programs capable of sophisticated multiapplication program automation and scheduling.

Terminating the Command-Prompt Window

Command-line windows you execute by clicking the Command Line icon don't terminate until you intentionally kill them. To remove the window and thus the memory it consumes, just type **exit** and press Enter at the command prompt.

Terminating a window this way isn't necessary when you're running a DOS program from an icon in the Start menu or if another application has spawned the DOS window. Say you choose Start | Run, type **c:\ws\ws**, and press Enter to run WordStar. When you quit WordStar, the DOS window disappears.

Terminating Crashed Applications

When an application dies in NT, an error message is usually generated. NT kills the application itself, brushing it aside and freeing up the memory it was using. If this process doesn't happen automatically, you have to take the following steps:

1. Open the Task Manager by right-clicking the task bar at the bottom of the screen (avoiding any tasks listed there), and choose Task Manager from the pop-up menu. The Task Manager window, shown in Figure 3.12, then appears.

FIGURE 3.12.

The Task Manager window.

2. Select the program you want to terminate, and click End Task.

Another approach, if you can't seem to get to the Task Manager, is to press Ctrl+Alt+Delete. Pressing this key combination brings up a box with a button you can click to get to the Task Manager.

If the program is running in an NT command-prompt window, you have another option. You can terminate the application by opening the Control menu and choosing Close or Terminate.

Running Multiple Programs Simultaneously

You can run many applications simultaneously under NT. Windows NT's thread dispatcher takes care of slicing up CPU time between the applications, at least making them all appear to run at the same time.

To run multiple programs at once, simply continue launching them using any of the techniques explained previously in this chapter. The actual number of applications you can run is determined by the combined amount of RAM and virtual memory available. If you have 16M of memory or more, you can run several applications at once without NT issuing messages about low memory. If you begin seeing error messages about low memory, you need to increase your virtual memory allocation or add more physical memory.

No More System Resource Shortages

In Windows 3.1, an enigmatic feature called *system resources* often is responsible for error messages about low memory, even when plenty of physical and virtual memory is left. System resources are a small amount of memory (64K) set aside for applications to use for certain internal functions, such as tracking small graphics like those in application toolbars.

NOTE

The seemingly arbitrary size of 64K is a limitation of the 16-bit architecture of the Intel 8086 and 80286 CPUs and the associated code required for compatibility. Even enhanced-mode Windows 3.1 on 386 and higher processors uses 16-bit code and, therefore, suffers the same problem.

WARNING

Because Windows NT has no noticeable resource limit, a problem might occur if you commonly migrate data files from Windows NT to Windows 3.1. For instance, I have used the Microsoft Office products (Word for Windows, Excel, Access, and PowerPoint) as front-end and analysis tools using custom macros. Using products this way can cause a problem if you do it under Windows 3.1, which normally doesn't have enough system resources to execute all these applications simultaneously and display the applications' associated data. A large PowerPoint slide show might also demonstrate this portability issue.

After you run only a few programs in Windows 3.1, system resources often can run low, triggering low-memory messages. Checking the available memory by choosing the Help | About command in My Computer or Explorer or using other programs that list this data may often send you off scratching your head because, typically, plenty of memory is left. What you might not understand is that your system resources are low, not your system memory. The computer can have a great deal of physical and virtual memory available but still be unable to run more programs. This fact is particularly bad news if you just dropped big bucks to purchase extra RAM, thinking it would solve the problem.

The good news is that NT doesn't allocate system resources the same way Windows 3.1 does. It's much more intelligent. Because NT doesn't run on top of DOS, the 64K limit isn't an issue; for all intents and purposes, NT's WOW environment subsystem simply never runs low on system resources. If, in fact, you run Windows 3.1 utilities that measure system resources when in NT, they report that you have used none whatsoever, regardless of the number of Windows 3.1 applications running.

Running Multiple Instances of the Same Program

When you're running multiple applications, remember that each one does use up some memory. Eventually, you will run out of application space if you keep launching programs or opening documents. You should limit the number of open applications, or at least experiment with the program mix if you're running out of space. Some POSIX applications, for example, might be quite large and might precipitate memory shortage messages when you run them. You might have to close an application or two to load a new large one.

Switching between running applications in Windows NT is as simple as it is in Windows 95. You have several choices:

■ Click the window you want.

■ Press Alt+Tab to go to the application.

■ Bring up the Task Manager.

■ Press Ctrl+Alt+Delete, and choose the Task Manager option from the resulting dialog box.

The most natural approach is to click the window containing the application you want to activate. This technique assumes that you have a mouse and that all your applications aren't maximized (that is, with the window taking up the whole screen).

Personally, I usually have my applications maximized, so my preferred switching technique is to press Alt+Tab. Each press of the Tab key (while you hold down the Alt key) advances you to the next application. A box in the middle of the screen reports the name and displays the application's icon.

Release the Alt key when you see the name of the application you want to switch to. When you do, that application's window jumps to the foreground. This process is called *fast application switching*.

Often with the Alt+Tab technique, you pass the application you're looking for because the tendency is to press these keys quickly. Rather than pressing Tab to move your way around the applications circle again, hoping to stop at the right one, press Shift+Alt+Tab. Each press moves you backward through the same list of applications. This technique is like putting a car in reverse to back into a parking space.

Another alternative is using the Task Manager. TASKMAN.EXE presents the Task Manager, which lists all the currently running applications—well, usually. Actually, many NT services and certain applications designed to "hide" in the background don't show up in the list. You have to use a craftier program if you really want to see a complete list of what's running. A program called PVIEWER.EXE, included in the NT Resource Kit and in the Win32 Software Developer's Kit (SDK), displays a complete list.

Just double-click the name of the program you want to jump to, or select it and click Switch To. Note that you can use the Task List for other purposes, such as ending the task (quitting the application) or cascading and tiling running applications to organize them neatly.

TIP

As I mentioned earlier, the Task List also has a RUN line in it. This line is functionally equivalent to the command-line interpreter explained earlier. Therefore, another quick way to run a program whose name you know is to press Ctrl+Esc, type in the name, and click the Run button.

Because NT is a networking multiuser system, some additional considerations not affecting single-user systems can crop up when you're running applications. In general, issues arise around shared resources. At any time on a network, two or more people might be sharing the same applications, files, or physical devices (such as a printer). Although NT is quite capable of precluding networked device and application conflicts, it's useful for users as well as administrators to understand the process of data, application, and device sharing.

For anyone accustomed to local area networking on PCs, this discussion is elementary and therefore may be skipped. However, if you're new to networking or you're upgrading from a more casual system (for example, a pure peer-to-peer system such as Windows for Workgroups or LANtastic), these issues will be more germane.

Network Software, File Locking, and Record Locking

Networking a number of PCs does not, by itself, magically transform your current software—for instance, database managers such as dBASE, Access, or Paradox—into multiuser software. Usually, more than one person can run single-user programs at the same time (for example, two people can run the same copy of Excel stored somewhere on an NT server), but when it comes to opening and sharing the same data file simultaneously, look out. If NT let you do that, you could have what I call a "data collision."

If NT were to allow two people to, for example, open and modify the same letter at the same time, what would happen? Figure 3.13 gives the answer.

FIGURE 3.13.

Flow diagram of a data conflict if two users have write privileges and the operating system doesn't support file locking.

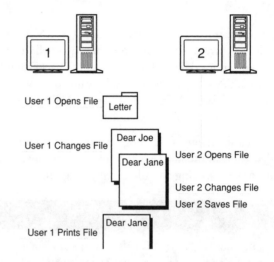

Whoever saves the letter last wipes out the earlier version. Losing a letter is enough of an inconvenience, but the effect can be far worse when single-user databases are used simultaneously from a number of network stations. Invaluable data records can be lost if the last saved version of the file doesn't include changes made by another user.

With correct network management (implementing a data protection scheme called *file locking*, which prevents more than one person from using a file at one time), this type of data collision scenario can be prevented. Windows NT (as well as Windows 3.1 and Windows for Workgroups) applications typically implement file locking, so when you try to access a file that has been opened by another user (whether on your computer or on a remote one), you receive a message. The actual message you receive may vary from program to program.

When you try to open files with other programs, you might see a dialog box that asks about opening the file as read-only. Opening the file as read-only means that you can display the file onscreen (or possibly print it), but you can't make changes to it. Not until the other user has closed the file does NT make it available to you for changes. So, if you answer Yes to such an interrogative, don't expect to be able to save any changes you've made to the file. One way around losing changes you've made is to choose File | Save As and give the file a new name.

Sharing Applications

Sharing application programs is much simpler than sharing data files. Several people can use most programs simultaneously because these programs are simply read into your computer. Merely using a program doesn't alter its program file. Occasionally, however, the changes you make to a program's settings or performances are written to disk, but they usually go into an initialization (.INI) file stored in the Windows directory or elsewhere.

As a rule, multiple users can use most non–network-aware programs on networks. If multiple users have trouble running a program simultaneously, contact the manufacturer of the program to determine a possible fix. When purchasing new programs for use on your network, look for Windows for Workgroups or NT compatibility statements in the advertising or on the product box. Also, buy networking products when possible, or products that give you a discount on upgrades as they become available.

> **NOTE**
>
> System administrators have the option of denying read-write privileges and assigning read-only privileges to any user on an NT system. Attempting to change a file for which you have read-only rights results in a dialog box announcing that what you're attempting to do isn't possible. The message doesn't necessarily mean that the file has been opened by another user.

Groupware to the Rescue

Some applications are written specifically for network use and are intended for multiuser platforms such as NT, Novell NetWare, or UNIX. Such programs implement more advanced data-sharing schemes devised for networks—schemes enabling many users to have access to the same data file, rather than limiting it to a first-come, first-served basis.

The software protocol that manages multiuser data access is often called *record locking*. Instead of locking a user out of a file altogether, record locking allows any number of users into the file but limits their access to one record (a discrete portion of the file) at a time. The most obvious application of record locking is in databases, where files are actually broken into discrete records. As long as users edit different records, no conflict occurs. If simultaneous access to the same record is attempted, an error message is generated, typically advising the user to wait a few seconds until the record is unlocked.

Until recently, few attempts had been made to write multiuser word processors or spreadsheets. However, a rash of multiuser groupware programs, ranging from games to messaging software such as MS-Mail and Lotus Notes, have gained attention in the network software market. These products are setting the stage for a new class of network software that allows network users to modify documents interactively while sitting in different offices.

3

WORKING WITH
WINDOWS NT

Pointers for Sharing Files Across the NT Network

The main points to keep in mind when sharing applications and document files across the NT network are as follow:

- If you intend to run applications stored on a remote machine, consider whether the remote machine is always going to be turned on and connected to the network when you need the application. If not, copy the application onto your local workstation's hard disk and run it locally.

- Are the data files you plan to use stored on a mainframe that you intend to connect to by using NT's TCP/IP capabilities or other connectivity add-on modules? If so, do you need to use NT's remote access services, or is the mainframe local? How many users can connect at once, and which NT machine or domain provides the gateway to the mainframe? Talk with the network administrator about scheduling such complex activities.

- Do you need access to the same data files that other workers are using? If so, are those files accessible through multiuser software? If not, you need to arrange a schedule with coworkers for file access and coordinate management of the files. You might want to create and maintain an audit trail listing times, dates, and the nature of changes made.

> **TIP**
>
> The NT Administrator's utility program is called Event Viewer. It keeps track of a wide variety of system events, including the date and time any file on an NT machine is opened, read, or modified, and by whom. You can use the Event Viewer log as a means of tracking file access. Although it's not an elegant solution to the problem of tracking a workgroup's access to files, it works.

- As a rule, if more than one person is going to work on an evolving document, keep only one copy of the file and store it in a central location. Duplication of files leads ultimately to confusion among people in a workgroup. If necessary, keep another file, such as a simple text file that contains a log of changes made. Better yet, add a section for such a log at the beginning of the file in question (for example, in a large text cell in a spreadsheet, or on the first page of a report) so that users on the network know what's going on with the file. This way, whenever the file is opened, the user sees the notes.

- Consider buying a groupware version of the programs you use for group activities. Some of the newer programs are intelligent in design and might even improve a workgroup's efficiency by facilitating communication between workers.

- Remember that even though users at DOS-based workstations can access files stored on shared NTFS or HPFS partitions, filenames are truncated to the "8.3" format for those users. Check and possibly modify filenames for the DOS-based workstations.

- Make use of your network's e-mail program to send notes to other users about modifications you make to files. A simple note such as "Sharon, I added the latest sales figures to the monthly balance sheet on the NT server" is often all that's needed to prevent mishaps.

- Make backups of vital shared files on a regular basis.

- Don't shut down your computer if you know that others have files open on your system.

Using My Computer

Like Windows 95's, the NT My Computer is much improved over its Windows 3.1 predecessor. For example, the NT My Computer has a user-configurable toolbar to speed up common tasks, and it also sports new icons that indicate shared directories and networked drives. Additional menus and menu options also have been added to supply needed networking functions—for instance, connecting to and disconnecting from network resources, determining who is using files on your system, declaring security levels for directories and files, copying a file to the Windows Clipboard, and viewing proprietary information about programs that manufacturers store in the file's NTFS file header (such as an application's version number).

General Operation

In general, the operation of My Computer is identical to that in Windows 95. Running the program from the desktop icon results in the dialog box shown in Figure 3.14 (or a reasonable facsimile).

FIGURE 3.14.

The My Computer dialog box.

The My Computer dialog box shows all the drives the NT system knows about (including networked drives), as well as some icons for Dial-Up Networking, if configured on your system. Clicking one of the drive icons displays a list of that drive's contents, as shown in Figure 3.15.

FIGURE 3.15.

You can see a drive's contents by clicking its icon in the My Computer dialog box.

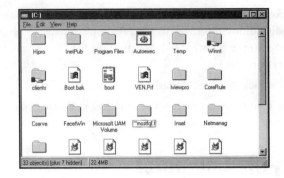

Notice that the layout of the window (the directory and file panes, the tree, and the file icons) is almost identical to Windows 95. NT has a configurable toolbar, some new icons, and some new commands. Note the icon for shared directories (the little hand under the file folder). It shows up after you share one of your directories, meaning that other users have access to it. All drives are case sensitive and support longer filenames. Case sensitivity is for display purposes only. You can access a file or directory with any combination of upper- and lowercase letters.

Functionally, however, many features are not new. As with Windows 95, you can do the following:

- Drag and drop files into new destination directories, or drag and drop from the file windows to a drive icon.
- Drag entire directory branches to new destinations, effectively grafting entire sections of a hard disk.
- Drop a document icon on top of an executable file to open the file.
- Display the contents of multiple drives at once in separate windows, which can be sized, cascaded, or tiled.
- Print from My Computer or Explorer, by either choosing the File | Print command or dragging and dropping to pull a file onto the printer icon (you have to open the Printers folder first).
- Format and label disk volumes.
- Save your window setup for future sessions.

Because most of these features are identical to NT's Windows 95 cousin, I'll spare you the details.

> **NOTE**
>
> Advanced options, such as NTFS security options prevent copying or moving files, allow changing ownership of files, and let you keep an audit list of who uses your shared drives and directories. These and other security features are covered in Chapter 8, "Using the Control Panel to Configure Windows NT."

Before you can use someone else's directory, that person has to share it intentionally, and you have to connect to it. Sharing and connecting are both done by using Properties sheet options. In general, this process is called *making connections.*

> **NOTE**
>
> Actually, a user with Administrator status can connect to any machine's hard disk, even if it's not shared. The user can do so because all machines create a hidden share for each root directory in the machine. For example, in a two-drive machine called SRV, an administrator can connect to the hidden shares \\SRV\C$ and \\SRV\D$. NT automatically creates these hidden shares.

After connections are established between workstations on the network, they are, by default, remembered (although this capability can be defeated) both by NT and some other network types, such as Windows for Workgroups. The next time you boot up, the operating systems will try to reestablish the connections. With NT and WFW, this is true even if your system powered down unexpectedly (because of, say, a power outage or an inadvertent flip of the switch) or a system crash occurred. The reconnection is simply part of the boot-up sequence.

Before you can use files stored on other network workstations, you have to connect to the drive and directory where they're stored. You perform this operation in the Network Neighborhood window, as shown in the following steps:

> **NOTE**
>
> Some applications, such as Notepad, are UNC file–aware and can be accessed without mapping a drive to a remote drive. You can specify the UNC name \\ROADTRIP\C\AUTOEXEC.BAT in the File Open dialog box to open a remote computer's AUTOEXEC.BAT file.

1. Open Network Neighborhood by clicking on its icon on your desktop. Figure 3.16 shows a simple network of two machines to make the example clear. Click the icon for the machine you want to connect to.

> **NOTE**
>
> Your station also appears in the listing of workstations on the network when you select your workgroup in the list. Any directories you might have shared also appear. At first, connecting to your own directories over the network doesn't make sense, although NT allows you to do so. However, being able to connect to one of your own shares can be quite useful.

continues

> continued
>
> You can use it like the MS-DOS ASSIGN command, or you can use it to copy or back up data from your CD-ROM drive. Normally, you can't back up a CD-ROM to tape, for instance, but if you share it and then connect to it, it becomes a regular network drive and can be accessed as such. You never know when this feature might come in handy.

Figure 3.16.

The Network Neighborhood window.

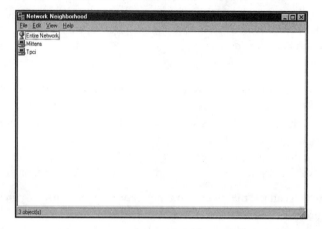

2. You might be able to look at the resources available on the remote machine by double-clicking the machine name.

NOTE

On some systems, you might have to log onto the remote machine you want to connect to as a user. If this is the case, the dialog box shown in Figure 3.17 appears, and you can enter the logon name and password for the remote system. If you don't log on properly, you cannot connect to the remote machine's drives.

Figure 3.17.

Use this dialog box to log onto a remote machine, if your logon is not automatic.

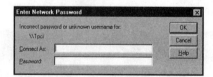

3. After connecting to the remote machine, you see the machine's drives and resources, as shown in Figure 3.18. This window shows directories and printers on a remote UNIX server.

FIGURE 3.18.

*After you connect to a
remote machine, you
should be able to see all
its shared resources.*

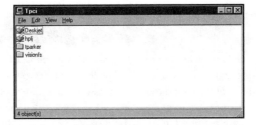

4. After you select the name of the remote machine or the name of a resource, right-click to bring up the pop-up menu. Choose Map Network Drive. The dialog box shown in Figure 3.19 then appears.

FIGURE 3.19.

*Use Map Network
Drive to connect the
remote resource to your
system.*

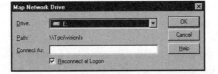

3

WORKING WITH
WINDOWS NT

NOTE

The volumes available to you, as well as the exact layout of dialog boxes, might look different if you're using Novell NetWare or another network in addition to Windows for Workgroups.

5. Windows NT assigns the next available drive letter to any new connection, so the top line of this dialog box is filled in. You don't have to change it unless you want to. You can choose a new drive from the drop-down Drive list if you want, but leaving it alone is usually fine.

6. Normally, when a connection is made to another machine, the network uses your current username to identify who is making the connection. (This information is stored in the workgroup or domain's user database, and it determines the level of accessibility to remote directories you have.) The current username is the name you logged in with and is the default unless you fill in the Connect As text box in the Map Network Drive dialog box. If you want to connect to a remote NT system's directory and have higher privileges than those assigned to the current username, enter a different username in the Connect As text box. (Of course, you must already have an account under this alternative name for this procedure to work.)

> **NOTE**
>
> The last point I made in the preceding steps might be academic, but remember that what appears as a network drive is, in reality, the directory on a remote drive. It typically is a subdirectory, not the root directory, so you're not really seeing everything on the drive—just selected portions that the owner decided to share. Also remember that drive letters on your workstation are assigned in the order that you connected to remote directories. If you set up some icons that point to files on a network drive, you should make sure that the drives are reconnected in the same order, or at least that you give the connections the right drive letter assignments when you reconnect.

A special type of shared directory called an *administrative root share* is restricted to those users logged on as administrators or backup users (two types of user groups that have a high level of permissions). Administrative root shares aren't displayed in the big dialog box that lists available directories on the network. To connect to such a root share, you have to manually type in the pathname, such as \\SERVER1\C$.

In Microsoft-based networks, the path for a network drive is preceded by a double backslash (\\), followed by the workstation name and the sharename. To connect to a share called PROJECTS on a server named SALES, for instance, you would enter the path as **SALES**\ **PROJECTS**.

Disconnecting from a Network Directory

After you finish using a network directory, you might want to disconnect from it. To disconnect from a network directory, do the following:

1. Finish any work you're doing with that drive, such as editing files and running programs.
2. Select the drive or resource icon from the list of available drives.
3. Drag the icon to the Recycle Bin or press the Delete key. This way, you can remove the resource from your windows.

Sharing Directories with Others on the Network

Before other workgroup or domain members can use your files, you have to share the directory containing those files. Shared directories can have passwords, and they also can have specific privileges (read-only or read-write). If you have a bunch of files that you want people to be able to see but not alter, just put them into a new directory and share it as read-only. If you want only specific people to be able to alter the files, share the files protected by a password by following these steps:

TIP

You can also use NTFS-enhanced security features to restrict directory and file access to individual groups and users. For instance, you can set up a share called SALES that contains monthly reports. By using the Security menu option, you can specify read-only access for management while providing read-write access for accounting. Permissions are explained in greater detail in Chapter 10.

1. Click the directory name in either My Computer or Explorer.
2. Choose File | Properties. Then click the Sharing tab to open the Sharing page, as shown in Figure 3.20.

FIGURE 3.20.

The Sharing page for a directory or folder.

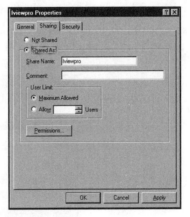

3. Fill in these text boxes according to your needs. The Comment text box is optional.

    The Share Name is, by default, the same name as the directory itself. If the directory has a long filename, a dialog box alerts you that DOS (and therefore Windows 3.1) workstations cannot see the entire name and asks whether you want to shorten it. Note that other NT and Windows 95 workstations can see the long name.

CAUTION

Because publishing the root of a disk allows network users into all directories on the disk, doing so can be dangerous. Be cautious when publishing. As I mentioned, NT automatically creates root shares, but only administrators can access them, as you can tell by the $ after the drive letter.

TIP

Because MS-DOS applications are limited by the DOS eight-letter file-naming convention, you might want to elaborate on a FAT directory name that you're sharing. Still, you have only 12 spaces to work with here, and the name must conform to DOS file-naming conventions (spaces and some characters are illegal). You might, for example, lengthen REPORTS to REPORTS.94.

4. You can limit the number of users who can simultaneously access the directory because your system's local performance, or even its ability to service remote users, might bog down if too many users connect to the directory at once. If you share a popular directory and notice significant system sluggishness, or if you find that other workers complain of slow service from your server, try decreasing the user limit.

5. You can set specific permissions to restrict the use of the directory by others. Click Permissions to display the dialog box shown in Figure 3.21.

FIGURE 3.21.

Use this dialog box to set access to your shared directories.

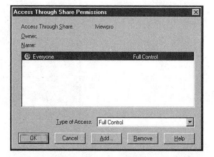

NOTE

The protection to set from this Access Through Share Permissions dialog box is available regardless of whether the volume is of the FAT, HPFS, or NTFS type. However, these permissions apply only to directories and files accessed over the network. Recall that NTFS partitions also can have special permissions already set on them by the particular NT system's administrator. If they do, these permissions operate in addition to the ones set here. The NTFS permissions are covered in Chapter 8.

CAUTION

If you don't set the permissions, anyone can access the directory, and eve
full access (meaning read-write access and even the ability to delete files i
they want).

Change the general permission level by opening the Type of Access ~~drop-down list~~
box. You have four choices:

No Access: If you select this option, nobody can get into the directory. You can use this setting to block access temporarily.

Read: This setting allows users to view filenames, change the shared directory's subdirectories, run applications in the directory, and open document files.

Change: This setting gives users all permissions listed previously, plus adding files and subdirectories, altering data in files, and deleting subdirectories and files.

Full Control: This setting gives users all permissions listed previously, plus changing permissions and taking "ownership."

These last two permissions apply only to NTFS partitions. You can find a more in-depth discussion of permissions and security as it pertains to directory and file sharing in Chapter 10.

CAUTION

Note that a user has the same rights to all the subdirectories of a shared parent directory. Be careful not to share directories that have subdirectories unless you want them to become accessible with the same level of restriction. However, you can manually set the access rights for each subdirectory on NTFS partitions only.

6. The permission level you choose applies to all groups of users shown in the list at the top of the dialog box. Normally, this level is set to "Everybody," encompassing all classes of users (from administrators to guests). If you want to fine-tune which groups have access to the directory or directories you're sharing, click Remove (to remove everyone) and then click Add (to add select groups of users).

> **NOTE**
>
> NT comes with a standard set of 10 groups. However, the system administrator can create new groups. By creating a group that includes only certain employees, such as "Finance Group," the system administrator provides an easy way to let a user limit directory access to just a few individuals.

7. Click OK. The directory becomes available to any other users who are attached to your workgroup. It appears in the window with a little hand under it—a reminder that you're making an offering to the public.

You can change permissions or other settings pertaining to the share afterward, if necessary. For example, you might decide to limit the number of connections to the share.

Unsharing a Directory You've Shared

When you want to remove a workstation's directories from the network, follow these steps:

> **NOTE**
>
> You can stop the sharing of files or directories only if you're a member of the Administrator or Power Users groups.

1. Choose Properties | Sharing.
2. Click the Stop Sharing button in the toolbar.

Finding Out Who's Sharing What

If you want to know what's really going on with a directory (that is, who's using it and whether files are open), do the following:

1. Run Server from the Control Panel.
2. Click the In Use button. The In Use dialog box appears displaying information about each file currently being shared, its location, and its user.
3. Click Close, and then click Cancel.

CAUTION

Be careful not to click Close Resource or Close All Resources unless you mean to immediately cut users off. The list shown in this dialog box is just to help you make a decision about terminating the connection using this procedure.

Working with Long Filenames

In this section, I cover naming files with long filenames. In Chapter 2, I explained briefly what happens to long filenames when they're saved under the different disk file systems that NT supports. The following are the NTFS and DOS file-naming rules and some hints for using them.

The following rules apply to long filenames:

- NTFS and FAT enable you to give files and directories names of up to 256 characters in length.
- You can include an extension, separated from the rest of the name by a period, such as 1994 Sales Reports.WK3.
- You can include spaces.
- Special characters not allowed are ?, ", \, /, <, >, *, |, and :.
- Uppercase and lowercase are both allowed, and they do appear in listings. However, they aren't interpreted by NT or NT applications as being different from one another.

NT automatically generates shorter DOS-compatible filenames for every long name you create by using the following methods:

- Removing illegal characters and replacing them with an underscore (_)
- Removing any spaces in the name
- Using only the last period that has three consecutive letters after it as the extension
- Truncating the first name to six letters and adding a tilde (~) and a single-digit number as the last two characters of the first name

Here are some examples of how NT generates shorter filenames:

Long Filename	DOS Name
Quarterly Sales Reports.WK3	QUARTE~1.WK3
Quarterly Sales Reports.Atlanta.Georgia.WK3	QUARTE~1.WK3
Qrtr[Sales]Reports from Atlanta,Georgia.WK3	QRTR_S~1.WK3

> ## TIP
>
> Recall that DOS programs having files with long filenames can be used in two ways: in a DOS window under NT or by sharing the directory they're on. (If you boot up with DOS on the NT machine, NTFS partitions are invisible.) After a directory is shared for the network, NT does its magic on the filenames. Even DOS-based workstations, seeing their shortened names, can connect to the directories and use the files. Of course, 32-bit programs cannot run, but document files and 16-bit executables work fine.
>
> In any case, you might want to adopt a naming convention that makes sense to you when the longer names are converted to shorter DOS names. Try to use only one period and use the extension that the application expects. Because the first six letters are the ones that are retained, pack as much description into them as possible. For instance, SALES for Frambo Computers 1994.WK3 would convert to something like SALES~1.WK3.

Just in case you're a bit rusty on DOS file-naming conventions, here are the rules:

- Eight letters maximum in the first part of the name
- After the first name, a period and up to three letters as the extension
- No spaces
- Any characters except <, >, +, *, ?, ,, =, |, ;, :, [,], /, \, ", or .
- Illegal names include PRN, COM1, COM2, COM, COM3, CON, LPT1, LPT2, LPT3, LPT4, NUL, and AUX

Finally, if you're working with long filenames and you want to see the MS-DOS filenames, follow these steps:

1. Switch to the relevant drive window.
2. Choose View | Partial Details. The dialog box shown in Figure 3.22 appears.

FIGURE 3.22.

Changing the viewing details to display short filenames.

3. Enable the checkbox to select MS-DOS filenames.

Using the Control Panel

Like My Computer and Windows Explorer, the Control Panel is almost identical to its Windows 95 relative.

TIP

All Control Panel settings are stored in the Windows NT Registry. The Registry is NT's analogue of Windows 3.1's WIN.INI, SYSTEM.INI, and several other .INI files, along with settings specific to NT (for example, usernames, passwords, auditing options, and other security features). Each user on a system has a separate batch of Registry settings. Most Control Panel settings a user makes don't carry over to all other users of a system. This rule has some exceptions, notably Fonts, which, when modified, affect all user sessions on that workstation.

Table 3.1 lists the major Control Panel subprograms (applets) and their respective functions.

Table 3.1. Control Panel subprograms.

Applet	Description
Color	Customizes the colors Windows uses onscreen
Fonts	Adds or removes type styles from Windows and Windows applications
Ports	Initializes serial communications ports
Mouse	Fine-tunes mouse speed and button assignments
Desktop	Sets desktop background, icon spacing, screen saver, fast Alt+Tabbing, full drag, and cursor blink rate
Keyboard	Sets key repeat rate and delay before repeat
Printers	Runs Print Manager to install/remove printers, assign printer ports, select network printers, and manage print queue
International	Makes settings that vary between countries, such as formats for currency, date, and keyboard special characters
System	Sets virtual memory paging size, DOS Window environment variables, default boot-up operating system, and tasking priorities
Date/Time	Sets the computer's internal date and time
Network	Joins a workgroup/domain, adding, removing, and configuring network drivers for different types of network cards

continues

3

WORKING WITH
WINDOWS NT

Table 3.1. continued

Applet	Description
Cursors	Fine-tunes the system cursors
Display	Selects the video driver, resolution, refresh frequency, font size, and color palette
Sound	Assigns sounds to system events and disables or enables sounds
MIDI Mapper	Adjusts MIDI key and patch assignments for non-Microsoft standard synthesizers attached to your computer
Drivers	Adds, removes, and configures software drivers for add-in cards such as sound and video cards
Server	For network administrators: Allows observing who is connected to the local system's directories and what local resources are shared or open; manages directory replication and system alert routing (such as impending power-down)
Services	Manages system software services by individually starting and stopping them and by configuring which ones automatically start at bootup
Devices	Controls when hardware device services (drivers) start and stop
UPS	Sets how an optional uninterruptible power supply (UPS) alerts the NT machine of a power failure, and how NT powers down and warns users without loss of data

You might notice several interesting (and possibly confusing) additions here, particularly those for system services and devices. If you've experimented with them at all, or at least opened their dialog boxes, you know what I mean. The distinction between devices and services, what you can start and stop, and so forth, can be confusing to anyone familiar with DOS's way of loading device drivers at bootup. After a device driver is loaded in DOS, it's in memory and running, period; there's no control after that. If you're familiar with UNIX, you might be more at home with the notion of being able to load, start, or stop devices while the operating system is running.

You can find details of all the Control Panel settings in Chapters 9, "Windows NT Administration," and 10 "Optimizing Windows NT: Performance Determinants."

Aside from the self-explanatory Cursors, which lets you change some of the cursor shapes a bit, the other new Control Panel choices primarily concern NT system administration. These options aren't available to all users, but only to those with higher-level privileges. Therefore, coverage of them has been relegated to Chapter 9.

Locking Your Workstation

All the computer security in the world is of no value unless you take advantage of it. It doesn't take a "back-door man" or a hacker to get into your computer files if you just walk away from your desk. When you get up to take a break, think about the value of your files and take precautions. You probably don't need to be paranoid about computer crime, but being safe can't hurt.

NT has a built-in, easy-to-use trick for locking your computer without logging off and having to restart again. It's also good protection from prying eyes. Just follow these steps:

1. Press Ctrl+Alt+Delete. A dialog box with a Lock button in it appears.

> **NOTE**
>
> Your network or system administrator might ask you to change your password from time to time. You do so by using this dialog box.

2. Click Lock. A message dialog box reports the time you locked (so people can see when you were last physically present at the station) and reminds you how to get back in.

3. To unlock the station, press Ctrl+Alt+Delete as instructed. You see a box similar to the original logon dialog box you see when you start an NT session.

4. Enter your password, and you're back up, happy in the knowledge that nobody accidentally (or intentionally) messed with your system.

You must remember to tell users (and remember yourself) that correct NT session termination is imperative. It's also done differently than it is in Windows 3.1. Correct termination of a session is more important for NT machines than for Windows 3.1 machines, partly because of the possibility that other users are connected to resources on your system. You certainly don't want to just press the power switch while other users are in the middle of a print job or editing files when your NT machine is acting as a server.

But that's only part of the story. The other pivotal point is that a typical NT multiuser machine supports a number of separate users from one single machine. Recall that a complex file called the Registry stores numerous settings pertaining to each user's work habits and a host of other preferences and administrator-declared permissions. Shutting down an NT session improperly can cause damage or loss in the Registry. You have only one Registry, and it contains information about all the users on the system, so loss of or damage to the Registry can make the system completely unusable, which sometimes requires a complete reinstallation. In some cases, even the NT Emergency Repair Disk can't help you recover your configuration unless you update the repair information periodically.

WARNING

The primary problem in just shutting down the system with the on/off switch is that data is cached in NT's dynamic disk cache. This cache includes the Registry files. Just turning off your machine instead of performing an orderly shutdown can make NT completely unusable. Many NT installations have had to be redone because the user forgot this single point. Always use the Shutdown command before powering down.

TIP

You can use the RDISK utility to update your repair information and create a new repair disk to help prevent catastrophic loss because of a power failure or accidental shutdown.

Logoff Versus Shutdown

Before I get into the actual procedure of logging off and shutting down, a little theory is in order—particularly for anyone raised on DOS and Windows.

As you might have gathered along the way, NT's executive kernel offers certain services: resource sharing, screen and keyboard I/O, and so forth. These functions are internal to NT, and they run as long as NT is up—and NT is running as long as the NT logon screen is up. This means that even if nobody has logged onto an NT machine, its services still are running over the network and are available to network users. All the shares that were last made (typically by an administrator) become available as soon as the machine boots.

Therefore, when a user logs off, this process isn't really analogous to terminating a Windows or Windows for Workgroups session. You aren't cutting off users who might be connected to your workstation, and you don't really have to think about other users unless you're considering a shutdown of the system.

A true shutdown, on the other hand, closes all open files and terminates all service on the NT machine, so you should consider who's using what before running one. If, however, you want to take the lazy approach, NT will cover you. If network users are connected to the station's resources, an alert box notifies you and asks you to confirm the shutdown.

NOTE

Incidentally, a shutdown can take a little time. Be prepared to wait a minute or so for it to finish.

> **CAUTION**
>
> If nobody is logged onto the system and the Ctrl+Alt+Delete message is displayed, it doesn't mean you can power down. If you're working on a Windows NT Server system, someone must log onto the system and either choose Shutdown from the Startup menu or press Ctrl+Alt+Delete again and choose Shutdown.

Shutting Down

Here are the steps for shutting down your Windows NT system:

1. Close any open applications, especially if you haven't saved files you've been working with.

> **CAUTION**
>
> Most applications are good at warning you if you've forgotten to save edited files, but don't count on it.

2. Choose Shutdown from the Start menu, or open the Task Manager and choose Shutdown.
3. Click OK to end your session and shut down the system.

Wait until a dialog box appears that says it's OK to turn off the computer before you actually do so.

Summary

This chapter has covered NT's basic operational procedures. Typical NT workstation users reading this chapter will have gained enough knowledge to organize their documents and applications, run applications in a variety of ways, manage files and directories over the network, and make some changes to their Windows environment.

The next chapter covers using the Print Folder for setting up, sharing, and managing printers, both locally and over the network.

3

WORKING WITH WINDOWS NT

Printers

IN THIS CHAPTER

CHAPTER 4

In Chapter 7, "Installing Windows NT," I discuss the installation of printer driver software during the Setup process. If you stipulate a local printer type at that time, the NT system has a default printer driver already installed.

Windows NT prevents any application from writing directly to the printer port. Any such attempt by applications to write directly to hardware is trapped by the Security Manager and either is rerouted to the NT printer driver or simply fails. Windows NT automatically takes control of print jobs, whether from OS/2, POSIX, Win32, Win16, or DOS applications. Windows NT's printer routine receives the data, queues up the jobs, routes them to the correct printer, and, when necessary, issues error or other appropriate messages to print job originators.

In Windows 95, printer driver installation and configuration (making connections) are done through the Printers applet in the Control Panel, but print job management is done through a Manager application program. Windows NT combines both functions into Printer folders. (The Control Panel still has a Printers icon, but it simply calls up the Printer folder.) Menus allow you to install, configure, connect, disconnect, and remove printers and drivers.

In this chapter, I explain these features, as well as procedures for local and network print queue management. I also discuss some basics of print management, offering a primer for the uninitiated or for those whose skills are a little rusty.

Adding a Printer

Adding a printer to a Windows NT 4 system is much simpler than in earlier versions of NT or Windows. Windows NT 4 can handle directly connected, remote, and networked printers with the same ease. Most of the procedures for adding a printer are handled through a wizard that gently guides you through the process.

Adding a Local Printer

To add a local printer (one connected to the Windows NT machine either by serial or parallel cable), start by displaying the Printers window. You can do so by selecting the Control Panel Printer icon or by choosing the Start menu's Settings option, which has a direct link to the Printer window. When you choose this option, the window shown in Figure 4.1 appears.

Clicking the Add Printer icon starts the Add Printer Wizard. In the first window, shown in Figure 4.2, you indicate whether the printer is local or remote. For a local printer, leave the default setting alone. You learn about adding a network printer in a moment.

Clicking the Next button moves to the port selection window, shown in Figure 4.3, where you can choose the port the printer is attached to. If the port you're using is not listed, you can add a port to the list either through the Port icon under the Control Panel, or through the Add Port button on this screen. If you're using a serial or parallel port, chances are the ports are listed already and you can simply choose the port your printer is connected to.

FIGURE 4.1.

The Printers window for Windows NT 4.

FIGURE 4.2.

In the first window of the Add Printer Wizard, you can indicate whether the printer is local or remote.

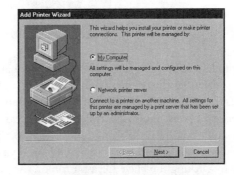

FIGURE 4.3.

Choose the port your printer is connected to.

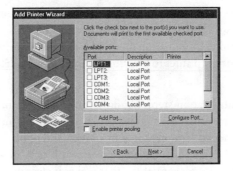

4

If you're using a serial port, you might need to set the port speed and other communications settings. You can adjust these characteristics through the Configure Port button, or through the Ports icon on the Control Panel. Incorrect port settings are most common with serial printers, where the number of bits, the baud rate, and the parity are often incorrectly set. Parallel ports are usually properly set for all printers.

After you choose the port, the Select Printer window appears. This window, shown in Figure 4.4, is composed of two scrolling lists. The left side holds a list of manufacturers. Select the manufacturer from the list (you can type the first few letters of the manufacturer's name to get through the list quickly), and the list of supported printers is shown on the right. From that list, select the printer model you're connecting.

FIGURE 4.4.

Select the manufacturer and model of the printer from this window.

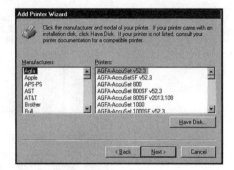

If the printer model you're using is not on the list, you have a number of options. The easiest is to use a driver disk that the printer manufacturer supplies. These disks are usually included with the printer, or available from a BBS or Web site sponsored or supported by the manufacturer. Some generic drivers are also available from sources such as CompuServe. In many cases, older drivers that are readily available do not work properly under Windows NT 4, although Windows 95 drivers should work without a problem. If you have a driver, you can read it into the printer file by clicking the Have Disk button on the printer selection window.

Another option is to configure the printer in an emulation mode. Many printers support the command sets of popular, widely used printers, such as Hewlett-Packard lasers and deskjets. Putting the printer in emulation mode and selecting a compatible printer should provide enough instructions for the printer to function properly, although some advanced features of the printer may not be available.

As a final configuration step, Windows NT asks for a name for the printer. This window is shown in Figure 4.5. This step is necessary because Windows NT lets printers be used anywhere on the network or on shared machines, and figuring out which "HP Laser" is the closest of the 40 "HP Laser" printers on your network that are listed on the printer screen can be a pain. Name the printer something that makes it clear where and what it is. Of course, if you're running standalone or on a very small network, naming it is not necessary.

FIGURE 4.5.

Each printer on the system should have a descriptive name.

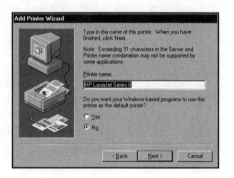

If the printer you're configuring is to be treated as the default printer for your workstation or server, make sure you select the default option at the bottom of the naming screen. The default printer is the one that all print requests are sent to when a destination is not specifically given.

The next window that appears through the Add Printer Wizard, as shown in Figure 4.6, asks if the printer is to be shared with others. If you intend to keep the printer for yourself, then you don't need to do anything on this window. If you're allowing others to use the printer, click the Shared radio button and fill in a name for the printer. This name then appears on the Network Neighborhood window of other network users who are looking for your printer.

FIGURE 4.6.

If the printer is to be shared with other users, use this window to indicate who has access.

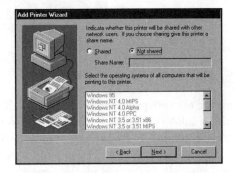

Finally, Windows NT asks whether you want to print a test page. If you select Yes, Windows NT tries to send a test page to the printer after the drivers have been loaded. Loading the drivers may require you to insert the distribution CD-ROM or disk, as prompted by the wizard. After you add the driver, the printer is ready to go. You don't need to reboot the machine to make the printer available.

Adding a Remote or Network Printer

Windows NT can handle two kinds of printers that aren't directly connected to your machine. Both types can be connected directly to the network cables themselves, or can be attached to another machine on the network but used by others. They are called *network* and *remote* printers, respectively. A network printer is managed by another machine (such as a print server or UNIX workstation) that your Windows NT machine talks to but does not manage. A remote printer is one attached to another machine or to the network that's managed by the Windows NT machine on which you're configuring the printer.

Adding a remote printer is almost as easy as adding a local printer. The only real difference is the way the printer is accessed. On many systems, network and remote printers have a unique ID such as an IP address. If the printer you're adding is network-connected and has an IP address, the process is almost trivial. For some other networks, you have to identify the printer uniquely to the Windows NT system using whatever method your network uses.

4

PRINTERS

To add a network printer, begin with the Add Printer icon in the Printers folder. In the first window, shown in Figure 4.7, choose the network printer option (this window is from the NT Server 4 release).

FIGURE 4.7.

To add a network printer, select the network option from the first Add Printer Wizard window.

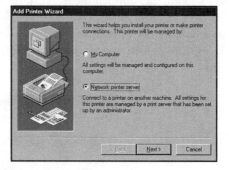

After you choose the network printer option, a network browser window appears, as shown in Figure 4.8. In this window, you should find the printer you want to configure on your system. For a printer to be recognized by the browser, it must be turned on and properly acknowledging network probe requests. If the printer you want to add isn't shown on this window, make sure the printer is properly configured for the network protocol and has a proper identification. For example, to connect a printer to an Ethernet TCP/IP network, the printer must be connected to the network and must have a valid IP address set before Windows NT can find it. The rest of the configuration for a network printer is similar to the process you've just seen.

FIGURE 4.8.

On this network browser window, you can identify the printer to be attached to your system. Select the printer from the display.

You set up a remote printer (one attached to another machine or the network to be managed by your Windows NT machine) in the same manner, except using the My Computer option on the first screen (shown earlier in Figure 4.2). You might easily confuse the My Computer and Remote Computer buttons on this window, assuming that remote printers should be configured with the Remote button. That's not the case, as the text in the window indicates. If the printer is to be managed by this machine, use the My Computer button.

After you select My Computer, the second window that lets you choose ports on the system appears (as you saw in Figure 4.3). If the remote printer is attached to the network or to another machine, it is unlikely the port it uses is on the list of ports in this window. To add the port, you should click the Add Port button at the bottom of this window, to display the Printer Ports window shown in Figure 4.9. If none of the port descriptions on this window match the type of port the printer is attached to, click the New Port button to display the dialog box shown in Figure 4.10. If the type of port you want to use is listed, select it from the list and ignore the following information about adding a port.

FIGURE 4.9.

To add a remote printer to the system, you need to identify the port in this window.

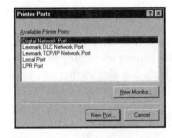

FIGURE 4.10.

To add a new port to the system, use this window. It lets you configure a wide variety of ports that printers can use.

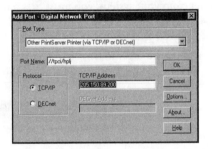

When the Add Port window appears, as shown in Figure 4.10, you need to specify the method by which Windows NT can access the remote printer. Using the drop-down list at the top of the window, you can choose the access method (in this case, through TCP/IP). The figure shows the printer's IP address or the name of the machine the printer is attached to. (In Figure 4.10, it is //tpci/hplj, showing that the printer "hplj" is attached to the machine "tpci.") After you add the remote printer port, you are returned to the printer port selection window.

When the port selection window reappears after adding a remote printer port, the port should be on the list (usually at the bottom), as shown in Figure 4.11. Select it as the remote printer's port, and click Next to move to the next window.

From this point on, the procedure is exactly the same as for a local printer. You select the type of printer, indicate a name and sharing characteristics, and are given the option of printing a test page. Especially for remote printers, you should print a test page to make sure your computer can access the remote device.

FIGURE 4.11.

Select the proper port for the remote printer from the port list.

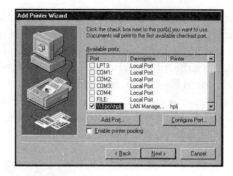

Whenever you add a new printer, whether local or remote, a new icon with the name of the printer appears in your Printer folder. If you're using a lot of printers over the network, clearly naming the printers is a good idea so that you know which ones are which.

Removing a Printer

To remove a printer from your system, you must first remove any print requests that are queued. To do so, double-click the printer icon in the Printer folder to open the Printer Manager window, shown in Figure 4.12. (You look at the Printer Manager in more detail in the section "Using the Printer Manager" later in this chapter.) Under the Printer menu is the option Purge Print Documents. When you choose this option, any print requests that were queued are removed.

FIGURE 4.12.

Using the Printer Manager window (one for each printer on the system), you can manage and manipulate print requests.

Close the Printer Manager and select the icon in the Printer folder. Press the Delete key, and a dialog box asking whether you're sure you want to delete the printer appears, as shown in Figure 4.13. If no printer requests are queued for the printer, the icon is removed from the Printer folder. If the icon still remains in the folder, some print requests are probably still queued. When you remove them, the icon disappears.

FIGURE 4.13.

Before Windows NT removes a printer, it confirms that it should. This confirmation prevents accidental deletion of printers.

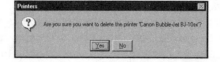

Finally, you might see a message about a new default printer being assigned by Windows. You get this message if you delete a default printer (one you chose as default). Windows NT likes to have a default printer defined, so it chooses another of the printers as a default. If you don't like Windows' choice, you can manually alter the default printer inside the printer's Properties sheet.

Setting Printer Properties

Each configured printer has a Properties sheet associated with it (as do most objects in Windows NT). You can display the Properties sheets by selecting the printer name in the Printer folder and then right-clicking to bring up the pop-up menu and choosing Properties. Alternatively, you can choose File | Properties to bring up the same window, shown in Figure 4.14. The Printer Properties window has six pages, mostly mirroring the information added during the initial configuration of the printer.

FIGURE 4.14.

The Printer Properties window.

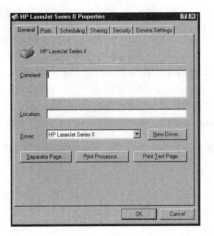

On the first page, shown in Figure 4.14, you can add comments about the printer, such as where it is or a maintenance history for future reference. Maybe you need special drivers or have to remind yourself about paper problems. These comments can all go in the Comment box. In the Location field, you can specify exactly where the printer is ("floor 4, pillar 2B," for example). The Driver field indicates which driver Windows NT is using for that printer. When new drivers are released, you can update them using the New Driver button, which reads the driver from a disk or file and updates the printer configuration for you. As most printer manufacturers update drives with each release of Windows, you might not have to update drivers often, but occasionally a new driver is released to fix bugs or add features. The New Driver option saves you from having to delete and add the same printer again.

You can use the three buttons at the bottom of the first Printer Properties sheet to add extra functionality to the printer. The Separator Page button lets you add a page separator of some type between print requests. This page may be necessary on heavily loaded printers to identify whose print request is being printed or perhaps to add a different color page between each request. Click this button to pop up a dialog box that lets you select the file to be printed as a separator.

The Print Processor button lets you choose a different processor for print requests on this printer. Usually, the default is what you want, but some remote printers might need different handling. You can choose the processor you want to use from the list displayed when you click this button, as shown in Figure 4.15.

FIGURE 4.15.

Most printers work well with the NT print processor, but in this dialog box you can change the processor.

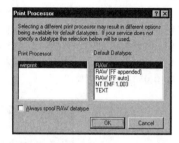

The Print Test Page button, not surprisingly, prints a test page. You should use this button when you have made changes to the driver or other major configuration modifications, just to make sure the printer is working properly. The Test Page is a single page with a quick summary printed on it.

The second page of the Printer Properties window is the Ports selection, shown in Figure 4.16. It shows the port you selected when you added the printer, but you can easily change the port by clicking the new port in the list. All identified ports on the Windows NT system are shown, including network ports. You can add, remove, or configure ports using the buttons at the bottom of the page.

FIGURE 4.16.

On the Ports page of the Printer Properties window, you can add or change the printer port.

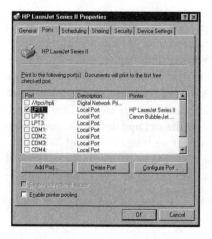

The third page in the Printer Properties window is for scheduling the printer, as shown in Figure 4.17. This Scheduling page lets you decide when the printer is available and any special requirements it has. Most printers are available all the time, but if you are in the habit of turning off a shared printer when you leave the office, for example, you may want to embed the operating times in this window. Most of the options on this page are self-explanatory. You should be careful adjusting the printer priority slider, as too high a priority can cause serious performance effects on other tasks you're doing.

FIGURE 4.17.

Through this page, you can set availability times for the printer, as well as some handling characteristics.

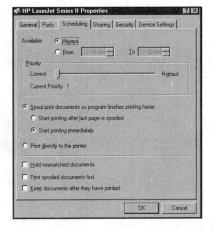

The Sharing page of the Printer Properties lets you keep the printer to yourself or make it available to others. This window, shown in Figure 4.18, is much the same as the Sharing page you filled out when you created the printer. On this page, you can change the sharing at any time, as well as select which types of machines have access to a shared printer. The shared name is the name others see when they browse the network for a printer.

FIGURE 4.18.

The Sharing page lets you share your printer or keep it to yourself.

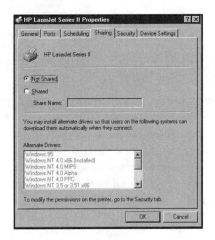

4

PRINTERS

The Security page, shown in Figure 4.19, lets you control access to the printer. The security settings are broken up into three parts. The first, called with the Permissions button, displays a list of users whom you want to allow to access the printer for management purposes. These users can modify the printer configuration or manage the printer queue. This window is shown in Figure 4.20. By default, the administrator groups are the only ones with full control, but you can easily change that by selecting a group and using the pull-down list box to change the type of control they have.

FIGURE 4.19.

You can use the Security page to control access to the printer, especially when it's shared.

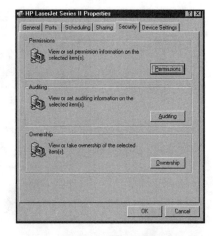

FIGURE 4.20.

You can control access to the printer configuration and queue managers by using this window.

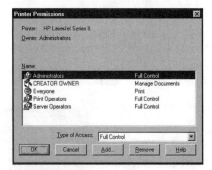

Using the Auditing button on the Security page, you can set up an audit log that can record who does what and some conditions on the printer. By default, auditing is off. To activate it, use the Add button to select the group or users to audit and the types of records to be maintained in the bottom part of the screen. Print audit logs can become very large, so take care when using auditing. Most users want to record only failures with the printer for debugging purposes, but if you have a special user printer (such as a color laserjet or wide-bed scanner) which is costly to use, you might want to record who uses it.

Using the Ownership button on the Security page, you can decide who owns the printer for administrative purposes. In most cases, the owner is the person who set up the printer, but with changes in workstation users, you might need to update this information.

Finally, the Device Settings page, shown in Figure 4.21, lets you see and manage some printer characteristics. If the printer has a number of print trays or automatic feeders, the current settings are displayed on this page. Also shown are any devices attached to the printer (assuming the printer can report their use back to the printer driver) such as sorting trays and special input feeders such as envelope feeds. Fonts, memory, and other aspects of the printer are also reported. As you would expect, a red circle with a bar through it means that the device isn't in use.

FIGURE 4.21.

The Device Settings page shows what the Windows NT printer driver knows about the current configuration of the printer.

Using the Printer Manager

When a printer is created, a new icon is added to the Printer folder. When you double-click a printer icon, the Printer Manager for that printer is displayed, as shown in Figure 4.22. Each printer on the system has its own Printer Manager. (This is a major change from the last release of NT in which a single print manager process handled all the printers on the system.) As you can see in Figure 4.22, each print request that is queued to the printer has a separate entry in the manager.

If a problem occurs while printing one of the requests (which are taken in order from the top of the list down), Windows NT displays a warning dialog box like the one shown in Figure 4.23. At this point, you can either select Retry to have the Printer Manager try to reprint the request, or Cancel to ignore the request and remove it from the printer queue.

An Introduction to Windows NT

FIGURE 4.22.

The Printer Manager lists all the print requests that are still queued for each printer.

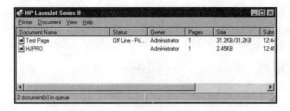

FIGURE 4.23.

When Windows NT can't print a request, it displays this warning dialog box.

Through the options on the Printer Manager window, you can perform a number of different tasks. The Printer menu lets you pause and restart the printer, as well as change defaults and sharing. You can also bring up the Properties sheets from this menu.

The Document menu lets you pause or hold a document in the printer queue, or restart it when a problem has occurred such as a paper jam. You can also cancel the request, removing it from the queue. You can see the properties of a print request from this menu, too.

Summary

In this chapter, you have learned how to configure local and remote printers and how to change their properties. Each printer has a Printer Manager of its own in Windows NT 4, and you've seen how you can use this manager to handle the print requests.

## CHAPTER 5

Sharing Data Between Applications by Using Clipboard, ClipBook, DDE, and OLE

IN THIS CHAPTER

In a perfect world, operating systems would provide a seamless meshing of applications. Although this is only an ideal that has yet to be completely realized by any operating system, Windows has bridged a few significant gaps. The ability to run several programs at once and switch between them at will is a strong move in this direction. This chapter considers a common issue that results from this new freedom: sharing data between these applications.

Because of developers' conformity with the Windows API and Microsoft's vision of a world where dissimilar applications can communicate, thousands of applications now can easily share data through cutting, copying, and pasting—that is, by using the Windows Clipboard. The Clipboard is a major advancement in PC programs that previously couldn't even come close to performing these types of functions.

Still, today's applications often continue to use proprietary file and data formats—a move that often seems promoted by developers' marketing departments in hopes of establishing their own industry standards. Whatever their motives, the result seems to be that actually sharing data files (as opposed to copying portions of data between programs) seldom is easy. Just try to open and publish a dBASE data file in Microsoft Word, for example. Things become even more complicated as multimedia applications gain popularity. Competing formats for live-motion video, audio recording, and MIDI files now are emerging.

As time passes, more conversion programs and input filters are built into programs as solutions to application intercompatibility. Word for Windows enables you to read and write numerous text and graphics file formats, for example. Similarly, database management programs (such as Paradox) and desktop publishing programs (such as Ventura Publisher) offer a plethora of conversion options. Standards such as *Rich Text Format* (RTF) now are emerging to facilitate data transfers between programs, and more elegant solutions will appear in the future.

Aside from actual file swapping, which is not discussed here, Windows NT offers three internal vehicles for exchanging data between programs: the *Windows Clipboard* (and *ClipBook*, an extension of Clipboard), *dynamic data exchange* (DDE), and *object linking and embedding* (OLE). If you're a veteran Windows user, you're certainly familiar with at least the Clipboard, and you know that both DDE and OLE are built into "vanilla" Windows as well. So why discuss them here, in a technical book about NT, you might wonder. After observing Windows users over the years and writing books on the topic, I've found that, aside from the very basics, people are confused about Windows data sharing. As a result, its many possibilities are widely underused. Also, Windows NT introduces some new wrinkles due to the inclusion of network DDE and OLE capabilities, the capability to share Clipboard material via ClipBook, and NT's security system, which can affect how and when data can be shared. This chapter reviews some Windows Clipboard, OLE, and DDE concepts and procedures, and it presents a thorough discussion of how Windows NT's treatment of them differs from Windows 3.1's treatment. Some special considerations for data sharing across the NT network also are discussed here.

Using the Clipboard

Although it's not capable of significant data conversions between file formats (such as .TIF to .PCX or .RTF to WordPerfect) or any radical sleight of hand to miraculously render all programs compatible, the trusty Windows Clipboard comes in handy for many everyday tasks. As a result, virtually all Windows programs that let you edit data use the built-in functionality of the Clipboard.

By using the Clipboard, you can move text, graphics, data cells, portions of multimedia files, and OLE objects from one location to another. The Clipboard works with a number of data formats, on both 16-bit and 32-bit Windows programs, and with non-Windows programs. Certain limitations pertain to non-Windows applications, however, which are explained throughout this chapter.

The Clipboard uses system memory (RAM and virtual memory) to temporarily hold information that is in transition. The data waits in suspension until the user is ready to copy or move it to its new location—typically a document that is open in a window. The data remains on the Clipboard until you delete it, replace it, or exit Windows. This feature lets you paste the information any number of times. You can paste into several documents or into the same document several times.

The Clipboard's contents can be viewed, stored to disk, and later retrieved by using the Clipboard Viewer utility. Clipboard data is stored in .CLP files.

Selecting, Copying, and Cutting in Windows Applications

In Windows NT, the Windows 95 standards and procedures for copying, cutting, and pasting apply, because NT's WOW supports all the Windows 95 calls for these services. Also, because the WOW subsystem shares a common clipboard with the Win32 subsystem, data can be passed between 32-bit and 16-bit applications.

In a nutshell, when running NT, you use an application's Edit menu and the Edit menu's shortcut keys to perform cutting, copying, and pasting tasks, just as you've done before, minus a few limitations imposed by standard mode operations in Windows 95.

When selecting parts of documents for copying or moving to another document, these steps still hold true:

1. When working with text in NT, techniques such as dragging across the text, using the Shift key with the arrow keys, and double-clicking in the left margin to select complete lines still apply. These techniques vary from application to application.

   For graphics, the techniques for selection vary—even more so than for text-based programs such as word processors. Typically, users have to consult the application's instructions or Help files for tips on selection procedures.

2. After selecting text or graphics, choose Edit | Copy or Edit | Cut, depending on whether you want to copy the material or delete the original and paste it later.

3. Reposition the cursor (in the same document or in another document) and choose Edit | Paste. The material then appears in the new location.

NOTE

Some programs might have shortcuts for copying, cutting, and pasting, so you should read the manual or the Help screens supplied with the program.

Copying Text or Graphics from Non-Windows Applications

You can copy a selected area of graphics or text from non-Windows programs, such as DOS applications. You might want to copy something in order to paste text data or graphics into a Windows document. You can do this only when the non-Windows program is running as windowed (not as a full screen). If the program won't run in a window, you're out of luck.

POSIX and OS/2 applications run in character-based screens, because NT can't run graphics programs in those environments. The information you copy from these windows therefore is character-based. When you're running DOS applications, the story is different. NT knows whether the application is running in character mode or graphics mode and processes the grabbed (copied) data accordingly. If the data is detected as text, it's copied as a character stream. If the data is detected as graphics, it's pasted into the destination application as a bitmapped graphic. You then can paste the data into any Windows program that will accept text or graphics from the Clipboard (for example, Notepad, Write, Cardfile, Paintbrush, Terminal, Word, and so on).

TIP

Some DOS programs might appear to be in text mode (because they are displaying text) when, in fact, they are not. If this is the case, copying text might not work as expected. Sophisticated DOS-based word processing programs such as WordPerfect or Microsoft Word for DOS can run in graphics mode to better represent the final printed page. If you copy text from the DOS window when a program is running in text mode, you might be surprised to find that what was copied to the Clipboard is a graphic rather than text. You won't be able to paste it into another text file, so switch the DOS program back into text mode before copying and then try again.

To copy text and graphics from a DOS-based program window (the command-prompt window), follow these steps:

1. If your DOS application is currently full screen, make it a window. (Some applications can't run in a window. See the coverage of the PIF Editor in Chapter 8, "Using the Control Panel to Configure Windows NT," for DOS application quirks.)

2. In the DOS application, open the document from which you want to copy. Scroll it so that you can see the item you want to copy. (You can copy only what's actually on-screen.)

3. From the Control menu, choose Edit | Mark to place the window into select mode. Select the text or graphics area to be copied by dragging the mouse pointer as explained earlier in this chapter. Start in the upper-left corner of the target area and move down to the lower-right.

4. Release the mouse button. The selected area is highlighted. Figure 5.1 shows some highlighted text in an ASCII file.

FIGURE 5.1.

To select text or graphics from a DOS application, window the document and then select the text with the mouse.

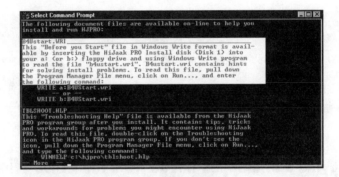

> **NOTE**
>
> As soon as you click in the window to begin selecting, the menu bar changes. The word `Select` precedes the window name, indicating that you're in select mode. You can't use your application again until you finish the selection process or press Esc.

5. From the DOS application's Control menu, choose Edit | Copy to place the text on the Clipboard. (Note that there is no Cut command.) The text or graphic now is on the Windows NT Clipboard.

6. Switch to the destination Windows application, position the cursor, and choose Edit | Paste to paste the Clipboard's contents at the cursor position, as shown in Figure 5.2.

FIGURE 5.2.

Using the Paste command.

Copying a Bitmapped Image from the Active Window

To create documentation or marketing information about software, you can capture the screen or portions of it, such as the active window, by using the Clipboard. The screen or window you capture can contain a Windows or a non-Windows application.

> **TIP**
>
> If you write a great deal of documentation, remember that some 16-bit Windows screen-capture techniques that work in NT are superior to using the Clipboard. Collage and HiJaak PRO were used to capture the screen shots in this book. Other programs of note are Tiffany, PixelPop, and Hotshot. These programs tend to be very flexible in their capture modes and file formats, including gray-scaling capabilities.

To copy the active window's image to the Clipboard, follow these steps:

1. Open the application in a window.
2. Adjust and size the window as needed. Note that if a dialog box is open, this window usually is considered the active window.
3. Press Alt+Print Screen to copy the image in the active window to the Clipboard.

> **TIP**
>
> If pressing Alt+Print Screen doesn't seem to copy the image, try pressing Shift+Print Screen. Some older keyboards use this key combination instead.

4. Follow the steps in "Pasting Information from the Clipboard," later in this chapter, to paste the copied information.

Copying a Bitmapped Image of the Entire Screen

If you want to capture an image of the entire screen, follow these steps:

1. Set up the screen appropriately. For DOS applications, the screen can be windowed or full screen.
2. Press the Print Screen key. (On some keyboards, this is called Prt Scr or something similar.)

> **TIP**
>
> If pressing Print Screen doesn't work, try pressing Shift+Print Screen or Alt+Print Screen. Some older keyboards use this combination.

The image is copied to the Clipboard. See "Pasting Information from the Clipboard," later in this chapter, and the sections that follow it for information on pasting the Clipboard's contents.

Copying a File to the Clipboard from My Computer

You can use My Computer to embed or link files into other files by using the Clipboard as an intermediary. Follow these steps:

1. Select the source file from My Computer.
2. Right-click in the active window and choose Copy from the pop-up menu that appears.
3. From the Copy dialog box, choose Copy to Clipboard. The entire file is copied to the Clipboard as an object.
4. Return to your destination document, position the cursor at the point where you want to insert your document, and choose Edit | Paste Special | Paste Link. The document then is embedded.

Pasting Information from the Clipboard

As soon as you've copied or cut a graphic, some data, or another type of object (such as a portion of sound or video) to the Clipboard, you have three choices:

- Paste it into a document you're working with (or that you open later)
- Save it to a Clipboard file
- Save it on a ClipBook page

- Pasting information into Windows applications
- Pasting information into full-screen, non-Windows applications

Pasting Information into Windows Applications

The vast majority of Windows applications have a Paste command on their Edit menus. If nothing is on the Clipboard, though, this option is grayed out, indicating that you can't choose it. Also, some applications have their own internal clipboard, so even though you've copied something, it might not be on the systemwide Windows Clipboard. Such setups are for use only between separate documents created in the same application. Word for Windows's Clipboard is an example of this.

> **NOTE**
>
> Some Windows applications can provide more than a single data format when material is cut or copied to the Clipboard. This feature gives you more flexibility when you're pasting to the destination document, and it can provide live data conversions (instead of storing actual data in ClipBook) for particular formats. When you paste, the destination document and the Clipboard figure out which stored format to use. See the section "Changing the View Format," later in this chapter, for more information.

In any case, to successfully paste information, all you have to do is set up the right conditions and issue the Paste command. Just follow these steps:

1. Copy or cut the desired text or graphics onto the Clipboard.

2. Switch to the application and document to receive the information and position the cursor or insertion point. The exact technique for positioning differs from application to application.

3. Choose Edit | Paste or press Ctrl+V. (Pressing Ctrl+V doesn't work with all applications, however.) The Clipboard's contents appear in the destination window.

The Clipboard's contents remain static until you copy or cut something new, so you can paste the same material repeatedly.

Pasting Information into Non-Windows Applications

Pasting into non-Windows applications is a little trickier, and the results might not be what you expected, because all non-Windows applications do not accept data in the same way.

> **CAUTION**
>
> Keep in mind that any formatting contained in text is lost when you paste data into non-Windows documents.

You can paste only text (not graphics) into non-Windows applications. To paste graphics, you have to cut or copy the graphic into a program such as Paint or CorelDRAW! and save the graphic in a file that can be read by the DOS graphics program. Because so many graphics programs are Windows-based these days, you're probably not using DOS-based graphics programs anyway, so this shouldn't be a common problem.

The easiest way to paste into a non-Windows application is to follow these steps:

1. Make sure that the application is in a window rather than full screen.

2. Using the method suitable for the destination application, position the cursor at the location where you want to insert the Clipboard's material.

3. From the destination application's Control menu, choose Edit | Paste. (Make sure that you're not in select or mark mode, or the Paste option is grayed out. Press Esc if you are in one of these modes.) The text then is copied to your document.

The Clipboard's contents are sent to the portion of the environment subsystem responsible for buffering keyboard data entry, so the data is dumped into the keyboard buffer for the non-Windows application. The result is that the application thinks that you have typed the text from the keyboard. For the procedure to work correctly, though, the recipient program must be written in such a way that it doesn't balk at receiving information faster than a human can type it.

Working with Clipboard Viewer

After you put data on the Clipboard, you might not want to paste it immediately. The ClipBook Viewer program in the Accessories group facilitates other Clipboard-related activities you might need. With it, you can perform these tasks:

- View the Clipboard's contents.
- Save the Clipboard's contents to and retrieve the Clipboard's contents from a file.
- Clear the Clipboard's contents.

Viewing the Clipboard's Contents

Sometimes, you forget what information is on the Clipboard. Every time you cut or copy, the Clipboard's contents are replaced with the new material, so you might forget what's there. Pasting the wrong thing can be a hassle, so viewing the contents in advance can be useful. Viewing also is useful when you're trying to get a particular item onto the Clipboard, but you can't quite see how well you're doing. If you bring up Clipboard Viewer and position it in the corner, you get instant feedback when you cut or copy.

To view the Clipboard's contents, follow these steps:

1. Run the ClipBook Viewer program by selecting it from the Start menu.
2. The ClipBook Viewer window appears. Double-click the rectangular icon in the bottom-left corner of the window. A window then appears that displays the Clipboard's contents.

Changing the View Format

The contents of the Clipboard might look different in the viewer window than in the source application. Text line breaks might be in new positions, or graphics might be mottled or distorted. Graphics and text can have a considerable amount of formatting material associated with them, such as font type and size, as well as graphics settings for resolution, color, aspect ratio, gray-scaling, and so on. The application from which you cut or copy is supposed to inform Windows NT, and thus Clipboard, of the nature of the material. The NT Clipboard does its best to capture all the relevant information, but it doesn't necessarily display all of it in the viewer window.

Based on this information from the source application, Clipboard knows in which formats the data can be viewed and accepted. A Paintbrush picture, for example, can be passed to another application as a bitmap-enhanced metafile, a picture-enhanced metafile, or a Windows-enhanced metafile. Other information that relates to OLE also can be included in an item placed on the Clipboard, but these aspects don't appear in the viewer window.

In any case, check the View menu for display options. The options don't affect the Clipboard's contents—only its display. The default setting returns the view to the original display format in which the material first was shown.

> **NOTE**
>
> When you paste into another Windows application, the destination program does its best to determine the optimal format for accepting the information. This isn't determined by the Display menu's setting or the current Clipboard window display. If the destination's Paste option is grayed out, the contents are not acceptable.

Saving the Clipboard's Contents to a File

When you log off, shut down, or place new material on the Clipboard, its current contents are lost. Also, because the Clipboard isn't network-aware, its contents can't be shared with other users. You can save Clipboard contents to disk in .CLP files and reload them later, however. If you do much cutting and pasting of specific items, you might want to use this technique. Additionally, if network users have access to the drive and directory containing the .CLP file, they can, in effect, use your Clipboard.

> **NOTE**
>
> .CLP files use a proprietary file format that is unreadable by virtually all other popular programs. ClipBook Viewer provides what you might consider a more elegant technique for achieving the same results.

To save the Clipboard's contents to a file, follow these steps:

1. From the Clipboard Viewer utility, choose File | Save as. The Save As dialog box appears.
2. Type a name in the Save As field. As usual, you can change the pathname and extension. You should leave the extension as .CLP, however, because Clipboard uses this as the default when you reload the file.
3. Click OK.

The file is saved. You can load the file again, as described in the next section. You can save in 16-bit or 32-bit format.

Retrieving the Contents of a Stored Clipboard File

You can reload a .CLP file into the Clipboard. Note that when you do so, anything currently on the Clipboard is lost. Follow these steps:

1. Run ClipBook Viewer from the Start menu.
2. Click the Clipboard icon.
3. Choose File | Open in Clipboard Viewer's window. The Open dialog box appears.
4. Select the file you want to place on the Clipboard. (You can open only legitimate .CLP files.)
5. If something is already on the Clipboard, a message box appears, asking whether you want to erase it. Click OK.
6. If you want to, change the display format by using the View menu (assuming that options are available on the menu).
7. Paste the contents to the desired destination by using the pop-up menu's Paste option or most applications' Edit | Paste menu choice.

Clearing the Clipboard

Although NT machines tend to have a great deal of RAM and sizable hard disks, system requirements are likely to consume significant amounts of these resources. Memory and application management therefore can be important. Keep in mind that information stored on the Clipboard can affect the amount of memory available for use by the system and other applications. If you're cutting and pasting small bits of things, as most people do during the course of a workday, you have no cause for concern. Some items, however, such as graphics, video, sound samples, or large amounts of formatted text, take up considerable space on the Clipboard. This is especially true of items stored on the Clipboard in multiple formats.

If you're running into memory shortages, you might occasionally want to clear the Clipboard's contents.

TIP

In Windows 95, you can get an idea of how much system memory an item on the Clipboard is occupying by referring to Program Manager or My Computer's Help | About boxes before and after copying (if you clear the Clipboard first). NT's dialog boxes don't report free memory, so it's harder to know what's happening. You'll need to use the NT Performance Monitor to determine the amount of free memory. Performance Monitor is covered in Chapter 19, "Optimizing Your Network."

To clear the Clipboard, follow these steps:

1. From ClipBook Viewer, select the Clipboard view by double-clicking the Clipboard icon or by clicking in its window.
2. Choose Edit | Delete. Click the X button on the toolbar or press Delete.
3. Click OK. The Clipboard's contents are deleted.

Using ClipBook

The Clipboard has some downsides. The three most glaring disadvantages follow:

■ You can't store more than one item at a time. Copying a new item erases the previous one.

■ You can't share Clipboard data with network users.

■ It's a hassle to store and retrieve Clipboard files. Saving a number of small clip-art bitmaps, for example, means naming multiple files and remembering their names when you reload them.

A Clipboard enhancement called *ClipBook* first appeared in Windows for Workgroups and is also in Windows 95. A 32-bit version is included with NT. ClipBook offers a number of key advantages:

■ ClipBook offers up to 127 pages of Clipboard storage. Each page is like a separate Clipboard.

■ You can give each page a description of up to 47 characters.

■ You can display pages as thumbnails for easy reference.

■ Network workstations can share individual pages.

■ ClipBook contains enhancements for network OLE that make linking to objects on another computer easy.

Running ClipBook

To run ClipBook, choose it from the Start menu. The toolbar offers a number of useful options. Figure 5.3 shows the ClipBook Viewer main window. Table 5.1 lists the toolbar's buttons and their meanings.

FIGURE 5.3.

The ClipBook Viewer's main window.

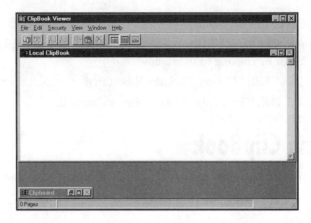

Table 5.1. ClipBook Viewer toolbar buttons.

Button	Function
Paste	Pastes the contents of the Clipboard to the ClipBook
Copy	Copies a selected ClipBook page to the Clipboard
Table of Contents	Lists the named pages in the ClipBook
Thumbnails	Displays small images of the ClipBook's pages
Full Page	Displays a full screen of a selected ClipBook page
Delete	Deletes the contents of a selected page (or the contents of the ClipBook, if they're showing)
Connect	Connects to a ClipBook on a remote (networked) computer
Disconnect	Disconnects from a ClipBook on a remote (networked) computer
Share	Shares a page of your ClipBook for network users to access
Stop Sharing	Stops sharing a page

Pasting into ClipBook

ClipBook doesn't replace Clipboard. Instead, like many of the Clipboard enhancements from third-party software developers, ClipBook works with Clipboard. Cutting, copying, and pasting into applications is still done with the Clipboard. ClipBook is simply a convenient storage tank for Clipboard items.

When you want to add an item to the ClipBook, follow these steps:

1. Put the information on the Clipboard by using the source application's Edit menu.
2. Switch to ClipBook Viewer if it's already open, or start it from the Start menu.

3. Choose Edit | Paste. A Paste dialog box appears, asking for a name for the new page. Each time you paste into ClipBook, you have to name the page.

4. Enable the Share Item Now checkbox if you want to make the item immediately available to network users.

Pasting from ClipBook

As soon as items have been copied to the ClipBook, you can paste them into documents on the NT workstation or share them with networked workstations. Follow these steps to paste an item from ClipBook to the Clipboard for use in other applications:

1. Open ClipBook Viewer from the Start menu.

2. Select the page containing the information you want.

3. Click the Paste button on the toolbar, or choose Copy from ClipBook Viewer's Edit menu. This places the material on the Clipboard.

4. Switch to the application into which you want to paste. Place the cursor where you want to paste the information and choose Edit | Paste.

Sharing ClipBook Pages for Network Use

When you want to share a ClipBook page so that others on the network can link to it or copy it into their documents, do the following:

1. Select the page in ClipBook Viewer.

2. Click the Share button or choose File | Share. (See Figure 5.4.)

FIGURE 5.4.

The Share ClipBook Page dialog box.

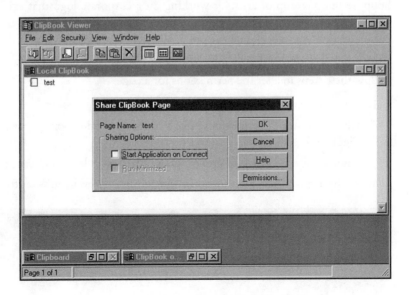

5

SHARING
DATA BETWEEN
APPLICATIONS

3. Notice the Start Application on Connect checkbox. You have to enable this checkbox if the data on the ClipBook page is more complex than a bitmap or unformatted text. If you don't enable it, network users won't be able to access the data.

> **TIP**
>
> When the Start Application on Connect checkbox is enabled, the source application will run when a remote user accesses the specific page. If you don't want the running of the application to interrupt your work by opening a window on the serving workstation, enable the Run Minimized checkbox in the Properties window.

4. Unless specified otherwise, pages are shared with a permission level that allows others only to link to it or read it. Only the creator has permission to change, erase, or share the data.

Setting Permissions for Shared ClipBook Data

Each page of ClipBook can have separate permission levels assigned to it. If you created the ClipBook page, or if you've been assigned a high enough permission level on the system, you can adjust the permissions assigned to the page. This means that you can control who has access to the page. Normally, all users have read and link access to pages, but you might want to limit access to power users or administrators, or to another group of users set up by an administrator, such as art personnel, finance personnel, and so on. Alternatively, you might want to extend the access to allow some users to alter ClipBook data by giving them write access.

Suppose that a group of artists is working on a corporate logo that exists on one system's ClipBook but that has been linked to a number of documents in the network, such as the company letterhead, envelopes, and memos. You might want to allow any of the artists to alter the logo to update it as it evolves. This requires changing the default rights.

Follow these steps to alter the permissions for a page:

1. Select the ClipBook page in question.
2. Choose Security | Permissions. The Permissions dialog box appears, as shown in Figure 5.5.
3. Choose the individual (or group) whose permission level you want to alter.
4. In the Type of Access area, choose the permission level you want to assign.

> **TIP**
>
> If you want to prevent any access to the page by a group or individual, select the group or person and click Remove.

FIGURE 5.5.

The ClipBook Page Permissions dialog box.

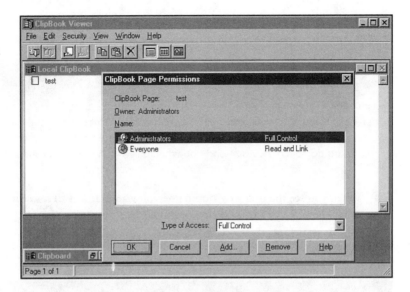

Instead of changing permissions for an existing user, you might want to add a new user to the list. You also do this from the Permissions dialog box. Follow these steps:

1. Choose Security | Permissions. The Permissions dialog box appears.
2. Click Add. The Add Users and Groups dialog box appears, as shown in Figure 5.6.

FIGURE 5.6.

The Add Users and Groups dialog box.

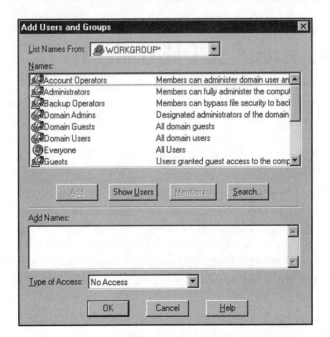

3. If the person's name isn't showing, choose a new domain or computer in the List Names From section.

> **TIP**
>
> You can use the other options in the Permissions dialog box to find users and groups on the network, including in which domain they're located. Most often, you'll click the Show Users button after you select a computer or a domain from the List Names From section. If you've selected a domain or a group and you want to see who's in it, click the Members button.

4. When you see the user or group name you want, click it to select it, and then click Add. The Type of Access dialog box appears.

5. Choose the permission level you want to assign to the groups or users.

6. Click OK.

> **TIP**
>
> You can set the NT ClipBook server to create an audit trail, which records the use or attempted use of your ClipBook pages. Your audit report can list a variety of variables, such as day and date of access, users' names, and so on. Auditing is covered in Chapters 9, "Windows NT Administration," and 11, "Maintenance and Troubleshooting."

Understanding OLE Under NT

One of the big draws to Windows was that it enabled users to run multiple programs at the same time, almost as if they were designed as a single piece of software. Even die-hard DOS users have been caught using Windows 95 simply as a task switcher, running multiple DOS sessions so that they didn't have to quit one to start another. The additional advantages of a consistent user interface across applications and Clipboard's data-transfer capabilities have converted some hard-core DOS users to the GUI world of Windows despite the issues of speed and stability.

As you learned earlier, you can use the Clipboard to pass information—text, numeric data, sounds, drawings, charts, and so on—from one program to another. But post-Windows 3.0 products (Windows 3.1, Windows for Workgroups, Windows 95, Windows NT Workstation, and Windows NT Server) have gone a step further with the information-sharing system OLE, which allows the information passed to other programs to remain linked to its source program.

As a power user or a system administrator, you are undoubtedly aware of the existence of OLE. You might even use it regularly. Maybe you've set up complex arrangements on your network based on OLE protocol. On the other hand, many veteran Windows users have only a cursory knowledge of OLE and don't understand its nuances, so they stick with the tried-and-true Clipboard for interapplication data passing. Because not all applications are OLE-aware or implement OLE in the same way, it sometimes seems to some users like opening a can of worms. Add to this some confusion over the differences between DDE and OLE, as well as additional confusion over rules governing the use of OLE over a network, and you've got a rich topic that could use some clarification! This section offers a short OLE primer, followed by a discussion on the use of OLE under Windows NT.

Looking at the Advantages of OLE

Take a minute to look at a classic business application of OLE. Suppose that you're starting a business and you want to construct a convincing, professional-looking business plan using a Windows word processor such as WordPerfect, Word, or Ami Pro. You want to include financial projections for the new company, substantiating them with financial data taken from a spreadsheet. You could cut and paste numbers from your spreadsheet into the document, but the projections change daily as you update your spreadsheet input. Instead, you link the relevant cells from the live spreadsheet directly to the document. When you change the numbers in the spreadsheet, they automatically change in your business plan.

Even simpler, when you need to enter new figures in the spreadsheet, you don't need to manually locate and open it. Windows knows which document and program the numbers came from, so you can bring up the spreadsheet and edit it just by double-clicking it in the word processing document. This causes the source application (such as 1-2-3) to run and automatically load the spreadsheet, ready for your changes. As soon as your changes are entered, you close 1-2-3. The changes appear in the Word document and in any other document linked to the spreadsheet.

By using this same technique, you can link charts, graphics, sounds, and even video to documents. You might want to add a chart from that same spreadsheet program to your business plan to communicate the numeric information graphically, for example, or a sound clip that explains a concept when you click it. In the case of a chart, you want the chart to be redrawn automatically to reflect any changes in the underlying data.

Using OLE Versus DDE

Although OLE is the more powerful of Windows' data-sharing devices, the older and less-nimble DDE still is included in Windows NT, so you should become familiar with it. With earlier versions of Windows, you can achieve some of the same results you get with OLE by using DDE. (NT and Windows for Workgroups include an updated network version of DDE called *NetDDE*.)

The drawback of DDE is that it leaves much of the work of sharing information to each individual application. As a result, the steps you have to go through to ensure that data is updated in linked documents varies greatly from program to program. Because OLE came out with Windows 3.1, and because it has been updated since then (with OLE 2), most major Windows applications support OLE rather than DDE for user-related data sharing.

Understanding OLE Concepts

It's important to have a thorough understanding of the basic OLE terms and concepts before you try to create documents by using OLE. Otherwise, you might end up creating a mess, especially over the network.

First, take a look at the differences between the terms *linking* and *embedding*. With OLE, you have the option of using either one. They're different in functionality and in how you work with objects that are linked as opposed to embedded.

In the case of linking, two separate files exist. Spreadsheet data can be edited from a word processing document or separately from its source file in the spreadsheet application. With OLE, a graphics file is more intimately connected to the word processing document. An embedded picture can be edited only from within the document and doesn't need to have a separate source document.

With both linking and embedding, both documents are categorized as compound documents. A *compound document* is any document composed of two or more dissimilar document types joined with OLE.

Examining Servers and Clients

To refine this discussion a bit, consider a few other concepts. Programs play two distinct roles in the process of sharing information via OLE:

- One program originates the object that is to be embedded or linked. This is called the *OLE server*.
- The other program accepts the object. This is called the *OLE client*.

NOTE

An *object* is any chunk of information passed as a bundle from one program to another. An object can consist of as little as a single spreadsheet cell, a database field, or a graphics element, or as much as an entire spreadsheet, a database, or a complete picture.

High-end applications often work as both OLE servers and clients. A spreadsheet program might supply charts and worksheet objects to a word processor or a desktop publishing program, for example, but it also might be able to accept embedded database objects from a *database management system* (DBMS). Client/server capability in a single application isn't always the case, however. Some programs, such as Sound Recorder and Paintbrush, can act only as servers. Others, such as Write and Cardfile, can function only as clients.

Two other OLE terms that are fairly self-explanatory refer to the documents with which an object is associated. The *source document* is the document in which an object is created. The *destination document* is the document into which you place the object.

Using Packages

In addition to the two basic OLE options of linking and embedding, a third variation of OLE packaging is available. You can use packaging to essentially wrap a server document in a bundle represented by an icon. As soon as the package is embedded, the icon (rather than the document itself) appears in the destination document.

You can perform packaging from My Computer or by using the Packager program.

> **NOTE**
>
> It's worth mentioning that DDE and OLE functionality require that there be enough memory to load both involved applications (server and client) simultaneously. I've known several users who have forgotten this fact and have been seriously discouraged when using DDE and OLE, particularly in very complex compound documents. Also, note that very complex documents created under NT might not function properly if the same document is loaded under Windows 3.x, because of differences in system resources.

Looking at OLE Methodology Variations

Despite a greater consistency among OLE-aware programs relative to DDE, idiosyncrasies and slight variations in the way you work with OLE still exist in different applications. You might have to snoop through an application's menus or consult its manual to determine how to edit OLE items. In Cardfile, for example, you don't have to place the cursor over a linked picture before you edit it, because Cardfile knows that the picture is in the upper-left corner. Similarly, because you play a linked or embedded sound object in a destination document by double-clicking the Sound Recorder icon, you can't use the double-click method to edit the object. Instead, you choose Edit | Sound Object and then choose Edit from the submenu.

Embedding Objects

Embedding an object is almost identical to pasting a static copy of it from the Clipboard into an old-style, non-OLE application. These two processes—embedding and plain old pasting—are very similar, because neither involves a link to any external files. The only difference between standard Clipboard cutting and pasting and OLE embedding is that, when you embed an object, you easily can edit it by clicking it or by choosing an Edit menu option. This is possible simply because the embedded object contains a pointer to its source application.

Here are the basic steps for embedding an object into a document:

1. Open the source application and document. Make sure that the application can perform as an OLE server.
2. Select the portion of the document you want to embed in the other document.
3. Switch to the destination application and document. Position the insertion point and choose Edit | Paste. If the application is OLE 2.0-compliant, position the insertion point and choose Edit | Paste Special.

TIP

When using some OLE applications, you can embed an object by using a command choice, such as Insert | Object. This command accesses a dialog box that allows you to choose the type of object. (All the OLE-aware programs on your system are listed.) After you choose the type, the source application runs. You then can create the object and exit, returning to the calling application. When you exit, the object is placed in the destination document.

Editing an Embedded Object

To edit an item you have embedded, follow these steps:

1. Double-click the item. The source application runs, and the object is loaded into it.

TIP

In some applications, double-clicking an embedded file doesn't have any effect until you change modes. In Cardfile, for example, you have to choose Edit | Picture first.

2. Choose File | Update and then File | Exit, and answer Yes to any resulting message boxes about updating. (Alternatively, you can just choose File | Exit.)

TIP

As an alternative to this technique, an application might have an Edit menu option for editing the object. Select the object and check the Edit menu.

Linking Objects

As I mentioned earlier, linking an object is similar to embedding it. An important difference does exist, however. When you link, the connection between the source and the destination document is maintained. So, instead of copying the object's data to the destination document, the link tells the destination application where to find the original source file.

The user can open the source document in the original program without leaving the destination document. Any changes made to the object are stored in the source file and reflected in the destination document. Similarly, editing the source document the ordinary way also works—the changes are reflected in the destination document the next time it's opened.

Remember that you can drop the same object into multiple destination documents. Changes to the source object are reflected in all destination documents. As a result, linking is the technique to use when you want to use data that always must be identical in two or more documents.

To link two files, follow these steps:

1. Create or find the server document you want to link (the source document). You can open Paintbrush and draw something, for example.

TIP

Before you can link a file, you must save it on disk. You can't link a file that's still called Untitled. Also, if you make changes to the document, be sure to save it before linking.

2. Select the portion of the document, drawing, and so on that you want to link.
3. Choose Edit | Copy to place the selected area on the Clipboard.
4. Switch to the destination document, such as a word processing document.
5. Place the insertion point at the location where you want to insert the linked item.
6. Choose Edit | Paste Link (not Edit | Paste).

TIP

You also can choose Edit | Paste Special, choose a specific data format, and then click Paste Link. (See "Changing the View Format," earlier in this chapter, for a discussion of choosing data formats.)

7. If you want to establish a second link, repeat Steps 4 through 6, selecting a different destination document in Step 4.

5

SHARING
DATA BETWEEN
APPLICATIONS

The linked item should appear in the correct position in the destination document. If all goes well, the object appears in its original form. That is, a graphic looks like a graphic—not like the server application's icon. In some cases, though, you'll see the source application's icon instead. If you're trying to link some Word for Windows text into Write, for example, you'll see a Word icon instead of the text. If you really just want the text, you should use the Paste command. Otherwise, you get essentially a packaged object. (See "Linking and Embedding with Packages," later in this chapter.)

Editing a Linked Object

After you link an object to one or more destination documents, you can edit the object starting from any of the places it appears. The technique for doing the editing is the same technique you use to edit an embedded object. The result is different, however, because changes you make to a linked object appear in all the documents to which you've linked it.

Here's the basic game plan for editing a typical linked object:

1. In any of the documents the object has been linked to, double-click the object. The source application opens with the object loaded.

> **TIP**
>
> As an alternative, check the Edit menu. If you click the object and open the Edit menu, it might have an option such as Edit Object on it. Choosing this also works.

2. Make your edits.
3. Choose File | Save, and then choose File | Exit. Changes you made should appear in any destination documents containing the link.

Linking and Embedding with Packages

So far, you've learned about embedding and linking objects by placing the objects themselves into destination documents. As an alternative, you can embed or link an object in the form of an icon that represents the object. This type of icon is called a *package*. After the user double-clicks on such a package, the object contained in the package opens in the application that created it (or, in the case of sound or animation objects, the object plays).

Why use packages instead of the ordinary embedding and linking method? Packages provide a simple yet powerful means of allowing access to supplemental information in documents designed primarily to be used onscreen rather than printed.

So, instead of presenting users with a confusing document displaying many pictures, charts, or tables, you can give users the option of clicking icons that open to reveal only what they choose. Each package can be labeled with a helpful description, such as `For more about ostrich eggs, double-click here`. Packages are a good way to include support documents in e-mail sent over the network.

Remember to use packages when you want to give the user the option of skipping over or ignoring the object, or of opening or running a program, batch file, or multimedia event by double-clicking the object.

You can create a package in several ways:

- From My Computer
- From Explorer
- From the Object Packager application
- From My Computer and Object Packager together

TIP

Because you can embed .EXE, .PIF, .BAT, and .CMD files, you can easily construct what amounts to a graphical menu of options in a document, with instructions next to each one. Write your comments and instructions to the user in an OLE-aware text processor such as Write. Then embed the appropriate file after each description, such as `Double-click here to back up the data files`. You should create non-Windows applications' packages by using the Object Packager program discussed in the next section.

Packaging an Entire Document

A program called *Object Packager* is included with Windows NT (as well as with Windows 3.1, Windows for Workgroups, and Windows 95). It's used specifically for creating packages. You'll find it in the Accessories group.

NOTE

Packages can contain an embedded or a linked object. Object Packager can package only embedded objects. To package a linked object, you must use My Computer, as explained in the next section.

To package a document, follow these steps:

1. Open Object Packager. Object Packager has two windows: Content and Appearance.
2. Select the Content window by clicking it.
3. Choose File | Import to display the Import dialog box.
4. Click the Browse button to select the document you want to package.
5. Click OK. The filename of the document you chose in the Content window and the icon for it are displayed in the Appearance window.
6. Choose Edit | Copy Package to place the document on the Clipboard.
7. Run the destination application and open a document.
8. Place the insertion point where you want to place the package.
9. Choose Edit | Paste. The package appears in the document in the form of an icon labeled with the document's filename.

You now can bring up the document, run the program, and so on by double-clicking the package. Some Edit menus have other options, such as Edit | Package.

Using My Computer to Package Document Objects

For packaging complete documents, My Computer is actually easier to use than Packager, and it's also more flexible. If you make a habit of keeping My Computer open, you might as well rely on it for packaging documents. You might remember that you must use My Computer to prepare packages containing linked objects.

My Computer packaging is very flexible. You have three ways to package documents (although all three aren't available with all programs):

- Drag the document to the destination document.
- Use the Clipboard to copy the document from My Computer, pasting it into the destination document as a package.
- Use the Clipboard to copy the document from My Computer to Object Packager, from which you can copy it to the destination document and paste it as a package.

Packaging an Entire Document from My Computer by Dragging

You can easily create packages by dragging documents to their destinations with the mouse. Follow these steps:

1. In My Computer, open the directory that contains the source document, batch file, and so on.
2. Open the destination document and position the cursor.

3. Arrange the My Computer and destination document windows so that you can see the source file and its intended destination.

4. Drag the file into the destination document window. This creates an embedded object. To create a linked object, press Ctrl+Shift while dragging the source document icon to the destination window.

5. Release the mouse button to place the package at the insertion point.

> **TIP**
>
> A plus sign (+) should appear in the document pointer when the cursor is over the destination document. If, instead, you see the international No symbol cursor (as in No Smoking, No Turkeys, and so on), the destination application isn't OLE-capable.

Packaging an Entire Document by Using My Computer and the Clipboard

Here's how to use My Computer with the Clipboard to package an entire document:

1. In My Computer, select the file you want to package.

2. Choose File | Copy. The Copy dialog box appears.

3. Choose Copy To Clipboard and click OK.

4. Open the destination document.

5. If necessary, position the cursor or insertion point where you want to place the package.

6. Choose Edit | Paste Link to place the document package as a linked object. Choose Edit | Paste to place the package as an embedded object.

Creating a Package by Using My Computer with Object Packager

You can transfer a document from My Computer to Packager by using the Clipboard as an intermediary. This method involves an extra step, but it offers some advantages. With this approach, you can change the icon or label used to represent an embedded package, and you also can create linked packages. Follow these steps:

1. In My Computer, select the source document.

2. Choose File | Copy.

3. In the Copy dialog box, choose Copy To Clipboard and click OK.

4. Run or switch to Object Packager. Select the Content window.

5. Choose Edit | Paste Link to create a linked document package; choose Edit | Paste to create an embedded document package. The filename of the source document appears in the Content window. The Appearance window displays the icon of the source application.

6. Choose Edit | Copy Package to place the package on the Clipboard.

7. Open the destination document, move the cursor to the location where you want to insert the package, and choose Edit | Paste. The package appears in the document.

Packaging Part of a Document

When you're creating packages, the primary advantage of Object Packager over My Computer is that you can limit the package to just a specific portion of the source document. You might want to limit the package to a few cells of a spreadsheet or a paragraph of text, for example.

Here's how to package just a portion of a document and place it in a document as an embedded or linked object:

1. Create or open the source document. In this case, the object must have been created by an OLE server—an application designed to originate linked or embedded objects. As always, if you want to link the object rather than embed it, you must first save the source document on disk.

2. Select the document section you want to package.

3. Choose Edit | Copy.

4. Open Object Packager and select the Content window.

5. In Packager, choose Edit | Paste if you want to embed the object, or choose Edit | Paste Link if you want to link the object. The Content window shows the path and filename for the source document, and the Appearance window shows the source application's icon.

6. In Packager, choose Edit | Copy Package.

7. Open the destination document. Position the insertion point or cursor where you want to insert the package, and choose Edit | Paste. The package's icon appears at that spot.

Packaging .EXEs, .PIFs, .BATs, and Command Lines

As mentioned earlier, you can package an application just as easily as you can package a document. You might place the Calendar program at the top of your To Do list for easy reference, for example. You also can package a DOS or other command line (POSIX or OS/2, for example) in a package.

Just use any of the techniques outlined earlier to package the documents. Simply select the filename or icon of the application or batch file during the process. The application's icon appears in the destination document, labeled with the program's full filename. Double-clicking the package runs the application just as though you typed it at the command prompt or chose it from My Computer or Program Manager. When you quit the application or batch task, Windows returns you to the original document.

Creating an MS-DOS Command Package

Object Packager has a little feature that facilitates creating a command-prompt package. Such a packaged command line might execute a single program or a number of commands from a batch file you have created. You can use this feature to package a series of NT-compatible command-prompt commands.

> **NOTE**
>
> Remember that because NT can execute any mix of programs from its command-prompt window, Object Packager can be a rich feature. You can mix Windows, POSIX, OS/2, and DOS commands in a batch file.

To create a command-prompt package, follow these steps:

1. From Object Packager, choose Edit | Command Line.
2. Enter a command acceptable to the command prompt in the dialog box that appears. If you're typing the name of a batch file or a program file, enter the full pathname of the batch file.
3. Click OK. The command you entered appears in the Content window.
4. Before you can package the command, you must assign an icon to it. Click the Insert Icon button in the Appearance window. The Insert Icon dialog box appears.
5. Select an icon from the scrolling display. Choose Browse if you want to change the icon. Find a file containing icons and choose one. Click OK.
6. Choose Edit | Copy Package.
7. Insert the new package into your destination document in the standard way.

Managing OLE Links

Windows NT normally takes care of managing, linking, and updating all linked files and packages when alterations are made to OLE server documents. At times, though, you might want to make manual changes or set some features of a link.

Manually Updating a Linked Object

Normally, any changes you make to the original version of a linked object appear immediately in all the linked copies of that object in other documents. When circumstances dictate, however, you can set up a link so that the changes appear only in destination documents when you manually execute an update command. You might want to do this when a source document is in flux and the destination document would read inaccurately or appear unfinished if the source were being updated before your work is done.

Here's how to set a link for manual updating:

1. Open the destination document.
2. Click the object to select it.
3. Choose Edit | Links. The Links dialog box appears.

TIP

If the Links dialog box lists two or more links, you can select multiple consecutive links by holding down the Shift key while you click the links. You can also select multiple links that don't appear consecutively by pressing Ctrl while you click the links.

 The Links dialog box lists all the links in your document, identifying each link by the source document's filename.

4. Click the Manual button at the bottom of the Links box, and then click OK.

You can return to automatic updating for any link whenever you want. Repeat this process, but in Step 4, click the Automatic button in the Links dialog box.

CAUTION

As soon as a manual link is declared, no changes will occur in the destination document until you manually update it. Just open the Links dialog box again and choose Update Now.

Using the Links Dialog Box to Manage Links

You can also use the Links dialog box to break or delete links, to fix broken links, and to alter existing links to refer to different source documents. Repairing broken links, especially on a network, is not an uncommon need. Source files can be lost or moved to other directories if they're scattered across the network or if they're under the supervision of many users, and source machines can be offline.

Sometimes, you'll want to break or cancel a link, destroying the connection between the source and destination documents. In this case, the object continues to appear in the destination document, but it can't be edited from within that document. A static copy of the material exists in the destination document, as though it were simply pasted in it. Two separate copies of the material now exist: one in the source document and one in the destination document, assuming that the destination document actually can display that type of material in the source file.

> **TIP**
>
> You probably can still edit the object if you need to by copying it to the Clipboard and pasting it back into the originating program.

You probably will want to break a link only when you're fairly certain that you'll never be revising the object as it appears in the destination document.

In contrast to breaking a link, deleting a link goes a step further by actually removing the object from the destination document. The source document is left intact, of course.

You use the Links dialog box to break or delete links. Follow these steps:

1. Start from the program containing the object with the link you want to break or delete.
2. Select the object and choose Edit | Links to display the Links dialog box.
3. Highlight the object in the list of links.
4. To cancel the link, click the Cancel Link button. To delete the link, press Delete.
5. Click OK.

Working with Objects Located on Other Computers

Although you can use My Computer, the Link dialog box, or possibly commands in some programs to create links based on source objects stored on drives in other people's workstations across the network, the ClipBook application can make linking objects easier.

As mentioned earlier, other network users can make information available to you by placing it on the pages of their ClipBooks and then publishing the pages that contain that information.

Similarly, to allow you to link to a source document stored on their computers, users can put the file or a portion of it on a ClipBook page and share it. You can then copy that information to your Clipboard and paste the link into your document. Follow these steps:

5

SHARING
DATA BETWEEN
APPLICATIONS

1. Run ClipBook and choose File | Connect.

2. Choose the computer and ClipBook page containing the information you want to link.

3. Choose Edit | Copy in ClipBook Viewer. This puts the information on your local Clipboard.

4. Switch to your destination document, position the cursor, and choose Edit | Paste Link (or Edit | Paste Special if you need a specific data format and the command is available).

Coping with Server Error Messages

If a destination document contains links to source documents on a remote workstation, errors can occur if that computer is unavailable for some reason—maybe the computer is busy, dead, or offline. Or maybe the directory containing the document hasn't been shared, the file has been moved, the server application is busy printing, or a dialog box is open.

In such instances, you might see a `Server Unavailable` error message when you try to open a link or a package in hopes of playing, editing, or updating it. Here are your options:

- Just wait. The server might get it together after some process is completed. Your computer will keep calling for the information as long as the dialog box is onscreen.

- Click the Cancel button in the message box to cancel the box, and then alert the other computer's user that there's a problem. Make sure that the server application and document are shared and available and that your permissions allow you access to the directory.

Looking at OLE Security and Permissions

Keep in mind that users on NT networks have certain rights and privileges applicable to all files, directories, and disks to which they're connected. Complex documents present a particular challenge to NT's security system because they can combine elements supplied from various sources. The text in a document can come from a file the user has read-write (full) access to, for example, but an embedded portion of a spreadsheet is supplied by a workstation or a directory to which the user has only read privileges.

As far as security goes, there's an important distinction between embedded and linked documents. In the case of embedded documents, there is really only one document. Therefore, the access restrictions assigned to that file apply to all portions of the complex document. In other words, when you embed an item, it takes on the security level of the destination document.

By contrast, when you link a document, there are still two documents, each with its own access restrictions. These restrictions might be identical, or they might be different. If users try to edit a portion of a complex document to which they don't have access privilege, NT doesn't allow it, and a message box issues an appropriate message.

Summary

This chapter has discussed the different methods available for sharing data between applications and workstations. Note that many of the procedures explained here can apply equally well to Windows for Workgroups because that platform supports network OLE and ClipBook page sharing using the same techniques described here. The information in this chapter should make it clear that data sharing is not limited by the simple Cut, Copy, and Paste commands most Windows (and even Mac) users are familiar with.

With OLE, complex and rich documents that combine the talents of seemingly disparate programs can be pulled together, calling on elements spread across even huge, NT-based networks. It's not inconceivable that a company report could contain live spreadsheet data from the Houston office, a newly updated logo from the San Francisco art department, and freshly edited text from the New York office, all pulled together and updated when you open the document first thing in the morning. Changes that the remote offices made the day before would appear immediately in the document as NT reached across the network to load the document's objects.

Remember that you can use the Windows Clipboard to create screen captures to illustrate user documentation and that ClipBook pages make sharing bits of clip art, spreadsheet sections, pages of text, bits of sound, or even whole files a simple task. You rarely have to copy material onto a floppy disk and walk it around the office to another workstation just to share a little data with a coworker.

## CHAPTER 6

Improvements, Enhancements, and Additions in NT Workstation Version 4

IN THIS CHAPTER

Windows NT 4 offers many improvements over NT 3.51. Some of the changes are directly visible to you, the user, and others are embedded deep in the system to offer more compatibility, better performance, or more flexibility. This chapter takes a quick look at the major changes Microsoft made to Windows NT 4. You'll look primarily at Windows NT 4 Workstation, but you'll also learn about changes to the Server version.

Changes in NT 4

This chapter takes a look at the major changes introduced with Windows NT 4. The following list reflects the changes Microsoft made since the last version of NT. The improvements in NT 4 follow:

- A GUI similar to Windows 95
- The addition of Windows NT Explorer
- A simpler installation routine
- Improvements to the Task Manager
- Accessibility options
- New accessories
- An updated Internet Explorer
- Client support for PPTP, WINS, and DNS
- A better Network Control Panel
- Client support for NDS
- Improved dial-up networking
- Better user profiles
- Improved printer management
- Internet and TCP/IP tools and services through Internet Information Service (explained in Chapter 28, "Internet Information Server")
- Multimedia and telephony APIs

It's worth taking a look at each of the major improvements in a little more detail.

A GUI Similar to Windows 95

Windows NT 4 uses the same Windows GUI as Windows 95. The Windows 95 look and feel has been kept, and NT's security and robustness have been integrated without compromising the GUI behavior. The Windows 95 GUI is a major change from that of Windows 3.11 and Windows NT 3.51; it eliminates the Program Manager windows and introduces a Start button that leads to all applications on the machine.

Windows NT's GUI uses Windows 95's Start button, its task bar for quick application switching, and its feature that allows you to create shortcuts quickly and easily. (See Figure 6.1.) The desktop icons from Windows 95 remain, including My Computer (which replaces the File Manager), Network Neighborhood, and Recycle Bin.

FIGURE 6.1.
The Windows NT 4 GUI is similar to the Windows 95 GUI.

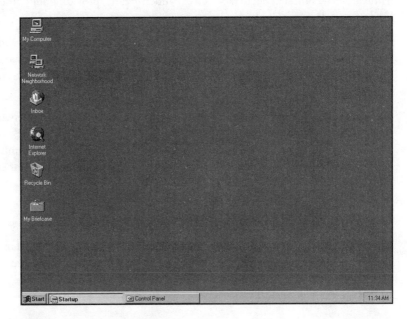

The Addition of Windows NT Explorer

Windows NT Explorer is a tool you can use to display the contents of drives and to browse not only your own machine's resources, but those accessible over the network as well. Explorer displays your machine's resources as a tree, which lets you see the contents of any drive or directory with just a few clicks of the mouse. (See Figure 6.2.)

FIGURE 6.2.
The Explorer shows a tree-like display of all your system's resources.

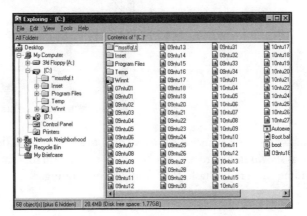

A Simpler Installation Routine

The entire setup and installation process for Windows NT 4 has been simplified. A new interface makes setting up and configuring your system much easier than it was with NT 3.51. The hardware-detection subsystem has been expanded greatly, providing support for practically every kind of popular peripheral.

A new set of tools to provide networking support makes setting up a networked NT workstation or server much easier, too. During the setup process, network cards and network characteristics are detected automatically, making the configuration of the network as easy as possible.

NT 4 also allows you to install NT from one machine to others on a network, which is especially useful in corporate networks. After you install NT on one machine, you can use the network to install NT on any other machine connected to the server (remember that legally you need to have a license—either a site license or multiple copy license—for each machine running NT).

Improvements to the Task Manager

The Task Manager has been improved since NT 3.51. The new Task Manager lets you manage your applications much more easily and offers important ways to measure your NT system's behavior. You can use the Applications tab to switch between tasks and end them if they're locked up. (See Figure 6.3.)

FIGURE 6.3.

You can use the Task Manager to control or switch between running applications.

You can use the Task Manager's Processes tab to see a list of all the processes running on your system, as shown in Figure 6.4. You'll find this list useful for examining the system's behavior and finding background tasks that shouldn't be running.

FIGURE 6.4.
*You can use the Task
Manager to see all the
processes running on
your NT system.*

Finally, you can use the Performance tab to view statistics and measurements that reflect how well your system is functioning. In Figure 6.5, you can see displays for CPU and memory usage, as well as summaries for several other aspects of the kernel. You should occasionally check this screen to find out whether your system is running low on memory or pushing the CPU too hard.

FIGURE 6.5.
*The Performance tab
displays system statistics
and measurements.*

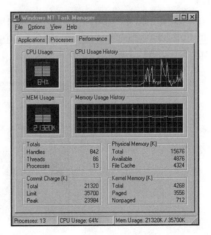

Accessibility Options

Microsoft added a number of accessibility options to improve NT's usability by people with disabilities. These options are also useful for those who want to tailor their systems to make them easier to use.

You can double-click the Accessibility Properties icon in the Control Panel to select features for special key assignments, alternative input devices, scalable user interface elements (such as enlarged fonts and icons), or sound cues to indicate system behavior. (See Figure 6.6.)

FIGURE 6.6.

Accessibility options have been expanded greatly to accommodate the growing number of NT 4 users.

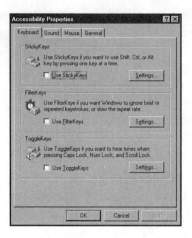

New Accessories

Several new applications and utilities have been added to Windows NT 4 to make it easier to use and to provide greater functionality.

HyperTerminal

HyperTerminal is a 32-bit communications software package that allows users to connect to other machines and offers access to online services. HyperTerminal comes preconfigured with wizards for CompuServe, MCI Mail, AT&T Mail, and several others, as Figure 6.7 shows.

FIGURE 6.7.

HyperTerminal is a 32-bit communications package with advanced functions.

WordPad

WordPad is an improved 32-bit editor that supplements the older Notepad (which is still in-cluded with NT 4 because it provides a slightly faster editor for small documents, and probably to provide backward user compatibility with earlier versions of NT). WordPad has removed many of Notepad's limitations and provides basic word processing capabilities for many users. Figure 6.8 shows the WordPad window.

FIGURE 6.8.

WordPad is a small, fast word processor that supplements the older Notepad.

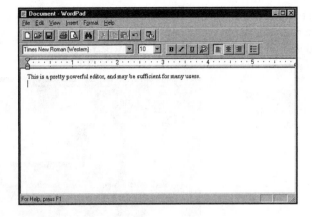

Paint

Paint is a 32-bit update of the veteran graphics application that can handle PCX and BMP files. (See Figure 6.9.)

FIGURE 6.9.

Paint has been updated to a 32-bit application.

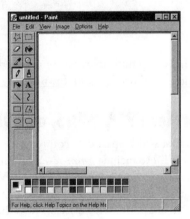

Quick Viewer

The Quick Viewer enables you to view files in many popular file formats without opening the application used to create the file. If you want to check on the contents of a Word document but don't want to go through launching Word and then opening the document, for example, you can use Quick Viewer to look at the document's contents. It's much faster and easier.

An Updated Internet Explorer

Microsoft's latest version of Internet Explorer (its competition against Netscape's popular browser) is included in NT 4 and is designed for World Wide Web access. (See Figure 6.10.)

Internet Explorer is very easily configured and quite flexible. You can use it to configure your modem and easily access the World Wide Web. Internet Explorer works with the modem Setup Wizard and Dial-Up Networking to supply better functionality.

FIGURE 6.10.

You can use Microsoft's Explorer to browse the World Wide Web.

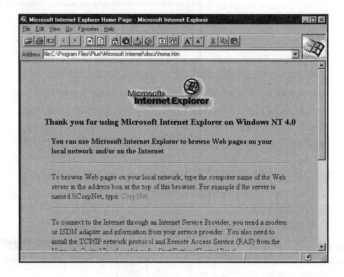

Internet Explorer has many built-in extensions, including inline sound and video, support for shopping applications, and background downloading capabilities.

Client Support for PPTP, WINS, and DNS

For NT machines that will be part of a corporate network, Microsoft extended the network clients offered with NT 4 to include *Point-to-Point Tunneling Protocol* (PPTP), and it expanded *Windows Internet Name Service* (WINS) and *Domain Name System* (DNS). PPTP provides more secure communication between machines, thanks to encryption methods built into the protocol. WINS and DNS are popular network services that make tracking machine names much easier.

A Better Network Control Panel

The Network Control Panel in NT 4 greatly expands on and simplifies the Control Panel in 3.51. (See Figure 6.11.) By using page tabs, NT 4 consolidates much of the information that a network administrator needs into one location. Setting up network protocols and services is also much easier, thanks to a more logical layout of the pages.

FIGURE 6.11.
The NT 4 Network Control Panel is much easier to use than the 3.51 Control Panel.

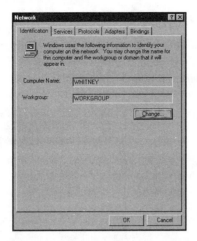

Client Support for NDS

Novell NetWare remains a popular networking protocol; one of the features of NetWare is *NetWare Directory Services* (NDS). NDS enables an NT workstation to log onto a NetWare server and access the server's files and printers. Windows NT 4 includes an NDS client that makes this connection much easier than it is when installing third-party drivers.

Improved Dial-Up Networking

Dial-up networking, a feature borrowed from Windows 95, supports fast and simple configuration of a modem or network connection to other machines. Windows NT's Dial-Up Networking Wizard includes support for bonded ISDN B channels, with throughput to 120Kbps. This wizard makes setting up network connections fast and simple, as shown in Figure 6.12.

FIGURE 6.12.
The Dial-Up Networking Wizard makes network or modem access much simpler than before.

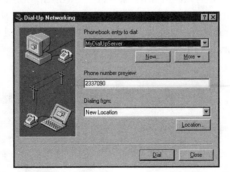

Better User Profiles

Windows NT 4 takes the concept of user and system profiles used in NT 3.51 and expands on it. System profiles and policies are easy to set up with NT 4, and you can configure user profiles in minutes with the User Manager. (See Figure 6.13.)

FIGURE 6.13.

With NT 4's User Manager, you can easily set user profiles and system policies.

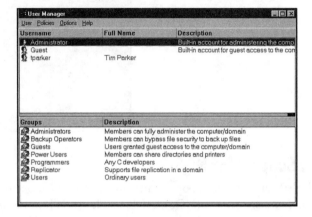

A user profile contains all the settings users require when they log onto a system, letting several users have different profiles on one machine. Windows NT 4 Server allows user profiles to be placed on the server machine, so that users can get the same desktop look and layout, regardless of which network workstation they log onto.

Improved Printer Management

Printer management in NT 4 is greatly improved over Windows NT 3.51. Printers now can be managed remotely from other servers or workstations. A useful addition to the printer system is the ability to store printer drivers on the server for all network shared printers, removing the need to install drivers on each machine that might need to use the networked printer. Printer installation wizards make installing new printers on the system or the network much easier. (See Figure 6.14.)

FIGURE 6.14.

Wizards make installing new printers a snap.

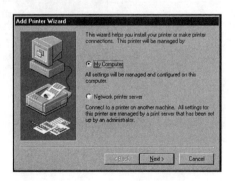

Printing performance is improved in NT 4 by using better spooling—especially for non-PostScript print requests. This results in a shorter wait for applications to return control to users after they submit a printer request.

Multimedia and Telephony APIs

Windows NT 4 includes many *application programming interfaces* (APIs), which means that it can easily be integrated with many up-to-date applications developed with these APIs in mind. The multimedia APIs in Windows 95 are included in NT 4, for example. These APIs improve the behavior of games and applications that use sounds or video when run under NT 4. The *Telephony API* (TAPI) lets you integrate telephone applications into Windows NT 4, including many of the new *Computer-Telephony Integration* (CTI) applications that offer voice mail and messaging on an NT platform.

What You Won't Find in Windows NT 4

If you have used Windows 95, you might expect some of the Windows 95 applications and functions to be included in NT 4; in many cases, this is true. Some Windows 95 features aren't included in NT 4, however, because of porting or support reasons.

Here are the primary features found in Windows 95 that aren't included in Windows NT:

- **Power management:** NT 4 doesn't include support for battery-driven laptops with special power-management requirements.
- **Plug-and-Play:** The idea of Plug-and-Play is to reduce the need to interact with the hardware. Because NT 4 is a much more complex operating system than Windows 95, Plug-and-Play could not be implemented properly.
- **Microsoft Fax:** The Microsoft Fax application in Windows 95 isn't included in Windows NT 4.
- **Infrared communications:** Windows NT 4 has no support for infrared ports.

The Floating-Point Division Problem in Pentium CPUs

As you probably know, some early Intel Pentium processors exhibited a floating-point calculation error under rare circumstances. Some experts argued that the possibility of this affecting the work of the average user was about as likely as being hit by lightning. Still, it was shown to be possible, and it did affect computations in some banking spreadsheets and the work of academic mathematicians who use many decimal places. Intel found and fixed the problem, so later Pentium chips' floating-point units (sections in the Pentium) no longer calculate erroneously.

The manual Setup program was updated to detect whether your Pentium processor's floating-point hardware has the much-dreaded division error. If, during setup, the malfunction is detected in the computer's CPU, the Setup program alerts you. You then have the option of disabling the *floating-point unit* (FPU) on the processor. When this is disabled, calculations that normally would be performed by the FPU are handed off to the CPU, where they are done in "long-hand." Such calculations might take a bit longer to complete, but at least you can be assured that they will be correct to more than 100 decimal places. You don't have to decide during setup to disable the FPU; you can do it later by using the command-line utility called *pentnt*.

PC Card Support

PC Cards (the little cards that plug into the side of laptop computers) have become very popular. (PC Cards used to be called *PCMCIA*.) If you have added a modem, SCSI controller, proprietary CD-ROM controller, Ethernet, or sound card to a laptop, you most likely have used a PC Card.

Windows 95 was the first operating system to provide Plug-and-Play support for PC Cards. Just inserting a card resulted in the card being detected. Powering down wasn't necessary, nor was rebooting. After the card is inserted, Windows 95 loads the proper device driver and configures itself accordingly so that the device can be used.

Now, with Windows NT 4, support for certain modem cards, *Small Computer System Interface* (SCSI) controller cards, network adapter cards, and hard disk PC Cards is also included. Unlike Windows 95's complete one-stop shopping, though, PC Card and socket support haven't been included. (*Card and socket services* are the low-level drivers needed to make your PC Cards work under an operating system.) This feature will come in time, of course, but not with NT 4. Microsoft recommends that you check the Hardware Compatibility List to determine which cards and computers are supported.

When you know that your card and computer are among those supported, using them is a little less elegant than under Windows 95. For one thing, you can't do "hot" inserting and removal, which means inserting or removing a PC Card while the machine is running and expect the machine to recognize the change (Windows 95 allows hot changes, but NT doesn't). Instead, you must follow these steps:

1. Shut down your computer.
2. Insert your card.
3. Restart your computer. Windows NT Workstation should detect the card in the socket.
4. To remove the card, you must also shut down Windows NT Workstation.

Here are a few additional notes about PC Cards:

■ You should insert *Integrated Device Electronics* (IDE) hard disks before you install Windows NT Workstation so that it can recognize the drive and write a signature on it. NT uses these signatures to keep track of the mass storage devices in each system.

■ For Windows NT Workstation to detect a supported SCSI or network adapter PC Card, you first must load the appropriate NT-compatible SCSI device driver or configure the network adapter card before shutting down to insert the card. Then, shut down, insert the card, and reboot. To install a SCSI device driver, for example, double-click the Windows NT Setup icon in the Main program group, then choose Add/Remove SCSI Adapters.

■ Before you insert a PC Card, you might want to check certain applications or system settings or look for a related key in the Registry. This enables you to verify whether NT detected the card after you inserted it. For more information about viewing and searching the Registry, see Chapter 11, "Maintenance and Troubleshooting."

Suppose that you're inserting a modem card and want to know whether it has been detected. You would follow these steps:

1. Before you shut down the computer, double-click the Ports icon in the Control Panel to display the number of communication ports you have.

2. Exit NT and shut down your computer.

3. Insert your modem PC Card.

4. Restart Windows NT Workstation.

5. After the computer restarts, repeat Step 1. If the PC Card is detected, an additional communications port is listed in the Ports dialog box.

Suppose that you want to know whether a SCSI card was detected. You would follow these steps:

1. After you have enabled and configured your SCSI PC Card, but before you shut down Windows NT Workstation to insert the SCSI card, check the Registry for the following key:

   `HKEY_LOCAL_MACHINE\HARDWARE\DEVICEMAP\SCSI`

2. Reboot and check the value again.

CAUTION

For additional information about using the Registry Editor, see "Editing Registry Values" in the README.WRI file. Using the Registry Editor can be dangerous to your system if you don't know what you are doing.

Summary

Although the list of new features in Windows NT 4 is quite lengthy, most of the features are apparent to users. This chapter has discussed the most important new features found in NT 4 and changes from NT 3.51 to NT 4. If you want more information about the NT 4 features, Microsoft's home page on the World Wide Web includes several documents with feature lists.

IN THIS PART

Windows NT System Administration

PART

II

Installing Windows NT

IN THIS CHAPTER

In general, the actual software installation of Windows NT is a self-explanatory and automated process. In some ways, it's much simpler than installing other major operating systems, GUIs (such as Windows 3.1), or even some Windows applications. This is especially true if you install NT from a CD-ROM or over a network.

You will still want to read this chapter before installing NT on your target system, though. You have some choices to consider (some of them new to PC users) before you start the installation process. An incorrect choice can lead to a great deal of extra work later.

> **NOTE**
>
> For the time being, most NT installations will be on Intel x86 systems because RISC-based MIPS ARC/R4000 or DEC Alpha systems are rather expensive and less available. This chapter (in fact, most of this book) assumes that you have an x86-based system. If you're installing on a RISC-based computer, see the section "Installing NT on a RISC Computer," later in this chapter.

Checking for NT Hardware Compatibility

Before attempting an NT installation, you should check your hardware for compatibility with NT. Keep these considerations in mind:

- **You need a speedy processor.** If you can afford a multiprocessor, such as a DEC or a MIPS machine, great. If you're planning to install on a uniprocessor 80486 or Pentium machine, make sure that the CPU and bus design are pretty fast. Microsoft says that you can run NT on an 80486, but I suggest that it be at least a fast speed in the 486DX class or, even better, a Pentium. Even with a fast 80486, NT can seem slow sometimes, especially when you're running Windows 3.1 applications on top of NT. When choosing a bus design, remember that any 32-bit I/O bus is superior to any 16-bit bus. EISA, MCA, PCI, and VLB are all 32-bit buses. If you already have an ISA machine and it has VLB (VESA local bus) slots, consider using them for your video and hard disk controllers. SCSI controllers typically are faster than IDE, but make sure the one you want to use is supported by NT.

> **NOTE**
>
> You can find more specific advice on system upgrades in Chapter 10, "Optimizing Windows NT: Performance Determinants."
>
> Hardware caching controllers are great in theory, but NT does software caching and, in some cases, requires hardware caches to be disabled. NT supports caching controllers, but only if the controller has an NT driver that supports caching, if write caching is disabled, or if caching by the controller is completely disabled.

■ **Be sure you have enough disk space.** You must have about 110M of free space on your target disk for an Express setup. This allows space for the NT files and a 20M paging file (virtual memory). You can get away with less if you use the Custom setup, but don't bother unless you're really pressed. If you choose the Custom Setup option, the required disk space is reported. This amount varies, depending on which NT components you choose to install.

If you're using an x86-based system and you don't have at least 16M of RAM, get ready for painfully slow loading, a great deal of hard-disk thrashing, and long periods of waiting for each dialog box to appear. Contrary to what Microsoft says, NT will load and run with only 12M of RAM. But do yourself a favor and get some more RAM first—it's less frustrating. RISC machines need at least 16M. There is no more important factor than physical memory in determining NT's performance.

NOTE

NT supports up to 4G of RAM. In 16-bit, ISA-based machines, the speed limitations of the 24-bit DMA hardware of these machines are overcome by NT's use of double buffering. Microsoft claims that this double-buffering process works almost as fast as 32-bit DMA. It warns, however, that on some ISA systems, adding memory above 16M actually degrades performance instead of improving it. You might want to borrow some memory and try it both ways if you're considering upgrading beyond 16M for your workstation or server, especially with memory prices going through the roof these days.

■ **Note or look up how your network card is installed.** What are the IRQ and base port addresses? If possible, make sure your system is working correctly under less demanding operating systems, such as DOS, Windows 3.1, or Windows for Workgroups. If your network, sound, video, and mouse cards are working correctly in Windows for Workgroups (WFW), NT will probably install smoothly. (See the next section for help with add-in card configuration.)

■ **You need a minimum of a VGA resolution video display adapter.** A generic VGA screen driver is used for the setup process. At the end of the installation, you can select a video driver based on the detection process or manually select and install a video driver. You can change this selection later by double-clicking the Windows NT Display icon in the Control Panel.

Checking Your Hardware Settings Before Starting

Often, configuration and installation problems are due only to incorrect settings on network, I/O, sound, and other cards. These incorrect settings can produce cards that conflict with one another for the same *interrupt request* (IRQ) line, base I/O port address, DMA, or base memory address.

Usually, you make these settings by changing jumpers or DIP switches on the board. The following cards typically require settings:

- Network cards
- Bus mouse cards
- Sound cards
- Tape backup controller cards
- SCSI cards
- Fax/modem cards

NOTE

There is a move afoot by VESA for manufacturers to design software-configurable cards when possible. Some cards (for example, Novell's NE2000 PLUS) use software programs to set the IRQ and port addresses. You might have to run a DOS program to make the settings before running NT Setup.

In case your understanding of board configuration settings is somewhat foggy, the next few sections give you a quick review.

IRQs

When an add-in card (or program) needs to grab the attention of the CPU, it issues a message called an *interrupt* directly to the CPU. The CPU then services the request accordingly. A common example can be seen when data targeted for a specific workstation arrives at its destination network card. The card "pulls" the predetermined interrupt line, and the CPU then jumps to the appropriate code related to that interrupt to service it. This is done by using an *interrupt handler*.

As a rule, no two boards should share the same interrupt request line or IRQ. When two devices try to use the same interrupt at the same time, a data collision can occur and the system can hang, or nothing happens at all.

TIP

With some operating systems, such as DOS and Windows, there's an exception to this case: Some IRQs can be shared. You might be familiar with this exception. Under DOS, for example, it's often possible to share the LPT1 (IRQ 7) with other devices, as long as you're not printing through that port at the time the second device tries to use it.

NT handles IRQ sharing differently. It doesn't share IRQs on ISA machines. (It does support sharing on EISA, MCA, or PCI machines, but only if no ISA card is sharing the same IRQ as another card.) Instead of IRQ sharing, if two devices are detected as sharing the same IRQ, NT switches to a polling mode; in this mode, the CPU regularly checks for and services I/O requests instead of waiting for IRQ lines to be activated. This process can slow down overall NT performance, because it creates another software loop that the operating system has to service. The bottom line is that NT hangs, fails to load a service or driver, or, at best, slows down a bit if boards have IRQ conflicts, so you need to do your homework on IRQ assignments.

The bad news is that there aren't a lot of IRQ lines to go around. You might have to decide to leave something out of your system if you have boards that aren't very flexible in their IRQ options. Older Novell NE2000 boards, for example, give you only a few IRQ options, and the Logitech Bus Mouse board lets you choose from only IRQs 1 through 5.

If you're configuring a network card, you probably can use IRQ 3 or 5. Take a look at Table 7.1 for help in setting IRQ and port addresses for your cards. Refer to the manuals with the cards to determine how to make the settings and to determine which IRQs already are in use.

Table 7.1. Typical IRQ assignments in 80286-based or later x86 systems.

IRQ	Typical Assignment	Availability
2	EGA/VGA video	Almost never available because it's redirected to IRQ 9.
3	COM2, COM4	Available sometimes.
4	COM1, COM3	Usually not available.
5	LPT2	If a second parallel port is installed, probably available. Not available if a Trantor or Future Domain 8-bit SCSI card is used, unless polling is used for one of the devices.
6	Floppy disk controller	Almost never available.
7	LPT1 (printer port)	Almost never available, but if it is, it is sharable only on EISA, MCA, and PCI devices. If an ISA peripheral is detected on the same IRQ, this prevents sharing.
8	System clock	Never available.
9	EGA/VGA	Seldom available, because devices using IRQ 2 are redirected here as well.
10		Available.
11		Available if no 16-bit SCSI card is in use and set to this default IRQ.

continues

7

INSTALLING WINDOWS NT

Table 7.1. continued

IRQ	Typical Assignment	Availability
12	PS/2 mouse	Available only on systems that don't have a PS/2-style mouse connector. Compaq and NEC, for example, have this connector, so this IRQ is not available on these systems.
13	Math coprocessor (if installed)	Never available.
14	Hard disk controller	Never available if an ST-506-compatible hard disk controller (MFM, RLL, ESDI, or IDE) is used. But possibly available if a SCSI hard disk controller is used.
15		Available.

TIP

Microsoft recommends that you disable COM2/COM4 in your ISA system's CMOS settings if you decide to use IRQ 3 for your network board. This prevents an interrupt conflict in case the two are being used simultaneously. Even if your system works properly under DOS and Windows 3.x, it probably won't work correctly under NT because of the way NT services interrupt requests.

DMA Channels

Your PC has eight DMA channels that can be used for rapidly transferring data between memory and peripherals, such as hard disks, sound cards, and so on. Some cards even use several of these channels at once. (The ProAudio Spectrum 16, for example, uses two DMA channels for high-speed transfer of digitized audio sound data.) The DMA numbers are 0, 2, 3, 5, 6, and 7. Typical users of DMA channels follow:

■ Tape backup controllers

■ Network cards

■ Proprietary printer cards, such as PostScript cards

■ Scanner cards

■ SCSI controllers

In general, you shouldn't share DMA channels. If you're really pressed, though, you can share certain channels. You should never share DMAs that are in use by network cards or hard disk controllers, however, because you might lose important data. As a rule, just try to make sure that no two devices use the same DMA channel at the same time.

Table 7.2 lists the typical DMA controller assignments in x86 (286 and higher) machines.

Table 7.2. Typical DMA controller assignments in x86 machines.

Channel	Typical Assignment
0	Generally used for DMA refresh
1	Available
2	Floppy disk controller
3	Available
4	NT's cascade channel (not available)
5	Available
6	Available
7	Available

7

INSTALLING WINDOWS NT

Base I/O Port

Some devices send and receive data through I/O ports rather than DMA numbers. In PC architecture, I/O ports are mapped into system memory and therefore are accessed by using memory addresses. Again, each device that uses an I/O port must have a different port address.

Table 7.3 shows commonly used and unused port addresses (given in hexadecimal notation).

Table 7.3. Commonly used and unused port addresses.

Port	Device	Port	Device
200 to 20F	Game port	300 to 30F	N/A
210 to 21F		310 to 31F	N/A
220 to 22F		320 to 32F	PS/2 model 30 hard disk controller
230 to 23F	Bus mouse	330 to 33F	N/A
240 to 24F		340 to 34F	N/A
250 to 25F		350 to 35F	N/A
260 to 26F		360 to 36F	N/A
270 to 27F	LPT3	370 to 37F	LPT2
280 to 28F		380 to 38F	N/A

continues

Table 7.3. continued

Port	Device	Port	Device
290 to 29F		390 to 39F	N/A
2A0 to 2AF		3A0 to 3AF	N/A
2B0 to 2BF		3B0 to 3BF	LPT1
2C0 to 2CF		3C0 to 3CF	EGA/VGA
2D0 to 2DF		3D0 to 3DF	CGA/MCGA; also EGA/VGA when operating in color
2E0 to 2EF		3E0 to 3EF	N/A
2F0 to 2FF	COM2	3F0 to 3FF	Floppy disk controller; also COM1

> **TIP**
>
> A common source of I/O contention exists among video cards, SCSI devices, and network cards. As soon as NT is up and running, a program in the Administrative Tools group reports such conflicts in a fairly understandable manner (quasi-English).

Base Memory Addresses

Similar to the I/O port address, the base memory address is the beginning memory address that some cards use to communicate with the CPU. Sometimes, this setting is called the *RAM starting address* (or *start address*).

Some cards (particularly network cards) must have their base memory address set by a jumper or software. Then a corresponding software setting in the NT driver must be set to match. A typical base memory address is D3000. Sometimes, the last zero is dropped, so the address is displayed as D300.

Another consideration with cards using base memory addresses is the amount of RAM space they occupy. Some cards use 16K of space, and others use 32K or more. Check the card's manual for options. Using more memory might improve the card's operation, but it decreases your system's memory availability because that space is occupied.

Note that most ISA cards use an upper memory address that falls somewhere between A000 and FFFF. Many EISA, MCA, VL-Bus, PCI, and some ISA cards, however, can use address space above 1M, or even above 16M in the case of 32-bit cards. If your card can use such an address, it's better to do so because it minimizes the chances of bumping into the operating system.

CAUTION

If you have an ISA computer, check the BIOS and video card shadow RAM addresses being used. These addresses have been known to conflict with the addresses of memory-mapped add-in cards. This kind of data collision definitely can cause a system to crash or at least cause major erratic behavior.

NOTE

Some cards don't specify a base memory address because they don't use RAM address space for data transfer.

Looking at NT Device Driver Availability

Windows NT 4's driver support is pretty impressive. NT 4 supports practically every kind of peripheral and many different models in each support category. All the basics are there. It's still possible that some of the devices in your system aren't supported by NT right out of the box, though.

A fax/modem, fancy monitor, sound card, video card, SCSI adapter, or network adapter board, for example, might not be recognized by NT and might not work.

Just as it took device manufacturers some time to come out with drivers for OS/2 and Windows 3.1, you might have to wait a bit or do some digging. On the upside, though, what Microsoft supplies at least gets NT booted on most systems.

TIP

Look for the NT Hardware Compatibility List if you're in doubt about whether your computer or hardware will work with NT. This booklet comes in the box with NT. Be aware that, even if your products aren't listed, NT still might work with them. A call to Colorado Memory Systems, for example, informed me that another of the supplied tape backup drivers would work with my unit. The same was true of a video card not named, but because it used the Tseng Labs ET4000 chip set, the generic ET4000 screen driver worked fine.

Examining README.WRI and SETUP.TXT

After you install NT, make sure you read the last-minute additions to your release of NT. These additions are listed in the Write files README.WRI and SETUP.TXT. README.WRI is dumped into the Main Program Manager groups. It's well worth scanning.

> **TIP**
>
> You can't easily read the README.WRI file until NT is installed. This is sort of a Catch-22 if you're having trouble with installing. If you think you might have a problem that's listed in the release notes, find a friend with NT installed and view or print the document. If you have a CD-ROM player, just look for README.WRI in the MIPS directory (assuming that your CD-ROM drive is functional under another operating system—preferably, Windows 3.1, because the file is in Write format).

Choosing a File Source for Setup

You can install NT 4 in a number of ways, depending on the source file location:

- From a CD-ROM
- From a network location (called a *sharepoint*)
- From floppy disks

Installing from a CD-ROM and across a network definitely are the preferred techniques. They don't require feeding in many floppy disks. If you don't mind inserting 20 floppy disks and waiting for dialog boxes, there's nothing inherently wrong with floppy disk installation. Using a CD-ROM or the network as a source, however, is much simpler and quicker. Considering all the other tweaking an administrator has to do later, not to mention the learning curve for getting up to speed on the advanced aspects of NT, you don't need the additional aggravation.

Deciding Where to Put NT Disk-Partitioning Schemes

As soon as you decide on the setup source, but before you install NT, one of the biggest issues to consider is the type of partition on which you want to install NT. Windows NT supports two file systems:

- DOS's *file allocation table* (FAT) format
- Windows NT's *NT file system* (NTFS) format

Table 7.4 lists the advantages and disadvantages of each file system.

Table 7.4. Types of partitions.

File System	Advantages	Disadvantages
FAT	Usable by DOS and Windows 3.1 without running NT, so you can boot NT or DOS from a FAT partition with the Boot Loader option that NT automatically installs on a drive containing an existing operating system.	Provides little security. No file or disk recovery features without add-on programs.
NTFS	Extensive file protection (security) and file/drive recoverability. Long filenames—up to 256 characters instead of eight characters or less, plus extension. Usable by DOS applications running in a DOS VDM under NT. (Long filenames are truncated to supply DOS with 8.3 filenames.)	DOS and Windows 3.1 can't see or work with NTFS partitions. DOS and Windows 3.1 applications running under NT can work with NTFS partitions, however.

CAUTION

FAT partitions also can support long filenames, but without the enhanced security and file-recovery options. Also, you should use extreme care when using MS-DOS utility applications that are not aware of long filename support. At worst, these applications can destroy the data on a FAT drive with long filenames. At best, they will convert the long filenames to truncated 8.3 filenames.

If you intend to make a major commitment to NT and you need the safety and security features of NT, you should lean in the direction of NTFS. Remember, though, that after a partition is reformatted as NTFS, DOS won't recognize it. Also, although you can convert a FAT partition to NTFS nondestructively, the reverse is not true. To convert an NTFS partition to a FAT partition without losing data, you have to perform a backup, reformat the disk, and perform a restore. In other words, it's a hassle.

The bottom line is this: The DOS-to-NT migration path that makes the most sense for DOS and Windows 3.1 users is to install NT on the existing DOS or DOS/Windows 3.1 FAT partition and preferably on top of the existing Windows 3.1 or Windows for Workgroups installation. Installing on top of the existing 16-bit Windows directory makes switching to NT easier, because it gives you the option of migrating various Windows 3.1 settings (such as application-specific WIN.INI settings, font settings, desktop settings, and Program Manager settings) to NT automatically. Just be sure to clear off 80M of free space before you run the NT Setup program.

You'll probably want higher security for some files or disks, so you should create an NTFS partition elsewhere to experiment with NT's security or to use for sensitive files or applications that require a higher degree of safety and protection. A common solution among beta testers of NT was to purchase another drive and to format at least part of that drive as NTFS.

Another solution, short of purchasing an additional drive, is to divvy up your existing drive into a couple of partitions (assuming that you have enough disk space). Leave the current system drive in its current format (typically, FAT) and create an NTFS partition for use with directories that need security.

NOTE

You have the option of migrating Windows 3.1 settings to NT only if you opt to upgrade Windows—that is, if you install NT on top of the existing Windows directory. If you do so, Setup adds several files to your Windows directory and adds a \WINDOWS\SYSTEM32 directory to hold additional support files that's similar to the \WINDOWS\SYSTEM directory used by Windows 3.1.

Another option you have is to install the basic boot files (about 2M worth) on the normal boot disk (drive 0), but to locate the NT support files elsewhere, such as on another partition or on another physical drive. If you can't figure out how to reclaim 90M of disk space on drive 0, you can instruct NT to install the support files on another drive while still performing the initial bootup from drive 0. The boot drive must have the NT boot sector, NTLDR, NTDETECT.COM, NTBOOTDD.SYS (if SCSI), and BOOTSECT.DOS in the c:\ directory. The rest of the files can go wherever you indicate.

Coping with DoubleSpace and Stacker

Simply put, NT doesn't recognize virtual drives created by compressing software. Before you can even begin, you must remove the disk-compression scheme, restoring all your files to a decompressed format on volumes you want NT to recognize. This can be a hassle, particularly if your hard disk is packed (and whose isn't?). Look in the manual that came with your disk-compression software for help with this process.

Here's the approach I took before installing NT. I had a 205M drive that, when compressed with DoubleSpace, gave me about 350M of files. It was gridlock city, because I had only a 40M decompressed portion on the drive—not enough to unsquish much data into. Short of performing a total backup and restore, you might try the following steps, using a new drive:

1. Install a second physical drive or locate a decompressed partition to copy to. (In my case, it was a new, 340M physical drive.)

2. Start copying directories to the second drive. (Dragging from the My Computer or File Manager drive icon is the easiest way.) Because your target drive isn't compressed, this process, in effect, decompresses the files.

3. Occasionally exit Windows and, from DOS, run DoubleSpace using its menu interface. Choose to resize the compressed volume, decreasing its size as much as possible. (You might have to defragment the compressed drive a couple of times by using the Defragment option before DoubleSpace allows you to decrease the compressed volume's size.)

> **NOTE**
>
> Be aware that, even with defragmentation, there can seem to be arbitrary limitations on how much you can decrease the compressed volume's size. These limitations don't always make sense and can prove frustrating. Often, the culprit is a file (or files) marked as hidden, system, or read-only. These files can't be moved, so they limit the minimum size of the compressed drive. Try using My Computer or another file-management tool to display file attributes, then look for such files and change these attributes. Then you can try to decrease the compressed partition size again.

4. Repeat Steps 2 and 3 as many times as you need to, depending on how much data you have to decompress.

5. If you're still out of space, zip or archive some directories. I use PKZIP (DOS) or QUINZIP (Windows). You can unzip the archives later when you get your compressed volume back in usable form. Eventually, you will get everything copied out of or backed up from the compressed volume.

6. Delete the compressed volume. With DoubleSpace, you can do this by erasing the hidden system volume file. The name of this file is in the form DBLSPACE.*XXX*, where *XXX* is a number—for example, DBLSPACE.000.

> **TIP**
>
> Another way to delete a DoubleSpace drive is to use this DOS command:
>
> ```
> dblspace /delete x
> ```
>
> In this command, *x* is the logical drive letter of the compressed drive. Note that you can't delete drive C in this way.

7. Unzip directories, move directories back to their original drive, and, in general, try to reestablish the same drive/directory tree structure you had before. (Many applications—particularly Windows 3.*x* programs—expect support DLLs, fonts, and other related files to be where they were when you installed them.) Try to arrange for about 90M of free space if you want to set up NT on the same disk.

> **TIP**
>
> An alternative to the preceding steps for gradually juggling files is to use a tape backup system and then do a complete backup and restore. Or, if you're on a network, find a hard disk with enough temporary space to hold your directories. A third alternative is to make sure your second hard disk is large enough to take everything on your compressed drive in one fell swoop. Remember, though, that files expand to approximately twice their compressed size when copied out of their volume.

Performing a Basic Installation

The following steps describe the basic installation procedure, regardless of whether the source is a CD-ROM or floppy disks. (Upgrading an existing installation is covered in "Upgrading an Existing Installation," and installation across a network is covered in "Installing NT over a Network with WINNT"—both located later in this chapter.)

> **NOTE**
>
> If you intend to load NT from a SCSI-controlled CD-ROM, make sure that the drive isn't set to device 0 or 1. If it is, Setup might report the CD-ROM as an active hard disk partition rather than removable media.

Before you start Setup, you have to know the type of display, mouse, printer, printer port, keyboard, network adapter address and IRQ, and computer name and domain name if you're going to connect the NT machine to a Windows NT Advanced Server domain.

To run Setup, follow these steps:

1. Insert the NT Setup Disk 1 into drive A.

> **TIP**
>
> Most Intel-based PC systems use a floppy disk data cable with two connectors—one for drive A and one for drive B. The drive A connector is the one that has a few of its wires twisted just before the connector.

2. Reboot your machine and, optionally, reset the CMOS BIOS settings to cause your system to read the floppy drive for startup if you've changed that in the past.

3. The boot disk takes over your system and loads enough of the operating system to bootstrap the Setup program and identify your SCSI disk controller. During this process, you need to insert the additional Setup disks as prompted.

4. You are asked several things about your system and your preferences for installation. First, Setup identifies your hardware. Next, it asks you to make choices regarding the file system you want to use and the directory for storing NT files.

5. Prepare a blank, high-density disk that's compatible with your drive A. NT uses the disk during installation to create an Emergency Repair Disk that you'll use in case NT has trouble booting in the future. (Typically, you might have trouble rebooting if you've made system modifications, such as adding drivers that just won't work with your system.)

6. You're asked to choose a Custom or an Express setup, just as with standard Windows. Express setup is a better choice in most circumstances, simply because it requires less intervention. Although Custom setup allows you to choose not to install certain modules of NT (such as Help, Accessories, and so on) and to declare system hardware settings manually, Express setup does its best to work around disk space shortages, bagging trivial components not necessary for NT to work. It then searches for applications and adds icons to the relevant NT program groups.

> **TIP**
>
> Custom setup lists your detected hardware and lets you modify the list. You can also change the target directory, configure network adapters, and join a workgroup. In addition, Custom setup gives you more control in setting up applications by allowing you to choose the paths and drives where you want it to look for applications. Again, Express setup is easier. But if, for some reason, the auto-detection capabilities of Express setup hang the Setup program (this can happen particularly if network cards or video cards are detected incorrectly), run Custom setup and manually scrutinize and modify the detected hardware settings as they are presented in dialog boxes. This might get you through the installation successfully.

> **NOTE**
>
> Custom setup presents a screen asking you to declare virtual memory (paging or swap file) settings. Express setup does this automatically. Virtual memory (paging file) considerations are covered in Chapter 8, "Using the Control Panel to Configure Windows NT." In the meantime, you can choose the default settings suggested by Setup.

7. Proceed with the installation. The program scans for SCSI adapters and examines the hard disk partition scheme on your system. If your NT CD-ROM is in the drive connected to the SCSI adapter that Setup finds, it assumes that this is the file source for the installation.

8. Setup looks for an existing Windows NT installation or a 16-bit Windows installation if no previous NT installation is found. If Setup finds a previous installation, it suggests installing NT in the same directory (C:\WINDOWS, for example). If you want to install NT on a FAT partition, you should accept this suggestion. NT system files will land in a new directory—C:\WINDOWS\ SYSTEM32—instead of in your Windows or \WINDOWS\SYSTEM directory, so don't worry about file collisions or more confusion in those already overloaded directories.

> **TIP**
>
> There's an advantage to installing in the existing Windows directory: Many of your existing Windows settings (notably, Program Manager groups, application .INI files, and so on) are maintained and still work with the existing pathnames. If you choose to put NT elsewhere, Win 3.1 applications are more likely to issue error messages, because they're less likely to find their related support files.

9. NT Setup performs a check of your entire disk to make sure there aren't any errors, and then it copies what seems like a zillion files to the hard disk. By using the CD-ROM, this process is painless and takes just a couple of minutes.

10. You now see a message about performing a reset; do it, and note that the bootup sequence is very different now. You see a message about the NT OS loader booting and a message about NT checking the hard disk media. NT is looking for broken chains, much like CHKDSK. NT doesn't boot until the volume is considered clean (free of errors). If errors are detected, NT tries to correct them.

> **NOTE**
>
> On most VGA screens, these messages are in a smaller-than-normal point size. Instead of 25 characters per line, you will see 48 characters per line.

7

11. During the installation, you are prompted to enter your name and your company's name and to verify them. As with other Microsoft products, this information shows up in NT-related dialog boxes, such as About boxes. It's Microsoft's way of recording who is supposedly the registered owner.

12. You're then prompted to give the computer a name. If you've been using the computer with another networking scheme, such as Windows for Workgroups, use the same name. This way, other stations on the network can connect to the new NT station, and they won't even know it has changed status from a WFW peer to an NT peer.

13. You are prompted to choose the language locale. Usually, English (American) is fine. This affects primarily date, currency, and time displays, just as in 16-bit Windows.

14. When you're prompted about printers, in the Model area, choose the type of printer attached to your system, set the correct port, and give the printer a name. This name is the name users on the network see when they're browsing around to attach to a printer. Use a name that makes sense, such as HP Laser Printer in Room 302. A name like this tells users where to pick up their printouts.

15. You are asked about the network card(s) in the machine. Set the IRQ, port address, DMA channel, or other relevant information if you don't want NT to search for these values. Defaults for the detected card are displayed (assuming that your card is installed and is detected properly). Change the defaults if necessary. (See Chapter 10 and this chapter for more details on network installation.) Setup now copies a significant number of files.

NOTE

If the network card isn't detected, you can still set up the driver for the card. Just stipulate the IRQ and base address, or whatever else you're asked about. Later, you can adjust the card's jumpers (or run a DOS-based software configuration program). Then try rebooting NT until the card is detected properly.

16. After some advertisements about how great NT is, and after the installation of other files, the network modules are started, and you're asked to declare the name of the workgroup or domain you want to join and to declare a password. If you want to connect to an already existing Windows for Workgroups workgroup, just enter the name of the group and click OK.

NOTE

If, at this point, your connection to the network doesn't start, it's probably because the network isn't running (check the other workstations/servers) or, more likely, because Setup didn't recognize your network card. You should try to reinstall NT using the Custom setup, because it lets you declare the network card and settings. Or, as soon as NT gets up and running fully, you can run the Network applet from the Control Panel and adjust the card and driver settings there.

17. You now see the Administrator Account Setup window. Each NT machine can have multiple accounts or sets of passwords, privileges, and so on for each user. Each NT machine you set up must have at least one administrator account, though. This is the account the system administrator will use to log onto the system and perform certain maintenance tasks, such as setting up and altering passwords, creating a post office for use with the Mail program, and controlling the sharing of directories and other resources. Setup assumes that the person doing the installation is an administrator and grants Administrator status by allowing him or her to enter the password. Enter a password and write it down somewhere so that you'll remember it.

NOTE

The default password is *Administrator*. If you don't enter a password and you are prompted for the administrator's password later, enter **Administrator**. It might work.

18. You now have the option of creating a local account for the user (as opposed to the administrator). Initially, the user has the same privileges as the administrator, but you can change this later by using the User Manager program. No two accounts can have the same password, so even if the same person is both the local user and the administrator, the accounts must have different assigned passwords.

NOTE

You can set up multiple user accounts on the same NT machine by using the User Manager applet (available only to those with Administrator status). At this point, though, you have the option of creating only one user account. Chapter 9, "Windows NT Administration," tells you how to establish new accounts with User Manager.

19. Check the Date and Time dialog box for accuracy. Normally, you just have to change the time zone.

20. After you're prompted, insert a high-density floppy disk into the boot drive for NT to make an Emergency Repair Disk. The disk is formatted and then written to with backup information.

NOTE

The Emergency Repair Disk contains the directory structure, the NT Registry information, and the computer name. (The Registry is NT's version of Windows 3.1's .INI files, among other things.) The disk can be used only with the computer it was created on. It can't be transferred to another machine unless the other machine is identical (physically and logically) to the machine the disk was created on. This isn't likely, but it's possible.

21. Remove the floppy disk and restart your computer. If you already had DOS on the system disk, your system tracks are modified so that the multiboot OS Loader runs at boot time. You then see an option for starting MS-DOS or NT.

22. Make sure that Windows NT is highlighted and press Enter. NT also boots by itself if you just wait 30 seconds.

23. The first time you log on as a user, if NT was installed in a directory with a preexisting Windows 3.1 or Windows 95 installation, you're prompted to take these actions:

   ■ Migrate Windows 3.*x* WIN.INI and CONTROL.INI files into NT.

   ■ Migrate Windows 3.*x* Program Manager group files into NT.

   As a rule, I suggest you take these actions if you want the smoothest migration path from 16-bit to 32-bit Windows. When you opt for this action, you'll notice some major disk thrashing. You suddenly have many groups, and your color settings, desktop setup, and so on are the same as they were under Windows 3.1. You still have to adjust the Program Manager windows, however (by choosing Arrange Icons). Also note that your WINFILE.INI file isn't migrated, so File Manager also needs to be arranged.

NOTE

If you install NT in an existing Windows for Workgroups installation with the Microsoft At Work fax support or other mail extension DLLs, MS Mail might report several error messages about invalid images. These error messages occur because the NT version of MS Mail doesn't support 16-bit DLLs. The easiest way to correct this problem is to use the Registry Editor to delete the undesired keys. Having experienced several problems trying to correct these situations, I suggest you delete all but the following key in HKEY_CURRENT_USER\Software\Microsoft\Mail\Microsoft Mail. The tree should be completely empty except for this single key. This key will restore the application to its initial state, ready for you to configure the application as desired.

Installing NT on an Unformatted Hard Disk

This section describes installation on a new hard disk or one that hasn't been formatted. Normally, NT assumes that you want to keep the existing partition type (FAT, NTFS, or HPFS) intact. On an unformatted disk, however, Setup gives you the option of formatting the disk as a FAT or NTFS volume. Follow these steps:

1. At the beginning of Setup, you see this message:

   ```
   Setup has determined that your computer's startup hard disk contains a
   nonstandard OS or has never been used. If a nonstandard operating system is
   installed, continuing Setup may interfere with or destroy the operating
   system's ability to start.
   ```

   If the hard disk has never been used, or you want to discard its current contents, choose to continue Setup.

   You then see these messages:

   ```
   Please select the partition where you would like to install Windows NT.
   ```

   ```
   The list below shows the existing partitions that Setup has found, as well as
   space available for new partitions. Use the Up and Down arrow keys to high-
   light your choice in the list.
   ```

   At this point, you can create a partition by pressing P. On a new disk, the default is to partition the whole disk. You can decrease the size of the partition if you want. Press Enter to continue. This just creates a partition; it doesn't format it.

NOTE

Sometimes, 1M or so of space is left unpartitioned. Older drives in particular list this unused 1M or so. This unused space is actually one cylinder on the hard disk that's reserved as a test track. Some newer drives, such as late-model SCSI drives, don't set aside a test track, so you don't see the unused space after you partition these drives. Some older SCSI drives (for example, Adaptec 154x drives) have a test track, but the newer NT drivers can be repartitioned to regain this extra 1M.

2. Now you have a choice to format the partition as FAT or NTFS.

NOTE

To take advantage of the security features of NT (such as recovery from media glitches and prevention of unauthorized access), you must use NTFS. As discussed earlier, be aware that you don't have access to NTFS partitions when you boot MS-DOS.

3. Setup warns you that formatting will erase data on the partition. After you choose to continue, a "gas gauge" appears, keeping you informed of the formatting progress.

4. After the format, you're asked in which directory you want to place NT. The default is \WINNT. This option is the best overall choice. If you later install another Windows version (such as 3.1 or Windows for Workgroups), its Setup program detects NT and suggests that you install into the \WINNT directory to allow a symbiotic relationship between the two versions and to allow the migration of settings.

> **NOTE**
>
> To force a Windows 3.1-to-NT migration after installation ends, you must create a new user account.

5. After installation is over, reboot. If there was another operating system on your computer before you installed NT, you see a Windows NT Boot Loader message asking which operating system you want to load: NT or MS-DOS (and, optionally, OS/2 if that was the previous system). Select NT, and NT starts. It checks the system first and then asks you to press Ctrl+Alt+Del to log on.

> **NOTE**
>
> You might wonder why NT makes you press the traditional three-key reset command keys to log on. In DOS, these keys are the "abandon ship" keys. Microsoft claims that pressing these keys prevents Trojan Horse viruses or "back doors" from being available after logon.

After the first boot, the volume check reports that your volume is a FAT volume. Don't worry. If you chose to create an NTFS partition, it is converted after the partition is determined to be "clean" by the OS Loader. The OS Loader then runs the convert program, converting the FAT to NTFS, and finally reboots.

Installing NT over a Network with WINNT

Network administrators might want to set up a number of NT machines along a network. You can easily do this by creating a shared directory on the network. This directory will hold the NT files. After the files are copied there by Setup, you use a supplied command-prompt program, WINNT.EXE, to install the NT files on the target machine. Setting up such a shared directory for NT installation is called (by Microsoft) *creating a sharepoint*. As soon as the sharepoint is created, an administrator can install NT for a user by using the WINNT32 command. These steps are covered in the next section.

Setting Up the Network Sharepoint for Subsequent Network NT Installations

To create a sharepoint, follow these steps:

1. Run NT on the machine on which the sharepoint will reside.

2. Make sure that the network is alive and functioning. Any kind of network will do, as long as all the workstations on which you want to set up NT can access the network via MS-DOS.

3. Check your directory permissions. The drive on which you're going to install the sharepoint must have read/write permission by you, because you're going to write files there.

4. From NT My Computer, switch to (or connect to) the target drive.

5. Create a fresh directory to receive the files—use the command md netnt, for example.

6. Open a DOS session (command prompt) from Program Manager, or choose File | Run from File Manager and type **COMMAND**.

7. Enter the following command:

   xcopy SourceDirectory\Platform DestinationDirectory

   To copy the files for the Intel platform, for example, you enter this command:

   XCOPY E:\I386 \\SRV\SETUP\I386

   Here, E: is the local CD-ROM (source files), and the destination directory \SETUP\I386 resides on the server SRV.

NOTE

If you're installing to a shared directory on another network, just specify the drive letter you used to connect instead of a UNC filename for the destination directory.

---

8. After all the files are copied to the sharepoint, you're ready to proceed with the client installations.

Follow the instructions in the next section to install NT on one of the workstations connected to the network.

Installing NT from a Network Sharepoint

As soon as the sharepoint is set up, you're ready to install NT on any workstation that can access the sharepoint. Microsoft says that it doesn't matter which *network operating system* (NOS) connects the stations, as long as each can access the sharepoint through MS-DOS or some operating system that can run an MS-DOS program from the DOS command line, such as Windows for Workgroups, OS/2, or Windows 3.1 with a compatible network link like Banyan VINES or NetWare. The only catch is that the DOS command-line interpreter must be running in an environment that allows only a single instance of MS-DOS; you can't be running Windows in enhanced mode—it must be running in standard mode. Also, you cannot be running OS/2 2.*x*; it must be 1.*x*. Obviously, just quitting OS/2 or Windows and running a plain old DOS session might be the easiest way to perform such an installation.

> **NOTE**
>
> Even though you can install NT across a non-NT network, that doesn't mean that NT will recognize that network after it's installed. NT recognizes only specific networks.

> **TIP**
>
> Instead of installing across a network, you could pass around a CD-ROM drive. However, network speed often is higher than that of a CD-ROM, so network installation is faster, with less hassle. Also, because all WINNT does is copy files, multiple workstations can be installing NT at the same time with no network conflicts.

To install NT from a network sharepoint, follow these steps:

1. Make sure that the sharepoint (NT file source directory) is shared for network access.
2. At the target workstation, log onto the network and connect to, or otherwise access, the sharepoint directory.

> **NOTE**
>
> If your target station is a Windows for Workgroups 3.1 machine, you have to follow a few more steps. As mentioned earlier, you can't run WINNT in enhanced 386 mode—only in standard mode. To start Windows for Workgroups in standard mode, you first must start the network manually. Follow these steps:
>
> 1. Boot the machine into DOS and type net start workgroup.
> 2. Enter your computer name and password, then type win /s.

NOTE

Windows for Workgroups 3.11 doesn't support standard mode. However, `win /t` provides the same basic functionality—with one exception. If your network driver is an NDIS 3.0 (a protected-mode driver), your network won't start. To solve this problem, use the Network Setup applet in the Network Group to install an NDIS 2.0 driver for your network adapter, or configure your current driver to support real mode and enhanced mode.

3. Use File Manager or My Computer to connect to and log onto the sharepoint.

4. An .EXE file should be in the sharepoint directory called WINNT. Run this program.

5. NT installs pretty much as explained earlier in the "Performing a Basic Installation" section, but with a few twists:

   ■ First, WINNT prompts you to insert a disk into drive A. It then creates three floppy disks, which are essentially the same NT installation floppy disks you use in a normal installation.

   ■ Next, WINNT copies the NT source files from the sharepoint into the target directory on the local machine, dropping them in a temporary directory called WIN_NT.~LS.

   ■ WINNT then prompts the installer to reboot the machine so that the boot floppy disk is read.

   ■ A standard installation takes place, except that Setup moves files from the temporary directory into the target directory (instead of copying them from a CD-ROM or floppy disk).

   ■ If less than 8M of RAM is detected in the target machine, Setup terminates.

NOTE

Because files are *moved* rather than *copied* between directories on the target partition, you don't need to ensure double the normal amount of hard disk space. Approximately 110M is still adequate.

TIP

Your company might have NT customization requirements or preferences. If you alter the source NT files at the sharepoint before network installation, all subsequent network installations reflect those changes immediately after installation without the need to fine-tune each workstation's setup. This feature can save workstation configuration time. See Chapters 8 through 11 for customization information.

Upgrading an Existing Installation

You can upgrade an existing installation of NT in several ways. You can use either of the setup methods just discussed, or you can use WINNT32. WINNT32 is a native NT application that can be configured to use a network sharepoint to upgrade an existing NT installation with or without any boot disks. My favorite method uses the No Floppy Boot option, because it's essentially a hands-off upgrade that requires minimal user interaction.

> **NOTE**
>
> You can't use WINNT to upgrade a RISC-based computer. Instead, follow the standard method of installation as described in the next section, "Installing NT on a RISC Computer," or use WINNT32.

To perform an upgrade and create the three boot floppy disks, follow these steps:

1. Make sure that the sharepoint (NT file source directory) is shared for network access.

2. At the target workstation, log onto the network and connect to, or otherwise access, the sharepoint directory.

3. An .EXE file should exist in the sharepoint directory called WINNT32. Run this program.

4. NT installs as explained in the preceding section, "Installing NT from a Network Sharepoint."

To perform an upgrade without creating the three boot floppy disks, follow these steps:

1. Make sure that the sharepoint (NT file source directory) is shared for network access.

2. At the target workstation, log onto the network and connect to, or otherwise access, the sharepoint directory.

3. An .EXE file should exist in the sharepoint directory called WINNT32. Run this program with these command-line parameters:

```
/s:\\ServerName\SharePoint /b /x
```

This specifies the source path and floppy-less operation and tells NT not to create the boot floppy disks, respectively.

4. NT installs pretty much as explained in the preceding section, "Installing NT from a Network Sharepoint," but with a few exceptions:

   ■ First, NT copies the NT source files from the sharepoint into the target directory on the local machine, dropping them in a temporary directory called WIN_NT.~LS. Another temporary directory called WIN_NT.~BT contains the boot files required for setup (basically, the same files contained in the three boot floppy disks).

- Next, an entry is added to BOOT.INI for the NT upgrade, and you're prompted to restart the computer or to exit to Windows NT. After the computer restarts, the upgrade process continues.

- A standard installation occurs, except that Setup moves files from the temporary directory into the target directory (instead of copying them from a CD-ROM or floppy disk). Also, as an upgrade to an existing installation, even if Custom setup is specified, there are no options to customize the exiting network settings, user account, domain, or other settings. In fact, the only configurable options are remote access (if the TCP/IP protocol has been installed) and the display settings.

Installing NT on a RISC Computer

There's some variation in the way you run Setup on RISC-based computers. First, you have to check that your hard disk has been initialized. It doesn't all have to be partitioned, but at least some of it must be. Unlike x86 systems, RISC systems can split the boot track and the NT system files between two partitions. Your primary partition (called the *system partition*) must be a FAT, and it must have at least 2M of space to handle the NT hardware-specific NT boot files. If you're not sure where the system partition is located or whether you have one, study the manuals or call the manufacturer.

NOTE

After you install NT, the system partition has a directory called \OS\NT, which includes two boot files: OSLOADER.EXE and HAL.DLL.

Next, you should check the manual to determine how to run a program found on a CD-ROM. As soon as you have that under control, the following instructions are typical of what you'll have to do:

NOTE

Because of differences between machines, these steps are approximate. The general principles are the same, however.

1. With the NT CD-ROM in the disk, restart the computer.
2. Choose to run a program. On an ARC machine, for example, choose Run A Program from the menu.

3. You should see a command prompt. Enter the following line (or something similar):

   `CD:\mips\setupldr`

   The gist is that you're trying to run the SETUPLDR program.

4. Now go through the basic installation as described earlier in this chapter, responding to the dialog boxes.

Summary

In this chapter, you've seen how to install and start the configuration process for Windows NT 4. The setup routine supplied on the NT 4 CD-ROM does almost all the work for you, showing you the best choices to make in most cases. If you haven't worked with Windows NT before, you should probably let the CD-ROM's setup procedure do the work for you. If you need to make configuration changes, the setup routine is flexible enough to let you, although previous NT experience is very handy.

If you're upgrading to Windows NT 4 from an earlier version of Windows NT or from Windows 95, the setup routine provided with NT 4 handles almost everything automatically. All you have to do is confirm the choices. This type of installation procedure makes working with Windows NT 4 much friendlier and easier than earlier versions!

7

INSTALLING
WINDOWS NT

Using the Control Panel to Configure Windows NT

CHAPTER

8

The basics of configuring Windows NT was explained in Chapter 7, "Installing Windows NT." For many typical NT systems, the Setup program oversees configuration quite well. As a result, in many cases, any adjustments needed are minor.

Because NT is based on an entirely different model from Windows running on DOS, configuration (although achieved in some cases through similar paths, such as the Control Panel) actually works quite differently in NT. For example, 32-bit applications written for NT no longer use traditional 16-bit Windows .INI files for saving their settings—neither does Windows NT. (Of course, 16-bit Windows applications running under NT still do.) No longer does Windows configuration entail laborious scrutiny of the WIN.INI, SYSTEM.INI, AUTOEXEC.BAT, and CONFIG.SYS files. In place of these files, NT relies on a totally new hardware and software configuration concept that helps MIS personnel locally or remotely configure and maintain hundreds or even thousands of computers and applications. Windows 95 uses a similar (but not completely compatible) system as Windows NT 4.

This new configuration is achieved through the *Configuration Registry*—a centralized database that stores information about hardware, applications, and operating system settings for each computer on the network.

Since the introduction of the Registry, a SYSEDIT program no longer exists for modifying your system files, and new applications are no longer allowed to run amok among your configuration files, potentially wreaking havoc on a finely tuned system. Instead, when absolutely necessary (which isn't often), you can use the Registry Editor to dig into things. (The Registry Editor is covered in Chapter 12, "An Overview of Windows NT Networking.")

Under most conditions, actual direct manipulation of the Registry isn't necessary or recommended. The supplied administration tools, such as the Control Panel, offer an easier interface and make sure Registry alterations are maintained properly.

This chapter covers the most likely avenues you can use to tailor Windows NT settings on the workstation or server.

NOTE

Settings specific to NT Server aren't covered here. Look for descriptions of these settings in Part III, "Networking Windows NT."

Using the Control Panel Applets

The NT Control Panel has extensions above and beyond those in Windows 3.1 or Windows 95. Aside from actual system administration involving passwords, user profiles, and disk management, the majority of NT configuration can be performed by using the Control Panel. Any Control Panel changes you make are stored in the Registry in the active account's section (tree).

This means that each user on any given system can have unique Control Panel settings, such as screen savers, mouse sensitivity, screen colors, and so on.

> **CAUTION**
>
> Some settings, such as fonts, are systemwide. Adding or removing fonts on a given workstation affects all users.

As with Windows 95, you open the Control Panel by choosing Start | Settings. (See Figure 8.1.)

FIGURE 8.1.

The NT Control Panel from NT Workstation.

8

CONFIGURING
WINDOWS NT

Table 8.1 lists the most important Control Panel options (applets) and their uses. You'll be familiar with some of the options, and others are new with NT. An asterisk indicates that the function is identical (or nearly identical) to Windows 3.1 or Windows 95. *Local* means that settings can be set individually for a specific user on a workstation. *Global* means that changes affect the accounts of all users on the workstation.

Table 8.1. Control Panel applets.

Applet	Local or Global	Function
Accessibility Options	Local	Sets some behavior options.
Add/Remove Programs	Global	Installs or removes software.
Console	Global	Sets the DOS window characteristcs.
Date/Time	Global	Sets the system's clock.

continues

Table 8.1. continued

Applet	Local or Global	Function
Devices	Global	Similar to Services, but apply specifically to devices like a CD-ROM drive. In fact, they are loadable device drivers, such as those you're used to loading with CONFIG.SYS in DOS. This applet allows you to interactively start, stop, and declare when each device driver is loaded (such as at boot time).
Display	Global	Installs and removes video drivers, video resolution, color palettes, font size, and refresh rate. Also sets wallpaper and screen savers.
Fonts*	Global	Installs, removes, and views installed TrueType fonts.
Internet	Global	Sets access routines for an Internet connection.
Keyboard*	Local	Sets key-repeat rate and delay before repeat.
Microsoft Mail Postoffice	Local	Controls mail preferences.
Mail	Global	Controls how NT gets mail.
Modems	Global	Configures the system's modems.
Mouse*	Local	Sets sensitivity, double-click speed, and left/right buttons.
Network	Global	Sets the network interface card. Sets card parameters, such as IRQ, DMA, and port address. Installs network drivers and software components. Joins workgroups or domains.
PC Card (PCMCIA)	Global	Configures PC Cards on the system.
Ports	Global	Configures serial asynchronous ports with settings such as Baud, Parity, Data Bits, Flow Control, Base Port Address, and IRQ.
Printers	Global	Runs Print wizards.
Regional Settings*	Global for language; local for everything else	Sets currency formats, special characters, and the date/time display format.

Applet	Local or Global	Function
SCSI Adapters	Global	Configures SCSI adapters on the system.
Server	Global	Lets you see who is connected to your local computer, which devices you share, and who is using them. You also can disconnect other users from these resources, as well as declare which users will get alert messages in case of a system emergency, such as an impending power-down. Also allows you to manage directory replication, described in Chapter 9, "Windows NT Administration."
Services	Global for administrators; local for other users. Specific services can be installed either way.	Many of NT's inner workings are divided into modules called *services*. The ability to act as an OLE server to others on the network and to browse the network for other machines are both services, for example. The Services applet lets you start or stop such modules without quitting and restarting NT. You also can declare when each service becomes active.
Sounds*	Local	Assigns system sounds if you have a sound card, or turns off the annoying beep if you don't want the computer to talk back to you.
System	Global	Sets virtual memory page size, system and application environment variables, system-recovery options (logging events, administrator alerts, and system reboots), and the startup operating system (OS/2, MS-DOS, or NT).
Cursors	Local	Configures cursor shapes, such as the pointer, the waiting hourglass, and others. Some animated cursors are supplied too, which can be fun.
Drivers*	Global	Allows you to install, configure, and remove software drivers for add-on multimedia sound boards, video boards, TV boards, and so on.

8

CONFIGURING
WINDOWS NT

continues

Table 8.1. continued

Applet	Local or Global	Function
UPS	Global	Lets you set certain options if you have an uninterruptible power supply. You can specify how long to wait before saving files and shutting down the system, which serial port its communication line is connected to, and so on.

Display

Earlier versions of Windows NT supported only the most popular graphics cards and monitors. That's changed with NT 4, as drivers for most video cards and monitors are now supplied with the CD-ROM. For newer devices that aren't included, you can usually use a compatible device from the same manufacturer or download an NT driver from the manufacturer's Web site or bulletin board system. In this section, you'll look at the basics of configuring your display system under NT 4.

Configuring Your Video Display

Windows NT includes a nifty new Control Panel applet to configure your video display. It's a significant improvement over its predecessor, the Windows NT 3.51 applet, which allows you to specify only the video resolution and refresh rate. With the new Display applet's Settings page, you can determine at a glance all the supported video resolutions and refresh rates your video driver supports. (See Figure 8.2.) You also can select your color palette, font size, display area (or video resolution), and refresh rate. You can change your video driver and even test a new video mode before final acceptance.

FIGURE 8.2.
Setting the display size.

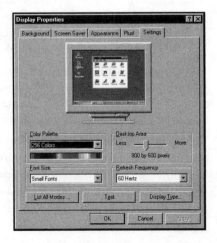

The most common use of the Display applet is to install and test a new video driver or display mode. To install a new video driver, follow these steps:

1. Start the Display applet in the Control Panel by double-clicking the applet icon.

2. Select the Settings tab from the list across the top of the window.

3. Click the Display Type button to open the Display Type dialog box, as shown in Figure 8.3.

FIGURE 8.3.

Changing the display type on the Display applet.

8

CONFIGURING
WINDOWS NT

> **NOTE**
>
> The Display Type dialog box contains several useful pieces of information. The Driver Information group lists the display driver's manufacturer, version numbers, and combined files. The Adapter Information group lists the video chip set, *digital-to-analog* (DAC) chip set, total adapter memory (which is useful knowledge to have when you're considering modifying a supported palette or resolution), and an identification string.

4. Click the Change button to display the Change Display dialog box shown in Figure 8.4.

FIGURE 8.4.

Changing the display type.

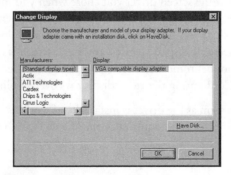

5. From the list of drivers shown on the window, select the video driver to install and click the Install button. If your video adapter isn't listed and no compatible driver exists (such as the Weitek P9000 Graphics Adapter, which also works for the Diamond Viper VLB), click the Other button. To remove a video driver from your system, click the Deinstall button.

6. Click OK, then click the Close icon in the Display Type dialog box. If you haven't tested this driver before, you are prompted to test the selected driver and resolution. A series of graphics is displayed for approximately five seconds. If the graphics are visible, click the OK button. If they aren't, select a different video driver, resolution, or refresh rate.

TIP

If, for some reason, the selected video driver doesn't work and you can't see the display, restart the computer and use the Last Known Good option (displayed on the Startup menu when you boot NT 4) to restore your previous configuration or the /basevideo boot option at system startup. This loads NT with the default VGA video driver.

Creating or Loading a Color Scheme

You can also use the Display applet to alter the colors assigned to Windows screen elements. Because colors on gray-scale screens (such as many laptops) are mapped to shades of gray, changing the color settings has some effect on those types of screens, too. The default setting (called Windows Default) is fine for most screens. Users can make modifications, however. Users' settings are stored in the Registry and are reactivated when they log onto the system.

You can modify the color setting of just about any part of a Windows screen—either manually or by choosing one of the predefined color schemes. You select manual color choices from a palette of premade color choices. If no color satisfies you, you can mix custom colors, just like in a paint store. After you create custom colors and color schemes, you can save them for later use.

It's possible that the screen driver you chose when you installed NT will have some effect on the color rendering on the workstation's screen. Experimentation is the key. Choosing the standard color VGA driver, even when you're using a noncolor VGA screen, for example, can give you a more agreeable display, particularly if the screen is capable of gray-scaling. Therefore, if you chose a monochrome VGA driver when you installed NT, you might want to switch to a color driver. Configuring the video display is covered a little later in this chapter.

In any case, as soon as the driver is installed and working, you can fine-tune the display in the Control Panel. After you double-click the Display icon, you see the Display Properties dialog box shown in Figure 8.5. Each Windows NT screen element is displayed in a sample area. When you select different color schemes, the sample area changes to display the effect.

FIGURE 8.5.

Setting screen and window colors.

To view an existing color scheme, follow these steps:

1. In the Display Properties dialog box, select the Appearance tab. Then click the arrow to the right of the Scheme box to view the drop-down Scheme list.

2. Select a scheme by using the arrow keys to select the scheme from the list, or by typing the first letter of the selection you want to move to and then making sure the selection is correct. The colors in the dialog box change, showing the scheme you have selected.

TIP

You can quickly cycle through the color schemes. Highlight the Scheme box and press the up-arrow and down-arrow keys. The sample screen elements change to reflect each color scheme as its name is highlighted.

3. Click OK, and the new colors go into effect.

The Plus! page in the Display properties dialog box lets you change the icons shown on your desktop. You can also select some options that alter the way the screen looks, although most users find the default settings are the best.

Some tips on color schemes for laptops follow:

■ If you have a gas plasma screen, you might want to use the Plasma Power Saver color scheme. It extends battery life by using darker shades, which draw less power.

8

CONFIGURING
WINDOWS NT

■ On many laptops, noncolor LCD screens appear in an unsightly reverse video when you run Windows NT. Some laptops have a program or a switch that reverses this (the ideal solution). If your laptop doesn't, try one of the LCD color schemes to rectify the problem.

Changing the Desktop Appearance

You can make several alterations to the Windows desktop. You can change the following:

■ Background patterns
■ Background wallpaper
■ Screen saver

You can use the patterns and wallpaper settings to decorate the desktop with something a little more festive. Patterns are repeated designs, such as the woven look of fabric. Wallpaper uses larger pictures created with a drawing program. You can create your own patterns and wallpaper or use the ones supplied. You can wallpaper by using a single copy of the picture placed in the center of the screen or by *tiling*, which gives you several identical pictures that cover the whole screen.

Follow these general procedures to adjust any of the display and desktop features; some are covered in greater detail later in this chapter:

1. Double-click the Display icon in the Control Panel and select the Background tab (usually the default when the window opens), as shown in Figure 8.6.

FIGURE 8.6.

Choosing a wallpaper and background color from the Display applet.

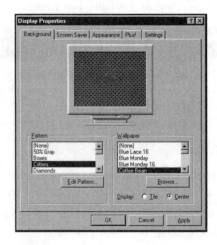

> **NOTE**
>
> As with color schemes, you can cycle through the choices in a drop-down list without opening the list. With the current selection highlighted, press the up-arrow and down-arrow keys to see the other choices.

2. Open the Pattern or Wallpaper drop-down list and select the pattern or wallpaper you want. You have to try each one to see the effect, because the choice doesn't go into effect until you leave the dialog box. You can have only wallpaper or a pattern showing at one time—not both. You can see a sample and a closeup of a pattern (called a *cell*) by clicking Edit Pattern. You then can edit the pattern by turning pixels on and off by clicking them.

3. If you make a wallpaper selection, select Tile or Center.

4. If you want a screen saver, select the Screen Saver tab and adjust the settings.

5. Click OK.

Unfortunately, Display Properties is one of those dialog boxes that you'll have to open, reset, and okay a million times to see all the patterns and wallpaper choices and to see the effect of changing the border size and granularity.

Changing a Pattern

If the supplied patterns don't thrill you, you can create your own with the built-in Bitmap Editor. You can change an existing pattern or design your own. If you want to design your own, choose None from the Name drop-down list in the Pattern Editor dialog box before you begin. Otherwise, choose a pattern you want to play with. To create a pattern, follow these steps:

1. In the Display Properties dialog box, select the Background tab and click Edit Pattern. The Pattern Editor dialog box appears, as shown in Figure 8.7.

FIGURE 8.7.

Editing a desktop background pattern with the Pattern Editor dialog box.

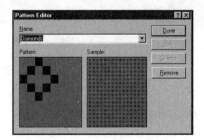

8

CONFIGURING
WINDOWS NT

2. From the Name drop-down list box, type a name for the new pattern.

3. Create the pattern by clicking in the Pattern box (this is the cell). Here, you're defining the smallest element of the repeated pattern; it's enlarged to make editing easier. Each click reverses the color of one pixel. The Sample box shows the effect when the pattern is applied across a larger area and in normal size.

4. When you are satisfied with the pattern, click Add, and the pattern is added to the list. You can select the pattern later from the Desktop dialog box.

If you want to remove a pattern later, select the pattern and click Remove.

Choosing a Specific .BMP File for Wallpaper

The images used in wallpaper are actually *.BMP files*—bitmapped files created by programs like Paintbrush. Because many other applications also create bitmapped .BMP files, you can use files such as scanned images for wallpaper. Note that wallpaper takes up more system memory than patterns, though.

You also can edit the supplied .BMP files with Paintbrush. Because Paintbrush reads .PCX files and converts them to .BMP files, you also can use virtually any .PCX file as wallpaper. Just load the file into Paintbrush and save it as a .BMP file by choosing File | Save As | Options.

To change the wallpaper, follow these steps:

1. Create the image with the program of your choice (it must be able to create a .BMP bitmapped file).

2. Copy the file into the Windows NT directory (\WINNT, for example). Only then does it appear in the list of wallpaper options.

3. From the Display Properties dialog box, select the Screen Saver tab and choose the file. (If you leave the desktop open while creating your .BMP file in Paintbrush, the Wallpaper drop-down list won't show the new file until you close the desktop and reopen it.)

TIP

You can choose a file in another directory if you enter its entire pathname in the Wallpaper drop-down list. This way, you don't have to copy the file into the Windows directory.

Setting the Screen Saver

Screen savers reduce the wear on your monitor by preventing static images from "burning" the phosphors into the CRT's inside surface. You can use the Screen Saver option to choose a blank screen or something more interesting when the system detects no mouse or keyboard activity for a preset period of time. You set the pattern and the time interval before the screen saver is activated.

To set the screen saver, follow these steps:

1. From the Screen Saver page of the Display Properties dialog box, choose a name from the Screen Saver drop-down list. (The default setting is None.)

NOTE

Before anyone actually logs on, the default screen saver is the Logon dialog box, which pops up in random locations onscreen. This screen saver is set to kick in after 15 minutes of waiting for a user to log on.

2. To see what the screen saver looks like, click Test. The screen goes black and the screen saver starts. Move the mouse or press a key to return to the selection window.
3. If you want to fine-tune your choice, click the Settings button. Depending on which screen saver you choose, you'll have a few possible adjustments, such as text for a message, speed, placement, and details pertinent to the graphic.
4. If you enable the Password Protected checkbox, every time your screen saver is activated, you have to type your password into a box before you can resume work. This option is handy if you don't want anyone tampering with your files or seeing what you're doing. It can be a pain if there's no particular need for privacy at your computer.
5. Set the number of minutes you want your computer to be idle before the screen saver springs into action. In the Delay field, type a number or click the increment or decrement button to adjust the minutes.
6. When all the settings are correct, click OK.

Keyboard

You can adjust several variables by using the Keyboard applet, although the only one most people will want to alter is the repeat rate. Most keys repeat when you hold them down. The Repeat Rate setting allows you to change the speed and how long a key has to be pressed before repeating begins.

To change the Repeat Rate setting, follow these steps:

1. Double-click the Keyboard icon in the Control Panel. The Keyboard Properties dialog box appears, as shown in Figure 8.8.

8

CONFIGURING
WINDOWS NT

FIGURE 8.8.

The Keyboard applet.

2. Drag the sliders to change the character repeat speed and how long it takes before any key goes into repeat mode. You want to increase the delay if you find that keys are accidentally repeating when you or other users don't really intend for them to repeat.

3. Test the settings by clicking in the test repeat rate area and holding down a letter key. If it's too slow or starts repeating too soon, adjust the speed and try again.

Fonts

As you probably know, the word *font* refers to type styles you set in a document. Fonts get your message across by adding visual impact, by spicing up your document, and by increasing readability. Fonts are specified by name, size, and style. Font names can be Helvetica or Courier, for example. Sizes refer to the point size of the font, such as 10 point or 12 point. Styles include bold, italic, underline, double underline, subscript, and superscript.

Windows NT comes with approximately the same set of fonts as Windows 95. The actual number and sizes of available fonts installed depends on the type of screen and printer you have. Font types also depend on whether you installed NT over an existing Windows 95 version. If you did, installed TrueType fonts migrate to NT.

Classes of Fonts

Now take a moment to look at the classes of fonts. You encounter several general classes of fonts in Windows:

■ *Screen fonts* control how letters display onscreen. Fonts come in predefined sizes, such as 10 point, 12 point, and so on, and they match the printed fonts as closely as possible. (A *point* is 1/72 of an inch.) The onscreen resolution is usually lower than the resolution of the printed output, however, because laser printers, bubble jets, and inkjet printers have a resolution of about 300 dpi or more, as opposed to about 72 dpi on a typical screen.

■ *TrueType fonts* debuted with Windows 3.1. These fonts solve many of the earlier Windows font problems, such as differences between how fonts appear onscreen and how they print. Depending on the printer and the font, TrueType fonts are generated as bitmaps or downloaded as font files. TrueType fonts are stored in .TTF files. Matching screen fonts are stored as .FOT files. Both types of files are necessary to print and view a TrueType font onscreen.

■ *Non-TrueType fonts* specific to your printer are called *printer fonts* by Windows NT. Typically, these fonts are stored in a printer—as a PostScript outline font or an HP bitmapped font, for example. The storage location can be a CD-ROM or a plug-in cartridge in the printer. These fonts also can be downloaded to your printer by Windows NT when you print. Downloaded fonts are called *soft fonts*.

■ *System fonts* are fonts used internally by Windows NT to display dialog boxes, menus, and so on. These fonts also are used for applications that don't support font choices, such as Cardfile and Notepad. System fonts are stored in .FON files, such as MSSERIF.FON, which is the generic Microsoft serif font. Windows NT sometimes uses system fonts when it can't find an exact screen font to match a selected printer font. If you have a PostScript printer installed and you set some selected text in Palatino, for example, an appropriate system font substitutes for it onscreen, indicating as closely as possible the correct size, line breaks, and so on.

■ *Vector fonts* are fonts that draw letters by using straight-line segments and formulas. Vector fonts are used mostly on plotters.

TrueType offers simplified font management and installation. Installing a TrueType font automatically takes care of both the screen and printer files. This wasn't always the case before Windows 3.1 and NT. A third-party font manager, such as Adobe's ATM, needed to be loaded as a separate program to coordinate screen and printer fonts and scale fonts on-the-fly for use by applications. Windows NT has an internal font scaler that, limited only by your printer's capabilities, provides applications with multiple font sizes from about 8 to 127 points. Additionally, TrueType fonts always look the same, regardless of the printer or screen you use (although they might have differences in smoothness). The TrueType Font Scaler Engine performs these services for 32-bit applications and those running in the 16-bit Windows 3.1 environment subsystem.

Adding New Fonts to the System

NOTE

Remember that fonts aren't user-specific. Fonts that one user installs are available to all other users on the same system.

To install TrueType fonts on your system, follow these steps:

1. Run the Fonts applet by double-clicking its icon in the Control Panel. Installed fonts are listed in the Fonts window that appears, as shown in Figure 8.9.

FIGURE 8.9.

The Fonts applet.

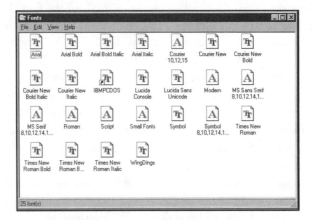

2. If you want to see what an installed font looks like, double-click on the font name. The font name and a brief description of the font appear in the Symbol dialog box, along with a look at the font, as shown in Figure 8.10. For bitmapped fonts, sizes are listed. For vector or TrueType fonts, no sizes are listed after the name, because they can be printed or displayed in any size (typically, up to a maximum of 127 points).

FIGURE 8.10.

Viewing a font.

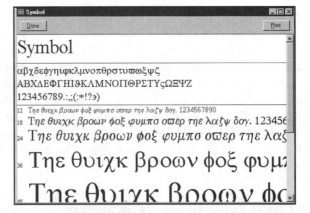

NOTE

A typical TrueType font file (.TTF) is approximately 30K to 50K. Its matching screen file (.FOT) is about 1.3K.

3. To add a new font, choose File | Install New Font. The Add Fonts dialog box shown in Figure 8.11 appears. Choose the source drive and directory containing the fonts. Click Network to choose a network drive that you're not currently connected to via File Manager. This brings up the Browser dialog box. You'll have to walk your way through the tree to find the fonts you want. This is a good way to snarf some TrueType fonts from other workstations, though. Typically, you'll want to look in the \WINDOWS\SYSTEM or \WINNT\SYSTEM directory on another person's workstation to find fonts. You need to have read privileges on the directory, and the directory must have been shared previously by its owner.

FIGURE 8.11.
Installing new fonts.

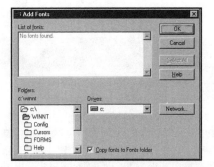

> **NOTE**
>
> Before you copy fonts from another person's computer, you might want to check on the legalities of that. Fonts typically have a single-CPU license associated with them. It's illegal to copy such a font to another machine.

4. Select the fonts to add. Make multiple selections by Shift+clicking (to select a range) or Ctrl+clicking (to select individual, noncontiguous fonts).

5. Note the "Copy fonts to Fonts folder" checkbox at the bottom of the Add Fonts dialog box. Normally, fonts are copied from the source drive and directory to the Windows NT system directory. (Typically, this is \WINNT\SYSTEM32\FONTS, but if you installed over an existing Windows 3.1, fonts might be copied into the \WINDOWS\SYSTEM directory.) If you're adding the fonts from a floppy disk, this makes sense. But if the fonts are already on the hard disk, why make additional copies and take up more disk space? Disable this checkbox if the fonts are already in a drive or directory that is available when you start Windows.

6. Click OK to add the fonts to your font list.

7. Close the Fonts dialog box. The new fonts should be available for your Windows applications. You don't have to restart Windows NT.

8

CONFIGURING WINDOWS NT

NOTE

The installer doesn't let you install a font that's already on your system, so don't worry about accidental redundancy.

TrueType .TTF font files are not only large, but when installed on the system, they take up system RAM space and tend to slow down processes such as loading applications that might use them. This occurs because the whole font list is read each time such an application runs. Windows NT already is memory-hungry, so to help avoid memory shortages caused by RAM cram and exacerbated by TrueType fonts, try not to load more than you need.

TIP

There's a case to be made for using non-TrueType fonts. Using printer fonts already built into your printer (not soft fonts) often increases print job efficiency, because the fonts already are in the printer and don't have to be downloaded at the start of each print job. Unless your printer setup specifies (in Print Folders or an application's Printer Setup box) a substitution table that maps certain TrueType fonts to printer fonts, printing is often faster when using built-in printer fonts, such as those in an HP cartridge or a PostScript font like Helvetica. (Editing the substitution table is discussed in Chapter 4, "Printers.")

Removing Fonts

Remember that removing fonts or font sets increases the available system memory. This means that you can run more applications simultaneously, or that processes will run more smoothly because of decreased paging. If you're having memory-limitation problems, check your font list. If you have many TrueType fonts installed, try removing the fonts you rarely use.

NOTE

Normally, removing a font doesn't erase it from the disk. You can add it back later.

CAUTION

Don't remove the MS Sans Serif font set. It's used in all the Windows dialog boxes.

Follow these steps to remove a font:

1. Open the Fonts window by clicking the Fonts icon in the Control Panel. This window lists all your installed fonts.

2. Select the font or fonts you want to remove. You can select several fonts at once by using the Shift or Ctrl keys to highlight contiguous or separate font names, respectively.

3. Press Delete. A confirmation box appears, asking you to confirm the removal.

CAUTION

If you didn't copy the font into the Windows directory when you installed the font, you have only one copy of the font on your hard disk. If you delete the font file, you'll have to reload the file from a floppy disk, the network, a CD-ROM, or another source if you want to use it again later.

TIP

If you're not sure how often you use the font, you might try deleting it without removing the file and then doing your work as usual. Do you or some applications miss the font? If so, reinstall it. If not, delete it from your disk later. You'll have to add it and then delete it again with the Delete Font File From Disk checkbox in the Delete Font window.

---

4. Click Yes to confirm that you want to delete the font.

Ports

You can always use the DOS MODE command to initialize COM ports on a PC, but it's a hassle because you have to remember the command syntax. Windows 3.*x* and later versions have an applet in the Control Panel to help you set up COM ports from a dialog box with baud, parity, flow control, IRQ, port ID, and so on. Windows NT supports up to 256 serial asynchronous ports—from COM1 to COM256. Of course, you need some sophisticated I/O cards to supply you with 256 COM ports, but it's possible. More likely, you'll have a fax/modem board or data-input devices that use no more than the standard COM1 through COM4.

Actually, every communication, mouse, or fax program I've seen has built-in COM port initialization, rendering the Port applet rather useless. Initialization from such programs overrides settings you make in the Control Panel. If you have to configure a port for a program that doesn't check the port status before trying to send and/or receive data across a serial port, you'll have to use this. You might by using a serial printer connected to a COM port, for example, and the printer driver doesn't initialize the port.

NOTE

Parallel (LPT) ports can't be altered, because they aren't serial ports and don't have settings.

Follow these steps to initialize a serial port:

1. Double-click the Control Panel's Ports icon. The Ports dialog box appears, as shown in Figure 8.12.

FIGURE 8.12.

The Ports applet.

2. You can set up the parameters of any of the four basic COM ports from here. Click the port you want to alter, then click the Settings button. The Settings dialog box shown in Figure 8.13 appears.

FIGURE 8.13.

Changing the settings for a port.

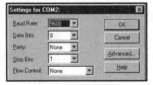

3. Each item in the Settings dialog box has a drop-down list. Your settings should match the settings of the equipment you're connecting to the port. If you're in doubt about requirements, consult the manual supplied with the external equipment. You might also want to refer to a book that covers the use of asynchronous serial communications interfaces.

4. Normally, you don't have to go any further. But if you're working with COM5 or higher, or if your physical serial ports are addressed oddly and you need to alter the port address or change the IRQ request line (hardware interrupt), click Advanced. Make your settings in the dialog box that appears, then click OK. Chapter 7, "Installing Windows NT," lists common IRQ and port addresses.

CAUTION

These settings require an understanding of the interrupt and port assignments of your hardware and possible conflicts with other ports or cards, such as network interface cards in the system, so make sure that you do your homework first. Otherwise, leave these settings alone.

5. Click OK. You are returned to the Ports dialog box. Change other ports if necessary, and then click Close when you're finished. The port is initialized immediately. The next time you boot NT, the ports are initialized to the new settings.

Mouse

You can adjust three aspects of your mouse's operation:

- Tracking speed
- Double-click speed
- Left/right button reversal

TIP

The Mouse Trails setting was left out of NT because Microsoft assumes you aren't going to use NT on an LCD screen. This is a mistake on Microsoft's part, in my opinion. You can use an animated cursor (by using the Cursors applet in the Control Panel) to get a similar effect, however. Microsoft's 9.x mouse driver for NT offers many of the features laptop users want.

To change your mouse properties, follow these steps:

1. Double-click the Mouse icon in the Control Panel. The Mouse Properties dialog box shown in Figure 8.14 appears.
2. Drag the slider to adjust the mouse-speed parameters.

   This dialog box has four pages you can use to change aspects of your mouse's performance and behavior.

3. Click OK.

Now take a minute to look at the mouse options. *Tracking speed* is the speed at which the mouse pointer moves in relation to the movement of the pointing device—whether it is a track ball, pen, mouse, or other device. Mouse motion is measured in *Mickeys*, which equal 1/100 of an inch of mouse movement. You use the Tracking Speed setting to adjust the relationship between Mickeys on the desktop and pixels (dots) onscreen. Decrease the tracking speed to increase your exactitude, requiring more hand motion for the same corresponding cursor motion. If you're especially coordinated or you have a large screen, you might want to increase the speed (fewer Mickeys per pixel). Notice that the tracking speed changes instantly as you move the slider in the dialog box. Move the cursor around to test the new speed. Double-click in the Test area to try out the new double-click speed.

FIGURE 8.14.

The Mouse applet.

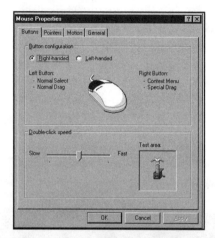

> **TIP**
>
> If you use the mouse with non-Windows programs (such as Ventura Publisher or AutoCAD), you might want to match mouse speeds in the two environments. This way, you don't need to mentally adjust when you use non-Windows programs.
>
> When you run a DOS window in NT, the mouse driver is supplied to the DOS environment automatically, unlike in Windows 3.1, which requires that the mouse driver be loaded as a TSR or a device driver before loading Windows. Tracking speed in the DOS environment is controlled by the Control Panel setting—another nifty feature of NT.

Double-click speed determines how quick double-clicks have to be to register with NT. If the double-click speed is set too fast, many users will find it difficult to run programs from icons, select a word in a text file, and so on. If the speed is set too slow, you will end up running programs or opening and closing windows unexpectedly. I find that the slowest speed works well for me. Double-click in the Test area to test a new speed. The button should change color each time you successfully double-click.

Left/right button reversal simply switches the function of your mouse's buttons. (If your mouse has three buttons, the middle button isn't affected.) If you're left-handed, being able to switch the mouse buttons might be a boon. If you use non-Windows programs outside of Windows or on other computers that don't support button-swapping, however, you might be adding some ergonomic confusion to your life. If you use the mouse only in Windows programs and you're left-handed, it's worth a try. Changes take effect immediately.

You might want to change the way the cursor looks when you are performing different tasks. Select the Pointers tab, as shown in Figure 8.15. Select the pointers you want from the list; they are applied when you exit the window.

FIGURE 8.15.

Customizing the way the cursor looks.

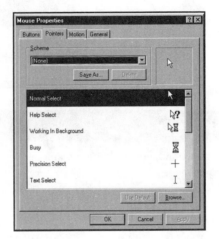

8

CONFIGURING
WINDOWS NT

Printers

Running the Printers applet in the Control Panel simply runs the Print Wizard. The Printer applet is in the Control Panel as a convenience and to offer as much similarity with Windows 95 as possible. To alter printer setups or to add and remove printer drivers, see Chapter 4.

Regional Settings

You use the Regional Settings applet to customize Windows NT for use in countries other than the one targeted by Microsoft when it sold you your copy of NT. It's likely that nothing needs to be changed. Note that the settings made from this box pertain exclusively to Windows NT and Windows applications. POSIX, MS-DOS, and OS/2 applications don't take advantage of these settings. Even some Windows applications don't use them. You should experiment with the settings to see whether they make any difference, or read the application's manual for information about how to set the formats.

Double-click the Regional Settings icon in the Control Panel to display the Regional Settings Properties dialog box shown in Figure 8.16. Note that this dialog box has several tabs.

FIGURE 8.16.
The Regional Settings applet.

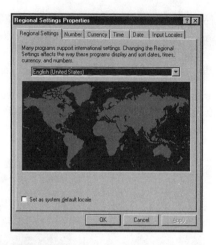

NOTE

If driver files are needed, you might be prompted to insert Windows NT floppy disks when you're making changes.

To change any settings, follow these steps:

1. Double-click the Regional Settings icon in the Control Panel to open the Regional Settings Properties dialog box.
2. Select the relevant page.
3. Set date, time, currency, and number formats by selecting the relevant pages. Examples of the current settings are shown in each section, so you don't need to change them unless they look incorrect.

System

You use the System applet for five activities:

- Specifying which operating system boots (when your computer has two or more operating systems) if there's no user input
- Viewing or changing the system environment variables and viewing or changing the user environment variables
- Setting the virtual memory (paging) file size
- Setting the system-recovery options for STOP (blue screen) errors
- Setting the amount of CPU resources the foreground application gets in relation to background applications

Changing the Default Bootup Operating System

If you installed NT over an existing copy of DOS or OS/2, you had the option of wiping out the preexisting operating system or having NT live with it harmoniously. If you chose the latter, NT relocated the first 512 bytes of the existing boot track (the boot sector) to a new location on your hard disk as a file called BOOTSECT.DOS (regardless of whether the preexisting operating system was DOS or OS/2) and wrote the boot portion of the NT operating system into the normal boot sector.

After you turn on the machine, press Reset, press Ctrl+Alt+Del, or shut down and restart NT, the NT Boot Loader goes into action and presents a menu of the operating systems you can boot. By default, the NT operating system starts, but you can change this. You or a user on the network might prefer to boot right into the MS-DOS or OS/2 environment rather than NT, for example.

To change the default bootup operating system, follow these steps:

1. Double-click the System applet icon in the Control Panel. Then select the Startup/Shutdown tab, as shown in Figure 8.17.
2. From the Startup drop-down list box, select the operating system that will boot by default unless you intervene by selecting the alternative operating system.
3. You can optionally set the time-out that determines how long the Boot Loader waits for you to choose the alternative operating system. By default, it's 30 seconds.

The next time you boot, the operating system you chose is highlighted in the Boot Loader menu and loads unless the keyboard is touched.

8

CONFIGURING
WINDOWS NT

FIGURE 8.17.

*Changing the default
operating system to be
booted.*

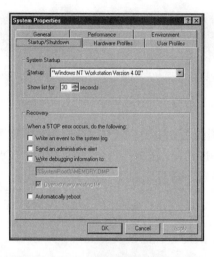

NOTE

During the Boot Loader countdown, if any key on the keyboard is pressed, the countdown stops, which causes the boot-up process to pause.

Setting the Environment Variables

Just as DOS has provisions for setting system variables such as the \TEMP directory, prompt, and search path, NT provides a similar service that closely complies with the DOS variable definitions. The difference is that there are two sets of variables in NT: system and user. The Environment page of the System Properties dialog box lists both sets, as shown in Figure 8.18.

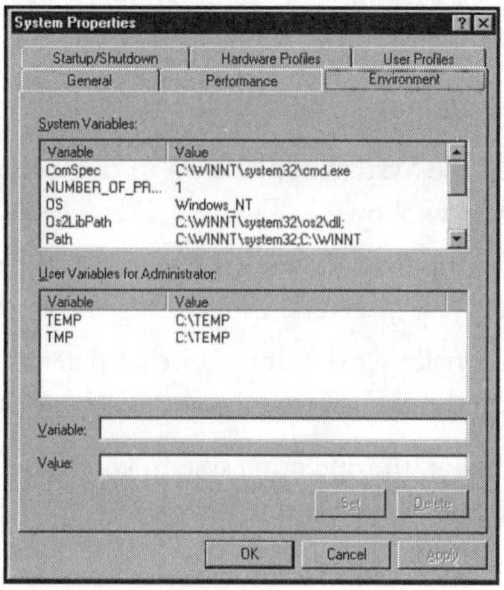

FIGURE 8.18.

*The Environment page
of the System applet.*

The *system* variables apply to all users, but the *user* variables pertain to the logged-on user. These variables allow users to set up personalized environments for their applications or command-prompt (DOS) sessions.

It's important to know how NT processes and prioritizes each of these groups of settings. First, the system environment settings are loaded. Then, the user settings are loaded. Whenever there's a conflict between the settings, the system settings take priority over the user settings.

Because user settings take precedence over system settings, you can, in essence, edit the system settings by declaring a user setting for the same system variable, effectively overwriting it. If the system variable for temp (the temporary directory) is set to \WINDOWS\TEMP, for example, and you want to change it to E:\TEMP, you just enter this line in the User area of the System Properties dialog box. Note that an exception to this rule applies to the path statement, which isn't overwritten by the user or system commands. If you have different search paths declared in each section, NT adds them to one another, resulting in a cumulative path setting.

To change an existing system or user setting, follow these steps:

1. Select the variable line in the System Variables or User Variables for Administrator box.
2. Edit the variable line in the Variable field at the bottom of the dialog box.
3. Click Set. (If you want to delete the variable, click Delete instead.)

Follow these steps to enter a new variable:

1. Select an item in the System Variables or User Variables for Administrator box.
2. Type the new variable in the Variable field and the value in the Value field.
3. Click Set. The variable is added to the existing User Variables list, but it doesn't go into effect until the user logs off and then on again, or the computer is rebooted.

Setting the Virtual Memory File Size

If you're familiar with Windows, you probably know about the swap file. The *swap file* temporarily stores data from the computer's RAM. This file is treated by the operating system and applications as actual physical RAM. Swap files (sometimes called *paging files*) fool the operating system and applications into thinking that there's more physical RAM in the computer than what actually exists, which allows more programs and operating system services to run than would otherwise be possible. Paging files have been around almost as long as digital computers. They were especially necessary back in the days when mainframes often ran with little more than 8K or 16K (not megabytes) of RAM. Whether the paging files were stored physically in the form of paper tape, punch cards, or magnetic tape didn't matter. The upshot was that only a very small amount of data was actually in RAM at any one time for processing, while the rest was offloaded momentarily until it was needed. The idea of swap files grew from this technology.

NT creates a swap file when it's set up. This file, which typically is stored on the NT boot partition, is called PAGEFILE.SYS. When NT runs out of RAM to dish out to applications or internal services, some of what's in memory is paged out to this file for a moment. The result is that NT can continue to operate smoothly, while all you know is that some hard-disk activity is occurring.

NOTE

If you try running NT with only 12M of RAM, you'll see some very heavy disk activity caused by intense paging.

Setup calculates the optimum size of the file when NT is set up. You might want to experiment with this setting, because your application mix might benefit from having a larger paging file (especially if your application is giving you low memory messages even when you don't have many other applications running).

Here's another reason for changing your paging file setup. NT is pretty smart about paging files and can use more than one. Each hard disk can have its own file. If you have a smart disk controller (or separate controllers for each drive), NT can actually use the paging drives simultaneously. NT could be reading from one drive and writing to the other drive, for example, which speeds up paging operations. Even if you don't have such a setup, having paging files on multiple disks gives NT more breathing room and an option in case one drive suddenly fills up. (Paging files can expand dynamically (up to a limit declared by the user), unlike the permanent swap files in Windows 3.1 in enhanced 386 mode.)

NOTE

You have to have administrator privileges to alter the paging file settings.

Here's how to modify the paging file sizes and locations:

1. Double-click the System icon in the Control Panel. In the System Properties dialog box, select the Performance tab, as shown in Figure 8.19. Click Change to display the Virtual Memory window shown in Figure 8.20.

2. To change a value, click Set, and then select the drive with the file size you want to alter.

3. Specify the sizes for the drive in the Initial Size and Maximum Size fields and click Set. If the paging file size specified is less than the size of the physical RAM installed on the computer, and the recovery option to create a dump file is allowed, an error message appears.

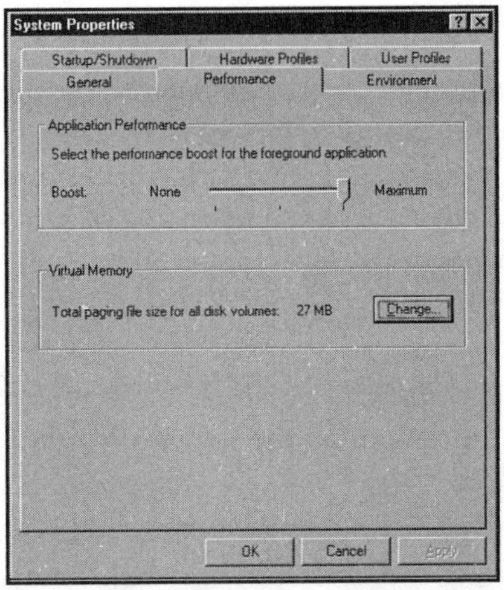

FIGURE 8.19.

The Performance page of the Systems applet.

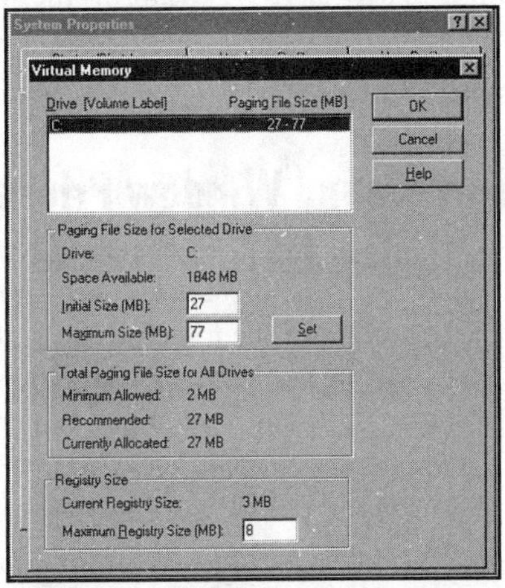

FIGURE 8.20.

You can change the Virtual Memory settings to alter the swap file size.

TIP

Notice the information in the bottom part of the Virtual Memory dialog box. It might be helpful when you're making sizing decisions. You will want to allocate at least the minimum amount, and possibly more than the recommended amount, if you're having low-memory trouble.

Setting the System-Recovery Options

No matter how robust an operating system is, the potential to fail (encountering a marginal static RAM chip, for example) does exist. If such a failure is detected with Windows NT, a blue screen with white text appears with a brief error message, a CPU register dump, and a stack dump. This type of error is known as a *STOP error* or the *blue screen of death*, as some people frequently refer to it.

To set your system-recovery options, follow these steps:

1. In the System Properties dialog box, select the Startup/Shutdown tab.

2. Configure the options for the action you want:

Write an event to the system log	Creates an event message in the system Event Log, listing the error. Useful in isolating intermittent system failure.
Send an administrative alert	Informs the system administrator of the failure and cause.
Automatically reboot	Reboots the computer after a system failure.

Setting the Foreground Window Priority

Because Windows NT is a multitasking operating system, each running application receives CPU slices and is serviced in a round-robin fashion. The NT scheduler assigns more CPU cycles to the program that's running in the foreground window (the active window) than to background windows. This scheme is sensible, because you usually want the fastest reaction time in the window you're currently using. You might be performing a spreadsheet recalculation, a database sort, or a word-processor spell check, for example, and you don't care whether NT is servicing a drawing program or a PIM's phone dialer in the background.

If the way you work involves a lot of background processing that you want to speed up, the Tasking button in the System Properties dialog box lets you alter (somewhat) the tasking priority level assigned to the foreground window in relation to others. In other words, you can relinquish some CPU cycles from the foreground to speed up the background.

To speed up processing, follow these steps:

1. In the System Properties dialog box, select the Performance tab, as shown in Figure 8.21.

2. Slide the marker to the option that best fits your needs and click OK.

FIGURE 8.21.

Setting the foreground application performance.

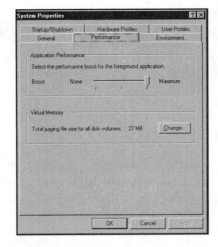

Date/Time

You can use the Date/Time applet to adjust the system's date and time. These settings date-
and time-stamp the files you create and modify, and they specify other time-related operations,
such as calendar alarms, automated backups, and so on. This applet doesn't change the *format*
of the date and time—just the actual date and time. To change the formatting, double-click
the International icon in the Control Panel.

Follow these steps to adjust the date and time:

1. Double-click the Date/Time icon in the Control Panel. The Date/Time Properties
   dialog box shown in Figure 8.22 appears.

FIGURE 8.22.

You can use the Date/Time applet to set the date and time.

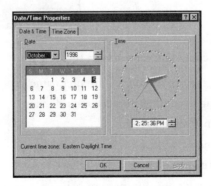

2. Adjust the time and date by typing the changes, selecting the month from the drop-
   down list, or clicking the increment or decrement arrow to change the year.

8

CONFIGURING
WINDOWS NT

> **TIP**
>
> You also can adjust the time and date by using the TIME and DATE commands from a command-prompt session.

Network

Aside from connecting to and sharing printers and directories (tasks done from Print Folders and My Computer), all other essential network-related configuration is done through the Control Panel. The Network applet is rich in features. If you're a system administrator, you should take time to become familiar with the many options. After you double-click the Network icon in the Control Panel, the Network dialog box shown in Figure 8.23 appears.

FIGURE 8.23.

The Network applet.

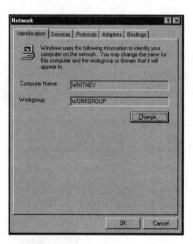

Some of the functions you can perform by using the Network applet follow:

- Changing the workstation's computer name
- Connecting to another workgroup or domain
- Adding a network adapter
- Configuring network software and hardware
- Adding network software
- Removing cards or software from NT

Changing the Workstation's Computer Name

When you move a computer to another office, change administrators, or just decide that a computer's name is inappropriate for some reason, you can use the Network applet to change a name. It's sort of like changing the volume label on a hard disk. You should remember four things when you change a computer's name:

■ When you change a workstation name, the official network path required to access the computer changes. This can throw off printer, disk, OLE, ClipBook, and any other connections that other workstations might have made to that particular workstation.

■ A computer name must be unique on the network; no two computers can have the same name.

■ The workgroup name can't be the same as the machine name.

■ If you're connected to a domain, you should be extra careful before changing the name. Each workstation on a domain has an account based on the workstation name. If you change the name to something the domain server doesn't recognize, you won't be able to access the domain. You should have the domain administrator add an account under the new name and then change the workstation name, or vice versa.

To change the workstation name, follow these steps:

1. In the Network dialog box, click Change. The Identification Changes dialog box appears, as shown in Figure 8.24.

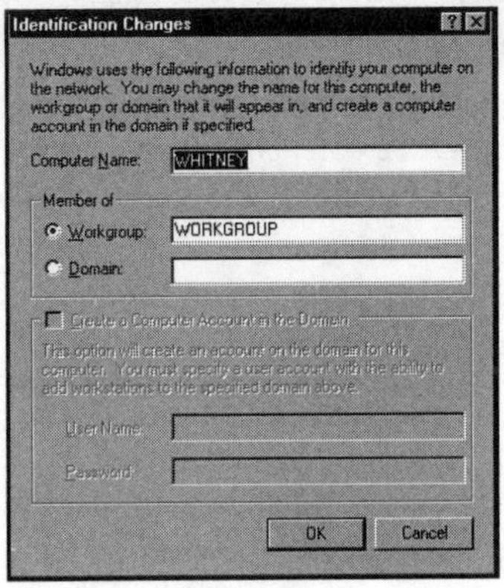

FIGURE 8.24.

Changing the machine name.

2. Enter a unique name and click OK.

8

CONFIGURING
WINDOWS NT

Connecting to Another Workgroup or Domain

Domains and workgroups are covered in more detail in Part III, "Networking Windows NT." Briefly, though, when you set up NT on a workstation, and a network card is detected, the networking interface software is set up and you're asked whether you want to join an existing workgroup or domain.

If you're joining a network after NT is installed, or you want to connect to a new domain or workgroup, follow these steps:

1. In the Network dialog box, click Change. The Identification Changes dialog box appears.

2. Select Workgroup or Domain. (If you're connected to an NT Server-based network, you should select Domain.) Then enter the name of the workgroup in the field beside the option you have selected.

TIP

If you don't know the workgroup or domain name, you can browse the network by using My Computer or Explorer. Choose Disk | Connect Network Drive. The NT browser scours the network and lists workgroup and domain names.

NOTE

If you just changed your computer name and haven't rebooted NT so that it logs on with the new station name, you can't change the domain you're connected to; the Change button is grayed out. As a rule, you should change the domain name before the workstation name.

In the lower half of the Identification Changes dialog box, an administrator can create an account on the domain and join it simultaneously. Just follow these steps:

1. Make sure the computer's name is unique for the domain.

2. Select Domain.

3. In the Domain field, enter the domain to connect to or on which you want to create an account.

4. Enable the Create a Computer Account in the Domain checkbox.

5. In the User Name field, enter the administrator account name, and enter the password in the Password field. At this point, your dialog box should look similar to the one shown in Figure 8.25.

6. Click OK.

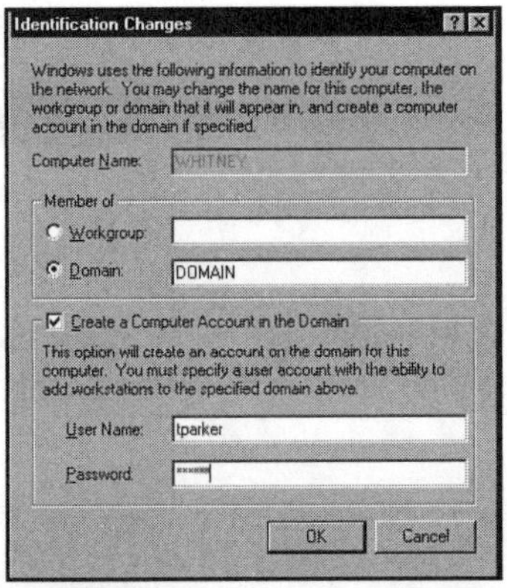

FIGURE 8.25.

Setting a computer account for a domain.

TIP

The process is a little different if you don't directly have an account on the domain, but instead have an account on a trusted domain connected to the domain where you're trying to set up a new account. In the User Name field, enter the trusted domain's name, a backslash, and your account name (for example, `marketing\johnd`). Note that `marketing` must be a trusted domain and that the account `johnd` must have administrator status.

You also can connect to a domain if you're on the road or at home by using the *Remote Access Service* (RAS). You first have to log onto the network from your remote computer. Also, you must have administrator privileges for your local computer and/or domain administrator privileges for the domain you're trying to create an account on. See Chapter 17, "Internetworking: Remote Access Service and TCP/IP," for more about RAS.

Adding a Network Adapter

If you want to add an additional network card or change the type of card you have, the procedure is simple:

1. Double-click the Network icon in the Control Panel. The Network dialog box appears.
2. Select the Adapters tab, as shown in Figure 8.26.
3. To add an adapter, click Add. Then, from the list that appears, choose the type of adapter. If it's not listed, and you have a disk from the manufacturer, scroll to the bottom of the list and choose Other.
4. Click Continue.

   If the driver files for the particular card aren't in the NT system directory, you're prompted to insert a disk or to enter the path where the files are located, such as a CD-ROM drive.

8

CONFIGURING
WINDOWS NT

FIGURE 8.26.

The Adapters page of the Network dialog box.

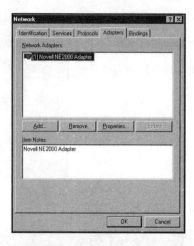

> **NOTE**
>
> You might be prompted to specify other settings for the card, such as IRQ, base port address, DMA channel, and so on. If you're in doubt about settings, see Chapter 7's discussion of network card installation.

5. Close all dialog boxes. You might be prompted to restart the computer before the network card becomes activated.

Configuring Network Software and Hardware

Sometimes, you'll add a new card such as a fax/modem or a sound card to a workstation and find that it conflicts with an installed network card. The most common solution is to adjust the DIP switches, jumpers, and/or software configuration programs for the different cards to try to create a peaceful coexistence among them. You'll have to tell the NT network driver what you've done when you change settings for a network card, however.

To add a new card to a workstation, follow these steps:

1. Double-click the Network icon in the Control Panel. Click on the Adapters tab, then click the Add button. Choose the card from the Adapter Card section.

2. Click Configure. A dialog box for the card appears.

3. Make your changes to the settings and click OK.

Some network software can also be configured. Just click the software you want to configure in the Protocols or Services pages of the Network applet, then click the Configure button. The most likely software items you'll want to configure (although this is pretty technical stuff, and meant for administrators) follow:

- Server
- RPC name service provider
- Remote Access Service
- NetBIOS interface

A majority of the network software items can't be configured and display a message to that effect if you try to configure them.

Adding Network Software

Installing the network board and configuring it is only half of what a board needs to communicate with the network. It also needs a protocol driver. Protocol drivers fit between the network card's driver and the higher-level network software, and they control how data is packaged and sent across the network. Setup installs the most popular small-network protocol: IPX/SPX. For modest networks, this is all you'll need, so installing additional software isn't necessary. If you want to interact with UNIX or IBM mainframes, set up a *wide area network* (WAN), or connect printers directly to the network for sharing, you might need to load other network protocol software.

To add network software drivers, follow these steps:

1. In the Network dialog box, select the Services tab (or, to add protocols, select the Protocols tab). (See Figure 8.27.)

FIGURE 8.27.
The Services page of the Network dialog box.

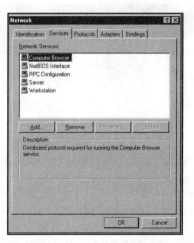

2. Click Add.
3. Choose the software you need from the list of vendors and their drivers, and click Continue.

8

CONFIGURING
WINDOWS NT

Removing Cards or Software from NT

Suppose that you decide to switch network cards from one brand to another, or you decide that you no longer need a particular piece of network software—such as Remote Access Services—on a workstation. It's a good practice to eliminate unused software or hardware drivers from an NT configuration. Additional services often consume CPU cycles and tie up system memory. Also, if you remove a piece of hardware and leave in the driver, you get an error message at boot time, informing you that at least one service couldn't be started.

TIP

Whenever possible, you should install the new driver before you remove the old one. This can spare you the trouble of several reboots.

To remove a network card driver or a piece of network software, follow these steps:

1. Double-click the Network icon in the Control Panel to open the Network dialog box. Select the Adapters tab.
2. In the Network Adapters box, select the software or adapter card you want to remove.
3. Click Remove.
4. Click OK.

NOTE

If you remove an adapter card, the associated software driver listed is removed automatically. You don't have to remove both.

Sounds

You can use the Sounds applet to turn on or off system sounds, such as the ubiquitous beep you hear when you've made an error or when NT or an application wants to get your attention. If you have a sound card installed, you can assign more interesting sounds to system events. In this case, system events are categorized so that distinct types of events (such as system startup, logoff, questions, information boxes, and so on) can each be assigned a separate sound. Something more than the simple beep is not only more entertaining, but it's also more informative.

You can record your own sounds for system events by using the Sound Recorder program, or you can purchase sound files (which must be in the .WAV format) and use those instead of the somewhat limited offering of sounds supplied with Windows 3.1, Windows 95, and NT. If you have an audio-capable CD-ROM drive and the right software (such as the mixer supplied with the Pro-Audio Spectrum 16 board), you can record snippets from your favorite CDs, edit them, and use them for system sounds.

> **NOTE**
>
> To use .WAV files for system sounds, you must install and configure an NT-supported sound card and install a suitable device driver for it by using the Device applet from the Control Panel. Pay special attention to the sound card's IRQ, memory, and port addresses to make sure they don't conflict with other devices and cards—particularly, your network adapter. See Chapter 7 for a discussion of such conflicts and typical device assignments.

To assign sounds for system events, follow these steps:

1. Double-click the Sound icon in the Control Panel. The Sounds Properties dialog box appears, as shown in Figure 8.28.

FIGURE 8.28.

Setting system sounds.

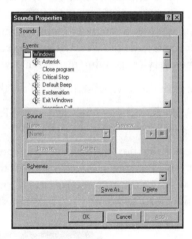

8

CONFIGURING
WINDOWS NT

2. Assign different sounds to system events by selecting them from the Events list.
3. Click OK to finish.

Server

The Server applet displays resource connections, the number of users connected to the workstation over the network, the names of files that are open, and who should be warned in case of administrative alerts. Because these items relate to system administration more than to configuration, see Chapter 9, "Windows NT Administration," for details.

Services

As mentioned in Chapters 1, "What Is Windows NT?" and 2, "The Architectual and Operational Design of Windows NT," Windows NT's design is very modular. This modularity has many advantages—especially the fact that individual components can be added, removed, and updated with little upset to the remainder of NT. It also turns out that NT is designed to allow many individual internal components to be activated or deactivated without upsetting the rest of the apple cart—even in the middle of a workday while the workstation or server is attending to users' tasks.

Many of NT's inner housekeeping chores are classified as *services*. The feature that lets you create and share a ClipBook is a service, for example, as is the *Event Log*—a feature that records every major activity on the workstation for administrators who want to monitor network use.

Windows NT offers several services. You can start and stop many of these services by using the Control Panel. Also, many of these services can be configured to start at a specific time, such as at NT boot time, or you can specify that a service wait until an administrator starts it manually. Because services consume memory and CPU time, turning off a service might supply some additional computing power or memory room for particularly demanding applications. Also, if an administrator wants to deny a workstation or certain users access to specific services, he or she can turn off these services pending manual intervention by the administrator.

To view and work with the services' settings, follow these steps:

1. Double-click the Services icon in the Control Panel. The Services dialog box shown in Figure 8.29 appears.

2. In the Services dialog box, notice the Status column. Unless a service has been started, this column is blank. After a service is started, the word Started appears in the Status column. Now notice the buttons. You can start, stop, pause, continue, or configure the startup time for a service.

FIGURE 8.29.

The Services applet.

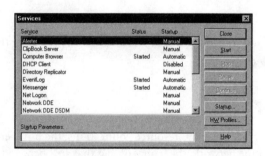

The Services dialog box includes a list of services, along with their status and some buttons for working with them. Table 8.2 describes the primary services.

Table 8.2. Services offered in Windows NT.

Service	Function
Alerter	Along with the Messenger service, generates warning messages to administrators about problems on the local computer.
ClipBook Server	Allows network users to share ClipBook pages.
Computer Browser	Allows users to browse the network for resources shared by other workstations.
DHCP Client	Configures the DHCP client to get IP address information from the DHCP server.
Directory Replicator	Performs directory-replication service for administrators to easily copy complete directories to multiple workstations.
EventLog	Monitors the workstation's use by local and remote users, recording events of significance. Also reports internal error conditions, such as malfunctioning hardware, drivers, and so on.
Messenger	Handles bidirectional communication between administrators. Also sends alerts generated by stations.
Net Logon	Verifies the authenticity of users logging onto a workstation, workgroup, or domain, depending on the system configuration.
Network DDE	Required for dynamic data exchange between workstations.
Network DDE DSDM	Stands for DDE Shared Database Manager. Used by Network DDE.
NT LM Security Support Provider	Supplies Windows NT security to RPC applications that don't use LAN Manager named-pipe transports.
OLE	Supplies OLE support to applications.
Remote Procedure Call Locator (RPCL)	Used by the RPC to find available workstations to process remote procedure calls.
Remote Procedure Call (RPC)	Used primarily to support client access to the NT machines. Also allows specialized NT applications to offload subroutines to network workstations to increase efficiency.
Schedule	Required for prescheduled commands, such as automated backup, to run at a specified time.

8

CONFIGURING
WINDOWS NT

continues

Table 8.2. continued

Service	Function
Server	Allows a workstation to share files, printers, named pipes, and RPCs.
Spooler	Allows a workstation to spool printer files.
UPS	Monitors the uninterruptible power supply and instructs the system to issue warnings, save files, and shut down prior to power outages.
Workstation	Gives a workstation the ability to connect to and interact on a network and to let multiple users access a single, standalone workstation.

Starting, Stopping, Pausing, or Continuing a Service

Follow these steps to start, stop, pause, or continue a service:

1. In the Services dialog box, select the service you want to affect. If you're starting it, it should be one that isn't already started.
2. Click Start, Stop, Pause, or Continue.

You can use the Startup Parameters field in the Services dialog box to enter a startup command that will be passed to the service as it's started. Startup parameter details vary based on the service. Most services use Registry settings for startup options, but startup parameters entered here will override those Registry settings.

> **CAUTION**
>
> Exercise caution when you stop the Server service. As explained in Table 8.2, this service is responsible for managing shared resources, such as files and printers. If you shut down this service, any users connected to your workstation are disconnected from those resources. This can lead to data loss or a crashed application. The solution is to pause the Server service, then warn users that they should stop using resources on the particular workstation; only then should you stop the service. Pausing the service keeps it running for users who are already connected but prevents new users from gaining access to the shared resources.

Specifying the Startup Time

As a final option, you can stipulate whether a service starts automatically when you start Windows NT on the workstation, or whether it must be started manually. In general, this area of settings is better left alone unless you regularly need to stop a particular service. In that case, you can set the service to manual startup and then start it only when you need it.

The Startup column of the Services dialog box indicates the startup status of each service. Many of these services are set to automatic, meaning that they start at boot time. To change a service's startup status, follow these steps:

1. Select the service.

2. Click Startup. The startup dialog box for the particular service appears. Figure 8.30 shows an example of one of these dialog boxes.

FIGURE 8.30.

Setting a service's startup option.

3. In the Startup Type area, choose a startup option:

Automatic	Starts at boot time.
Manual	Starts only after the Start button in the Services dialog box is clicked or an application or other service requests the service.
Disabled	Doesn't start when an application or service requests it. Doesn't start after the Start button is clicked. Must be reset to Manual or Automatic to be started.

NOTE

You must have at least 12M of memory in a computer, or the Server service won't start automatically—it must be started manually.

Devices

As you probably know, the Windows NT operating system supports loadable device drivers just as DOS does. The advantage with NT is that many drivers can be loaded (started), stopped, and configured from within NT by using dialog boxes. This is a far cry from having to exit Windows, carefully edit your CONFIG.SYS file, reboot DOS, and run Windows again.

8

CONFIGURING
WINDOWS NT

> **NOTE**
>
> Unfortunately, not all devices and drivers can be loaded or unloaded without rebooting. Whether a particular one can be depends on where it's located in the startup chain (System, Automatic, or Manual), as well as what other devices and drivers it relies on.

You use the Devices applet in the Control Panel to work with device drivers. The dialog box you see looks similar to others discussed so far in this chapter, such as the Services box. Remember the distinction between devices and services, however. *Devices* control physical hardware, such as network cards, video cards, pointing devices, and CD-ROM drives. *Services* are higher-level software modules in NT that supply a complex ability, such as sharing resources like directories or printers. After you double-click the Devices icon in the Control Panel, you see the Devices dialog box shown in Figure 8.31.

FIGURE 8.31.

The Devices applet.

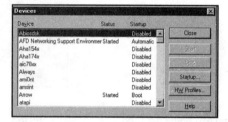

Just as with the Services dialog box, the Devices dialog box has three columns. The first column lists the name of the device. Unfortunately, the name is rather cryptic. It takes some sleuthing to determine what a device name actually does. With some guesswork, however, you can often figure it out. The VGA item is the screen driver, for example. The second column indicates whether a device driver has been started. If this column is empty, the device hasn't been started. The third column indicates when the device is set to start (there are four options, as explained later in this section).

Starting or Stopping a Device Driver

To start or stop a device driver, follow these steps:

1. In the Devices dialog box, select the device you want to stop or start.
2. Click Start or Stop. NT displays a message box telling you that it's trying to start or stop the device driver.

NOTE

Sometimes, a device can't be started or stopped. At least NT informs you that it can't do what you asked. In some cases, you're informed that the selected device is not something that supports being stopped or started. If you try to stop something integral to system functioning, such as the screen or a mouse driver, you won't succeed. The Stop button is grayed out when some devices are selected for the same reason.

Configuring the Startup Time for a Device

You can set a device to start at several different times, as shown in Table 8.3. To set a startup time, click the Startup button to display the dialog box shown in Figure 8.32.

FIGURE 8.32.

Setting a device's startup options.

8

CONFIGURING
WINDOWS NT

Table 8.3. Startup time settings.

Setting	Effect on Device Driver
Boot	Starts the device as soon as NT begins to boot, just as with the old CONFIG.SYS. This is the first class of devices to be loaded. Used for starting drivers that are required for system startup—generally, hard disk controllers, video drivers, keyboard drivers, and so on.
System	Starts the device after boot devices are loaded. Use the System setting for devices a notch less critical for early boot processes but still critical for bringing up the system. This setting generally is for software drivers that rely on a specific piece of hardware, such as the CD-ROM services.

continues

Table 8.3. continued

Setting	Effect on Device Driver
Automatic	Starts the device after boot and system devices are loaded. Use this setting for less critical items not required for system boot-strapping or intermediate stages of operating. Also for basic services required for general operation, such as Server, Workstation, SQL Server, FTP, and so on.
Manual	Starts the device after the Start button in the Devices dialog box is clicked or when a calling service or application specifically requests it.
Disabled	Doesn't start under any circumstance. Its startup status must be reset from this dialog box before it can be started.

A quick examination of the startup settings for your system's devices shows you which device drivers are critical for system bootup. Be careful not to change the startup settings for anything initially set to Boot or System. These devices are needed to bring up the system. If you set them to Automatic, for example, the system probably won't boot. Then you'll have to use the Last Known Good boot technique, explained in Chapter 10, "Optimizing Windows NT: Performance Determinants."

Follow these steps to change your startup settings:

1. In the Devices dialog box, click a device driver.
2. Click Startup to open the Startup dialog box. Choose the radio button for the startup type.
3. Click OK.

UPS

An *uninterruptible power supply* (UPS) is an AC-powered box containing a battery with enough power to keep a computer running for a short time after the AC input power has been lost. The UPS is plugged into the wall, and the computer is plugged into the box. A communications link using one of the computer's COM ports connects the UPS and the computer. When the UPS detects a power outage, it sends a message to the computer. Windows NT receives an interrupt on the COM port and responds to the alert by issuing messages to administrators (and, optionally, users) that the computer is going to shut down within a certain number of minutes unless the power is revived. Then, after a preset period of time, NT begins an automated, safe shutdown. When power is restored, the NT machine resumes where it left off, with no loss of data.

Typically, a UPS will be added to a server station (such as an NT Server station), but it also can be set up for any individual's workstation responsible for maintenance of crucial data and where valuable work would be lost if the station were to go down unexpectedly.

If a UPS is installed on a workstation, the UPS settings from the Control Panel are used to inform NT of the characteristics of the UPS. Many brands and models of UPS devices exist, and each has its own power-life capabilities, recharge times, and interface voltages. Also, you might want to specify the types of actions NT should take when a power outage does occur.

> **NOTE**
>
> Not all UPS devices interface with NT in such a way as to trigger an automated shutdown. Any UPS keeps the machine going after a power outage (at least for some time), so all PC-compatible UPSs will work with NT to some degree. But if you need unattended shutdown capability, you need to check with the manufacturer to make sure the device and its cable are NT-compatible. The Hardware Compatibility List includes the appropriate settings for supported UPSs.

To configure your Windows NT–compatible UPS, follow these steps:

1. Read the manual supplied with the UPS and connect the AC lines and COM lines as instructed.
2. From the Control Panel, double-click the UPS icon. The UPS dialog box appears, as shown in Figure 8.33.

FIGURE 8.33.

The UPS dialog box.

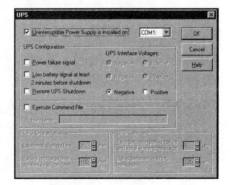

3. Fill in the settings in the box to indicate how the UPS is connected to the NT machine, and how NT should behave in case of notification of a problem.
4. After you fill in the options, click OK. NT asks whether you want to start the UPS service. (Remember that the UPS service is the internal software module that monitors

8

CONFIGURING WINDOWS NT

the state of the UPS and performs the requisite messaging and automated shutdown when necessary.)

5. Click Yes, and the UPS service is set to automatically start whenever NT starts.

If you want to remove the UPS device and service from the machine, disable the first checkbox that indicates a UPS is attached, and click OK. You are asked whether you want to stop the service. Click Yes.

Three other services must be running if you want the UPS and the NT UPS service to alert users of impending shutdowns and keep a log of what happened: the Messenger, the Alerter, and the Event Log. See the earlier discussion of the Services applet to review how to determine whether these services are on. Ideally, they should be set to start automatically at NT bootup. You also might want to set who is to be notified in case of a shutdown. You can do this with the Server applet, which was discussed earlier.

Of course, if your whole company's power goes out, everyone with a UPS should know better than to keep computing. They should choose Shutdown from the Program Manager or Task List and log off their computers quickly. Users without a UPS will be dead in the water, of course, and they will have to take their losses. Sometimes, these losses will be minimized with help from the application software being run. Some better programs are fairly compassionate when it comes to power loss, for example, because they keep track of temp files and recover them gracefully when you power back up.

Windows NT Administration

IN THIS CHAPTER

CHAPTER 9

Administrative management of Windows NT is, in many ways, a system administrator's dream. Even in the best of circumstances, supporting PCs in a corporate setting is typically a nightmare. Novell has earned its market share in the PC networking niche largely because of its adept addressing of the manageability issues alone. Microsoft, no doubt based on its own experience in the corporate setting (which includes huge networks), has learned this lesson well. As a result, NT is quite rich in administrative tools and built-in security, which often precludes the need for those tools.

Unless users have the proper authority, they can't alter files, directories, or important NT settings. Internal Access control lists and transaction logging make network and workstation management of critical data a reasonable (instead of an impossible) chore. Permissions can be modified over the network. That way, you don't have to visit the workstation in question. Even so, users still have the feeling that their PC is theirs because they still have control over desktop attributes, such as color, fonts, program groups, and My Computer preferences.

When using NTFS partitions, managers can selectively lock out users to prohibit them from altering or even seeing specific files, directories, and even entire partitions. Also, lower-level users are not given access to administrative tools used for disk partitioning and formatting, or for setting up and altering user profiles, passwords, and permissions.

Many of the NT system-administration techniques were discussed in earlier chapters. In particular, Chapter 8, "Using the Control Panel to Configure Windows NT," dealt with configuration issues that could be classified as system management. Topics such as font management, network software and hardware configuration, and system services and devices were discussed in that chapter. You might want to review Chapter 8 if you're managing a workstation or network.

> **NOTE**
>
> Relatively effortless installation of NT on new workstations over the network is covered in Chapter 7, "Installing Windows NT."

This chapter discusses system-related applications and techniques that are specifically administrative in nature, including the following:

- The best methods for organizing program groups and icons
- Replicating directories across the network
- Managing shared workstation resources
- Managing your users by using permissions, passwords, access rights, and groups
- Working from a distance: using remote workstation administration
- Managing the hard disk: partitioning and converting between file formats

Using these techniques with the Control Panel, My Computer, and Print Manager commands covered in previous chapters should give you a pretty good handle on the basics of local and network administration of NT. (Part III, "Networking Windows NT," covers network installation, usage, and optimization in more technical detail.)

> **NOTE**
>
> The Performance Monitor application (located in the Administration group), which helps locate network bottlenecks, is covered in Chapter 20, "Troubleshooting Your Network."
>
> Windows NT includes versions of User Manager, Server Manager, Print Manager, Event Viewer, and other tools that can be installed on any Windows NT or Windows 3.1 (or higher) workstation running in enhanced mode to aid in remotely administering the network. These tools are located in the CLIENTS\SRVTOOLS directory on the installation CD-ROM.

Organizing Programs and Document Groups Effectively

I discussed the details of setting up application groups on the local machine in Chapter 3, "Working with Windows NT." There, I reviewed the procedures for creating new program groups, adding applications to them, and setting the application icon properties. That and subsequent chapters covered additional techniques for running programs—from both the command prompt and My Computer. If you're a veteran Windows user, you're sure to know the basics of running applications and organizing My Computer to work the way you like best. A few quirks exist in NT and NT networking, though, that are worth keeping in mind. These could be seen as pertaining to system administration—especially when you're setting up working environments for others.

Organizing Local Workstation Applications

How you organize your groups depends on how many users are going to use the local workstation. Obviously, if you're the only person using the station, configuration is straightforward; simply set up your groups as you want them. If you imported your groups from a previous Windows 3.1 setup, they are already arranged according to your preferences (assuming that you were using Programs as your shell in 3.1). If you were using Norton Desktop or one of the many other better alternatives to Programs, you have some work to do until you can buy your favorite shell for use under NT.

If you've added an NTFS partition to your hard disk, this might cause trouble with the pointers in your Programs icons. I added an NTFS partition on my second physical drive, for example, which comes up in NT as drive D, pushing my original drive D to logical drive E. Under DOS, the NTFS partition isn't seen, so the FAT partition on Drive 0 comes up as C, and the FAT partition on Drive 0 is D.

These drive reassignments are OK, except that under NT I now have three partitions: C, D, and E. Therefore, program icons that were imported from Windows 3.1 might not point to the correct drive letter to find the application; therefore, when you try to run some programs, you get an error message. Changing the property settings (from D:\123\123.EXE to E:\123\123.EXE, for example) fixes the problem in NT, but because the changes sometimes are reflected in Windows 3.1 settings, you also get an error message when you try to run the programs under Windows 3.1. The section "Disk Administrator," later in this chapter, offers partition-management tips that can solve this problem of dealing with reassigned drives.

In a nutshell, if you're running dual operating systems, you want to add any NTFS partitions in such a way that they're logically the highest letter drive—even above the CD-ROM drive, if possible. All Programs icons pointing to your FAT, HPFS, or CD-ROM drives then work fine in both operating systems. When you boot NT, NTFS partitions are added to the end of the drive list rather than to the middle.

TIP

One workaround solution for erroneous pointers is to use environment variables in CONFIG.NT and AUTOEXEC.NT startup files, as explained in Chapter 8. Use a declared variable as part of the application or document's pathname in the Programs icon's Path property field.

Administration-wise, if you're the only user on the workstation and your network administrator believes that you're fit for the job, you want to set yourself up with full privileges. Create a new account for yourself (don't use the Administrator account—you should reserve that for emergencies) and give yourself Administrator status. Then set your desktop colors, fonts, My Computer preferences, Programs groups, and so on.

Even if you're the only user on the workstation, you might want to create a few Common Programs groups anyway, instead of having them all local to you. Sometimes guests might come over to use your computer, or you might want to log on using the real administrator's account (in case yours gets messed up, for example). If you have your most-used programs (such as a word processor, communications program, or whatever) in a Common group, it appears in Programs when you log on under these other accounts.

NOTE

Some application installation programs (VCNT++, for example) create Common groups but still allow you to set user-specific details, such as environmental settings. So, although the program group might appear for all users, other relevant settings created during installation might not appear for users other than the one who installed the program.

Setting Up Multiuser Workstations

If you're going to be sharing a workstation with other users, you have to coordinate who's going to be the big cheese on the workstation—whether it is one or several people. In any case, you might want to share access to some programs and documents. You should discuss this with your coworkers and decide which programs should go in Common groups.

Set up your applications in directories that are available to each person with access to the group. Take special note of whether the applications in question must have write access to their own directories, because this can affect the type of permission you assign the directory. You don't want people erasing the application's files, so if it can run with read-only privileges, all the better. Many applications write to an .INI file when you change preferences or quit the program, however, so you might have to set the directory's permissions a notch higher.

> **NOTE**
>
> See "Security Options with My Computer," later in this chapter, for details on setting permissions for directories and files.

Each user on the station probably will want to set up his or her own personal directories, permissions on those directories, and network connections (if networking) as well. Don't forget that you can set up a home directory for each user with User Manager, explained later in this chapter in "User Manager."

If the workstation is running regularly on a network, you have an additional headache when it comes to application organization. Again, two major issues—drive names and directory permissions—arise. But on top of this, you have share contingencies on the other workstations to consider. Take a look at these considerations one step at a time.

First, the problem of shifting drive letters becomes even worse than it is on a single workstation when you are working with two operating systems and NTFS partitions. As you know, when you connect to a network drive, NT assigns it the next available drive letter unless you specify otherwise. If your Programs application or document icons point to Drive F, for example, and you or the user connect to a number of network drives in the wrong order, Drive F might be on Joe's computer instead of Jane's computer. The application you want to run might not be on Jane's computer, and the directory structure is probably different on Jane's computer anyway. The result is an error message.

Second, you need to look at the issue of directory shares. If you set up Programs icons for yourself or a user, and those icons point to an application or a working directory that is on another machine (or if the user is accustomed to saving files on a drive with a particular letter), you have to be careful. When you set up an icon for an application on removable media or on the network, Programs warns you that you might not be able to access the application in the future, and the point should be well taken. If the network workstation (in this case, you could call it an application server) containing the application isn't up and running, or the directory holding the application(s) isn't shared, you also get an error message when you double-click a Programs icon pointing to an application in that directory.

The moral of the story is twofold. First, consider whether using network workstations as application servers makes sense. Maybe it doesn't. Often, it's less of a headache for an administrator to copy entire application directories to each workstation (especially in a peer-to-peer network) than to deal with users who can't get their applications to run. Although this arrangement consumes more disk space, at least the user always has access to the application.

Second, if you're going to use remote workstations to hold applications, make sure each user's My Computer is set to restore the necessary connections at boot time and that connections are assigned the correct drive letters. Also, explain to users that an error message probably means that the remote workstation isn't up or that the directory isn't shared, and tell them how to handle that. If you want to set up a dedicated application server (a computer just for dishing out applications and possibly data files), that's another solution. But just make sure that the server is always on and that permissions allow an adequate number of users access to the files and directories if you're expecting a heavy traffic load.

> **TIP**
>
> Set the user limit on a directory by choosing My Computer's Disk | Share As command.
> You can automate the process of restoring shares in the appropriate order by using a logon script. Logon scripts can be generic (for group-specific configurations) or user-specific.

Using the Control Panel's Server Applet

The Control Panel's Server applet displays resource connections, the number of users connected to the workstation over the network, names of open files, and who should be alerted in case of administrative alerts.

The Server applet is mostly for use by system administrators or those administering their own standalone systems. Server provides several important views of your network and allows you to control aspects of network operations, called *server properties*. You can perform these tasks by using the Server applet:

- See who's connected to the local system's directories
- Disconnect network users from the workstation
- See which local resources are shared
- See which local resources are open by others

■ Manage directory replication

■ Control who receives important system alert messages—for example, when a power outage occurs

To run the Server applet, double-click the Server icon in the Control Panel. The Server dialog box appears, as shown in Figure 9.1.

FIGURE 9.1.

Using the Server applet.

In the Server dialog box, you see a report of several key factors of your server's usage, as listed in Table 9.1.

Table 9.1. Key information in the Server dialog box.

Item	Description
Sessions	Number of users connected
Open Files	Number of files users have open
File Locks	Number of files currently locked by users
Open Named Pipes	Number of named pipes currently open
Description	Description for your computer

In the Server dialog box, you can change the description of your computer. To reach the other functions, you have to click one of the five buttons at the bottom of the dialog box, as described in Table 9.2.

Table 9.2. Server dialog box buttons.

Button	Function
Users	Examines who's using your system resources, which resources are open by each user, and (if you want) disconnects any user from such resources.

continues

9
WINDOWS NT
ADMINISTRATION

Table 9.2. continued

Button	Function
Shares	Performs the reverse of the Users button. Instead of showing a listing organized by user, Shares lists your shared resources (printers or directories, for example) and shows who's using each resource. Again, you can disconnect any or all users from the shared resource.
In Use	Displays which shared resources are open.
Replication	Manages the importing of a fixed set of directories and their files from an NT Server machine. NT Server machines can export and import directories and files.
Alerts	Specifies a list of computers to be notified when administrative problems crop up on your machine.

Managing the Users Connected to Your Machine

Earlier in this chapter, you learned about the need to know who's connected to your computer—especially when it comes to shutting down the computer or turning off sharing of a directory in which others might have files open.

Administrators have a particular need to closely observe the number and nature of connections remote users have to a machine, especially before performing a system shutdown. Because not all users have the right to shut down the system or share directories and printers, this type of activity is rarely of concern to them. But even from a security perspective, an administrator might want to know at any given time just how many users are connected, who they are, and the number of files they have open. If, for some reason, the user poses a threat or fails to terminate his or her connection when asked, you can use the Server dialog box to force such a disconnection.

In any case, here's how to see who's connected to the workstation:

1. Run the Server applet from the Control Panel.
2. In the Server dialog box, click Users. The User Sessions dialog box shown in Figure 9.2 appears, listing the connected users and the resources they're using.
3. After you click a username in the Connected Users box, the resources that user is connected to are displayed in the Resource box. Note in Figure 9.2 that some unnamed person on the ENGINEERING computer has five files open on the shared directory called WINWORD and is printing something to a shared printer called QMS-PS-8. Fred Johnson on the FINANCE computer also has five files open. Also listed are the elapsed time the user has been connected, how much time has elapsed

since the user did something that affected this connection (such as saving a file), and whether the user is logged on as a member of an account other than Guests.

FIGURE 9.2.

Seeing who is connected and which resources they are using.

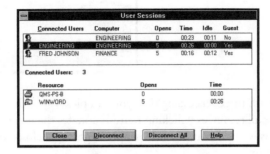

4. You only have two real choices here if you're going to take action (besides closing the box, of course, if you're just observing):

   You can select a user by clicking that name and then clicking Disconnect.

   You can click Disconnect All to get everyone off your system in one fell swoop.

   In either case, you're prompted to confirm your choice.

TIP

If you want to know more about which files are open and how to close only specific files, be sure to read the next section.

WARNING

You will probably cause a loss of data if you disconnect users who have files open. Warn them first with a phone call, a visit to their office, or the Chat program, and give them time to close files and disconnect from your computer.

Seeing Which Specific Resources Are Being Used

Before you disconnect a user, you might want to know more than just he or she has five or 10 files open. Viewing a listing might be useful, even if it's just to examine network traffic flow and specific file demand.

To see a listing, follow these steps:

1. Run the Server applet from the Control Panel.

2. In the Server dialog box, click the In Use button. The In Use dialog box appears, listing all open resources (those in use by another user), as shown in Figure 9.3.

FIGURE 9.3.

Checking out the resources open by other users.

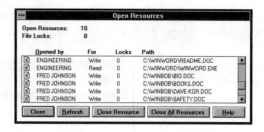

3. As with the Users dialog box, you can pick a specific resource to close, or you can close all resources. Clicking Refresh updates the box to display the latest situation. (This is important, because people might have closed or opened files since you opened the box.)

After you get in the sharing mood, it's sometimes hard to remember what you've offered to the world. How many directories have you shared? What are their sharenames? Which printers or other devices (such as fax modems) have you made available to other users? Which named pipes are available to others? The Shares button can tell you; just follow these steps:

1. Run the Server applet from the Control Panel.

2. In the Server dialog box, click Shares. The Shared Resources dialog box appears, which is similar to one shown in Figure 9.4.

FIGURE 9.4.

Checking the list of your shared resources.

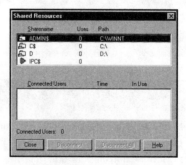

3. Scroll the list to see what is shared. In some cases, you probably didn't even know that some of these items existed, much less that they were shared. Some of the items are *special shares*—shares the computer arranged all by itself. Don't worry about these; each item has an icon that indicates the type of item, as shown in Table 9.3. Table 9.4 lists the other items you can view in the Shared Resources dialog box.

4. Click the shared item you want to investigate. The names of the current users appear in the Connected Users column, and an indication of how much time has passed since each user connected to the resource appears in the Time column. Also, the total number of users is listed in the Connected Users field, and a Yes or No appears in the In Use column to indicate whether the user of the resource has files open at the current time.

5. To disconnect a user, select the user and click Disconnect. To disconnect everyone, click Disconnect All.

CAUTION

Note that disconnecting users disconnects them from any and all resources they have open, which could cause a loss of data, particularly if data files are open for the users' applications. You are reminded of this by a confirmation dialog box, and you must choose OK before NT executes the disconnection.

Table 9.3. Viewing special-share items.

Description	Represents
Hand holding a file	Shared directories
Plug	Shared named pipes
Printer	Shared printers
Question mark	Miscellaneous: Other types of shares that NT can't classify for some reason

Table 9.4. Items in the Shared Resources dialog box.

Item	Lists
Sharename	Items available to others on the network. Remember that a share with a dollar sign ($) after its name is an administrative share. Only other NT administrators can access it.
Uses	The current number of connections to the resource.
Path	The pathname of the resource. Typically a drive/directory path, although it can be a printer path—that is, the name the printer was given when it was created.
Connected Users	Users connected to the selected resource. When information about the user isn't available for some reason, the connecting computer's name appears.
Time	The length of time the user has been connected to the resource.
In Use	Whether a user actually has a file open on the resource or is just connected to it. You might want to know, for example, whether a user is likely to lose data if you disconnect him or her. If this column has the word No in it, your user won't lose data.
Connected Users	The total number of users connected to the highlighted resource.

Table 9.5 lists some common types of special shares that you might see in the Shared Resources dialog box.

Table 9.5. Types of special shares.

Share	Description
driveletter$	The default setting when sharing the root directory of a drive. It gives administrators and backup operators access to the drive (unless the machine is an NT Server, in which case server operators can access it as well).
ADMIN$	A resource used by NT's internals for its own purposes. The path of such a share always points to the directory where NT is stored. Only administrators, server operators, and backup operators are allowed access. Administrators use these resources heavily to access and troubleshoot user-related problems.
IPC$	An internal NT resource used for sharing named pipes. It is used for remote administration of a workstation.
PRINT$	An internal NT resource used for remote administration of printers.
REPL$	Only on NT Server. Pertains only to systems set up to act as replication export servers.
NETLOGON$	Only on NT Server. Used by the system to manage a remote logon from another domain.

Importing Replicated Directory Groupings

Directory replication is an NT Server option that makes it easy to maintain (synchronize) identical directories of files on multiple computers, based on a single source computer called an *export server.* This topic is covered in Chapter 15, "NT Server."

Managing Alerts

The final administrative option on the Server applet is the Alerts button. Clicking this button allows you to view and manage who will be alerted to important system developments, such as an impending powerdown or other system alerts originating at the specific workstation. Messages typically appear in these situations:

- Access problems
- Printer problems

- Security violations
- User session problems
- UPS-controlled shutdown

Alerts don't appear unless two conditions exist:

- The source computer (the one you're configuring) must have the Alerter and Messenger services running.
- The destination computer(s) must have the Messenger service running.

> **NOTE**
>
> To see whether these services are running, use the Control Panel's Services applet. The Messenger service typically is started automatically at NT boot time. Alerter is normally started manually, which means when an application or the operating system calls it or when you manually start it from the Services applet. If your alerts aren't being sent and received properly, make sure that the correct services are running. You might have to start Alerter manually with the Start button or change its setting to Automatic and then reboot.

To manage system alerts, follow these steps:

1. Run the Server applet from the Control Panel. The Alerts dialog box appears, as shown in Figure 9.5.

FIGURE 9.5.

Specifying the recipients of alerts.

2. Type the name of the computer or user you want to be a recipient of alerts. If you enter a computer name, any user on that system receives the alerts. If you enter only names of specific users on a computer, only those users receive alerts.
3. Click Add. (To remove a recipient or computer, highlight the name in the Send Administrative Alerts To box and click Remove.)
4. Click OK in the Alerts dialog box, and then click OK in the Server dialog box.

9

WINDOWS NT ADMINISTRATION

> **NOTE**
>
> Although you can add Windows for Workgroups computers to the list of recipients, these computers won't receive alert messages unless they're running Windows for Workgroups 3.11 and also are running WINPOPUP, which can be enabled with their Control Panel's Network Logon button.

Working with User Manager

User Manager is one of six applications found in the Administrative Toolsgroup under the Programs menu displayed by the Startup button. As a system administrator, you'll rely on User Manager to perform these tasks:

- Add new user accounts to the workstation
- Modify existing user account settings, such as name and password
- Set a logon script or batch file that executes when the user logs on
- Delete user accounts from the workstation
- Assign a user to one of several permission sets, called *groups*
- Assign or reassign the permissions given to each group
- Set workstation policies, such as minimum password length and account locking
- Define which items you want in an optional audit trail of system activity

When you run User Manager by selecting its name from the Administrative Tools menu, you see the window shown in Figure 9.6. The number of users varies, depending on your system.

FIGURE 9.6.

The User Manager window.

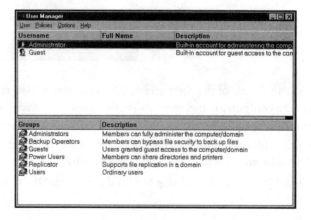

Note the upper and lower panes. The upper pane lists the accounts that already exist on the system. Each account has a username, a full name, and a short description for identification purposes. The bottom pane lists the groups or categories of users that exist on the system. All accounts must fit into one of these groups. A group is defined by a set of rights and privileges. Assigning people to a group means that you don't have to construct their privileges from scratch. Because NT has so many security features, this would be a formidable job.

NOTE

If none of the existing groups meets your needs, you can fine-tune one of them or create your own group definition. You'll learn how to do this in the section "Adding, Deleting, and Renaming User Accounts" later in this chapter.

Knowing Who Can Do What

Not all users can operate User Manager equally (Table 9.6 shows a breakdown of who can do what). Because the program is primarily an administrative tool, it makes sense that its use is restricted to classes of users with higher privileges. Depending on your privilege level, you might not be able to execute all the menu commands. In other cases, it might look as though you're executing the command, but changes you make won't actually go into effect.

Table 9.6. User Manager rights.

Class of User	Rights
Users	Users in this group can assign themselves membership in the Administrators or Power Users group in order to give themselves all rights on the computer. They can create only more Users-level groups.
Power Users	Create, modify, and delete accounts and groups. This includes adding and removing accounts from the Power Users, Guest, and Users groups.
Administrators	Create, modify, and delete accounts and groups, assign passwords, set audit trails, set systemwide policies, and set user rights for each group.

Adding, Deleting, and Renaming User Accounts

The User Manager functions you're likely to use include adding or deleting user accounts. When NT is installed on a workstation, two accounts are created: Administrators and Guests. At install time, you also have the option of configuring one user account (called the *initial user account*) by supplying a logon name, full name, and password. Therefore, the typical newly installed system has two or three accounts. The Guests account is serviceable for occasional use by visitors to the system. You should create separate accounts for any users who use the system regularly, however, so that they can be given individual Programs groupings, My Computer connections, security privileges, and so on.

The initial Administrators account is created at setup, when you're prompted to enter a name and other information. By default, the name on this account is Administrator, and the password is admin. You can change this password by using User Manager.

TIP

If you forget your password, you're in trouble, because you won't be able to administer the system. You can work around this problem, though. First, the default Users account added at installation time also has Administrators privileges, so logging on as a member of that account lets you alter passwords. Second, you can use the Emergency Repair Disk to boot the system and change the password then. Finally, if you're on a network, another administrator can log onto the machine remotely and change the password.

As a rule, however, it's a good idea to create an Administrators account for each person who will have administrative privileges. Don't just let each administrative-level user use the built-in Administrator account, because if one account password is lost, another user with a different administrator account can access the administrative tools and commands reserved for administrators. Also, if each administrator has a unique account, you can use auditing to determine whose activities are adversely affecting system security.

TIP

If the Domain Admin group is removed from the local Administrator account, the computer can't be administered by any domain administrator except for one with local administrative accounts. If a new group is created and added to the local Administrator account, only members of this group can administer the computer. You can use this feature to prevent access to sensitive computers or data on the network.

The Guests account is a convenience that gives a casual user access to the computer but not the right to wreak havoc. The Guests account is created during setup and can't be removed, although it can be renamed to something like Visitor. Its rights can be altered by the administrator, however, so a nefarious (or unwitting) administrator could conceivably give away precious rights to any passerby who logs on by typing `Guest` and entering no password. As a protection, an administrator might want to disable the Guests account. On NT Server systems, the Guests account is disabled by default.

Adding a New Account

To add a new account, follow these steps:

1. Choose User | New User. The New User dialog box appears, as shown in Figure 9.7.

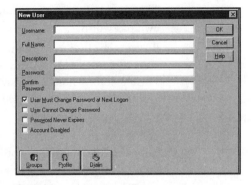

2. Fill in the Username, Full Name, Password, and Confirm Password fields. The Description field is optional. The username can be as long as 20 characters, but it must be unique and can't be the same as a groupname for the workstation (administrators, users, and so on). Also, you can't use the following characters in the name:

```
< > ? * + , = ¦ ; : [ ] / \ " or a space
```

NOTE

Passwords can contain up to 14 characters. Remember that uppercase and lowercase letters are treated differently. If you create a password of ABRACADABRA, for example, entering **abracadabra** won't log you on.

TIP

Use a standard formula for usernames, because people will see them listed on the network or in various dialog boxes. The popular fashion is to use the first name followed by the first letter of the last name, such as Johnd for John Doe.

3. Fill in the appropriate checkboxes, which are described in Table 9.7.
4. Click OK in all the necessary dialog boxes; the new user then is added to the list of accounts.

9

WINDOWS NT
ADMINISTRATION

Table 9.7. New User checkboxes.

Checkbox	Description
User Must Change Password at Next Logon	Enable this checkbox if you're setting up an account for which you don't want to be the creator of the user's password. This is typically the case because users should choose their own passwords.
User Cannot Change Password	Prevents the user from altering the password. Normally, you want to do this only with accounts that aren't personal, such as Guests, for whom the password is, by default, blank (although this can be changed).
Password Never Expires	Prevents the password from expiring after the time set by the policies for the workstation. Usually, you set this time by using the Maximum Password Age setting in the Account Policy dialog box (which you open by choosing Policy│Account). You normally use this only with an account assigned to a service rather than an individual. (The Scheduler and Directory Replicator services are typical services with which you might want to use this. Custom services are another example. You can assign them to an account with the Control Panel's Services applet.)
Account Disabled	You can disable any account except the administrator's. Other accounts might call for disabling if a user is on vacation, for example. Or, you might want to create and disable a standard user account template that you easily can copy for future new users by choosing User│Copy. When you copy the template account, everything about the account is copied, but it's activated rather than disabled. You have to fill in the username, full name, and password for the new account.
Groups	Specifies to which group(s) the user will be assigned.
Profile	Sets the optional logon script (batch file) that will run when the user logs on, and the optional home directory (default directory) that the user's File Save and File Open dialog boxes default to for saving data files from applications.

Deleting an Account

Deleting an account is simple. You'll want to delete an account when a user moves to another department, leaves the company, or no longer needs access to the computer.

To delete an account on the workstation, follow these steps:

1. Bring up User Manager from the Administrative Tools group in the Startup menu.

2. Select the account by clicking it in the upper pane. You can select multiple accounts if you want, which allows you to delete multiple users in a single operation.

3. Choose User | Delete. The warning box shown in Figure 9.8 appears. You might have to confirm your choice several times.

FIGURE 9.8.
Confirming that you want to delete a user.

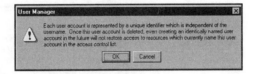

Renaming an Account

After an account is created, you might want to rename it. You can't do this from the Properties dialog box. Renaming is really nothing more than changing the username. You might want to change Guest to Visitor or Joe to Joseph, for example.

To rename an account, follow these steps:

1. Select the account in the upper pane of User Manager.

2. Choose User | Rename. The Rename dialog box appears, as shown in Figure 9.9.

FIGURE 9.9.
Renaming an account.

3. Enter a new name (containing up to 20 characters) and click OK.

Modifying Account Properties

Each account has a set of properties, just as files and Programs icons have properties. Modifying the properties for an account allows you to redo everything you declared when setting up the account (except the username, which you change as explained in the preceding section).

To modify an account's properties, follow these steps:

1. Select the account in the upper pane of User Manager. (You can select several accounts at once and change settings for all of them. Select multiple accounts just as you select multiple files in My Computer—by pressing Ctrl+click or Shift+click.)

2. Choose User|Properties. If you selected only a single account, the User Properties dialog box shown in Figure 9.10 appears. If you selected two or more accounts, the User Properties dialog box shown in Figure 9.11 appears.

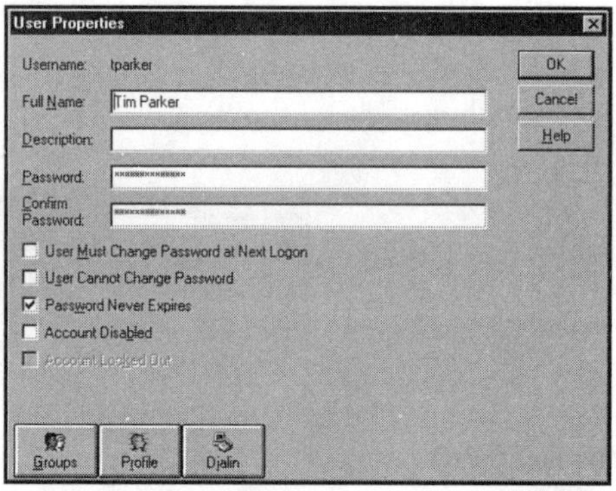

FIGURE 9.10.

The User Properties dialog box for a single account.

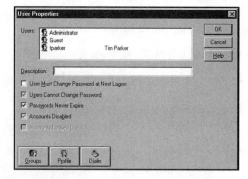

FIGURE 9.11.

The User Properties dialog box for multiple accounts.

3. Change the properties as needed, and use the Groups and Profile buttons as necessary.

Note that, if you're changing a group of users at once, the box has fewer settings. (This is useful when you want to change the description or the password requirements, or you want to disable a group of accounts quickly.) You can't change the username, full name, or password, for example, because they're different for each user.

> **NOTE**
>
> Property changes don't take effect until the next time the user logs on.

Managing Account Groups

Every account must be assigned to a group. The advantage of groups is that, by defining a set of privileges for a group, you make it easy to add a user to the system and assign those privileges to the new user. Simply add the user to the group that has the rights you want to assign to that user.

As explained earlier in this chapter, NT sets up several groups at install time: Administrators, Power Users, Users, Guests, Backup Operators, and Replicators. You can create additional groups as you find the need. You might want a group that has more rights than Users but fewer than Power Users. You also can redefine a group's rights and privileges so that all the members of that group have more or fewer powers when using the system. When you redefine a group's rights (properties), all accounts that are members of the group are quickly updated to reflect the changes.

Two types of groups also exist in NT: local and global. You usually deal with local groups when administering a workstation. *Local groups* are sets of privileges that can be used only on the local workstation. *Global groups* have a different icon and can be used anywhere in the domain or by trusted domains connected to your domain. (See Part III for more information.)

Assigning an Account to a Group

When you bring up User Manager, all existing groups are displayed in the lower pane. Based on this information, you then can decide to which group you want to assign a new user.

Suppose that you're creating a new user account. To assign its group membership, follow these steps:

1. Bring up the New User dialog box from the User Manager window. After you fill in the upper section of the New User dialog box (username and so on), click Groups. The Group Memberships dialog box appears, as shown in Figure 9.12.

FIGURE 9.12.

Assigning a new account to a group.

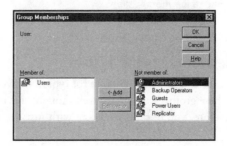

9

WINDOWS NT
ADMINISTRATION

2. By default, new accounts are made members of the lowest empowered group: Users. You can then add groups to or remove groups from the list. The existing groups from which you can choose are listed in the "Not member of" box. Click any groups to which you want to give the new user admission, and then click Add.

> **NOTE**
>
> An account can be a member of more than one group. You can be a member of Administrators and Users, for example. Because the rights of Users are a subset of Administrators, though, there's no need to be a member of both groups. For this reason, if you're upgrading a user's rights, you typically remove them from the previous assignment by clicking the Remove button. Some exceptions to this rule exist. Some groups have capabilities that others do not, and these capabilities can't be added to or removed from that group. The Backup Operators group, for example, has some capabilities that other groups don't, so you might want to assign an account to the Users group and to the Backup Operators group. (See Table 9.9 in "Managing Security Policies," later in this chapter, for a list of existing group rights and capabilities.)

3. Click any group in the "Member of" box from which you want to remove membership, and then click Remove.
4. Click OK.

> **TIP**
>
> You also can drag groups between the "Member of" and "Not member of" boxes to reassign them.

> **NOTE**
>
> As explained in the section "Modifying Account Properties," earlier in this chapter, you can alter the group assignment of an existing account or accounts by using the Properties dialog box. Just select the account(s) in question and choose User | Properties. Then click Groups and make the modifications.

Adding a New Group to the System

Normally, the canned groups are enough for typical networks and workstations. The rights and capabilities of these groups were pretty well thought out by Microsoft, based on their in-house networks. Therefore, you're probably okay with just the Users, Power Users, Administrators,

Backup Operators, and Replicators groups. Table 9.8 provides a brief breakdown of each of these groups.

Table 9.8. The default groups used by Windows NT.

Group	Description
Administrators	Can do anything on the system. The person who installed NT and the initial account are both assigned to this group. If the machine is connected to an NT Server domain, all administrators on the domain are, by default, given this status on this workstation.
Power Users	Can add program groups to the Startup menu; set the system clock; share directories; and install, share, and manage printers. Can create and manage User Manager groups, except the Administrators group.
Users	All new accounts are automatically given this level of permission. It supplies all the necessary rights to run programs. If the workstation is connected to an NT Server domain, all users on the domain are, by default, given this status on this workstation. Can't share or stop the sharing of directories and printers.
Backup Operators	Can use the Backup and Restore commands in the Backup utility supplied with Windows NT.
Replicators	Not usually used by users. This group is used with the Control Panel's Services applet to set up the Replicator service.
Guests	Limited access only, such as logging on and using specific directories and files, but not changing any system settings, creating accounts, or managing and sharing resources.

9

WINDOWS NT
ADMINISTRATION

If you're not happy with the supplied groups, create your own. Although the Microsoft manual suggests that copying an existing group saves you some legwork, it really only copies the account names, not the permissions and other settings, so you might as well start from scratch.

To create a group, follow these steps:

1. Choose User | New Local Group. The New Local Group dialog box appears, as shown in Figure 9.13.
2. Click Show Full Names to see the full names of any users you add or who are by default already added (such as Administrators). This step is optional.
3. Fill in the Group Name and Description fields.
4. Click Add to add members to the group. The Add Users and Groups dialog box appears, as shown in Figure 9.14.

FIGURE 9.13.

Creating a new account group.

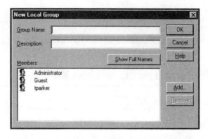

FIGURE 9.14.

Adding users to the new group.

5. Click a username in the Names box, and then click Add. The account is added to the Add Names list box.

TIP

If you want to search the network for a particular user or group of users, click Search. This brings up the Find Account dialog box, from which you can type a user or groupname and specify in which domain or workgroup to look. You use this process to add a remote user to a group on your workstation. Searching a large network can take some time, so use this command with care. For a large network, if you know the user's domain or workgroup name, select it first and select Search Only In in the Find Account dialog box.

---

6. Repeat Step 5 until all the desired names are added. When the list is complete, click OK.

7. Check the members by double-clicking the new group name in the bottom pane of the User Manager window. The Properties dialog box appears, which lists all members.

Changing a Group's Properties

You use the Properties dialog box to change the members in a preexisting group. You also use Properties to change the description of the group. Follow these steps:

1. In User Manager, select the group whose properties you want to examine or alter.

2. Choose User | Properties. (Actually, the menu name User is a misnomer in this case; there should be a Group menu, but there isn't.) The Local Group Properties dialog box appears, which lists the current description and members roster, as shown in Figure 9.15.

FIGURE 9.15.

A Local Group Properties dialog box showing the Users groups.

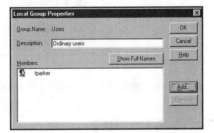

3. Type a new description or edit the existing one.

4. Edit the members list by clicking Add, which brings up the Add Users and Groups dialog box, or click an existing member and then click Remove.

5. Click OK, and the properties are altered.

9

WINDOWS NT
ADMINISTRATION

Deleting a Group

You can easily delete a group by choosing User | Delete. Remember that, just as when you delete a user, you can't reinstate a group. Even if the new group has the same name and members as the old group, it won't have the same properties and access rights. You have to re-create the group from scratch.

Follow these steps to delete a group:

1. Highlight the groupname in the User Manager window.

> **CAUTION**
>
> Don't delete any of the NT-supplied groups: Administrators, Backup Operators, Guests, Power Users, Replicators, and Users.

2. Choose User | Delete. The message box shown in Figure 9.16 appears, reminding you that after you delete the group, you won't be able to reinstate it.

FIGURE 9.16.

Use care when deleting a group.

3. If you're sure that you want to delete the group, click OK to confirm the operation.

Managing Account Profiles

Each user account has special settings, which make up its *profile*. This profile contains some useful (although optional) settings:

■ A logon script, which runs when the user logs on. This can be a .BAT file (DOS batch file), a .CMD file (NT batch file), or an .EXE file. Running this script is similar to putting such a program in the Startup group. The advantage is that the administrator can easily assign the startup script to a number of users.

■ A home directory, which is the default directory that Save As and Open dialog boxes use when saving or loading files for use with applications. This makes work easier for administrators who want to back up or delete data files belonging to an individual user, because chances are good that the user's files will be in one directory. The home directory setting also determines the active directory when a command-prompt session is run. This directory can be a local or network directory.

To set up the profile, follow these steps:

1. Select the user's account in the upper pane of the User Manager window. If you want to set the profile for a number of users, Shift+click to select contiguous accounts and Ctrl+click to select noncontiguous accounts.

2. Press Enter or choose User|Properties. The Properties dialog box appears, listing the selected accounts.

3. Click Profile. The User Environment Profile dialog box appears, as shown in Figure 9.17.

FIGURE 9.17.

Setting several account profiles.

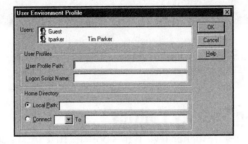

4. Enter the logon script name in the Logon Script Name field. By default, NT looks in the \SCRIPTS directory—WINDOWS\SYSTEM32\REPL\IMPORT\SCRIPTS. You can use another directory if you specify it exactly as part of the file's pathname.

5. Set the home directory (this is optional). This can be on a local or network path. Select the setting that applies (Local Path or Connect). If you choose a local path, enter the directory name. For example, c:\users\fredg stores Fred G.'s files. NT creates the \FREDG directory under the existing \USERS directory for you. If you want to use a network directory, you must specify the logical drive letter to which the network directory will connect, as well as the network path. This is similar to connecting to a remote directory in My Computer, but it happens before My Computer runs (right as the user logs on), so it doesn't interfere with My Computer. This method just bumps up the drive letters a notch. Click Connect, choose the drive letter from the drop-down list, and type the network path in the To field (for example, `\\accounting\user\fredg`).

WARNING

If you're setting the profile for several accounts at once, you might not want to modify the Home Directory setting unless you want the whole group to have the same directory. It's better to modify the accounts separately.

9

WINDOWS NT ADMINISTRATION

TIP

You can have NT supply the directory name by using one of its internal environment variables: %username%. Just enter this into the path (for example, `c:\users\%username%`). If the user's name is FREDG, the result is C:\USERS\FREDG. If the username contains more than eight characters, NT tells you that it can't create the directory and that you must create it manually.

NOTE

If you don't enter a home directory, NT uses the default home directory, which is \USERS\DEFAULT on the NT drive.

Managing Security Policies

Security policies are higher-level rights policies that are systemwide in influence or, at the least, affect an entire group of users. You can set three security aspects from User Manager (by using the Policies menu): the account policy, the user rights policy, and the audit policy, as shown in Table 9.9.

Table 9.9. Setting security policies.

Policy	Function
Account	Sets details about passwords: how long before they have to be changed, minimum and maximum password length, number of bad logon attempts before locking the account, and how long old passwords are remembered.
User Rights	Sets the system rights (such as shutting down the system) assigned to a group of accounts. You can use this command to keep all Power Users groups from changing the system time, for example.
Audit	Sets what type of security-related events (such as system logons and logoffs, user rights changes, and system restarts) are monitored and stored in an audit file, which can be reviewed later by an administrator to see what users have been up to. (You can read the audit file by using the Event Viewer application, which is covered in Chapter 11, "Maintenance and Troubleshooting.")

Account Policy

Follow these steps to change the account policy:

1. Choose Policies | Account. The Account Policy dialog box appears, as shown in Figure 9.18.

FIGURE 9.18.

Setting the account policy for the entire workstation.

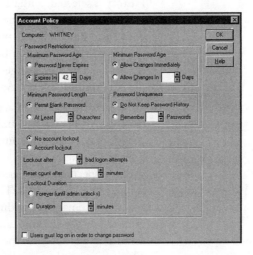

2. Make settings as desired. Remember that these settings apply to all users on the workstation. Table 9.10 describes these settings.

Table 9.10. Account Policy settings.

Setting	Notes
Maximum Password Age	How long can a user keep the same password? The range is 1–999 days. If you never want to require a change of password, select Password Never Expires.
Minimum Password Age	How long must a person use a new password before changing it? The range is 1–999 days. If Allow Changes Immediately is selected, the user can change the password as often as desired.
Minimum Password Length	All passwords must be at least as long as specified in this setting. Longer passwords provide greater security. The range is 1–14. Selecting Permit Blank Password allows some accounts (such as Guests) to have a blank password.

continues

Table 9.10. continued

Setting	Notes
Password Uniqueness	How many password changes must occur before you can use a previously used password again? If Do Not Keep History is selected, a user being prompted for a new password can just enter the same old password. This doesn't do much for security. If Remember is selected, you have to choose a number from 1–8. This doesn't work unless Allow Changes Immediately is not selected in the Minimum Password Age section.
Account Lockout	How many times can an account be accessed with a bad password before the account is locked? The range is 1–999. If Account Lockout is selected, you can further limit the lockout counter to the number of attempts within a specified number of minutes. This setting ranges from 1–99,999 minutes. The locked account can be enabled automatically within the range of 1–99,999 minutes, or the account can be disabled until an administrator manually enables the account with User Manager. This option can prevent local hackers from entering your system. I highly recommend it.

User Rights Policy

To set the user rights policy, follow these steps:

1. Choose Policies | User Rights. The User Rights Policy dialog box appears, as shown in Figure 9.19. This box is a little confusing. This is where you set the rights that each *group*, not each user account, has on the system. Of course, all users in a given group are affected, but you aren't setting rights for individual users.

FIGURE 9.19.

Changing the rights for each group account.

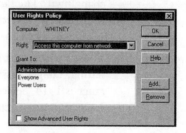

2. From the Right drop-down list, select the right you want to grant to a particular group. Suppose that you want to grant the right to back up files and directories. Open the Right drop-down list and click that right. In the Grant To box, the names of groups that already have that right appear, so don't bother giving that right to them again.

> **TIP**
>
> Some rights are pretty bizarre, and their meanings aren't immediately obvious. Create Permanent Shared Objects is a pretty obscure right, for example. Normally, the rights displayed in the Right list make more sense, and complex rights aren't listed. You can show and grant the rights that are more advanced if you want, however. Just enable the Show Advanced User Rights checkbox and reopen the Right drop-down list. You then see the new items.

3. Suppose that you want to give the selected right to a new group not listed. Click Add. The familiar Add Users and Groups dialog box appears. Click the group(s) you want to add to the list and click Add; then click OK. The groups are added to the Policies box. If you click Show Users, you can assign rights to individual user accounts.

4. Click on OK to give the new right to the group(s).

Follow these steps to remove a right from an account group:

1. Choose Policies | User Rights. The User Rights Policy dialog box appears.
2. From the Right drop-down list, select the right you want to remove.
3. Click the group from which you want to take the right.
4. Click Remove.

Audit Policy

To set the audit policy, follow these steps:

1. Choose Policies | Audit. The Audit Policy dialog box appears, as shown in Figure 9.20.

FIGURE 9.20.

Setting the auditing policy.

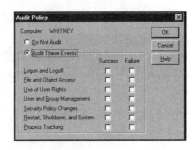

9

WINDOWS NT
ADMINISTRATION

2. By default, auditing is disabled. You might want to choose certain items to keep track of—for example, whether users are making security policy changes or whether a hacker has been trying to log onto the system. To activate auditing, enable the Audit These Events checkbox.

3. Now the checkboxes in the Audit These Events group become available. Check one or both of the Success and Failure boxes for the event(s) you want to audit. Table 9.11 lists the events you can monitor.

4. Click OK.

TIP

You should curtail your monitoring choices, because the audit log's size is limited. Some events (such as File and Object Access) occur so often that they can fill up the log quickly. You set the size of the log by choosing Log | Log Settings from the Event Viewer. (You learn about the Event Viewer in Chapter 11.)

Table 9.11. Auditing events.

Event	Description
Logon and Logoff	Makes entries when users log on or off the station. Also keeps track of remote users making a network connection to this station.
File and Object Access	Makes entries when users access files, directories, or printers for which auditing has been set. Auditing of files and directories is set from My Computer's Security menu. You set printer access auditing from Printer Manager's Security menu.
Use of User Rights	Makes entries when any user takes advantage of an assigned user right.
User and Group Management	Makes an entry when a user changes a user account or group—for example, when an account is created, deleted, renamed, disabled, enabled, or has its password changed. Also monitors when a group is altered by adding or deleting accounts or deleting the group totally.
Security Policy Changes	Makes a log entry when the audit policy or user rights policy is changed.
Restart, Shutdown, and System	Makes an entry when anyone restarts or shuts down the system. Does the same when any event happens that might jeopardize the system's security, including attempts to alter the Security (Audit) Log.

Event	Description
Process Tracking	NT has many types of processes (covered in Chapters 1 and 2). Many simpler applications consist of only a single process; some contain multiple processes. The creation of filehandles is considered a *process*, as are some accesses of objects (if done indirectly). In any case, entries are made indicating such processes. Some managers might find it useful to track the launch of and exit from applications. More obscure process tracking might be of lesser value.

Using Disk Administrator

Disk Administrator is the last of the major administration applications covered in this chapter. You'll find it in the Administrative Tools group (visible only to administrators).

With Disk Administrator, you can perform these tasks:

- Display facts about your partition sizes and setup
- Change drive-letter assignments
- Create and remove disk partitions of various types
- Create, enlarge, and delete volume sets
- Create and delete stripe sets

From the command prompt, you can perform these tasks:

- Change volume labels
- Convert a partition's format

None of these actions is likely to be necessary unless you find that you need to rearrange your partitions, decide that you want to convert FAT or HPFS partitions, or have a great deal of extra room on your disks and want to improve performance or accommodate huge files with stripe and volume sets. Another possibility is that you've installed a RAID 5 disk controller and you want to set up stripe sets or volume sets on your machine (typically, only on an NT Server machine).

When you install NT, Setup performs disk formatting and system transferal automatically, essentially performing the same functions as the FDISK, FORMAT, and SYS commands in DOS. When you use Disk Administrator, the program partitions the disks for you. Then you can choose Tools | Format to format the partitions.

Many of the changes you can make from Disk Administrator can erase entire volumes or hard disks. The good news is that the changes don't take effect until you exit Disk Administrator, at which time you're asked to confirm changes. The changes are recorded only if you choose Yes. Make sure that you want to save the changes you've made before you click Yes.

You must be logged on as an administrator to be able to run the Disk Administrator program and make changes.

To run Disk Administrator, follow these steps:

1. Double-click the Disk Administrator icon in the Administrative Tools group under the Startup menu. If this is the first time you've run Disk Administrator, or if Disk Administrator determines that your physical hard disk setup has changed since the last time it was run, you see the message shown in Figure 9.21.

FIGURE 9.21.

Confirming that you want Disk Administrator to update its configuration information.

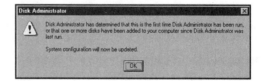

2. Click OK if you want Disk Administrator to update the configuration information. Disk Administrator examines your disks and partitions, and then a window similar to Figure 9.22 appears.

3. You wil see a color key at the bottom of the screen that explains what each color in the diagram represents. You will notice that divided disks have a primary partition and secondary partition(s). Also, it's likely that there's a little free space, especially if a disk is broken into several partitions. Disk Administrator displays unformatted free space as different from free space in an extended partition.

If you can't read the color key easily, you can assign different colors or patterns to partitions. Choose Options | Colors and Patterns. Choose a partition from the list that appears, and then choose a color or a pattern.

Note that early SCSI adapters maintained a test track (1M in size) when the drive originally was partitioned, but NT can format that one extra megabyte if you want. Early
Adaptec 1542bs and earlier have test tracks. NT and newer SCSI controllers don't reserve
this test track.

FIGURE 9.22.

*The basic Disk
Administrator screen
with a single disk drive.*

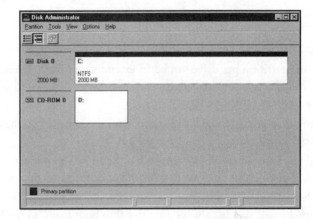

4. To work with a partition, simply click on it in the figure. A box appears around the
   partition, and the status line reports a few facts about it—for example, whether the
   partition is the active partition (the partition that contains the operating system and
   starts the bootup process), the size of the partition, the type of file system, the letter
   assignment, and the volume name. This information also appears in the drive's
   representative box.

TIP

If you have more disks than can be displayed at one time onscreen, scrollbars appear,
enabling you to scroll down to the additional drives. Also, the program decides initially
how to best display the sizes of drives and partitions relative to one another. You can
change this for each separate drive by choosing Options | Region Display. You might want
to display partitions with bars representative of their relative sizes, for example.

9

WINDOWS NT
ADMINISTRATION

Working with Partitions

As you might know, hard disks often are divided into partitions. Until a hard drive is partitioned, the operating system can't use it. Partitions come in two types: primary and extended.
Primary partitions can't be subdivided into logical drives; extended partitions can. (See Figure
9.23.) Extended partitions are generally more flexible to use than primary partitions. Most
operating systems require at least one primary partition, however.

FIGURE 9.23.

Extended partitions are more flexible than primary partitions.

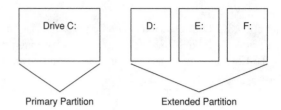

Here are some rules about disk partitions under NT:

- Each drive can have up to four primary partitions or as few as zero.

- One partition per drive can be an extended partition. Each extended partition can be divided into many logical drives, each with its own letter, or none. Free space can be used for NT volume sets.

- If you're going to use DOS and NT on the same drive, the two operating systems can coexist only on a FAT partition—not NTFS.

- If you want operating systems other than DOS to coexist with NT, each needs its own partition. Check the manuals for the operating system to determine which type of partition is required.

- Intel-based systems always use drive 0 to boot from, so the boot tracks have to be on that drive. RISC systems can have more than one system partition, enabling you to switch between them.

NOTE

Although you have to put the boot files on drive 0 on an Intel-based machine, NT allows you to put the system support files and directories (\WINNT\...) on another drive or partition.

- Before a disk partition can be used, NT reboots, and you have to format the partition from the command prompt.

To create a new primary partition, follow these steps:

1. Click on any section of a drive's bar labeled as Free Space. Note that only two types of free space exist: disk free space and extended partition free space. You want disk free space.

TIP

Disk free space is represented by a bar with lines that slant to the right. Extended free space has lines that slant to the left. If you're in doubt about which type of space you have, click on the bar and read the status line.

2. Choose Partition | Create. The Create Partition dialog box appears.

3. The program reports the minimum and maximum sizes that can be assigned to the partition. You don't have to use all the space. Remember that a disk can have up to four partitions, so you can leave one for use by another operating system, or you can assign some free space to an extended partition later. Adjust the size using the small arrows, or enter the desired size from the keyboard. Typically, the size can't be less than 1M.

4. Click OK.

You have to format the partition before it can be used, as described in "Preparing New Partitions for Use," later in this chapter.

Creating Extended Partitions

If you have room on the disk, and if you don't already have an extended partition on the drive, you can create one by following these steps:

1. Click on a free space bar. (This must be disk free space, not extended partition free space.)

2. The Create Partition dialog box appears, asking for the size of the partition you want to create. Enter the size and click OK.

If you want, you can create a logical drive in the new extended partition so that you can use it to store directories and files. Otherwise, you must use the partition for fault-tolerance purposes within NT, such as volume sets and stripe sets. If you want to use some or all of the otherwise unused extended partition for setting up a logical drive, follow these steps:

1. Click on the extended partition space in the drive bar.

2. Choose Partition | Create. The Create Partition dialog box appears, in which you specify the size of the logical drive. Choose the size and click OK.

3. Move to the next section to format the partition for use.

Preparing New Partitions for Use

As mentioned earlier, you must format a partition before the operating system can use it. You can do this by choosing Tools | Format from Disk Administrator or by using NT's `format` command, which is functionally identical to DOS's FORMAT command (with a few added capabilities):

1. Reboot the machine into Windows NT. This is imperative, because NT won't recognize any new partitions otherwise.

2. Log on using an administrator-level account.

3. Run a command-prompt session.

9

WINDOWS NT
ADMINISTRATION

4. At the prompt, type **format x:** and press Enter, where *x* is the logical letter of the drive you just created. For more information about the syntax of the format command, type **format /?** or see Figure 9.24.

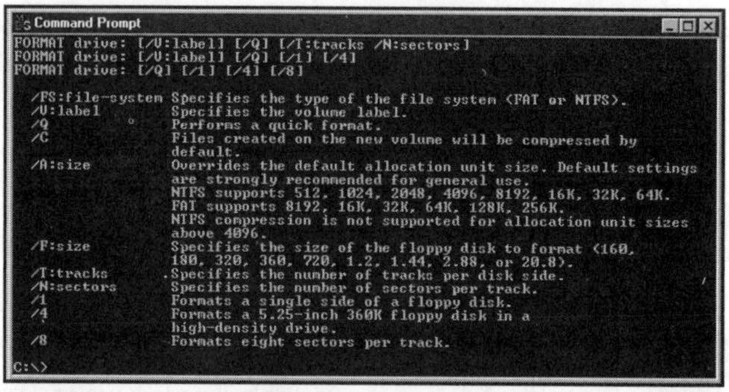

FIGURE 9.24.

The format *command's syntax and arguments.*

NOTE

If you created a partition but didn't give it a letter, go back to the preceding section and follow the instructions about assigning logical drives to a portion of an extended partition.

CAUTION

As usual, don't format a logical drive that already has data on it, unless you really want to trash the data. You'll be warned against this when you format.

---

5. After the partition has been formatted, you're prompted to enter a volume label.

TIP

To relabel the partition, choose Tools | Properties from Disk Administrator or type the **label** command at the command prompt. The Properties dialog box appears, as shown in Figure 9.25. Use the command syntax label *x:* (where *x* is the drive letter). You are then prompted to enter a volume label. If you change your mind about wanting to alter the label, press Ctrl+C. To display the current label from the command prompt, type **vol** and press Enter.

FIGURE 9.25.

You can relabel a partition from the drive's Properties dialog box.

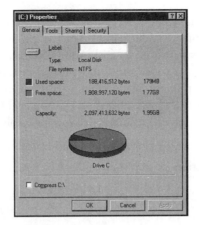

Setting the Boot and System Partitions

So much for creating, formatting, and labeling partitions. Now for the story about which partitions boot the operating system.

As I mentioned in Chapters 7 and 8, NT boots by first reading the boot track from the boot partition. The *boot partition* is the partition that the ROM BIOS points to for booting; it's sometimes called the *active partition*—for example, by FDISK. The information in the boot partition is responsible for bootstrapping NT and getting it started. Assuming that this process is successful, numerous data files stored in the load partition are loaded. These are the files stored in the NT directory (for example, \WINNT and \WINNT\SYSTEM32).

> **NOTE**
>
> Both the boot and load partitions can be in the same partition or in separate partitions. They can be on separate disks and even accessed by different controllers. They can be on partitions formatted as FAT, HPFS, or NTFS, and they can be on mirrored disks. Both boot and load partitions can't be located on a volume set, a stripe set, or a stripe set with parity, however.

Although the boot partition and the load partition don't have to be the same, they often are. If you installed NT on drive C of an Intel-based machine, the machine boots from drive C and gets all its system files from it as well. By contrast, if you installed NT on a drive other than C, the system and boot partitions aren't different. This is fine, and it offers you additional flexibility at install time—especially if you don't have 90M of free space on your boot drive.

9

WINDOWS NT
ADMINISTRATION

The boot partition *must* be active. Being *active* means that the computer knows to use the boot partition to start up. Only one partition can be active at any one time, and the active partition must be a primary partition. In Disk Administrator, the active partition is the one with the asterisk (*) in its color-coded bar. On Intel machines, the active disk is always drive 0. Only if you have multiple primary partitions on drive 0 can you set another partition to be active. The active partition on RISC machines is set by using software that comes with the computer. To set the active partition on an Intel-based machine, follow these steps:

1. Select the partition from Disk Administrator.

2. Choose Partition | Mark Active. The Mark Active Partition dialog box appears.

3. Click OK.

4. Close NT and reboot. The operating system on the active partition loads.

NOTE

If there is only one partition on drive 0 of an Intel-based machine, the Make Active command in the Mark Active Partition dialog box is grayed out because no other possible active partitions exist.

TIP

System partitions on RISC machines must be FAT partitions. Therefore, you can't set security on just the NT system directories because FAT doesn't support this feature. If you want security on the system partition of a RISC machine, you must lock the whole partition for use by administrators only. Choose Partition | Secure System Partition and then reboot to enable security. Choose Partition | Secure System Partition again and reboot to unlock the partition.

Assigning a Drive Letter to a Partition

Disk Administrator can perform an interesting and useful stunt. You can reassign logical drive letters permanently. DOS allows you to reassign letters by using the ASSIGN command, but this method isn't permanent. When NT boots up normally, it checks your hard disks and partitions and names them the same way DOS does. The first primary partitions on each drive are named first, starting with drive 0, moving to drive 1, and so on. These drives are named C, D, and so on. Next, logical drives are named, continuing down the alphabet. Finally, additional primary partitions on each disk are named.

Disk Administrator makes a record of the disk partition and logical drive assignments and stores them in a small database that doesn't change, even if you add a new hard disk or another piece of hardware—a CD-ROM drive, a Bernoulli Box, or what have you—that might bump up the drive letters. This method is called *static drive letter assignment*. (This is one solution to the troubles mentioned earlier in this chapter about Programs icons pointing to the wrong drives.)

You can alter the static drive letter assignments if necessary. Follow these steps:

1. Run Disk Administrator from the Administrative Tools group of the Startup menu.

2. Click on the partition or logical drive you want to reassign.

3. Choose Tools | Drive Letter. The Assign Drive Letter dialog box appears, as shown in Figure 9.26. If you want to change the drive letter for a CD-ROM drive, choose Tools | CD-ROM Drive Letters to open the dialog box shown in Figure 9.27.

FIGURE 9.26.

Reassigning a logical drive to a new static letter.

FIGURE 9.27.

Reassigning a CD-ROM drive to a new static letter.

4. Choose the letter from the Assign drive letter drop-down list and click OK. Alternatively, you can decide not to assign a letter at all by selecting Do not assign a drive letter. Then the partition isn't usable for storage of files and directories, but it still can be used by the operating system for stripe and volume sets.

5. Quit Disk Administrator by clicking Close. You're asked whether you want to save the changes you made. Choose Yes, unless you've changed your mind. (Choosing No abandons all the changes you made this session.) You should see a message box informing you that the disks were updated successfully and that you should restart the computer. The message box implies that system shutdown occurs automatically, but I have had to do it manually. As the reboot process occurs, the NT Loader reports your partitions in the newly assigned order.

9

WINDOWS NT
ADMINISTRATION

TIP

You can't name more than 24 logical drives (C through Z). This is one of the reasons why you can create volumes. You simply concatenate several physical drives into a single logical drive and give it one letter.

TIP

If you want to reverse the letters of two partitions, you must do a little shuffling. To reverse drives D and E, rename drive E to F. Then rename drive D to E. Then rename drive F to D.

CAUTION

Be careful not to assign a new letter to the load partition (the partition that holds the bulk of NT's files—for example, the \WINNT or \SYSTEM32 directory). If you do assign a new letter to the load partition, NT has trouble finding the files. Also, be aware that reassigning logical drive names might require adjusting Programs icons, some Windows program .INI files, and some MS-DOS application pointer or initialization files.

Deleting Logical Drives, Partitions, and Volumes

You can delete drives, partitions, and volumes, with a few restrictions. On x86 machines, you can't delete the partition containing NT's files. Also, you can't delete just a portion of a volume or stripe set. Another restriction is that logical drives and volumes in an extended partition must be deleted before you can trash the partition; just follow these steps:

1. Select the item you want to delete, whether it is a partition or a logical drive.
2. Choose Partition | Delete. A warning appears, alerting you to the loss of all the data on that partition.

CAUTION

Make sure that you really want to erase the partition, volume, or drive. You can't restore it if you change your mind, unless you first save the current configuration by choosing Partition | Configuration | Save while in Disk Administrator.

3. Click Yes to confirm that you want to delete the partition or drive. The item is deleted, and free space becomes available on the disk.

Converting Partitions Between NTFS and DOS

In a typical Microsoft move to get you hooked, Windows NT makes it easy to convert existing FAT and HPFS partitions to NTFS format—much easier, in fact, than performing the reverse operation. You might want to do this as you become more comfortable with Windows NT and the available 32-bit Windows application mix grows richer. Eventually, I suspect that most power users will bag their 16-bit applications and Windows 3.1 in favor of the more robust Windows NT. Obviously, this is what Microsoft is banking on too. The added security of file protection and the convenience of long filenames offered by the NT file system are additional charms that might woo you away from the FAT system.

Whatever the reason, you can upgrade to NTFS by issuing the `convert` command at the command prompt. The syntax is relatively simple:

```
convert drive: /fs:ntfs
```

Here, `drive` specifies the drive to convert to NTFS, and `/fs:ntfs` specifies to convert the volume to NTFS.

NOTE

You can't convert the drive you're logged onto. Switch to another drive first.

Oddly enough, you have to specify the file system to convert to, even though the program only converts to NTFS. This suggests that later versions of the convert program will change a volume to additional file systems.

Converting an NTFS volume to FAT is not so easy; follow these steps:

1. Back up the partition to whatever extent you feel is necessary. You can use the NT backup program (covered in Chapter 11, "Maintenance and Troubleshooting") if you want, or you can use any other means, such as borrowing some temporary space on a network hard disk and copying all the files there.

2. Format the partition to the desired file system by issuing the `format` command at the command prompt. Type **format /?** at the command prompt for the syntax.

3. Restore all the files and directories to the partition.

9

WINDOWS NT
ADMINISTRATION

NOTE

There is one exception to this procedure. If the NTFS partition you want to convert has NT on it, neither the `format` command nor Disk Administrator allows you to reformat it. You can get around this problem by running the Setup program from the original NT CD-ROM.

Setting Up Volume Sets

A *volume set* is a means of combining free space on a drive or a number of drives (up to 32) to form a single volume. In a sense, it fools the operating system into thinking that the volume is a single drive.

There are two primary advantages and one secondary advantage to using volume sets. The first advantage to using volume sets is that they provide a means of using otherwise wasted disk space by combining small amounts of free space into a volume large enough to be useful. The other primary advantage is that volume sets allow you to create huge volumes (in the gigabyte range, for example), combining several large partitions on separate disks. Such large volumes allow you to store huge files, such as large databases. Finally, volume sets can improve disk I/O performance, because data more often is read and written to several drives instead of just one drive. Because a disk controller can redirect data more quickly than a single disk can access the correct track and sector, using multiple disks effectively decreases the average access time of the volume.

NOTE

The downside of using volume sets is that only NT can use them. Other operating systems don't recognize volume sets.

Windows NT fills up a volume set from the first drive in the set and moves along the chain. If a set consists of partitions A, B, and C, partition A is filled up first, then B, and then C.

Creating a Volume Set

Follow these steps to create a volume set:

1. Choose several areas of free space, either on one drive or across as many as 32 drives. Ctrl+click each area, just as you do to select multiple files in My Computer.
2. Choose Partition | Create Volume Set. The Create Volume Set dialog box appears, advising you of the size range possible. Enter the size you want for the total volume set.
3. Click OK.

The volume set is created and assigned a drive letter. You must format the volume from Disk Administrator or the command prompt before you can use it to store files and directories.

Enlarging a Volume or a Volume Set

You can enlarge a volume or a volume set to incorporate free space that might become available over time as your disk arrangement changes. Unfortunately, you can't shrink a volume. This would be a great feature, but Microsoft didn't build it in—at least not in NT 3.5. To decrease a volume size, you must create a new volume, copy files to it, erase the original volume, and rename the new volume.

To enlarge a volume or a volume set, follow these steps:

1. From Disk Administrator, select the volume or volume set.
2. Choose Partition | Extend Volume Set. The Extend Volume Set dialog box appears.
3. In the Size field, enter a value within the range of acceptable values displayed in the dialog box.
4. Click OK. The requisite free space is added to the volume and subtracted from the free space pool.

Deleting a Volume Set

You might want to delete a volume set to reclaim or reassign space or to remove a drive from the set. Unfortunately, you can't just remove one of the partitions from the set and keep on using the rest. Because data sectors are spread over the volume set as the set is used, this would be functionally similar to removing one of the platters of a hard disk and expecting it to continue being serviceable.

To delete a volume set, follow these steps:

1. In Disk Administrator, select the volume set to delete.
2. Choose Partition | Delete. The Delete Partition window appears along with a message warning you of the loss of all your data.
3. Confirm that you want to delete the partition by choosing Yes. All the data in the set will be lost, so you might want to back it up, copy it elsewhere, or check to make sure that nothing of value is stored in the volume.

Setting Up Stripe Sets

Stripe sets are similar in concept to volume sets. Free space on a number of disks (at least two, and up to 32 physical disks) is combined to create a large volume. The advantage of stripe sets over volume sets is that overall throughput can be increased. Therefore, a datastream destined for storage is broken up and striped across a number of drives almost at once, rather than filling the volume from the "bottom up" (recall the discussion in "Setting Up Volume Sets," earlier in this chapter).

In stripe sets, all the partitions must be the same size. When you select a number of free areas across several disks, the smallest free space determines the common size for all the portions of the stripe set. Leftover space is returned to the system as free space that you can use in a volume set or a separate partition.

Stripe sets available in standard NT (not NT Server) are compatible with the industry standard known as RAID 0 (redundant array of inexpensive disks). RAID 0 is striping without parity, as opposed to RAID 5, which does record parity information and thus is less prone to catastrophic data loss in the event of a single drive failure. RAID 0 has no fault tolerance, so if one drive fails, you lose all the data in the set. The improved throughput might be worth the gamble, though, and regular backups might be all the security you need.

Creating a Stripe Set

To create a stripe set, follow these steps:

1. Open the Disk Administrator. Select multiple free space areas, starting with the first disk that has free space. Ctrl+click free space on subsequent disks (disks 2, 3, 4, 6, and so on).

2. Choose Partition | Create Stripe Set. The Create Stripe Set dialog box appears, listing the maximum and minimum sizes that you can set. Specify the size of the stripe set.

3. Click OK.

Deleting a Stripe Set

Deleting a stripe set is like deleting a volume set. Follow these steps:

1. Select the set in Disk Administrator by clicking one of its portions.

2. Choose Partition | Delete. A message box appears, asking you to confirm that you want to delete the partition.

3. Choose Yes.

CAUTION

Errors in volume and stripe sets are serious; when parity isn't used, the system can't recover from such a fault. If an error occurs while NT is booting, the set won't come online, and an error message is recorded in the Event Log. If the error occurs during the running of NT, you see a message reporting a severe disk error. Use the Event Viewer to examine the log for a description of the fault. You will probably have to delete and re-create the set.

Summary

In this chapter, you have looked at a lot of administration issues, including handling your system users and groups, as well as the hard disks. The User Manager makes handling users and groups much simpler and is straightforward to use.

Windows NT is flexible when it comes to disk drives, allowing you to manage most of your disk partitions through a utility instead of from a DOS prompt using FDISK and FORMAT. Changes to the file system and disk partitions are, therefore, much less troublesome, and chances of a major error are reduced.

## CHAPTER 10

Optimizing Windows NT: Performance Determinants

IN THIS CHAPTER

If you're reading this chapter, chances are good you're either the type of user who wants to squeeze every drop of performance from your machine, or you're hoping to resolve some specific NT performance shortcoming. NT's performance is determined by where the bottlenecks are and how your application mix and hardware affect your system efficiency.

To improve your system's performance, you must first determine your possible workstation optimization strategies. The approach you take depends somewhat on your system type. Fine-tuning an x86 machine differs from fine-tuning a DEC Alpha or a MIPS machine. Even within a class of machine, such as the x86, there are variations in hardware appointments, such as RAM caching, disk caching controllers, video accelerators, CPU upgrades, and so forth.

> **NOTE**
>
> Network optimization, and therefore server performance tuning, is covered in Chapter 19, "Optimizing Your Network," which discusses the Performance Monitor program.

> **NOTE**
>
> This chapter focuses only on the x86-based systems currently common in the workplace. For fine-tuning other machine architectures, consult your manual or manufacturer.

This chapter organizes system optimization approaches from the bottom up—that is, from the cheapest to the most expensive. CMOS BIOS adjustments are discussed first because they're free. CPU, video system, and motherboard replacements are discussed last because they tend to cost big bucks.

> **TIP**
>
> Study the manual supplied with the computer hardware. Often, important proprietary performance-tuning features go unnoticed until they're discovered buried deep in the manual somewhere—for example, the hot key that turns on turbo mode to double the CPU's performance.

A Few Thoughts on NT Optimization

If you're a veteran PC power user, you'll feel somewhat constricted when it comes to optimizing NT. As a writer who has pounded out hundreds of pages about supercharging Windows 95, I feel somewhat limited when writing about it. Because NT is a corporate animal, heavy modifications to a workstation setup are discouraged. I've already discussed this issue in earlier chapters, but it's worth repeating: Unless you're tweaking a single-user workstation (you're not going to share the machine), nonstandard shells, freaky hardware, and other novel arrangements can cause more headaches for your users than they're worth.

In other words, the cost/benefit ratio of tweaking Windows might be more attractive in theory than in reality. Yes, you can pore over your Windows 95 configuration files until the wee hours or scan magazines weekly for the latest hot-rodding techniques, hoping to squeeze that additional ounce of performance from your speed-demon system. Overall, though, the time you spend usually isn't worth the reward.

Microsoft knows this too. Windows 3.*x* systems that have crashed because of programs that toyed with the .INI files or enthusiastic hobbyists have caused many technical support headaches. One reason why the analogs to the Windows 3.1 .INI files in NT are protected from accidental hacking is to prevent this sort of technical support problem. You have to dig into the Registry to get at the .INI files, and even then the Registry Editor helps prevent erroneous entries into the Registry.

> **NOTE**
>
> The other reason for protecting NT's internal settings is that Microsoft's design goal was to have Windows NT meet government C2-level security—something that, by definition, must preclude easy tinkering with system settings.

Of course, not everyone running NT needs to be concerned with optimization as it's discussed in this chapter. Other chapters of this book cover everyday NT operations, often with an eye toward efficient and effective organization of workstation and network operations. Efficiency tips for everything from application and user organization to workgroup appointment scheduling have been discussed in previous chapters. Even purely performance-oriented settings, such as tasking priority adjustments or the use of stripe sets, are discussed elsewhere. This chapter, by contrast, focuses on tricks for optimizing the hardware in your computer system.

Is optimizing of this sort something you need? Maybe not. If you've already bought a state-of-the-art system, such as a multiprocessor Compaq, a DEC Alpha, or a top-notch Pentium, and this system has a fast video accelerator, a SCSI drive, and lots of memory, there isn't much more for you to do. You might want to consider NT's peculiarities and give it as much RAM as possible, adjust the paging file sizes, or convert as many partitions to NTFS as you can, but that's all. By the same token, if you're a single NT user doing common tasks like word processing and you're satisfied with the performance of your computer as a whole, you probably don't need to worry about performance boosters either.

However, if you're on a budget, working with 486s upgraded from DOS/Windows to NT, or a systems administrator who suddenly has the task of upgrading a slew of machines to NT for networking (and who has to concoct a machine to perform as a server), there might be a few tricks in this chapter worth considering.

BIOS Adjustments

The typical manual supplied with your common Intel CPU-based clone usually mentions the CMOS setup routine. Upon bootup, pressing Delete (or following some other onscreen instruction displayed at boot time) brings up a CMOS setup program that lets you view and change an extensive array of internal settings affecting memory usage, CPU speed, activation of the math coprocessor, video and BIOS shadowing, RAM wait states, hard-disk specifications, floppy disk drive capacities, and often much more.

These settings are called *BIOS settings* because they alter the basic input/output system. When the operating system needs to write to the hard disk, floppy disk, or screen, receive keyboard input, or perform other input and output tasks, it calls the BIOS. The BIOS, in turn, performs the requested action.

The BIOS is software stored in ROM that's plugged into the computer's motherboard. Although the BIOS's duties are standardized for each class of machine, particularly IBM PC compatibles, the BIOS manufacturer varies. For example, two popular BIOS manufacturers for IBM clones are Phoenix and American Megatrends Inc. (AMI). Because manufacturers of BIOS chips are legally prevented from copying each others' (and IBM's) software exactly, the user interface for setting BIOS parameters isn't identical for all PCs on which NT might be running. Usually, though, you see a menu listing several options, such as "standard CMOS settings" and "advanced CMOS settings." You also have a couple of options for saving the settings or quitting without saving. When you save the settings, they're stored in a CMOS chip (a chip whose contents can be modified and whose settings can be maintained even when the power to the computer is turned off) that's powered by a small battery inside the computer.

> **NOTE**
>
> With RISC-based machines, such setup screens are available through a supplied program, as was the case with the old IBM AT (80286-based) computers and most AT compatibles.

The available BIOS options depend on what's built into the motherboard (for example, what type of bus, CPU, and video). Some fancy motherboards let you tweak the technique the system uses to refresh the RAM chips, specify blocks of memory that shouldn't be used by the operating system because a plug-in card needs that memory block, or set the internal clock source (tick rate) or CPU type and speed.

Be careful when adjusting BIOS options, however. If your machine is working fine, there probably won't be any problems that need addressing. If you're inexperienced in such matters, avoid making changes to BIOS settings. You can view them, but leave the setup program without saving the changes. How you do this varies from machine to machine, but usually a series of Esc key presses gets you out safely.

You should be concerned with the following BIOS optimizing options:

- Setting the floppy disk drive sizes and types
- Making sure the hard-disk types are correct
- Setting the CPU to the highest possible startup speed
- Enabling or disabling the RAM checking
- Setting the RAM wait states as low as possible
- Enabling BIOS and video shadowing if possible

With some BIOSs, you can configure all these settings from the "standard" settings screen rather than from the "advanced" one. The following sections examine these options one at a time.

Setting the Floppy Disk Drives

The floppy disk drives are usually set up when the drives are installed, so unless the machine's battery has run down and the CMOS settings were erased as a result, the floppy disk drives are set to the correct size and density. More important, some BIOSs let you declare the order of boot drives. Should the computer boot from drive C without looking for a floppy disk in drive A first? I like to set the boot order to C and then A so that I don't have the inconvenience of having to remove a disk I've accidentally left in drive A. Changing the boot order prevents the resulting error message and makes NT boot faster because the floppy disk drive isn't scanned first.

Hard-Disk Type

The hard-disk type is in the standard settings. A typical BIOS supports 47 different types of drives, each with its own specifications for heads, tracks, sectors per track, landing zone, precompensation, and so forth.

> **CAUTION**
>
> Don't change this setting unless you know what you're doing.

If your system has been working fine, you don't need to adjust this setting. If you make the wrong modification, your system won't be able to boot until you reset it correctly. Most BIOSs have a feature, sometimes called *auto-detect hard disk*, that sleuths out the hard disk's specifications by examining the disk. This feature can save you some problems if you're adding a new hard disk and you don't know its specifications or if you accidentally change the hard-disk type on an existing drive. With most machines, you can't do anything to the BIOS to speed up hard-disk performance. You can, however, buy a faster drive and then use the BIOS to set the drive type. (Disk upgrading is discussed in the section "Upgrading Your Hard Disk.")

> **NOTE**
>
> The Gateway 2000 does let you make hard-disk speed improvements from the BIOS. This PC and others with the RIDE (rapid IDE) BIOS have three speed settings for hard-disk data transfers. The highest speed is 5M/second, which works fine with NT.

Turbo Mode

Some x86-based PCs, whether workstations or servers, have a speed or "turbo" switch. This switch is a throwback to the original IBM PCs and the 80286-based IBM AT, which had much slower processor speeds. On most PC clones, this switch gives you the option of slowing down the system to properly run older PC games. Some older games used the CPU clock signal (rather than the real-time clock) to determine how fast events occurred in the game. On super-fast systems, the games became unplayable, or they just bombed. In any case, there are few reasons these days to slow your system to a snail's pace by turning off the turbo switch, but you might want to make sure the machine is running in turbo mode and starting in that mode. Some BIOSs let you set the motherboard to start in slow mode for the memory check or for another purpose (such as initializing cranky cards) and then go into high speed. Anyway, check this setting to make sure that the computer comes up full-speed ahead. Booting takes long enough without the processor running in slow motion!

Memory Amount and Memory Checking

Most systems ensure that the physical memory installed in the computer and the CMOS setting agree. If they don't, you usually get an error message, and you're forced to enter the Setup program to make adjustments. After the comparison is made, a memory check follows, which can be annoying if it runs too slowly or if you have tons of memory in the machine (for example, 16M or 32M). Some CMOS setups let you turn off the checking, enable or disable the click noise that emanates from the speaker as the check is executed, or opt to check only the system memory (the first 640K). If you want to speed up booting, turn off as much as possible. IBM PCs and clones use a parity checking scheme that reports memory errors if they crop up. I have yet to have one on a modern clone (although I have had them on old original IBM PCs). I've even turned off parity altogether, with no ill effects, when I was short on RAM SIMMs and had to use 4M by 8 SIMMs, which means SIMMs without parity checking, rather than 4M by 9 SIMMs.

NOTE

Although the RAM check at bootup isn't anywhere close to an exhaustive test that will turn up all kinds of errors (you should buy a specialized program for RAM testing if that's what you want), at least it's something. If the computer in question is highly critical to your corporate or other needs, a 15–30-second wait is no big deal. Leave it on.

Wait States

Most PCs have a CMOS setup option for setting the number of RAM wait states, usually anywhere from zero to two. *Wait states* cause the system to insert the specified number of clock cycles (thumb twiddling) between processes involving the RAM chips (reading or writing). A wait state allows the data to settle reliably into the chip before another action is taken, such as writing another byte to a series of chips.

More expensive chips can read and write data as fast as the processor can dole it out, so they need zero wait states, but cheaper ones can't. Typically, the slower chips were intended to perform up to snuff, but they didn't, so they were stamped as such and sold at a cheaper price. Slowness is often due to slight manufacturing imperfections.

Inserting wait states might be necessary if your RAM can't keep up with your CPU. Determining whether they're necessary isn't always easy. You might have to consult the manufacturer or systems integrator.

TIP

RAM chips are stamped with their reliable speed. Look for a number such as 70, 80, 90, or 100 on the chips.

You don't usually need wait states for 70ns (70 nanosecond) RAM chips. Slower RAM chips (over 80 or 90ns) might need one or two wait states with fast processors, such as 66MHz 486s or Pentiums, but not always. I've used some 80ns chips at that speed with no adverse effects. If you're in doubt about whether your RAM can operate reliably with no wait states, try the wait state setting at zero. If you start getting lots of errors, such as programs crashing, the system memory check reporting errors, or the operating system not loading, add a wait state and try again.

How much performance loss do wait states contribute? From my experience, not much. The major bottlenecks on most systems are threefold: processor, video, and hard disk. RAM speed comes in fourth. But if you're really trying to fine-tune performance, wait states are something to consider. Benchmark programs that measure memory data transfers do show an improvement in system efficiency when fewer wait states are used.

> **NOTE**
>
> See the discussion on memory caching in "About RAM Caches" for another approach to RAM optimizing that can be very effective.

BIOS and Video Shadowing

Most systems let you "shadow" the BIOS and video subsystem ROM software. As I mentioned, the BIOS is a small amount of software stored in ROM (read-only memory) chips on the computer's motherboard. When the operating system needs to execute a low-level operation, such as writing to the hard disk, getting data from the keyboard, or sending data to a port, it makes a "call" to the software in the ROM (actually called firmware) to execute it. Having the BIOS in a chip means that the operating system itself (typically MS-DOS or NT) doesn't have to know about the machine's physical structure. An application makes a call to the operating system, the operating system passes the call to the BIOS, and the requested service is performed. This modularization allows the BIOS to be upgraded without altering the operating system.

> **NOTE**
>
> In the early days of microcomputers, people had to write their own BIOS code to handle the keyboard, screen, printer, and I/O ports, assemble the code using a software assembler, carefully patch it into the operating system, reboot, and hope it worked. BIOSs are now standardized enough so that you can often pull a BIOS chip out of one clone machine and drop it into another. (This works only if the chip sets—the CPU and support chips—of the two machines are identical, though.)

The bad news is that ROM chips are slow by design. They simply can't dish out the data very fast. Even with a screamer of a machine, when the operating system makes a BIOS call, the CPU is still waiting for the BIOS code. The same is true of the firmware stored in ROM on your video card.

The solution is to copy the firmware code from the ROM into some of your much faster system RAM. Then fool the operating system into redirecting calls to the video card and BIOS to the code's new location, where it will execute much more quickly. This is what shadowing does.

Most CMOS BIOS setup routines let you turn BIOS and video shadowing on or off individually. Make sure both are on, if possible. Sometimes you have the option of choosing the location of the RAM used to hold the relocated code. This specification might be necessary when you have an oddball card or another device that's mapped into a portion of system memory normally used for shadowing. I've never had to bother with this specification, and you probably won't either. Just check to see that the setup routine has video and BIOS shadowing enabled.

Optimizing Virtual Memory

Windows NT, like Windows 3.1, incorporates a virtual memory scheme. The virtual-memory manager gives the NT operating system more apparent RAM for use by applications and the operating system than is physically present in the computer. This is done by using hard-disk space to simulate RAM, with the advantage that more applications and services can run simultaneously than would normally be the case. Data is temporarily shifted out of RAM and into one or more files called PAGEFILE.SYS.

When you install NT, settings controlling the virtual-memory manager are automatically adjusted to reflect your hard-disk space and drive designations. In NT, the virtual-memory files (called paging files) created on the hard disk are dynamic. As available hard-disk space decreases, the paging files shrink in size, making room for your data files or applications. Also, under NT, each logical drive can support a single paging file (if you choose to set up this option), so if you have several disks, NT might decrease the size of a paging file on one drive and be intelligent enough to shift paging onto another drive.

> **NOTE**
>
> If the paging drives are physical (instead of logical), throughput can be increased for both paging and application services because multiple requests can be processed simultaneously.
>
> Paging files can't be removed while NT is running because important data could be lost if this were allowed. However, you can remove them under another operating system. Just look for the file PAGEFILE.SYS on each of your hard disks. Another way to remove them is from NT, if it's not in use. Just remove the paging file by using the Control Panel's System applet, reboot, then delete the inactive file.

Paging files are central to system optimization. NT is a huge operating system for a PC to run, so tons of paging goes on. You've probably noticed that the hard disk, even in a simple workstation, can get very busy thrashing around with the simplest of operations. The moral is this: Make sure that not only does your system have a lot of RAM, but also that you have ample paging file room for NT. See Chapter 8, "Using the Control Panel to Configure Windows NT," for details about setting paging file locations and sizes, which you do from the Control Panel.

> **TIP**
>
> Also consider compacting your hard disk and upgrading your hard disk, hard-disk control-
> ler, and/or motherboard for faster disk performance. All these options are explained in the
> following sections.

Upgrading Your Hard Disk

There are several approaches to upgrading your hard disk system:

- Delete unnecessary files
- Repair fragmented files
- Defragment the hard disk
- Optimize the hard-disk interleave
- Upgrade the disk controller
- Get a faster disk drive

Deleting and Managing Files

As you know, hard disks are never large enough. This is particularly true of NT. By the time
you have NT on a disk, you're already pushing 100M of used disk space. Add the almost infi-
nite number of document files, electronic junk mail, applications, support files, help files, and
temporary files, and pretty soon you're dreaming about gigabyte-sized drives. Because NT 4
doesn't work with disk-compression programs, you can't easily double your capacity with
DoubleSpace, Stacker, or SuperStor, either.

What to do? Regularly sift through your files and delete old ones you don't use frequently.
Back up important files to floppy disks. Erase programs you don't use, including accessory
programs such as Paintbrush and Notepad and their associated help files (which have the same
first name, but an .HLP extension instead of .EXE).

> **TIP**
>
> If you're sharing your workstation with other users, remember to clear the removal of an
> application with them.

When you're searching for files to kill, remember that many applications (especially Windows
applications) create and use temporary files while they're running. For example, when you edit
a Word for Windows document, Word creates a file with a name like ~doc1b2e.tmp to store

the file as you edit. If such a program bombs, or if the computer loses power or is turned off before you properly exit the application, aside from probably losing your work, you'll also be left with a dead temporary file. Such files can take up considerable room and will never be used again. Neither NT nor the application automatically deletes them.

The location of your temporary files varies, depending on your system and the applications you use. Often they'll be in the \WINDOWS\TEMP directory. If they're not there, they might be in the same directory as the application or document you're working on.

Temp files often use names that start with a tilde (~) and have the extension .TMP. Others start with the characters ~WOA and can have any extension. You can search for them by using Find.

> **NOTE**
>
> Some temp files might be hidden or system files and therefore won't appear in listings unless you opt to display such files (for example, by using My Computer's (or Explorer's) View | By File Type command).

To simplify cleanup, you might write a batch file that deletes temporary files. If you run DOS regularly, you could add the following lines to your AUTOEXEC.BAT file or have your autoexec file call the batch file:

```
del c:\windows\temp\~*.tmp
del c:\windows\temp\~woa*.*
del c:\windows\win386.swp
```

> **CAUTION**
>
> Be careful when deleting temporary files from NT. Ideally, such files should be deleted only when you're not running Windows or Windows NT (that is, preferably from DOS), because this will ensure that the files aren't in use. However, if you simply close all applications in NT and delete the files, you should be okay. For most applications, NT alerts you if the file is still in use, because it will be locked by another process. However, this might not always be the case.

> **TIP**
>
> You also can use the Windows NT Setup program to quickly and easily erase classes of programs, such as games, wallpaper, help files, and accessory programs.

10

OPTIMIZING WINDOWS NT

Repairing Fragmented Files

Occasionally, a faulty program or a system crash causes chunks of otherwise related data to lose their relationship to one another. When a disk is newly formatted, even large data files are written across the disk in their totality using consecutive sectors. As the disk fills up and files are erased, moved, copied, and so forth, "holes" of erased data open up, leaving sectors available for storing files. Disk operating systems (OS/2, DOS, NT, or UNIX) use this space by breaking large files into pieces and fitting them in wherever possible. The disk directory (file allocation table, or FAT) remembers which pieces (or sectors) go with each other to constitute the letter to Uncle George, the business plan, and even the NT Registry file.

When a program or the system crashes, however, the directory might not be updated correctly, resulting in "lost" or orphaned sectors. The result is not only a corrupted file, but also sectors that are marked as unavailable even though they're serving no purpose. Such sectors are hidden, and they don't even display in a directory listing because they don't have names.

As you may know, DOS's CHKDSK program is the cure for lost sectors (or, more typically, groups of sectors, called *clusters*). CHKDSK is a program in your DOS directory (assuming that you have an Intel-based machine with DOS on it) that, when used with the /f option (chkdsk /f, for example), searches your hard disk for lost clusters and reclaims them. If clusters are found, you're asked whether you want the data collected into files you can later edit. If you type Y (for yes), files with names such as FILE0000.CHK and FILE0001.CHK are created in the root of the checked drive. If you type N (for no), the clusters are immediately deleted and returned to the pool of available disk space.

NT does a cursory CHKDSK when it first boots up. It's not exhaustive, but it detects cross-linked files or confused directories and tries to make repairs. For more exhaustive checking, NT includes a CHKDSK program that's much like the one that comes with DOS. In fact, it has the same name and can be executed from the command prompt from within NT. It can be used on any active drive (to fix problems) and causes a more thorough automatic CHKDSK at boot time.

Also note that NT's CHKDSK sometimes fails, particularly if there's an error in one of the system boot files. This book's technical editor commented that this has happened to him several times. He used SCANDISK (an MS-DOS 6.2 utility) to correct the errors found in the system Registry and Event Log files.

> **NOTE**
>
> See Chapter 11, "Maintenance and Troubleshooting," for details on maintaining and repairing damaged hard disks.

One way or another, make sure you don't have lots of lost clusters hanging around on your hard disk. If you run DOS regularly, do a CHKDSK once in a while on your FAT partitions. OS/2 has a similar program. As NT matures, you'll see more disk maintenance programs that sleuth out all types of errors, including lost clusters, cross-linked files, bad disk media, and so forth.

Defragmenting the Hard Disk

As mentioned, over time your files get broken into pieces so that they can most efficiently be fitted into available sectors on the hard disk's platters. However, your system pays a speed penalty for this ingenuity. When a file is read from or written to, the hard-disk heads must physically move around on the platters to reach sometimes far-flung tracks that otherwise might be consecutive. It's as if a song on an LP were broken up across the bands of the record, requiring the tone arm to jump to play one piece of music. Obviously, the song would be interrupted while the arm moved between portions. On a hard disk, such an interruption might be miniscule (perhaps 20 milliseconds), but it adds up—especially in NT, which does so much disk accessing.

You can prevent these interruptions by defragmenting each hard disk on your system or on the network once in a while. Defragmenting rearranges all the data on a disk so that files are written on consecutive sectors and tracks. As a result, the heads have less moving to do when reading from or writing to a file, so overall system efficiency increases.

Defragmenting programs for DOS, Windows 3.1, and OS/2 are widely available and a few are now available for Windows NT. A good program (such as Windows NT's Defragment utility, or those supplied with Norton Utilities, can prevent disastrous data loss in case the power goes out during the process and can even be aborted in the middle of the process if you change your mind. Be aware that disk defragmenting (sometimes called *compacting*) can take quite a long time. It's the kind of thing you let the computer do overnight.

> **TIP**
>
> You can defragment NTFS partitions by backing up and restoring the partition.

Optimizing the Hard-Disk Interleave

Another approach to hard-disk optimizing is to make sure the interleave is set to its optimum value. Some hard-disk controllers don't have electronics fast enough to read consecutive sectors as they pass by the heads on the hard disk. (Such a hard-disk controller isn't likely to be on an NT system, but it's possible if you're just now upgrading.) Instead, they read one sector of information, and then need a bit of time to prepare for the next sector. Hard disks spin very fast, and as a result, magnetically recorded data flies by the head rapidly. To accommodate slower electronics, hard-disk controllers can be set to number the sectors nonconsecutively. Spacing out the sectors gives the electronics more time to work between reading from or writing to each sector's data. Imagine numbering a pizza's sections with gaps between the numbers. Figure 10.1 illustrates this concept.

FIGURE 10.1.

A disk's interleave determines the order in which the sectors are numbered. This illustration compares an interleave of 1:1 to that of 2:1.

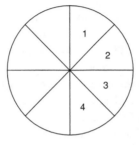
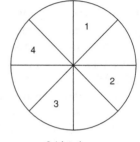

1:1 Interleave   2:1 Interleave

The fastest possible interleave is no interleave at all, meaning that sectors are adjacent. This is called 1:1 (one to one) interleave. On many computers, the interleave is set higher than it needs to be, such as 3:1, which would mean that there are two added sectors between sectors 1 and 2. You might want to check your interleave setting with a good hard-disk utility program. Such a program tells you the current setting, recommends a new optimum setting, and reorders the sectors for you. Some good DOS-based programs are Power Disk (Multisoft Corp.), SpinRite II (Gibson Research), and OPTune (Gazelle Systems).

NOTE

As with defragmenting, resetting interleave can take quite a long time because major shuffling of data is required. Be prepared for a couple of hours of hard-disk activity. Also, you should make a backup of any important data before resetting the interleave. You might lose something important.

Upgrading the Disk Controller

As you may know, the two elements of the disk subsystem are the disk itself and the controller that connects it to the computer. (There's also the bus that connects the controller to the computer, but that's covered later.) Several types of controllers have been available over the years, such as FM, MFM, RLL, ESDI, IDE, and SCSI. Each of these is an improvement over its predecessor, and each type of controller requires a drive of the same type. (An RLL controller requires an RLL drive, for example.) As of this writing, the bulk of current drives are either SCSI or IDE. Anyway, you can't just mix and match any drive and any controller.

Some disk controllers are smarter than others. The two prime considerations are the data path and the ability to cache data on the controller card itself rather than doing caching in system RAM with programs such as SmartDrive. Because there's always a delay (no matter what type of drive) when reading and writing, a caching disk controller speeds up processing by storing data in RAM on its card until the drive or the operating system can process it. An intelligent controller uses sophisticated algorithms to figure out which sectors or tracks are likely to be read by analyzing recent activity. It then reads in data (typically a whole track or two) and stores it in the card's RAM, making it available for the operating system to grab.

Likewise, during a write, the operating system can quickly dump a large amount of data on the controller, believing that the data has been written to the disk when actually it's only been absorbed by the disk controller's RAM cache. The cache then hands it off to the disk while the operating system goes about its business. Good caching controllers have all the necessary hardware (including an on-board processor) to shuffle data to and from the hard disk without intervention by the main CPU or the operating system.

Aside from the inescapable mechanical slowness of hard drives (compared to the almost speed-of-light performance from RAM), the other classic bottleneck for drives is the bus. The *bus* is the data path through which the CPU communicates with the drive. Typically, on an x86 machine, this path is a 16-bit ISA (industry standard architecture) bus running at the standard 8MHz data transfer rate popularized by the IBM AT-class machines. CPUs and plug-in cards, such as disk controllers and video cards, can now operate well beyond this, so individual manufacturers like IBM and vendor consortiums, such as VESA, have given customers faster alternatives. MCA, EISA, and VLB are new and competing bus standards, each of which at least doubles the old data transfer rate.

If your budget allows it and your system board supports it (changing the system board is discussed in the section "Upgrading Your CPU and Motherboard"), consider upgrading your disk controller to take advantage of a faster bus. In some cases, you can make this upgrade for a very small outlay. For example, nowadays many system motherboards have at least one VLB connector—often two. This connector is a 32-bit high-speed data path designed principally for video and disk controllers. A clone IDE floppy/hard disk controller that plugs into a VLB slot costs about $50, and it will work with your existing IDE drives (IDE controllers support up to two hard drives and two floppy drives). The cost/performance benefit ratio of this upgrade is very high.

Most pundits agree that for fastest throughput and greatest flexibility, SCSI is the way to go. SCSI is an industry-standard, high-speed parallel interface designed for small computer peripherals. The Apple Macintosh has supported SCSI for years because it lets you daisy-chain many dissimilar devices (printers, modems, scanners, hard disks, removable media drives, CD-ROM drives, and so on) on the same cable. Each device gets a device number, and each device driver is assigned to its respective number. Only one controller card is necessary, leaving more slots in your computer free for other uses. SCSI drives typically are faster (and more expensive) than their counterparts, such as IDE. Assuming that the SCSI specification doesn't change, buying SCSI devices also means you don't have to keep buying controller cards. You buy one card and then just an extension data cable to add each new device to the chain.

In reality, though, SCSI has been an evolving standard, which is why some wary consumers (including me) have opted for IDE. Now in its third major iteration (SCSI III), the specification is settling down, and most devices seem to be working fairly reliably.

Getting a Faster Disk Drive

Replacing drives is expensive, which is why I discussed upgrading your system by changing controllers first. However, plummeting hard-drive prices mean that you can now find controllers that outprice the drives.

As you probably know, hard disks are rated primarily by type (SCSI, IDE, and so on), capacity (120M, 300M, 1G), and speed (12ms, 18ms, 20ms). Over the years, I've experimented with many speed upgrades to my systems, and I've concluded that one major Achilles' heel of a GUI system like Windows is the hard disk itself. Regardless of whether you change the controller card, upgrade the CPU, or even upgrade the video controller card, getting a fast disk can seem to double your system's speed. I had read this assertion in magazines, but I didn't believe it. It seemed wrong, and I thought it was just another industry ruse to sell expensive products. After all, a hard disk transfers data across its ribbon cable at about 5 megabits per second, and the platter is flying past the head at several hundred miles per hour. What could be slow?

Recall my earlier LP analogy. Even though the disk is spinning quickly and the data on it is always available, the heads that read and write the data have to be positioned on the track and then locate the right sector before any data is transferred. The time this takes is called *access time*, which is one major area where drives take a speed toll on your system. A drive's access time is averaged using a random pattern of track accesses. A drive with an average access time of 28ms will perform much slower than one with 12ms, for example.

As with controllers, some drives have smart electronics. They might keep tabs on which tracks are being used the most, for example, and buffer (cache) data from those tracks into their on-board RAM. Typically, the cheaper drives don't have these features and are relatively dumb. However, drives with fast access times and relatively high storage capacity are so cheap that it doesn't matter.

Drive technology changes quickly. Currently, the market is offering 3-inch and 1 1/2-inch drives and removable-media drive technologies, such as "floptical" drives, 8mm tape drives, and so forth. Hard-disk prices continue to drop, and capacities are hitting the multigigabyte range. (A gigabyte equals one billion bytes or a thousand megabytes.)

NOTE

See the previous discussion on disk economizing for alternatives to huge drives. Remember that having huge drives means losing huge amounts of data in case of a disk failure and that crashes are more prevalent with new technology.

Because of the rapidly changing nature of hardware, I can't offer too many specific recommendations, so remember to use time-tested, reliable media formats for mission-critical work, whether at home or in the office. If the choice is between buying new and flashy technology or a popular, boring drive, go for the latter. Also remember that new operating systems (NT is a good case in point) tend to ship with drivers for only the popular, "vanilla" hardware.

If you must have a new whiz-bang toy, carefully compare specifications on drives, including the MTBF (mean time between failure) ratings. Check magazines for the latest scoop on drive recommendations, noting that long-term testing usually is beyond the reviewers' ken. If you're setting up stripe sets, consider upgrading from NT to NT Server and using stripe sets with parity. This way, if one drive of an array fails, you can still recover the data. Recovery isn't possible with standard stripe sets. Also remember to use backup disks with tape, as described in Chapter 11.

Upgrading Your Memory Subsystem

You should take full advantage of your machine's physical endowments, not to mention NT's great capabilities. Like its little brothers, NT screams for extended memory (not expanded memory or anything else, incidentally). Give NT as much memory as possible. You might as well forget all the other fine optimizations mentioned earlier if you're short on RAM.

NT 4 Workstation is remarkable in that it boots and appears to run with less memory than the recommended amount. However, it runs at a snail's pace while sending the hard disk into conniptions and probably wearing out the stepper motor controlling the hard-disk heads way before its time. What's going on is almost continuous disk swapping, because the operating system components don't have room to load into RAM.

Microsoft says 12M will run NT on an x86-based client well enough. This is true. However, I suggest that this is also marketing hype based on the negative press about NT's hardware requirements. Splurge for the additional 4M and run with at least 16M. Certainly an NT server should have 16M or more, and RISC clients need a minimum of 16M. For NT Server machines, I recommend a minimum of 20M and preferably 32M or more if SQL Server is running. The extra memory helps a lot!

How you install memory depends on your system. How much it costs depends on the position of the moon, the state of the economy, the current laws governing international import tariffs, and the whims of those in a position to concoct stories about the trickle-down effects of destroyed Japanese plastics plants. Check the manual that came with the computer or motherboard. Do you need proprietary cards and/or chips? If you do, expect to pay twice what a generic SIMM or SIP would cost. It's unfortunate, but true.

Next, what speed should the chips be? As a general rule, buy the fastest chips you can, because you might end up plugging them into a new, faster motherboard or machine later, particularly as system prices fall.

TIP

Consider running Windows for Workgroups, DOS, Novell, Windows 95, or another operating system on lower-priority workstations and just waiting for system prices or RAM prices to come down before you install Windows NT. Windows for Workgroups, despite some negative reviews, is now actually something to write home about. For starters, it's Plug-and-Play with NT. Second, because it's from Microsoft, it's been thoroughly tested with NT in-house. Finally, it's cheap.

Be careful when installing memory. RAM chips are static-sensitive. If you rub your feet across a carpet while carrying RAM chips, and then discharge the buildup through the chips to something like the computer's chassis, the chips can be blown. This has never happened to me, but I don't live in a dry climate. Stay in one place while doing your installation (don't walk around the room with the chips in your hand). Also, touch the computer chassis before picking up the chips, and try to touch only the fiberglass circuit board the chips are mounted on rather than the metallic circuit or chip legs themselves.

Most chips come three or nine to a card (called a SIMM—single inline memory module) that plugs into a holder on the motherboard. You must line up the chips in the right direction and line up little holes that engage with pins in the holder. Then the board snaps into place. The trick is to first insert the SIMM board at about a 45-degree angle and wiggle it to make sure the contacts on the bottom of the board are fully inserted in the bottom of the connector cage. Then lift the SIMM, seeing that it stays fully seated.

NOTE

When you power up again, be sure to set the CMOS settings to reflect the memory upgrade. Otherwise, NT probably won't take advantage of the new memory. See the section titled "BIOS Adjustments" for details.

If you're using an EISA system, make sure the EISA settings for memory amount and SIMM type are correct. Failure to do this can cause the ISA settings to be used, which might lead to NT not recognizing all of the installed memory.

CAUTION

Of course, memory should be inserted only when the power to the computer is off. Otherwise, you're likely to blow it out. This caution applies to all system upgrades. Unplugging hard disks with the power on, for example, isn't particularly dangerous, but it can trash the data on the drive. The voltages on a computer tend to be low (for example, +5, −5, +12, −12 volts), but the power supply box has high voltage. Even though the power supply is shielded from contact with users, to be extra safe you should unplug the computer before opening it and making modifications.

Upgrading Your Video Subsystem

The computer press has given Windows video a great deal of attention. Innumerable video system reviews, fancy benchmarking tests, and conflicting "editor's choices" appear monthly. It's impossible to keep up. One thing is for sure, however: Video system performance greatly affects most Windows (or other highly graphical) tasks. Even if the computer is already endowed with a fast processor and hard disk, sluggish video performance can make it seem to crawl when you move or resize a window, display a chart, or scroll a page of text.

Any version of Windows runs the video card in graphics mode, as opposed to the zippy character mode used by most DOS applications. Character mode is fast because it requires just pushing letters on the screen. A hardware-based character generator defines what an *A* looks like, and pushing it around just requires telling the generator where to put it. Pushing a line of text down the screen or scrolling requires simply sending the video controller the appropriate command for line-down or line-up. Because the hardware knows that this command means shifting everything up or down *x* number of pixels, it's fast. This is why DOS applications running in character mode (WordPerfect 5.1, PC-Write, WordStar, dBASE IV, and Lotus 1-2-3 version 2) run fast, even on an old clunker like a 286 or an old original IBM PC with a prehistoric 8086 processor. I still use some of these machines with DOS applications because, believe it or not, they're still darn fast at what they were designed for.

> **NOTE**
>
> The sad thing is that people throw out perfectly useful computer hardware instead of recycling it or giving it to schools or third-world countries, but that's another story.

Windows became a hardware marketeer's heyday. Machines suddenly came to a crawl, mostly because of all the video overhead required to run in "graphics" mode on dumb VGA cards. Whenever you scroll a window, open a menu, or close a dialog box, Windows must redraw pixels on the screen. This process takes time, and the finer the screen's resolution, the more dots that have to be moved or redrawn. On a 1024×1280 monitor, that's 1,310,720 pixels! Each pixel on a monochrome monitor (purely black-and-white) equals one bit in the video board's memory. These bits typically are moved around and turned on and off (to create a black dot or a white dot) by the computer's CPU. On a color screen, the number increases dramatically.

Imagine being the CPU in a typical computer. The user has a document running full-screen and scrolls up a line. Suddenly, in addition to whatever else you're doing, you have to move a million bits of data around on the video board. This could get tedious and slow your system down a lot. The CPU in your computer has better things to do than redraw dots. And if the video card is drawing in color, there are many more bits per pixel, as many as 24 if you want "true color," which gives you 65 million colors. So, on a standard VGA screen at 480×640 resolution, in true color, there are 7,372,800 bits per screen. You get the idea.

There are four ways around the video bottleneck:

- Use fewer colors or lower resolution
- Get a faster CPU
- Get an accelerated video board

First, if you don't need true color, don't use the true-color driver. Move back to a 256-color driver, or even 16. At 16 colors, you can use a totally dumb video card available for about $50 (maybe even less) and run in 800×600 or 640×480 at high speeds. For many employees, this system will be enough. An entire color video subsystem can then be had for a song (maybe $200 to $300).

A similarly marked speedup results from decreasing the resolution. If you're running at 1280×1024, scale back to 1024×768 or 800×600. Sure, you see less on the screen, but the system response time speeds up considerably, and the text is larger, which is easier on the eyes.

> **NOTE**
>
> You change video drivers through the NT Display applet in the Control Panel. This procedure is discussed in Chapter 8.

If you've just got to have high resolution or lots of colors, then what? Using a faster main processor helps, but the results are marginal, contrary to what you might hope. I recently moved up from a 25MHz 486 to a 66MHz one and didn't notice one bit of difference on my 1024 × 1280 gray-scale (16 levels of gray) 21-inch monitor's performance. The card for it doesn't have an accelerator chip, so the main CPU in my computer is doing all the work. Benchmark tests showed far less than the more than 100 percent improvement I had expected. The bottleneck was elsewhere, obviously.

As with hard disks, the bottleneck is sometimes in the bus. The CPU just can't move data to and from the screen fast enough on the slow 8MHz ISA bus. Proprietary systems, such as the DEC Alpha, shine in the video department because they're designed for high-speed video I/O, as are EISA and VLB systems.

> **NOTE**
>
> VGA is the common name for 640 × 480 resolution, and Super VGA is the common name for 800 × 600 resolution. The remaining two higher resolutions are referred to as 1024 × 768 and 1280 × 1024. The first number is the number of pixels from left to right; the second number is the number of pixels from top to bottom.

Choosing a Monitor

Although this chapter primarily covers optimizing NT's performance in terms of speed, I'm going to digress a bit and discuss video displays—something a bit more aesthetic. Because video displays are the primary conduit through which you interact with computers and because they must dovetail with your video card choice, they deserve attention.

As with video cards, many magazines have devoted special issues to monitors. I suppose this is because monitors, especially with the advent of color graphical computing, are so nice to look at and can make boring old computing visually exciting, or maybe it has something to do with the nation's obsession with television. Anyway, color is here to stay, and with Windows, OS/2, and now NT, graphical interfaces are also here to stay. As a result, big, clear, easy-on-the-eyes monitors are on the rise. The problem is, how do you choose a monitor, especially a monitor for use with NT?

As you know, monitors come in all shapes and sizes. Well, they're all mostly square, but some are deeper than others, and certainly screen dimension varies. Most monitors these days are 14 or 15 inches and are used to display SVGA resolution. However, the days are numbered for this size of monitor. Users are slowly becoming dissatisfied with the limitations imposed by a monitor this size.

> **NOTE**
>
> Recall that this measurement is taken diagonally across the screen's surface area. Often the image on the screen isn't even this large, so the figure can be misleading.

Standard VGA isn't enough if you want to see more than a third of a page of text (although I'm writing this on an LCD laptop with a standard VGA screen) or if you abhor the "jaggies" when you're writing a play, designing a house, or doing anything else that has you staring closely at screen details for any length of time. On the other hand, upping the resolution on a 14-inch or 15-inch monitor (for example, by using a Super VGA driver—800 × 600—if your video card supports it) will likely result in a blurry image and letters too small to read easily. Therefore, the move to a larger monitor makes sense. Displaying 800 × 600 on a 17-inch monitor looks pretty good and increases your desktop by about 30 percent. A display of 1024 × 768 is also rendered nicely on a 17-inch monitor. I wouldn't want to work in 1280 × 1024 on one, though. You'll probably want a 20-inch or 21-inch monitor for that.

If you're in doubt about the wisdom of buying a larger monitor, check one out in a store. Be sure to ask questions about how it works with your system, particularly with the video card you have now and ones you might upgrade to. Shopping for monitors is something I've made sort of a hobby of, and writing about the ergonomics of them is something I've made a profession of. I once wrote a long article for *PC Week* about the ergonomics of CRT (cathode ray tubes) and the possible negative effects of long exposure to them at close range.

Here's my personal list of points to consider when choosing a monitor:

- Decide what screen size you want. As I mentioned, 17-inch is probably the best bet for serious day-in-day-out work by a power user. For a server that doesn't get much direct attention, this size is overkill and a waste of money. Use an old clunker monitor there. Ditto for workstations where simple tasks or character-based DOS, OS/2, or UNIX applications are being run.

- Do you need color? Color is nice, but it blurs the image. Three dots (red, blue, and green) make up each pixel instead of one dot on a gray-scale or black-and-white monitor. If you don't need color, you can enjoy a lower price and a cleaner image on a gray-scale monitor. Most gray-scale monitors work with color cards. The monitor just turns colors to shades of gray. Check with the manufacturer. For typesetting and technical drawing particularly, gray-scale monitors are preferable. I have a 21-inch monitor I use for typesetting books.

- Peruse the magazines and note whether they all agree on one model as the best in the size category you want. Typically, they won't. You'll find that maybe three models vie for the editor's choice among, for example, *Windows Magazine*, *PC World*, and *PC*. Typically, the best models are an NEC, a Nanao, and a Viewsonic (or a Mag). Note the names and exact model numbers (for instance, an NEC 5FG is not the same as an NEC 5FGe).

- Often magazines have extensive tables listing features. Save these articles. You'll be glad later when you have to compare one little detail, such as refresh rate or front panel adjustments.

- Check the front panel adjustments for each. Are they easy to set? You should have the following adjustments:

  Vertical height
  Horizontal width
  Horizontal and vertical position
  Brightness
  Contrast
  Pincushion
  Barrel
  Focus

  Optionally, you might want a color-matching control that lets you fine-tune color rendering to a standard color system, such as Pantone. Some NEC monitors have this option. Also, you should be able to save settings for each video mode (character mode, graphics mode, and each resolution), digitally stored in the monitor. The monitor should effortlessly sense the mode the card is in, switch to that resolution without blinking and making noise, and activate the appropriate presets. This feature prevents you from having to adjust the screen each time you run a full-screen DOS application, for example.

- Compare the screen's specifications with those of your video card. Specifically, decide which resolution you're going to be doing most of your work in, then figure you might want to move up a notch to a higher resolution at some time. Take that higher resolution and determine whether the card/monitor combination will work at a high enough refresh rate not to bother you with flicker. You should be able to run at 70Hz or higher; 60Hz is too slow for prolonged use. You can most easily detect flicker out of the side of your eye because the retina has less persistence outside of its focal area. Try looking just past the monitor. When you find that it doesn't flicker much when looked at this way while it's running in the desired resolution, you're doing well.

- Check the monitor's dot pitch. *Dot pitch* is a measurement of how focused the dots on the screen are. The smaller, the better. A dot pitch of .31 is too large. Look for .25, if possible. Monitors using Sony Trinitron tubes don't use dots. Instead, they use a grill whose aperture is about .26. A Trinitron tube doesn't always give a better picture than a conventional tube, but it's usually quite good. You often pay a premium for them. They aren't fully flat; they curve in the horizontal plane, like a vertical cylinder.

■ Observe the monitor, possibly even borrowing one to try in your office or at home for a day or two. Or buy it with a no-questions-asked return privilege. Ask yourself these questions:

Does it flicker?
Is the image clear?
Are the colors vibrant?
Is it well-focused in the corners and in the center?
Can you adjust it easily to your liking?
Does it make a high-pitched, bothersome noise?
Would you prefer a fully flat screen?
Does it look good at all resolutions you might use?
Does it have a decent warranty?

NOTE

Speed of video performance has nothing to do with the monitor.

Finally, consider a couple more features:

■ Most monitors have an antireflective etched tube. The etching prevents annoying, eye-straining glare, but it blurs the image just a bit. If you want the clearest image possible, buy a nonetched tube monitor, such as the 5FG or 5FGe from NEC. You might have to adjust the room's lighting to prevent glare.

■ Some studies suggest that long-term exposure to CRT-based monitors might be cause for health concerns. Specifically, even very low levels of electromagnetic radiation of various frequencies absorbed by the body over long periods of time may increase the risk of eye disease and possibly birth defects and cancer. The jury is still out, even after years of research, but there is some evidence to suggest a possible problem. As a result, better monitors are now designed to meet the stricter standards being imposed in some European countries. If you're concerned about this, buy a monitor meeting the Swedac II low-emission standard. Magazine reviews in which monitors' radiation levels were tested seem to bear out manufacturers' claims of meeting this standard.

■ Finally, consider buying "green." Some monitors power down to a fraction of their usual energy consumption level when they sit idle for a preset period of time. Instead of consuming a typical 200 watts, for example, a monitor might power down to 30 watts. When you move the mouse or press a key, it wakes up. Such "green" monitors are becoming more prevalent, but not all manufacturers make them yet. Also, be aware that they fall into two categories: those that don't power down unless used with a "green" video card that complies with the new standard, and those that power down by detecting a blank screen caused by a screen saver like After Dark. You'll probably want the latter kind of monitor.

Before buying, shop around carefully. You can save several hundred dollars by checking the magazines for competitive pricing.

> **TIP**
>
> CompuServe's Ziffnet has a buyer's guide that lets you enter a model name and number and quickly see a listing of the cheapest mail order prices in the country. There's also lots of useful information about how to purchase equipment by mail order without losing your shirt. Log in and then type **Go Ziffnet** at the ! prompt. Then follow the instructions for the Ziff Buyer's Market. Even if you don't buy from one of the vendors listed, it's a great way to get an idea of the latest street price of an item. You can also find Ziffnet at http://www.zdnet.com.

Upgrading Your CPU and Motherboard

Aside from buying a whole new computer system (which is often the easiest choice at upgrade time, considering the rock-bottom prices of many integrated systems these days), you might want to upgrade just the CPU or the motherboard. A new computer might cost you a couple of thousand dollars, but getting a new CPU or motherboard might cost only $500 to $1,000.

> **NOTE**
>
> In case you don't know, the motherboard is the main circuit board in the computer. It contains the edge connectors that the cards plug into, and it also contains the CPU, BIOS chip(s), and other support chips that make the computer work.

You have to consider whether you want the hassle of installing a motherboard. It takes skill and know-how. I won't go into details here, but power connectors, screwdrivers, and removing all the boards and possibly the disk drives are involved. It can take a couple of hours or more.

Decide what you're looking for:

- Faster CPU
- PCI slots
- ISA slots

As a rule, you'll find that CPUs alone are expensive, almost as expensive as a complete new motherboard. What's more, a new motherboard often incorporates new technology that's worth investing in. You'll get a new BIOS, for example, with some fancy CMOS settings. You might also get some extra slots, a fast memory subsystem, or some RAM cache that your older board didn't have.

If you're starting with a motherboard that has a zero-insertion-force Pentium upgrade slot, and the motherboard is pretty up-to-date, then purchasing a new processor alone might make sense. You just pop out the old one and pop in the new one. But remember that the old processor you'll be chucking might be worth more than you realize. Relatively fast processors alone (a notch down from top-of-the-line) cost about $400, and you can almost always find a complete motherboard with CPU for this price. An added advantage is that you'll then have the old motherboard as the basis for another system.

Motherboards fall into two basic categories, just as complete systems do: clone and name brand. The name brands cost a bit more, but they tend to have slightly better performance. That is, for the same speed of CPU and RAM, you'll get faster performance. Often this difference is because of the design of the circuitry surrounding the CPU, particularly the memory subsystem. How fast the CPU can communicate with the RAM is a crucial determinant in system efficiency. If you already have a fast CPU, it's not even out of the question to buy a fast motherboard without a CPU, plug your old CPU into it, and discard the old motherboard.

One trick I've used in choosing a motherboard is to check the magazines for reviews of clone computers. Some reviews have an accompanying chart listing performance and, if you're lucky, which brand of motherboard is used in each system. Look for fast performers and note who makes the motherboard. Often it will be a name brand like Micronics, AIR, or Mylex. Then check your local systems integrator or supplier or scan magazines for your board of choice. Most companies also have a Web site, so check their home pages (usually mentioned in their documentation) or use a search engine like AltaVista or Yahoo to find them.

Choosing a CPU

Choosing a new motherboard can also be confusing because of all the CPUs around, not to mention clock speeds. Ever since Intel was busted for monopolizing CPUs for PCs, the industry has bombarded consumers with confusing literature and ads. Everyone claims that their CPU is faster, smarter, and more compatible. Some are cheaper than others. Some use lower voltages so that they'll run longer in a laptop. Some are clock-doubled, and others are not. Some have math coprocessors, and others don't. You'll have to do some research to determine what's best for your application mix. Because new processors seem to be born weekly, I'm not going into extensive detail here, but I have a few suggestions.

The first big decision is whether to go with a Pentium or an 80486 class of chip. This depends on your budget. If price is no object, you should get a DEC Alpha or one of the multi-CPU machines (for example, the AcerFrame 3000 MP50). Stepping down a notch, Pentium machines are now becoming affordable, and NT is no speed demon. If you can afford a good Pentium motherboard, or if your current board allows a Pentium to be plugged in, consider it.

Then there are the non-Intel chips. IBM has a manufacturing agreement to make their own chips using the 486 name, and Cyrix makes the SLC (486, 586, and 686) chips. AMD also makes chips. Look for performance specifications that compare these chips with the Intel chips. Clone CPUs, which are a little cheaper, usually are fine. Many complete systems, including laptops, use these renegade CPUs, helping to keep the free-market system alive and kicking. Make sure you're not getting something without a math coprocessor, though.

Internal caches are yet another fertile field of battle in the war between the CPUs. Processors have varying amounts of internal speedy RAM that temporarily holds data being used repeatedly, just as a disk cache does. This caching can increase overall processing speed; the larger the cache, the faster a certain processor can run. Caches typically range from 1K to 16K. A 486 CPU with only a 1K cache (some Cyrix CPUs, for example) might run almost as slowly as a fast 386. IBM's chips typically use 16K internal caches these days.

Next, consider processor speed, an important determinant of performance. The faster the better, obviously. Some CPUs, however, are clock-doubled internally. This means that the CPU is working double-time on its own computations, and communicating with the board at one-half the speed it's working at inside. The clock-doubled chips are a cheap way of upgrading existing motherboards without having to install new timing crystals and high-speed support circuitry. It was a great idea on Intel's part to get PC makers to buy their new chips because the computer makers didn't have to change the circuitry in the computers.

About RAM Caches

When you're shopping for motherboards, you'll see listings in magazines with descriptions like this one:

> 486/66DX2
>
> 128K
>
> 0K
>
> no CPU

The first part means that the motherboard is set up for a 486DX/2 chip running at 66MHz. The speed is determined by a crystal on the board. Often, such a board will also run a 33MHz 486 because the crystal speed is the same for each. Some boards list a number of CPU chips (for example, 386/386SX/486/486SX/Pentium) and a number of speeds. These boards have a couple of sockets for the different CPUs and jumpers for setting the clock speed.

The 128K refers to RAM cache, an important asset when running Windows. The CPU must do a significant amount of memory accessing with Windows, so a fast memory system is crucial. Although dynamic RAM is fast as opposed to a hard disk, it isn't as fast as it could be. A

70ns wait for a chip to settle down after being written to, for example, can add up because the CPU executes millions of instructions every second. Just as hard disks use RAM caches to simulate hard-disk storage and allow the CPU to get back to work sooner, the memory system can have a cache of super-fast RAM, too. This cache is also called RAM cache.

RAM cache uses static memory chips that typically have a speed of 20ns (normal memory chips are of the dynamic variety). Without going into the structural and operational differences between static and dynamic RAM, static RAM is, quite simply, really fast and really expensive. You probably don't want to buy more than 256K, even though it would be nice if your whole 16M (or more) were of this variety. A good board will have at least 128K of cache that's set up for both read and write-back operations. Avoid boards that don't have write-back cache.

> **NOTE**
>
> If you buy a board or a machine with a write-back cache, make sure you can turn it off if you need to. Some machines with write-back caches have been known to disagree with NT. Turning off the write-back caching action (but leaving the read cache on) is the only solution to the problem of random NT crashing.

The 0K reference in the ad listing means that no RAM is installed in the board. Shop for RAM carefully (as discussed elsewhere in this chapter) and comparison shop aggressively. Make sure the RAM you're buying is fast RAM.

Finally, if a board listed in a magazine or a flyer says "no CPU," you have to buy the CPU separately. "No CPU" boards are usually inexpensive, for good reason. Try to get one with a CPU, if possible. Installing a CPU isn't always easy, and you'll want to know that the board/CPU combination works before it leaves the factory or store anyway.

Slots

Even if you're not upgrading a machine yourself but are buying it new, you have to decide about slots—what kind and how many. As you probably know, the old standard is the ISA (industry standard architecture), a 16-bit slot. More cards are made for this format than for any other, and they're cheap. Clone ISA cards are plentiful, so if you're fabricating systems for the office and trying to keep costs down, this is the way to go. However, you should get a couple of VLB (VESA local bus) slots as well. Those slots will be for the hard disk or SCSI controller and/or video card.

Some power users opt for EISA (extended ISA) bus machines. Some EISA motherboards have both ISA and EISA slots, so you can still plug your old I/O, sound, mouse, or other ISA cards into the EISA motherboard instead of chucking them. Others have PCI slots in addition to the

ISA or EISA slots. The EISA bus is a wider bus (32-bit), just as PCI and IBM's MicroChannel are. The other downside is that far fewer EISA cards are available, and they're much more expensive. Some industry experts think that EISA is dead and that an ISA machine with PCI slots for I/O-intensive devices is the way to go.

In any case, you'll need enough slots to accommodate your arsenal of cards, with a few left over for future expansions. Typically, you'll want about six to eight slots. Make sure that the slots are spaced properly for the computer chassis you have and that the board fits in the chassis. Take some measurements. Although slot spacing is standardized for ATs and all machines after that, some older boxes (such as original PC boxes) don't accommodate today's motherboards.

General Buying Points

Some benchmark tests are useful in determining how well a motherboard will perform when running Windows NT. Before settling on a particular motherboard, you might ask how it performs by using popular benchmarks, such as *PC Magazine's* Winmark. Of course, video and hard-disk performance measures don't apply because those depend on the disk and video subsystem you plug into the board. You're interested only in the memory and CPU performance.

If you're going to upgrade the motherboard in your system, be ready to find someone who will put it in, or expect to spend the better part of the day doing it yourself. You will have few instructions (perhaps only a small block diagram and a cryptic translation), so you'll have to know something about how to disconnect and reconnect lots of wires, connectors, LED lights, ribbon cables, speakers, and so forth.

You can figure most of this out by observing how the wires are connected to the existing motherboard. Although the layout of the new board will be different from the old one, most connectors (such as those for the reset switch and LEDs) are marked on the board to help you.

CAUTION

Pay extra attention to the power connectors, marked P8 and P9. They go back on with the black wires on each connector facing each other (all black wires grouped together). You don't want to blow out your new motherboard by doing this backward.

Summary

This chapter has discussed different approaches to upgrading your NT system to optimize its performance. It has covered the cost-free approaches of BIOS adjustments and hard-disk maintenance with interleave adjustment, defragmenting, and using CHKDSK. It has also discussed the more costly variations you can make, such as upgrading your video and hard-disk subsystems or upgrading the motherboard and CPU. All these changes have been discussed with an eye toward the particular computational needs of Windows NT. Armed with this information, you should now be better equipped to make system purchases or optimization decisions. Keep in mind that system hardware is always changing in the competitive PC hardware market. You must refer to the industry magazines often if you want to keep abreast of what's new.

Maintenance and Troubleshooting

IN THIS CHAPTER

This chapter presents an assortment of topics pertinent to Windows NT maintenance and troubleshooting. General system problems are covered first, and then more specific problems—those concerning video, networks, and hard disks—are discussed. The following topics also are discussed:

- Using the Event Viewer
- Using the Tape Backup program
- Looking at specific MS-DOS and Windows 3.*x* applications notes
- Recovering from a system crash
- Trying to recover crashed hard disks
- Converting partitions between file formats
- Reinstalling NT from scratch
- Using the Registry Editor

Looking at General System Issues

This section addresses general system maintenance issues that might be useful if you're administering an NT machine or network.

Understanding the NT Booting Process

Understanding how NT boots might help you diagnose system startup problems. If you're having trouble booting, you first should make sure that the computer's system is set up correctly; use the CMOS Setup utility or another program supplied with the computer. The computer needs to know which drive to boot from, and you must enter the hard-disk type into the setup information. NT must be installed as explained in Chapter 7, "Installing Windows NT," and no IRQ, DMA, or other bus conflicts can exist. In particular, the video card must be set correctly; otherwise, NT might boot, but you might not know it because nothing recognizable appears onscreen.

Assuming that all is well with the physical system and that NT installed without incident, the boot-up drive's boot record was modified to cause the computer to load the NT Loader (NTLDR) program. When you boot, the following things happen:

1. NTLDR runs and then calls NTDETECT.COM. This program announces itself onscreen and checks out the computer's hardware attributes (type of video card, hard disk, ports, memory, and so on).

2. Based on the results of the search, NTDETECT compiles a list of hardware. This information is placed in the Registry under the appropriate hardware keys.

Maintenance and Troubleshooting

CHAPTER 11

317

11

MAINTENANCE
AND TROUBLE-
SHOOTING

3. NTLDR reads an ASCII text file called BOOT.INI to determine which other operating systems are on the hard disk. (This file, created during Setup, is located in the root directory of the boot partition.) Typically, the list is MS-DOS and NT, or OS/2 and NT.

4. After the countdown period ends, the default operating system (typically, Windows NT) is loaded.

TIP

If you intervene by pressing the up-arrow or down-arrow key (not Enter, because that boots the highlighted item), the time-out clock stops. You then can take as much time as you need to decide which operating system to boot.

---

5. NT starts the booting process by loading the low-level drivers and services. You can alter which services start at boot time by changing settings in the Services dialog box, which you access from the Control Panel; these settings are stored in the Registry. A stock set of default services is started (unless you tinker with these settings, of course); these are the services necessary for typical NT functionality.

6. The GUI and higher-level drivers load, and NT appears onscreen, waiting for a user to log on.

Examining the Structure of BOOT.INI

Listing 11.1 shows a typical BOOT.INI file.

Listing 11.1. A BOOT.INI file.

```
[boot loader]
timeout=30
default=multi(0)disk(0)rdisk(0)partition(1)\WINNT
[operating systems]
multi(0)disk(0)rdisk(0)partition(1)\WINNT="Windows NT Server Version 4.00"
multi(0)disk(0)rdisk(0)partition(1)\WINNT="Windows NT Server Version 4.00 [VGA
➥mode]" /basevideo /sos
```

The [boot loader] section indicates that the default operating system is WINNT, located on partition 1. This section also indicates the time (in seconds) the startup program waits before starting the default system.

The [operating systems] section lists all the operating systems that are bootable and will appear on the startup menu. All text between the quotation marks is the text that appears on the menu.

NOTE

Currently, NT can boot multiple versions of NT, or NT Server and one previous operating system.

NOTE

At first glance, Listing 11.1 looks as though two duplicate entries exist for starting Windows NT. Although they're similar in appearance, they're not similar in functionality. The second instance, which includes the /basevideo switch, starts Windows NT with a default VGA driver. This entry can be used to start Windows NT if the user-installed video driver fails for some reason. Selecting a video card refresh frequency that is higher than the monitor can handle, for example, results in an unreadable display.

TIP

You can change the default operating system by using the System applet from the Control Panel. See Chapter 8, "Using the Control Panel to Configure Windows NT," for details. You can also change the default by editing the BOOT.INI file in the root directory of the boot drive after you change BOOT.INI's attribute to read-write.

Backing Up Configuration Information

As you add new users and make other changes to NT, you will want to update the repair information stored in the %SystemRoot%\System32\Repair directory and on the Emergency Repair Disk. To update this information, you run the Repair Disk Utility, RDISK.EXE. Figure 11.1 shows the opening screen of this utility.

FIGURE 11.1.

Updating the system recovery data with the Repair Disk Utility.

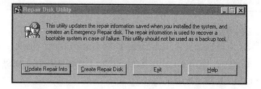

TIP

Some of these subsystem configuration settings are stored in the file \SYSTEM32 \CONFIG.NT. You should back up this file (put it on a floppy disk) periodically. You might have to use this file if the system crashes and you use the Emergency Repair Disk to resuscitate it. The Emergency Repair Disk contains only the configuration information from when NT was installed or last updated with the Repair Disk Utility.

Note that, because the Registry files are always in use, you can't just copy them to or from a floppy disk unless they're stored on a FAT partition and the currently running operating system is MS-DOS. Otherwise, these files are locked.

You can use the Repair Disk Utility to update the recovery information stored on the hard disk or to create a new repair disk. I recommend that after each major change (after you install and test new software, for example), you update the repair information stored locally on the hard disk. After a hardware upgrade, or once a month, you should create a new repair disk. Don't just keep updating the existing repair disk; create new ones. This method gives you the option of restoring a configuration that you know is good. If you label your repair disks, you can keep a running history of your changes and have the option of restoring any of your configurations.

TIP

Use the RDISK utility to update the local copy of the repair information before you install new software on the system, just in case the software doesn't live up to the manufacturer's claims. If you have a tape drive attached, make a backup, too.

Booting Another Operating System

Most NT users have had previous versions of MS-DOS or OS/2 on their machines; NT supports almost any previously installed operating system. If you decide to keep your current operating system, the installation process simply grabs the boot record and relocates it in the file BOOTSECT.DOS. This file then is jumped to and used as the boot record when the optional secondary operating system is selected. Note that you can have only one alternative operating system.

For a second operating system to boot (as an option from the menu displayed at boot time), a file called BOOTSECT.DOS must exist in the root directory of the boot partition. During NT installation, NT creates the BOOTSECT file and copies into it the preexisting operating system boot record it found on the computer (such as DOS or OS/2).

When you choose to boot the alternative operating system, the NT Boot Loader must be able to locate the BOOTSECT.DOS file, and it uses the statement in the BOOT.INI file to do so. If the pathname declared in BOOT.INI points to an incorrect or nonexistent directory, the alternative operating system won't boot. Typically, BOOTSECT.DOS is in the C:\ directory, so the line in the [operating systems] section of BOOT.INI should read like this:

```
C:\="MS-DOS"
```

NOTE

To run MS-DOS, NT needs to find the AUTOEXEC.BAT and CONFIG.SYS files. If you don't have these files in the root directory of the boot partition, add them by using a plain text editor.

Solving Problems with Logging onto NT

Occasionally, you or a user might have trouble logging on. Check the following items to determine the cause of this problem:

- Have you entered the password correctly? Remember that NT is case-sensitive; it does not see BEGIN.htm and Begin.htm as the same file.

- Does the account require you to change the password every so often? If so, perhaps the password needs to be updated. You can set the password expire, as well as a new password, by using the User Manager program (see Chapter 9, "Windows NT Administration," for details). After you log on successfully, you can change the password by pressing Ctrl+Alt+Del.

- Is the workstation locked? A previous user might have locked the station in the middle of a session (to attend a meeting or to get a cup of coffee, for example). Only that user (or anyone who knows the user's password) can unlock the station. You can lock your session by using the Ctrl+Alt+Del sequence, which displays a dialog box with Lock as an option.

- Is your account still active? Some accounts expire after a preset period of time. Again, you can check this expiration setting and change it with User Manager.

- Is your account locked? If the account lockout policy has been set, you can't log onto the system until the administrator resets your account or the lockout duration expires.

- Have you forgotten the password? This is a common problem, particularly when users are required to change their passwords frequently; it becomes difficult to remember them. Because there is no way to display the current password, the only solution is to assign a new one. Again, User Manager is the vehicle. See the next section for the exact steps.

- Recall from Chapter 9 that accounts can be assigned a property that limits logon to times that fall between certain hours. Perhaps you are trying to log on at a time that doesn't fall within the assigned range.

- If the login service fails to start, no authentication (and therefore no logon) is permitted. Sometimes, a reboot solves the problem. At the worst, you might have to invoke the Last Known Good option or reinstall NT. Administrators and users should be aware that this service should never be disabled by using the Control Panel applets or the Registry Editor.

- If the workstation with the logon problem is on a network, an administrator can remotely connect to it and possibly fix the problem.

If you're trying to log onto a remote station over the network, other gremlins might be preventing this. Ask yourself these questions:

- Is the network up and running?

- Is your station communicating correctly with the workgroup(s) or domain(s) containing the station you're attempting to log onto?

- Are you attempting to log onto the correct domain? A domain that doesn't have a trust relationship won't allow you to log on.

Dealing with a Lost User Password

Suppose that one of the users on a station you administer has forgotten his password. Here's exactly how to deal with the problem:

1. First, a little lecture is in order. Users should choose passwords that make sense to them but that aren't too obvious to anyone trying to break into the system. For example, JOED isn't a good password for Joe Derek. It's an acceptable username, but it's not a good password. Use something that's memorable, though, to prevent having to hassle the administrator. DEOJ (JOED backward) is better. The name of the user's dog, wife, or something else memorable certainly beats ERJ#(+p!, which means nothing.

2. Log onto the system as someone with administrative powers.

3. Run User Manager.

4. Locate the user account for which the password has been lost, and highlight it.

5. Choose File | Properties.

6. In the Properties dialog box, enter a new password and confirm it.

7. At this point, you have a choice: You can opt for the new password to become official until it's changed at some future date, or you can require the user to change the password the next time he logs on. For the latter option, choose the User Must Change Password at Next Logon checkbox option in the Properties dialog box.

TIP

A third option, which gives the user an additional feeling of security, is to turn your back or leave the room while the user enters the new password at your computer. You might want to make sure that you don't leave the room long enough to allow the user to change privileges, though. Also, this works only for local workstations. Network workstations require that the administrator modify the domain account rather than the local account.

Handling Video Problems

Some video adapters are not very graceful when it comes to switching video modes, particularly from character mode to graphics mode or vice versa. When you run an MS-DOS application, the application might run fine in a window, but when you switch back to a full screen, the display might become an indecipherable mess. The application still might be running, but you can't see anything recognizable. This is a known bug on a small number of video cards.

TIP

If you experience such a video problem, check the Hardware Compatibility List for notes on your video card. Also, see whether your video manufacturer has an updated video ROM or an exchange policy.

If you experience display problems when switching modes, you can try some things to solve your problem. First, you can switch back to windowed mode, save your work, and quit the application (or continue working if the application displays and responds correctly). If you can't get back into windowed mode, you must terminate the application from the Task List or issue the necessary keyboard commands blindly (if you know them).

Second, you can try other refresh modes. Some video adapter and monitor combinations just don't work as expected, particularly those that push the hardware past its rated capacity.

Handling Network Problems

Chapter 7 and Part III discuss network installation and some troubleshooting issues. If you're having difficulty with your network, you might want to look in those parts of the book for specific discussions of network card and software installation, as well as I/O port, DMA, and IRQ assignments. This section includes some additional general troubleshooting hints.

If your network isn't operating properly, you should consider several issues: user settings, network card settings, conflicting computer names, conflicting protocols, and conflicting IRQs. Another possibility is physical cabling anomalies.

Maintenance and Troubleshooting

CHAPTER 11

323

11

MAINTENANCE
AND TROUBLE-
SHOOTING

NOTE

Many of these typical problems—such as conflicting protocols, network card conflicts, and IRQ conflicts—are reported in the Event Log. Check the Event Log by using the Event Viewer (as described later in "Working with Event Viewer Logs") for possible entries explaining the problem.

In terms of general system maintenance, remember that if you physically replace a workstation's network card, you might have to install an appropriate device driver. You can do this by using the Control Panel, as described in Chapter 8. Make sure that the IRQ settings are set properly on the board and that the software driver in the Control Panel is configured to that DMA (and/or other settings that the driver lets you change in its dialog boxes). Note that, even if you're replacing a card with a so-called "compatible" card, such as a Novell NE2000-compatible card, the methods for setting up a card's IRQ, port, and so on might differ. One card might use hardware jumpers, whereas another card might use a software setup program.

TIP

If you make hardware changes to a system, try to configure the software drivers before you switch the hardware. That way, the system stands a better chance of booting up properly the next time you reboot.

If you rearrange cabling, make sure that you observe all rules pertaining to the network topography and the system used. Did you use the proper repeaters, terminators, hubs, and cables? Did you exceed the maximum run length for your type of cable? You get the idea.

Finally, if you've upgraded to a network that uses a different protocol, you have to load the new protocol driver as well as the card driver. (Again, see Chapter 8 for instructions on how to do this from Control Panel.)

Finally, a problem can result from computers and domains not having unique names. Even with the most intelligent computer software, it's wise not to tempt fate by creating duplicate names. This applies to files and directories as well as workstations, workgroups, and domains. If, as NT is booting, it detects an existing domain, workgroup, or workstation that has the same name as the workstation, the network connection will not start. Check the workstation's name, or go to another workstation and browse the network for workstation, workgroup, and domain names to try to determine whether a name conflict exists. Note that some characters are illegal when naming computers, workgroups, and domains. The most frequently used and illegal characters are the bullet, pipe (vertical bar), and any currency symbols. These characters prevent the network from recognizing the name and can cause unexpected results.

If network problems don't clear up and the station won't come online, check the Event Viewer for hints. Possible interrupt conflicts, as well as missing or inappropriate card drivers and software protocols, might be reported in the System Log.

Working with Setup Utilities

Windows NT uses a number of applets in the Control Panel to program a number of system-maintenance functions. As with Windows 3.1, the primary function is for installing basic system drivers to control the screen, mouse, and keyboard. Typically, you need to modify only the mouse and screen drivers, because most keyboards have the same specifications.

You also can use applets in the Control Panel to install and remove SCSI and tape backup devices; to add and remove large portions of related NT components, such as Help files, accessories, and so on (typically to free up disk space); to delete user profiles; and to set up applications.

Changing Screen, Keyboard, and Mouse Drivers

Generally, you'll use the setup applets when you install a new mouse (or a keyboard designed for another language) or delete user profiles that have accumulated from temporary users of the workstation.

Changing your keyboard or mouse doesn't necessarily require that you change the driver. If you change the keyboard or mouse, you have to change the driver only if the new device isn't compatible with the driver you formerly installed. Many keyboards are generic keyboards, for example, that work with the standard NT keyboard driver even if they offer extended functionality (extra keys or a built-in calculator). Likewise, many mouses are Microsoft Mouse–compatible.

> **CAUTION**
>
> Remember that you can't use Windows 3.1 drivers with Windows NT. You must get a special NT-compatible driver for your multimedia hardware, fax modem, and so on, or they won't work from NT. Some Windows 95 drivers will work with Windows NT 4, but you should be careful when using any drivers not specifically tested for Windows NT.

NT comes with a good number of drivers; some already are installed in the \WINNT\SYSTEM32\DRIVERS directory. If you choose to install a driver that isn't, you're prompted to insert a source disk containing the driver (and possibly other support files, such as screen fonts).

Maintenance and Troubleshooting

CHAPTER 11

325

11

MAINTENANCE
AND TROUBLE-
SHOOTING

NOTE

Setup isn't used for printer, language, network, or multimedia driver alterations. You use Print Folders to install printer drivers, the International applet to change language settings, the Network applet to install network drivers, and the Devices applet to install multimedia drivers (for sound cards, for example).

To install a new driver, first run the respective applet from the Control Panel. The Keyboard Properties dialog box shown in Figure 11.2 appears when you want to change your keyboard, for example.

FIGURE 11.2.

You can use Control Panel applets to customize machine settings or to add new drivers. This window controls the keyboard type.

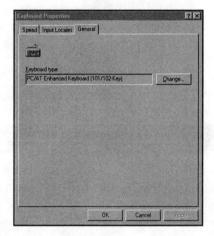

To change a driver, you have to be logged on with administrative privileges. Whether you install the new hardware first depends on the hardware. You want NT to be able to run while you make the alterations. If changing the hardware (for example, installing a completely different SCSI adapter that wouldn't run with the old setting) would prevent the system from running, installing the new hardware first won't cut it. You have to make the software changes first, then power down, install the hardware, and reboot.

Suppose that you're installing a new mouse driver. First, make sure that the new hardware (if any) is installed properly. Then follow these steps:

1. Double-click the Mouse applet in the Control Panel. The Mouse Properties dialog box appears.

2. Select the General tab.

3. Click Change. In the Select Device dialog box that appears, select the description that matches the new hardware you want to use. You might select Logitech Serial Mouse,

as shown in Figure 11.3, for example, instead of Microsoft Mouse Port. If the correct device isn't listed, you're out of luck unless you have a driver from another source, such as the hardware manufacturer. In this case, click Have Disk.

FIGURE 11.3.

Selecting a description for your new hardware.

TIP

Microsoft maintains a regularly updated library of NT drivers. You can download drivers by calling (206) 936-MSDL between 6:00 a.m. and 6:00 p.m. Pacific time Monday through Friday. You also can find this library on CompuServe and GEnie, as well as the Internet at the Microsoft home page or FTP site. Microsoft will mail you the library on disk if you call (800) 227-4679.

---

4. Click OK. If you clicked Have Disk, or if the driver isn't already in the drivers directory, a dialog box will appear, prompting you to insert a disk or to specify a drive and directory where the driver is located. You can specify a location across the network, on a CD-ROM, or on a floppy disk. You can also grab a driver from another networked workstation. If the needed driver already is on your system, a message box appears, informing you of this and asking whether you want to use the existing driver or load a new one. Choose to load a new one only if you're updating the driver. Otherwise, opt to use the existing one.

5. In most cases, you must restart the computer before the changes go into effect.

NOTE

You can't restart the system until you properly exit the applet. Otherwise, you get a message telling you to exit the program properly.

TIP

If you think that you'll want to be able to easily switch between different drivers (for example, so that you can switch between various keyboards to test your foreign-language skills), install them all by repeating Steps 2 through 4 for each driver. (Do not reboot each time.) Then you'll have all the necessary support files on the system's hard disk. Next, choose the driver you currently want to work with (Setup asks whether you want to use the driver already found in the drivers directory, so choose Yes), and then reboot. The next time you want to change drivers, just run Setup, choose the driver, and then reboot.

Adding and Removing Tape and SCSI Drivers

You can set up tape and SCSI drivers by using a Control Panel applet. When you install NT initially, the Setup program scans for SCSI devices and installs the correct one for the device it finds if an Express installation was chosen. For a Custom installation, Setup lets you choose the drivers to test. Assuming that your SCSI device is one that Setup detects, you're in business; the driver already is installed. You need to use Setup as described here only if you change your brand of SCSI controller or if your controller wasn't detected in the first place.

NOTE

This note pertains to users of the Media Vision Audio Spectrum 16 sound/SCSI card if used with other SCSI controllers.

If NT detects a SCSI device upon booting, it installs the device's driver, even if the device isn't used. I have a Media Vision Pro Audio Spectrum 16, for example, but I don't use the SCSI on the card because I also have an Adaptec 1742a controller installed. The problem is that the Media Vision driver expects the SCSI device to be used for something, and its sound driver doesn't load (for wave, MIDI, and so on) unless the SCSI driver loads. Because I have no SCSI devices connected to the Media Vision SCSI port, though, the driver fails to load. The solution is to use the Control Panel's Drivers applet to disable the TMV1 driver. Alternatively, you can remove the driver from the system. Users of the Media Vision Basic cards without SCSI ports also must disable this driver to be able to install the sound driver. Just select Polled I/O for the SCSI device in the dialog box for configuring the card.

The process of installing a SCSI or tape device works essentially the same as that described for installing mouse and keyboard drivers. Follow these steps:

1. If you are using a SCSI tape drive, you must install the SCSI adapter first (if it isn't already) by double-clicking the SCSI Adapter applet in the Control Panel.

2. When the SCSI card has been configured, you can install the tape device. Double-click the Tape Devices applet in the Control Panel. The Tape Devices dialog box appears.

3. Click Detect to tell NT to try to find your tape drive. If it locates your drive, continue to Step 4. If it doesn't locate your drive, skip to Step 5.

4. You're prompted to choose a directory or drive where the tape driver resides. Enter the proper location of the driver (usually supplied with the tape device or on a SCSI adapter's software disk. Click on OK to load the driver.

5. After the driver is installed, click Continue in the Tape Devices dialog to get back to the NT Setup program.

TIP

Some devices—notably, SCSI devices such as CD-ROM readers, removable media units, or tape units—don't come online when NT boots unless they're powered up before booting. Check the power switch on external SCSI units before booting NT.

Dealing with an Incorrect Driver Installation

Instead of remembering only one setup configuration of system drivers, NT remembers two: the last configuration that worked successfully (as far as NT knows, anyway), and the configuration you just created by adding, changing, or removing drivers. Therefore, when you reboot, NT knows whether something didn't pan out. If the system doesn't boot properly (typically, because of the wrong screen or mouse driver), the next time you reboot, NT reverts to the last known functional setup configuration.

If the system doesn't boot after you make driver changes from the Setup program, just reboot a second time. NT tries to fix itself. Then try making your driver changes again.

CAUTION

Keep one thing in mind when correcting a driver installation. Each time you log on, the Last Known Good configuration is updated. So don't log on if there is a serious problem and you want to use the Last Known Good option.

Removing User Profiles

User profiles are collections of settings that apply to certain users. Each profile stores Explorer and My Computer settings, desktop settings, mouse settings, and network and printer connections for a certain user, for example. If the user no longer uses the system, you should remove the user profile from the Registry.

To delete a profile, follow these steps:

1. Double-click the System applet from the Control Panel. The System dialog box appears.
2. Select the User Profiles or the Hardware Profiles tab, depending on what you want to delete.
3. Highlight the profile you want to delete.
4. Click Delete.
5. Repeat the process for other profiles, if applicable.
6. Click Close when you're finished deleting profiles.

> **NOTE**
>
> If the user currently is logged on, you can't delete that profile. Setup issues an error message if you try. Also, you must have administrative privileges to delete a profile.

Adding and Removing System Components

You can use the Add/Remove Programs applet in the Control panel to install or remove applications and Windows NT components. If you didn't choose a complete installation when you initially set up NT, you might want to use this option after the fact to load Help files, README files, wallpaper files, games, or screen savers, for example.

By the same token, if you performed a complete installation and are running tight on disk space, you might want to delete a class of files (or at least selected files in a class). If you don't use the accessory Help files, for example, deleting them frees up a fair amount of space.

Follow these steps to add or remove components:

1. Double-click Add/Remove Programs in the Control Panel. The Add/Remove Programs Properties dialog box appears.
2. Select the Windows NT Setup tab, as shown in Figure 11.4.
3. Notice that some components have their checkbox enabled, meaning that they're already on the system. If you want to remove a component, disable its checkbox. If you want to add a component, enable its checkbox.

FIGURE 11.4.

*The Windows NT
Setup tab of the Add/
Remove Programs
Properties dialog box.*

4. If you want to remove or add selected portions of a component, click the Files button for that component. A Details dialog box appears, listing the currently included files on the right side and the files you can add to the list on the left side. If you're adding files, keep an eye on the Space available on disk number. Make sure that you have enough disk space to accommodate the new files. Click OK when the correct files are listed.

5. Click OK in the Add/Remove Programs Properties dialog box. You're prompted to insert disks containing the source files (or to specify the location of the files, such as on a CD-ROM) or to confirm the deletion of files. Respond accordingly.

Setting Up Applications

The Control Panel's Add/Remove Programs applet sets up or removes applications. This option often is used when an application is designed specifically for Windows NT or Windows 95, or when no setup program is included.

Using the Add/Remove Programs applet has some drawbacks, however. Although the applications themselves might be installed, for example, file associations, Registry information pertaining to DDE and OLE, and other such details aren't necessarily incorporated into the NT environment. Typically, if an application has a setup program, that's the better way to go.

To set up or remove an application, follow these steps:

1. From the Control Panel, double-click the Add/Remove Programs applet. The Add/Remove Programs Properties dialog box appears, as shown in Figure 11.5.

2. To add a program, select the Install/Uninstall tab and click Install.

FIGURE 11.5.
*Installing an
application.*

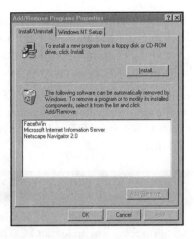

3. When the application's media (floppy or CD-ROM) is in the drive, click Next, and NT searches for the application's installation files. NT Setup uses an internal lookup table (database) of filenames to figure out which program an .EXE file is. You might be asked to confirm the names of applications if Setup is confused by the executable filename. Installation proceeds after you confirm the installation. You might be asked for configuration information as the application installs.

4. Click OK to finish the installation.

Maintaining Your Hard-Disk System

This section covers hard-disk maintenance and troubleshooting issues.

> **NOTE**
>
> Disk optimization and upgrading are discussed in Chapter 10, "Optimizing Windows NT: Performance Determinants."

Dealing with SCSI Drives

Windows NT requires special attention to support more than two non-SCSI drives per machine. As I mentioned in Chapter 10, this is one of the primary limitations of IDE and other non-SCSI drive setups (such as ESDI). When you need more space than is available on two such drives (for example, when setting up stripe, volume, or mirrored sets), you have two choices.

If you have a machine that supports additional IDE cards or has additional controllers built in (such as some models from Compaq and Gateway), acquire and install the appropriate boards and drives, and then reboot. NT recognizes up to six such drives. If you're in doubt about the compatibility of the hardware, ask the supplier or call Microsoft Product Support Services.

Another, perhaps easier, solution is to upgrade to SCSI drives. NT supports as many as seven SCSI drives, while at the same time allowing two non-SCSI drives to coexist in the same computer. Therefore, you can keep your IDE or ESDI drives, for example, add a SCSI controller, and start buying SCSI drives.

> **NOTE**
>
> The latest SCSI specification allows multiple SCSI drives in each computer, with up to 15 drives per card, and NT recognizes up to four SCSI controllers with 15 drives per adapter at this point. If you're shopping for SCSI controllers and devices, the SCSI II specification is the preferred way to go.

SCSI drives have some peculiar requirements not characteristic of other types of drives. If you're having trouble installing or maintaining a SCSI drive, consider the following:

The README file supplied with NT contains information about particular brands and models of SCSI devices, such as those from NEC, Adaptec controllers, Compaq, Future Domain, and others. Special instructions for approximately 2,115 products are discussed in this file. I won't repeat them here, because you have the file already. If your SCSI adapter isn't working, you might have to change a switch, disable the adapter's BIOS, or alter the termination in some specific manner, as explained in that text file.

Two general rules pertain to SCSI cabling. First, SCSI cables (like some network cables) must be terminated properly at both ends in order to work. Second, the SCSI device or the SCSI adapter must supply termination power to the SCSI bus. You have to make sure that these two requirements are met.

> **TIP**
>
> SCSI termination comes in two flavors: passive and active. Active terminators supply a more constant voltage to the SCSI bus and help eliminate noise. Most SCSI I adapters use passive termination, and most SCSI II adapters use active termination. You can use active termination on either SCSI bus, however. If you suspect a problem, use active termination when possible.

Additionally, you should make sure that SCSI devices are turned on before you boot NT, and that a CD-ROM drive is set to a SCSI ID number other than 0 or 1. Those numbers are reserved for bootable media (typically, hard disks, but this could include removable media). If you assign a CD-ROM drive to a SCSI ID number of 0 or 1, NT might think that the CD-ROM has multiple partitions. You can add or modify the SCSI adapter configuration by using the SCSI Adapter applet of the Control Panel, as shown in Figure 11.6.

FIGURE 11.6.

*The SCSI Adapter
applet lets you configure
or add SCSI adapter
cards.*

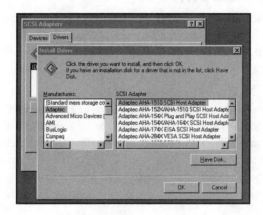

Recognizing a Hard Drive

Windows NT has stricter rules than MS-DOS for determining whether a hard drive has legitimate partitions. If sectors, boot tracks, or partition tables aren't encoded with absolute conformity to MS-DOS rules, NT might not recognize the drive even though DOS might. This can be unnerving, but the upside is that it offers more protection against viruses that alter the partition tables, FATs, or boot tracks. Such an altered drive simply won't come online.

To deal with an altered drive, you have to reuse the MS-DOS FDISK and FORMAT commands on it. First, make sure that the problem isn't the result of another issue, such as SCSI settings, cabling, hard-disk termination, or hard-disk jumpers.

CAUTION

Some devices might not work after you perform an FDISK and FORMAT command under DOS. Check the drive or controller's manual to determine whether this is the case. If it is, attempt a reformat by using Disk Administrator instead of following the next steps.

Follow these steps:

1. Back up all important data, including the DOS directory and related files (such as AUTOEXEC.BAT and CONFIG.SYS).

2. Boot DOS.

3. Use the FDISK command to prepare the disk for formatting.

4. Use the FORMAT command to format the drive.

5. Repartition as necessary, and restore the files to the drive.

Adding a Hard Drive

When you add a new drive to an NT system, you actually can get away with not running Disk Administrator or declaring the addition of a new drive. Assuming that the controller and the system setup (CMOS or other BIOS-related settings) are correct and that the drive is formatted in a file system that NT can recognize, the drive simply comes online and is assigned the next available filename.

If you want to assign a static letter name to the drive that will not shift when new drives (such as CD-ROMs or additional hard disks) are dumped into the system, you should run Disk Administrator. When you do, the program detects that a new drive has been added since Disk Administrator was run last and prompts you to okay the process of updating the internal settings. Go ahead and do this. Then, if you want to assign a static letter name to the drive, use Disk Administrator commands to do so (as outlined in Chapter 9).

NOTE

As soon as a static label has been assigned in Disk Administrator, MS-DOS also recognizes the modified disk letter scheme. This can be a useful attribute, but it can wreak havoc for the uninitiated when they boot DOS and wonder how their hard drive or CD-ROM letters became rearranged.

Removing a Hard Drive

If you remove a hard disk from the system, you might not get past the startup screen the next time you boot up. NTDETECT runs as expected (see "Understanding the NT Booting Process," earlier in this chapter) but then can hang up. This is true especially if you remove the data cable from a drive but leave the power cable on, and you don't change the CMOS BIOS settings to indicate that a drive is missing. Apparently, your BIOS settings must agree with your actual physical hardware for NT to work properly.

NOTE

This problem of the system hanging when a drive is removed occurs only for Seagate ST-506/Western Digital 1003-compatible media. SCSI drives don't suffer from this problem (unless the removed drive is the boot drive). In many cases (IDE in particular), the master/slave arrangement is the cause of the problem.

In any case, the solution is to change the BIOS settings and then reboot. To be completely conscientious, you should inform NT that you have physically removed a hard disk from the system—particularly if you've assigned a static drive letter to that drive. To do this, run Disk Administrator, let it update itself, and make sure that drive letter assignments and partition information agree with your physical setup and that your disk letters are as you want them.

> **TIP**
>
> Think ahead when removing or reassigning drive letters. If you have drives C, D, and E, for example, and you remove physical drive D, you might not want to have drive E fall back to drive D's position. Pointers in Program Manager icons and shared directories in File Manager might expect to find specific files on logical drive E. Just leave the hole where D was, and perhaps assign the CD-ROM drive to D (unless you want to adjust other settings, such as Program Manager icon properties, other workstation connections, and so on).

Recovering Disk Configurations with Disk Administrator

NT is savvy in how it stores information about hard-disk volumes, stripe sets, volume sets, mirrored sets, and partitions. Much of this information is discussed in other chapters. Recall that a given machine's disk appointments are recorded in the NT Registry. A DISK section in the Registry contains the details of your disk partitions, their logical letter names, physical drive locations, and the role each partition plays in the NT system (for example, standard volume, volume set, and so on).

What's intelligent about this system is that it stores most of this information (everything except static drive letters) in the Registry, instead of in each partition or the disk's boot sector. This way, if the boot sector becomes nonfunctional or is corrupted, you don't lose advanced partition information such as volume set and stripe set arrangements and each partition's role in running NT. Therefore, you're more likely to be able to recover from disaster without losing data.

What's bad about this arrangement is that if the Registry becomes corrupted and trashes the partition map, you're out of luck. Unless you've backed up the repair information (as explained earlier) or the disk information by using Disk Administrator (as explained in the following numbered list), you won't be able to recover such advanced disk-utilization information.

Disk Administrator offers a security backup option that lets you make a copy of the disk partition arrangement on a floppy disk. Then, if you have to reinstall NT, you easily can reset the partition map from the floppy disk and thus gain access to your files and mirrored, volume, and stripe sets. Here's how to use it:

1. If necessary, update the map using Disk Administrator. (See Figure 11.7.) If you've added drives since running it the last time, you're alerted to this fact, and you must allow the program to update the Registry.

FIGURE 11.7.

The Disk Administrator main screen.

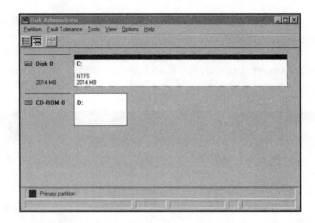

2. Exit Disk Administrator and save any changes.

3. Restart the computer, NT, and Disk Administrator.

4. Choose Configuration | Save. Some information appears in a Save dialog box, and you're asked where you want to save the partition information. Indicate a floppy disk and insert a blank disk, a disk you use for saving disk configurations, or even the Emergency Repair Disk you made when you installed NT.

5. Click OK. The disk configuration information is stored on the backup disk. Mark the disk appropriately (including the date), and store it in a safe place.

NOTE

You should follow this procedure whenever you change partition arrangements with Disk Administrator so that you have a current copy on a floppy disk.

You can restore the partition information at any time. Simply follow these steps:

1. Run Disk Administrator again.

2. Choose Configuration | Restore. The Restore dialog box appears.

3. Indicate the source of the partition information (for example, floppy drive A) and insert the proper disk.

4. Click OK.

If you have additional installations of NT on your hard disk(s), you can have Disk Administrator search for partition information in such setups. Just choose Configuration | Search. All preexisting configurations are listed, allowing you to choose one.

CAUTION

Changing configurations can be very dangerous if you don't know what you're doing. Obviously, you can render your system inoperable (and potentially lose data) if you activate a partition map that's out of date. Before restoring a configuration, save the current one in case you need to revert to it. Not only should you save the current configuration, but you should also back up the data when possible. After all, if the NT partition is destroyed, you can't boot NT to run Disk Administrator and fix the problem. In that case, you will have to reinstall NT and then restore all your data before NT returns to its previous state.

Repairing a Corrupted Volume

This section explains how to try to repair a FAT, NTFS, or HPFS volume that appears to be corrupted. Corruption often occurs because of broken chains or a disagreement between the FAT and the physical disk sectors. When you boot NT, the AUTOCHK program runs and tests the validity of your volumes. It also attempts to repair them. If the volume is NTFS, the repairs probably will cause less loss of data than on a FAT or HPFS volume. If problems continue, the solution is to run the CHKDSK program on the questionable volume by using the following sequence, regardless of the partition's file system:

1. Boot NT.
2. Run a command-prompt session and issue the CHKDSK command on the volume in question.
3. If errors are reported, run CHKDSK again—this time with the /f option (for example, chkdsk c: /f), unless the volume in question contains the Windows NT files. If it does, jump to Step 1 of the next procedure.

NOTE

The /f option causes CHKDSK to fix broken chains and dump lost clusters into files in the root directory. You can read these files with a text editor. These files are given names such as FILE0001.CHK.

4. If you're informed that CHKDSK can't correct the errors, look to see that no files are open on the volume. Close all applications except the command-prompt session and try running chkdsk /f again. If the errors still can't be fixed, restart the computer, reboot NT, log on, and try again.

If the volume in question contains NT, and CHKDSK reports that errors exist, follow these steps:

1. Perform a shutdown and then restart NT. AUTOCHK runs and possibly fixes the problems. If it doesn't, go to the next step.

2. Run a command-prompt session and run chkdsk /f on the volume in question. CHKDSK knows that you're attempting to run it on the NT volume and gives you the option of scheduling an AUTOCHK at the next bootup. This should clear up the trouble.

3. If even this fails, consider this. NT won't fix all problems—particularly on files that NT accesses before the AUTOCHK program starts. The final solution is to boot another operating system (MS-DOS or OS/2) and run CHKDSK or SCANDISK on the NT partition to correct the problem.

Using the Tape Backup Application

NT comes with a tape backup system to help administrators manually or automatically back up important directories and files and then restore those items if and when needed. NT's backup program is surprisingly competent, considering Microsoft's history of backup programs supplied with DOS. Backups can be performed on local or remote FAT, HPFS, or NTFS partitions. The Backup program looks and works much like File Manager, so if you understand File Manager, you should find the basics of the Backup program easy to understand.

NOTE

The Backup program included with NT was written by Arcadia Software. Like many programs derived from third parties, a more complete package is available from the manufacturer.

You also can perform these tasks with the Backup program:

- Automate backups with batch files
- Examine a backed-up tape directory just as if it were a hard-disk directory
- Back up huge directories or files across multiple tapes because file size is unlimited
- Organize backups into backup sets—sets of files on a single tape
- Choose for backup sets to be updated incrementally so that only modified files are backed up, or to have the entire set backed up again and appended to the tape as a new backup set
- Verify accuracy of all files copied to tape during a backup
- Create an Audit Log of backup operations for review by backup or system policy makers to ensure that data is regularly protected

11

As with any backup system you should put some forethought into developing a backup schedule and tape-rotation scheme. You need to decide which directories or files are crucial and which can be skipped because they easily can be replaced from other sources (application programs, for example). You should consider quite carefully the value of your data and the time required to re-create it if it is lost. You might also want to consider making duplicate tapes from different locations on a network, and also how other data risk-reduction techniques (such as fault-tolerant disk schemes) play into your overall information management policy.

Using Tape Backup Units

To use the Backup program, you need an NT-supported *tape backup unit* (TBU). Check the NT Hardware Compatibility List or the documentation supplied with the drive to determine which unit you need. Initial support is included for inexpensive minicartridge QIC 40/80 tape drives as well as high-capacity SCSI 4mm, 8mm, and 1/4-inch drives. Other formats probably will follow in the future. You can install drivers for multiple devices, but only one will work at a time. Choose the target device from the Tape Backup program's Operations menu before performing the backup. This is similar to choosing a printer before you print a document.

Making a Tape Backup

This section walks you through the basics of making a tape backup. Note that the program has ample online help, so you might want to refer to it for additional details.

Backing Up Files

Here are the steps for backing up specific files:

1. Run the program by typing **ntbackup** in a command-prompt session or launching the tape backup program from the Start menu.

NOTE

To back up everyone's files, you must be logged on with Backup Operators Administrators privileges. No special privilege is required to back up files, directories, or volumes to which you normally have access.

2. Choose which files you want to back up. Double-click to select a drive from the Drives window, and then click a directory in the resulting directory window to see its files. Note the checkbox beside each drive, directory, and filename. When the checkbox is enabled, the item is set for backup.

NOTE

Check out the Tree and View menus for viewing options that are identical to those in File Manager.

If you want to select all the files on a disk, simply enable the drive's checkbox. When you select a whole drive or directory, note again that only files accessible to the backup operator will be backed up. If a file is hidden, or if the user doesn't have read permission for a file in the selected drive or directory, this file is skipped during the backup.

NOTE

Minicartridge tape must be formatted before you can use it. If your tape is new and unformatted, you must choose Operations | Format to format it. Formatting some tapes takes much longer than formatting a disk, so be prepared to wait. 4mm DAT drives take a few seconds to format because only the initial label is replaced and the rest is performed on-the-fly. In striking contrast, QIC 40/80 tapes can take hours to format.

3. Choose Operations | Backup to begin the backup process. The Backup dialog box appears, asking for more information.

   Fill in the dialog box as required; Table 11.1 lists the options you'll see here.

4. After setting the options, click OK. A Backup Status dialog box appears, reporting the status of the backup.

5. Click OK, and the backup process starts. If a tape runs out, you are prompted to insert another tape.

Table 11.1. Tape backup dialog options.

Setting	Function
Current Tape	Shows the name of the tape currently in the drive. If no name appears, check to see whether a tape is in the drive. A blank tape does not have a name.
Creation Date	Specifies the date of the first backup made on this tape, or the date when the first set was replaced (overwritten) by a new set.
Owner	Displays the name of the person who created the first backup.
Tape Name	Changes the name of the tape (see Current Tape). Not available if you're appending.

Setting	*Function*
Append	Adds the backup data, beginning at the end of current data on the tape.
Replace	Starts backing up the data at the beginning of the tape and overwrites what's already there.
Verify After Backup	Determines whether files are verified for accuracy after they're copied to tape. Enabling this option slows down the backup process, but I recommend that you do it. After all, an unreliable backup is not really of any use. If a file fails the verification, it is listed in the CORRUPT.LST file.
Restrict Access to Owner or Administrator	Not available if you're appending rather than replacing. If this option is enabled, it protects the tape's contents from being used by anyone other than thetape's creator, an administrator, or a backup operator. Also, if it's secured in this way, the tape must be used on the same computer on which it was created.
Hardware Compression	Enables hardware compression on supported SCSI tape drives.
Backup Registry	Gives you the choice to include a copy of the Registry files for the machine as part of the backup. You might want to enable this option to ensure that you have a backup of Registry settings, especially if you do a daily backup. Note that the Registry can't be backed up unless at least one file also is selected to be backed up.
Description	Specifies a description of up to 32 characters for a backup set. (A *set* is a set of files on a single drive that will be or has been backed up.)
Backup Type	Lets you choose a backup type for each set you have chosen to back up. Five backup types are available: *Normal* backs up all the selected items and marks the archive bits accordingly. *Copy* has the same effect as Normal but doesn't mark the archive bit. *Incremental* backs up selected files that have been modified since the last backup and marks the archive bit. *Differential* is the same as Incremental, but it doesn't mark the archive bit. *Daily* backs up only selected files that are changed on the day the backup is run. The archive bit is not marked.

continues

Table 11.1. continued

Setting	Function
Log File	Specifies the name of a text file log you want to have Backup create for you, in case you need to audit backup activity later on the system. Click the ellipsis (…) button to browse for a filename of an existing log.
Full Detail	Logs all backup events, including which drives, directories, and files were backed up.
Summary Only	Logs basic Backup events: when the tape was loaded, when a backup was made, and whether files fail to back up.
Don't Log	Prevents a log file from being created.

Restoring Data from a Tape

When you realize that you need to restore some data from a tape, follow these steps:

1. Locate the tape that you think has the latest version of the volume, directory, or file contents, and insert it into the tape drive. Note that, when you restore data, you're restoring a whole tape's contents, individual files you select, or a backup set (a set of directories or files that were backed up during the same session).

2. Run the Backup program from the Startup menu.

   Now things get a little tricky, because you might have to do a little work to locate the backup sets or files you want to find. Normally, when you insert a tape, only the first backup set appears. If you want to look at other backup sets on the tape, you have to look at the tape's catalog, go to the desired backup set, and view that set's catalog to select the desired files (or you can use the whole set). In other words, each tape has a catalog of sets, and each set has a catalog of directories and files.

3. To see the catalog of backup sets on a tape, double-click the tape's name in the Tapes window. After a while, the list of sets on the tape appears in the window. A question mark icon next to the set's name means that its catalog hasn't been loaded yet, so its contents aren't available for viewing.

   To see the catalog of the set's contents, double-click the set's icon. A list of all the directories and files in the set appears. A red X in a file or directory means that it's corrupted. A corrupted file or directory won't be restored.

4. Select the tape, backup set, or files to restore.

5. Click Restore. The Restore dialog box that appears has options similar to those described in the preceding numbered list. Note the following, however:

   ■ If you're restoring items from an NTFS partition to an NTFS partition, you can restore file permissions. Do this only if you're restoring to the same computer

Maintenance and Troubleshooting
CHAPTER 11

343

11

MAINTENANCE
AND TROUBLE-
SHOOTING

from which the files were backed up; NTFS file permissions from one computer won't work on another computer.

■ If you want to restore to a drive or directory other than the original source of the files, enter the alternative target in the appropriate box(es).

6. Click the Log Options button. See the preceding numbered list for descriptions.

7. Click OK. A status box appears, updating you on the progress. You might be prompted to confirm the replacement of files in case conflicts arise.

TIP

If the backup set you created uses two or more tapes, it is called a *family set*. Family sets have the set's catalog on the last tape rather than the first tape. Sometimes, when you use such a set, you're prompted to insert the last tape of the series. If the last tape is lost, or if you ran out of tapes when you were doing a backup and then canceled the process, the first tape won't have a concise catalog. You'll have to rebuild the catalog. The easiest way to do this is to run Backup from the command prompt with the command

```
ntbackup /missingtape
```

A new backup set catalog is created. Be aware that this process can take quite a while, because the tape must be scanned slowly.

NOTE

If a disk drive crash causes you to have to reformat and reinstall NT, you will want to restore the NT system files from your backups (if you have any). Check the README file under "Restoring Data after Reformatting the System Volume" for details.

Using the Event Viewer

Many internal system occurrences trigger the display of error message boxes while NT is running. If a user tries to access protected files or remove a printer over which he doesn't have control, for example, a message usually appears.

Because of NT's intelligent internal security design, many other subtler events internal to NT are equally well noted by the operating system, but they're not directly reported. Events such as applications running, drivers loading, or files being copied between directories are common examples. Such events typically are not reported in message boxes. These events are stored in a log available for later examination by a system administrator, though. Many events are stored in the log by default. Other events, as earlier chapters discussed, are optional. You can set these optional events in My Computer, Print Folders, and User Manager.

NT generates three separate logs (files): the Security Log, the Application Log, and the System Log. The Security Log records events that might affect system security, such as logging on and off. The Application Log is used only by applications that know about it and are coded to report to it. An application that can't find a support file or that runs out of disk space, for example, might report an error in the Application Log. The System Log contains numerous entries for system events, such as bootup, shutdown, loading drivers, and errors with hardware conflicts (such as conflicts between ports, CD-ROMs, SCSI cards, or sound cards).

Event Viewer is the application that displays each of the log files. Aside from simply displaying a log file, the Event Viewer also lets you do the following:

- Apply sorting, searching, and filtering that makes it easier to look for specific events
- Control settings that affect future log entries, such as maximum log size and when old entries should be deleted
- Clear all log entries to start a log from scratch
- Archive logs on disk for later examination and load those files when needed

> **NOTE**
>
> Only a user with Administrator privileges can work with the Security Log. Other users can view the Application and System Logs, however.

Working with Event Viewer Logs

To use the Event Viewer to open the three available logs and more easily view specific events, follow these steps:

1. Run the Event Viewer program from the Administrative Tools group. When you run it, the basic Event Viewer window appears with the System Log loaded by default; Figure 11.8 displays a typical example.

> **NOTE**
>
> The first time you run Event Viewer, the System Log is the default log. After that, the last log you view will be the default log.

2. Choose the log you want to view by choosing System, Security, or Application from the Log menu.

FIGURE 11.8.

Using the Event Viewer to display the System Log of the local computer.

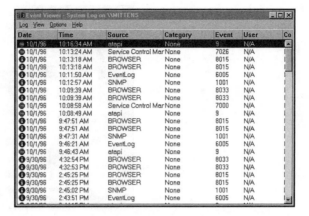

3. By default, the local computer's log is displayed. If you want to examine a networked computer's log, choose Log | Computer and use the Browse box to choose the workstation or server log you want to view from the Log window that appears.

   Normally, the list is sorted with the most recent events at the top of the list. You can reverse this order by choosing View | Oldest First.

> **TIP**
>
> Changes to the log that occur while you're examining it aren't always immediately reflected. Press F5 to update the log if you suspect that some system activity has occurred while you've been running the program.

4. Filter out any events that you don't want to wade through. You can show events that occurred only during certain times of the day, events pertaining to a specific user or event ID, or certain event types (such as errors or warnings). Choose View | Filter and fill in the Filter dialog box. (The options are explained in "Filtering Events," later in this chapter.)

5. If you want to search for a specific event, choose View | Find and enter the relevant information in the Find dialog box.

6. To see more information about an event, double-click it. An Event Detail dialog box appears, listing details about that event. (Figure 11.9 shows an example.) Details of your Security Log won't make much sense if you're not a programmer. Even then, the messages are cryptic. The System and Application Logs offer more in the way of understandable English. Most useful is information about drivers failing to load (often leading you to IRQ and port-conflict resolutions).

FIGURE 11.9.

*Viewing details of
an event.*

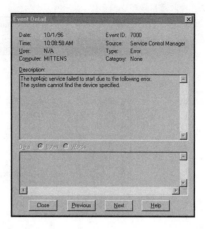

Essentially, each log file consists of a database with eight fields, as listed in Table 11.2.

Table 11.2. Log file fields.

Field	Displays
Date	The date the event was logged (according to the system clock). This is another reason to ensure that the workstation or server internal clock is set correctly.
Time	The time the event occurred. Note that, if it's necessary, you can synchronize all workstation clocks by using a command that pulls the time from the server machine for use in the log and other activities. Add the line **net time *server* /set** to the startup file for the machine, replacing the word *server* with the server's name. You can even include this line in the logon script for the user (see "Adding a New Account" in Chapter 9).
User	The name of a user related to a certain event. A user might be using the application that logs an error or other event to the Application Log, for example. This is useful particularly for tracking down attempted security breaches.
Computer	The computer where an event happened. Of course, this almost never changes. The only time it is different is if you export the log data into a comma-delimited format, merge it with exported data from other logs, and then read it back into the Event Viewer. In this case, you might need to see which computer generated which entries. (You can export logs by choosing Log | Save As.)

Maintenance and Troubleshooting

CHAPTER 11

347

11

MAINTENANCE
AND TROUBLE-
SHOOTING

Field	Displays
EventID	An event number assigned to the event, based on a coding system designed by Microsoft. Event numbers help technical-support people figure out what's wrong with an errant system.
Source	The name of the application software or device driver that reported the problem to NT, which then logged it.
Type	The type of event. There are five kinds of events (see Table 11.3); they appear in the left margin of the Event Viewer window.
Category	The classification under which this event falls. Each of the three logs has different categories of events.

Table 11.3 lists the icons displayed in the Event Viewer.

Table 11.3. Event Viewer icons.

Icon	Type	Indicates
Stop sign	Error	Serious trouble of some sort, such as the device driver not loading, IRQ or other hardware conflicts, missing network cards, and so on.
Exclamation Mark	Warning	Less serious trouble, but worthy of attention soon, such as being low on hard-disk space (which can bring down the system).
i sign	Information	Typically, successful operations achieved by applications.
Key	Success Audit	The success of a procedure. If you chose to audit successful operations from Print Folder or File Manager's Security menu, for example, a successful attachment to a shared printer or a successful drive connection by another workstation is reported as a success audit.
Padlock	Failure Audit	The failure of a procedure. Failures typically occur because the user making the attempt doesn't have the correct privileges.

Filtering Events

As mentioned in the preceding section, you can exclude all but the events you're interested in examining. When logs get quite large, or if your server supports a high density of workstation activity, this might be the most effective technique for ferreting out what you need to examine. You can access the Filter dialog box by choosing View | Filter Events. (See Figure 11.10.)

FIGURE 11.10.
The Filter dialog box.

See Tables 11.2 and 11.3 for descriptions of the options in this box. It's worth noting that, just as in File Manager, a filter remains in force until it's reset. Don't be alarmed if all your entries suddenly seem to have disappeared; they're probably just being filtered. Check the Event Viewer's title bar. You will see Event Viewer—Filtered if a filter is active. Also, if you choose Options | Save Settings on Exit, the filter will be activated the next time you run the program.

Setting Logging Options

You can use the Options menu to stipulate a few settings that affect how log entries are recorded. These settings are most useful in managing the size of your logs so that they don't eat up too much disk space. So many loggable events exist that even a typical day on a busy network server could produce far larger log files than you would want to wade through, or to which you'd want to devote that much disk space.

To view or change options settings, choose Log | Log Settings. The Event Log Settings dialog box appears, as shown in Figure 11.11.

FIGURE 11.11.
Altering or viewing log settings.

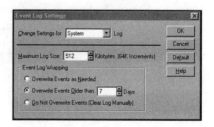

The default log settings shown in Figure 11.11 suffice for most systems. Table 11.4 lists some changes you can make.

Table 11.4. Event Log settings.

Setting	Function
Change Settings for	Specifies one of the three logs for which you want to alter settings.
Maximum Log Size	Declares the largest size of the log file (before old events are overwritten or entries cease to be written to the log).
Overwrite Events as Needed	Specifies that, when the log fills up, a new event takes the place of the oldest preexisting log entry.
Overwrite Events Older than	Specifies that new entries replace old events only after the number of days you specify here.
Do Not Overwrite Events	Prevents events from being overwritten (and therefore lost). The selected log might fill up if you enable this setting. If so, you have to choose Log | Clear All Events to make room for new entries.

Using Archived Log Files

A final option in the Event Viewer lets you create archives of log files and reload those files for later examination. As a rule, archiving log files isn't of much use unless you're running a very secure operation in which extensive background records of system or network use are mandated by the government or the corporation where you work. Most likely, in such a secure operation, you'll be performing regular tape backups or other forms of backup (which might include backups of the log files anyway), and this regimen might meet your security requirements, depending on your tape-rotation scheme. If it doesn't, you'll want to archive your event logs. It's a relatively simple process.

TIP

One case to be made for archiving is this: Logs can be useful in isolating network or machine failures. By keeping copies of past logs, you have something to compare with current versions that list new failures. By comparing logs, you perhaps can notice how and when the errors began to accumulate. Generally, a network failure starts as a simple error and then increases in frequency until a catastrophic failure occurs. Old logs can help here.

NOTE

The file created by the archiving process isn't affected by any filtering active at the time. All events in the log are written to the archive file.

To create an archive of a log file, follow these steps:

1. View the log you want to archive. Run the Event Viewer and open the Security, Application, or System Log. Only the log that's showing will be archived.

2. Choose Log | Save As. The Save As dialog box appears.

3. Choose the drive and directory in which you want to place the archive, and give your file a name.

4. The standard extension for log archives is .EVT. At the bottom of the dialog box, you have the option of choosing an alternative format for the file. You can save the file as an ASCII text file or as a comma-delimited text file for use by a database or spreadsheet program that can import that format. (*Comma-delimited* format separates columns with commas instead of tabs or spaces. Both text file formats omit nontextual, binary information from the event.) By default, both alternative formats are given the .TXT extension.

5. Click OK.

NOTE

After you click OK, the log is archived, but the current log isn't cleared. Its contents are unaffected. If your log was full, you'll have to clear it manually.

To recall an archived log for later examination, follow these steps:

1. Run the Event Viewer.

2. Choose Log | Open. The Open Log dialog box appears.

3. Specify the file. Be sure to specify the type of file in the File Type section before actually opening the file. This setting determines how the Event Viewer displays event detail data. Click OK and the log is opened for you.

Repairing a Crashed System

You can repair a nonfunctional NT system in several ways. You should consider the following approaches, in this order:

■ Alter system settings from dialog boxes if you still can run NT.

11

■ Revert to the Last Known Good configuration if NT won't start but recently was running before you made changes in the last session.

■ Resort to the NT Emergency Repair Disk to attempt an NT recovery.

■ Install another copy of NT on the system and boot it. Then use the NT Backup program to perform a restoration of the last system backup you made. This procedure lets you restore all the security and administration settings from the previous installation rather than starting from scratch. Then delete the temporary NT installation.

■ Reinstall NT from scratch.

NOTE

Dealing with crashed applications (rather than the operating system itself) is covered in the next section, "Using the NT Emergency Repair Disk."

Windows NT is a complex animal. Aside from the stringent physical requirements NT places on your hardware (disk space, CPU speed, and RAM), NT's complexity can tax your system. NT's many features offer the PC user a very rich mix. As with any software application, however, NT's complexity also can lead to problems.

Part of the original design plan for NT was for it to be less error-prone than DOS-based Windows, and in some important respects, Microsoft succeeded in its goal. NT certainly is less prone to catastrophic crashing, for example. NT also is good at detecting system failures, logging errors in files for later examination, and, in many cases, recovering on-the-fly—for example, from a downed hard disk, a bad sector, or even a power outage (with the aid of a UPS, of course).

Still, serious problems might crop up from time to time. A system you work with might refuse to start, for example, or it might become so bungled from mismanagement that reinstalling NT seems a less daunting task than sorting out all the user accounts and profiles. Or perhaps you've installed new hardware and made changes to the system as you thought appropriate, but NT just won't start. In any case, you might want to consider some of the following troubleshooting points in such circumstances. I suggest that you read them all before deciding which approach to take. Consider reinstalling NT as a last resort. Not only does a total reinstallation take time, but you'll lose a great deal of user account information and preference settings in the process. Consider these possible solutions:

■ Try simply rebooting.

■ Try logging on as a different user. The problem might lie in the user's profile or Registry settings. If you can log on as an administrator, try adjusting the defective user settings with User Manager or other accessories.

■ Run the Control Panel and make sure that the Workstation and Server services are running properly (refer to Chapter 8). These two services are required for all users and for basic NT functionality.

■ If NT booted fine the last time but won't boot now, try the Last Known Good Configuration trick. Do a cold reboot. When you see the words OS Loader, press the spacebar. You then can choose one of these options:

Current Startup Configuration

Last Known Good Configuration

■ Choose Last Known Good Configuration. NT always keeps two sets of configuration information on disk: the current one and the last one it perceived as being functional—at least functional enough to let you interact with the screen and with NT. Note that NT overwrites the Current setup when you revert to the Last Known Good setup. Also, of course, if you've changed your hardware (upgraded the video card, hard-disk controller type, and so on) since NT stored the Last Known Good Configuration setup, and then you revert to Last Known Good Configuration, the system still might not work because NT tries to use the old drivers with the new hardware! You might have to reinstall the old hardware and then invoke the Last Known Good Configuration option. After you're up and running again, try reinstalling the new drivers (through NT Setup, the Control Panel, an installation program, and so on), power down, install the new hardware, and power up. Don't overlook the possibility that the software driver you're trying to install isn't correct for the new hardware.

Using the NT Emergency Repair Disk

If none of the options in the preceding section is successful in solving your problem of a crashed system, the next approach is to use the Emergency Repair Disk you created at installation time. Follow these steps:

1. Insert the same NT installation disk you used to set up the system in the first place. If you used WINNT.EXE for installation (in other words, if you installed over the network), you should have another set of disks that WINNT made at that time for just this purpose—unless you performed a floppyless installation, in which case you should get the original setup disks from the system administrator. In any case, insert the proper disk and reboot.

NOTE

If you installed across the network with WINNT, this procedure has limited usefulness. This is because, among other things, the Emergency Repair procedure compares the system files with the source files. Unless you have access to the installation floppy disks or a portable CD-ROM drive, this part of the process won't work. This is the main reason why I advised you in Chapter 7 to set up network workstations with a local CD-ROM or floppy disks.

Maintenance and Troubleshooting

CHAPTER 11

353

11

MAINTENANCE
AND TROUBLE-
SHOOTING

2. A text screen appears, allowing you to do a complete installation or just to attempt repairs. If you're having some trouble with NT options that might not require a complete reinstallation, you might consider the second approach.

   If you choose to repair the current installation (by pressing R), you have the option of using your Emergency Repair Disk or the repair information stored on the local hard disk. Then the Repair program offers you the following options, which might be effective in repairing the damage:

   - Check the boot disk for a corrupted boot track. If the boot track is corrupted, or if the boot partition accidentally was reassigned with the Disk Administrator program, the program reassigns the partition using the configuration stored on the floppy disk.

   - Check the boot hard disk and the disk containing the system files for broken links (use CHKDSK).

   - Check the system directory to make sure that all the necessary system files are present and okay. If a corrupted file is detected, it's replaced. (You are prompted to insert a disk containing the needed file.) If you've deleted some NT components since your last repair information update (wallpapers, fonts, games, and so on), these unfortunately are re-added to your system directory. You'll have to delete them manually.

   - Check the Configuration Registry for errors. If errors are detected, you can replace the Registry with the Registry file that was stored on the Emergency Repair Disk.

   CAUTION

   Replacing the Configuration Registry effectively wipes out the security and user account settings, and probably some application initialization (.INI) settings for the workstation made since you installed NT. This is one important reason to be certain that the Repair Disk Utility (RDISK.EXE) is used regularly to update the repair information.

   - As a final measure, the Repair program removes security blockages from the NT system files (only if they're stored on an NTFS directory) to make sure NT can access its own system files. It's possible that you or someone accidentally restricted permissions on the files to prevent even NT from reading them; this prevents NT from running.

3. If you go ahead with repairs, you see a screen with various options. Follow the prompts. You're prompted to insert the Emergency Repair Disk into drive A and, if needed, NT disks along the way.

NOTE

If you don't have enough space on your hard disk, the repair program warns you after doing a media check. You have to eliminate some files and try again. If you can't even boot NT, you're stuck. You have to boot from a DOS disk in the floppy drive, or from another operating system on the hard disk (for example, DOS or OS/2) if you have two systems on the disk. You might be able to continue to the next screen anyway, but you will probably see an error message later saying that the repair couldn't be completed.

If the repair does bomb, you could end up with two or more Windows NT items in the Boot Loader menu. This also could happen after a reinstallation. One or more of these items might not work. At the least, they're redundant. You can edit the Boot Loader startup choices by editing BOOT.INI with a text editor and eliminating the redundant line(s), as described in "Booting Another Operating System," earlier in this chapter.

CAUTION

Often, a repair replaces the disk-partition information as set in Disk Administrator and as detected by NT when you first installed. If you have changed your disk partition setup by adding or deleting partitions or hard disks, or by converting partitions to another file format, you'll want to keep a copy of that information on a floppy disk for use after the repair or reinstallation. Make sure that you haven't caused the problem in the first place by reassigning the boot partition to a partition that doesn't contain the NT boot tracks. Recovering such a setup only causes the NT bootup failure to recur. See Chapter 9 for more information about saving partition setups.

4. After performing the options you select, such as running CHKDSK and checking the validity of the boot and system files (which easily can take about 10 minutes), the program asks which major items you want restored from the Repair Disk's copy of the Configuration Registry:

    System

    Security

    SAM

    Default

    Software

> **CAUTION**
>
> As the message warns, restoring a configuration file is a last resort, because existing configuration information will be trashed.

Each item has a Help screen. Press F1 to read about each one before opting to replace any or all of them. If you don't enable any item's checkbox, you still can complete the repair and system validation by pressing Enter.

5. Reboot. NT should come up, at least in some form. If you replaced many files, you need to check the user profiles, accounts, disk partitions, security and auditing settings, program groups, and so on. If you opted not to change too much but just to verify the disk media, system files, and boot track, NT should look pretty much the way it did before it bombed.

Reinstalling NT from Scratch

If you decide that you just can't cope with the old copy of NT, run Setup again and choose the directory where you want to install the new copy of NT. You'll be told that a copy of NT exists, which is especially likely if you notice that you're short on disk space, because NT installations are so large. It's not likely that you'll want to install two copies of NT on the same drive. Setup therefore suggests that you remove one of the NT installations and indicates where they are—in C:\WINDOWS, for example.

> **NOTE**
>
> If the \WINNT\SETUP.LOG file has been deleted, NT won't be able to remove the previous version and/or files. SETUP.LOG contains the list of replaceable files.

You're reassured that removing the existing NT installation won't jeopardize your Windows 95 installation. This is because only the NT-related files will be wiped out (Setup has a large internal database listing its own files). Any files with the same names as earlier Windows files, such as WINFILE.EXE, reside in the \SYSTEM32 directory to prevent collisions. You're asked to confirm that you want the files removed. Removal takes some time (about five minutes), because there are so many files. You're then told how much disk space was freed (typically, about 45M).

Windows NT System Administration

If, after the files are deleted, there still isn't about 90M of free space, you can reboot and delete some files or choose a new path. If you choose a new path (for example, a different disk drive or partition), you're presented with a list of the detected partitions and the available space on each partition. You have a choice of reformatting the partition in a different file format (NTFS or FAT) or leaving it as is. Typically, you'll leave it as is.

Follow the installation instructions, and reboot the computer when prompted.

> **TIP**
>
> If you lose the Boot Loader menu and the computer boots right into NT instead of giving you the choice of NT or the preexisting operating system, you have to run the Control Panel's System applet and make settings there. You also might have to examine or modify the BOOT.INI file stored in the root of the boot disk. The alternative operating system is stored in the file BOOTSEC.DOS (even if it's OS/2 and not DOS), typically in the root of the boot drive. NT itself always gets the real boot sector of your boot disk. The OS Loader and BOOT.INI enable you to branch to BOOTSEC.DOS to load the alternative operating system.

Dealing with Crashed Applications

If you're running a potpourri of Win16 applications, you'll encounter unexpected or erratic behavior from time to time. Contrary to bad press, NT generally is not at fault; instead, the application developers are to blame. Many developers don't follow the Microsoft guidelines for developing applications. Instead, to maximize performance, they use undocumented APIs or nonstandard coding methods.

When your system dies due to such a runaway 16-bit application, you see a dialog box. If you choose Ignore, the application might continue to run. Save your work, if possible, and then close the application. If the program doesn't let you run more than one copy of it, when you try to run the program again, you get a message to that effect. The internals of NT don't thoroughly close out the application, so when you try to rerun the application, the application thinks that one instance of itself still is running, even though the Task List doesn't show it. You should log off and then log on.

Sometimes, when a WOW application crashes and you click Ignore, the Task List doesn't indicate that it's running anymore, but the application thinks that it is. You can't run it again. You might think that shutting down all visible WOW applications would allow you to start from scratch by having NT reload the WOW subsystem, but this doesn't always work. You might have to actually restart NT. Oddly enough, you might be able to run other WOW applications just fine, even with the crashed or invisible application apparently still in memory.

TIP

If you have enough paging file space, you might want to consider running your 16-bit applications in separate memory spaces. This method prevents one 16-bit application from pulling down all 16-bit applications.

Running DOS and Windows 3.x Applications

As you know, in most cases, Windows NT will run DOS and Windows applications with little configuration changes necessary. Changes you make to .INI files associated with the programs when running them in other Windows products (such as 3.1 or Windows for Workgroups) carry over and are used in NT. The only real adaptation you have to make with most Windows 3.x and DOS products is simply to expect them to run slower, and to realize that this is the price of security and robustness.

When running non–32-bit programs under NT, remember the cardinal rule: If the program accesses hardware directly, it probably won't run under NT. Windows NT traps the hardware access, displays a dialog box, and probably kills the program. The exception to this is when an NT device driver has been written to support such access. For example, NT includes some video device drivers that support MS-DOS applications that directly access the video hardware. But even these don't work in all video modes or with all programs that directly access video, such as all DOS-based games. Certainly, any program that attempts to access the hard disk will fail.

Also, remember that all Windows 3.x programs run in one *virtual DOS machine* (VDM)—this is the default; you can change this in the application's Property Setting dialog box)—and if one program bombs, it can (but doesn't always) pull down other Windows 3.x programs that are running. DOS programs, on the other hand, each run in separate VDMs; if one program crashes, it doesn't pull down others.

NOTE

It wouldn't make much sense for this book to cover known bugs on existing programs, because vendors constantly update their software. Since the release of NT, many software developers have been busy updating their 3.1 applications to work with NT and, of course, Windows 95. Anything printed here likely would be out of date by the time you read this. Therefore, you should read the README.WRI file for details on specific applications.

This section includes some general notes about running non-NT applications—specifically DOS and Windows 3.1 applications, which are the bulk of applications that are run under NT.

continues

> *continued*
>
> See Chapter 8 for notes about creating PIFs for your DOS applications. See the following section for a discussion of tips and tricks that pertain to running memory-resident applications and specific DOS and Windows applications.

Dealing with Windows 3.x Program Errors

You might already have had a few cases of Windows 3.1 and Windows 95 programs bombing under NT. In general, NT is very stable. Some Windows programs aren't all that happy with NT, though. As mentioned in Chapter 3, "Working with Windows NT," just as Windows has some quirks (such as running out of resources), you might have to experiment with NT a bit to locate its quirks. Although Microsoft states that most Windows applications that don't access hardware should run just fine, this isn't actually the case. I've had a number of programs, especially Windows communications programs, behave unacceptably one day but run just fine another day. Clearly, the program mix loaded at the time has something to do with this effect; in my case, loading WinCIM or WinCIS (communications packages used with CompuServe) without loading PC-Kwik's Toolbox program seemed to clear things up.

TIP

You should use only communications programs that support dual-ended data flow control. Otherwise, data might be lost or the program might hang. Most protocols (such as Kermit, XMODEM, and CompuServe B+) use flow control. Flow control also is available for YMODEM-g and ZMODEM. Plain ASCII transferring routines often do not use flow control.

When NT traps a program error, a dialog box appears, reporting the offending error and offering several choices—none of which is very useful to the end-user. You can cancel the program, generate a Dr. Watson Error Log for dispatch to Microsoft or a programmer, or click Ignore and continue with the program. Clicking Ignore is supposed to allow you to save your work and exit the program gracefully; with some programs, though, none of the options actually allows you to do so. In reality, you can save your work if (and this is a big IF) the application hasn't corrupted its internal memory management. If the program becomes very unstable and you continue to try to use it, you probably can kiss your work goodbye. But, as in Windows 3.x, sometimes the application restores to a known good state and allows you to save your work.

With some programs, some invisible internal stack continues to inform NT that the program is still alive. The application's name might or might not show up in the Task List, but even if it does, clicking the End Task button in Task List doesn't always clear the application from the

Maintenance and Troubleshooting
CHAPTER 11
359

11

MAINTENANCE
AND TROUBLE-
SHOOTING

Windows 3.*x* subsystem. If you're trying to rerun a program that allows only one instance of itself in memory at one time, you might be stuck, because terminating the program isn't completely successful. When you try to run the program again, you might see a message from the application that says You can only run one copy of *the program* at a time. Sometimes, I've found that I have to log off (or possibly even shut down NT), reboot, and then try the application again. As I mentioned earlier, this is one way to clear the WOW subsystem. The other way is with the PVIEW.EXE program, which kills the NTVDM session. Closing all Windows 3.*x* applications and then running one application in hopes of launching a new WOW subsystem doesn't seem to help. Also, no Control Panel applet allows you to terminate and restart the WOW environment.

With a little experimentation, you soon will discover which Windows 3.*x* programs are finicky under NT. The real causes of these bugs will take a while to iron out, but you might as well relax and let the programmers do it. Improvements continually are being made in the compatibility arena. If you find major problems, you should ask the application's manufacturer for possible fixes, updates, or workarounds.

As a final note, installation routines for Windows 3.1 applications might occasionally bomb when run under NT. Microsoft claims that this is due to NT's "more stringent" floppy-disk and hard-disk formatting rules. The installation programs might work fine under DOS or Windows. One fix is to boot Windows 3.*x* (or DOS, if that will work) and install under one of those environments. If you don't have DOS or Windows 3.1 on your machine, find a machine that does. Format some blank disks on your NT machine using File Manager or the command prompt. On the other machine, boot DOS and use XCOPY to copy your original application installation disks' files onto the new blank disks. Then rerun the installation on the NT machine.

One of NT's great features is that system resources no longer are limited. Also, with the amount of memory you probably will install in NT systems and the dynamic use of hard-disk virtual space NT is capable of, memory shortages might be less common. So, you might wonder what's going on when you get an out of memory or out of resources message from a Windows 3.*x* application under NT.

To fix the problem, run Print Folder and specifically set an existing printer (create one if necessary) as the default printer. Also, you might try choosing this new default printer from the application's Print Setup dialog box, if it has one.

Dealing with DOS Problems

The DOS emulator in Windows NT is pretty reliable. Again, don't forget that, unless they're supported by device drivers that allow such access, any programs that attempt to directly access hardware will bomb. Therefore, DOS applications supplied with sound cards, communications programs, or anything else that circumvents standard DOS systems calls will display an NT-generated dialog box that announces an error.

Handling Mouse-Pointer Conflicts

One particular conflict occurs when you try to share the mouse. The command-prompt window does supply mouse capability to DOS programs that request it. Although NT usually surrenders the mouse cursor to such applications gracefully, sometimes a conflict occurs. To handle such conflicts, follow these steps:

1. Resize or minimize the application so it doesn't take up the full screen.

2. Open the application's Control menu by using the mouse or by pressing Ctrl+Spacebar.

3. Choose Hide Mouse Pointer. Now the pointer is exclusively under the control of the DOS application.

4. To return the mouse to use by NT, open the Control menu again and choose Display Mouse Pointer.

Handling DOS Memory-Resident Programs

As you probably know, many DOS programs rely on or are themselves memory-resident or *terminate-and-stay-resident* (TSR) programs. Most DOS-based, remote-control programs (such as PC-Anywhere) load a memory-resident portion, for example. SideKick is the perennial example of a TSR.

The NT User's Guide is pretty confusing on the issue of how to run TSRs. This is partly because there are so many different ways to do it and so many caveats. Here's the gist, in plain English.

The easiest way to run a TSR is to run it just as you would from DOS. First, run a command-prompt session. In the resulting command-prompt window, run the TSR as usual. The program should pop up or otherwise work as expected. If you want to run another program in the same session (typically, one that works with the TSR), run that too by entering its name at the command prompt. Note that the TSR is available only in the current window—not in every command-prompt window that you open from NT.

If you want to easily load a TSR and a DOS application in the same window at once, just follow these steps:

1. Create a batch file, including the lines necessary to run both programs.

   The following code loads a thesaurus program that I use, and then it loads PC-Write on top of it:

   ```
   thes ed
   ```

2. Save the batch file and create an icon for it in Program Manager.

3. Run the two programs simply by double-clicking the icon.

So much for the simple approach. What if you want every command-prompt window to automatically have the same TSR loaded? You can do this, but be aware that each command-prompt window uses up that much more precious memory. To add the TSR to each command-prompt window you launch, follow these steps:

1. Edit the CONFIG.NT or AUTOEXEC.NT file (depending on how the TSR normally is loaded—typically, AUTOEXEC.NT is used) to include a line such as this:

   SK2

   Then save the file.

2. Check the System applet in the Control Panel to be sure that the startup files for command-prompt sessions actually match the names of the file(s) you edited.

TIP

If you need to set additional aspects of the DOS environment for a DOS application, such as reserving pop-up keys or requesting expanded memory, you have to create a PIF instead of just running the application with its usual name. You can use the same batch file or keyboard-command techniques explained earlier, but use the file's PIF instead; just cite the PIF's name in the batch file (for example, ED.PIF).

Additionally, you can set up the PIF to load a particular set of startup files (analogous to AUTOEXEC.BAT and CONFIG.SYS). Each PIF can stipulate its own set of startup files. Click Windows NT in the PIF Editor to edit the name of the file. The AUTOEXEC startup file can include the name of the TSR you want to run before the main application runs.

Finally, here's one caveat with respect to TSRs; they might cause your application to hang. Most pop-up TSRs (and even some standard programs) let you "shell out" to DOS to run DOS commands. For example, X-TREE has a command that brings up a DOS prompt. Or, you might pop up SideKick and then close its window. In both cases, the idea is for the DOS prompt to appear. NT meets your expectations by running the MS-DOS command interpreter COMMAND.COM when you shell out from an MS-DOS program. This is in contrast to what NT normally supplies as a command-line interpreter, which is the 32-bit program CMD.EXE. Using COMMAND.COM speeds up a TSR's response time, which is good. The downside of this arrangement is that you accidentally might try to run an unsupported type of program (such as an NT, POSIX, or OS/2 application) and cause COMMAND.COM, the TSR, or your MS-DOS application to hang. You can prevent this problem by being careful about which commands you enter in such a window, of course. But to be extra cautious, you can alter the CONFIG.NT file (or another startup file, if you've specified it in a PIF) by adding this line to the file:

dosonly

This allows only DOS programs to be run from the prompt.

Similarly, if you want the TSR or DOS application to shell out to NT's command interpreter so that you can use its extended commands, add the following line to the CONFIG.NT file (or to another startup file, if you've specified it in a PIF):

```
ntcmdprompt
```

This might prevent a pop-up program from appearing after you press its hot keys, though.

Solving General Printing Problems

Some of the solutions discussed here apply to problems other than those listed under the specific headings that follow. If you don't see your particular problem listed in one of those headings, check out the following points. These are the most common causes of printer problems:

■ Make sure that you installed the correct printer driver, port, and printer name when you created the printer in Print Folders.

■ Check the cable between your printer and your computer. Is it seated firmly? Are the little screws or clips that hold the connector secured?

■ Check the switch settings and the power to your printer. Is it really on? If it's a laser printer, did it print a startup page successfully? Try powering it down and then up again.

■ If you're using a docking station with a portable or other pass-through connection, check your parallel port settings. The Toshiba DeskStation IV, for example, requires the parallel port settings to be configured to output only instead of to the bidirectional default in order to print with an HP DeskJet 310.

Nothing Prints

If nothing at all prints, there might be a fast fix, because it means that something's really wrong. Here are some possibilities:

■ Make sure that the printer has paper.

■ Some printers have an online switch. Check for it.

■ Is there an error light or indicator to alert you to a problem with the printer? If so, check the manual to see what it means, and try to correct the problem. It could be a paper jam, a dead ribbon, a toner cartridge that needs replacing, or a font cartridge that needs to be plugged in.

■ Check the application from which you're trying to print. Is the correct printer selected from the application's Printer Setup dialog box? If the application doesn't have a Setup dialog box, it assumes that you want to use the default printer. Check Print Folders to make sure that the default printer is the one you're trying to print to. (See Chapter 4, "Printers" for more information.)

Maintenance and Troubleshooting

CHAPTER 11

363

11

MAINTENANCE
AND TROUBLE-
SHOOTING

■ Is the printer driver set up to print to the correct port? Check the Configure dialog box. (Again, see Chapter 4 for details.)

■ If the printer is connected to a serial port (COM1 through COM4), are the communications settings correct? They must be the same on both sides (printer/computer). For the computer, make settings by using the Ports applet from the Control Panel. For the printer, check internal switch or software settings.

■ Does the printer work with any application? Does it work outside of Windows? If it does, the problem is with your Windows setup.

■ Are you trying to print to a networked printer? If so, check that the printer is really currently shared. Your workstation might have connected to the printer when you booted, but the printer's workstation might have powered down since then or unshared the printer. The printer might have limited permissions, preventing use by others or limiting it to certain hours of the day.

An Indecipherable Mess Prints

Another common printing problem is the appearance of garbage, as this example shows:

```
!^&*(ghAU"YeW*%^#$!!
```

If garbage appears on your screen, consider the following items:

■ Severe garbage invariably results when a serial printer's communications settings are configured incorrectly (although other causes might be at work). Check the port settings from the Control Panel and the switches on the printer. Baud rate, stop and start bits, and parity must all be set identically for the printer and computer. Try running the printer at a slower baud rate. Note again that if a slower baud rate is used, both printer and COM port must be set identically.

■ If, on a serial printer, output is correct for a few lines or pages, but is followed by a lot of garbage, the flow control probably is incorrect. The printer is being overrun by data faster than it can print it. The garbage starts because data is being lost. Check the flow control for the printer's COM port by using the Ports applet in the Control Panel or use the Print Fodler's Properties dialog box. The Xon/Xoff method is software flow control. The Hardware setting uses voltages on specific wires in your cable to control handshaking. Your printer and Windows NT must use the same flow-control method.

■ Your serial printer cable may be wired incorrectly and therefore isn't relaying the handshaking information to the correct pin on the computer's serial port. Make sure that the cable is intended for use with an IBM PC and that your serial interface card is configured with the correct port and handshaking.

■ Try another cable. (A cable that's too long also can be the culprit.)

■ Try another printer driver that's similar, or, for simple printing, try the Generic/Text Only printer driver.

■ Turn your printer off and on again. Data might be left over in the buffer.

> **NOTE**
>
> A batch file or another command that ejects the current page often flushes the buffer.

■ If the printer has an emulation mode, is it in the correct mode? It might be set to emulate another type of printer. Some laser printers can emulate both PostScript and Hewlett-Packard printers, for example.

■ Try the printer's self test (if it has one). Maybe the printer is defective.

Incorrect Fonts Appear in the Printout

Sometimes, downloaded fonts or font cartridge fonts don't print correctly. Other times, even TrueType fonts won't appear correctly.

■ If you're using a cartridge, did you install the cartridge properly?

■ If you bought TrueType fonts or another brand of fonts, did you carefully follow the instructions supplied with the fonts? Fonts often have to be installed in the correct directory, and you must tell Windows NT where the fonts are located. Read the "Fonts" section in Chapter 8.

■ If the fonts are of the downloaded soft font variety, they're dumped from the computer into the printer. They'll be lost when the printer's power is turned off. You must download the fonts again if the power was turned off at any time after the fonts were downloaded.

■ Is the printer's RAM already full of fonts? Perhaps you downloaded more fonts than it can handle, so the last few fonts weren't actually installed. Use a utility program to determine which fonts were downloaded successfully.

Only a Portion of a Graphics Page Prints

If only a portion of a page prints when you're printing graphics, consider the following:

■ If your printer lets you add memory and it's likely that you've run into a memory limitation, you might have to install more memory. Typical laser printers have 3M or more of memory. This amount of memory easily can support extra fonts and full pages of graphics. If you do a lot of complex printing, it's worth the price.

■ Some laser or inkjet printers have limited internal RAM that prevents them from printing a whole page of graphics in the highest resolution. Select a lower resolution and try printing again.

■ Does the paper size selected in the printer's setup box match the paper you're using? Check this and adjust it if necessary.

Maintenance and Troubleshooting

CHAPTER 11

365

11

MAINTENANCE
AND TROUBLE-
SHOOTING

Using the NT Registry

The Registry is a database that contains information on system and application configuration. It replaces the multitude of .INI files used in previous versions of Windows. Some 16-bit Windows applications directly access .INI files, however, instead of relying on the services provided with Windows 3.*x* for this purpose. Therefore, Windows NT continues to support .INI file use for compatibility.

The Registry is divided into multiple sections, referred to as *hives*. To maintain hive integrity, modifications first are written to a backup of the current hive. Only after the system confirms that the changes have been written successfully to disk is the primary hive file modified. If a system crash occurs before the primary hive is modified, the system uses the alternative hive to update the primary hive. The files are stored in the *SystemRoot*\SYSTEM32\CONFIG directory, where *SystemRoot* is the directory where NT is installed. Table 11.5 lists the normal hives in a Windows NT system.

Table 11.5. The normal hives in a Windows NT system.

Hive	Located In	Files
SAM	HKEY_LOCAL_MACHINE	SAM, SAM.LOG
SECURITY	HKEY_LOCAL_MACHINE	SECURITY, SECURITY.LOG
SOFTWARE	HKEY_LOCAL_MACHINE	SOFTWARE, SOFTWARE.LOG
SYSTEM	HKEY_LOCAL_MACHINE	SYSTEM, SYSTEM.ALT
DEFAULT	HKEY_USERS	DEFAULT and DEFAULT.LOG
HKEY_CURRENT_USER	HKEY_USERS	USER###, USER###.LOG or ADMIN###, ADMIN###.LOG

A hive consists of keys, subkeys, and value entries stored in a hierarchical manner similar to directories, subdirectories, and files. Although .INI files can't contain nested entries as a hive can, the same basic relationship for section, entry, and value still exists. The WIN.INI file's [windows] section contains the run entry, for example, which lists the applications to be executed at Windows startup. This same value appears in the Registry in the HKEY_CURRENT_USER hive under the Software\Microsoft\Windows NT\Windows subkey for the run value entry. Consider the Registry subkey the .INI section and the .INI value the Registry value entry.

A Registry value entry is composed of three parts separated by colons: the name, the data type, and the actual data value. For the preceding example, the name is run, the data type is REG_SZ, and the data value is a null string. Therefore, the subkey Software\Microsoft\Windows NT\Windows would appear as run:REG_SZ:. Table 11.6 lists the data types for value entries.

Table 11.6. Data types for value entries.

Data Type	Description
REG_BINARY	An uninterpreted binary data field.
REG_DWORD	A 32-bit numeric field.
REG_EXPAND_SZ	A text string that contains an insertion string. This insertion string is expanded to its actual data representation before the string is used. For example, ComSpec:REG_EXPAND_SZ: %SystemRoot%\system32\cmd.exe.
REG_MULTI_SZ	A multiple null-terminated text-string field.
REG_SZ	A standard text string.

Using the Registry Editor

You can use the Registry Editor to directly edit the Registry hives on a local or remote computer. I find the Registry Editor to be so useful for system administration that, in every installation, I automatically install the application in Program Manager's Administrative Tools group for the Administrators account. The interface is very similar to that used in File Manager. Instead of directories, subdirectories, and files, though, the Registry Editor displays keys, subkeys, and value entries. This interface also includes the option to set permissions, audit, or take ownership of a Registry key.

> **CAUTION**
>
> Editing the Registry manually with the Registry Editor can be a dangerous task, because a miskeyed value might prevent Windows NT from loading. Whenever possible, use the Control Panel or other provided applications to modify the Registry.

Starting the Registry Editor

To start the Registry Editor, follow these steps:

1. From a console window, type **start regedt32.exe** and press Enter.
2. Double-click regedt32.exe, located in the SystemRoot\SYSTEM32 directory, or choose File | Run and enter **regedt32.exe**.

3. Create an application icon in your favorite group or choose Run and enter
   `regedt32.exe`.

> **TIP**
>
> If you're only interested in browsing the Registry, be sure to choose Option | Read Only Mode so that inadvertent modifications aren't recorded in the Registry.

Examining the Primary Registry Keys

When you launch the Registry Editor, five separate window panes, each containing a single root key, are displayed:

Key	Contains
HKEY_LOCAL_MACHINE	State information for the local computer system
HKEY_CLASSES_ROOT	OLE
HKEY_CURRENT_USER	Current user profile
HKEY_CURRENT_CONFIG	Current configuration information
HKEY_USERS	All loaded user profiles

Adding and Deleting Keys and Value Entries

To add a new Registry key, follow these steps:

1. Select the primary key in the left window pane where you want to add the new key as a subkey of the primary key.
2. Choose Edit | Add Key or press Ins. The Add Key dialog box appears.
3. Enter the name of the key in the Key Name field and leave the Class Name field blank; it is reserved for future use by Microsoft.
4. Click OK or press Enter. The new key then is displayed.

Follow these steps to remove a key:

1. Select the primary key in the left window pane where you want to add the new key as a subkey of the primary key.
2. Choose Edit | Delete or press Del. A message box appears, warning you that the key will be removed from the Registry and asking you to confirm the operation.
3. Click OK or press Enter. The key then is removed from the Registry.

To add a value entry, follow these steps:

1. Select the key in the left window pane where you want to add the new value entry.
2. Choose Edit | Add Value. The Add Value dialog box appears.
3. Enter the value name in the Value Name box and scroll through the list box to select a data type (for example, REG_SZ, REG_MULTI_SZ, REG_EXPAND_SZ, REG_BINARY, or REG_DWORD).
4. Click OK or press Enter. The Resource dialog box appears so that you can enter the initial value of the entry.
5. Enter the appropriate value and click OK or press Enter. The new value is displayed.

To edit a value entry, follow these steps:

1. Double-click the value entry in the right window pane, or select the value entry and press Enter. Alternatively, select the value entry and choose Edit | String, Edit | Multi String, Edit | Expand, Edit | Binary, or Edit | DWORD to display the Resource Edit dialog box.
2. Enter your changes in the dialog box and click OK or press Enter. The new value is displayed.

Saving and Restoring Registry Hives

Registry hives (a key, subkey, and value entries) can be saved and loaded to and from disk. I recommend that, before you make any changes to a hive, you save it first so that you can restore it if necessary.

To save a Registry hive, follow these steps:

1. Select the primary key in the left window pane.
2. Choose Registry | Save Key. The Save Key dialog box appears.
3. Select the drive and directory where the file is to be stored, and enter the name of the file in the File Name box.
4. Click OK or press Enter. The Registry hive then is saved for later use.

To restore a Registry hive, follow these steps:

1. Select the primary key in the left window pane.
2. Choose Registry | Restore or Registry | Restore Volatile. The Restore Key dialog box appears.

NOTE

The Restore Volatile option works exactly like the Restore option, except that the modifications remain in effect only until the computer is restarted.

3. Select the drive, directory, and filename to which the hive file will be restored.

> **NOTE**
>
> When you're restoring a key on a remote computer, drive C listed in the Drive box is the remote computer's drive C—not the local computer's drive C.

4. Click OK or press Enter. The new entries are displayed.

Accessing a Remote Registry

Follow these steps to access a remote computer's Registry:

1. Choose Registry | Select Computer. The Select Computer dialog box appears.
2. Enter the computer name in the Computer box, or select a computer name displayed in the Select Computer box.
3. Click OK or press Enter.

> **TIP**
>
> If the computer is on another domain, preface the computer name with the domain name—for example, WORK\SRV.

Using Registry Keys

Now that you've learned the concepts of the Registry database and Registry Editor, it's time to consider putting this knowledge to use. From a user standpoint, the interface to the Registry is the Control Panel applets or another application. An administrator, however, occasionally might need to delve deeper into the Registry to solve a problem. This section discusses a few of the more useful Registry keys that do not have a Control Panel interface and why an administrator might need to modify them.

Modifying the Windows NT Logon Process

Many corporations need to display a warning to unauthorized users to legally protect themselves from computer hackers. With a character-mode network client, the most commonly used method is to display a splash screen when the user signs onto the network. Windows NT and NT Server machines can accomplish the same task by displaying a dialog box with a custom caption and message with a single OK button to acknowledge a user's acceptance of the message. The Registry key HKEY_LOCAL_MACHINE\SOFTWARE\Microsoft \WindowsNT\CurrentVersion\Winlogon value entries include the following value entries:

LegalNoticeCaption: The caption to be displayed in the dialog box's title bar.

LegalNotice: The actual message to be displayed.

NOTE

To display a message, you must set the `LegalNoticeCaption` value entry to a non-null value.

If Windows NT or NT Server computer security is not an issue, you can automate the logon process. This bypasses the normally required logon dialog box at system startup. To accomplish this task, modify the following entries:

DefaultPassword: The user password to be used in the logon process.

NOTE

You must add this value manually by choosing Edit | Add Value from the Registry Editor. This value cannot be a null value.

DefaultUserName: The username to use in the logon process. By default, this is the current user.

AutoAdminLogon: To enable automatic logon, set this value to 1. To disable it, set it to 0. The default is 0.

Normally, the logon dialog box displays the Shutdown button on NT Workstations but not on NT Servers. You can modify this by editing this `Winlogon` entry:

ShutdownWithoutLogon: To enable the Shutdown button, set this value to 1. To disable it, set it to 0.

Locating .INI File Entries

If a Windows 3.x migration occurred during the Windows NT installation, or if an application is installed under Windows NT, the application's .INI file entries are located in the Registry key HKEY_LOCAL_MACHINE\SOFTWARE\Microsoft\WindowsNT\CurrentVersion\ IniFileMapping. Generally, these values are pointers to another key that contains the actual .INI entries. If you look for MSMAIL32.INI, for example, you will find the value entry `<noname>USR:Software\Microsoft\Mail` and the actual .INI entries in HKEY_CURRENT_ USER\Software\Microsoft\Mail. Normally, there is little reason to modify these settings directly. If the application fails to execute after a modification, however, you can modify or delete the settings manually in their entirety to reestablish the default settings.

Maintenance and Troubleshooting

Chapter 11

371

11

MAINTENANCE
AND TROUBLE-
SHOOTING

NOTE

Additional entries can contain the SYS: prefix, which directs the request to the HKEY_LOCAL_MACHINE\Software key.

Only applications that use the Registry APIs will create an entry. Applications that directly access the .INI file will continue to do so and will not use any entries under this key.

Modifying Setup-Specific Information

When Windows NT is installed initially, certain information is stored in the Registry and no longer is available to the user for modification. You might need to update some of this information throughout the life cycle of the installation, though. This information is located in the HKEY_LOCAL_MACHINE\SOFTWARE\Microsoft\Windows NT\CurrentVersion Registry key. Table 11.7 lists some of these entries.

Table 11.7. Entries in the HKEY_LOCAL_MACHINE\SOFTWARE\Microsoft\Windows NT\CurrentVersion Registry key.

Entry	Description
CSDVersion	The service pack version if the installation has been upgraded by using the Microsoft Service Pack.
CurrentBuild	The build number of the current installation.
CurrentType	The type of installation. Lists the uniprocessor or multiprocessor and whether the build is a free (nondebug) or checked (debug) installation.
CurrentVersion	The version number of the installed product.
RegisteredOrganization	Contains the registered organization of the software.
RegisteredOwner	Contains the registered owner of the software.
SourcePath	The default source path used during setup.
SystemRoot	The root directory where NT was installed.

NOTE

You can display the data in these first four entries by executing WINVER.EXE. This data shouldn't need to be modified, though. It's included for informational purposes only.

Configuring the WOW Subsystem

The HKEY_LOCAL_MACHINE\SYSTEM\CurrentControlSet\Control\WOW Registry key contains configuration information for the MS-DOS and Windows 3.*x*-compatible subsystem. Although you'll rarely have any need to modify these values, some unique software might benefit from a modification of these value entries:

LPT_timeout: Indicates the number of seconds that NT waits before reusing the port. If your MS-DOS or 16-bit Windows applications have garbled print jobs, increasing the default value of 15 seconds might solve the problem.

Size: Lists the default amount of memory to be allocated in megabytes for an MS-DOS application. The default value of 0 lets NT determine how much memory to give an application based on the current memory configuration.

Wowsize: This entry isn't used on Intel platforms, but it's used on RISC systems to determine the amount of memory in megabytes to be allocated for use by the WOW subsystem. For each megabyte specified, NT actually uses 1.25M. The additional .25M is not available to applications.

CAUTION

Setting Wowsize to less than 3 generally causes the application to fail when launched.

Summary

This chapter has covered a great number of maintenance and troubleshooting issues. Topics have ranged from the rather mundane (although never to be overlooked) chore of making backups to the elaborate—such as editing the Registry, troubleshooting networks, and dealing with crashed hard disks and applications. This chapter has a wealth of information—information compiled from a number of writers' and consultants' experience, and information that probably is difficult to absorb in a single reading. You might want to stick a bookmark at the beginning of this chapter and revisit it from time to time as problems pop up on your NT systems.

IN THIS PART

Networking Windows NT

An Overview of Windows NT Networking

IN THIS CHAPTER

CHAPTER 12

Networking is one of Windows NT's great strengths. A PC running NT can, without shells or other add-ons, act as a LAN workstation accessing data on file servers, as a server sharing data with the network community, and as a Remote Access Service (RAS) point, allowing you to dial in from home so you can use the data on your machine at the office. Throw in a few machines running Windows NT Server, and you can easily build a secure network with sophisticated domain-based naming.

Installing a LAN card driver into Windows NT automatically loads a group of other programs and drivers that handle jobs like carrying data across the network, making requests of file servers, and responding to requests from other workstations. Each of these programs includes instructions for Windows NT to use a specific protocol to handle each task.

A *protocol* is an agreed-upon way to do things. For example, the protocol for a telephone call requires you to dial a 7-digit or 11-digit number, then wait for the person at the other end to answer and say hello. If you don't follow the protocol—by dialing only 5 digits, for example— you can't make a call. Computer protocols work the same way. For a workstation to open a file on the file server, it must send the right kind of request.

Besides the default protocols automatically loaded when you start, Windows NT also includes support for protocols that might have advantages over your network's default protocols. To help you understand Windows NT protocols and choose the right combination for your network, this chapter briefly covers how LANs work.

Most books, including this one, use the ISO (International Standards Organization) open system interconnect (OSI) as a model to describe how communications networks work and as a comparison with other specific networks. The Computer Book Act of 1974 requires that any book discussing computer networking include a description of the OSI model or bear a warning label on its front cover, so I included the following section to avoid interfering with this book's fine cover art.

The OSI Model

The OSI model divides a computer network's (either LAN or WAN) processes into seven layers. The bottom (or physical) layer specifies the network's wire and other physical attributes, and the top (or application) layer defines how the network interacts with the user. The model calls for each layer to communicate just with the layers immediately above and below it; this allows each layer to be well-defined without getting out of control with "featuritis." Each layer's protocol is responsible for shielding the higher layers from knowing how the layers further down work.

Although the ISO has standardized protocols for each of the seven layers, most local area networks use older protocols that aren't OSI-compliant. The OSI model shown in Figure 12.1 is still useful for comparing these protocols.

FIGURE 12.1.
The OSI model defines seven layers of network communications.

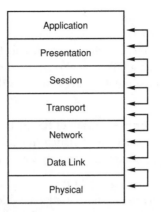

Application
Presentation
Session
Transport
Network
Data Link
Physical

One good way to remember how the OSI model works is to think of a message, a request for data, a response, or an e-mail message as a letter. This letter needs to be delivered to Aunt Matilda, who's waiting for it impatiently. The letter passes through several layers of handling, each of which puts the message inside a container: the envelope, the mail bag, the air freight container, and so forth. Similarly, each OSI layer adds a layer to the data it's sending and, as it receives a packet, removes a layer of wrapping and passes the data up.

The Physical Layer

The physical layer is responsible for sending data from one end of the cable to the other. A physical layer specification, such as 10Base-T, defines the network's tangible aspects, including the type of cable, the *topology* (how the cables are connected), and how many pins are in the connector and how they're used. Physical-layer protocols also define the cable voltages, the bit rate, and the encoding method.

The Data Link Layer

The data link layer packages the data bits from the physical layer into *data frames*—structured packets containing data. A frame is a group of data bits that includes network control information, such as addresses.

A data frame's structure changes for different types of networks. As shown in Figure 12.2, each frame has several fields that carry important data about this packet for the network.

FIGURE 12.2.
An example of a data frame in a data link layer.

Type	Source Address	Destination Address	Data	ECC

The *source address* is the address of the workstation that sent the frame; the *destination address* is the address of the workstation the packet is being sent to. The *frame type* is the type of data being carried in the frame, and the *data* is the data being transmitted over the network's physical connections. The data link layer also adds error-correcting code (ECC) information, typically a CRC (cyclical redundancy check) that lets the receiving station make sure the data was sent properly.

This layer provides error-free transfer of frames between computers over the physical layer. If a frame's CRC doesn't calculate to match the CRC in the packet, the packet is discarded so that the upper-layer protocols don't get data with errors.

The *media access and control (MAC)* sublayer is the upper half of the data link layer that handles how workstation addresses are formatted and which station has access to the network at any given time. You might hear a product described as a MAC layer bridge, which is a device that links two networks at the MAC layer.

The Network Layer

The network layer's primary job is to route data packets through the network, moving them from their source to their destination along the best route. To handle this task, the network layer adds a network address to the address used by the data link layer; think of the network address as a street name and the MAC layer address as a house number. The network layer also manages switching and packet congestion on the network.

The network layer bundles data frames into single packets that can be transmitted over the network, as shown in Figure 12.3. These packets, with their additional address and ECC information, are inserted into the data field of a data link layer frame. If packets are too large, the network layer protocol restructures them into smaller packets. On the destination computer, the network layer converts packets into their original structures.

Figure 12.3.
A network layer packet.

Type	Source Address	Destination Address	Source Net	Source Node	Dest. Net	Dest. Node	Data		ECC	ECC

Windows NT supports IPX and IP as network layer protocols. The default NetBEUI (NetBIOS extended user interface) protocol has some of the features of a network layer protocol, but it doesn't actually support routing.

The Transport Layer

The transport layer manages error recognition and recovery. If the ECC information in a packet indicates an error, or if a packet isn't acknowledged, the transport layer tries several times to deliver its message before reporting a transmission error. This layer ensures the delivery of messages originating at the application layer. Like the network layer, the transport layer collects data frames and assembles them into packets. On the destination computer, the layer reassembles the packets into their frame structure.

Windows NT supports TCP, UDP, and SPX as transport layer protocols. Again, NetBEUI has some (but not all) transport-layer protocol features.

The Session Layer

The session layer allows applications on different computers in a network to establish, use, and end a connection or session. This layer manages security measures and name recognition between computers.

The session layer synchronizes user tasks and manages the communication between processes. It regulates which computer transmits, when it transmits, and for how long. Functions like remote file and print services are usually considered to be session layer services.

Windows NT uses the server message block (SMB) protocol as its primary session layer protocol. SMB supplies message types for remote file and print services. By adding a NetWare requester, Windows NT also can use Novell's NetWare Core Protocol (NCP). Third parties, such as NetManage and Sun, also provide Network File System (NFS) support for Windows NT.

The Presentation Layer

The presentation layer determines how to exchange data between two computers. First, it translates the data sent from the source computer's application layer into an intermediary format. Next, on the destination computer, it translates this intermediary format message into something the destination computer's application layer can use. The presentation layer is also responsible for data encryption.

The Application Layer

The application layer is at the top of the OSI model; it supplies the means by which application processes can access network services. This layer directly supports user applications for e-mail, file transfers, and database access. Windows NT offers Mail, Schedule+, File Manager, and many other application layer services.

Using the OSI model as a framework for describing the network connections in your computer will help you understand the Windows NT protocols as you install them. These protocols are the "languages" Windows NT uses to communicate with other computers running the same protocols.

Windows NT's Network Architecture

Windows NT's networking functionality was designed from the ground up, unlike earlier PC operating systems, such as DOS and OS/2 1.*x*, that tacked on networking as an afterthought. Incorporating networking early on allowed Microsoft's programmers to make Windows NT's networking more efficient and elegant. To make Windows NT the platform of choice for networked applications, they built transparent file and print services into each Windows NT workstation and supplied a variety of powerful interprocess communications facilities to support client/server applications.

Microsoft also realized from its experience with OS/2 that users weren't going to just toss out all their current networking applications and software. Therefore, it used several technologies allowing Windows NT to support standard network protocols so that Windows NT workstations could communicate with existing networks. The layered architecture that Windows NT uses, shown in Figure 12.4, mirrors the OSI model quite well.

FIGURE 12.4.

Windows NT's networking architecture.

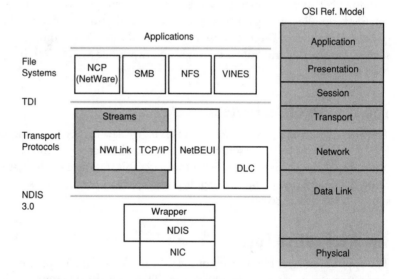

NDIS

The foundation of Windows NT's networking architecture is the NDIS (Network Device Interface Specification) 3.0 device driver. Early PC LANs used monolithic device drivers that not only interfaced with the LAN card but also carried out the network and transport layer protocols used by the LAN operating system. IBM's PC Network went so far as to implement NetBIOS in ROM.

The problem with this monolithic approach is that it allows a LAN card to use only a single network layer protocol. If you use Novell's IPX.COM to talk to your Ethernet card, you can send only IPX data through that card. If you want to also send TCP/IP (Transmission Control Protocol/Internet Protocol) data to your UNIX machine, you're out of luck.

By 1989, the industry realized that the monolithic driver approach was a technological dead end. Microsoft, in cooperation with 3Com, developed NDIS as a solution to this problem. Rather than create a single piece of software serving as both device driver for the LAN card and network layer protocol implementation, NDIS defines a data link layer interface so that multiple network layer protocols can access the same LAN card at the same time. (See Figure 12.5.)

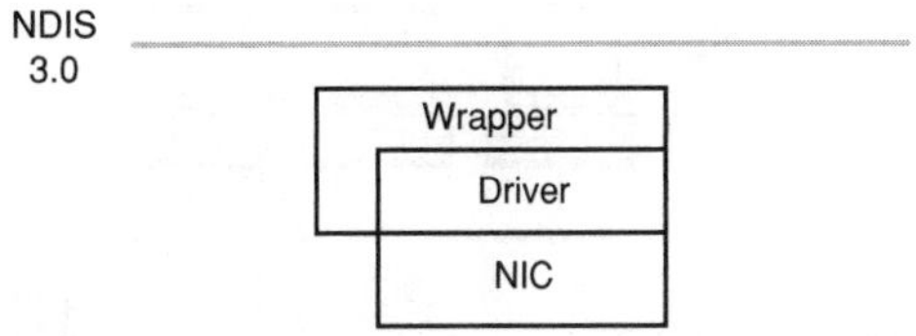

FIGURE 12.5.

The NDIS device driver allows multiple protocols to be used at the same time.

NDIS 3.0 conforms to the device driver standards established for Windows NT. It specifies a C-call interface; NDIS drivers have access to the helper routines and are 32-bit, portable, and multiprocessor safe. Windows NT 4 includes NDIS 3.1, which adds a few extra features.

Unlike previous NDIS implementations used in OS/2 and Windows for Workgroups, Windows NT doesn't use a protocol manager or PROTMAN module to link the components at each layer. Instead, the bindings (or relationships) between protocols are stored in the Registry, and a small piece of code, or *wrapper*, around the NDIS device driver supplies a uniform interface between protocol stack drivers and NDIS device drivers. The NDIS wrapper also contains supporting routines, which makes developing an NDIS driver easier.

In addition to the usual LAN systems, such as Ethernet and Token Ring, Windows NT also can use a serial port as a physical/data link layer protocol through the Remote Access Service. With RAS, users can dial into a Windows NT network and access data as though they were on a workstation connected to the network.

RAS is discussed in Chapter 17, "Internetworking: Remote Access Service and TCP/IP."

Multiple LAN Cards

One of the advantages of the NDIS approach is that it allows you to have multiple LAN cards in your system. (See Figure 12.6.) By adding a second, third, or even sixteenth LAN card to your file server, you can extend your network beyond the distance limitations of your LAN technology by running, for example, 100 meters of thin Ethernet cable from each of four LAN cards. Multiple LAN cards also let you support different LAN technologies for different users. Your CAD group, for example, can run FDDI (Fiber Distributed Data Interface) or some other high-performance network while the front office uses plain old Ethernet. Finally, you can provide greater bandwidth in and out of a system using conventional Ethernet or Token Ring cards by spreading the load over multiple cards. This can improve your network or server's performance.

The one thing Windows NT doesn't do for multiple LAN cards is forward data from one network to another. NetWare users are familiar with *internal routing,* in which a NetWare file server forwards traffic from one network to another. As a result, the users on all the workstations in Figure 12.6 can access Server 1, but users on the A1 through A3 and B1 through B3 workstations can't access data on Server 2 unless another bridge or router is added to the network.

FIGURE 12.6.

Windows NT supports multiple LAN cards.

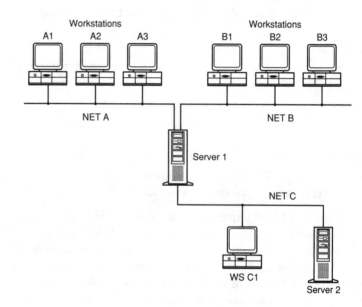

Transport Protocols

Even though it's confusing, network people often use the term *transport protocols* to describe not only OSI transport layer protocols but also their associated network layer protocols. These combinations of protocols are collectively called transport protocols because their responsibility is to transport data across the network. The higher layers relate more to specific applications than to just carrying data here and there. In the Windows NT architecture, these protocols are just above the NDIS wrapper, and they use it for access to the LAN hardware. (See Figure 12.7.)

FIGURE 12.7.

Transport protocols sit directly above the NDIS software and use it to access the network hardware devices.

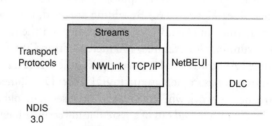

Windows NT ships with four sets of transport protocols. NBF, a simple protocol derived from NetBEUI, offers compatibility with existing LAN Manager, LAN Server, and MS-Net installations. TCP/IP is a popular routable protocol for wide area networks and communication with UNIX machines. NWLink is Microsoft's implementation of Novell's IPX/SPX protocols for communicating across NetWare networks and with NetWare file servers. Finally, DLC (data link control) gives you an interface for access to mainframes and printers attached to networks. NT Server also provides Apple's AppleTalk protocol stack as part of its Services for Macintosh.

NetBEUI

The NetBEUI protocol is automatically loaded and bound to your adapter card when you install your LAN card into Windows NT. It's a self-tuning protocol that doesn't use very much memory, and it's fast because it has little overhead, compared to data.

NetBEUI is a good choice for regional sales offices or other small networks. It's also used by Microsoft's LAN Manager and Windows for Workgroups. If you already run WFW or have LAN Manager, you can share those resources.

Although NetBEUI is fast for small networks, it's a bad choice for larger networks. Because NetBEUI uses your computer's name as its address, you can't use it effectively if you have several computers with the same name on your network. NetBEUI doesn't add a network address to your computer's name, so it can't be routed as a true network layer protocol can. This means that as your network grows, so does NetBEUI's overhead, because all messages that get broadcast by a station looking for the computer named Shlomo, for example, get forwarded across all your network links.

NetBEUI Isn't NetBIOS

When I talk about NetBEUI, it's important for you to understand that means the transport layer protocol, not the programming interface NetBIOS. Most people think of NetBEUI and NetBIOS as being one and the same because earlier implementations of NetBEUI on MS-DOS and OS/2 used the NetBIOS programming interface as part of the NetBEUI device driver.

Remember, the programming interface NetBIOS can be used in higher layer programs, such as Windows NT's file and print services, by protocols other than NetBEUI. Therefore, you can remove NetBEUI from your system and still take advantage of the higher layer services.

Data Link Control

The data link control (DLC) protocol is used primarily by IBM Token Ring networks. Strictly speaking, DLC isn't a transport protocol but a sophisticated data link layer protocol. Windows NT's file and print services don't use DLC, but NT offers DLC to allow connectivity to IBM mainframe computers. DLC can also be used to communicate with printers attached directly to the network, such as the HP LaserJet IIISi, instead of through a print server's parallel or serial port.

NWLink

NWLink, or NetWare Link, is Microsoft's implementation of Novell's IPX (internetwork packet exchange) network layer and SPX (sequenced packet exchange) transport layer protocols. These protocols were originally developed by Xerox as part of their XNS protocol suite.

NWLink also includes a NetBIOS interface, which Microsoft calls NWBlink, that allows your Windows NT systems to communicate over networks using Novell NetWare and routers.

Contrary to popular opinion, NWLink alone doesn't let you access data on a NetWare file server. For that, you must have a NetWare-compatible transport protocol and a NetWare requester. Connecting Windows NT to NetWare networks is discussed in more detail in Chapter 18, "Integrating Windows NT with Other Networks."

TCP/IP

TCP/IP actually refers to a whole suite of protocols first developed for the U.S. Department of Defense in the 1970s as part of the ARPAnet (now Internet) development project. TCP/IP is the most widely supported protocol suite in the world, partly because the Department of Defense required all its computers to support TCP/IP. Because these are the people who think $600 is a reasonable price for a hammer, no computer manufacturer wanted to write them off as a customer. TCP/IP is also the standard suite of protocols used by UNIX systems for their LAN and WAN applications.

Windows NT's TCP/IP support has two advantages for you, the user. First, TCP/IP is the protocol suite of choice for large networks linked by routers. It's efficient on wide area and complex networks and well supported by router manufacturers, WAN providers, and, of course, the Internet. Second, TCP/IP lets you connect easily to UNIX and other non-PC systems.

Not only do users benefit from Windows NT's TCP/IP support, but system administrators and network architects will also appreciate the Microsoft Dynamic Host Configuration Protocol (DHCP) and Windows Internet Name Service (WINS). These two services make it easier to manage large networks and are explained in more detail in Chapter 16, "Setting Up Trust Relationships in NT Server."

Streams

Windows NT's TCP/IP and NWLink use another multiple protocol support facility called Streams, derived from AT&T's UNIX; it's a popular method of implementing the TCP/IP protocol on UNIX-based systems. Instead of being a single device driver bound directly to the NDIS device driver, these protocol drivers reside "inside a wrapper." You can think of TCP/IP or NWLink as being surrounded by the Streams device driver. Calls to the TCP/IP or NWLink transport protocol driver must first go through the upper layer of the Streams device driver, then to the NDIS device driver through the lower end of the device driver.

Streams is a definite departure from the way protocol stacks were developed for MS-DOS and OS/2, and there are several reasons for using it. Streams makes it easier to port existing protocol stacks to Windows NT. It also encourages protocol stacks to be organized in a modular, stackable style, thus moving closer to the OSI model's original vision. Novell uses Streams similarly in NetWare 3.*x* and 4.*x* file servers.

Transport Data Interface

Above the transport protocols, Windows NT uses another boundary layer similar in function to NDIS called *TDI* (*transport data interface*), shown in Figure 12.8. This layer supplies a common interface for file system and I/O manager processes to communicate with network transports. It's a "thin" layer, with very little code involved. TDI helps other vendors develop their software, and it allows software developed above and below a level to be mixed and matched without reprogramming.

FIGURE 12.8.

The transport data interface (TDI) is used to simplify the development of third-party applications.

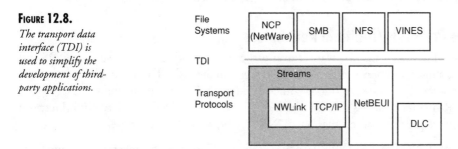

TDI is based on 32-bit–wide handles, which increases the connection capacity between upper layers and protocols like NetBEUI, which supports only an 8-bit Local Session Number—a real problem if you need to create a network with more than 256 stations.

The Session Layer and Above: File and Print Sharing on the Network

If all you wanted to do was pump data into a cable and receive it at the other end, transport protocols would be all you'd need. If you're not a programmer and you want to get work done using your computer rather than just sending packets back and forth, you need higher layer protocols.

For most users, networking means file and printer sharing, and these features are key parts of Windows NT. The most important components for providing these file and print services are the server and redirector, or workstation, service. These two components provide most of the functionality of the OS/2 version of LAN Manager available today. Both of these modules execute as 32-bit services.

The redirector service, which takes requests from applications, formats them into server message block (SMB) protocol messages, and sends them across the network to the server, is a file system driver (FSD) that actually does the interaction with the protocol stack's lower layers through the NetBIOS API. The server accepts the SMB messages, gets the requested data, and sends it back across the network to the requesting station.

When you access a resource on another system, you must refer to the resource's UNC (universal naming convention) name. First used by Microsoft in MS-Net and the PC Network Program, UNC is used to describe servers and sharepoints for those servers on a network. UNC names start with two backslashes (\\), followed by the server name. All other fields in the name are separated by a single backslash. Here's the format for a typical UNC name:

```
\\server\share\subdirectory\filename
```

A *share* or *sharepoint* is the name assigned by the server's administrator to a disk drive or directory he or she wants to make available to other users to share.

Multiple Protocols/Multiple Requesters

One of Windows NT's major advances over earlier PC operating systems, such as DOS and OS/2, is its ability to support multiple requesters simultaneously. This feature lets you use the default Windows NT requester to access other Windows NT workstations and servers, Novell's NetWare Requester to access data on NetWare file servers, and a third-party NFS (Network File System) requester to access files on a UNIX server, all at the same time.

The Multiple UNC Provider (MUP), shown in Figure 12.9, is responsible for managing these multiple requesters, or UNC providers. Think of the MUP is as a UNC name locator. It can identify the right requester from a partial name; \\server is enough for the MUP to find a server and get a list of its sharepoints.

FIGURE 12.9.

The Multiple UNC Provider is used to resolve machine names.

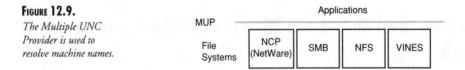

Unlike the NDIS and TDI boundary layers, which really just define how the protocols above and below them should communicate over specifically defined paths called *binds*, the MUP is actually a program. Like NDIS and TDI, it has defined paths to redirectors, but it also must know which requester to send any given request to.

When the MUP receives a command from an application, it checks the UNC name in that request against the table it keeps of UNC names and their associated requesters. If the MUP has seen this UNC name in a request during the past 15 minutes or so, the UNC name will be in the MUP's local name table, and the MUP just passes it on to the right requester.

If it's is a new UNC name, the MUP sends it to each requester, essentially going around the room asking, "Is this your mitten, Timmy? Is this your mitten, Joey?" until a requester 'fesses up. The redirector with the highest registered priority response that claims it can establish a connection to the UNC is passed the command and the security context of the application generating the request.

For applications that don't make UNC requests but instead make Windows networking calls directly, Windows NT also has a multiple provider router (MPR), which functions similarly to the MUP but for different function calls.

Additional Network Services

In addition to the workstation and server services, Microsoft ported a few other services from its older OS/2 LAN Manager. Alerter, Messenger, Browser, and Replicator all offer important services for network users.

The Alerter is used to forward alerts generated by events like a full disk drive to remote computers or usernames. The Messenger receives messages and alerts and displays them onscreen in a dialog box. The Browser collects information about the machines in this domain or workgroup for use by other applications. Windows NT uses the Browser's information to list the available sharepoints on another system, which allows you to connect to a new drive. The Replicator service automatically copies the contents of a directory from an NT Server to another machine to create a real-time background backup.

Distributed Applications

It seems that all you need to do today to attract a big crowd at a seminar is to put "client/server" on the brochure's cover. Consultants can also make big bucks by using these magic words. However, don't get snowed by all the buzzwords. A *distributed* (or client/server) *application* is simply a program that has two parts. One typically interacts with the user and runs on one computer (called the *client*), and the other (called the *server*) typically offers some service, ranging from a database backend to a computing or communications service. These two parts of the program need to communicate with each other, and this is where Windows NT's interprocess communications features come in.

Just as with transport protocols, Windows NT has a wide variety of interprocess communications (IPC) features, ranging from old and primarily historically interesting ones, such as NetBIOS, to the latest industry standard features, such as remote procedure calls.

Windows NT actually gives you six different IPC mechanisms: named pipes, mailslots, NetBIOS, Windows sockets, remote procedure calls (RPCs), and NetDDE (network dynamic data exchange). Named pipes and mailslots were first introduced as part of LAN Manager. They're included in Windows NT to provide backward compatibility with existing LAN Manager installations and applications like Microsoft's SQL Server. NetBIOS is the oldest of Windows NT's IPCs and is also offered for backward compatibility. Windows sockets is a

Windows-based implementation of the Berkeley sockets APIs, which are popular in the UNIX world. Windows NT's RPC is compatible with the OSF/DCE (Open Software Foundation/ Distributed Computing Environment) specification for remote procedure calls. NetDDE allows even the nonprogrammer to build distributed applications by extending standard DDE connections between Windows applications across the network.

Named pipes and mailslots, unlike the other IPC mechanisms, are written as file systems, so they share common features with other file systems, including security access controls, which are part of NTFS and other file systems. In addition, processes can use named pipes and mailslots to communicate with other processes on the same machine, besides using them to communicate with processes on other machines on the network.

The named pipes' APIs, although based on the OS/2 API set, have been ported to the Win32 base API set and extended, making support for client/server applications easier to implement. As a file system, named pipes can take advantage of the cache manager, improving the performance of some named pipe applications by reducing the number of frames (and network overhead) generated.

Windows NT extends the named pipes support from OS/2 by adding an *impersonation*, which allows a server to change its security identity to that of the client on the other end. If, for example, you have a database server system that uses named pipes to receive read and write requests from clients when a request comes in, the database server program can impersonate the client before trying to perform the request. Even if the server program does have authority to perform the function, the client doesn't, so the request is denied. If not for this impersonation, a client could send a request to a server and have it fulfilled if the server had enough access rights, thus fooling the system. With impersonation, the server pretends to be the client, but the client can't get a beer by asking the 21-year-old server to go to the liquor store for it.

Mailslots in Windows NT are only a subset of full OS/2 LAN Manager implementations. LAN Manager supplies both first-class and second-class mailslots, but Windows NT provides only second-class mailslots. Mailslots give you so-called connectionless, basic broadcast messaging, but delivery of the message is not guaranteed.

Mailslots are most useful for discovering other machines or services on a network or for advertising a service's availability. Because of the mailslots' broadcast nature, they can easily clog your network with traffic, slowing down other important functions. Because most wide area networks don't forward broadcast messages across bridges or routers, mailslots are useful only for local communications.

NetBIOS has been used as an IPC mechanism since the introduction of the interface in the early 1980s. Even though higher level interfaces, such as named pipes and RPC, are superior in their flexibility and portability, many applications use NetBIOS because of its wide acceptance in the PC network arena. The NetBIOS entry point in Windows NT's registry defines a common interface point from which many possible transport protocols can take the data across your network. Windows NT comes with NetBIOS interfaces to the NetBEUI transport protocol through the NBF driver; a device driver called Nbt provides NetBIOS support for the TCP/IP protocol stack and a NetBIOS interface to the NWLink IPX/SPX protocol stack.

Note that neither the NWLink nor the TCP/IP NetBIOS interface uses packet encapsulation or tunneling to put a NetBEUI packet inside an IP or IPX packet. Instead, they use the accepted methods defined by Novell in its NETBIOS.COM program for NWLink or RFC (request for comment) 1001/1002, which defines how to use TCP/IP to carry NetBIOS traffic. This allows a workstation running Windows NT and, for example, NWLink NetBIOS to communicate with a workstation running DOS and Novell's IPX and NetBIOS.COM.

The sockets interface for TCP/IP was created at the University of California at Berkeley in the early 1980s. Since then, it has become a popular interface for developing distributed applications in the TCP/IP and UNIX environments. Microsoft, in cooperation with several other software vendors, developed the Windows Socket API set to migrate the sockets interface into the Windows and Windows NT environments and standardize the API set for all platforms. WinSockets is now used by almost all the TCP/IP products for Windows 3.*x*, including Novell's LAN Workplace for DOS and NetManage's Chameleon. The Windows Socket interface for Windows NT runs as a layer above TCP/IP and uses TCP/IP as its transport. WinSockets isn't available if you haven't installed TCP/IP support.

Remote Procedure Calls (RPCs) are one of Windows NT's most sophisticated interprocess communications facilities. First designed by Sun, RPCs are a transport protocol–independent medium. The basic concept is that a programmer can define a function that, rather than actually execute on the user's workstation, calls another program on a remote machine.

The RPC definition has been taken over by Open Software Foundation (OSF) as part of their Distributed Computing Environment (DCE) specification, which is supported by most of the major computer vendors. The Microsoft RPC implementation is compatible with the OSF/DCE standard RPC. Windows NT RPCs are completely interoperable with other DCE-based RPC systems, so a program running on a Windows NT workstation can call an RPC on an IBM RS/6000 or another DCE-compatible machine.

The RPC mechanism is unique in that it uses the other IPC mechanisms to establish communications between the client and the server. RPC can use named pipes, NetBIOS, or TCP/IP Sockets to communicate with remote systems. If the calling function (the client) and the actual program (the server) are on the same machine (as they may be for very small or test systems), the RPC mechanism can use the LPC (local procedure call) system to transfer information between processes and subsystems. This makes RPC the most flexible and portable of the IPC choices available.

A typical program has main (or backbone) logic, which defines what the program does, and a series of functions that actually do the "grunt work" of calculating pi or locating George Tirebighter's record in the "Shoes for Industry" database. In traditional programs, the functions and core logic are all statically linked into an executable program by the developer and then distributed.

In a multitasking environment like Windows, these monolithic programs have a few disadvantages. First, because the functions and core logic are linked, a computer running five or six different programs has five or six different copies of common functions like "Display a File Open dialog box" in memory at the same time, which takes up valuable space. If you use DLLs (dynamic link libraries) instead, you can save memory and update the functions without updating the program's main logic. With DLLs, the functions and main logic are stored in different modules.

RPC takes the concept one step further and places the main logic and the functions on different machines. A client application using RPCs is developed by using a specially compiled "stub" library. The functions (or *stubs*) in this library actually transfer the data and the function to a module called the *RPC Runtime*. The RPC Runtime finds a server that can process the function and sends the function and data to the server, where they're picked up by the RPC Runtime module on the server. The server loads the DLL for the function, runs it, and sends it back to the client through the RPC Runtime module. When the function returns to the client application, it either has the appropriate returned data or indicates that the function failed in some way.

This is where distributed applications can make a big difference. If you build these applications with services in mind, you can do some interesting things with NT machines.

Summary

Like the OSI model, Windows NT uses a layered structure to give each workstation networking functions, from simple file and print sharing to sophisticated IPCs such as remote procedure calls. The layered structure—together with boundary layers and structures like NDIS, TDI, and Streams—allows a single Windows NT workstation to run several transport protocols and requesters simultaneously to access servers and resources on the network.

The following chapters look at many of these networking features in more detail to help you design a Windows NT–based network and connect Windows NT to your existing computing infrastructure.

CHAPTER 13

Designing and Installing Your Windows NT Network

IN THIS CHAPTER

In this chapter, you learn about designing a local area network (LAN) with Windows NT, installing Windows NT's networking features, and configuring Windows NT to use your LAN card. If you're planning to use Windows NT as the basis of a new local area network, one of your first decisions will be which LAN technology to use.

If you've already started installing network hardware or if someone else in your company is concerned about hardware installation, you can skip ahead to the section on setting up your LAN card or configuring NT for your network card. If someone else is responsible for installing and maintaining your network and you just want to know how to use it, you can skip to Chapter 14, "Windows NT Networking Out of the Box: Peer-to-Peer Networking."

If you're planning a network with more than 30 or 40 workstations, you should divide your network into segments connected by bridges or routers. However, details on setting up this kind of design are beyond the scope of this book. Although there are several excellent books on this kind of enterprise-wide networking, as a network consultant, I believe a large network should be designed by a network professional.

Network Cabling and Technologies

Over the past few years, two technologies—Ethernet and Token Ring—have emerged as the best choices for most users. Older technologies, such as ARCnet and StarLAN, have fallen by the wayside because of their limited data-carrying capacity.

> **NOTE**
>
> Some people use the term *topology* to describe LAN technologies like Ethernet and Token Ring. Strictly speaking, a LAN's topology defines only how the stations are connected. Most networks use a bus or star topology.

After talking to LAN installers and managers, you might think that Ethernet and Token Ring are completely different technologies and that choosing one over the other could be a fatal error. In reality, Ethernet and Token Ring have a lot in common. Both are widely supported by hardware and software vendors and have been recognized as international standards by the 802 committee of the Institute of Electrical and Electronic Engineers. Either can be used to build a stable network for your NT users.

New multimedia applications, such as desktop video conferencing, and the overall growth of network use have started to push Ethernet's 10Mbps capacity and Token Ring's 16Mbps capacity past their limits, making the network cable the data bottleneck. Several new network technologies, including FDDI (Fiber Digital Device Interface), 100VG AnyLAN, and Fast Ethernet boost performance to 100Mbps. Alternatively, switching technology gives each user his or her own Ethernet to eliminate the bottleneck.

FDDI products are available (if quite expensive) now. Both 100VG AnyLAN and Fast Ethernet products are available and reasonably priced now, and can use your existing cabling.

> **NOTE**
>
> Wireless network adapters (using either radio or infrared communications links) have been entering the market. They can be useful for small departments or low-traffic networks.
>
> When you're choosing a LAN technology, you need to balance cost, reliability, and performance. Local area networks differ in what type of cable they use, how fast they run, how easy it is to troubleshoot the system, and how easily they connect to larger computers.

People often make a big deal out of one of the least important differences between networks: the access method. Most LANs allow only one network station to send data at a time. The *access method* is the set of rules governing how a station is allowed to transmit.

CSMA/CD networks, such as Ethernet, control access to the network by making a station wait until the cable is quiet before sending. When the network gets busy, two stations may try to transmit their data at the same time. If this happens, they both stop transmitting; each waits for a random period until the cable is quiet again.

Token-passing networks use a special message called the *token* that's sent from station to station. When a station receives the token, it can either send a message to another station or pass the token—and, therefore, permission to send—to the next station.

Cable Types

Over the past 10 years, vendors have developed LANs that can run on just about any type of cable. I wouldn't be surprised to find that some small Texas company has a LAN that runs on barbed wire for the computing cowboy market.

Luckily, the popular local area networks all use one of four types of cable:

- Unshielded twisted pair
- Shielded twisted pair
- Coaxial cable
- Optical fiber

Unshielded Twisted Pair

The unshielded twisted pair (UTP) cable used by local area networks is similar to the cable used by telephone companies, only better. An unshielded twisted pair cable is made up of pairs of wires twisted around each other. (See Figure 13.1.) This twisting causes the magnetic fields in the two wires to interact, which improves the wire's ability to carry a signal. All other things being equal, cables with more twists, say 10 twists per foot, carry data better than cables with fewer twists.

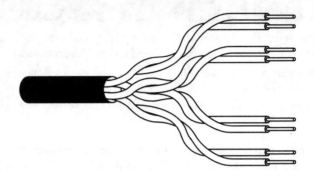

An unshielded twisted pair cable can vary in how it's made, which affects how well it carries high-speed data. Many early 10Base-T Ethernet and Token Ring network installations were disasters because users discovered that their telephone installers just didn't know what was needed to make a LAN work. Telephones can run on just about anything, but a high-speed LAN needs cable that won't scramble its data bits too much. Using just one 6-foot length of the flat wire typically used between your home phone and the wall (telephone installers call it "silver satin") in a LAN cable system often prevents LAN data from passing through the entire cable segment.

Because computer networks are much less forgiving of poor-quality cable and poor installation practices than voice applications are, the EIA/TIA (Electronics Industries Association/Telecommunications Industry Association) recently came up with a grading system that ranks unshielded twisted pair cable in levels from 1 to 5. Higher-grade cables can carry progressively faster data traffic.

Levels 1 and 2 are rather low quality and should be used only for telephone systems. Most commercial telephone systems installed before 1990 use these lower-quality cables that can't be used for LAN data.

Level 3 cable is good enough to use for 4Mbps Token Ring or 10Base-T Ethernet, but that's all. If you want to run 16Mbps Token Ring, you'll need to use at least Level 4.

Level 5, the top grade, can be used for 10Base-T, Token Ring, and all the new 100Mbps LANs. Well-installed Level 5 cable can handle data at rates of up to 100Mbps and is the cable new network technologies like Fast Ethernet are designed for.

Because a cable plant should be designed to last 10 years or more, and because up to 80 percent of a cable plant's cost is labor, any new UTP cable you install should be Level 5. The small initial cost will save you money later because you can upgrade your network without pulling new cable.

NOTE

I occasionally hear that a LAN vendor has told a customer that Level 5 cable can't be used for 10Base-T Ethernet, which requires Level 3. This isn't true. Each of the levels specifies only the *minimum* quality needed. All Level 5 cable exceeds the Level 3 specifications. Here are the specifications for the UTP levels:

Level	Maximum Data Rate
1	0Mbps
2	1Mbps
3	10Mbps
4	10Mbps
5	100Mbps

Shielded Twisted Pair

To reduce the cable's sensitivity to electrical noise, the shielded twisted pair (STP) adds a foil or copper braid shield around the wires just under the outer jacket. (See Figure 13.2.) The shield stops any noise that would cause a problem in unshielded pairs. Some cable also adds a shield around each pair in the cable to prevent signals on one pair from creating induced voltages in another pair.

FIGURE 13.2.

A shielded twisted pair cable.

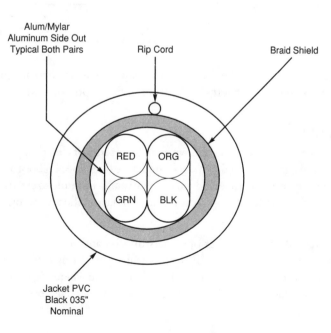

The only shielded twisted pair cable in wide use today is the IBM Type 1 cable used with Token Ring. Some manufacturers of 10Base-T Ethernet cards also supply adapters that allow them to run on shielded cable.

Shielded twisted pair cable is more expensive to buy and install than unshielded twisted pair. It's a good choice for Token Ring installations, especially those in electrically noisy environments, such as factory floors. Shielded twisted pair use has been declining since IBM endorsed UTP for Token Ring.

Coaxial

Before 1990, almost all LANs used coaxial cable that was similar to the type used for cable TV. Coaxial cable is made of a single conductor centered in a foil or copper braid shield.

Coaxial cable is simple to install and relatively inexpensive. Unfortunately, each local area network technology that uses coaxial cable uses a slightly different type. Coaxial cable is a dead end for LANs because none of the new standard LAN technologies are designed to use it. Figure 13.3 shows Thick Ethernet cable, the most sophisticated and expensive coaxial cable in common use for LANS.

Figure 13.3.

Thick Ethernet coaxial cable.

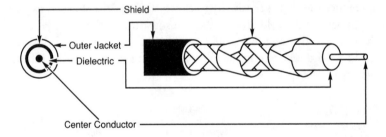

Coaxial cable should be used only in small networks, where it can be cost-effective. For large networks (and in networks of the future), fiber-optic and twisted pair cables are preferable.

Optical Fiber

Rather than send your data down a wire as a series of electrical pulses, fiber-optic networks use pulses of light running down a glass or plastic fiber. (See Figure 13.4.) Because fiber-optic cables don't use electricity to send data, they are totally immune to electrical and magnetic noise. This makes them perfect for applications used in factory floors and other electrically noisy environments.

The real advantage of fiber-optic networks is bandwidth. Twisted pair and coaxial cables currently max out at about 100Mbps, but fiber-optic long distance lines can carry several Gbps. For this reason, you should run fiber-optic cable where high traffic levels are expected in the future or where installation costs far outweigh materials costs, as in the case of vertical risers.

FIGURE 13.4.

Light follows a fiber-optic cable.

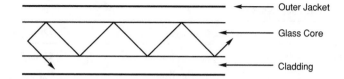

Fiber-optic LANs typically need a pair of fibers for each link, one for each direction the data travels in. (See Figure 13.5.)

FIGURE 13.5.

Typical fiber-optic cable.

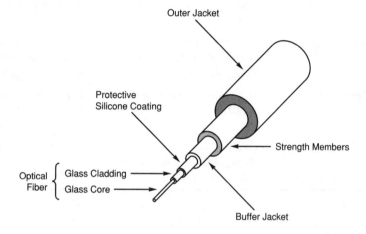

13
INSTALLING YOUR
WINDOWS NT
NETWORK

Fiber-optic networks have developed a reputation of being hard to install, fragile, and very expensive. However, over the past few years, fiber-optic components have become less expensive. Several vendors, including 3M and AMP, have developed connector systems that are much easier and faster to install. Fiber-optic networks also have a security advantage over copper networks. Some of the electrical signal pumped into a cable gets radiated out into the environment.

If you must run your LAN from building to building, you should always use a fiber-optic link. A Texas school learned this lesson when it ran coaxial cable between two buildings. One day a thunderstorm wandered over the school, looked down, and called out to its thunderstorm buddies, "Look boys, lunch!" After the lightning strike, more than 30 feet of cable was completely vaporized. Two active hubs, five PCs, a printer, and an electric typewriter were severely damaged, too. Because fiber-optic cables don't conduct electricity, the thunderstorm wouldn't have had a target.

A less dramatic, but more common, problem with copper cables between buildings is ground differentials. If copper cables are used to connect two buildings, a current (called a *ground loop*) may flow through the cable, interfering with the data.

Table 13.1 summarizes the differences between the types of cables used in most LANs.

Table 13.1. Cable types.

Type	Advantages	Disadvantages
UTP	Low cost Very flexible High performance Good management tool	Sensitive to RFI/EMI Cable lengths limited
STP	Flexible Less sensitive to electrical noise	Cable lengths limited Moderately high cost
Coaxial	Less sensitive to electrical noise Moderate cost	Different cable needed for each network Easily damaged
Optical Fiber	Completely immune to RFI/EMI Very high performance bandwidth Long distances supported No ground loops	Expensive to install Limited card choices Patch panels very expensive

Ethernet

Ethernet was developed in the mid-1970s by a team headed by Robert Metcalf at Xerox's legendary Palo Alto Research Center (Xerox PARC). Ethernet was just one of the computing breakthroughs developed at PARC, but it was never well exploited by Xerox. (PARC also developed the laser printer and the concepts behind the Windows user interface, including icons and pull-down menus.)

What's called the *Ethernet* is usually a network that's compliant with the IEEE 802.3 standard; this standard was based on the Ethernet product Digital, which Intel and Xerox introduced in the early 1980s, but it's slightly different. Almost all current products sold as Ethernet are 802.3-compliant.

Over the years, vendors have developed a variety of cabling schemes, standardized by the IEEE, for Ethernet. You can now run Ethernet on coaxial, twisted pair, or fiber-optic cable. With Motorola's Altair, you can get rid of the cable altogether. Regardless of the cable used, Ethernet is always a 10Mbps network using CSMA/CD as its access method.

Ethernet's strengths are its low cost, its good performance, and its availability for most systems—most minicomputer and UNIX workstations have Ethernet ports built in. Ethernet cards and other hardware are available from many vendors at reasonable prices.

Thick Ethernet (10Base5)

The first Ethernet networks linked expensive minicomputers, workstations, and laser printers. The cable system design stressed performance, reliability, and flexibility, but didn't emphasize cost as a factor. Thick Ethernet is expensive because of the cost of the special cable and transceivers. Currently, it's used most often in university environments.

This original cabling system has become known as Thick or "Yellow" Ethernet, after the special 50 ohm impedance coaxial cable it uses. The IEEE has designated Thick Ethernet as *10Base5*. Thick Ethernet cable, which is usually yellow, is very thick compared to other LAN cables and quite expensive to install because of its .4-inch diameter size and 10-inch minimum bend radius. To protect the signal from electrical noise, the cable is extensively shielded with two copper braid shields and two foil or metallicized mylar shields.

Computers are connected to the trunk through transceivers—small metal boxes with electronics—connected directly to the cable. Workstations are connected to transceivers through a DB-15 AUI (attachment unit interface) or a DIX (Digital, Intel, Xerox) connector and a length of AUI or transceiver cable. A transceiver cable can be up to 50 meters (164 feet) long.

A single Thick Ethernet trunk, shown in Figure 13.6, can be up to 500 meters (1,640 feet) long and have up to 100 transceivers. Each trunk must have a 1W 50 ohm (±1 ohm) resistor at each end. Multiple Thick Ethernet segments can be connected with repeaters to create a single *collision domain*—that is, a single logical network up to 2,500 meters long (8,200 feet, or approximately 1.5 miles) with no more than four repeaters in the longest path between the two most distant nodes.

FIGURE 13.6.

Thick Ethernet connects machines to the network, and subnetworks to each other through transceivers.

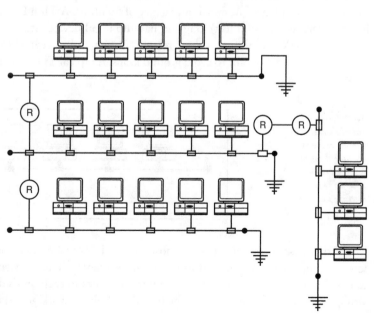

Thin Ethernet (10Base2)

By 1982, Bob Metcalf had left Xerox and started his own company, 3Com. At 3Com, he and his team realized that $600 was a lot to ask someone to pay for a cable connecting two PCs in an office. For these smaller networks, they set out to make a variation of Ethernet that would be more cost-effective than Thick Ethernet.

When they first unveiled their creation, they called it *Cheapernet* because it was cheaper than the traditional Ethernet. After they hired a few marketing people, they started calling it *Thin Ethernet* because it uses a thinner cable than the traditional, or Thick, Ethernet.

To make Thin Ethernet less expensive, the engineers made two major changes. Instead of using special cable that costs a dollar a foot, they used RG-58A/U, a stock item that costs about 12 to 30 cents a foot. They also decided to build the transceiver right into the network adapter, saving the AUI cable and the transceiver's separate packaging.

Because the transceiver is part of the network interface card, you attach a PC to a Thin Ethernet segment by attaching a T-connector to the BNC (bayonet nut connector) on the back of the workstation's network interface on its base and attach the trunk cable to its arms.

Using drop cables between the BNC on the LAN card and the T-connector or main bus cable is a big mistake because it can cause unforeseen problems. For example, in one case, adding a drop cable to one PC didn't affect that PC's access to the cable, but did disable several other PCs on the network.

Thin Ethernet cable can be RG-58A/U, RG-58C/U, or specifically designed for use with Thin Ethernet; it must have a nominal impedance of 50 ohms. A Thin Ethernet cable segment can be up to 185 meters (600 feet) long and have up to 30 devices attached. Each segment trunk must have a $^1/_2$W 50 ohm ($\pm$1 ohm) resistor at each end. A segment should be grounded at one—and only one—point to avoid ground loops. A typical Thin Ethernet is shown in Figure 13.7.

FIGURE 13.7.

Thin Ethernet runs from machine to machine through T-shaped connectors attached to each machine's network port.

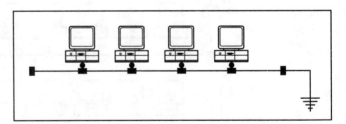

Thin Ethernet is currently one of the most popular LAN technologies because of its simplicity, low cost, and relatively high performance. Unfortunately, Thin Ethernet has a few problems, too; its biggest problem is that the main bus cable goes to each user's desk. If something goes wrong with the cable anywhere on the bus, the whole network goes down.

Thin Ethernet is a good choice for small networks, but larger networks are better served by 10Base-T.

Twisted Pair Ethernet (10Base-T)

For many years, running Ethernet over twisted pair cable seemed like an unattainable technical goal. In 1986, Synoptics, a Xerox PARC spin-off company, shipped its first products which allowed Ethernet to run on shielded twisted pair cable. By 1988, several companies were selling products that allowed users to run Ethernet on telephone-style unshielded twisted pair cable. These Ethernet products used a star topology with multiport repeaters (called *hubs* or *concentrators* by manufacturers) in the wiring closet on each floor.

The IEEE 802.3 committee decided that if there was this much demand for an Ethernet over a twisted pair cabling system, they should add a 10Base-T chapter to the specification. A 10Base-T workstation is connected to its hub by up to 100 meters (330 feet) of UTP cable that meets Level 3 specifications.

The network uses two pairs of wires: one to send data from the workstation to the hub and the other for data going from the hub to the workstation. It's wired using the RJ-45 style 8-pin connector, so most people install a four-pair cable, which allows some room for broken wires and future growth. A typical 10Base-T network is shown in Figure 13.8.

FIGURE 13.8.

A 10Base-T network.

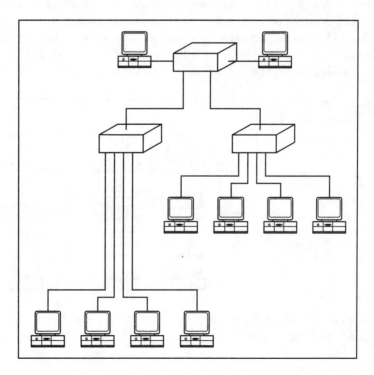

You can get 10Base-T hubs with anywhere from 8 to 128 ports. Several manufacturers, including Intel, have developed 12-port 10Base-T hubs on PC bus cards for use in a file server or router. Small unmanaged hubs are available for $50 to $100 per port. Typically, they include an AUI connector so that you can use fiber-optic or Thick Ethernet cables to connect your hubs. Hubs with expandable card cages and management features usually cost more.

All in all, 10Base-T has proved itself a reliable and cost-effective LAN technology, so I recommend it for any Ethernet system with more than 10 workstations. Larger networks with more than 50 stations should use hubs with management features that let you get status information and control the hub from your desk.

Token Ring

Token Ring was first developed by IBM and released in 1985 as a 4Mbps LAN running on shielded twisted pair cable. In 1988, IBM increased Token Ring's speed to 16Mbps, and the IEEE issued a formal specification—number 802.5—for Token Ring.

Each workstation is connected to a hub or MAU (multistation access unit), which connects that station to the next one on the ring. Token Ring is usually wired with twisted pair cable, but both fiber-optic and coaxial Token Ring products exist.

Each hub or MAU (sometimes written MSAU) has a number of ports for cables running to machines on the network and a pair of connectors marked RI (for *ring in*) and RO (for *ring out*). MAUs are connected by running a cable called a *main ring cable* or a *patch cable* from the RI connector on one MAU to the RO connector on another MAU. Using shielded twisted pair cable, a single Token Ring can have up to 260 nodes. (See Figure 13.9.)

FIGURE 13.9.
A Token Ring network.

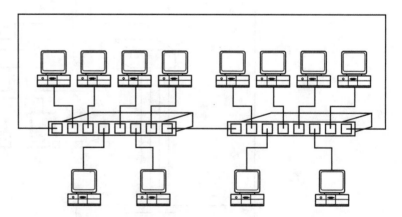

The rules for wiring Token Ring are rather complicated. If you have a small network, your cables can be up to 100 meters (330 feet) long between workstations and their MAUs.

The Token Ring architecture connects each station to the stations next to it on the ring. A Token Ring card listens to the station on the network just before it and transmits that data to the next station. (See Figure 13.10.) An IBM 8228 MAU, IBM's basic Token Ring hub, has a mechanical relay behind each port. When the MAU sees a DC phantom voltage of 3.5-7Vdc from the workstation, it opens the relay to connect the workstation to its neighbors. If the phantom voltage disappears, the MAU closes the relay connecting this station's neighbors.

FIGURE 13.10.

The Token Ring data flow.

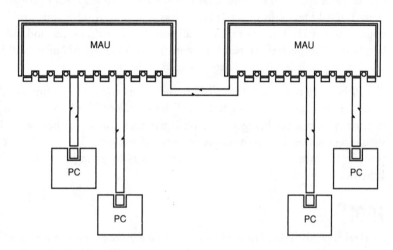

Token Ring's greatest strength is that it can be easily connected to IBM host computers, such as 3090s and ES/9000s. The downside is that Token Ring is fairly expensive, at least twice the cost of an equivalent 10Base-T setup. It also has a well-deserved reputation as being difficult to troubleshoot.

Cabling System Pointers

If you need to make a quick decision about cabling systems for your network, use the following guidelines:

- If you must connect to an IBM mainframe, choose Token Ring.
- If you need to connect to Sun or other UNIX systems, use Ethernet.
- Thin Ethernet is good for networks with up to 10 stations.
- 10Base-T with four-pair Level 5 cable is best for larger networks.
- Ethernet costs at least 50 percent less than Token Ring.
- Unless you have a lot of support staff and some Ethernet and Token Ring specialists, try to use just one technology.

Going Faster

If you have a very large network and an unlimited hardware budget, or if you're working on applications, such as desktop video, that need more than a shared 16Mbps data pipe, you have two ways to give your users the bandwidth they need.

The obvious approach is to use a faster network. If 10Mbps isn't enough, get 100Mbps. The Fiber Digital Device Interface (FDDI) was designed to solve your problems. Unfortunately, upgrading to FDDI means replacing all your LAN cards, cables, and hubs at a cost of several hundred dollars per station. Fast Ethernet and 100VG AnyLAN offer 100Mbps at a much lower cost, usually only involving a network card replacement.

The alternative is to use 10Base-T Ethernet cards and replace some or all of your hubs with Ethernet switches, such as the Kalpana Etherswitch or SMC ES/1. These switches, which are essentially high-speed bridges, effectively give each user his or her own 10Mbps data path by switching packets between multiple ports simultaneously. Using a 12-port data switch lets you provide 120Mbps total bandwidth to your users by giving each user or workgroup its own Ethernet segment.

FDDI

At 100Mbps, the Fiber Digital Device Interface is the fastest standard LAN on the market and is currently the best choice for the real power user. The ANSI (American National Standards Institute) standard for FDDI specifies a dual counter-rotating ring wired in a star, using hubs like 10Base-T or Token Ring.

Several vendors, led by Crescendo Communications with its CDDI product, have developed products that let you run FDDI on shielded, or Level 5 unshielded, twisted pair cable. By the time you read this, an ANSI committee should have issued a standard for running FDDI over copper cable.

Because of its high cost (over $1,500 per station) and limited software support, FDDI is best suited to backbone networks that connect smaller workgroup networks.

Fast Ethernet

In early 1993, several vendors announced products they claimed were the next logical step from Ethernet. They were soon divided into two camps: The 100Base-T group, led by Grand Junction Networks and 3Com, proposed a system using two pairs of Level 5 UTP cable to build a 100Mbps Ethernet, and the 100Base-VG group, led by Hewlett Packard and AT&T, replaced the CSMA/CD access method with a demand protocol. It used a signaling system that could support sending 100Mbps data across the Level 3 cable most users had installed for 10Base-T by using all four pairs of wire in the RJ-45 jack.

When these groups went to the IEEE 802.3 committee to ask them to decide which product would become a standard, the IEEE, in an act of unique mediocrity, decided not to endorse one plan over the other, but to standardize both approaches. The 802.3 committee is defining specifications for 100Base-T, and 100Base-VG, which now has Token Ring support added because IBM joined the group, will be defined by a new 802.12 committee.

Choosing Your Cards

As soon as you've chosen Ethernet, Token Ring, or FDDI, you still need to choose LAN cards for all your workstations. Don't agonize too much over this decision. Unlike three or four years ago, when a slow Ethernet card could be two to three times slower than a fast one, there are now few differences between competitive cards from different vendors.

Just make sure that the card you pick has an NDIS 3.0 or NDIS 3.1 driver available for it. Microsoft ships Windows NT with drivers for most popular Ethernet and Token Ring cards. You can get drivers for other LAN cards from the manufacturer or from Microsoft's Windows NT Driver Library (WNTDL).

The Hardware Compatibility List available with the Windows NT software, or through the Microsoft World Wide Web home page, lists all the supported network cards. You can download a list of the hardware devices tested by Microsoft in Library 1 of the CompuServe's WINNT forum. This list is periodically updated by Microsoft as new drivers are added to the library. You can download the files from CompuServe, Microsoft Download Services, or GEnie. If you don't have a modem, you can get an individual driver from the WNTDL on a disk by calling Microsoft Product Support Services at (206) 637-7098.

You also need to make sure you match your LAN card to your system's bus, which can be identified fairly easily. Most PS/2 systems, including any machine that has a reference disk, use IBM's 16-bit or 32-bit MicroChannel Architecture (MCA), which was designed as a faster successor to the 16-bit ISA (industry standard architecture) or AT bus slots used in most PCs. If you have a MicroChannel machine, you have to use MicroChannel cards. IBM's probably are the best choice.

EISA (extended industry standard architecture) systems, generally used for file servers and other I/O-intensive tasks, have slots that can take a standard 16-bit ISA card or a 32-bit EISA card. If you have an EISA system, you should take advantage of it and use EISA Ethernet or Token Ring cards.

Newer systems might have ISA, or even EISA, bus slots and additional local bus slots that meet either the VESA VL-Bus or Intel PCI specification. VL-Bus cards interact very closely with the processor and require many processor resources to manage. If your system has VL-Bus slots, you still might get better overall system performance by using an ISA or EISA LAN card.

Pentium systems with PCI bus are just coming on the market. The 64-bit PCI bus shows great promise for disk controllers and LAN cards, in addition to the video cards most often used with VL-Bus. PCI doesn't share VL-Bus's limitations when multiple cards are used, so if you have a PCI system and find a PCI LAN card from a major vendor with NT drivers, buy it.

Most PCs connected to Ethernets use cards from 3Com, SMC, or Intel or use cards compatible with Novell's original NE-2000, such as those from National Semiconductor or Eagle. These cards have the widest variety of drivers available. You can't go wrong if you stick with one of these brands. It's not worth the $10 to $30 you might save by using a Taiwanese clone card.

When it comes to Token Ring, most systems use IBM cards. This is a safe choice, especially if you might need to use IBM products, such as AS/400 PC Support or PC3270, to access your host computer. SMC, Madge, Intel, and Olicom also make good Token Ring cards.

You should also consider the card's flexibility. The latest cards from SMC, Intel, and 3Com have both BNC and RJ-45 connectors, so they can be used for both 10Base-T and Thin Ethernet. They're also software-configurable, so you don't need to fiddle with jumpers and switches to set the card up. Cards also differ in the number of I/O ports and the amount of memory they take up, which can be important if you're also going to be running DOS on your system.

TIP

If at all possible, get a software-configured network card. It's much easier to set up and test because you don't have to remove the card to change the jumper or DIP-switch settings.

Choosing a Network Card Configuration

CAUTION

This chapter discusses setting up and configuring a network card in very general terms. It covers procedures and common concerns, but it's not meant to be a substitute for your network card manual.

WARNING

Installing a network card is easy enough that just about any user can do it. However, electrostatic discharge, or static electricity, can destroy your motherboard, cards, and other components. Therefore, you should take some simple precautions if you're installing a

network card. Touch a grounded metal surface—such as your computer's power supply—
before you handle the card or do *any* work inside the PC.

Most LAN cards use one interrupt line, between 1 and 16 I/O ports, and up to 64K of upper
memory. Some older cards might also use a DMA (direct memory access) channel. Before you
install a LAN card on your system, you need to make sure it won't have a resource conflict
with a device that's already in your system. Check the resources already in use, then set your
adapter to a set of unused resources.

If you have a PS/2, here's where you get off easy. You can just stick the reference disk in your
machine and view what kind of card is in each slot and the resources it's using. When you
configure your LAN card, the reference disk even tells you when you have a conflict with another card. If you have an EISA machine, the configuration utility can give you the same information for slots that have 32-bit EISA cards installed. Unfortunately, it can't tell you anything
about any ISA bus cards your system might have.

Most people have ISA bus systems and must find some other way to figure out what resources
are available. If you're setting up a new system or working on a system that has just the standard I/O devices, such as COM ports, you can use Tables 13.2, 13.3, and 13.4 to determine
what resources are available. If you can't remember whether you have fancy cards, such as a
SCSI host adapter or sound board, you can try using a diagnostic program like CheckIt, Mani-
fest, or the WINMSD program that comes with Windows NT. These programs do a good job
of identifying the I/O ports and memory addresses used by cards in your system. However,
sometimes these programs tell you that an interrupt is free when it's actually being used by a
card in your system. This can happen if you haven't loaded the device driver for the card before running the diagnostic.

Table 13.2. Uses for PC interrupt request (IRQ) lines.

IRQ	Typical Use	Availability
0	System clock	Never available
1	Keyboard	Never available
3	COM2 and COM4	Usually available; disable motherboard port if present
4	COM1 and COM3	Sometimes available; disable motherboard if present
5	LPT2	Usually available; disable motherboard port if present
6	Floppy disk controller	Never available

continues

Table 13.2. continued

IRQ	Typical Use	Availability
7	LPT1	Usually available via sharing
8	Real-time clock/calendar	Not available
9	Really IRQ 2 cascaded	Not available
10	No standard use	Usually available
11	Often used by SCSI adapters	Usually available
12	PS/2 mouse	Available if system doesn't have PS/2 mouse port
13	Math coprocessor	Sometimes available
14	Disk controller	Not usually available
15	No standard use	Usually available

Table 13.3. Uses for PC I/O ports.

I/O Ports	Common Use
200-20F	Game port
230-23F	Microsoft bus or inport mouse
270-27F	LPT2
2E8-2EF	COM4
2F8-2FF	COM2
280-29F	SMC/Western Digital Ethernet card default
300-31F	Novell and 3Com Ethernet card default
320-32F	XT hard-disk controller (including PS/2 model 30)
330-33F	Commonly used by SCSI adapter and sound cards
378-37F	LPT1
380-38C	SDLC adapter
3B0-3BB	Monochrome adapter and LPT0
3C0-3CF	EGA
3D0-3DF	CGA and EGA/VGA when in CGA mode
3E8-3EF	COM3
3F0-3F7	Floppy-disk controller
3F8-3FF	COM1
A20-A27	IBM Token Ring card default

Table 13.4. Uses for PC high memory addresses.

Memory	What It's Used By
A000-C400	VGA
CC00-CDFF	Token Ring default
D000-DFFF	Default EMS page frame
D800-DBFF	Token Ring default
E000-FFFF	PS/2 extended BIOS or Plug-and-Play BIOS
F000-FFFF	AT and PS/2 ROM BIOS

> **TIP**
>
> If you're going to be running Windows 3.x or other DOS environments in addition to Windows NT on this system, it's a good idea to configure all your cards that use upper memory to keep all the used upper-memory regions together. This makes it easier for memory managers like EMM386 to load device drivers into upper memory.

If you can't use the default settings, the safest settings for an Ethernet card are IRQ 5, base I/O port 300, and base memory address CC00.

> **TIP**
>
> It's easier to use the default settings recommended for your LAN card whenever possible. Change the settings only if they conflict with another device in your computer.
>
> If you can't find the manual for your LAN card, you can find the default settings for some common network adapter cards in the *Windows NT Installation Guide* manual. See the section "Network Adapter Card Settings" on pages 50–56.

Connector Settings

When you're setting up your card, don't forget to set its option for which connector to use. Most Ethernet cards have at least two connectors for Thick Ethernet, Thin Ethernet, and/or 10Base-T. Besides setting your card's IRQ, I/O ports, and memory address, you must also tell it which connector option you're going to use. Some Token Ring cards have both STP and UTP connectors and need to be told which to use.

Speed Settings

Most Token Ring cards support both 4Mbps and 16Mbps operation. When you set up a Token Ring, all the stations on that ring must have their adapters set to the same speed because each station repeats data to the next station on the ring. If you add a 4Mbps adapter to a 16Mbps ring, or vice versa, the whole ring will go down.

Most Fast Ethernet cards also have speed jumpers to adjust them from 10 to 100Mbps.

> **TIP**
>
> It's a good idea to make a list of the cards in your system, along with the resources they use, and tape it to the inside of your computer's case. That way, the next time you need to change anything, you'll have all the information handy.

Changing the Card Settings

If you're lucky, you can run configuration programs or reference disks to set your LAN card to the configuration you've selected. However, if you have older or more basic LAN cards, you must venture into the world of DIP switches and jumpers.

Jumpers are groups of small pins sticking out of the card and the plastic covers that fit over a pair of pins, connecting them electrically. To change your card's configuration, you have to pull the cover off the pins it's currently connecting and move it to another position. Jumpers are harder to work with than software-configurable cards or even DIP switches, especially when there isn't enough finger room to get a good grip on the jumpers.

The other problem with jumpers is that they're easy to lose. Those little black pieces of plastic have a truly perverse nature. They jump out of your hand at the worst possible times. In an emergency, I've soldered the two pins together when I couldn't find a jumper. Some cards, such as the Ansel Ethernet card, control all the settings by using jumpers, so these cards are tedious to set up and reconfigure.

Your network card might also use *DIP switches*, which are banks of tiny switches that take up about the same space as a small chip. As soon as you've found the DIP switches on your card, the first thing you need to do is find the mark on the switch bank that shows which way to flip the switch to close it. Most DIP switches say either "on" or "closed" at one edge. When each switch is flipped toward the mark, it connects its two traces on the card. To change DIP switch settings, move the switch to its alternate position (either on/off or open/closed). Make sure you move the switch all the way. Luckily, most switches click to let you know they've moved.

> **TIP**
>
> Don't use a pencil to change your DIP switches. Little pieces of pencil lead could fall into the switch and cause short circuits. Use a paper clip instead. You can use a pen in a pinch, but it makes a mess.

Software-Configured Cards

If you're lucky (or smart), your cards don't have huge numbers of DIP switches or jumpers, but instead are software-configurable. Some cards, such as the Intel Ether Express 16 that Microsoft uses in the Windows for Workgroups starter kit, have no jumpers at all. Others, such as SMC's Elite 16, have one or two jumper-selectable configurations and a jumper setting that lets you set their configuration by using software.

Software-configurable cards come with a DOS-based application that allows you to tell the card how to behave. These programs range from well-written applications that scan your PC and recommend a configuration that doesn't conflict with any of the other devices in your system to crude command-driven setup programs.

For example, you can configure an SMC Elite 16 card by installing it in a free slot in your system, setting its jumper for software configuration, and running SMC's EZSETUP.EXE. EZSETUP shows you the current adapter settings and lets you change them, as shown in Figure 13.11.

FIGURE 13.11.

The interactive screen in EZSETUP.EXE.

```
Board Type:    8013EWC
Node Address:  0000C02A5F70

                         Current Setup

I/O Base Address       320
IRQ                    5
RAM Size               16 K
RAM Base Address       0D0000
Add Wait States        Yes
Network Connection     BNC or 10BaseT

ROM Size               Disabled
ROM Base Address       Disabled

Do you want to change the setup ? (y) -> y

I/O base address ? (320) ->
IRQ ? (5) ->
RAM base address ? (0D0000) ->
Network Connection:
   1= BNC or 10BaseT
   2= AUI or 10BaseT
   3= Twisted Pair - No Link Integrity      ? (1) ->
```

After you change the card settings, you usually need to save your changes and reboot your computer. With some cards, you must turn your computer off for a few moments. After that, you're ready to test the card to make sure it works. Remember to record your card's settings in your computer settings table.

> **TIP**
>
> Don't connect your card to a production network until after you've carefully configured it. A misconfigured card can take your network down, especially on a Token Ring.

After the Installation

As soon as you've installed your network card, you should test it to make sure it's working properly. Most LAN cards come with a disk containing device drivers for popular network operating systems and a diagnostic program to test the card. Most LAN card diagnostics test the card's memory and configuration, verifying that the card is working and that it's configured the way you think it is. The better diagnostics can also send data between two machines running the diagnostic, which will also test the transceiver and cable system.

For example, SMC Ethernet cards come with the program DIAGNOSE.EXE that tests the RAM on the network card and tests connections to a remote station. When you run DIAGNOSE.EXE, you select your adapter card in one menu, then choose the tests you want to perform in another menu. The Basic Adapter Test determines whether the adapter is properly installed and configured. This test will fail if there are hardware or software conflicts with the IRQ, I/O base address, or RAM base address or if the network isn't properly terminated.

If you have another computer on the network with the adapter card correctly installed and configured, you can run DIAGNOSE.EXE and select the Respond to Test Messages option. On the computer where you're configuring the card, select the Initiate Test Messages option. When you run the test, the responding computer echoes the messages, and the initiating computer checks to make sure it received the same message it transmitted.

If your adapter didn't come with diagnostic software, you'll just have to go ahead and install NT on your station, or add the LAN card to your existing NT, and hope it works. If it doesn't, see Chapter 14 for troubleshooting tips.

Installing Windows NT After the Card

If you've set up and installed your LAN card before installing Windows NT on your system, the Windows NT Setup program makes installation easy for you. Right after Setup asks you about your local printer, it scans the system for popular LAN cards. If you have a common card, such as a Novell NE2000 or an SMC Elite 16, Setup will find it and ask you how it's configured.

If, for instance, you have an NE2000 card installed, Windows NT will find the card, check the card settings, and display them in the Adapter Card Setup dialog box. (See Figure 13.12.) If you have another LAN card or you want to use another set of settings, you can change the settings by clicking in the field and entering a new value or by selecting a value from the drop-down list.

NOTE

Because different LAN cards have different sets of configuration options, the dialog box for your card might look quite different from the one in Figure 13.12.

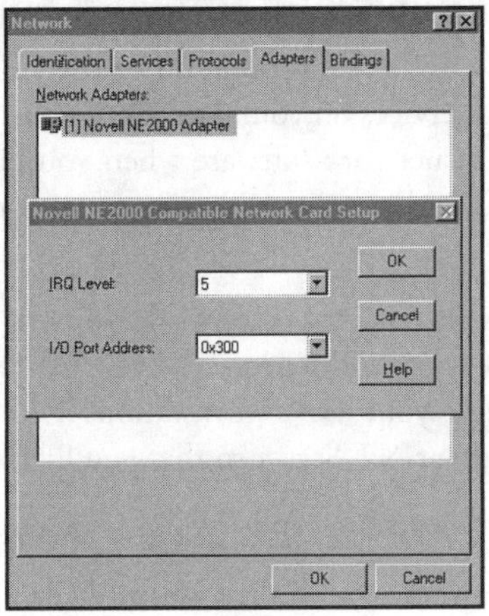

FIGURE 13.12.

The Adapter Card Setup dialog box for a Novell NE2000 network card.

If the information you enter isn't actually how your LAN card is set up, you won't be able to finish configuring your network, communicate with other workstations, or join a Windows NT Server domain. After you finish the installation, you need to change the settings by using the Control Panel, as described in the next section.

Installing a Network Card After Installing Windows NT

If you're installing your network adapter card after you've installed Windows NT, you need to use the Network option in the Control Panel to tell NT how to talk to your card. You also can use the following steps to add a second LAN card to your Windows NT system so that you can access more than one network:

1. Open the Control Panel and double-click on the Network icon to open the Network dialog box. Click on the Adapter tab at the top to display the Adapter page, then click the Add button to add the driver for a new LAN card.

2. When the Select Network Adapter dialog box appears, choose the type of card from the list if it's supported with a Windows NT–included driver. If you have a driver from the manufacturer, click the Have Disk button.

3. Click the Continue button. NT checks your card's settings and displays the Adapter Card Setup dialog box.

4. Check the settings to make sure they reflect how your card is actually configured. If they don't match, you should correct them. You can then click the OK button for both the Adapter Card Setup dialog box and the Network Settings dialog box. Windows NT then installs the drivers and binds the default protocols to each card.

If you have trouble installing the software for your adapter, refer to Chapter 14.

Installing and Removing Network Software

Although Windows NT's Setup program or the Control Panel can install a basic set of network protocols and services on your workstation automatically, you might need to add or remove a few pieces of network software when you install your LAN card. The protocols you choose to install depend mostly on the size of your network and what you're planning to do with it.

If your computer is part of a larger network, you might need to add TCP/IP support or install a requester to allow your workstation to access UNIX servers. You might also want to remove the server service from your user's workstations if you're using a sophisticated server operating system like NetWare or NT Server so that you'll have better control and security.

To add a network protocol or service, follow these steps:

1. Click the Network icon in the Control Panel.

2. Click the Protocols tab at the top of the window to display the list of installed protocols. If the protocol you want to use isn't listed, click the Add button to open the Select Network Software dialog box.

3. From the list, select the protocol you want to add and click OK. If you're adding a protocol other than those that come with Windows NT, click the Have Disk button.

4. You might see a dialog box asking for the path to the files needed to install the protocol or service; if not, Windows NT uses the default information to copy the drivers it needs. When Windows NT has finished copying files, you return to the Network dialog box.

5. Click OK. Windows NT displays a progress dialog box as it binds the protocols to your adapter card.

Some network protocols, such as NWLINK and TCP/IP, prompt you for more configuration information, typically network addresses. For details, see the discussion of these protocols in Chapter 14.

You'll have to restart your computer so changes to your network configuration can take effect. After you've made changes, Windows NT gives you an opportunity to restart the system.

The files that make up your new protocol or services are copied to your \WINNT\SYSTEM32 directory. To remove a network component, follow these steps:

1. Click the Network icon in the Control Panel.
2. In the Network Settings dialog box, select the protocol, adapter, or service you want to remove in the list.
3. Click the Remove button and let Windows NT remove the drivers for you.
4. Restart your computer.

Summary

In this chapter, you've seen the types of networks that are available to a Windows NT machine, and you should be able to decide which one will suit your needs if you don't already have a network in place. Usually, the overriding criteria are the number of machines on the network and the cost per station, followed by the transfer speed. For most small networks, one of the standard Ethernet 10BaseT or 10Base5 networks works well.

This chapter has also looked at how to configure your network card and negotiate the confusion of setting the card's configuration parameters properly. Choosing the correct IRQ, DMA, and memory address can be difficult, but by using the tables in this chapter, you should be able to find a setting that works.

13

INSTALLING YOUR
WINDOWS NT
NETWORK

CHAPTER 14

Windows NT Networking Out of the Box: Peer-to-Peer Networking

IN THIS CHAPTER

If you're planning to build a small network—especially if the vast majority of the workstations are going to be running some version of Windows—you'll probably find all the networking software you need right in the Windows NT box. With just the standard Windows NT networking software, you can share data and printers across the network with other Windows NT and Windows for Workgroups workstations, as well as allow DOS machines access to shared resources.

Because all the Windows NT, Windows 95, and Windows for Workgroups stations on the network can act as equals or peers, both offering their resources to be shared and accessing resources on other stations, this type of network is generally called *peer-to-peer networking*. In the DOS world, this kind of peer networking is provided by products such as Artisoft's LANtastic, Novell's NetWare Lite, and, of course, Windows for Workgroups.

This chapter takes a good look at how Windows NT's peer-networking features help you build workgroups that allow users to share resources with other systems. If you've used Windows for Workgroups (WFW), the concept of workgroups will be familiar to you because Windows NT workgroups and WFW workgroups work the same way, as do Windows 95 workgroups.

Defining Workgroups

A *workgroup* is a collection of two or more computers that share files or printers across a network. You might, for example, create workgroups on your network that correspond to your organization's structure.

Members of these departments can exchange data among themselves and share printers. When you need to retrieve files from a computer in your workgroup, you can easily find the shared directory and link a drive letter to it by using File Manager. If Windows NT didn't make you organize your computers into workgroups, or if you made the mistake of creating only one workgroup for a large organization, you'd have to scroll through a list of all the computers in your company to find your data. With workgroups, My Computer or Explorer displays a directory tree of the networks, workgroups, and servers available on the network, which makes finding your data much easier. Organizing computers into workgroups makes it easier to browse network resources.

Your workgroups should have more to do with the logical organization of computers than with a network's physical structure. Creating workgroups for the first floor, second floor, and third floor makes a lot less sense than setting up departmental workgroups.

If your company advocates the modern management practice of interdisciplinary teams, in which designers, engineers, and marketers all work together to bring a new product to market, you can (and probably should) create a workgroup for each active team rather than each department.

Although workgroups help you organize network resources, they don't really simplify network administration. Each server, which can mean each PC on the system, is still administered individually. If the user WGATES needs to access secure data on four, or 400, different machines, someone (and that means you) needs to create the user WGATES on each of those servers—one at a time. With a large number of computers, this can be an onerous task, about as much fun as having large, hairy men force burning bamboo shoots under your fingernails.

Users with large networks should use Windows NT Server, which goes beyond the workgroup concept to a domain-based naming and security scheme. Unlike servers in a workgroup, servers in a Windows NT Server domain are administered as a group. A *domain* is a group of file servers that share a common user and group definition file. Because these servers all share the same user file, if you want WGATES to have access to data on 30 file servers that are all part of the same domain, you need to create an account for him only once.

Because servers in a domain are usually running Windows NT Server, or some version of Microsoft's LAN Manager or LM/X (LAN Manager for UNIX), Chapters 15, "NT Server," and 16, "Setting Up Trust Relationships in NT Server," discuss domains. Workgroups, as opposed to domains, are the unit of organization in peer-to-peer networks.

Setting Up the Peer Network

Installing the LAN card driver into Windows NT automatically installs the server service (which lets you give users at other computers access to your disk data and printers), the workstation service (which allows you to access other computer files and printers), and the computer browser service (which keeps a list of the other computers on the network). You then tell Windows NT your computer's name and the name of the domain or workgroup this computer will be a member of.

Although it's tempting to just rip off the shrink wrap and get that new software toy installed as quickly as possible, that's probably not a good idea. My experience has shown that organizations that spend a little bit of time and energy planning their installation spend much less time maintaining their system than organizations that allow their networks to grow piecemeal.

First, you need to come up with a convention for naming your computers, domains, and workgroups. A naming convention isn't just a way to keep people from using silly names, such as our NetWare file server Shlomo. It's also an important way to prevent people from creating duplicate names, which can keep either of two objects with the same name from working, and add some valuable information, such as the location of a computer or its most frequent user's name, which makes it easier to find and fix problems that crop up.

What naming convention you use is less important than simply developing a convention. The most successful conventions are the simplest and most understandable when viewed. I had one client who successfully used the most common convention: the user's ID, made up of the user's

14

PEER-TO-PEER
NETWORKING

first two initials and last name truncated to eight characters, plus -COMP for PCs and department names, plus -DOM for domains. Another client came up with a system that in eight characters included the company division, the user's initials and employment status, and a two-digit counter to ensure uniqueness. This code was so complicated that I was hired to create a client/server application to generate the codes and increment the counters as Jean-Paul Marat and John Patrick Murphy were assigned accounts.

> **NOTE**
>
> A computer's name can't be the same as any other computer on the network—even if they're in different workgroups—or the same as a Windows NT Server domain. In addition, your workgroup name can't be the same as your computer name.

Joining a Workgroup

After you have everything installed, you might want to make your computer a member of a new workgroup. To change workgroups, follow these steps:

1. Open the Network applet in the Control Panel.

2. In the Network dialog box, shown in Figure 14.1, the first page shows the current workgroup and machine name.

FIGURE 14.1.

The Identification page of the Network dialog box identifies the machine and workgroup names.

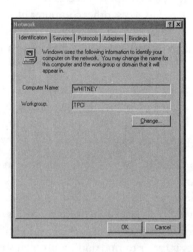

3. To enter a new name for either the workgroup or machine, click the Change button. Enter the new information in the Identification Changes window that appears, shown in Figure 14.2. The computer name entered at the top of the window must be unique on the network. Below the computer name, you can enter either a workgroup or a domain name, depending on the type of network you're using.

FIGURE 14.2.

From this window you can enter a machine and workgroup name, or a domain name, depending on the type of network.

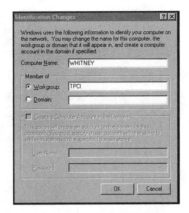

4. Click OK to save the new values.

> **NOTE**
>
> A computer can be a member of only one workgroup at a time.

Joining an NT Server Domain

Joining a domain is similar to joining a workgroup. The difference is that anyone can join a workgroup at any time, but only computers and users who have accounts created by the network administrator can join a domain. As you can see from Figure 14.2, when you enter a domain name in the Identification Changes dialog box, you get the option of entering the domain's administrator account name and password.

If the computer's account already exists on the domain, or if you enter the correct administrator name and password so that the program can create one, your computer becomes a member of the domain. If not, you are rejected.

> **NOTE**
>
> A computer can be a member of only one domain at a time.

To join a domain, follow these steps:

1. Open the Network applet in the Control Panel.
2. Click the Change button next to the current workgroup or domain name.
3. Enter the name of the domain you want to join, as shown in Figure 14.3.

14

PEER-TO-PEER NETWORKING

FIGURE 14.3.

When entering a domain name, you can specify account information at the same time.

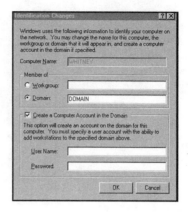

4. If the domain administrator has created an account for this computer, you can click OK to join the domain.

Creating a User Account in a Domain

If you're the domain administrator, you can save a step by having the Control Panel create the computer's account as you install Windows NT on the system. All you have to do is enter your username and password.

1. In the Identification Changes dialog box, click on the Create a Computer Account in the Domain checkbox.

2. Enter the name of the domain administrator in the User Name field, and then enter the domain administrator's password in the Password field.

3. Click OK.

This creates an account for the user and logs this computer onto the domain as a workstation.

Setting Up a Workgroup

After you've configured a set of computers into a workgroup, your next step is to decide which computers are actually going to make their resources available for other users to share (called *sharing* in Redmondtonian)—that is, which ones will be servers and which will be only client workstations accessing the data on the servers. You don't have to make every Windows NT workstation a server.

There's a constant debate between network experts who feel that a small number of servers is better (the client/server camp) and those who advocate the freedom of a network in which each user's machine is a server (the peer-to-peer camp). On a bad day, you might hear them call each other "fascist" or "anarchist."

The client/server camp argues that having fewer servers is better because you can back them up and make sure they have better disk subsystems, UPSs, redundant disk drives, and plenty of memory so that users working with shared data get good performance. Even more important, they argue, a single administrator can manage a few file servers, creating users and setting up their security. They claim that users administering their own servers are slipshod about security, forget to make backups, and otherwise don't do the job as well as a professional administrator.

The peer-to-peer camp argues that they save the cost of additional dedicated server machines and a full-time administrator while empowering users, thereby building esprit de corps and boosting productivity. They also point out the advantage of not having a single point of failure at the file server. If one of 50 servers fails, you can get more work done than if the one and only server fails.

The truth is somewhere in between, and which approach you should take depends on your corporate culture, personal temperament, and users. If you're putting in a five-station network for a group of software developers, making all of them servers and letting those sophisticated users administer their own systems is a good idea. If, however, you're setting up a system to support a new airline's reservation system, you're probably better off with a single big server or multiple NT Servers in a domain.

Sharing Resources

After you've decided which machines are going to be servers, you must set up their resources to be shared. Windows NT allows you to offer printers that are attached to your computer and directories on your local hard drives to be shared by other users. Whenever you want to offer a resource from your system, you need to give it a name—called a *share, sharename,* or *sharepoint*—that other users can then use to access the printer or directory.

14

> **NOTE**
>
> You can share a CD-ROM just as though it's a directory on your local computer. However, to prevent clients from getting errors, always make the share read-only; otherwise, a network client might try to write to this share (on your CD-ROM). I have seen a few programs try this and fail, sometimes causing the Windows or MS-DOS client to freeze, requiring a reboot to restore. If this happens, you can be sure that there's an accompanying data loss.
>
> One other point to consider when sharing a CD-ROM is that any client software needing local access to the CD-ROM will fail as well. This type of software uses MSCDEX (Microsoft CD-ROM Extensions) and will be unable to find its data files. In such a case, contact the manufacturer to see whether there's a network-aware version of the application.

When you first install Windows NT, it automatically creates sharenames for the root directory of each logical drive on your server and the directory you installed Windows NT into. The sharenames to the root directories are the drive letter with a dollar sign ($) added. So the share to C:\ is C$, you can access D:\ as D$, and so on. The Windows NT directory (typically C:\WINNT) is given the sharename ADMIN$. These shares are created to make administering the system easier. A network administrator can automatically update all of his or her servers by accessing just these administrative shares. Only members of the Administrators and Backup Operators groups can use, and only administrators can change, the properties of these sharenames.

Follow these steps to share a directory:

1. In My Computer, select the drive or directory you want to share.

2. Choose File | Sharing, or select the drive or directory and right-click to display the pop-up menu and select Sharing.

3. In the Properties window's Sharing page, shown in Figure 14.4, enter the name you want to use to share the drive or directory in the Share Name box. For a directory, the default sharename is the directory's own name. The sharename can be up to 12 characters long and should have some relation to the data the directory holds to make finding the right data easier.

FIGURE 14.4.

You can share a drive or directory by entering information in the Sharing page.

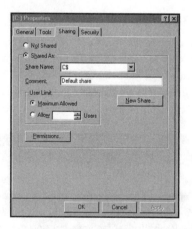

4. Enter a description of the data or the sharename's purpose in the Comment field; users can see this description when they're browsing for data.

5. Now you can enter information in the User Limit box to set a limit on the number of users who can simultaneously access your data through this or click the Permissions button to set the permissions for this share. The next section, "Securing Your Data: Setting Share Properties," explains what, if anything, you should do with these parameters in terms of security.

6. Click OK to make the drive or directory available for others to use.

7. You can set up several different names for each drive or directory, depending on how you want the shared item to appear to others. To set up another name besides the default, click the New Share button.

> **NOTE**
>
> To share a directory, you must be logged onto the server machine as a member of the Administrators or Power Users group.

Securing Your Data: Setting Share Properties

Each sharename has a user limit and a permissions filter associated with it. You can set the user limit to reduce the performance effect of other users accessing your hard disk or to serve as a primitive form of application metering. If, for example, you have five licensed copies of WinWord, you can set the WinWord sharename user limit to five. When the sixth user tries to link to that share—that is, assign a drive letter on his or her machine as an alias for the data in the server's directory—this attempt will fail. However, the user limit isn't really adequate as a software metering device because most users try to share the directory as they log on, instead of when they want to run the application. Therefore, 10 users need 10 shares, even if only two of them are running WinWord.

To limit user access to the data, you can set share permissions, in addition to user permissions you might have already set up for this directory. A user is allowed to link to a directory only when that user, or a group the user is a member of, has permission to access the share or directory. When you link a drive to a directory on a Windows NT server, your station sends a series of messages to the server that essentially says, "Hi, this is IBM686. My local user WGATES really would like to use your SECRET_STUFF directory, okay?" If WGATES has permission to use the directory, the server acknowledges the request; if not, it sends a negative acknowledgment.

You can give a user one level of access when he or she is sitting at the local keyboard, and a lower level of access when coming in over the network, by granting both directory and share permissions. The directory permissions act as the limit to rights, and the share permissions can then reduce access further. The user has any given permission only if he or she has that permission through both the share and directory permissions.

> **NOTE**
>
> The default NT user group Everyone automatically has the Full Control permission to each sharepoint when the sharepoint is created. Unless you want everyone to have access to all your data, get in the habit of deleting this permission.

To create a set of share permissions, click the Permissions button in the New Share dialog box to open the Access Through Share Permissions dialog box, shown in Figure 14.5. Select the name of the user or group you want to share the resource with, and then select a permission from the Type of Access list box.

FIGURE 14.5.

Creating a set of share permissions in the Access Through Share Permissions dialog box.

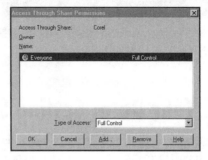

You have a lot less flexibility when setting permissions for a sharename than you do with a directory. You can set a user's or group's rights to only Read, Change, Full Control, or No Access. Table 14.1 shows the effect of each of these permissions.

Table 14.1. A list of directory permissions under Windows NT.

Permission	Rights Granted
No Access	No access rights.
Read	Read files, list subdirectories, and view file properties.
Change	Write to file, create file/subdirectory, delete file/subdirectory, and change attributes.
Full Control	Write to file, create file/subdirectory, delete file/subdirectory, change attributes, change permissions (NTFS), and take ownership (NTFS).

Because you have more detailed control over users through directory permissions, you should use directory permissions (explained in more detail in Chapter 3) as your primary data protection screen. Share permissions should be used to protect very sensitive data that should be accessed or updated only from the local console.

WARNING

Giving your users full control over a directory can be dangerous. Not only can they delete all your files, they can also lock you out. You would then have to use an administrator-level account to take back ownership of the directory.

After you set the permissions for the directory, click OK to close the Access Through Share Permissions dialog box and save your changes. Your directory is now available on the network for other users to connect to. In My Computer or Explorer, you can see a shared directory icon next to the directory's name, which lets you know it's being shared.

Stopping Drive or Directory Sharing

If you decide that you no longer want to allow other users to share your computer's resources, you can choose to stop sharing a particular resource. You should make sure no users have any files open before you stop sharing (through the Server applet in the Control Panel), or you'll start getting phone calls from annoyed users. If a user has a file open to read, he'll get errors when he tries to access the file. Even worse, if a user has the file open to write, he might not be able to save the data, and you might end up destroying the whole file. You can learn how to use the Server applet in Chapter 8, "Using the Control Panel to Configure Windows NT."

Just as you must be a member of the Administrators or Power Users group to share a directory, you must be a member of one of these groups to stop sharing. To stop sharing a drive or directory, follow these steps:

1. Open My Computer and highlight the drive or directory you want to stop sharing.
2. Choose File | Sharing, or right-click and select Sharing from the pop-up menu to display the Sharing page of the Properties window.
3. Select the Not Shared radio button. The Not Shared button affects all names, but the Remove Share button affects only one sharename at a time.
4. Click OK. If users are connected to the shared directory, the system asks you to confirm that you want to leave these poor slobs high and dry.

> **WARNING**
>
> Remember not to stop sharing if users have files open; it could lead to data loss or job loss.

14

PEER-TO-PEER
NETWORKING

Sharing Printers

If you haven't already read Chapter 4, "Printers," now would be a good time to do so because it concentrates on the network-related aspects of working with Print Folders. If I've skipped something here, it most likely applies to both networked and standalone Windows NT systems and is discussed in Chapter 4. Some features that are available only on PCs connected to networks, such as usable print spooling, are integral to Windows NT, even for single-user systems.

In addition to sharing your data, you can allow other users to send their print jobs to any printers you have on your system. Just as you do with directories, you can set permissions to control which users can access each printer or maintain the print queue for a printer.

As with any local area network, Windows NT provides shared printers by spooling data intended for the printer on the print server computer. When you tell an application to print on a remote printer, it sends the data across the network to the print server, which then sends it to the printer.

Windows NT's printer sharing differs from what you might have become used to with networks such as NetWare or LANtastic, which primarily have DOS workstations. First, you can print directly from Windows 16-bit or 32-bit applications to network printers. With DOS and Windows 3.*x* networks, you must link a network printer to one of DOS's logical printer ports (LPT1: through LPT3:) before you can send the data to a network print queue. This feature makes it a lot easier to have different printer definitions for high-priority and low-priority print jobs, different output trays, or other printer configuration settings, because users have to select just the printer definition.

Second, because printer definitions include not only the printer's logical location on the network but also the printer's driver, users at Windows NT stations that have been properly set up can't send a print job to a printer using the new driver. No longer do users send their print jobs to bit heaven by selecting LaserJet III as the driver for your LaserJet III with the PostScript cartridge, nor do they print reams of PostScript code by selecting the reverse.

Windows NT goes even one step further, saving you from driver-mismatch migraines and from the print driver–distribution blues. On most PC LANs, users must have the appropriate Windows print drivers for each printer on the network they might print to. When you get PageMaker 5.0 and discover that it works only with the newest version 99.99.99.22.9.9 of the driver for your Gutenberg WonderPress 10,000-page-per-minute printer, you might have a good day's work copying the Gutenberg WonderDriver to each machine on your network. With Windows NT on both the print server and the user's workstation, you just install the print driver on the print server; workstations simply use the server's driver.

If you've been working with NetWare and you're getting a bit confused by the new terminology, just bear in mind that what Windows NT calls a printer is actually more like a NetWare print queue (which can be serviced by one or more printers) than a NetWare printer (which is a specific port on the network, and therefore is really just one printer).

Sharing Your Printer with Other Network Users

You can share a printer that's attached to your computer for others to print to. Before you share a printer, it must be connected to one of your printer ports and have the printer drivers installed. Note that your workstation must be running the Server service to share a printer.

To share a printer, follow these steps:

1. Use the Control Panel's Printer icon to display the Printers folder. If you've already created the printer you want to share, highlight it and choose File | Sharing. If you're creating a new printer to be shared, use the Add Printer wizard and follow the instructions. To enable sharing of a printer, use the Sharing page of the Printer Properties dialog box shown in Figure 14.6.

FIGURE 14.6.

To share a printer, use the Sharing page of the Properties dialog box.

2. Enable the Shared radio button on the Sharing page. Windows NT then creates a sharename for the printer in the Share Name box by truncating the printer's name and making it fit the DOS sharename conventions, removing spaces and other forbidden characters. If you don't like the name it comes up with, you can edit it, but it can't be longer than 12 characters, and it must follow MS-DOS naming conventions or those for MS-DOS and Windows for Workgroups.

3. If your printer-naming convention doesn't tell users where to go to pick up their print jobs, you should enter a description of the printer's location in the Comment or Location boxes on the General page of the Properties dialog box.

4. Click OK on the Sharing page to share the printer.

Sharing a Networked Printer

Connecting printers directly to the local area network rather than to a network PC's serial or parallel port has really taken off in the TCP/IP and NetWare worlds. Directly connected printers have some important advantages over PC-connected printers; the biggest one is that the print stream is no longer at the mercy of the user whose printer is being shared. With a networked printer, you don't have to worry that Bill will try to run every TSR on his hard disk at the same time, or even that he'll just turn his PC off to go home in the middle of that 300-page report.

The other problem with PC-connected printers is the bottleneck at the parallel port. As laser printers that print at 15 to 20 pages per minute have become common, the standard (or even enhanced) BiTronics parallel port can't keep up, especially on graphically complex documents. A 10Mbps EtherNet or 16Mbps Token Ring can deliver data to the printer a lot faster than a parallel port.

Windows NT includes support for the most common networked laser printers—HP LaserJets with HP Jet Direct cards. You can use a Jet Direct card with LaserJet IIs and LaserJet IIIs; more sophisticated printers, such as the LaserJet IIISi and LaserJet IV, come with JetDirect cards as standard equipment. HP's Jet Direct card is available in EtherNet and Token Ring versions. Both use the DLC (data link control) protocol to communicate with Windows NT print servers.

If you're planning to use JetDirect cards, you need to install the DLC protocol on the machines that will be acting as print servers for the networked printers. (Refer to Chapter 12, "An Overview of Windows NT Networking," or Chapter 8.) The *print server* is the machine that has the printer definition for the networked printer and shares that printer definition with other users.

Follow these steps to set up a networked printer that's attached to one of your server's ports (and not accessed through the network cable):

1. Select the Printer folder from the Control Panel. If you're configuring a newly attached printer that hasn't been defined on your system before, click the Add Printer icon to start the Add Printer wizard. Follow the wizard's steps to add a printer until you reach the window that deals with Sharing, shown in Figure 14.7. If the printer already exists and you want to change its status to allow sharing, highlight the printer in the Printer window, and choose File | Sharing.

FIGURE 14.7.

Use this window to indicate whether the printer you're adding will be shared.

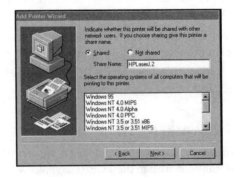

2. Enable the Shared radio button and either accept or edit the printer's shared name. This is the name others on the network see when they try to share this printer.

3. Click Next. The printer is now accessible to others on the network.

To share a printer that's attached to the network, such as an HP JetDirect-equipped printer for example, you need to configure your machine to provide printing services over the network. In many cases, you will be using TCP/IP as the network protocol, so that's the protocol used in the following steps:

1. If necessary, install the Jet Direct card or other network adapter in your printer. Connect the printer to the network, and turn it on.

2. Open the Network window from the Control Panel and select Services. If you have Microsoft TCP/IP Printing already loaded, move to the next step. If this service is not listed, click the Add button and select Microsoft, then Microsoft TCP/IP Printing to install the service. Microsoft TCP/IP Printing should be in your Network Services list, as shown in Figure 14.8. Once the TCP/IP Printing service is installed, click OK to move to the next step.

FIGURE 14.8.

You must have Microsoft TCP/IP Printing installed to use a network printer.

3. Select the Printer folder from the Control Panel. If you're configuring a newly attached printer that hasn't been defined on your system before, click the Add Printer icon to start the Add Printer Wizard. If you're modifying an existing printer, use the Properties menu brought up with a right-click.

4. If the network port isn't displayed in the window, click Add Port and select either the LPR port or TCP/IP port (if one is shown).

5. In the field for the name of the server-providing host, enter the printer name or IP address (usually supplied as part of the printer network card setup routine). Enter a name for the printer. Because DOS applications must send their data to this port and can accept only names similar to LPT*x*, you might want to call the printer by a short name. After you have entered this information, close the New Port dialog box and you should see the printer port on the list of available ports. Select it and click Next. Figure 14.9 shows the Port dialog box with a newly defined IP address selected.

14

PEER-TO-PEER
NETWORKING

FIGURE **14.9.**
*Adding a new port lets
you select it from the list
of available ports.*

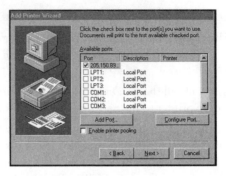

6. Continue with the Add Printer Wizard to select the type of printer on the network. When you get to the Sharing window, you will probably want to enable the Shared radio button to allow others to access the printer through your Windows NT machine, as shown in Figure 14.10.

FIGURE **14.10.**
*Enable sharing if you
want other users to
access the network
printer through your
NT machine.*

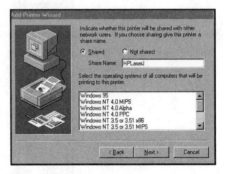

7. You can select a test page to be printed to make sure everything is working well. If there's a problem, check the IP address or server name, and reconfigure the printer.

NOTE

To use a TCP/IP network printer, your Windows NT machine must have both TCP/IP and Microsoft TCP/IP Printing installed. In addition, the network printer must support LPD (line printing daemon), which most printer network cards provide automatically.

Linking to Shared Printers

To use a printer on another user's computer, the procedure is much the same as setting up any other kind of printer:

1. Click the Printer folder in the Control Panel, and select Add Printer to start the wizard. In the first window, enable the "Network printer server" radio button to indicate you're using a printer connected to another machine. (See Figure 14.11.)

FIGURE 14.11.
In this step of the Add Printer Wizard, you can choose to use a printer on someone else's machine.

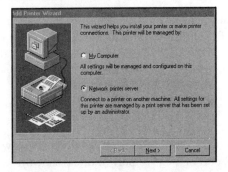

2. In the Connect to Printer dialog box that appears next, find the machine the printer is attached to, then expand it to find the printer. Select the printer name and click OK to link to it, as shown in Figure 14.12.

FIGURE 14.12.
Select the printer you want to use.

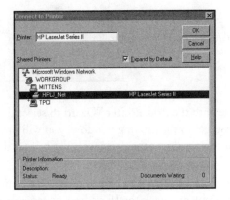

If you have enough permissions, you're now connected to the printer.

Connecting to Shared Printers on UNIX Servers

Many large networks include a mixture of print servers, including Windows NT Server, Windows NT, Windows for Workgroups, Windows 95, LAN Manager, NetWare, and UNIX servers. All of these servers except UNIX support browsing. To connect to a UNIX printer, you need to know the printer name and IP address. Contact your system administrator if you don't have this information.

14

PEER-TO-PEER
NETWORKING

After you have the printer name and IP address, connecting to the UNIX printer is relatively trouble-free. The procedure is the same as accessing a network printer, except instead of the network printer name or IP address, you supply the host machine's IP address or name. Follow these steps to connect to a remote machine's shared printer:

1. Open the Network window from the Control Panel and select Services. If you have Microsoft TCP/IP Printing already loaded, move to the next step. If this service is not listed, click the Add button and select Microsoft, then Microsoft TCP/IP Printing to install the service. Once the TCP/IP Printing service is installed, move to the next step.

2. Select the Printer folder, and then click the Add Printer icon to start the Add Printer Wizard.

3. If the network port is not displayed in the window, click Add Port and select either the LPR port or TCP/IP port (if one is shown).

4. In the field for the name of the server-providing host, enter the printer server name or IP address. Enter a name for the printer. Figure 14.13 shows the naming dialog box. After you have entered this information, close the dialog box and you should see the IP address on the list of available ports. Select it and click OK.

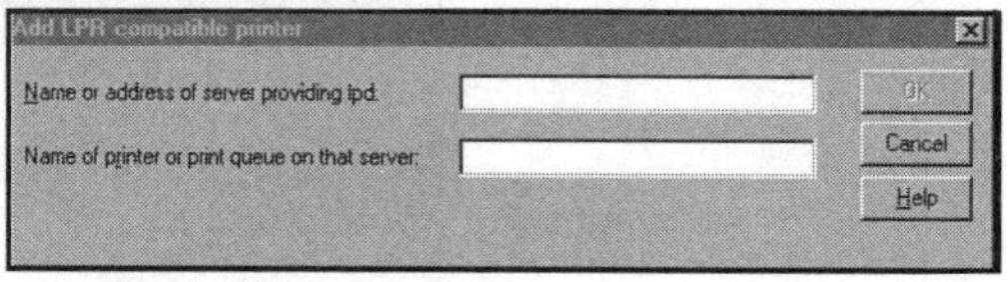

Figure 14.13.

Enter the name of the server and the printer in this dialog box.

5. Continue with the Add Printer Wizard to select the type of printer on the network. When you get to the Sharing window, you will probably want to enable the Shared radio button to allow others to access the printer through your Windows NT machine.

6. You can select a test page to be printed to make sure everything is working well. If there's a problem, check the IP address or server name, and reconfigure the printer.

TIP

If you share the printer you have created, other computers can then browse your computer and connect to it without having to know the printer name and IP address. From a system management viewpoint, it makes more sense to create and share these types of printers on a Windows NT print server.

Controlling Access to Printers

> **NOTE**
>
> Details about setting up printer permissions can be found in Chapter 9, "Windows NT Administration."

Securing a printer on a single-user system seems strange to most people. If George can use the computer, he should be able to print. In the network environment, however, you can see a good reason for setting printer permissions. Even if every user is allowed to print to every printer, you might not want all 500 students in your university to have the power to move their print jobs to the top of the queue or to delete other users' print jobs.

There are also good reasons for preventing users from accessing a printer at all. Color, large format, and high-resolution printers have a high cost per page and a high "potential for abuse" for personal uses, such as birthday party invitations. Printers with specific forms, such as invoices, should be protected to prevent accidents, and the printer with check stock in it just begs for a little late-night PageMaking.

You also can restrict printer access to printers at remote locations to keep wide area network traffic down.

For most network printers, the default set of printer permissions (in which the administrators and power users have full control over the print queue, everyone gets to print, and users get to control their own print jobs) is just about the right combination. It wouldn't hurt to give a user whose desk is physically close to the printer the ability to manage the printer so that he or she can handle the occasional stopping and starting of the printer for a paper change or jam.

Network Printing Tips

If you follow these hints, your network printing will be relatively trouble-free:

- Make sure that print servers have enough disk space to hold all their print jobs.
- Use separator pages if print jobs are distributed to users. Skip them if users pick up their own jobs.
- Networked, high-capacity printers make life easier.
- Assign a key operator for each printer. This user is responsible for changing paper, clearing jams, and so forth. Give him or her full control over the printer definition.
- If you have both high- and low-priority users, create separate printers with different priorities rather than have users change their priorities.

14

PEER-TO-PEER NETWORKING

NT and Windows for Workgroups/Windows 95

Even Bill Gates doesn't expect you to switch all your workstations to Windows NT right away. Most users' needs are met perfectly well by Windows 3.*x* or Windows 95, so they don't need Windows NT. Even more important, many users can't afford the 486 processor and 16M of memory that NT needs to run well. Windows for Workgroups can run comfortably on a 386 with 8M of memory. Windows 95 works better with a 486, but 8M of memory is still OK.

Microsoft designed Windows for Workgroups 3.11 to be the best 16-bit client software for accessing Windows NT and Windows NT Server file servers. Even with Windows 95 available, this is still the case because, technically speaking, Windows 95 is a mixture of 16-bit and 32-bit code. At this point, Windows 95 is probably the best low-end client for NT. Graduation would be to NT Workstation, of course, but WFW itself graduated up to Windows 95. When you can afford the upgrade to your workstations, it makes sense to advance to Windows 95 on your low-level workstations. Why? Windows 95 shakes hands with NT a little better, dishing up and understanding long filenames and folder names, for example; using 32-bit drivers whenever possible—such as for printers, the screen, and of course, network cards—speeds things up as well.

I'm not going to delve into the differences between how the two operating systems interact with NT because on this level, they're minimal. If you know how to use WFW on the NT network, you can easily understand Windows 95. Users on Windows for Workgroups or Windows 95 machines can link to resources on Windows NT machines as though they were other Windows for Workgroups or Windows 95 systems. Users on Windows NT stations can also access data on Windows for Workgroup and Windows 95 machines.

If you want Windows for Workgroups or Windows 95 stations to access your Windows NT machines, make sure they all use the same protocol. If the WFW or Windows 95 systems will be accessing only Windows NT system resources on the same network, Microsoft's NetBEUI is the best choice. If these systems need to access servers across routers, you might have to configure Windows for Workgroups to use IPX/SPX-compatible transport with NetBIOS or an optional TCP/IP. As a default, Windows 95 stations are set up with both NetBEUI and IPX/SPX. In my experience, it seems to be OK to leave the IPX/SPX drivers loaded even if they aren't being used, although it hasn't affected things when I've removed them, either.

> **NOTE**
>
> Although Windows for Workgroups/Windows 95 can support multiple transport protocols, such as NetBEUI, IPX/SPX, or TCP/IP, simultaneously, using a single transport protocol is more efficient and causes fewer problems. Always try to use a single protocol for your network clients who use MS-DOS or Windows for Workgroups.

Windows for Workgroups can access resources on a Windows NT or NT Server through the File Manager or Print Manger. The same holds true of Windows 95—just use the tools built into Windows 95 to access the NT or other WFW resources. Typically, you access resources on another machine through the Network Neighborhood icon on the Windows 95 Desktop; however, you can also use Windows Explorer.

Windows for Workgroups doesn't have a field for entering a different username to access this resource. If you're supporting Windows for Workgroups users, you must make sure that all users can get to all the resources they need from a single user ID.

When you access a Windows for Workgroups or Windows 95 system's data, you might see the dialog box shown in Figure 14.14.

FIGURE 14.14.

The Enter Network Password dialog box opens if there's a password-protected share on a WFW or Windows 95 station.

Unlike Windows NT and NT Server, Windows for Workgroups and Windows 95 don't manage file access permissions by user account. Windows for Workgroups uses a less sophisticated system called *share-based security*. When you share a directory on a Windows for Workgroups or Windows 95 station, you get to assign a password that the user must enter to access the data. If a user at a Windows NT station tries to access the data in a directory that has been protected this way, he or she sees the dialog box shown in Figure 14.14 and must enter the resource's password.

If you're running Windows NT Server, you need to tell Windows for Workgroups or Windows 95 machines to join a domain when the client machine is started; otherwise, they can't access resources on the servers in a domain. To do this on a WFW station, follow these steps:

1. Open the Network applet in Windows for Workgroups' Control Panel and click the Startup button to open the Startup Settings dialog box. (See Figure 14.15.)
2. Enable the Log On to Windows NT or LAN Manager Domain checkbox.
3. Enter the name of the domain and set the password.

Procedures for adding a Windows 95 workstation to an NT network are explained in the following section.

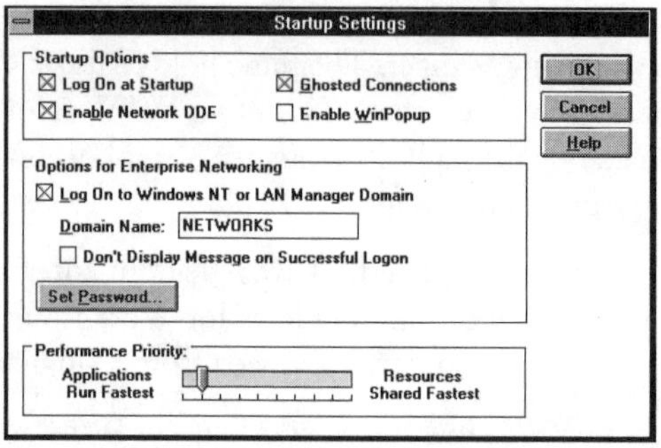

FIGURE 14.15.

Joining a domain from Windows for Workgroups.

> **NOTE**
>
> Because of limited security and performance with Windows for Workgroups and Windows 95 machines and, even more important, because a remote user accessing your hard drive slows a Windows for Workgroups or Windows 95 station much more than on a Windows NT station, you're better off keeping all your shared data on Windows NT systems. I would go so far as to recommend that you disable file sharing on Windows for Workgroups or Windows 95 machines.

Adding a Windows 95 Workstation to the NT Network

Because of slight differences between Windows 95 and WFW, I'll outline the steps for getting a Windows 95 station on the NT network. First, make sure the Windows 95 machine is set up for one of the networking protocols installed on the NT server, usually NetBEUI or IPX/SPX. On a huge network, however, it might be TCP/Internet provider. NetBEUI is the best choice for a Microsoft-only small network—it's lean and mean. Remember that your client stations—Windows 95 or other—must be speaking the same language as the NT server machine. Use the Control Panel in Windows 95 to check out the protocols installed.

After you've checked out the protocols, follow these steps to share resources on the network:

1. Right-click on any item you want to share on the network, such as printers, disks, or folders. Simply find the item with Explorer or My Computer, right-click, and choose Sharing. In the resulting box, activate the Shared As button and fill in the share name, comment, optional password, and possible security type and restrictions. Note that you have to be part of an NT Domain to take advantage of user or group-level access rights.

2. On the NT machine, of course, you'll have to share any drives, directories, or printers you want to give the Windows 95 stations access to. Use My Computer or Explorer and Print Folders on the NT machine to do this, using the Share As command. Remember that an NT machine can share not only local printers, but also any printers on other NT stations it has access to.

3. If the NT sever is a domain server, each Windows 95 client must have a user account set up for it on the NT server if it's to have access to resources on that server. Use the NT User Manager for Domains to set these up, and then use NT's Explorer or My Computer and Print Folders to declare any specific sharing restrictions that might apply to those accounts.

4. Next, choose one of these options, as appropriate:

   If you're using NT Workstation, make sure you have the same workgroup name specified on the NT workstation as you do for each Windows 95 station that will be part of this workgroup.

   If you're using NT Server, set each Windows 95 station to log onto the NT domain and enter the correct domain in the domain field at each station. To do this, open the Control Panel, choose Networks, and double-click on Microsoft Client for Windows Networks. Enable the Domain checkbox and enter the name of your NT domain.

Now you should be able to open Network Neighborhood on any Windows 95 stations in the workgroup or domain and see an icon for the NT machine. Also, with the server browsers in NT's Print Folders or My Computer, the Windows 95 stations should show up as additional servers in the workgroup or domain.

TIP

If your office has one or more Novell print servers around, you can use NT Server's Print Folders to share those printer servers. Using this technique, Windows 95, DOS, and WFW stations won't need NetWare-specific network drivers loaded to print on the Novell print server. (You will need to install a printer driver for each printer, though.) This approach can be done only with Server, not NT Workstation. First, install and configure the NetWare Gateway Services software that's supplied with NT Server, and second, connect to the NetWare print queue and share it.

Using Shared Printer Drivers

One important difference between WFW and Windows 95 connections with NT is this: Windows 95 (like NT) offers the ability to connect to a network printer without installing a printer driver. WFW doesn't support this feature. You need to install a printer driver only on the computer that has the local printer attached to it; then your NT and Windows 95 clients don't need to have a printer driver installed on their individual computers.

When NT or Windows 95 access the remote printer, the driver on the computer that's sharing the printer is used, which eliminates unnecessary redundancy in drivers and allows drivers to be updated more easily as new ones become available. Only when connecting to a WFW, UNIX, or Novell NetWare printer server do you need to make sure you've installed the requisite printer driver on Windows 95 or NT machines.

14

PEER-TO-PEER NETWORKING

Mapping Drives in Windows 95

After you have your Windows 95 stations online, using network resources is a snap. You might want to refer to a book specifically on Windows 95 for details; however, Windows 95 makes it easy for users to gain access to files and folders on remote machines, often without mapping them to logical drive letters. You just click on Network Neighborhood and work your way down the tree to the drive, folder, and files you want, then use them as though they were local. Windows Explorer can be used instead of Network Neighborhood, if you prefer that interface (which I do).

At times, you might need to map a network drive or shared folder (directory) to a logical drive letter; for example, a program you're using might require a conventional disk drive name for storing or opening data. Older 16-bit non-Windows 95 programs in particular can give you trouble because their File | Open dialog boxes and network browsers don't let you point to a remote folder as though it were local. In that case, you might want to set up at least a temporary, and possibly a persistent, logical drive allocation to a networked drive.

Follow these steps to map a network drive or shared folder to a logical drive letter:

1. Find the drive or folder in question through Network Neighborhood and right-click on it. (A folder/directory has to be formally shared from the server before it can be mapped to a drive letter.)

2. From the pop-up menu, choose Map Network Drive. The next available logical drive letter is automatically chosen and indicated in the box. Change it if you want to.

3. Click Reconnect on Login if you want the remove drive/folder to be assigned this drive letter each time you bring up the workstation in question.

4. Click OK; now you're mapped, and a new drive will show up in My Computer and Windows Explorer.

5. To disconnect from the network drive while at the Windows 95 workstation, right-click on the drive icon through My Computer or Windows Explorer and choose Disconnect.

Managing Your Network from the Command Line

The fashion in operating system design nowadays is to create Mac-like graphical user interfaces. Although systems with graphical user interfaces, such as Windows NT, are easier to learn than cryptic, old-fashioned, command-line systems like DOS and UNIX, a command-driven system is better at times. Luckily, the designers of Windows NT have recognized this need, so Windows NT, unlike Apple's System 7, does have a command-line interface that can be used to manage your network.

The biggest advantage commands have over graphical applications, such as Explorer and Print Folders, is the ability to string a series of commands together in a batch file to automate some procedure you perform on a regular basis (such as backing up your server). If you run a college computer lab or a similar network where you regularly need to create user accounts in batches, you might find it easier to write a batch file that creates the users, their home directories, and sharepoints rather than to use User Manager.

Table 14.2 lists the commands (along with their syntax) you can use to control your network. If you're moving up to Windows NT from a LAN Manager or MS-Net (PC LAN program) environment, many of these commands will look familiar. Each command is discussed in the following sections.

> **NOTE**
>
> Remember, you can also use these commands in user logon scripts.

Table 14.2. Commands for controlling your network.

Command	Description
NET ACCOUNTS	Displays and controls password and account restrictions on a server or domain.
NET COMPUTER	Creates a computer account in a domain (NTAS only).
NET CONFIG	Displays workstation or server configuration information.
NET CONTINUE	Reactivates suspended services.
NET FILE	Displays information on file shares and locks; can be used to close shares and unlock files.
NET GROUP	Maintains global groups.
NET HELP	Offers help with these commands.
NET HELPMSG	Gives a detailed description of an error message's meaning.
NET LOCALGROUP	Maintains local groups.
NET NAME	Maintains a workstation's messaging name list.
NET PAUSE	Suspends a service or printer.
NET PRINT	Displays and controls print queues.
NET SEND	Sends a message.
NET SESSION	Lists and disconnects user sessions.
NET SHARE	Makes resources available to share.
NET START	Starts a service.

continues

Table 14.2. continued

Command	Description
NET STOP	Stops a service.
NET STATISTICS	Displays network statistics.
NET TIME	Sets the workstation's clock to match the server and displays the time.
NET USE	Creates a link to a shared resource.
NET USER	Maintains user account information.
NET VIEW	Displays a list of servers or shares.

Using NET ACCOUNTS

The NET ACCOUNTS command is used to maintain the accounts database. You can use it to set password and logon requirements for all accounts. Changes you make with NET ACCOUNTS take effect only if user accounts have been set up (by using User Manager or the NET USER command) and if the Net Logon service is running on the server(s) you're trying to update. Net Logon is started automatically when Windows NT starts. NET ACCOUNTS changes affect all users on your server or domain.

If you type NET ACCOUNTS without any parameters, you'll see the current settings for password, logon limitations, and domain information.

Syntax:

```
NET ACCOUNTS [/FORCELOGOFF:{minutes ¦ NO}]
  [/MINPWLEN:length][/MAXPWAGE:{days ¦ UNLIMITED}]
  [/MINPWAGE:days][/UNIQUEPW:n] [/DOMAIN]
NET ACCOUNTS [/SYNC] [/DOMAIN]
```

Parameters:

/SYNC	Updates the user accounts database.
/FORCELOGOFF:{minutes ¦ NO}	Sets the amount of grace time a user can be logged on after his or her account expires or valid logon hours expire. Set this to NO if you don't want your users forced off.
/MINPWLEN:length	Sets the minimum password length from 0 to 14 characters. The default is 6 characters.
/MAXPWAGE:{days ¦ UNLIMITED}	Sets the maximum password age from 1 to 49710 days (136 years). Set to UNLIMITED to prevent passwords from expiring. MAXPWAGE can't be less than MINPWAGE. The default is 90 days.

/MINPWAGE:*days*	Sets the minimum password age from 0, for no minimum, to 49710 days. Must be less than MAXPWAGE.
/UNIQUEPW:*n*	Requires that a user's passwords be different than the last *n* passwords the user has used. The maximum value is 8.
/DOMAIN	Performs the operation on the domain controller of the current domain. Otherwise, the operation is performed on the local workstation if NET ACCOUNTS is run on a Windows NT machine that's part of a domain. By default, Windows NT Server computers perform operations on the domain controller.

Using NET COMPUTER

Using the NET COMPUTER command, you can add or delete computers from a domain. The NET command must be run from an NT Server machine that's a member of the domain.

Syntax:

```
NET COMPUTER \\computername {/ADD ¦ /DEL}
```

Parameters:

computername	Specifies the computer to add to or delete from the domain.
/ADD	Adds the specified computer to the domain.
/DEL	Removes the specified computer from the domain.

Using NET CONFIG

The NET CONFIG command displays the configuration of the workstation or server service. NET CONFIG with no parameters displays a list of services that can be configured.

Syntax:

```
NET CONFIG [SERVER ¦ WORKSTATION]
```

Parameters:

SERVER	Displays information about the configuration of a server.
WORKSTATION	Displays information about the configuration of a workstation.

Examples:

```
C:\users\default>net config workstation
Computer name                       \\AST
User name                           Administrator
Workstation active on               Nbf_SMCISA01 (0000C0295F70)
Streams\NWNBLINK (0000C0295F70)
Software version                    Windows NT 3.10
Workstation domain                  NAOL-DOM
Logon domain                        AST
COM Open Timeout (sec)              3600
COM Send Count (byte)               16
COM Send Timeout (msec)             250
The command completed successfully.
C:\users\default>net config server
Server Name                         \\AST
Server Comment
Software version                    Windows NT 3.10
Server is active on                 Nbf_SMCISA01 (0000c0295f70)
<C2>Streams\NWNBLINK (0000c0295f70)
Server hidden                       No
Maximum Logged On Users             Unlimited
Maximum open files per session      2048
Idle session time (min)             15
The command completed successfully.
```

Using NET CONTINUE

The NET CONTINUE command restarts a service that's been suspended by NET PAUSE.

Syntax:

```
NET CONTINUE service
```

Parameter:

service   The paused service, which can be one of the following:

                 FTP Server

                 Microsoft DHCP Server

                 Net Logon

                 Network DDE

                 Network DDE DSDM

                 Remote Access

                 Schedule

                 Server

                 Simple TCP/IP Services

                 Telnet

                 Windows Internet Name Service

                 Workstation

Using NET FILE

The NET FILE command displays, and optionally closes or removes, shared files and file locks. The listing includes the identification number assigned to an open file, the file's pathname, the username, and the number of locks on the file. Type this command from the server where the file is shared.

WARNING

Closing a file that's actively in use might make the data in the file unrecoverable or corrupted. Use NET FILE to close files as a last resort.

Syntax:

```
NET FILE [id [/CLOSE]]
```

Parameters:

id	The identification number of the file.
/CLOSE	Closes an open file and removes file locks.

Example:

```
C:\users\default>net file
ID       Path                            User name            # Locks

22       C:\FAX                          administrator        0
25       C:\FAX                          administrator        0
27       D:\WINWORD                      administrator        0
29       D:\WINWORD\CONVINFO.DOC         administrator        0
34       D:\WINWORD                      administrator        0
The command completed successfully.
```

Using NET GROUP

The NET GROUP command allows you to maintain global groups on servers. If you type NET GROUP without any parameters, it displays the group names on the server.

Syntax:

```
NET GROUP [groupname [/COMMENT:"text"]] ¦ groupname {/ADD
    [/COMMENT:"text"] ¦ /DELETE} ¦ groupname username
    [...] {/ADD ¦ /DELETE}
```

Parameters:

groupname	The name of the group to add, expand, or delete. The NET GROUP groupname displays a list of users in the group.
/COMMENT:"text"	Adds a comment up to 48 characters long for a new or existing group. You must enclose the text in quotation marks.

/DOMAIN	Performs the operation on the domain controller of the current domain. Otherwise, the operation is performed on the local workstation if NET ACCOUNTS is run on a Windows NT machine that's part of a domain. By default, Windows NT Server computers perform operations on the domain controller.
username [...]	A list of the users to add to or delete from a group, separated by spaces.
/ADD	Adds a group, or adds a user to a group.
/DELETE	Removes a group, or removes a user from a group.

Examples:

This example creates a group called AR:

```
NET GROUP AR /add /Comment:"Accounts Receivable Group"
```

This line adds John, Paul, George, and Ringo to the group Beatles:

```
NET GROUP Beatles john paul george ringo/add
```

This command kicks Pete Best out of the group:

```
NET GROUP BEATLES peteB /Delete
```

Using NET HELP

The NET HELP command expands a network help message.

Syntax:

```
NET HELP command
```

or

```
NET command /HELP
```

Help is available for the following commands:

NET ACCOUNTS	NET HELP	NET SHARE
NET COMPUTER	NET HELPMSG	NET START
NET CONFIG	NET LOCALGROUP	NET STATISTICS
NET CONFIG SERVER	NET NAME	NET STOP
NET CONFIG WORKSTATION	NET PAUSE	NET TIME
NET CONTINUE	NET PRINT	NET USE
NET FILE	NET SEND	NET USER
NET GROUP	NET SESSION	NET VIEW

The NET HELP SERVICES command lists network services you can get help on. NET HELP SYNTAX explains how to read NET HELP syntax lines. NET HELP|MORE, for example, displays Help one screen at a time.

Using NET HELPMSG

The NET HELPMSG command displays extended information about Windows NT error network messages when you type NET HELPMSG and the error number (for example, NET HELPMESSAGE NET2182). Windows NT tells you about the message and suggests action you can take to solve the problem.

Syntax:

```
NET HELPMSG message#
```

Parameter:

message#	The four-digit number of the Windows NT message you need help with.

Example:

```
C:\users\default>net helpmsg 2182
The requested service has already been started.
EXPLANATION
You tried to start a service that is already running.
ACTION
To display a list of active services, type:
NET START
```

Using NET LOCALGROUP

The NET LOCALGROUP command is used to maintain local groups on servers. When used without options, it lists the local groups on the server.

Syntax:

```
NET LOCALGROUP [groupname]
groupname {/ADD ¦ /DELETE}
groupname name [...] {/ADD ¦ /DELETE}
```

Parameters:

groupname	The name of the local group to add, expand, or delete. Typing just NET LOCALGROUP [groupname] results in a list of the users or global groups in a local group.
name [...]	A list of one or more users or groups, separated by spaces, to add to or delete from the local group being maintained. Names can be users or global groups, but not other local groups. If a user is from another domain, preface the username with the domain name (for example, SALES\RALPHR).
/ADD	Adds the users or global groups listed to the local group.
/DELETE	Removes users or global groups listed from the local group.

14

PEER-TO-PEER
NETWORKING

Using NET NAME

The NET NAME command adds or deletes a *messaging name* (*alias*) at a workstation. When used without options, NET NAME displays the names accepting messages at the computer.

A workstation can accept messages from three types of names:

- Message names, which are added with NET NAME.
- A computer name, which is added as a name when the Workstation service is started. This name can't be deleted.
- A username, which is added as a name when you log on (if it's not being used at another workstation). This name can be deleted.

Syntax:

NET NAME [*name* [/ADD ¦ /DELETE]]

Parameters:

name	The name, 1 to 15 characters long, to receive messages.
/DELETE	Removes a name from a computer.

Using NET PAUSE

The NET PAUSE command suspends a Windows NT service or resource. Pausing a service puts it on hold but doesn't remove it from memory. Typing NET PAUSE NET LOGON before you back up your system prevents a user from logging on and interfering with the backup.

Syntax:

NET PAUSE *service*

Parameter:

service	The service to be paused; can be one of the following:
	FTP Server
	Microsoft DHCP Server
	Net Logon
	Network DDE
	Network DDE DSDM
	Remote Access
	Schedule
	Server
	Simple TCP/IP Services
	Telnet

Windows Internet Name Service

Workstation

Using NET PRINT

The NET PRINT command is used to manage print queues. It lists jobs for each queue, showing the size and status of each job and the status of the queue.

Syntax:

```
NET PRINT \\computername\sharename
 [\\computername] job# [/HOLD ¦ /RELEASE ¦ /DELETE]
```

Parameters:

`\\computername`	The name of the server sharing the printer queue(s).
`sharename`	The name of the shared printer queue.
`job#`	The identification number assigned to a print job. A server with one or more printer queues assigns each print job a unique number.
`/HOLD`	Prevents a job in a queue from printing. The job stays in the printer queue, and other jobs bypass it until it's released.
`/RELEASE`	Reactivates a job being held.
`/DELETE`	Removes a job from a queue.

Using NET SEND

The NET SEND command sends a real-time message to other users, computers, or messaging names on the network. You can send a message only to a name that's active on the network. If the message is sent to a username, that user must be logged on and running the Messenger service to receive the message.

Syntax:

```
NET SEND {name ¦ * ¦ /DOMAIN[:name] ¦ /BROADCAST ¦ /USERS} message
```

Parameters:

`name`	The user, computer, or messaging name to send the message to. If the name is a computer name that contains blank characters, enclose the alias in quotation marks.
`*`	Sends the message to all the names in your group.
`/DOMAIN[:name]`	Sends the message to all the names in your domain. If `:name` is replaced by a list of names separated by spaces, the message is sent to all the names in the specified domain or workgroup.

/BROADCAST	Sends the message to all the names on the network.
/USERS	Sends the message to all users connected to the server.
message	The text to be sent as a message.

Using NET SESSION

The NET SESSION command lists or disconnects sessions between the server and other computers on the network. When used without options, it displays information about all sessions with the server of current focus.

Syntax:

```
NET SESSION [\\computername] [/DELETE]
```

Parameters:

| \\computername | Lists the session information for the named computer. |
| /DELETE | Ends the session between the server and computername and closes all open files on the server for the session. NET SESSION /DELETE with no computername closes all sessions. |

Example:

```
C:\users\default>net session
Computer            User name       Client Type     Opens Idle time

\\DELL              administrator   NT              5     01:34:02
The command completed successfully.
```

Using NET SHARE

The NET SHARE command makes a server's resources available to network users by creating a sharepoint for the resource. NET SHARE without parameters lists information about all resources being shared on the server. For each resource, Windows NT reports the device names or pathnames and the associated comment.

Syntax:

```
NET SHARE sharename
sharename=drive:path [/USERS:number ¦ /UNLIMITED] [/REMARK:"text"]
sharename [/USERS:number ¦ /UNLIMITED] [/REMARK:"text"]
{sharename ¦ devicename ¦ drive:path} /DELETE
```

Parameters:

| *sharename* | The name that the resource is shared by. Type NET SHARE *sharename* to display information about only that share. |
| *drive:path* | Specifies the absolute path of the directory to be shared. |

/USERS:*number*	Sets the maximum number of users who can simultaneously access the shared resource.
/UNLIMITED	Specifies that an unlimited number of users can simultaneously access the shared resource.
/REMARK:"*text*"	Adds a comment to the sharename. You must enclose the text in quotation marks.
devicename	One or more printers (LPT1: through LPT9:) shared by sharename.
/DELETE	Stops sharing the resource.

Examples:

```
C:\users\default>net share temp45=c:\temp45 /users:4 /remark:
"This is a test. This is only a tes..."
temp45 was shared successfully.
C:\users\default>net share temp45
Share name        temp45
Path              c:\TEMP45
Remark            This is a test.  This is only a tes...
Maximum users     4
Users
The command completed successfully.
```

Using NET START

The NET START command starts one of the Windows NT networking services or lists started services.

Syntax:

```
NET START [service]
```

NOTE

To get more help about a specific service, type NET HELP START *service*.

Parameter:

service	Starts one of the following services:
	Alerter
	Computer Browser
	Directory Replicator
	Event Log
	Locator

Messenger

Microsoft DHCP ServerNBT

NBT

Net Logon

Network DDE

Network DDE DSDM

Remote Access

RPCSS

Schedule

Server

Simple TCP/IP

SNMP

TCPIP

Telnet

UPS

Windows Internet Name Service

Workstation

NOTE

NET START also can start network services provided by third parties, such as an NFS client or server.

Using NET STATISTICS

The NET STATISTICS command displays statistics for the server or workstation service.

Syntax:

```
NET STATISTICS [WORKSTATION ¦ SERVER]
```

Parameters:

SERVER	Displays server statistics.
WORKSTATION	Displays workstation statistics.

Examples:

```
c>net statistics server
Server Statistics for \\AST
Statistics since 12/17/93 4:00PM
Sessions accepted              1
Sessions timed-out             1
Sessions errored-out           0
Kilobytes sent                 130
Kilobytes received             30
Mean response time (msec)      142
System errors                  0
Permission violations          0
Password violations            0
Files accessed                 45
Communication devices accessed 0
Print jobs spooled             0
Times buffers exhausted
Big buffers              0
Request buffers          0
The command completed successfully.
C:\users\default>
C:\users\default>net statistics workstation
Workstation Statistics for \\AST
Statistics since 12/17/93 4:00PM
Bytes received                           751060
Server Message Blocks (SMBs) received    1285
Bytes transmitted                        97926
Server Message Blocks (SMBs) transmitted 1196
Read operations                          7
Write operations                         1
Raw reads denied                         0
Raw writes denied                        0
Network errors                           0
Connections made                         2
Reconnections made                       2
Server disconnects                       0
Sessions started                         6
Hung sessions                            0
Failed sessions                          0
Failed operations                        0
Use count                                54
Failed use count                         0
The command completed successfully.
```

Using NET STOP

The NET STOP command stops the selected service from running and denies access to any users accessing the resource or open files. Because some services (NBT, for example) are dependent on others (such as TCP/IP), stopping one service might stop other services.

Syntax:

```
NET STOP service
```

14

PEER-TO-PEER
NETWORKING

Parameter:	
`service`	Stops one of the following services:
	Alerter
	Computer Browser
	Directory Replicator
	Event Log
	Locator
	Messenger
	Microsoft DHCP Server
	NBT
	Net Logon
	Network DDE
	Network DDE DSDM
	Remote Access
	RPCSS
	Schedule
	Server
	Simple TCP/IP
	SNMP
	TCPIP
	Telnet
	UPS
	Windows Internet Name Service
	Workstation

NET STOP also can stop network services provided by third parties for use with Windows NT.

NOTE

You must have administrative rights to stop the Server service.

Using NET TIME

The NET TIME command displays the time at a server or the time server for a domain, and it optionally synchronizes your system's clock with the time at the server or domain's time server.

Syntax:

```
NET TIME [\\computername ¦ /DOMAIN[:domainname]] [/SET]
```

Parameters:

`\\computername`	The name of the server you want to check or synchronize with.
`/DOMAIN[:domainname]`	Specifies the domain to synchronize time with.
`/DOMAIN`	Performs the operation on the domain controller of the current domain. Otherwise, the operation is performed on the local workstation (if NET ACCOUNTS is run on a Windows NT machine that's part of a domain). This parameter applies only to Windows NT computers that are members of a Windows NT Server domain but that don't have Windows NT Server software installed. By default, Windows NT Server computers perform operations on the domain controller.
`/SET`	Synchronizes the computer's time with the time on the specified computer or domain.

TIP

Although it's not documented in the online Help, you can also specify the /YES switch, which prevents the system confirmation prompt. This feature can be quite useful in logon scripts to synchronize all the computer clocks as users log onto the network.

Using NET USE

The NET USE command creates or deletes links between local aliases to shared resources. If you type NET USE with no parameters, you get a list of the resources you're currently linked to on other systems on the network.

Syntax:

```
NET USE [devicename] [\\computername\sharename [password ¦ *]]
  [/USER:[domainname\]username]
  [[/DELETE] ¦ [/PERSISTENT]:{YES ¦ NO}]]
NET USE [devicename] [/HOME [password ¦ *]] [/HOME[/DELETE]
NET USE [/PERSISTENT]:{YES ¦ NO}]
```

14

PEER-TO-PEER
NETWORKING

Parameters:

`devicename`	Assigns an alias to link to the resource, or specifies the device to be disconnected. There are two kinds of aliases: logical disk drives (D: through Z:) and printers (LPT1: through LPT3:).
`\\computername`	The name of the server containing the printer or directory you want to use. If the computer name contains a space, enclose `\\computername` in quotation marks. The computername can be from the same (or different) workgroup as the machine where the command is run.
`\sharename`	The network name of the shared resource.
`password`	The password needed (if any) to access the shared resource.
`*`	Produces a prompt for the password. The password is not echoed as you type it at this prompt.
`/USER`	Specifies a different username to make the connection with.
`domainname`	Specifies another domain. If `domainname` is omitted, the current domain is used.
`username`	Specifies the username for logging on.
`/HOME`	Connects a user to his or her home directory.
`/DELETE`	Cancels a network link connection and removes it from the list of persistent connections.
`/PERSISTENT`	Controls the use of persistent network connections. Persistent connections are reestablished automatically each time you log on.
`YES`	Saves connections as they are made and restores them at the next logon.
`NO`	Does not save the connection being made.

Using NET USER

The NET USER command is used to maintain the user accounts database on a server or domain. If you enter NET USER with no parameters, you see a list of the users on this server.

NOTE

This command works only on servers.

Syntax:

```
NET USER [username [password ¦ *] [options]] [/DOMAIN]
username {password ¦ *} /ADD [options] [/DOMAIN]
username [/DELETE] [/DOMAIN]
```

Parameters:

`username`	The name of the user account (up to 20 characters long) to add, delete, modify, or view.
`password`	Assigns or changes a password for the user's account. A password must be at least as long as the minimum length set by the system administrator and no more than 14 characters long. (See the NET ACCOUNTS command for more information on password restrictions.)
`*`	Produces a prompt for the password. The password isn't echoed when entered at the prompt.
`/DOMAIN`	Performs the operation on the domain controller of the current domain. Otherwise, the operation is performed on the local workstation (if NET ACCOUNTS is run on a Windows NT machine that's part of a domain). This parameter applies only to Windows NT workstations that are members of a Windows NT Server domain. By default, Windows NT Server computers perform operations on the domain controller.
`/ADD`	Adds the user account to the database.
`/DELETE`	Removes the user account from the database.
`/ACTIVE:{YES ¦ NO}`	Activates or deactivates the account. A user can't log on with an inactive account. The default is YES.
`/COMMENT:"text"`	Enters a comment for this user (for example, Sammy "The Bull" Provano) up to 48 characters long. Remember to enclose the text in quotation marks.
`/COUNTRYCODE:n`	Uses the operating system country code to activate the specified language files for the user's help and error messages. A value of 0 signifies the default country code.
`/EXPIRES:{date ¦ NEVER}`	Causes the account to expire if date is set. NEVER sets no time limit on the account.
`/FULLNAME:"name"`	A user's full name (for example, John Fitzgerald Kennedy as opposed to ThePrez) in quotation marks.

14

PEER-TO-PEER
NETWORKING

/HOMEDIR:*pathname*	Sets the path for the user's home directory. The path must exist.
/HOMEDIRREQ:{YES ¦ NO}	Is a home directory required? If so, use the /HOMEDIR switch to specify the directory.
/PASSWORDCHG:{YES ¦ NO}	Can this user change his or her own password? The default is YES.
/PASSWORDREQ:{YES ¦ NO}	Must this account have a password at all times? The default is YES.
/PROFILEPATH[:*path*]	Sets a path for the user's logon profile.
/SCRIPTPATH:*pathname*	The location of the user's logon script.
/TIMES:{*times* ¦ ALL}	The logon hours. TIMES is expressed as day [-day][,day[-day]],time[-time][,time [-time]], limited to one-hour increments. Days can be spelled out or abbreviated.
	Hours can be 12-hour or 24-hour notation. For 12-hour notation, use am, pm, a.m., or p.m. ALL means a user can always log on, and a blank value means a user can never log on. Separate day and time entries with a comma, and separate multiple day and time entries with a semicolon.
/USERCOMMENT:"*text*"	Lets an administrator add or change the comment for the account.
/WORKSTATIONS: {computername[,...] ¦ *}	The list of up to eight workstations that the user is allowed to log on from. If you don't enter a list, or if the list is *, the user can log on from any workstation.

Examples:

```
C:\users\default>net users howard
User name                   howard
Full Name
Comment
User's comment
Parameters
Country code                000 (System Default)
Account active              Yes
Account expires             Never
Password last set           12/3/93 8:57AM
Password expires            1/15/94 7:44AM
Password changeable         12/3/93 8:57AM
Password required           Yes
User may change password    Yes
Workstations allowed        All
Logon script
```

```
User profile
Home directory
Last logon                  12/16/93 11:01AM
Logon hours allowed         All
Local Group Memberships     *Administrators
Global Group memberships    *None
The command completed successfully.
```

Using NET VIEW

The NET VIEW command displays a list of resources being shared on a server. When used without options, it displays a list of servers in the current domain.

Syntax:

```
NET VIEW [\\computername | /DOMAIN[:domainname]]
```

Parameters:

\\computername	The server whose shared resources you want to view.
/DOMAIN:domainname	Specifies the domain for which you want to view the available servers. If domainname is omitted, displays all domains in the local area network.

Examples:

```
C:\users\default>net view
Server Name        Remark

-------------------------------------------------------------------
\\AST
\\DELL
The command completed successfully.
C:\users\default>net view \\dell
Shared resources at \\dell
Share name   Type         Used as  Comment

-------------------------------------------------------------------
NETLOGON     Disk                  Logon server share
The command completed successfully.
```

Summary

In this chapter, you've looked at a lot of material dealing with sharing your resources, such as your printers, as well as setting up a peer-to-peer network for your NT server and workstation. You've also seen how other Windows machines on your network recognize your NT machines, and how they can share the machine's resources. Finally, you've learned about the NET command, which is sometimes useful from the DOS command line to control network services.

NT Server

IN THIS CHAPTER

CHAPTER 15

Windows NT is a good platform for a small workgroup network supporting word processing, e-mail, and other back office applications. Once you start talking about the so-called "mission critical" applications, from simple accounting to electronic data transfer and customer support, plain old NT just isn't a robust enough platform. For the real, industrial-strength file server, Microsoft has Windows NT Server, a superset of Windows NT with several enhancements to make it a better file server.

What's Different About NT Server?

NT Server's most important advanced feature is its domain-based naming and logon system. By combining your NT Servers into a domain, you can greatly enhance your control over access to your data and also simplify administering your file servers. All the servers in a domain share a single user database. You need to create a user (using the User Administrator or Net Accounts command) only once for all the servers in your domain, whether you have 2 or 200.

If you have a large network, you might want to divide it into multiple, separate domains. You could create multiple domains to allow departments, divisions, or subsidiaries to manage their own networks without granting too much administrative control to anyone outside the business unit. Multiple domains are also a good idea if you have a large, geographically distributed, wide area network; they help reduce traffic over the slow WAN lines.

Once you create multiple domains, you'll discover that some of your users need access to data not only in their home domain, but also in another. Rather than building walls between domains, or creating a separate user ID in each domain a user needs data from, and making him choose which domain's data he wants to access, NT Server allows you to define trust relationships so users from one domain can access resources on another without logging out of one domain and into another.

If you've tried to manage a network of Windows workstations, you know the difficulties of allowing users to log onto the network from any station and still get their familiar Windows Desktop and Program Manager groups. With Windows NT Server, you can save users' desktops into user profiles on a file server. Once you've set up a profile for a user, she will have the same desktop regardless of which Windows NT system she's using.

NT Server has additional connectivity features, including AppleTalk and Macintosh client support. Users on Macintosh computers can access resources, including shared directories and printers on NT Servers, without any special software; they see NT Servers as AppleShare file servers and can access them by using the same software and techniques.

Windows NT's Remote Access Service (RAS) is an invaluable tool for logging onto workstations and networks from remote locations. Unfortunately, it's useful only for remote network administration or users accessing their office machines from home, because a Windows NT system can support only one RAS session. NT Server adds support for intelligent serial cards, such as Digiboards and IBM ARTIC cards, to allow a single NT Server system to support multiple remote users.

NT Server's data integrity features are important enhancements, too. NT Server supports disk mirroring and RAID Level 5 disk arrays with error correction to protect file server data from loss if there's a disk failure. In both schemes, redundant data is stored on additional disk drives so that a file server can have a drive failure but still continue operating and serving its users.

The replication service lets you protect your data from server failures, as well as drive failures. When you tell NT Server to replicate a directory, it automatically copies any files that have changed in that directory and its descendants on the tree to another Windows NT system on the network as soon as the changes have been made. You can think of the replicator as either a file distribution system, sending the latest copies of a new driver to each Windows NT machine in the network, or as an automated backup system that runs transparently to the user. Windows NT systems can receive replicated files, but only NT Servers can distribute files.

The network administration tools let you easily configure and maintain your TCP/IP network with the Dynamic Host Configuration Protocol (DHCP) Manager and Windows Internet Name Service (WINS) Manager. The DHCP Manager can dynamically issue IP addresses to client workstations from a pool of IP addresses. The WINS Manager associates computer names with IP addresses. NT Server also includes the Network Client Administrator, which creates installation disks to install network software, and the Remote Boot Manager, which configures diskless workstation clients.

Of course, NT Server is still Windows NT, so it has all the advantages of a true 32-bit, multithreaded, preemptive multitasking operating system with memory protection and a red racing stripe. However, some of Windows NT's base features, such as support for RISC processors and especially symmetrical multiprocessing, are more likely to be used with machines running NT Server than users' workstations.

In fact, symmetrical multiprocessing and portability are NT Server's greatest strengths over competing LAN operating systems, such as Novell's NetWare and IBM's LAN Server. With Windows NT, you can build a test server for a client/server database application on a simple PC and scale it up to a system with two 486s, four Pentiums, and more. Windows NT—and, therefore, NT Server—currently supports more than 30 multiprocessor computers from a dozen manufacturers ranging from ALR, AST, and Compaq to Siemens-Nixdorf and NCR. Some of NCR's multiprocessor systems can have up to 64 486 processors. How's that for a database server?

NT Server Domains

Domains, and domain management, are the most important advance in NT Server. An NT Server domain is a group of NT Servers and LAN Manager 2.1 servers that all have the same user database along with the workstations they serve.

Sharing that common database means that, unlike operating systems such as NetWare 3.*x*, users don't have to log onto each file server on the network individually; they just have to log onto the domain as a whole. As soon as users are logged onto the domain, their access to all the file servers in the domain is established.

Even more important, the system administrator doesn't have to create an account on each server in the domain for each user. The user database for each domain is stored on every NT Server in the domain. When you set up your domain, the first file server in the domain becomes the *domain controller*, which stores the master copy of the user database.

NOTE

Although NT Server supports TCP/IP, NT Server domains and TCP/IP domains (that is, compuserve.com or whitehouse.gov) are completely unrelated. A Windows NT Server running TCP/IP is a member of both an NT Server domain (Accounting, for example) and a TCP/IP DNS (domain naming service) domain. All the servers in an NT Server domain need not be members of the same DNS domain, and vice versa.

When you add or change a user account on an NT Server that's a member of a domain, it updates the master copy of the user database on the domain controller. All you have to do is select the name of the domain. Because the domain controller holds the master user database, User Manager for Domains won't let you edit the user database on NT Servers in a domain unless they are domain controllers.

The other NT Servers, and LAN Manager 2.*x* servers, that are members of the domain poll the domain controller about every five minutes, looking for changes to the user database. If the database on the domain controller has been changed, the domain controller sends the changes to the other server. To keep network traffic down to a reasonable level, NT Server doesn't send the entire database, just the changes since this server's last update.

User logon requests can be processed by any NT Server in the domain and normally are handled by the "nearest" file server to the user (the first to respond to a broadcast request). Because other servers can handle logon requests, if the domain controller should go down, it won't affect network availability except for the resources on the domain controller itself. Until you bring the domain controller back up or promote one of the other NT Servers in the domain to domain controller, you can't add or edit user accounts.

NOTE

Although LAN Manager 2.1 file servers can be members of a domain and can validate logons for OS/2, DOS, and Windows for Workgroups stations, they can't validate Windows NT stations' logon attempts. I recommend upgrading your LAN Manager servers to NT Server as soon as possible.

> If you're going to mix LAN Manager and NT Servers in the same domain, you should have at least two NT Servers to prevent a failure at the domain controller from stopping your Windows NT users from logging on.

Large networks and networks with departments that insist on managing their own servers (human resources, for example) can have more than one domain on the same network. You can create links, called *trust relationships*, between domains to allow users and Windows NT workstations from one domain to access servers in another domain.

This chapter concentrates on how to manage a domain. Chapter 16, "Setting Up Trust Relationships in NT Server," looks at multiple domain systems and how to plan your large network.

Domains Versus Workgroups

Windows NT servers and workstations can be members of workgroups that, like domains, group servers together in users' dialog boxes so users can easily find the resources they're looking for. (Refer back to Chapter 14, "Windows NT Networking Out of the Box: Peer-to-Peer Networking.") Now you also have NT Server domains. I'm sure you're asking, "Just how are domains and workgroups different, and why should I use either management approach?"

Workgroups are a casual affiliation of servers. Like a commune or co-op, they share their resources on an informal basis. To allow a user to access all the servers in a workgroup, you need to create the user's ID on each server individually. Workgroups can be made up of both Windows NT and Windows for Workgroups servers. Windows NT Servers can't be members of a workgroup; they must be members of a domain.

Domains are a more formal and somewhat more secure grouping of servers. Domain servers share a common user database that's replicated for fault tolerance and security, which makes domains easier to administer. Domains can have trust relationships, so a single user ID can be used throughout a large internetwork, if you want. Domains are made up of Windows NT Servers and Windows NT workstations and, to some extent, Windows for Workgroups 3.11 workstations. Chapter 16 covers domains in more depth.

Creating a Domain

A domain is created whenever you install Windows NT Server on a computer and configure that computer to be a domain controller. It's a good idea to finish planning before you excitedly rip the shrink wrap off the CD-ROM and type setup. You should have already come up with a naming convention for domains (or at least a name for the domain that the server you're installing right now is a member of), users, workstations, and servers. I can tell you from sad experience that just naming things willy-nilly leaves you with file servers named Obi-Wan and

Kosher, or Moe, Larry, and Curly. You might have to ask yourself, "Are the accounts receivable files on Sleepy or Grumpy?"

It's a good idea for your names have some relationship to the function of the object you're naming. Domains named Accounting and Advertising with servers named AR, AP, and PAYROLL and Art, Media, and Research can help users find the data they're looking for quickly and with a minimum of intervention from you. Because it's simplest to use user IDs as e-mail mailboxes, you should also associate a user ID with the user (a real person). Wgates, WilliamG., and DaBoss are all user IDs that would clearly identify Bill Gates better than AA001WG would if they were used on a Microsoft e-mail system.

To set up a new domain, follow these steps:

1. Open the Network window from the Control Panel.

2. The current machine and domain name appear on the Identification page of the Network window. If you want to change the name, click the Change button

3. Type the name of the new domain in the appropriate box. When you click OK, your server sends a query over the cable to make sure that the domain you're creating doesn't already exist.

CAUTION

Be very careful when you type the domain name. Although you can change the name of a domain, you can't move a server from one domain to another without installing all over again.

As soon as you've configured the domain controller and verified that it's working, you can install NT Server on the other servers in the domain. Because these systems have to communicate with the domain controller to install NT Server, I recommend that you bring up the domain controller and then try to access it from a Windows NT or Windows for Workgroups workstation to test the installation and LAN hardware.

To configure a server as a member of a domain, select the Server in Domain option when Setup asks you to define this system as a server or domain controller. The domain controller must be available on the network to join a domain. To maintain the domain's exclusive nature, the domain adminstrator must create an account for a server before it can join the domain—just as you can't join a country club without a recommendation from the membership committee.

If, as is usually the case, you (the network administrator) are installing NT Server, you can just enter your user ID and password into the Setup program's dialog box to have it create the account as you install the system, saving you the effort of entering the account names ahead of time. If you're letting users install NT Server and you don't want to trust them with the administrator's password (and who could blame you?), you should set up the server names ahead of time. As a side benefit, setting up server names in advance prevents your users from being creative with their server names and makes them stick to the names you want.

As soon as you've given the Setup program a name for this computer and a domain name, it asks you to enter the password for the administrator's account. Because the administrator's account has a great potential for abuse, you should definitely set a password. Make sure it's one you can easily remember.

WARNING

If you forget the password for the administrator account, and you don't have another administrator-level account to use to change it, you'll have to reinstall Windows NT Server and create a new domain.

TIP

Write down the administrator's password and lock it away in a safe place after configuring your domain controller. You might want to keep the password in the same place you keep the Emergency Repair Disk.

TIP

Use User Manager for Domain to create one or two additional user IDs that are members of the Administrators group and record these account passwords right after you install NT Server on your domain controller.

Managing a Domain

If you go to an NT Server, log onto a domain with an administrative ID, and open the Administrative Tools group from the Program menu, you'll find that it's just a little different from a standard Windows NT machine. Some of your old friends, such as User Manager, have changed—in this case, into User Manager for Domains—and two new tools, Server Manager and User Profile Editor, give you better control of users, groups, and file servers than you had with workgroups.

These tools let you control which users have access to your domain, when they have access, and what their computing environment and desktop look like when they're logged in at a Windows NT workstation. With Server Manager, you can also control Windows NT Servers throughout your domain.

15

NT SERVER

User Manager for Domains

You'll probably run User Manager for Domains, shown in Figure 15.1, more than any other NT Server administrative tool. As you saw in Chapter 9, "Windows NT Administration," User Manager is the primary tool that administrators use for performing day-to-day administrative tasks, such as creating users and user groups, maintaining group memberships, and, most important, changing users' passwords when they forget them. User Manager for Domains does all these things, just as Windows NT's User Manager adds several new features to improve system performance and security.

FIGURE 15.1.

The User Manager for Domains window.

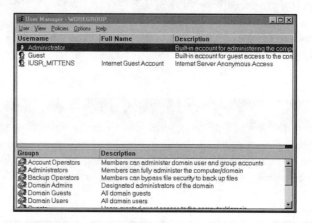

When you start User Manager for Domains, you'll notice two changes to the opening display. The first change is the addition of a View choice to the menu bar. The View menu lets you sort the list of user accounts by the user account name or the user's full name.

> **NOTE**
>
> This chapter covers only the features of User Manager for Domains that are new or different from the standard Windows NT User Manager.

Because NT Server is designed to support large networks, Microsoft decided that multiple administrators should be able to maintain a single domain's user database at the same time through User Manager for Domains. If you're not the only administrator working on the domain at any given time, User Manager for Domains periodically refreshes your screen to let you see what the other administrators are doing. If you need to refresh your screen immediately—to see whether someone else just created the Excel group, for example—you can choose View|Refresh.

> **NOTE**
>
> If the Low Speed Connection option on the Options menu is selected, you can't change your view or refresh it. When Low Speed Connection is active, the entire User Manager for Domains window changes, as shown in Figure 15.2. You can cancel this option from the Options menu.

FIGURE 15.2.

When Low Speed Connection is active, the User Manager display changes.

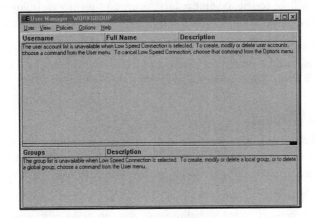

The other obvious change is that NT Server has several predefined groups that didn't exist in Windows NT. Two of those groups, Domain Users and Domain Admins, have an icon different from the one you're used to, as shown in Figure 15.3.

FIGURE 15.3.

The list of defined groups has some additions that Windows NT Workstation lacked.

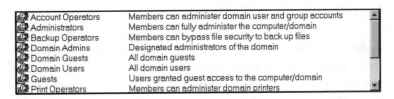

Global and Local Groups

NT Server supports not only the user groups supported in Windows NT, now called local groups, but also global groups. The new world and users icon represents a global group, and the computer and users icon you're familiar with represents a local group.

Both global and local groups make administering your network easier by allowing you to grant rights and permissions to, and perform actions and access resources for, groups of users instead of giving them to each user individually. During my years of managing networks, I've found that the network administrators who have the most hair left do careful planning and use groups extensively.

15

NT SERVER

After trying many theories and schemes for assigning users rights and permissions, I'm convinced that the easiest method is to create groups for logical workgroups—for example, users who need access to an application. With this method, you can set up a new user by simply making him or her a member of the groups that have access to the data this user needs access to. Because you can manage group memberships through User Manager for Domains, but you must set permissions for a single user through Explorer or My Computer, groups are generally easier to deal with. You can make sure that the group has exactly the right set of permissions, which will, of course, be granted to the group's members. If you try to assign file permissions to each user, occasionally you'll miss a permission and will get a support call.

I think all file permissions should be granted through groups, except when only two or three users will need access to the resource, such as when an assistant needs access to what is otherwise his or her boss's private data.

Global Groups

The members of a domain's global group are user accounts within the domain. Global groups can't contain other groups, but they can, of course, have members in common. They can contain only user accounts from within their home domain, so they can't have users from other domains as members.

These groups are called global because you can grant permissions not only in their own domain, but also in any other domain in your network that trusts your domain. Basically, a domain that trusts another domain gives rights to users from that other domain. If you need to know more about multiple domains, Chapter 16 covers trust relationships in more depth.

Local Groups

Local groups allow you to include global groups, from the domain you're managing or from any domain that your domain trusts, as well as users from your domain and any domain that your domain trusts. However, local groups can't contain other local groups, which means you can nest groups only two levels deep. A local group can contain global groups, but a global group can contain only users.

Besides being able to have global groups as members, local groups differ from global groups in two important ways. First, as their name implies, local groups are local to the servers that are members of a domain and aren't available to other domains, regardless of any trust relationships with other domains. In fact, Windows NT workstations in a domain can even have their own local groups. A domain's local group can be granted permissions on the servers in that domain, but not permissions to access resources on the Windows NT workstations. If you want to use a group to provide permissions to both servers and workstation resources, you need to create a global group. Second, local groups can be assigned rights—to create new users, for example—as well as permissions to access server resources.

Comparing Global and Local Groups

The following list shows the contrasts between local and global groups:

Group Type	Properties
Global	Can contain only users from the same domain it exists in. A global group can be used to grant permissions, and it can be used in its domain and domains that trust its domain.
Local	Can contain users and global groups from its domain and any domain its domain trusts. A local group can be used to grant permissions and rights, and it can be used only on servers in its domain.

Just as user groups make managing a file server easier, global groups make managing a multiple domain system easier by allowing you to grant access rights and permissions to users from outside your domain in groups. You can allow senior executives from the home office to access your accounting data just by granting permissions to the group HQ\BigBrass, for example. Any members of the global group BigBrass in the HQ domain can then access the resources you've given them permissions to, which means that the administrator in the HQ domain is controlling which users have access to your data because he or she has control over who's a member of the group.

Suppose you have a multidomain network and each domain has a WINWORD group composed of users allowed to run Word for Windows. If you make these groups global, it's easy to grant permissions to the WinWord directory in your domain to the WINWORD group of one or two other domains. If they do the same for your domain, you can back each other up, giving all the users access to the Word for Windows program even if the server in their domain has crashed or is otherwise unavailable.

The ability of local groups to have global groups as members also makes managing the network easier. For example, you could create a local group that contained your global WINWORD group as well as the WINWORD group for all the other domains you want to share data with. This way, only one group must have permissions, and adding new domains just means adding a member to the local group.

Built-In Groups

NT Server adds several new predefined groups to the set in Windows NT and changes how some others act. The Power Users group has been dropped. The following sections cover each of the built-in groups and how they should be used.

15

NT SERVER

Everyone

Everyone is not actually a group because it doesn't show up in User Manager for Domains's list of groups. It's a placeholder for all users accessing the domain. If you grant permissions through the Rights dialog box in User Manager for Domains, those abilities are given to every user in the current domain, users in trusted domains, and guests who access the server.

Guests

The least privileged group, Guests, is designed to allow unknown users—who could be any user from a domain you trust or the Clanton gang—access to your domain. The only right the Guests group has by default is to log onto the domain across the wire.

Users

This local group contains every user in the domain. As new users are created, they're added to the Users local group. Being a member of the Users group gives accounts the ability to do the following:

- Log on at a Windows NT workstation
- Lock and shut down the workstation
- Store a user profile on the workstation (user profiles are discussed later in this chapter)
- Create and delete local groups on the workstation
- Maintain the membership list for groups the user has created

Note that members of the Users group don't automatically get the right to log on at a machine running NT Server—just to log on across the network.

Domain Users

The Domain Users global group also includes all the members of the domain as they are created. The Domain Users global group gives an administrator in one domain a convenient way to allow all the users in another domain to access his system just by making, for example, HQ\Domain Users a member of his Users local group.

When a Windows NT workstation is made a member of a domain, that domain's Domain Users group is automatically made a member of the local Users group.

Backup Operators

The Backup Operators group can log onto a domain from a workstation or a server, back it up, and restore the data. Backup operators can also shut down servers or workstations.

Print Operators

The Print Operators group can log onto a domain from a workstation or a server and share, stop sharing, and manage printers on NT Servers. They can also shut down servers.

Because you want to have your file servers in centralized locations for security, power, communications, and environmental reasons, but you want your printers in the users' environment as a convenience to them, you'll probably want to connect your printers not to the printer ports on your file server but to selected workstations that will also act as print servers. If you do this, you'll probably want to give the Print Operators group the right to share printers on those workstations. Unfortunately, Print Operators is a local group, so you'll have to do a little extra work:

1. Create a global group in your domain that has as its members the users you want to have the ability to manage printers.

2. Make this global group a member of the Print Operators local group to give the users the rights they need in the local domain.

3. On each workstation whose printer you want these users to manage, add the new global group to the workstation's Power Users group.

Account Operators

Account operators are sort of junior administrators. They can create and modify local and global groups, except the built-in Administrators, Server Operators, Account Operators, Print Operators, and Backup Operators groups and the user accounts for the members of the Administrators accounts. Unlike administrators, account operators can't grant users rights.

If you're in the corporate MIS department, it might be a good idea to make a user in each department an account operator and delegate all the day-to-day password changes and new user account creations without giving him or her the power to lock you out.

Server Operators

If an account operator is a junior administrator who creates user IDs and changes passwords, a server operator is a technician maintaining the server itself. Server operators can share and stop sharing resources, make backups, format disks, and so on. Your departmental administrator should probably be a server operator, too.

Administrators

Members of the Administrators group have all the rights and abilities of users in other groups, plus the ability to create and manage all the users and groups in the domain. Only members of the Administrators group can modify NT operating system files, maintain the built-in groups, and grant additional rights to groups.

Unlike other operating systems, such as LAN Manager 2.*x* or Novell's NetWare, NT Server administrators don't have unlimited access to the data on the server. If an administrator is working at a file server, she can access data on NTFS partitions only if she has enough permissions. An administrator can access data she doesn't have permissions for only by taking ownership and granting herself permission, which can leave tracks a mile wide on the audit trail.

Domain Admins

The Domain Admins global group starts off with the Administrators account as its only member. Because the Domain Admins global group is a member of the Administrators local group, any users you add to the Domain Admins group automatically get any rights and privileges you might grant to the Administrators account.

When you create accounts that you want to be administrators on your domain, you should make those users members of the Domain Admins group, rather than the Administrators group, so they can also be administrators at each Windows NT workstation in the domain. When you make a Windows NT workstation a member of a domain, it automatically makes the domain's Domain Admins global group a member of its Administrators local group. Therefore, domain administrators are automatically administrators of not only the servers, but also the workstations in the domain. The Domain Admins group also allows the administrator of another domain to grant all your administrators access to his or her system by granting permissions to the Domain Admins group.

Working with the User Menu

When you start working with User Manager for Domains, you'll notice that the ability to sort your users and additional groups is just the tip of the iceberg. The User menu alone has several new choices, as you can see from Figure 15.4.

FIGURE 15.4.

The User menu in User Manager for Domains.

New Global Group

The first new option lets you create a new global group. As you can see from the dialog box shown in Figure 15.5, creating a global group is somewhat different from creating a local group. All you have to do is enter the new group's name and description and select the users you want to have as members of the group. You can select one or more users by using the Shift+click and Ctrl+click techniques. Click the Add or Remove buttons as needed.

Setting User Properties

When you create a new user or try to change a user's properties, you see the dialog box shown in Figure 15.6. The Hours, Logon To, Profile, and Account buttons give you tighter control over users in NT Server domains than you have on Windows NT workstations.

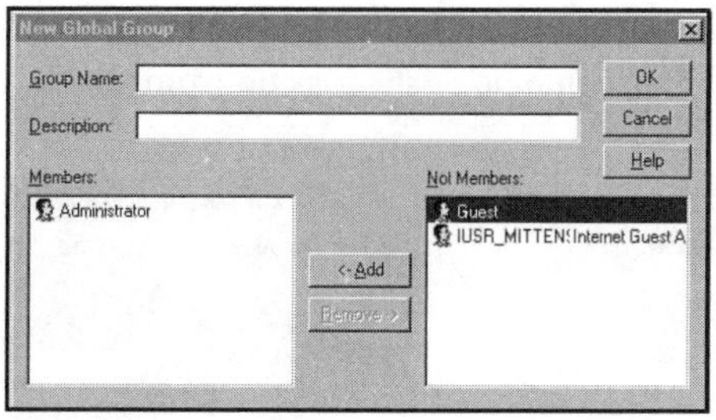

FIGURE 15.5.

Creating a global group.

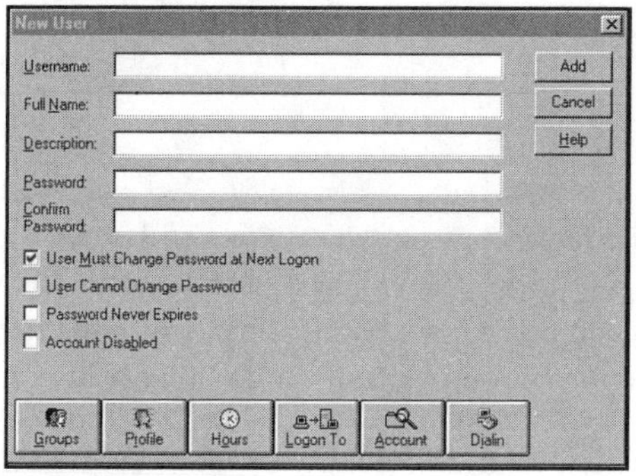

FIGURE 15.6.

The New User dialog box.

Profiles

Because you usually think of a PC as having a single, primary user, most managers of standalone NT machines probably haven't spent much time working with user profiles. After all, if Steve is the only person who ever uses his computer, why should I spend a lot of time making sure that users can log onto the system and have a unique working environment, down to Program Manager groups, color schemes, wallpaper, and finger-tapping mouse cursors? A user's profile is the user's Windows computing environment, including a home directory, logon script batch file that runs automatically every time the user logs onto the machine, and all the nuances of his or her Windows environment.

After you network your systems, you'll find that users often try to log onto the network from workstations other than the one on their desks. Bob might want to show Joe a report draft on the PC at Joe's desk, or you might log on from Susan's desk to troubleshoot her printing problems. Under Windows NT, the user's profile is stored on each machine he logs onto.

NT Server allows you to log on from any machine on the network and still get the same user profile. It also lets you, as the system administrator, control users' profiles so you can keep FreeCell and Tetris off the desktops of your game addicts. User profiles are discussed later in this chapter in the section "User Profile Editor."

Click the Profile button, and you'll see the dialog box shown in Figure 15.7. Here you can enter the filename for the logon script, the path or sharepoint, and the drive letter to use for the user's home directory, just as you do with Windows NT. You can also enter a path for the user profile file, which can be on an NT Server, which allows the user to have the same profile regardless of the machine he or she logs on from.

FIGURE 15.7.

The User Environment Profile dialog box.

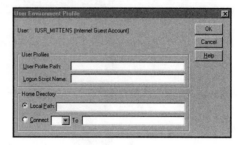

Hours

By clicking the Hours button, you can control when a user is allowed to log onto your network. (See Figure 15.8.) You might decide, for example, that you don't want students logging on between 4 and 6 a.m.; as a matter of fact, you might not want anyone logged on from 4 to 6 a.m. so that you can run backups or do other system maintenance.

FIGURE 15.8.

Setting the user's allowed logon hours.

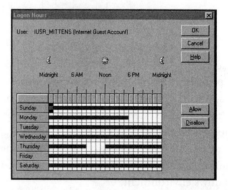

In the Logon Hours dialog box, you can control the user's allowed access times by selecting a block of time, in minimum half-hour intervals, during the week and then clicking the Allow or Disallow buttons. The times users are allowed to log on are indicated by blue bars, and the times they're forbidden access are shown as empty squares. Click on the box above a time slice to select that time slice for all seven days a week. If you want to allow or disallow access for a whole day, click on that day to select all 48 half-hour slices.

Unlike most operating systems, NT Server lets you decide how to handle users who are logged on when their allotted time runs out. You can either allow them to continue working until they log off or have them forcibly bounced from the system at the end of their allotted time. Set this option through the account's policy function, covered in the section "Setting Account Policies."

Logon To

You can also limit which machines on your network any given user can log on from by clicking the Logon To button. I've used this feature to limit Administrator accounts to be valid only from stations in the MIS department or the administrator's own workstations.

I got into trouble once with this feature, though. The human resources department in a brokerage firm was very concerned that a network administrator under NetWare automatically had access to every file on the file server (which isn't true of NT Server). They had us set up the system and show them how to change passwords and perform other basic administrative tasks. They got themselves in trouble by making the Administrator account valid only from the human resources director's workstation. That system was sick in bed with a nasty virus from Duke Nuke 'Em, which the director's son had downloaded from Larry's Pirate Paradise BBS. No one could administer the network.

You can limit the stations that a user or group of users can log on at by clicking the Logon To button to get the Logon Workstations dialog box. (See Figure 15.9.) Select the option User May Log On To These Workstations and enter the names of up to eight workstations the user can log on from. The workstations need not be defined as having accounts in the domain or be turned on for you to list them here. However, they need accounts if a user is actually going to log on.

FIGURE 15.9.

Setting the allowed logon addresses for a user.

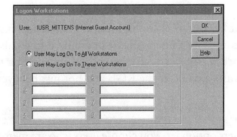

NOTE

Make sure you have allowed for a failed workstation. You should be able to log on as an administrator from at least two workstations.

Account

If you click the Account button, you can set a few more options for the user through the dialog box shown in Figure 15.10.

FIGURE 15.10.

*The Account
Information dialog box.*

Here you can set an expiration date for the account, a useful feature for summer interns, students, and temporary workers. It prevents them from logging on if they can finagle their way to a workstation. You don't have to remember to delete or disable their account. If they should return to work, you can just change the date to re-enable the account.

You also can declare this account to be a local account. Most user accounts you create will be global accounts, which allow users to log onto a server or a workstation, depending on their rights. Global accounts are also available in any domain that trusts your domain. You should use global accounts for your normal rank-and-file users.

However, suppose, for example, that a user has an account in another domain you don't trust, perhaps KGB\Sergi or Russia\BYeltsin. You can allow these users to access your domain across the network by either trusting their domain or creating a local account for the user on your domain.

You can grant local users access rights and permissions just as you can with a global user, but your local accounts won't be available in domains that trust your domain. That's actually how you want it, because the administrator of the domain that trusts yours should be able to decide whether he trusts anyone at the KGB and not just take your word for it.

Select Users

The Select Users option lets you choose users who are members of a global or local group. Once these users are selected, you can change their properties or delete them. Of course, you can also use the normal Windows selection methods to select several users at a time.

When you choose Select Users, you see the dialog box shown in Figure 15.11. If you want to select all the members of the Domain Admins group, click on that group and then click the Select button. If you want all the users who are members of the Domain Admins group or the Backup Operators group, select Backup Operators and click the Select button again. If you want users who are members of Domain Admins but not members of Backup Operators, click on Backup Operators and then click the Deselect button.

If you try to change users' properties after selecting more than one user, you'll get the dialog box shown in Figure 15.12 rather than the User Properties dialog box. Here you can change the properties for multiple users; for example, if you decide you don't want anyone from Accounting logged on from 3 a.m. to 6 a.m., you can just click the Hours button and change the allowed logon hours for all the users in that group. However, some properties, such as full names and passwords, can't be changed for more than one user at a time.

FIGURE 15.11.

The Select Users dialog box.

FIGURE 15.12.

The User Properties dialog box for multiple users.

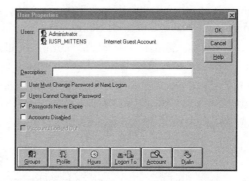

Select Domain

The Select Domain option allows you to manage other domains where your account is a valid administrator. When you click Select Domain, you get a list box with the names of all the domains active on your network, as shown in Figure 15.13.

FIGURE 15.13.

Selecting a domain to manage.

If you select another domain and click OK, you can see the user database for that domain—assuming, of course, that you have the correct security clearance. You can also enter the name of a domain, or a computer that has its own user database, such as a Windows NT workstation, in the domain box. If you enter the name of a Windows NT workstation, you can edit the local users and groups on that station. Because NT Servers don't have their own user databases but copies of the domain database, entering an NT Server's name in the domain box is the same as selecting the domain name.

If you're administering a domain that's across some low-speed (or especially busy) connection, such as a wide area link, you might find that User Manager for Domain's periodic user list updates and screen refreshes take a long time or clog the expensive low-speed link. If you enable the Low Speed Connection box, User Manager for Domains takes the following steps to minimize the required network traffic:

- The users in the domain aren't listed automatically, so you must enter a user's name in the appropriate dialog box to delete, rename, or otherwise modify that user's account.

- The groups in the domain aren't listed automatically; you'll have to enter the name of a local group in the appropriate dialog box to edit the group.

- You can't edit or create global groups. You can make users members of the group, or have them quit, by editing the user.

- Because there are no lists, the options on the View menu (Sort Order and Refresh) don't change how the list looks.

If you're not sure whether you should use the Low Speed Connection option, you can either rely on User Manager for Domains to remember whether you selected it the last time (it keeps the last 20 domains you've managed and remembers whether they were managed over high-speed or low-speed connections) or let User Manager for Domains automatically test the connection and see whether the connection is fast enough to use a high-speed connection. If it's not, the system automatically uses its low-speed option.

If the system chooses low speed, but you need to see the lists or modify a global group, you can change the connection speed through the Options menu.

Setting Account Policies

NT Server lets you set the same password information as Windows NT does. You can limit the minimum and maximum password age, minimum length, password uniqueness, and the maximum number of logon attempts to keep the hackers at bay by using User Manager's Account Policy dialog box, shown in Figure 15.14.

You can also decide what to do when a user stays logged on past the end of his allotted time. If you enable the "Forcibly disconnect remote users from server when logon hours expire" option, users logged onto the server when their allotted time ends are disconnected. (You set the allowed time by clicking the Hours button in the User Properties dialog box.) If you don't select this option, the user can stay on the system indefinitely as long as he's logged on; he just can't log back on if he logs off during one of his unauthorized periods.

FIGURE 15.14.

The Account Policy dialog box.

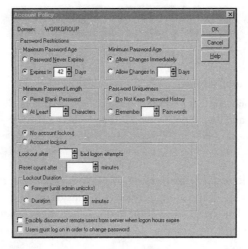

Another option forces users to log on before they can change their current passwords, so users with expired passwords must ask a system administrator to change their passwords, instead of logging on with an expired password and then changing it. This option is another tool that can help keep unauthorized people out of your system.

NOTE

If you're setting user time restrictions so you can do housekeeping (such as backups) when users aren't logged on and holding files open, select the Forcibly Disconnect option.

WARNING

With many DOS and Windows applications, forcibly logging a user out while he or she has a file open might corrupt the data in the file.

Establishing Trust Relationships

Chapter 16 covers trust relationships in more depth, but because you set them through User Manager for Domains, they are covered briefly in this chapter. A *trust relationship* is the ability of the administrator in one domain (the trusting domain) to use global users and groups from another domain (the trusted domain) to grant rights and permissions. By choosing Policies|Trust

15

NT SERVER

Relationships, you can have the domain you're managing trust other domains or have other domains trust yours.

NOTE

A trust relationship is a one-way path. If you want two domains to fully share users and groups, you must, for example, have the National Security Agency trust the CIA *and* have the CIA trust the NSA.

Trust relationships are nontransferable. If, for example, the CIA domain trusts the NSA domain, and the NSA domain trusts something so secret you're not even allowed to know its name (call it Project X), that doesn't allow the CIA domain to trust Project X's domain.

When you look at Trust Relationships, you see a list of the domains that this domain trusts and another list of the domains that trust this domain. Enter the name of the domain and set a password that the trusting domain uses when it tries to trust this domain. Next, you have to manage the trusting domain and add the trusted domain to its trusted domains list.

FIGURE 15.15.

Setting trust relation-ships.

NOTE

After the trusting domain logs onto the trusted domain for the first time, the systems agree on a new password, which is unknown to both administrators. If you need to break a trust relationship and reestablish it, you must remove both ends of the trust relationship and start from scratch so you can reset the password.

Creating User Profiles

As you've seen, a user's profile defines how the user interacts with Windows NT. His or her groups, network connections, and other information are all stored in the user's profile.

When a user logs onto a Windows NT workstation for the first time, the system makes a copy of the default profile for that user. Any changes the user makes during a session, such as changing the wallpaper, are saved to the user's profile on the system drive. The next time the user logs on, she sees the changes she made in her previous session.

So what gets saved in a user profile?

- Groups and their arrangement on the desktop
- Explorer and My Computer settings, including network connections
- The configuration of the command prompt, including colors and fonts
- Network printer connections
- Color scheme, mouse parameters, and desktop settings, including wallpaper and screen saver, keyboard, international, and sound options set in the Control Panel
- Additional user data from applications like Cardfile and Paintbrush

If you're still thinking in Windows 3.*x* terms, a user profile is made up of the .GRP files, most of WIN.INI, and most of the other .INI files, along with tasks Windows 3.*x* just doesn't do.

NT Server Enhancements

NT Server extends the user profile concept to allow users to store their profiles on the file server so they can have the same desktop whenever they log on at any workstation on the network. This feature lets Vice President Jane run her address book program from the Paris office or lets you log on at a user's workstation and use the diagnostic tools you've installed into your desktop.

You also get the ability to control users' profiles. You can have several users share a mandatory profile that they can't change. This option makes it easier to manage groups of reservation clerks, bank tellers, or other users with a well-defined set of tasks to perform because you can just set new users' profiles and know that all their options will be set properly. Users being unable to change their profiles can save you hundreds of technical support calls when users try to figure out how to install their new games, not to mention the productivity boost resulting from not playing games.

Even if you decide to allow your users to change their environments, you can control how much they can change settings and features. This option can protect you from users who have less technical acumen than they think they do.

Mandatory and Personal User Profiles

A Windows NT profile is actually the Registry hive of the user's information saved to a file on the local workstation or, with NT Server, on a file server. When the user logs on, his or her profile is copied from the file into the Registry to affect the current Windows NT session.

15

NT SERVER

NT Server divides user profiles into two categories: mandatory profiles for users whose working environment you want to control, and personal user profiles for users who can be allowed more control over their own environments. You can think of a mandatory profile as a read-only file. A user with a mandatory profile can rearrange icons or make other changes to his or her Registry during a Windows NT session, but he or she can't save any of those changes to the profile file. Personal user profiles, on the other hand, are read-write. Subject to the restrictions you set for him, each user with a personal user profile can change his computing environment and save those changes for his next session.

Assigning multiple users the same user profile sounds like a good idea. You need to create only one profile rather than 10 or 15 profiles. If you decide later that you want to change the profile in some way, such as adding a new application or changing the user's wallpaper to the new corporate logo, you need to make the change in only one place.

If, however, you set up several users to use the same personal user profile, you'll have a small problem. Any change that a user makes to the profile will show up on all the other users' desktops the next time they log on. You're almost guaranteed to have one user who loves an orange-and-black color scheme because of her Princeton days teamed with a diehard Harvard fan who insists on crimson.

The solution is to share only mandatory profiles. Because the users can't save their changes anyway, they can share a profile without any problems.

Creating and Editing User Profiles

Your first step in setting up user profiles is to run the Control Panel to set the workstation's computing environment the way you want it. You can then use the NT Server User Profile Editor to save the Registry hive to a file with the configuration information you've set up. Because you've spent the past three weeks getting your own account's configuration just the way you want it, you'll probably want to create a new administrator-level user ID to use while creating profiles. As soon as you've saved the profile, you can use User Manager for Domains to tell the user's account to use the profile.

Remember that some of the information in a profile, including icons, window locations, and sizes, depends on the workstation's video display. You should create user profiles on a system that has the same video subsystem as the users who are using the profile. Multiple users with different video displays might not be able to share a mandatory profile. You'll have to set up a mandatory profile for each resolution.

If you really want your users to be able to log on from different workstations and use the same profile, you have to make sure that all the application icons in the profile's groups access programs and working directories through the same paths from each workstation the user is likely to log on at. To do this, you might have to keep all your applications on NT Servers with the network connections stored as part of the profile or keep applications in exactly the same directory on each workstation so that the pointer to C:\WINAPPS\WINWORD is the Word for Windows directory for all the workstations your users are likely to log on from.

Default Profiles

If you log onto a Windows NT workstation using an account that doesn't have a user profile assigned to it, or if your profile is unavailable (for example, if the server you keep it on is down), Windows NT loads the local station's default user profile. Any changes you make to your configuration during that session are saved as a local user profile for the account you used to log on.

Each Windows NT system also has a default system profile that's used to define how the system behaves when no users are logged in. If your boss thinks your company logo is the highest form of art and should be displayed on every workstation on your network, even when the users aren't logged in, you can edit the default system profile for each station (a thankless task not worth the energy it takes to perform).

User Profile Editor

Besides letting you save your current configuration as a mandatory or personal user profile, the User Profile Editor also lets you control how much a user is allowed to change his or her configuration. By using the User Profile Editor, you get all the control that the Windows 3.*x* PROGMAN.INI restrictions section gave you and more.

1. Click on System in the the Control Panel.

2. Select the User Profiles tab to get to the page shown in Figure 15.16.

Figure 15.16.

The User Profiles page.

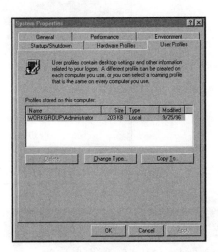

3. To create a new profile, click the Copy To button and enter a name for the new profile in the dialog box that appears. You can select the groups that can use this profile in the lower part of the window. After clicking OK, a new profile appears on the desktop.

4. Click on the new profile on the desktop to expand it. There will be several folders inside. You can move files and applications into the folders, and use the contents to properly configure the user profile.

Server Manager

NT Server's Server Manager extends the Control Panel's Server and Services applets to let you manage not only the server process on the computer you're now working at, but also other servers in your domain. Like the Control Panel, Server Manager allows you to control user connections, shares, open files, and the replication service.

Server Manager is also the tool you use to manage the members of your domain, both servers and workstations, adding and deleting members and promoting or demoting Domain Managers and servers. You can also remotely manage file sharepoints on Windows NT workstations and NT Servers in your domain.

When you start Server Manager, you see the dialog box shown in Figure 15.17. It lists the computers that are members of the domain you're currently logged onto. One, and hopefully only one, of the NT Servers is then identified as a Windows NT 4.0 Primary; this is your domain controller. Other NT Servers are identified as Windows NT Servers. Windows NT systems in the domain are identified as Windows NT Workstations.

Figure 15.17.

The Server Manager window.

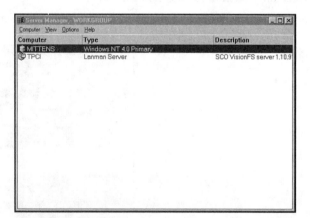

NOTE

In addition to Windows NT 4.0 Controllers, Servers, and Workstations, you might also see Windows NT 3.10 or 3.51 Controllers, Servers, and Workstations, as well as LAN Manager Servers and Windows clients.

Only members of the Administrators, Domain Admins, and Server Operator groups can run Server Manager. Members of the Account Operators group can run Server Manager, but only to add computer accounts to the domain.

If you double-click on a computer's entry in the list, select it and press the Enter key, or choose Computer|Properties, you'll see the familiar dialog box shown in Figure 15.18. Here you can view, and to some extent manage, user connections, shares, shared resources in use, the server's replicator, and how the selected server responds to events that need attention.

FIGURE 15.18.

The Properties dialog box for servers.

Except for the ability to manage these resources on any computer in the domain being managed, this dialog box provides the same functions that the Control Panel's Server applet does for the local system. See Chapter 9, "Windows NT Administration," for more information on the Server applet and this box.

Changing the View

When you first fire up Server Manager, you see a list of all the computers that have accounts in your domain. You can restrict the systems listed to just NT Servers or just Windows NT workstations. At any time, you can refresh the computer list by using the View menu. Refreshing the view adds any computer accounts that have been added since you started Server Manager and removes any computers whose accounts have been deleted.

The computer list changes even more if you disable Show Domain Members Only on the View menu. It shows not only the members of your selected domain, but also Windows for Workgroups and Windows NT systems on your network that might not be members of the domain. You'll also see each computer's status. If a computer isn't currently available on the network, its icon is grayed out and the version number isn't displayed; however, Windows for Workgroups systems never display a version number.

Server Manager automatically updates the computer display after some actions, such as changing the domain controller. These refreshes can cause a lot of network traffic because Server Manager polls all the computers in the list to check their status. If you're working on a domain across a low-speed or heavily loaded connection, such as a wide area link, you can reduce the traffic by selecting a low-speed connection from Server Manager's Options menu. As soon as you've selected the low-speed option, Server Manager stops updating the list automatically. Instead, it updates only when you choose View|Refresh.

15

NT SERVER

Managing a Domain or Peer Server

When you choose Computer|Shared Directories, you see the dialog box shown in Figure 15.19. You can use it to control the shared directories for a selected server or Windows NT workstation. If you want to stop sharing a directory, select it and click the Stop Sharing button. To change the number of users allowed to access the sharepoint or share level permissions on the directory, click the Properties button.

FIGURE 15.19.

The Shared Directories dialog box.

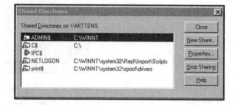

Click the New Share button to have the computer you're managing share another directory. Again, it works just like Explorer or My Computer, except that you can't browse for the directory on a tree display. You have to enter the directory you want to share in the Path field of the New Share dialog box. (See Figure 15.20.)

FIGURE 15.20.

The New Share dialog box.

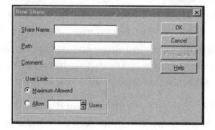

Choose Computer|Services to start and stop the Windows NT services running on the computer you're managing, such as the ClipBook server or replicator. This action is just like going to that machine and running the Services applet from the Control Panel. See Chapter 8, "Using the Control Panel to Configure Windows NT," for more information on managing services.

The Send Message option allows you to send a real-time message that pops up in a dialog box with an OK button to any user logged onto the selected computer. This option comes in handy for sending `Server going down in 3 minutes` messages to your users. Note that WFWG 3.11 machines need to be running Winpopup to receive messages.

Managing Your Domain

Every computer in a domain needs to have an account in the domain database. Normally, you create that account when you install Windows NT by entering the computer's name and the name and password of the domain's administrator-level account. If your users are going to be installing Windows NT on their own systems and you don't want to trust them with an administrative account, you can create the computer accounts for their machines by using the Add to Domain option on Server Manager's Computer menu. (See Figure 15.21.) Just enter the new computer's name and indicate whether it's running NT Server or Windows NT Backup Domain Controller.

Figure 15.21.

The Add Computer to Domain dialog box.

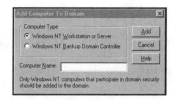

As you've seen, any NT Server in your domain can validate user logons, but only one computer in each domain—the domain controller—has the master copy of the domain database. If the domain controller goes down, you can't make changes to the domain database, such as adding users, until the domain controller is restored.

Because every Windows NT Server machine has a copy of the domain database, all you have to do to get your domain a working controller is promote that server to be the new domain controller. Just select the computer you want to promote and choose Computer|Promote to Domain Controller.

This choice causes the domain database on the computer you're promoting to be the master domain database for the domain. If you promote a computer in a domain that has a running domain controller, the controller is demoted to a server automatically. It's a good idea to synchronize one of your servers with the domain controller and promote it before taking the domain controller down for preventative maintenance or upgrades so that your network will never be without a functioning domain controller.

If you promote a server to domain controller while the previous domain controller is down, you might have to manually demote the previous domain controller when it rejoins the network. If a domain controller tries to join a domain that already has a domain controller, it won't validate logon attempts until it's demoted.

Synchronizing Servers

Theoretically, the domain controller automatically updates each of the other servers in a domain after each change in the domain database. If a server has been offline, it might have missed these changes in the domain database, which could mean some users might not be able to log on. Even worse, a deleted user might still be able to log on if the out-of-date server validates his or her attempt.

To synchronize a single server with the domain controller, select that computer and then choose Computer|Synchronize with Domain Controller. If your domain controller is offline and a new controller got promoted, or if you're not sure which server needs synchronizing, select the domain controller. That menu choice will change automatically to Synchronize Entire Domain. Remember that synchronizing a domain, or even a single server, can generate a large amount of data traffic and either take a long time or slow everything else happening on your network or both.

Data Protection and Fault Tolerance

If you've ever had the misfortune of a hard-disk error—or even worse, a complete disk crash—you know how much time and money you can spend reconstructing the drive and lost data. Even if you make regular backups, you have to go through the time and aggravation of finding your last backup and restoring the data from tape. Of course, any work you've done since the last backup goes directly to data heaven, never to return.

On your personal workstation, even a disk crash is a controllable disaster. If you have a recent backup, you have to reconstruct only a few hours of work. However, a disk error on a file server is another story. First, several different users will be saving their data to the disk, multiplying the amount of data you'll have to reconstruct (because it was created after the backup). Second, some users might not be technically astute (or just generally "with it") enough to know exactly what they've done on the system that day. You might end up sending out old versions of documents that haven't been spell-checked because Vice President Skippy found the file and forgot to redo the work he did on it that morning.

Even worse, you might have data that is simply irreplaceable. If you're developing an order entry system for L.L. Bean or J. Crew, in which a group of operators take orders over the phone and enter the data directly into their computers, a hard-disk error on the file server at 2 p.m., December 18th, could mean that hundreds of orders totaling thousands of dollars would be lost forever. There would be no record of the orders, or even of the customers' telephone numbers and addresses, other than the data on that disk.

Of course, data loss can be the least of your problems. If you have a disk error on your file server, you'll have to take the server down, leaving your users sitting around twiddling their thumbs until you can repair the drive and restore your data. The cost of this down time can easily add up to many thousands of dollars because your company must pay all those users and switch to manual procedures to deal with customers and suppliers. Add in any loss of goodwill resulting from customers not getting the level of service they're accustomed to, and you might be looking for a new job and cursing your disk vendor.

After reading all this, you'll be glad to know that NT Server has several fault-tolerance integrity features designed to allow your server to continue running right through a disk error, up to and including a drive crash. If you set up your servers right, your users will never know that your server just made one of its hard disks look like the Bee Gees album you used when you couldn't find a Frisbee.

Mirrored Sets

Data mirroring is the simplest of NT Server's fault-tolerance features designed to deal with a failed disk drive. Basically, if you configure two 500M disks to be a mirrored pair, they look like a single 500M drive to your users (whether they're sitting at the server or at workstations on the network). NT Server duplicates all disk writes so that the same data is written to both drives.

When one of the drives has an error reading some data, NT Server simply reads the data from the other disk and places a message in the Event Log. Users at their own workstations won't even know anything went wrong. Even if one of the drives fails completely, the file server will take a lickin' and keep on tickin' by using the other drive.

Unlike other PC operating systems, including Novell's NetWare, NT Server's data mirroring doesn't require you to mirror whole disk drives—you can mirror disk partitions. This means you can have different-sized drives in a mirrored pair without wasting the additional size on the larger drive. You can just create a mirrored pair of partitions the size of the smaller drive and an additional partition on the larger drive for the extra space.

If you're short on disk space or money, you can carefully segregate your data between mirrored and unmirrored volumes. Put your most valuable or least replaceable data on your mirrored drive E: and less important data, such as your collection of Leisure Suit Larry games or last year's accounting detail, on the unmirrored drive F:.

If you can, you should put the two partitions of a mirrored pair on drives that are connected to different disk controllers or SCSI host adapters. Using multiple controllers protects your data from drive failures *and* controller failures. You can also improve system performance with multiple controllers by supplying a higher bandwidth data pipe to the disk drives. Figure 15.22 shows examples of mirrored and duplex drives.

FIGURE 15.22.

Disk mirroring and duplexing.

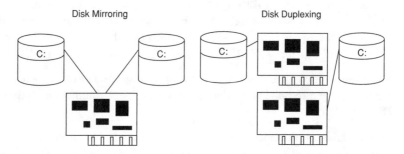

I've found that the protection against controller failure is less important than it seems at first glance because modern hard-disk controllers simply don't fail very often. Most of the controller failures I've seen have been so catastrophic that they take the server down by sending noise or excessive interrupt requests on the bus or by shorting out. The performance advantage alone is worth the extra cost of the second controller.

Creating a Mirrored Set

To create a mirrored set, use Disk Administrator to create the first partition of the pair, select that partition, and Ctrl+click on an unused area of disk space on another disk drive so that both the unused disk area and the first partition are selected. Next, choose Fault Tolerance|Establish Mirror. Disk Administrator then creates a disk partition out of the selected free space. This new partition will be the same size as the original partition and contain a copy of any data on the original partition.

Breaking a Mirrored Set

If one of the drives in your mirrored set fails, you might get desperate for disk space because your users insist on keeping every fax they've ever received online, or you're adding additional drives to your server and you need to rearrange your partitions. In cases like these, you'll need to break one or more of your mirrored sets. Breaking a mirrored set doesn't destroy the data on either partition; it just stops the process of duplicating data between the two partitions.

To break a mirrored set, simply select it in Disk Administrator and choose Fault Tolerance|Break Mirror. Because breaking a mirrored set reduces the data integrity of your server, Disk Administrator makes you confirm your decision.

Beyond Data Mirroring: Disk Arrays

Disk mirroring first appeared in the late '70s as part of special fault-tolerant computers, such as Tandem's NonStop. Disk arrays were first proposed in an article by three University of California, Berkeley professors as a solution to the problem of disk drive performance approaching theoretical limits and the growing cost of increasing drive speeds.

They proposed Redundant Arrays of Inexpensive Drives (RAID) as an alternative to a Single Large Expensive Drive (SLED). The article discussed five different methods by which an array of drives could emulate a single larger, more expensive drive, and it called these proposals Levels 1–5. The concept has since been extended by others, including vendors, at both the high and low ends; therefore, RAID solutions of Levels 0–7 are now available.

By using multiple disk drives and duplicating either data or error-correcting codes, RAID systems allow you to build very large (multiple gigabyte) volumes and improve your system's reliability.

RAID can be implemented in hardware, with special controllers, such as those from Compaq, Dell, or Ciprico, or in software. Windows NT Server has built-in support for several RAID schemes, including Level 5, without special hardware.

RAID Level 0 (Windows NT Stripe Sets)

Strictly speaking, Level 0 isn't RAID because it doesn't improve system reliability by storing redundant data. A Level 0 array simply distributes data across its drive. A typical Level 0 array writes the first stripe of data to the first drive in the array, the second stripe to the second, and so on. Data stripes typically are a sector, track, or cylinder in size.

Level 0 arrays, which Microsoft calls *stripe sets*, have a performance advantage over single, larger drives because more data is under the disk heads at any given time. This kind of array reduces the number of seeks required for any given data transfer, and multiple data paths from the drives to the processor can eliminate the disk interface as a bottleneck.

Both Windows NT and NT Server can build stripe sets out of standard drives. Because a failure of any drive in a Level 0 array leads to the effective loss of all data on the array, I don't recommend that you use stripe sets on your file servers.

RAID Level 1 (Windows NT Server Mirror Sets)

Level 1 is disk mirroring. In the original RAID paper, the authors assumed that mirroring would be on a disk drive basis as opposed to a partition or volume basis, but other than that, NT Server's mirror sets are a classic RAID 1 implementation.

For most systems, mirror sets give better performance than NT Server's other RAID options, especially when running with a failed drive. The downside to disk mirroring is that it requires you to buy twice the disk capacity you really need. This 50 percent capacity overhead can get expensive when you add additional gigabytes of disk to your servers.

RAID Level 2

Level 2 arrays stripe data across the drives of an array at the bit level. The first drive in the array contains the first bit, the second drive contains the second bit, and so on. Multiple additional drives contain error-correcting code (ECC) or parity information.

RAID 2 was designed for large computers with disk controllers that are as smart as, or smarter than, a typical PC rather than the microcomputers and technical workstations that run Windows NT. These controllers track drive errors through internal checksums on the disk and standard error flags performed by the drive and controller. As a result, RAID 2 systems are too complex and expensive for PC applications and generally aren't used on small systems.

RAID Level 3

Like RAID Level 2, RAID Level 3 systems stripe data across a series of drives. Level 3 differs from Level 2 by using only one parity or ECC drive. Data can be interleaved at the bit level, at the byte level (the most common), or at any other logical size. Level 3 arrays typically have from 20 to 25 percent error-correcting code overhead as opposed to the 50 percent overhead of a Level 1 or data-mirrored system.

Because data is interleaved across all data drives, a single read request is performed by multiple drives. Each drive reads a portion of the data, and all the drives transfer their portions to the controller in parallel. This process yields high transfer rates, making RAID 3 ideal for applications that need high I/O bandwidth. However, only one I/O transaction can be processed at a time because every drive is involved in each read or write transaction.

RAID 3's parallel data transfers often work well for workstations that require fast sequential access to single large files, such as image processing systems. It's generally not recommended for transaction processing systems or environments in which most I/O transactions involve small amounts of data.

RAID Level 4

RAID 3's primary disadvantage is its inability to perform simultaneous I/O transactions because even small blocks of data are interleaved across all drives. Writing even the smallest file to a Level 3 array requires that the system write to all the drives in the array.

A Level 4 array, on the other hand, places the entire first transfer block, or cluster, on the first data drive, the second transfer block on the second drive, and so on. This process improves disk performance by allowing multiple reads.

Level 4 arrays still have a dedicated parity drive that contains error-correcting information for all the data drives. Therefore, it's involved in every write, forcing each write to be performed one at a time.

A multitasking operating system accessing a Level 4 array can process independent read transactions for each data drive in the array. In an array with four data drives, for example, the array can perform three times as many reads as a single drive can in the same time period by accessing each of the data drives individually.

RAID Level 5 (Windows NT Server Stripe Sets with Parity)

The use of dedicated parity drives in RAID Levels 1–4 limits each of these architectures to one write transaction at a time. Level 5, which Microsoft calls *stripe sets with parity*, spreads the ECC information across all the drives in the array. Therefore, each drive in a Level 5 array contains both data and parity blocks. As in RAID 4, an entire transfer block is placed on a single drive, and the parity for that block of data is stored on another drive. When a drive fails, its data can be reconstructed from the remaining drives. Eliminating the dedicated parity drive removes the single-write bottleneck and lets RAID 5 perform multiple read and write transactions in parallel. (See Figure 15.23.)

Compared to a single drive, an array with four drives can perform four times as many reads and two times as many writes (because each write involves two drives) in a given time interval. In a combined read-write environment, the virtual transfer rates could be increased by a factor of one-half the number of drives in the array, compared to the single drive. As the ratio of reads to writes increases, the transfer rate increase factor approaches the number of drives installed. Theoretically, as you add drives to the array, performance increases, although not in linear proportion to the number of drives.

FIGURE 15.23.

A Level 5 disk array.

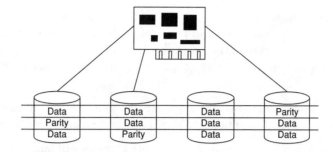

Eliminating the dedicated parity drive also reduces the performance effect of a drive failure. In any array that uses ECC instead of data mirroring to save disk space, the array's performance is reduced when reading from an array with a failed drive because calculating the original data from the ECC information takes time. In a Level 4 array with a failed data drive, every read requires that the original data be reconstructed. In a 5-drive, Level 5 array, 20 percent of the reads don't require the recalculation.

Hardware Arrays

In addition to the RAID features built into Windows NT Server, you can add a drive array to your file server by buying a hardware-based array, such as the Compaq Intelligent Drive Array or Micropolis Radiion. These hardware implementations have several advantages over software-based arrays. Because they have dedicated processors and cache memory on their controllers, these hardware arrays can be faster than software-based arrays.

Hardware-based arrays typically have cabinets that allow you to change drives in the array without turning the array off or bringing the server down. These systems can rebuild the array data onto a replacement drive in the background as users continue to access your array. These systems also feature dual redundant power supplies to protect your data from a power supply failure.

Configuring Your Server's Disk Subsystem

Designing the disk subsystem for any given file server requires carefully balancing cost, performance, and reliability. Any file server containing critical data, which includes the vast majority of file servers, should have some sort of data integrity feature. However, you shouldn't be lulled into a false sense of security because your data is protected from a disk or controller failure. Your data is more likely to be destroyed by user error, program bugs, or natural disaster than by a disk failure. In fact, the most important measure you can take to protect your valuable data is to have a regular schedule of backups.

The least secure option is to use volume sets or stripe sets. Because a failure of a single drive that's part of a volume set or stripe set causes the system to lose all the data on that set, increasing the number of drives in the set also increases the odds of losing your data. In fact, the odds of losing data on a four-drive array are four times greater than those of losing data on a single drive.

If you can't afford to make your system truly fault-tolerant, at least set up each volume to occupy only a single partition, limiting the amount of data you'll lose in a drive failure.

Mirrored sets improve your data integrity at the cost of buying twice as many disk drives as you need. However, mirrored sets typically have better performance than stripe sets with parity. If your drives are large enough to hold the largest volumes, mirrored sets are probably your best bet.

> **TIP**
>
> If possible, put the two drives in your mirrored set on separate controllers and connect them to different power supplies. This method protects your data against a controller or power supply failure, and multiple controllers speed things up.

Stripe sets with parity are a good solution if you need to create very large volumes or if you can't afford to buy enough disk drives to build mirrored sets. They give you a good level of data protection at a lower cost but are much slower than mirrored sets, especially for short writes. A short write to a stripe set means the system must read all the stripes to calculate the ECC information and then write to both the changed stripe and the ECC stripe.

> **NOTE**
>
> Stripe sets with parity require more memory to manage because the system needs to keep all the data described by a parity block in memory to calculate the error-correcting code. If you plan on using stripe sets with parity, figure on putting an additional 4M of memory in your server.

Hardware arrays can offer the best solution if your goal is to have the most reliable system possible. Their hot swap capability and improved performance over stripe sets with parity are big advantages if you can afford them.

> **NOTE**
>
> Although disk arrays and mirrored sets protect you against a drive failure, they are no longer fault-tolerant after such a failure. You should monitor your server's status regularly and swap a failed drive with a fresh one as soon as you notice it has failed.

If you choose to use NT Server's data mirroring or stripe set features, you should use SCSI disk drives. If you use IDE or ESDI drives to build your mirrored or striped set, you might have a rude awakening if there's a disk write error. Even though NTFS has a hot fix feature that automatically writes your data to an alternate sector if a write error occurs, this feature doesn't work properly for fault-tolerant sets because it's part of the file system. When using NTFS hot fix, a file is simply written to a different set of clusters on the disk if an error occurs, and the bad cluster is marked as unusable.

If you're using SCSI drives in your fault-tolerant set, NT Server takes advantage of SCSI's sector sparing to order the drive to assign the data to one of its spare sectors. From that point on, the drive makes it look to the system as though nothing ever went wrong. If you're using IDE or ESDI drives, NT Server disables the drive that has the error, thus breaking the set.

Setting Up a Stripe Set with Parity

To set up a stripe set with parity, install the needed drives and controllers, then follow these steps from Disk Administrator:

1. In Disk Administrator, select areas of free disk space on three to 32 drives by clicking on the first area and Ctrl+clicking on the others.
2. Choose Fault Tolerance|Create Stripe Set With Parity.
3. In the resulting Create Stripe Set With Parity dialog box, enter the size of the stripe set you'd like to create and click OK. The dialog box shows you the maximum- and minimum-size stripe sets you can create.

Disk Administrator then creates equal-size partitions on the selected drives. If the size you entered doesn't divide equally into the number of drives you selected, it's automatically rounded off.

Deleting a Stripe Set with Parity

To delete a stripe set with parity, select the stripe set and choose Partition|Delete.

> **CAUTION**
>
> Make sure you back up your data before you delete a stripe set. When you delete a stripe set, you lose all the data on it.

UPS Service

Windows NT's NTFS file system, which you should use on your file servers for security and performance reasons, holds some of your data in cache before writing it to the disk. Because writes to mirrored and striped sets take some time to complete, you should protect every file server with an uninterruptible file power supply and enable the UPS service, as described in Chapter 8, "Using the Control Panel to Configure Windows NT."

15

NT Server

Remember that the UPS service requires a serial cable from the UPS to your computer so that the UPS can tell your computer when it's running on batteries. Just plugging your computer into a UPS provides power monitoring. The UPS beeps when the power goes out, but it doesn't use an automatic shutdown sequence. If the UPS and server are locked in a wiring closet and an electrician turns off the breaker for that closet, you won't hear the beeping before the battery runs out. If you haven't set up the serial cable and UPS server when the battery runs out, poof—there goes the server. It's a shame, but many people think that just adding a UPS solves all their problems.

There's a continuing debate on the best type of UPS. Online UPSs give you better power filtering because the computer runs from the batteries all the time. However, online UPSs are much bigger and more expensive and seem to break more often than standby UPSs. I've had good experience with UPSs from Sola, Best, and American Power Conversion.

When you buy a UPS, make sure it's one that supports a true sine wave, such as the SmartUPS and the Matrix UPS from American Power Conversion. APC also offers software that can supply additional electrical line statistics, which might prove useful for long-term monitoring.

Directory Replication

With NT Server's directory replication service, you can automatically maintain duplicate copies of one or more directories on your Windows NT Servers. (See Figure 15.24.) When you change any files in the master copy of the directory, on the computer called the Export Server, the replication service copies the files that have changed to one or more import computers. Export Servers must be running NT Server, but import computers can be running either Windows NT or NT Server.

FIGURE 15.24.

The Directory Replication dialog box.

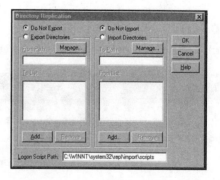

The replicator comes in handy for distributing files, from driver updates, for example, to multiple destinations to keep all the copies up-to-date and in sync. If you set up WordPerfect directories on five of your file servers to balance the load, the replicator lets you apply patches or copy new templates to only the master copy of the directory, which eases network administration.

If you have more than one server in a domain, you'll find that you have to use the replicator to copy users' logon scripts to all the servers in the domain so users can get the same logon script regardless of the system they log on from.

Some users use the replicator to extend NT Server's fault-tolerance, also. Setting up replication between multiple servers, they say, protects their data against not only disk drive failures, but also server failures. They'll tell you that even if a server fails, they'll have their system back up in seconds because users just have to access the backup data sets.

Although this sounds good, in practice you might find yourself in the same situation as a new client who called me recently. Their network consultant, who had years of experience with networks but was new to NT, set up their system to replicate their data directories to an import machine and then back up that import machine to DAT tape nightly. Being a network expert, he didn't actually test restoring a file from the tape; he was confident that everything worked right because there were no errors.

What our friend forgot was that the replicator copies files only after they're both changed and closed. The replicator won't do you any good if you want to protect your order entry database that's open by at least one user 24 hours a day. My new client had 24 tapes, none of which had their most valuable files.

Other users, such as law firms, who have many smaller files that get opened and closed as users work on them, can be well-protected by the replicator if they can live with the replication service's directory limitations.

How the Replicator Works

To copy files from the export server to the import computers, you need to run the replicator service on each system. When it's started, the replicator logs onto the systems using an account you've created just for that purpose. The service running on the export server then scans the subdirectories of the export directory (by default, C:\WINNT\SYSTEM32\REPL\EXPORT) for new or modified files and subdirectories. When it finds changed files, it copies them to each of the specified import computers, where it copies the data to their import directory (by default, C:\WINNT\SYSTEM32\REPL\IMPORT).

Although import computers must run Windows NT or NT Server, they don't need to be members of the same domain as the export server. In fact, cross-domain replications are a good way to distribute templates and other corporate master files.

When configuring the replicator, you can tell it to copy specific subdirectories of the export directory, but you can't tell it to duplicate C:\WINWORD\DOCS, for example. If you have applications that update groups of files, such as a data file and its related index files, you should tell the replicator to wait for the directory to stabilize—that is, for all the files in the directory to remain unchanged—for two minutes or so to make sure a synchronized set of files is duplicated.

You can even set up the replicator to copy from the export directory to the import directory on a single server to give you an instant backup copy.

Setting Up Replication

The first step in setting up the replication service, as it should be with anything, is to do a little planning. Figure out which of your NT Servers will be export servers, which data you want to replicate, and which machines will be import computers.

Remember that all this data being copied from one server to another adds to network and server traffic. If you put all your data directories under the export directory on all your servers, you'll flood your servers and Ethernet with so much data that users trying to get work done will feel like they're swimming through molasses.

Next, you need to create a user account on each domain for the replicator server to use when copying your data.

Creating the Replication User

You create the replication user with User Manager for Domains, described earlier in this chapter. You must set several options, such as allowing the replication user access to the data being copied and the ability to copy files whenever they're changed. To create the replication user, follow these steps:

1. Launch User Manager for Domains and create a new user by choosing User|New User.

2. In the New User dialog box, enter a user ID, full name, password, and description into the User Properties dialog box, shown in Figure 15.25, as you would when creating any other user. Make sure that the Password Never Expires option is enabled so that the replication service won't be locked out.

FIGURE 15.25.

Replication service users need passwords that don't expire.

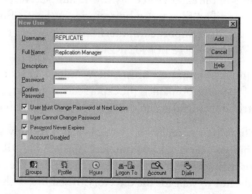

3. Click the Groups button. Make the user a member of the Backup Operators and Replicator groups by using the Group Memberships dialog box, shown in Figure 15.26. When you're done, click OK to go back to the New User dialog box.

FIGURE 15.26.

The replication user's group memberships.

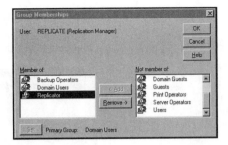

4. Back in the New User dialog box, click the Hours button. Make sure the user has access at all times by using the Logon Hours dialog box, shown in Figure 15.27.

FIGURE 15.27.

Replication service accounts should have access at all times.

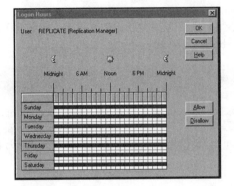

Setting Up an Export Server

Before you start configuring the replication service, you should create the appropriate user account and the directories you want to export. When planning your directory structure, keep in mind the following points:

- The directory replicator can copy only subdirectories of the export directory.
- An export server copies the same files and subdirectories to all its associated import computers.
- The total directory structure, from the export directory down, can be only 32 layers deep.

You don't have to copy the files into the subdirectories now. The replicator copies them whenever you get around to it.

To turn your system into an export server, follow these steps:

1. Launch the Server Manager, double-click on the server you want to configure, and click the Replication button to get the Directory Replication dialog box, shown in Figure 15.28.

15

NT SERVER

FIGURE 15.28.

*The Directory
Replication dialog box.*

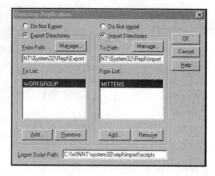

FIGURE 15.28.

*The Directory
Replication dialog box.*

2. Select the Export Directories radio button to enable your system's export function.

3. By default, the replicator exports the directory
   C:\WINNT\SYSTEM32\REPL\EXPORT\SCRIPTS and its subdirectories. You can
   change this path by editing the From Path field.

NOTE

A Windows NT Server can export only a single directory and its subdirectories. Although you can choose to export only some directories of the export directory, you can't have two independent trees. Therefore, you can't export data from more than a single volume.

---

4. If you want to add additional directories to export, click the Manage button to open
   the dialog box shown in Figure 15.29. In this dialog box, you can tell the system
   which directories you want to export. If you want to copy anything but the \SCRIPTS
   directory, click the Add button. The Add Sub-Directory dialog box opens so you can
   add another directory to the list.

FIGURE 15.29.

*The Manage Exported
Directories dialog box.*

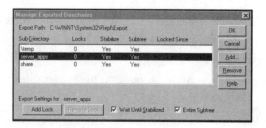

5. When you see the Add Sub-Directory dialog box, shown in Figure 15.30, enter the
   path to the directory you want to replicate, starting from the export directory. Because
   you have to do things the old-fashioned way and type the directory name, you'll long
   for a Browse button.

FIGURE 15.30.

The Add Sub-Directory dialog box.

6. After you add the directory, you can tell the replication service whether to copy its subdirectories and whether you want the directory to stabilize—that is, wait two minutes from the last file change to start the copy.

> **NOTE**
>
> Make sure the directory replication user has full control permissions to the source directories of the replication. If it has less than full control, you won't get the file's permissions copied properly.

7. When you've listed all the directories you want to copy, click OK to return to the Directory Replication dialog box.

> **NOTE**
>
> The Manage Exported Directories dialog box also allows you to apply a lock to a directory. To lock a directory, select it and click the Add Lock button. You can apply as many locks as you want, but only the first one matters. If a directory has one or more locks, the replicator won't copy its files until the locks are removed. To remove a lock, click the Remove Lock button.
>
> The directory replicator copies the same data to each import computer. There's no way to have the replicator copy one set of data to one import computer and a different set to another import computer.

8. Now you have to tell the exporters where to send the data by maintaining the To Path list. To add a system to the list of systems that can receive your data, click the Add button to get the Select Domain dialog box, shown in Figure 15.31.

FIGURE 15.31.

Selecting import computers.

9. Now you can choose another NT Server, Windows NT workstation, or domain to receive the data. For the data to actually be transmitted, the import computer must also be running the replicator and must be configured to receive data from this server or domain. As a result, if you use a domain name in the To Path list, the server exports data to every machine in the domain configured to import its data.

> **NOTE**
>
> If the To Path list is empty, the replicator exports its data to its entire domain. As soon as you add the first server to the To list, this replication ends unless you put the local domain back in the list.

You should avoid having a single import server receive the same data from more than one server. It wastes valuable network bandwidth and endangers data integrity, because a later version of a file can be replaced by an earlier version if the earlier version is replicated later. Loops, in which data gets back to its original server, are even worse, because they eat up network bandwidth.

Your export server is now configured. All you have to do now is configure the import servers and start the replicator.

Configuring the Import Server

Configuring an import server is almost exactly like configuring an export server. The right side of the Directory Replication dialog box works basically the same as the left side. Enter the directory you want your replicated data sent to into the To Path box, add servers to receive data into the From list, and so on. There are a few differences, though.

When you set up the import server, make sure that the replicator's user account has full access permissions to the data import directory so that it can write the data files and their properties.

You don't have to tell the import computer which directories are going to be copied, as you do with an export server. When you click the Manage button, you get the dialog box shown in Figure 15.32. It tells you the status of each directory that's been imported to this system.

FIGURE 15.32.

The Manage Imported Directories dialog box.

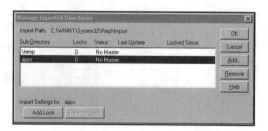

This dialog box can be useful for making sure that all your replications are still running. Each directory is listed, along with the number of locks on the directory, the date and time of the last update received, and the directory's status. A status of OK indicates that the system is receiving updates from the export server and has a current set of its data. No Master indicates that the export server hasn't been heard from lately, and No Sync indicates that the two sets of data don't agree. (This can result from an open file at either end or a communications failure.)

Although this dialog box has Add and Remove buttons, there's really no reason to use them. Directories are added automatically when they're received, even if you've removed them, so there's no way an import server can reject data from an export server. If you're getting data from an export server, you're getting it all, so make sure your import servers have plenty of free disk space.

The replication service import program treats an empty From list the same way the export program treats an empty To list. An empty From list makes the import program accept data from any server exporting to its domain. As with the export server, if you want to include your local domain and other servers, you'll have to select your local domain manually.

Replicating Logon Scripts

When you log onto a Windows NT Server network, your computer might run a logon script created by the network administrator. As you saw earlier in this chapter, a user logging onto the network can be validated by any NT Server in the network because each NT Server has a copy of the user database. As soon as a user logs onto the network, his or her workstation runs a logon script from the server where the user was validated.

A user's logon script is a batch file; it's stored in the file specified in User Manager for Domains's User Environment Profile dialog box in the path specified in NT Server's Server Manager Directory Replication dialog box. Because this batch file is loaded from the validating server, you need to have the same logon script on each NT Server in your domain to allow a user to log on from any workstation and get the same logon script each time.

You should declare one server in each domain to be the master logon script server. This server—which can be the domain controller—has the master copies of each user's logon script and replicates this data to all the other NT Servers in the domain. This way, you have to update the logon scripts on just a single server.

On a small network, you should probably use the domain controller to store the master copy of the scripts. As the network grows and the domain controller gets busier, you can move this task to another server to balance the load and, therefore, improve performance.

If you store your logon scripts in the default C:\WINNT\SYSTEM32\REPL\IMPORT\ SCRIPTS directory, your logon script replication will be all set up as soon as you start the service. If you want to make a change to a logon script, edit the file in the \SCRIPTS subdirectory of the export directory. The changes are automatically replicated to the \SCRIPTS subdirectory of the import directory on all the servers in the domain, including the master.

15

NT SERVER

Starting and Controlling the Replicator Service

As soon as you have the import and export parts of the replication service configured, you need to tell the replicator what user ID to use to log onto your system and start it. Because a service is just a special kind of program, starting a service is technically just launching another program. The replication service takes advantage of a service's ability to log on using a different ID than the user working on the station.

To configure the replication service, follow these steps:

1. Launch the Services applet in the Control Panel. You see the Services dialog box, shown in Figure 15.33.

FIGURE 15.33.

The Services dialog box.

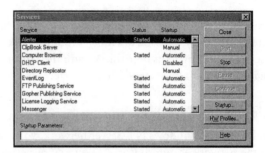

2. To configure the replicator, select Directory Replicator from the list of services installed on this system. You'll see the dialog box shown in Figure 15.34.

FIGURE 15.34.

The Service dialog box for the directory replicator.

3. To have the replicator start every time Windows NT is loaded, select Automatic as the startup type, which allows automatic copying on this system. If you want to run the replication service only occasionally, select Manual.

4. Select the This Account option in the Log On As section to specify the user ID that the replication service should use. Although most Windows NT services use the System Account to log on, this account has no permissions to use data. Therefore, it's useless for the replicator.

5. To select the user you created earlier, click the Browse button to open the Add User dialog box and select that account from the list of users in this domain. (See Figure 15.35.)

FIGURE 15.35.

The Add User dialog box.

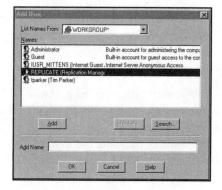

6. Select the user. Click Add, then click OK.

7. Make sure you enter the password correctly in the Directory Replicator dialog box, then click OK to get back to the Services dialog box.

8. Test everything by clicking the Start button to start the service. If you've forgotten the password, a dialog box tells you.

Network Administration Tools

Windows NT Server's Network Administration group includes four useful tools to help make an administrator's life less frustrating. These tools fall into two categories: TCP/IP network management and MS-DOS client management.

Normally, TCP/IP addresses are statically assigned by the system administrator and maintained by using either an online database of assigned IP addresses and computer names or a scratch piece of paper that lists IP addresses in use. When a new user is added to the network, an IP address is assigned to that user based on a free pool of unassigned IP addresses. Sometimes the documentation is updated and sometimes it isn't, depending on the maintenance method in use. Sometimes a duplicate IP address is assigned because the maintenance methods are inefficient; when this duplication happens, it can cause problems.

In addition to statically assigning TCP/IP addresses, the administrator also has to update some files to associate a name with an IP address. After all, how many people can remember the 12-digit IP address for the resource they want to access? If these files get out of sync or become damaged, a call to the system administrator is in order. To address these issues, Windows NT Server includes the Dynamic Host Configuration Protocol (DHCP) and Windows Internet Name Service (WINS).

To make network administration easier, Windows NT Server also includes the Network Client Administrator and Remoteboot Manager. The Network Client Administrator is used to create a network startup disk or network client installation disk set. The Remoteboot Manager is used for diskless workstation management. You can also use the remote boot capability on computers with local hard disks to provide increased security, better system performance, and easier software upgrades, yet still offer custom configurations.

Managing Your TCP/IP Network

The DHCP Server service automates assigning IP addresses, and the DHCP Manager is an interface for service configuration. The WINS service supplies name resolution services, and the WINS Manager provides configuration. Considering the complexity of these services, this section covers only some of the more basic issues. For additional information, see Chapter 4, "Installing and Configuring DHCP Servers," and Chapter 5, "Installing and Configuring WINS Servers," of the TCP/IP online Help files.

TIP

The online Help files for Windows NT Server are in the \SUPPORT\BOOKS directory on the installation CD-ROM. You can create a Common Group (Online Books) and use My Computer or Explorer to drag the Help files into the group. An icon is supplied (BOOKS.ICO) if you want to use a different icon than the default HELP.EXE question mark. I find the built-in search capabilities of the online books help interface to be quite useful during system configuration because the detail provided is better than the application's limited help facilities.

NOTE

DHCP Servers don't share a common database, so if you plan to use a single network segment, you should split the assignment of IP addresses between the DHCP servers. For example, if you have two servers in a single segment, you can set the first server to use IP addresses from 128.0.0.1 to 128.0.0.127 and the second server to use IP addresses from 128.0.0.128 to 128.0.0.254.

Installing the DHCP Server Service

You install the DHCP Server service through the Control Panel's Network applet. Follow these steps:

1. Launch the Network applet from the Control Panel and display the Service page.
2. Click Add to display the list of available services.

3. Select Microsoft DHCP Server Service and click OK.

4. DHCP Manager is then added to the installed services list, as shown in Figure 15.36.

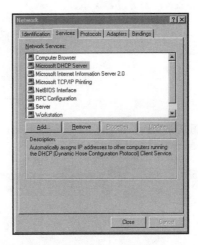

5. When prompted, restart the computer. If you intend to add more components, do so before restarting the computer.

Using the DHCP Manager

The first time you run the DHCP Manager, shown in Figure 15.37, it displays either the local machine—if it's run on an NT Server with an active DHCP Server service—or a message box prompting you for a computer with a DHCP Service to manage. After you select one of these options, the scopes for the service are displayed in the left window pane, and the right window pane displays configuration options for the selected scope.

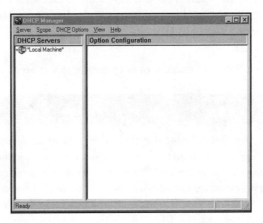

To create a scope, follow these steps:

1. Choose Server|Add to open the dialog box shown in Figure 15.38. Enter the IP address of the server and click OK.

FIGURE 15.38.

*Adding a DHCP
Server to the server list.*

2. Select the DHCP Server in the left window pane, then choose Scope|Create to open the dialog box shown in Figure 15.39.

FIGURE 15.39.

*Adding a scope to a
DHCP server.*

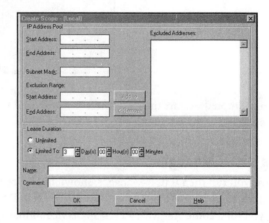

3. Enter the start address and end address of the IP address pool. Next, enter the subnet mask of the address pool. If you want to exclude a range of IP address from the pool, enter the start and end addresses in the Exclusion Range fields, and then click the Add button. Select your lease duration, enter a name and comment for your scope, and click OK.

4. If you have additional scopes to create, repeat Steps 1 through 3.

NOTE

A *lease duration* is the maximum time limit a workstation can use an IP address without renewing the lease from the DHCP Server. I recommend that you use a minimum lease time of twice your maximum DHCP Server offline time. For instance, if you routinely perform system maintenance over the weekend, your lease time should be four days. This lease duration prevents your DHCP clients from releasing their lease on an IP address and then not being able to find a DHCP Server to give them a new lease or IP address. If you have multiple DHCP Servers, lease duration isn't an issue, as long as a DHCP Server is available.

To configure a scope, follow these steps:

1. Select the DHCP Server scope in the left window pane. Choose DHCP
    Options|Scope to open the dialog box shown in Figure 15.40.

FIGURE 15.40.
*Configuring a DHCP
scope.*

> **NOTE**
>
> You can make global changes to all scopes by choosing DHCP Options | Global and set
> default scope options by choosing DHCP Options | Defaults.

2. Select the option to configure from the Unused Options list box and click the Add
    button. To change the default value, click the Value button and change the entry in
    the bottom of the dialog box. Do this for each option you want to configure, then
    click OK. Each option you select is then displayed in the Active Options list box.

> **TIP**
>
> If you have an active network with many floating workstations, you can reserve IP ad-
> dresses for them. Choose Scope | Add Reservations to open the Add Reserved Clients
> dialog box. (See Figure 15.41.) Enter the IP address to reserve, the adapter ID number, the
> client computer number, and a comment that describes the client workstation. Finally,
> click OK.

FIGURE 15.41.
*Reserving an IP address
for a workstation.*

Choose Scope|Active Leases to view active leases, including reservations. (See Figure 15.42.)
To display only reservations, enable the Show Reservations Only checkbox.

Figure 15.42.

Displaying the active leases.

Installing the WINS Service

You install the WINS service through the Control Panel's Network applet. Follow these steps:

1. Launch the Network applet from the Control Panel, and display the Services page.

2. Click Add.

3. Select Windows Internet Naming Services and click OK.

4. When prompted, restart the computer.

Using the WINS Manager

The WINS Manager has the look and feel of the DHCP Manager, and like the DHCP Service, the WINS service offers dynamic services. The primary purpose of the WINS service is to dynamically match NetBIOS computer names to IP addresses. Instead of requiring you to maintain a static list of computer names, the WINS service gives WINS clients dynamic name resolution. As each client makes its initial access to the WINS service, it registers itself; it updates this registration periodically.

The first time you execute the WINS Manager, there's nothing to display until you add your first WINS server. After that, the application displays the WINS servers in the left window pane and the WINS statistics for the selected server in the right window pane. (See Figure 15.43.)

Figure 15.43.

The WINS Manager.

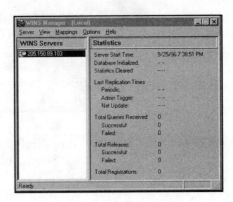

To add a WINS server, choose Server|Add WINS Server. When prompted, enter the computer name of the server providing WINS services.

To display detailed information about the WINS server, choose Server|Detailed Information to open the dialog box shown in Figure 15.44.

FIGURE 15.44.

*Displaying detailed
information about a
WINS server.*

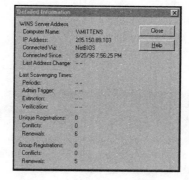

To configure a WINS server, choose Server|Configuration. To include advanced options, click the Advanced button, which displays the dialog box shown in Figure 15.45.

FIGURE 15.45.

*The WINS Server
Configuration dialog
box.*

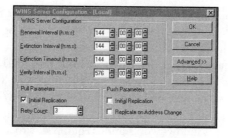

One advantage of the WINS service is that the database can be shared with other WINS servers. In fact, using multiple WINS servers can increase performance. Sharing the database is done by creating replication partners; each replication partner can send changes (push partner), request changes (pull partner), or make both requests.

To replicate the database, follow these steps:

1. Choose Server|Replication Partners to open the dialog box shown in Figure 15.46.
2. Before you can replicate a database, you need to add the WINS servers by clicking the Add button.
3. When prompted, supply an IP address and computer name (if requested), and then select the WINS server you added. Next, specify whether this WINS server is to be a push partner, a pull partner, or both. If you want the replication to occur immediately, click the Push or Pull button in the Send Replication Trigger Now section.

15

NT SERVER

FIGURE 15.46.
Replicating the WINS database.

> **TIP**
>
> If you're migrating an existing TCP/IP installation, you can migrate your host files by choosing Mappings | Static Mappings to open the Static Mappings dialog box. Click the Import Mappings button and load your host file.

Managing Client Workstations

A network administrator's life is tough enough without having to remember how to create installation disks for client operating systems and running around to each computer to install the software. Therefore, Windows NT Server includes the Network Client Administrator and Remoteboot Manager. The first can be used to create installation disks to install network client software for MS-DOS and OS/2, Remote Access for MS-DOS, TCP/IP-32 for Windows for Workgroups, and network administration tools for Windows NT Workstation and Windows for Workgroups. Remoteboot Manager can be used to provide remote boot capabilities to MS-DOS and Windows workstations equipped with a supported network card and remote boot ROM.

Creating Installation Disks

The Network Client Administrator, shown in Figure 15.47, has four options. Three of these options offer useful services to an administrator:

■ Make Network Installation Startup Disk

■ Make Installation Disk Set

■ Copy Client-based Network Administration Tools

The fourth option, View Remoteboot Client Information, displays the message shown in Figure 15.48, but otherwise, it performs no useful function.

FIGURE 15.47.

The Network Client Administrator.

FIGURE 15.48.

The View Remoteboot Client Information dialog box.

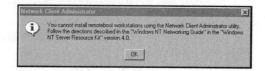

Creating a Network Installation Startup Disk

The easiest way to install software on a client machine is to create a *startup disk*—a bootable MS-DOS system disk configured for a specific computer configuration. By specifying the computer configuration beforehand, you can use a network sharepoint to contain the client software installation files.

To create a network installation startup disk, follow these steps:

1. Start the Network Client Administrator. Select the Make Network Installation Startup Disk radio button, and then click Continue to open the dialog box shown in Figure 15.49.

FIGURE 15.49.

The Share Network Client Installation Files dialog box.

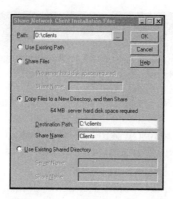

2. If your network has limited disk space, you can use the CD-ROM as the source media by selecting either Use Existing Path or Share Files. If you use the Existing Path option, the CD-ROM containing the installation files must already have been shared, or your users can't access the required files. If you have enough disk storage (at least 49M free), I recommend that you use the "Copy Files to New Directory, and then Share" option. Doing so copies the required files to a directory you specify and then shares that directory. If you have already copied the required files and shared the

15

NT SERVER

directory, you can use the Use Existing Shared Directory option. Once you've made your selection, copied the source files (if required), and clicked OK, the dialog box shown in Figure 15.50 appears.

FIGURE 15.50.

The Target Worksta-tion Configuration dialog box.

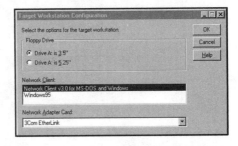

3. In this dialog box, select the floppy drive type, network client software, and network adapter to be used on the client workstation. Once you've made your selections, click OK.

NOTE

If you have multiple configurations (different floppy drives, client software, or network adapters), you need to create a disk set for each of these configurations.

NOTE

The adapter configuration is based on the manufacturer's defaults. If your configuration is different, be sure to modify the PROTOCOL.INI file in the \NET subdirectory to match the target workstation's configuration.

4. If you decide to install Windows for Workgroups, a message box informs you that you must have a legal license to use the supplied software. After you click OK, the dialog box shown in Figure 15.51 appears.

5. Enter the computer name, user name, domain name, and transport protocol to be used. If you select the TCP/IP protocol, you have the option of either assigning a static IP address or using DHCP to assign the IP address. You can also specify the default gateway IP address. When you're done, click OK.

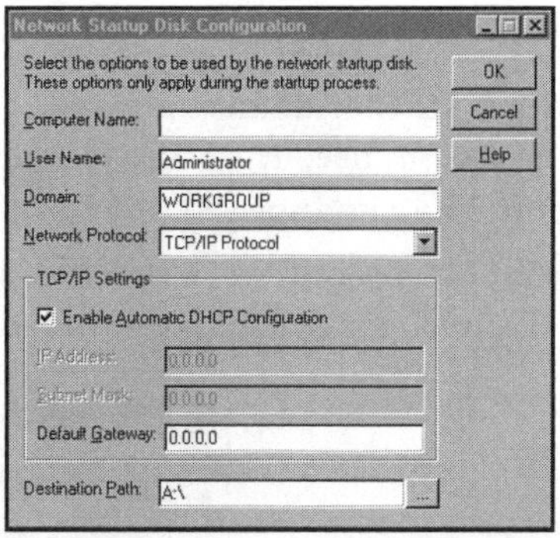

FIGURE 15.51.

Configuring the default client installation.

NOTE

If this installation startup disk is to be used for multiple installations, be sure to change the computer name on the client workstation after installation. Otherwise, a duplicate computer name message will be displayed the next time the installation disk set is used, thus preventing a successful installation.

---

6. You're then prompted for a formatted, bootable floppy disk of the selected type and asked to confirm your selections. Once you've accepted the configuration, the copy process is initiated, and your installation disk is created.

7. If you want to create another installation startup disk, repeat Steps 1 through 6. Otherwise, click Exit in the Network Client Adminstrator to terminate the application.

TIP

I recommend that you use DHCP to assign IP addresses if the installation startup disk is to be used for multiple installations. Otherwise, you'll need to change the IP address of the client workstation after installation to prevent duplicate IP addresses.

Creating an Installation Disk Set

Installation disk sets are used to create network client installation disks for MS-DOS and Windows, RAS for MS-DOS, TCP/IP-32 for Windows for Workgroups, LAN Manager for MS-DOS, and LAN Manager for OS/2. These generic installation disks , unlike a startup disk, can be reused without modification.

To create a network installation disk set, follow these steps:

1. Start the Network Client Administrator, select the Make Installation Disk Set radio button, and click Continue. The Share Network Client Installation Files dialog box, shown in Figure 15.49, is displayed.

2. Select your source media options, as specified earlier. Once you've made your selections and clicked OK, the dialog box shown in Figure 15.52 appears.

FIGURE 15.52.

The Make Installation Disk Set dialog box.

3. Select the network client or service and the destination floppy drive type. If you aren't using new floppy disks, enable the Format Disks checkbox. Once you've made your selections, click OK.

4. As prompted, label each floppy disk before inserting it into the requested drive.

5. If you want to create another installation disk set, repeat Steps 1 through 4. Otherwise, click Exit in the Network Client Adminstrator to terminate the application.

Copying the Client-Based Network Administration Tools

The client-based network administration tools include versions of User Manager for Domains, Server Manager for Domains, DHCP Manager, WINS Manager, Remoteboot Manager, Remote Access Administration, and User Profile Editor for Windows NT and Windows 3.1.

To copy the client-based administration tools, follow these steps:

1. Start the Network Client Administrator, select the Copy Client-based Network Administration Tools radio button, and click Continue. The Share Network Client Installation Files dialog box is displayed.

2. Select your source media options, as specified earlier. Once you've made your selections and clicked Continue, your users can connect to the specified share and run the appropriate setup program to install the administration tools. Windows users execute the SETUP.EXE program in the \SHARENAME\WINDOWS directory, and Windows NT clients use the SETUP.BAT program in the \SHARENAME\WINNT directory.

> **NOTE**
>
> Unfortunately, the Windows NT setup doesn't create a group or install any icons. Your users must do this for themselves.

Managing Your Remote Boot Clients

The remote boot service lets your client workstations boot MS-DOS and Windows 95 directly from the server. Instead of booting from a floppy or hard disk, a diskless workstation uses a Remote Program Load (RPL) ROM located on the network card. You can think of the RPL ROM as a replacement for your computer's disk controller ROM. Instead of initializing your disk controller ROM and reading the boot block from your hard disk, the RPL ROM is initialized and reads your boot block from a network server's hard disk.

Once the boot block has been executed by the client workstation, it loads either a common, or shared, configuration profile or a user-specific configuration profile. This configuration profile specifies the MS-DOS version to load and the CONFIG.SYS and AUTOEXEC.BAT to execute.

Installing the Remoteboot Service

You install the Remoteboot Service through the Control Panel's Network applet. Follow these steps:

1. Start Control Panel and launch the Network applet. Click on the Services tab.
2. Click Add and select Remoteboot Service, then click OK.
3. Once the Remoteboot Manager icon has been installed, click OK. Restart the computer as prompted.

Using the Remoteboot Manager

The Remoteboot Manager is used to create shared or personal profiles and workstation entries. A shared profile can be used by multiple workstations, and a change to a shared profile affects all users of that profile. A personal profile, on the other hand, is user-specific and can be customized without affecting other profiles.

The first time you run Remoteboot, you're informed that a profile must be created before you can create or edit workstation entries. A profile has a unique name, an operating system (which can be shared by multiple profiles), and a network adapter.

15

NT SERVER

To create a profile, follow these steps:

1. Choose Remoteboot|New Profile.

2. Enter a unique profile name—for example, MSDOS621—with no embedded spaces or backslashes and a maximum length of 16 characters. Also enter a description, such as MS-DOS 6.21 - Etherlink III, and select a configuration, such as DOS 6.22 Etherlink III. Configurations depend on the operating system software you have installed on the server.

> **NOTE**
>
> After you've installed new operating system software on the server, choose Configure|Fix Security to assign the correct file permissions. Then choose Configure|Check Configurations to update the available configurations for use by the Remoteboot Manager.
>
> Also note that until you install at least one MS-DOS operating system and execute the procedure just mentioned, you can't create a profile because no configurations are listed in the Configuration drop-down list box.

> **NOTE**
>
> Any version of MS-DOS 6.2x is displayed as MS-DOS 6.22 and must be installed in the \INSTALLROOT\RPL\RPLFILES\CONFIGS\DOS622 directory.

3. Click OK to create the profile.

4. If you have multiple profiles to create, repeat Steps 1 through 3.

Workstation entries, or records, require an active network adapter with the installed RPL ROM because each workstation entry uses the unique adapter identification number assigned by the manufacturer.

To create a workstation entry, follow these steps:

1. Choose Remoteboot|New Workstation.

2. If you know the 12-digit hexadecimal adapter identification number of the workstation's network adapter, enter it in the Adapter ID field. If you don't know the adapter identification number, restart the workstation (to create a remote boot record), choose View|Refresh (to update the display with the new workstation record), select the new record, and choose Remoteboot|Convert Adapter.

3. Enter the workstation's name, a description of the workstation, a password for the workstation computer account, a configuration type (either shared or personal), and a profile for the workstation to use. If TCP/IP is used as a network transport, select the appropriate TCP/IP settings.

4. Repeat Steps 1 and 2 for each workstation you configure.

Summary

In this chapter, you've looked at managing NT server domains and how they work with users and groups. NT domains are a powerful aspect of the Windows NT operating system and should be properly set up whenever you're using an NT server for a workgroup. You also covered fault tolerance and how to set up disk striping for your system. Implementing simple RAID techniques on your NT system is an excellent method for protecting your data.

Setting Up Trust Relationships in NT Server

CHAPTER 16

IN THIS CHAPTER

Most small-to-medium-size organizations will find that including all their servers in a single NT Server domain is the best way to set up their networks. A single-domain network is easier to design and administer than a multidomain network. When your network starts to include wide area links, more than 300 users, more than 15 file servers, or independent divisions that don't want central MIS to control their systems, however, you need to look seriously at dividing your network into multiple domains.

Dividing your network into multiple domains offers several advantages. First, you eliminate a performance bottleneck at the primary domain controller. In a very large network, the domain controller can end up spending so much time distributing user database updates that it can't simultaneously provide regular file services with a reasonable response time. The network traffic created as the domain controller updates each file server on a network also can cause performance bottlenecks, especially on slow wide area network (WAN) links.

Administratively, multiple domains let you group servers logically so that users browsing for data don't see lists of hundreds of servers. Multiple domains also let you easily assign the task of managing groups of users to different administrators.

Assigning Trust Relationships

Without trust relationships, dividing your network into multiple domains would limit a user's access to only the resources in his domain. If he weren't defined as a user in any of the other domains, he couldn't access data there without logging off his current domain and logging onto the new domain with another account. Trust relationships allow users in one domain to access data in another domain without creating two accounts—one in each domain. (See Figure 16.1.) Trust relationships allow the Human Resources department to manage its own network without allowing the MIS group any access, but it still gives everyone access to the corporate resources, such as e-mail.

FIGURE 16.1.

The Accounting domain trusts the Admin domain.

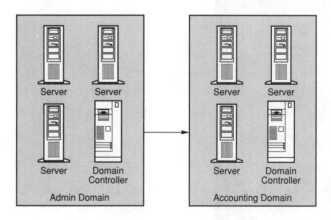

Establishing a trust relationship between two domains allows the users and global groups in the trusted domain to be recognized by the trusting domain; permissions to data and printer resources, therefore, are granted in the trusting domain. If you want the network administrators from the MIS group (who have their own domain) to be able to manage your Accounting domain, you can access User Manager for Domains to add the Domain Admins global group from MIS (domainadmins/mis) to your Domain Admins group, as shown in Figure 16.2.

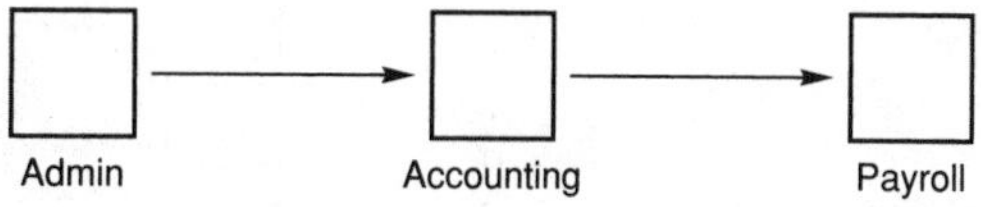

FIGURE 16.2.
The Accounting domain trusts the Admin domain, but the Payroll domain doesn't.

Admin → Accounting → Payroll

Trust relationships don't carry forward and aren't transferable. If the Human Resources domain trusts the MIS domain, and the MIS domain trusts the Audits domain, that doesn't mean that the Human Resources domain trusts the Audits domain. Each trust relationship must be explicitly defined. If you want the trust to work both ways, you have to establish a pair of trust relationships—one in each direction.

Organizing Your NT Servers

Microsoft suggests four methods for organizing NT Servers:

- Single-domain model
- Master-domain model
- Multiple-master model
- Complete-trust model

You should treat these models as just that—models from which you can borrow ideas to devise the most efficient configuration for your organization.

The single-domain model probably is best for you if these factors apply:

- You have a small network.
- You have fewer than 15 servers.
- You have the political power in your organization to be able to manage all the servers from a centralized MIS group.
- Your network doesn't have wide area or other low-speed links.

By sticking to a single domain, you can simplify matters dramatically.

The Single-Domain Model

In a single-domain network, any administrator can manage any of the servers in the domain. (See Figure 16.3.) Your only concern is creating one set of users and groups. You don't have to worry about which domains trust each other, and you don't have to create trust relationships.

FIGURE 16.3.

*A single-domain
network.*

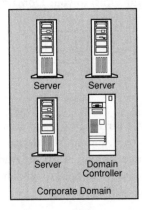

As your network grows, keeping everything in a single domain can start to cause problems such as these:

■ **Convenience problems:** Using and administering the network become more difficult as your network grows. The primary convenience problem is that, as the domain grows, the lists in the network become uncomfortably large. Users browsing for data have to scroll through long lists of servers and resources, and administrators have to scroll through huge user lists and group lists. Dividing the network into multiple domains makes these lists easier to manage.

■ **Performance problems:** As your network grows, simple domain-access tasks can create so much data traffic that the network becomes clogged. Performance problems rear their ugly heads often. Every time you create a new user or make some other change to the domain's user database, those changes must be replicated to all other servers in the domain. So, the domain controller can become the network's bottleneck if it can't transport that data to a large number of file servers fast enough. Performance problems can also occur as users browse the domain and the servers send their information to the user's workstation.

■ **Security or political problems:** Security problems are caused not by any technical factor in your network, but by the human factor in your organization. As your network grows, quasi-independent departments or divisions might want to join your network but not want you, the MIS group, to manage their servers or to have access to their data. Someone in the executive suite might decide that it's not a great idea for you to have access to all the data on all the servers on your company's network. I've found that most senior executives and human resources departments want their own domain under their own management to secure their sensitive data.

The advantages and disadvantages of the single-domain model follow:

Advantage	Disadvantage
Simple to administer.	No groupings of users into departments.
	No groupings of resources.
	Domain controller can be a bottleneck.
	Browsing resources can be slow and create large amounts of traffic.

The Master-Domain Model

If you're dividing your network into domains for convenience or to reduce the traffic on your backbone or a wide area link, you might want to set up your system with one master domain that all the other domains trust. (See Figure 16.4.)

In the NT Server documentation, Microsoft describes the master-domain model, in which all users and groups are created only in the master domain. Trusting, or *slave*, domains don't have any users defined. This model gives you centralized control and allows you to easily administrate the single-domain model, while shortening the browse lists and making the system easier to manage. If you have a central MIS department, it can run the master domain.

FIGURE 16.4.

A master-domain network.

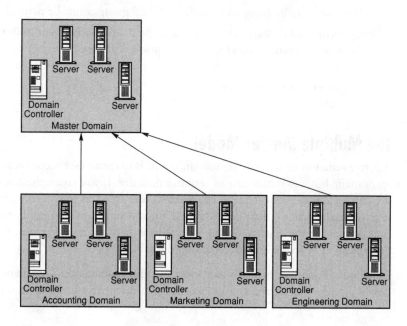

The servers in the slave domains refer all logon requests to the master domain, where all the users and groups are defined. If you have many users, this model still gives you long user lists and might create a bottleneck at the domain controller.

Organizations that follow the master-domain model typically create a master domain that's used only to contain the user accounts and subdomains that contain the actual resources to be shared. In fact, because only servers in the master domain contain the user database, if you don't put a second NT Server in the master domain, the domain controller becomes a single point of failure; if it goes down, no users can log onto the network.

The big advantage of the master-domain model is that the user divisions can decide for themselves who has access to their resources. Although the central MIS department creates all the user accounts, it doesn't actually need to have administrator-level access to the resource domains. Therefore, the administrators in the resource domains can keep the master domain administrators away from their data.

If you have a WAN, all user logon requests from sites other than the one that has the master domain have to travel across the wide area link. You can reduce the traffic slightly by distributing servers in the master domain throughout your network. The advantages and disadvantages of the master-domain model follow:

Advantage	Disadvantage
Central administration.	Poor performance on WANs or with large numbers of users or groups.
Resources can be grouped logically.	Local groups must be defined on each domain.
Departmental domains can have their own administrators for security.	The master domain controller can be a single point of failure.
Global groups must be defined only once.	

The Multiple-Master Model

A better variation on the master-domain model is to create user accounts not only in the master domain, but also in the slave or resource domains. If you create the resource domains on a departmental basis, you can create the user accounts for users who need access only to resources in their department on their departmental domain and users who need access to data in multiple domains in the master domain. This reduces network traffic because most logon requests don't need to be forwarded to the master domain.

As the number of users on your network grows, the single-master-domain model starts to break down. The domain database grows so large that resynchronizing file servers or adding a new server to the master domain takes a long time, and managing a list of 1,000 or more users can be quite difficult.

In the multiple-master model, instead of declaring a single domain as the sole repository of user and global group accounts, you declare as masters a small number of domains, each with a domain controller and preferably at least one other server to act as a backup. (See Figure 16.5.) All the user accounts are created in one of the master domains, which the central MIS department can manage.

As with the single-domain model, the multiple-master model places shared resources, such as directories and printers, in a series of subdomains, which can be organized departmentally or geographically. The resource, or slave, domains can be managed by the central MIS department or by local administrators.

FIGURE 16.5.

A multiple-master network.

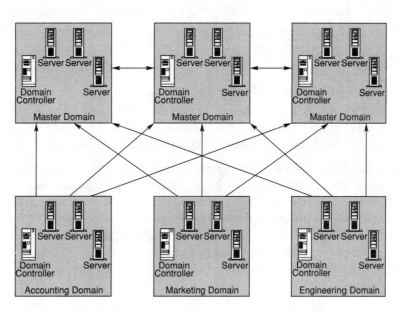

Each master domain trusts and is trusted by each of the other master domains. The resource domains trust all the master domains. Therefore, any user, regardless of the master domain of his or her account, can be granted permission to access resources in any of the resource's domains.

If you set up your network based on the multiple-master model without properly planning the distribution of users among the master domains, you might have some difficulty setting up global groups. Suppose that you want to group Excel users or the marketing staff by putting all users with accounts starting with the letters A–G in one master domain, those starting with H–Q in a second domain, and those beginning with R–Z in a third domain. To create a global group that contains users from multiple-master domains, you have to create a global group in each master domain for those users and then create a local group in the resource domains to contain all those global domains.

To simplify these groups, which is your best bet when running a multiple-master network, you should spend some time planning how to divide your users among the multiple masters. The best approach is usually to match the master domains to your company's organization, creating a master domain for each division or subsidiary and slave domains for each department in the division. The advantages and disadvantages of the multiple-master model follow:

Advantage	*Disadvantage*
Supports large numbers of users with acceptable performance.	Groups might need to be defined many times for different domains.
Resources can be logically grouped.	Many trust relationships to manage.
Resource domains can be managed independently for security.	Maintaining user accounts is more difficult, because they are in multiple domains.

The Complete-Trust Model

In the complete-trust model, all the domains on the network trust and are trusted by all the other domains. (See Figure 16.6.) Microsoft proposes this model for organizations that don't have a central MIS department to manage one or more master domains.

A fully implemented complete-trust network requires that you set up a large number of trust relationships, which can make it unsuitable for large organizations with more than a few domains. In fact, the complete-trust model requires that you create an $n(n-1)$ trust relationship, where n is the number of domains on your network. A network with five domains requires 20 trust relationships. By the time you're up to 15 domains, you need to establish 210 trust relationships. Just adding the sixteenth domain means adding 30 trust relationships to the other 15 domains on the network. The advantages and disadvantages of the complete-trust model follow:

Advantage	*Disadvantage*
Doesn't require central administration.	Lack of central administration can lead to chaos.
Can support a large number of users.	Requires creating very large numbers of trust relationships.
Resources are grouped logically into domains.	
Users are grouped logically into domains.	
Each department can manage its own resources.	

Setting Up Trust Relationships in NT Server

CHAPTER 16

531

16

SETTING UP TRUST
RELATIONSHIPS IN
NT SERVER

FIGURE 16.6.
*A complete-trust
network.*

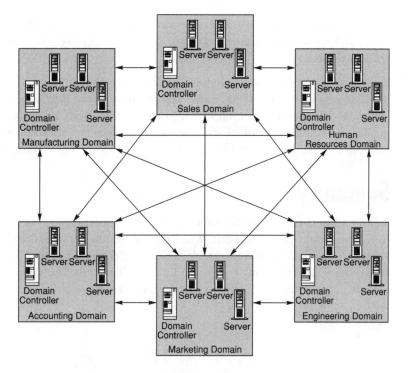

Choosing an Organizational Model

In my experience, real-world large networks aren't best designed by making them fit one of Microsoft's textbook models. True small networks are best set up as a single domain. Midsize networks might best be served by using a single master-domain model, but when the system grows beyond that manageable size, you're going to have to do some careful planning. I've found that, most of the time, a hierarchical structure best fits the organizational structure of the company and, therefore, is the most logical arrangement. You'll have to determine the best arrangement for your company, though.

Remember that when you trust another domain and grant rights and permissions to global groups in that domain, you're really trusting the administrator of that domain, because that person controls which users are members of that group and, therefore, which users have access to your resources. If you're implementing a multiple-domain network so that divisions or departments are in control of their own data, the administrators in the domains that contain your most sensitive data probably shouldn't use global groups from other domains.

If your network has any wide area links, you'll definitely want to use multiple domains. If you have multiple servers in your New York and Chicago offices, for example, the domain controller in New York sends each update to the domain database across the wide area link many times—once for each server on the Chicago side of the link. Because adding a user to a domain can send 1K to 2K to each server, a busy network administrator can really clog up a 9600bps or even a 56Kbps link, preventing real data such as e-mail messages and database requests from crossing the link.

You can reduce this network overhead by creating a domain in each office and having the domains trust each other. If you create user accounts for the users in each office on each domain, the only authorization traffic that passes across the wide area link consists of access requests (when a user in one office wants to access data from the other) and logon requests (when Joe from New York tries to log on from Chicago during his monthly trip to the Windy City).

Summary

In this chapter, you've looked at the use of trust relationships to set up cross-machine and interdepartment communications. When properly set up, trust relationships simplify a lot of network administration tasks and make a user's life easier. When poorly set up, though, trust relationships can open your systems up to abuse. Trust relationships are worth the trouble, though, as the advantages far outweigh the inconvenience of having to set them up properly.

CHAPTER 17

Internetworking: Remote Access Service and TCP/IP

There are basically two ways for users at remote sites to access data on your network. *Remote-control applications*, such as Carbon Copy and PC Anywhere, actually run the remote user's applications on a computer at your site. They send any data that the user's application sends to the screen across the phone line to the remote user's computer and send any keystrokes from the remote user's computer to the application. *Remote node systems* run the application on the remote user's computer and treat the phone line as an extension of the local area network, sending LAN-style traffic—including requests for file and print services—across the phone line. Each approach has its advantages and disadvantages, depending on the type of application you're trying to run across the phone line.

The main problem to be solved with any remote access system is that telephone lines, even with the fastest modems, have a very limited capacity to carry data. The 9600bps modem you thought was incredibly fast when you called CompuServe to download the latest games is more than 1,000 times slower than the Ethernet connecting your PC to your file server.

The solution is to keep the amount of data traveling across that link as small as possible. Back when everyone ran text-based DOS applications, remote-control packages performed much better than remote node systems because a DOS application just can't send that much data to the screen. After all, a full text-mode DOS screen is just 2K, but a graphics screen on a base VGA (640×480 in 16 colors) is well over 100K. If you use a high-resolution or high-color mode, a screen can contain well over a megabyte.

When you start running a graphical user interface, everything changes. Updating an 800×600 screen can send 250K of data across the line. If you use a remote node system, such as Windows NT's Remote Access Service (RAS), only the remote user's file access needs to go across the line.

Remote Access Service (RAS) Features

RAS is a remote node system that allows Windows workstations to access NT Servers across standard telephone lines or other asynchronous connections, X.25 packet switched networks, or ISDN lines. As soon as he's connected, a remote user can use resources on any Windows NT machine or NT Server that's connected to the RAS server he's dialed into, as long as they all use the same protocol to provide NetBIOS services.

A single RAS server running NT Server can support up to 256 remote users. Windows NT stations can act as RAS servers for a single dial-in line, so Windows NT users can dial in from home to their own workstations and access the rest of their network.

To maximize performance on limited-speed lines, RAS takes advantage of modem data-compression features or compresses data in software when you use modems that don't do their own compression.

Because RAS treats the phone line as an extension of the LAN, it fully supports NT's security model, complete with trust relationships and centralized domain administration. You can further improve security by using callback security, in which a user calls into the server, which identifies the user, disconnects the call, and calls the user back at the phone number the system administrator has stored as that user's valid location. RAS also supports extra security devices that can use cards, random-number generators, or other sophisticated techniques to validate users' identities.

Choosing Hardware for RAS

If you're like most PC system administrators, you've never given your system's communications ports much thought. You either ordered your systems with internal modems, which have their own COM ports built in, or worried more about the cables and connectors on your system's COM ports than how they worked. After all, you know that COM1 uses IRQ4 and that COM2 uses IRQ3, so all you have to do is plug in the modem.

If all you want to do is run Crosstalk under DOS to download Duke Nuke 'em from your local bulletin board, then that's all you really need to know about COM ports. However, if you want to use the latest modems at speeds above 9600bps, or if you want to do something else while your computer downloads Quake, you need to pay a little more attention.

Standard AT COM ports use 16450 UART (universal asynchronous receiver transmitter) chips to convert the parallel data on the PC's bus to serial data for the COM port. This particular chip has only a one-byte data buffer, so the COM port generates an interrupt every time a byte comes in. If the processor on your PC doesn't service that interrupt before a second byte comes in through the port, that first byte is lost. Supporting a single 9600bps modem for a file upload generates almost a thousand interrupts a second. A second full duplex communication, with data going both ways on the line simultaneously, requires the processor to deal with almost 2,000 single-byte data transfers every second.

Even a fast PC system loses characters if you try to run a modem faster than 9600bps through a standard serial port. Because even a single lost byte in a RAS session forces a retransmission of the whole data packet, losing every 200th byte would result in a net data transmission rate of 0bps.

Most good 486 and Pentium systems and most high-quality internal modems use the more advanced 16550 UART, which has a built-in 16-byte data buffer. Therefore, the processor can send data to the UART in blocks of 10 or more characters without having to pay attention to the port nearly as often. Similarly, when receiving data, the processor can empty the buffer 100—rather than 1,000—times a second. If you're investing good money in high-speed modems, you should make sure all your remote systems are equipped with 16550 UARTs.

Using a 16550 UART can relieve the interrupt overhead of one or two serial ports, but even systems running 16550s start to lose data when they run multiple high-speed data streams. The other problem with standard, or nonintelligent, serial ports is that the overhead of actually touching every byte as it comes into or goes out of the system can noticeably slow down other processes on the system because they get starved for processor time.

Conventional serial ports, even with 16550s, also limit the number of serial ports your system can support because each port needs its own interrupt request line and, if you're using internal modems, its own slot.

If you want, or need, to support more than one dial-in line on your server, you should consider using an intelligent serial I/O card, such as a Digitboard or an IBM Artic card. Rather than connecting the UART to the computer's bus and generating an interrupt for each byte received, these cards have from 2 to 256 serial ports connected to a dedicated processor, typically a Z-80 or an 80188 with 64K or more memory, to buffer the incoming and outgoing data.

By using an intelligent serial card and external modems, a single RAS server can support eight or more simultaneous connections without losing data or significantly slowing down the other processes on the server. The RAS server can send data to and receive data from the intelligent serial card in 100-byte or larger blocks, just like a LAN card, which greatly reduces the overhead on the server.

A Few Words on Modems

If you're like most PC experts (and you wouldn't be reading this book or be interested in Windows NT if you weren't already knowledgeable about PCs, would you?), you probably buy modems more out of habit and prejudice than because of any technical knowledge. Most PC managers buy the fastest modems they can afford from whichever vendor they've always bought them from. The biggest decision they're likely to make is whether to buy internal or external modems.

The internal modem supporters argue that internal modems are simpler to use and that the user is less likely to screw them up because the modems don't take up valuable desk space. External modem fans argue that troubleshooting is easier than it is with internal modems. I tend to agree with the internal camp for remote sites and for modem installations in users' PCs and with the external camp for servers and other central site applications.

You do have to watch the design and quality of your internal modems. Many use nonstandard UARTs, which can cause compatibility problems with NT or even MS-DOS. For instance, this book's technical editor has a client with an off-brand internal modem that won't work with Remote Control (from Microcom). Yet the same software on an external modem works flawlessly. You also have to be careful about installation on internal modems. You wouldn't believe how many times I've had to fix problems with machines that had two installed COM ports plus an internal modem. COM3 and COM4 aren't well-defined in the PC architecture, and even when you can set a modem to these addresses, they share interrupts with COM1 and COM2, which often causes more problems. If you need more than two serial devices in your system, you should consider either a bus mouse or a better serial port card, such as a Digitboard 2 port card.

I prefer modular or rack-mount modems for central sites. Rather than making you stack 10 or 20 regular modems on a table and find a way to plug in 10 or 20 annoying little plug transformers, rack-mount modems give you a rack, typically 17 inches wide and 6 8 inches high, which has a power supply and bus where you plug in up to 20 modem cards that have a serial port and lights like an external modem.

I developed this preference after working on a large bulletin board, where I discovered that Hayes used the aluminum case of their external modems as a heat sink. If you stacked more than two, the modems in the middle would fail because of the heat that developed in the stack. When I switched to rack modems, the internal fans kept everything working smoothly.

Actually, how well the modems work is more important than whether they're internal or external. Whether a modem is the right choice for your application depends on how fast it is, whether it understands the commands RAS sends it, and whether it sends back the status information in a way that RAS understands.

One of my first jobs as a writer was to evaluate high-speed modems for *PC magazine* in 1987. Back then, most modems that sent data faster than 2400bps used proprietary technologies and could communicate only with another identical modem. In addition, there were big differences in how well the modems handled noisy phone lines. If you chose the wrong 9600bps modem for your application, it might not have performed as well as even a 2400bps modem would.

Luckily, the International Trade Union (ITU), formerly the Consultative Committee on International Telephony and Telegraphy (CCITT), has established standards for how modems take the digital data from your serial port and convert it into beeps and squawks that plain old telephone lines can handle. Any two modems that are compliant with, for example, the V.32bis standard can communicate with each other at 14,400bps. The following table shows the modem standards commonly used with PCs and their transmission rates.

Modem Type	Maximum Speed Before Compression
V.22bis	2400
V.32	9600
V.32bis	14,400
V.32terbo	19,200
V.FAST class	28,800
V.34	28,800

17

REMOTE ACCESS
SERVICE AND
TCP/IP

Recently, AT&T proposed a new 19,200bps standard, which they called V.32terbo (a pun on V.32ter, which would be the next version of V.32 after V.32bis), and Rockwell, the leading manufacturer of modem chips, proposed a system, V.FAST, that would double V.32bis's 14.4Kbps speed. The ITU decided to reject V.32terbo because it wasn't a big enough advance to make a new standard worth it. They decided instead to make a few changes to V.FAST to turn it into V.34. As of this writing, you can buy V.34 modems for about $100.

Because I've been burned in the past by both new modem technologies and vendor-promised simple upgrades that turned out to require sending the equipment back to the factory for a month or buying a $200 ROM chip, I remain leery of V.32terbo and V.FAST class modems. If you can live with 14.4Kbps for now, I recommend buying V.32bis modems and waiting until the dust settles on V.34. Six months to a year from now, V.34 modem prices will have come down, so you can afford to buy V.34 modems and throw out the V.32bis modems you buy today without spending more than you'd spend for V.FAST class modems today. If you feel the need for speed now, skip V.32terbo and go all the way to V.FAST class.

Besides just sending data across a phone line, most modems also perform error checking/ correction and data compression. The ITU V.42 specification covers error checking and correction, and V.42bis defines a lossless data-compression algorithm that can compress some data up to 4:1. How much compression you'll actually see in the real world depends on the type of data you're trying to transmit. Bitmapped graphics files can be compressed the most—about 4:1—and text files, including most word processing files, can usually be compressed at about 2:1. Some data, such as .ARC or .ZIP files that have already been compressed, can't be compressed at all. Sometimes you see a modem vendor claiming to send data across a phone line at speeds of 50 to 100Kbps. Those claims apply only if you're trying to send 5,000 lowercase *M*s across the line. Typically, RAS users won't see more than a 2:1 compression ratio.

> **NOTE**
>
> In a 9600bps modem, the 9600bps refers to the speed at which data actually passes across the phone line. A modem with data compression, such as V.42bis, takes data in from your computer faster than its rated speed because it compresses the data after it gets it from your system. You should set your communications software, including RAS, to the highest speed at which your modem can accept data to get the best performance.

Regardless of the modem technology you choose, make sure you deal with a reputable vendor like Hayes, US Robotics, Multitech, or Intel. Off-brand modems generally aren't more than 10 to 15 percent cheaper than modems from the top vendors, and they can cause quite a bit more trouble. As usual, buying a product that's on CompuServe's current supported hardware list—which, by the way, had more than 100 modems listed the last time I looked—will make it easier to get technical support from Microsoft.

The MODEM.INF File

Although the ITU clearly defines how modems should communicate with one another across the phone lines, there's no standards-making body to define the commands computers should use to tell a modem to dial or answer the phone line or to control modem features like error correction or data compression. Almost all the modems sold to the PC market claim to be Hayes-compatible. Exactly what that claim means differs from vendor to vendor and even between different models of modems from Hayes itself. Just about any modem will dial when you send it an ATDT command, but at least half a dozen different sets of commands, used by different vendors, control the more advanced features.

If you're brave, if you think you know everything there is to know about modems, if you need to stick to the leading edge of technology, or if you're just an idiot, you'll decide to use a modem that's not on Microsoft's supported list. If you've chosen to do that, you'll have to tell Windows NT how to communicate with your modem by modifying the MODEM.INF file.

The MODEM.INF file has an entry for each model of modem that's supported by RAS. Each entry contains the modem's maximum data rate, the maximum port speed to use connected to the modem, and the character strings to send to the modem to make it dial, enable and disable data compression, and perform other tasks RAS might want it to do.

If you're lucky, your modem vendor can give you a MODEM.INF file, or at least the information you'll need to create one yourself. If not, see Appendix E of the Remote Access Service manual for more information.

When you get the latest model from Whizzo Datacomm, your regular modem supplier, you might try to take a shortcut and just tell RAS to use the same information for the new modem that it did for last year's Whizzo. To do this, just create an alias entry in MODEM.INF for the new Whizzo:

```
 [Whizzo228]
ALIAS=Whizzo9600
```

If you create an alias that points to a modem definition that's an alias, too, your system won't work. If, for example, you defined a Whizzo 3000 to use the Whizzo228 definition, it wouldn't work.

Beyond Modems: ISDN and X.25

Modems are a great way to let a few users dial in to your system at relatively low speeds. However, if you need to support many users, or if you need to give your users a faster connection to your RAS server, you should look past modems and plain old telephone lines at X.25 or ISDN alternatives.

ISDN (integrated services digital network) has been billed by the telephone industry as the future of telecommunications. Like plain old telephone lines, ISDN provides a circuit-switched service so that users with ISDN lines in their field offices or homes can dial into your RAS server just as they do with a modem. As with plain old telephone service (POTS), you pay the phone company a monthly charge plus a per-minute charge for the calls you make.

The big difference between ISDN and POTS lines is that ISDN lines are digital and can carry substantially more data. A primary-rate interface ISDN line supplies two 64Kbps data channels and a 16Kbps control channel for call setup and other communications with the phone company. When a user dials into your RAS server using ISDN, he or she can use one or both of the B data channels to get a 64Kbps or 128Kbps connection. That's at least twice as fast as the fastest modems on the market. RAS supports ISDN modems but requires a new digital telephone line to be installed.

X.25 is an older, better-established technology than ISDN. Unlike ISDN, it doesn't supply faster connections to your RAS server for users. Instead, it gives you more flexible, and possibly less expensive, connections from your remote sites to your RAS server. If you've ever used CompuServe or a similar service, your data traveled from the local access node you dialed to CompuServe's data center in Columbus, Ohio, across an X.25 network.

Your field sales or service force can access your RAS server without paying the outrageous long-distance surcharges most hotels tack on by connecting your RAS server to a public X.25 network, such as Sprintnet or the CompuServe network. Your users can then call the local node and, by sending a few commands to the X.25 PAD (packet assembler/disassembler), connect to your RAS server across the X.25 network.

X.25 connections are especially important if you're planning to build an international network. Just about every country in the world has at least one domestic X.25 network that's cross-connected to one of the domestic U.S. public data networks. In most countries, the telephone company is part of the government PTT (post/telephone/telegraph). The PTTs usually charge high rates for long-distance and international calls, but the PTT rates for X.25 connections can be as low as one-tenth the cost of a long-distance call.

X.25 is a packet-switched service, like a local area network, so multiple users' RAS sessions can share one 56Kbps leased line connection from the Eicon X.25 card in your RAS server to your public data network's nearest node. They can connect to the public data network by calling the local node in their city with a standard 9600bps modem or with another 56Kbps leased line and an Eicon card.

Before you rush right out and set up an X.25 network, you should know that the X.25 protocol's packet-switching and error-correcting overhead can substantially slow down communications with RAS.

Installing RAS

Installing RAS is a bit more complicated than installing a new network protocol; here are the basic steps:

1. Install and configure serial port hardware and modems.
2. Load the driver for the intelligent serial port card, if any.
3. Restart the system to start the intelligent card driver.
4. Add the Remote Access Service through the Control Panel's Network applet.
5. Select and configure the transport protocols you want to support (NetBEUI, TCP/IP, or IPX/SPX) for your dial-up users.
6. Grant users permission to use RAS through the Remote Access Administrator utility.

If you're planning to use standard serial ports or an internal modem, as you would for a typical RAS client or a Windows NT machine serving a single client, you don't have to worry about installing an intelligent serial card. If you're setting up an ISDN, X.25, or multiline server, you need to install the driver for your card through the Control Panel's Network applet. Because Windows NT treats RAS as an alternative network protocol, you install intelligent serial cards, ISDN, and X.25 cards the same way you install an additional LAN card.

You install RAS itself with the Control Panel's Network applet by clicking the Add Software button. When you configure RAS, you have to specify a modem type for each port you want to support and decide whether each port will be used for dial-in, dial-out, or both. (See Figure 17.1.)

FIGURE 17.1.
The Configure Port Usage dialog box.

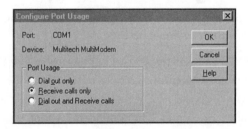

You can configure your transport protocols and select an encryption scheme with the Network applet, as shown in Figure 17.2. If you click the Configure button, you can limit users' access to just resources on the RAS server, or you can let them use the whole network. (See Figure 17.3.)

FIGURE 17.2.
*The Network
Configuration dialog
box.*

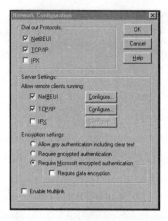

FIGURE 17.3.
*The RAS Server
NetBEUI configuration
dialog box.*

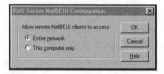

For best performance, enable modem error control, disable modem data compression, and just use RAS's software compression. Testing indicates that RAS's compression is somewhat better than V.42.

Configuring RAS

After you've installed RAS and restarted your computer, you'll notice that you have a new menu item for RAS with three programs in it:

- Remote Access: The program you use to call a RAS server
- Remote Access Monitor: Basically an external modem's lights, displayed as a window onscreen
- Remote Access Admin: The administrative tool

If the machine you're setting up will be a RAS server, start the Remote Access Admin application. Through this application's Server menu, you can start, stop, pause, and resume the Remote Access Service on any of the RAS servers on your network—assuming, of course, that you're a member of the server's Administrators group.

Your first step in administering your RAS server is to grant permission to use RAS to some, or all, of the users defined in your domain. When you choose Users | Permissions, you see the dialog box shown in Figure 17.4.

FIGURE 17.4.

Granting RAS user permissions.

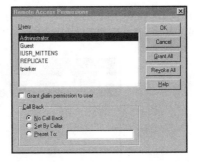

Here you can select the users who will have remote access to your network and grant them permission to use RAS. If you click the Grant All button, all the users in your domain will be allowed to use RAS. If you click the Revoke All button, the right to use RAS will be revoked for all your users, which could be a good idea if you're taking over a network that hasn't been managed well in the past. Start by revoking Remote Access permission from all your users, then give it back to those who need it.

RAS supports callbacks for security and convenience. When you enable the Call Back option, RAS will accept a call from a remote user, ask that user for his or her account and password, hang up the phone line, and call the user back.

If you want to limit your remote users to calling in from a single remote site—for example, their offices at home—to improve network security, select Preset To and enter the phone number RAS should call back for that user.

> **NOTE**
>
> Callback security is not absolute, especially if your RAS service is connected to your company's PBX (Private Branch Exchange—the telephone switch installed to handle all the company's calls). A skilled hacker can reprogram the PBX, or even the telephone company's central office switch, to redirect the callback number to another site.

If you want to support callback to prevent your field salespeople from running up big phone bills by having the server call back, and therefore pick up the cost of the call, you can select Set By Caller. When users with this type of callback call the system, RAS asks where they should be called back.

At first glance, the Set By Caller option seems to be a great way to avoid hotel long-distance surcharges, customer site phone bills, and other similar problems. Remember, however, that the user's modem must answer the phone automatically when the RAS server dials the number he enters. A hotel operator or other human intervention prevents you from using this callback option. An 800 number for your salespeople to call would probably work better.

To control how your users access your system and the network it's connected to, you should run the RAS administration program, shown in Figure 17.5.

FIGURE 17.5.

The Remote Access Admin program.

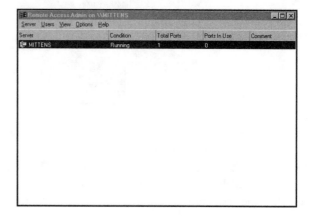

If you double-click on a server, or select a server and then choose Server | Communication Ports, you get a list of the ports and modems on this RAS server. You can use this screen to reconfigure the server's communications ports if you upgrade your modems. More important, you can double-click on a port and get the status screen, shown in Figure 17.6, to see how a session with a remote user is going.

FIGURE 17.6.

Checking a remote user's session in the Port Status screen.

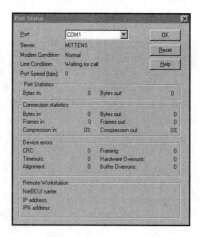

You can use the Active Users option in the Users menu to send messages to users and disconnect them from the RAS server.

Using RAS

When you want to call into a RAS server, open the Dial-Up Networking application. The first time you start Dial-Up Networking, you're prompted to create the first entry in your phone book. You will be asked what type of server you're connecting to, as shown in Figure 17.7, then asked for the phone number in the dialog box shown in Figure 17.8. Here you can enter the number of the RAS server and once again set the modem or other hardware settings. As soon as you've got entries in the phone book, choose Connect from the menu and log on. When you're done, log off and hang up.

FIGURE 17.7.
Choose the type of server from this window.

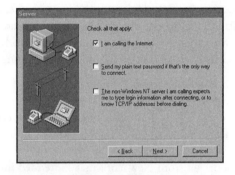

FIGURE 17.8.
Setting up a phone book entry.

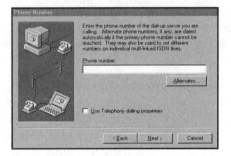

Connecting LANs

RAS is a good way to let users dial in to your network and access its resources from remote sites, such as homes or hotels. If you have sites—field offices, for example—that need continuous connections to your servers, or if you have more than one or two users who need simultaneous access, you'll be better off linking the LANs at these remote sites.

Bridges and Routers

To connect two networks, you'll need a bridge or a router at each site to connect the LANs to the wide area link. The bridge or router examines each data frame that comes across the LAN it's connected to and sends those frames intended for systems on the other side of the link across it.

Bridges and routers differ in how they determine which data should cross the link. A *bridge* works at the MAC sublayer of the OSI data link layer. It builds a table of all the node addresses it's seen as source addresses on each of its Ethernet ports and forwards those packets addressed to any port that hasn't been a source address on a frame so far.

Routers work at the network layer, examining the data packet's network address field and determining whether the packet is supposed to go to a different network. Routers, unlike bridges, rely on a particular network layer protocol. Routable protocols, such as IPX or TCP/IP's IP (internetwork protocol), divide the address of a node on the network into a network (think of it as the street name) and a node (think of it as the house number).

Rather than keeping track of which nodes have sent packets to determine which packets should be forwarded, all the routers on the network communicate with each other, exchanging information about which networks they communicate with. Routers are responsible not only for forwarding packets but also for determining the best route any given data packet should take.

If you have a small network, bridges might be the right choice for you. As your network grows, bridges become less efficient, however. The problem with bridges is that they forward broadcasts and other data packets that routers would be smart enough to know didn't really need to be forwarded. In addition, if you build a network that has multiple paths data can take—for example, your New York, Chicago, and St. Louis offices all connected in a triangle—your bridges will send a data packet from New York that's intended for one office to both of them, which ties up your valuable wide area bandwidth.

Because routers know how to get from New York to Chicago, they would send only the data actually intended for machines in the Chicago office. Routers, therefore, make more efficient use of the wide area network.

Routers do, however, have two disadvantages. First, any given router can route only protocols that it's programmed to handle. If you buy a TCP/IP router and later decide you also need to send IPX or AppleTalk traffic across that link, you might need to update or replace your routers. Some routers, called *bridging routers* or *brouters*, bridge any data packets that aren't in one of the protocols it knows how to route. The other problem with routers is that typically they're more expensive and more difficult to configure than simple bridges.

> **TIP**
>
> If you have more than two locations, or more than five separate networks, even if they're all in one location, routers are a better choice than bridges.

Now that you've decided to use routers to link your networks, you have to find a product to use. You can buy sophisticated routers from cisco, IBM, 3Com, or Wellfleet that can handle five or more local Ethernet or Token Ring connections and several high-speed WAN connections.

> **NOTE**
>
> If you're using DHCP or WINS, check with your router manufacturer for updates to support these services, if necessary. Not all routers support DHCP and WINS without software upgrades.

If your budget or your needs are more limited, you can build your routers from PC platforms you're familiar with. Novell's MPR (multiprotocol router), Newport's LAN2LAN MPR, and several other products turn a PC with one or more Ethernets and/or wide area interface cards into a full-fledged router. PC-based routers, as you might guess, are slower than cisco or Wellfleet's RISC-based routers, but they can usually keep up with a single WAN line at speeds up to T-1.

Phone Lines and Other Links

As you've learned, plain old telephone lines, even with the fastest modems, are much slower than the LANs you're used to. If you really want the users in your Chicago office to be able to get to the resources in New York without growing old and gray waiting for their applications to run, you'll have to set up a faster connection.

The traditional way to build a wide area network is to buy digital leased lines to connect your sites. Unlike dial-up or circuit-switched services, leased lines provide a continuous connection between two locations at a fixed cost per month. If you're going to be using the connection between your offices more than 60 hours a month, a leased line is generally cheaper than the equivalent dial-up service.

The basic building block of digital leased line services is a 64Kbps line called DS-0 (digital service-0). The telephone network was originally built to support voice communications. As AT&T started to change their system to use digital signals on the long-distance portion of a call to let them give better signal quality and send more voice calls across the same number of copper-wire pairs, they used a voice digitizing system that used 56Kbps of bandwidth to carry the voice signal and 8Kbps of call management overhead data. Therefore, here in the U.S. you can buy 56Kbps leased lines. In Europe, and in most of the world outside North America, the telephone companies give the user the full 64Kbps and use their own lines for the overhead.

Unless you've done a good job of designing your applications and you compress your data within an inch of its life, your users probably aren't going to be very happy with a 56Kbps connection. The next step up, which is usually available, is called T-1 or DS-1 in North America and E-1 in the rest of the world. At 1.544Mbps (or 2.048Mbps in Europe), a T-1 line supplies enough bandwidth for most applications, especially if you use bridges or routers with data compression.

Because T-1 lines can be quite expensive, up to several thousand dollars per month for a coast-to-coast line, customers started clamoring for something faster than a 56Kbps line that they

17

REMOTE ACCESS
SERVICE AND
TCP/IP

could afford. Some innovative long-distance carriers developed a series of services they called *fractional T-1*. Fractional T-1 lines provide from 122Kbps to 768Kbps in multiples of 56 or 64Kbps.

If you're building a huge network, or if you just have data-hungry applications like CAD/CAM or multimedia applications, you might find that even T-1 lines don't give your users the kind of response times you'd like. If you want to go even faster, you can buy T-3 (45Mbps) or fractional T-3 services.

The following table shows a summary of the common line options you can use to build your wide area network:

Line Type	North American Speed	European Speed
DS-0	56Kbps	64Kbps
Fractional T-1	112Kbps to 768Kbps	128Kbps
T-1/E-1	1.544Mbps	2.048Mbps
T-3 and fractional T-3	3 to 45Mbps	4 to 45Mbps

If 45Mbps isn't enough for you, this book isn't adequate to get you set up. I strongly recommend that you hire an expert to design your network.

Packet Switched Services

Because you're paying the telephone carriers to give you a 56Kbps or faster data link 24 hours a day, seven days a week, leased lines are a relatively expensive way to build your wide area network. Packet switched services allow you to share communications facilities with other users while sharing the cost.

In a *packet switched network*, also called a *public data network*, if users from several companies are allowed to send their data across the network, each of your field offices is connected through a leased line to the data network's closest node or point of presence. There the data is multiplexed (digitally combined) with the data from all the other network users at the network vendor's PAD (packet assembler/disassembler) or router and sent across the network to the point of presence where your other office is connected.

The first generation of packet switched networks used the CCITT X.25 protocol. X.25 networks were developed back when the long-distance locations were using analog technology and had relatively high data rates. To compensate, X.25 networks perform error checking as data crosses each router on the network. All this error checking can slow your data (or, in technical terms, increase latency), making X.25 networks unsuitable for most LAN-to-LAN traffic.

Frame Relay networks, now available in most parts of the U.S., assume that the lines making up the network have low error rates, so they perform error correction only at the data packet's final destination. Because modern fiber-optic lines have very low error rates, the slower end-to-end error checking done when errors occur is offset by how much faster it is when there are no errors. If you have more than three or four sites in your network, you should take a good hard look at Frame Relay.

Asynchronous Transfer Mode (ATM) is everyone's pick as the data communications medium of the 21st century. Like Frame Relay, it's a fast packet-switching system, but, unlike Frame Relay, it can be used for local area networks as well as wide area networks. ATM products are just now in the market and are still very expensive.

The following table shows the commonly available packet switched services and their relative merits.

Suitability for Network Type	*LAN-to-LAN*	*Speed*	*Cost*
X.25	Low	9600 to 56Kbps	Moderate
Frame Relay	High	9600 to 1.544Kbps	Moderate
ATM	High	T-1 to 155Mbps	High

Connecting Windows NT to Your WAN

You could just set up a default Windows NT or NT Server network at each of your offices and use bridges and leased lines to connect them, but this would be a big mistake. Although the NetBEUI protocol that NT uses by default to connect workstations to servers is very efficient on small networks, it's not really suitable for wide area networks. NetBEUI uses your computer's name as its address without any additional network address, which makes NetBEUI a nonroutable protocol.

NetBEUI uses broadcast messages to determine what computer names exist on the network. These broadcasts, combined with packets that get bridged in multiple directions, can quickly bog down your network.

TCP/IP

Luckily, Windows NT also includes support for the TCP/IP protocol suite. TCP/IP was first developed under a U.S. Department of Defense contract for use on the ARPAnet, which has grown into the Internet, and it's well-suited to wide area network use. As a result, these protocols are often called the *Internet protocol suite*.

TCP/IP's network layer protocol, IP, uses both network and node address fields, so it can be routed easily. In fact, almost all routers on the market support TCP/IP.

Unlike IPX or NetBEUI, the term *TCP/IP* doesn't refer to a single protocol, but to a set of protocols (also called a *protocol stack*) that performs the functions of all seven layers of the OSI model. In an effort to solve the problem of having at least one of every computer ever made and not being able to pass data between them, the DOD decided they would no longer buy computer systems that didn't support the TCP/IP protocol stack. No self-respecting computer manufacturer could let this opportunity pass, so TCP/IP became the common language of computing. The growth of TCP/IP was further accelerated by its inclusion in the 4.2bsd (Berkeley Software Distribution) version of UNIX.

The TCP/IP protocol stack is defined in a series of documents called RFCs (requests for comment) that are circulated on the Internet. The following are common TCP/IP protocols:

- IP: Internetwork protocol
- UDP: User datagram protocol
- TCP: Transmission control protocol
- SNMP: Simple network management protocol
- Telnet: A terminal emulation protocol
- FTP: File transfer protocol
- TFTP: Trivial file transfer protocol
- SMTP: Simple mail transfer protocol
- NFS: Network file system

The TCP/IP protocol suite isn't actually OSI-compliant, as you can see from Figure 17.9. The Internet protocol suite really defines three layers above the data link and physical layers. TCP/IP is commonly used on Ethernet, Token Ring, FDDI, and serial telephone line networks (called *SLIP* for serial line IP).

FIGURE 17.9.
The TCP/IP protocol stack.

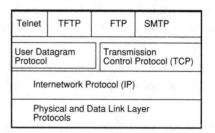

Internet Protocol

The Internet protocol (IP) operates as a network layer protocol responsible for routing, addressing, and packet delivery. Like most network layer protocols, IP doesn't handle assured delivery, packet division and sequencing, or error correction. These functions should be handled in higher layer protocols, such as TCP.

IP Addressing

Every computer or other device on a TCP/IP network, called a *host* in TCP/IP-speak because all computers were host computers when the protocols were designed, must have a unique 32-bit address. IP addresses are usually written with the value of each byte of the address in decimal, separated by periods from the other bytes in the address—for example, 234.34.222.123.

A 32-bit IP address includes both the address of the network the host is connected to and the unique address on that network for this host. If you plan to connect your network to the Internet, you have to get a network address assigned to you by the Defense Data Network-Network Information Center (DDN-NIC). If you're using a commercial Internet access provider, such as UUNET, Alternet, or PSI, they will take care of that for you.

To support both large and small networks, the Internet addressing scheme supports three different classes of networks. Class A network addresses have values from 1 to 126 for their first byte. The remaining three bytes are used for the host's address in the network. There are only 126 possible Class A network addresses on the Internet. A node with an Internet address of 46.23.42.243, therefore, is node 23.42.243 on network 46. Class A networks are designed for large networks, because each Class A network can have more than 16 million unique host addresses.

Class B networks use values of 128 to 191 in their first byte. The first two bytes of a Class B address identify the network, and the last two bytes identify the host address on that network. An IP address of 182.47.33.21, therefore, is host 33.21 on network 182.47. The 16,384 possible Class B networks can each have 65,534 hosts.

Class C networks have first-byte values of 192 to 223. The first three bytes of a Class C address represent the network number, and only the last byte is the host address. An IP address of 220.200.200.1, therefore, represents host 1 on network 220.200.200. Each of the more than 2 million possible Class C networks can have up to 255 hosts.

As you can imagine, this addressing scheme can result in some very inefficient uses of the possible address space. Because your routers work better if each Ethernet segment in your company has a different network address, you're unlikely to have enough hosts on your network to use even a small fraction of the addresses available on your Class B network.

To solve this problem, or some users would say to make things more complicated, an IP network can be further divided into subnets. To do this, you create a *subnet mask*—a 32-bit data structure typically written in the dotted digital notation used for IP addresses. Your subnet mask should have a 1 in each bit of the IP address to represent the network and subnetwork and a 0 for each bit of the host address.

A Class A network's default subnet mask is 255.0.0.0, a Class B network's is 255.255.0.0, and a Class C network's is 255.255.255.0. If you want to divide your Class B network into 16 subnetworks, you would use a subnet mask of 255.255.240.0, which would reserve the first four bits of the third byte for the subnet number.

> **NOTE**
>
> All the computers on a single network segment—that is, connected to the same router port—must use the same network address and subnet mask.

Transmission Control Protocol

The Transmission Control Protocol, or TCP, is the most common higher layer protocol in the TCP/IP stack. TCP is a connection-oriented, assured-delivery protocol with error checking and packet division and sequencing. TCP assures a transmitter that the data he or she is sending gets to its destination.

User Datagram Protocol

TCP's sophisticated features and error checking add some overhead and take time. If your higher layer protocol is going to do its own error checking, it can use *UDP*, the user datagram protocol, instead of TCP. UDP is a simple protocol that doesn't do much error checking, so it's somewhat faster than TCP.

Upper-Layer Protocols

FTP (file transfer protocol) and TFTP (trivial file transfer protocol) are used to exchange files between hosts. If you want to download a file from a site on the Internet, such as the latest patches to Windows NT from the Microsoft FTP server, you can use FTP or TFTP to make that transfer. TFTP uses UDP as its transport protocol and has less security checking than FTP, so it's frequently not supported on public access sites.

Telnet is a protocol designed to support terminal emulation programs, including the Windows NT Terminal. Because many TCP/IP hosts are UNIX systems, generally Telnet is used to allow a user at one host to emulate a terminal connected to another.

The network file system, or NFS, was first designed by Sun Microsystems. NFS, like Windows NT's SMB, is a file access protocol that allows users at one computer to access files on another.

SMTP, the simple mail transfer protocol, is used to send e-mail messages from host to host. Most UNIX e-mail systems use SMTP-based mail systems.

SNMP, the simple network management protocol, allows a user at an SNMP console to interrogate other nodes on the network—including hubs, routers, servers, and other network resources—and collect statistics from the device or control it. Typically, SNMP is used to collect error or traffic statistics and to control failed ports on hubs or routers. What information is available for controlling any particular device is defined by the MIB (management information base) for that device.

Domain Name Service

Although computers have no trouble with IP addresses, most people find it difficult to remember addresses like 137.14.14.14. They would rather deal with names that seem more meaningful in human terms, such as `ftp.microsoft.com`.

Internet names typically consist of the host name, domain name, and type of domain, separated by periods. Several domain types have been defined, including `net` for network control and management hosts, `gov` for U.S. government hosts, `edu` for educational institutions, and `com` for commercial users. International hosts typically use their country code for the domain type.

Here are some typical host names:

`whitehouse.gov`	Bill Clinton and friends
`FTP.microsoft.com`	Microsoft FTP Server
`compuserve.com`	The CompuServe information service

In early (or simple) TCP/IP implementations, each host on the network has a table listing the other host names and IP addresses known to this host. Because these tables must be maintained manually, it quickly gets to be a major administrative task to add the 100th host to your network.

The Domain Naming Service lets a single or small group of name servers store the host-to-address translation table. It allows other hosts to ask the domain name server how to find any given host.

Windows NT and TCP/IP

Windows NT can use TCP/IP as a transport protocol for its file and print services through the NetBIOS interface for TCP/IP, called NBT. This interface, defined in RFCs 1001 and 1002, doesn't encapsulate NetBEUI packets within IP but sends straight IP packets and communicates with other programs through the NetBIOS interface.

Windows NT users also can use TCP/IP to access other host computers across a TCP/IP network. Windows NT includes many of the usual TCP/IP applications.

Application	Description
Finger	Gets information about a host and its users
ARP	Converts IP addresses to Ethernet or Token Ring addresses
FTP	Transfers files
Ping	Confirms that a host can be communicated with
RCP	Remote file copy

continues

Application	Description
Rexec	Runs program on remote host
Rsh	Runs shell script on remote host
Terminal and Telnet	Terminal emulation
TFTP	File transfers
Route	Builds routing tables

Windows NT also includes an FTP server program to allow other FTP hosts to exchange files with the Windows NT system.

Windows NT supports the Windows Sockets API to allow third-party products, such as client/server database front-ends, terminal emulators, GUI file transfer utilities, and NFS clients or servers, to take advantage of its TCP/IP protocol stack.

Installing TCP/IP

Like most other networking software for Windows NT, TCP/IP is installed through the Network applet in Control Panel. Before starting your installation, you should assemble a few pieces of information:

- Your domain name
- Your default gateway (nearest router)
- Your primary and secondary WINS server IP addresses (if any)
- The IP addresses of any DNS servers in your domain (if any)
- The LMHOST file for your network (if any)

If you aren't using DHCP configuration, you also need to know the following:

- Your network number
- Your subnet mask
- The station's IP address

To install TCP/IP and related services, follow these steps:

1. Open the Network applet in Control Panel, click the Protocol tab, and click the Add button. Select the TCP/IP protocol and click OK. TCP/IP is then added to your list of installed components, as shown in Figure 17.10.

FIGURE 17.10.

TCP/IP has been installed on this system.

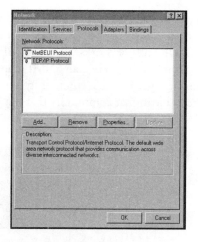

2. Click the Services tab and click Add. From the list that appears, select the Simple TCP/IP Services option and click OK to install basic TCP/IP family services.

3. If you want to run SNMP on your system, click Add in the Services page and select SNMP. When you click OK, you will see a window with three page tabs: Agent, Traps, and Security.

To configure the SNMP service, follow these steps:

1. The first page asks for SNMP administrator contact information and the services SNMP will apply to. (See Figure 17.11.) Usually the defaults are fine.

FIGURE 17.11.

Supplying administrator contact information and SNMP services in the Agent page.

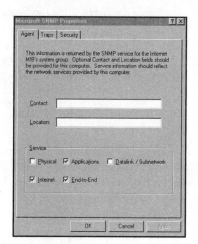

2. Click the Traps tab and enter the names of the SNMP communities that you want the SNMP station to send messages to if there's an error trap. This page is shown in Figure 17.12. On most networks, all the SNMP clients on the network are members of the public community. When an SNMP trap message is sent, the community name is part of the message. For each community, enter the IP address or the host name of the SNMP console in that community that the SNMP trap messages should be sent to.

FIGURE 17.12.

Specifying trap destinations in the SNMP Traps page.

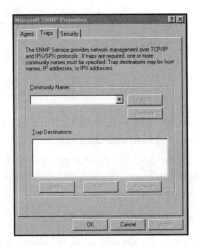

3. If you want to prevent unauthorized users from using the SNMP service and possibly resetting some valuable counters, click the Security tab. The dialog box shown in Figure 17.13 appears.

FIGURE 17.13.

Setting authentication traps in the SNMP Security page.

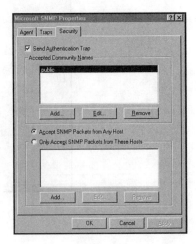

4. To limit access to the SNMP service to SNMP consoles in specific communities, enter the community names in the Accepted Community Names box. If security is really a concern, make sure the public community isn't in the Accepted list.

5. Enable the Only Accept SNMP Packets from These Hosts radio button to further limit SNMP requests honored by this station to the list of IP addresses you enter in the lower portion of the dialog box.

6. Check the Send Authentication Trap checkbox to have the system send out an error trap if an unauthorized host tries to use the SNMP service.

The FTP Service is installed with the Internet Server and is configured from there. When you open the Internet Service Manager from the Start menus, you see the window shown in Figure 17.14.

FIGURE 17.14.

The Internet Service Manager lets you control which TCP/IP services are running and which are stopped or disabled.

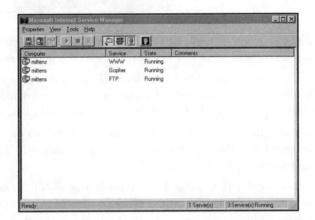

To configure the FTP service, double-click on the FTP line's server to display the FTP Properties sheets. There are five pages for configuring the FTP service. First, the Internet Service Manager informs you that FTP logons send their passwords across the network in clear text, so anyone on your network with a protocol analyzer, such as a sniffer, can discover a user's password. Next, the dialog box shown in Figure 17.15 appears; you can use it to configure the FTP service.

To configure the TCP/IP protocol itself, use the Network applet from the Control Panel, click Protocols, highlight TCP/IP, and click Properties. There are five pages to the TCP/IP configuration windows that let you modify your protocol. You can follow these instructions to configure the TCP/IP protocol:

1. Start on the IP Address page. If you're using DHCP to assign IP address, check the Obtain IP Address from a DHCP Server box. If you're not, enter the IP address for the network card shown in the IP Address field. Remember that every computer on the network must have a unique IP address, or it won't be able to communicate.

FIGURE 17.15.

Choosing configuration settings in the FTP Service page.

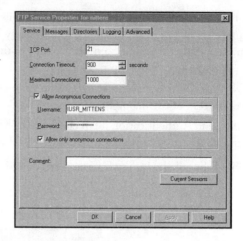

2. Enter your subnet mask into the appropriate field. Remember that all the hosts and routers on your network must be using the same subnet mask.

3. If this system is connected to an internetwork linked by routers, enter the IP address of the router port nearest to this station on the network into the Default Gateway field. A *gateway* is a TCP/IP term for what's usually called a router.

4. If you're using WINS to assign NetBIOS names, click on the WINS Address tab and enter the IP address of your primary and secondary WINS servers into the Primary and Secondary WINS Server fields.

5. If you're going to be using TCP/IP for Windows NT file and print services, select one of the network adapters in your system to use for that purpose. Windows NT can support multiple network adapters in any given system for NetBIOS by using TCP/IP, but each adapter must have its own IP address.

> **TIP**
>
> If you use multiple adapters with unique TCP/IP addresses, you can enable IP routing with the Enable IP Routing checkbox; click the Advanced button first.

6. While you're still on the WINS Address page, decide if this computer is going to be a member of an NT Server domain on a different IP subnet. If so, it must have an LMHOSTS file in its \WINNT\SYSTEM32\DRIVERS\ETC directory. If you click the Import LMHOSTS button, you'll be prompted for a path to an LMHOST file, which will be copied to the appropriate directory.

   If you're using NetBEUI as your transport protocol, your workstation will locate a domain server by sending out NetBIOS broadcast messages. Because IP broadcasts stay within the subnet they were sent in instead of crossing routers, a workstation can't find a server or domain controller on another subnet. The LMHOSTS file has a list of IP addresses and NetBIOS names to allow the station to find the NetBIOS names listed. A typical LMHOSTS entry looks like this:

```
122.22.22.3     AcctSrv
```

Any other systems on other IP subnets that this computer's replication service will import data from or export data to must also be listed in the LMHOSTS file.

7. If you have a Domain Naming Server on your network, click the DNS tab to configure your station to use DNS. (See Figure 17.16.)

FIGURE 17.16.

Entering domain information in the DNS page.

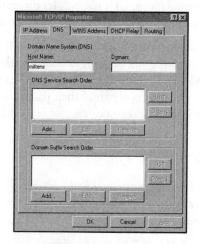

8. For DNS, you need to enter this system's DNS name. Put the host name, typically the same as the computer's NetBIOS name, in the Host Name field. Put the DNS domain name, which has no relation to any NT Server domain name, in the Domain Name field.

9. Next, you need to determine how you want your system to resolve host names into IP addresses. You can choose to use only the domain name service, to search the system's local hosts file and then the DNS servers, to search your DNS servers and then the local hosts file, or to use only the local hosts file.

   The local hosts file, which uses the standard UNIX file format, is used to resolve host names to IP addresses. Here's a typical entry:

```
133.33.4.21     powerpc.naol.com
```

10. In the Domain Service Search Order box, enter the IP addresses of the domain name servers on your network. Place the DNS server closest to this station on the network at the top of the list to speed address resolution.

11. In the Domain Suffix Search Order box, list the domains to search for host addresses. DNS servers will give you the address of the domain, which must then be searched. You can list up to six domains.

Third-Party TCP/IP Products

Although Windows NT includes all the basics for using TCP/IP, if you're installing TCP/IP to provide better access to UNIX or other host computers, you'll find that the standard tools are a little weak. The command-line–driven FTP, Ping, and other utilities aren't exactly user-friendly, and although Windows NT Terminal allows you to Telnet into your favorite host computer, it's pretty bare-bones.

Several third-party products, including Beame and Whiteside's NT/TCP, Net-Manage's Chameleon32, and the shareware QVT, have feaures such as improved terminal emulators with VT220 and 3270 emulations, GUI file transfer programs, and other improved user interfaces. Some also include Usenet news readers and other tools for Internet access.

The one feature missing from Windows NT's TCP/IP is any support for NFS—the network file system. Without NFS, you can only exchange, rather than share, files with UNIX systems, such as SCO UNIX and Sun workstations. Both Beame and Whiteside and NetManage include NFS clients and servers as part of their packages, so UNIX machines can access files on your Windows NT server and you can access files on UNIX servers.

Summary

This chapter has looked at installing and configuring Remote Access Services, which is very useful for connecting to a Windows NT server from anywhere else than being attached directly to the network. It has also covered TCP/IP and how to configure it for your network.

With RAS running, you will find the utility of your system increases enormously, allowing you to access your system from a hotel room across the continent, for example, or from home when you want to check your e-mail. Although RAS can pose a few security problems for a server, when properly configured, it works well and prevents almost all attempts to bypass it.

CHAPTER 18

Integrating Windows NT with Other Networks

IN THIS CHAPTER

In earlier chapters, you learned about networks made up primarily of Windows NT workstations and/or Windows NT Servers. This chapter covers using DOS workstations to access Windows NT and NT Servers. It also looks at adding Windows NT systems (as both servers and workstations) into networks that aren't dominated by Windows NT but might be running some other network operating system or systems.

Because the majority of large corporate sites already had local area networks in place before Windows NT was widely available, you can assume that most corporate MIS managers are thinking about using Windows NT in one of four ways:

- As a new operating system to replace the existing operating systems
- As a new workstation operating system integrating with their current network
- As an application server platform for new applications
- As a file server/application server in conjunction with their existing network infrastructure

Contrary to what you might hear from your Microsoft rep (that nerdy guy who has a picture of Bill Gates and a little incense burner in his office down the hall), your favorite columnist in *PC World in Review*, or anyone else, corporate America is not going to abandon overnight all the systems they've spent millions of dollars on. Even if Windows NT Server made its competition look out of date, inertia, budget cycles, depreciation schedules, and other business factors would slow its adoption; it would take from two to five years for NT to displace the previous generation of systems.

Given these truths and that NT Server, as nice as it is, isn't a vast technical leap over competing network operating systems, such as NetWare, IBM's LAN Server, or Banyan's VINES, you will probably have to deal with a mixed network at one time or another. Even if you've decided to replace your current network operating system with Windows NT and NT Server (which I strongly recommend if you're currently using Microsoft's LAN Manager), you might find that migrating to NT Server is much easier—and less stressful—than trying to make a massive conversion over a three-day weekend.

In this chapter, you look at the hows, whys, and especially the wherefores of integrating Windows NT as a workstation, file server, and/or application server into networks that predominantly run Novell's NetWare, Microsoft's LAN Manager, Banyan's VINES, or UNIX operating systems. I talk about the advantages, disadvantages, and pitfalls of some common techniques for allowing these varied systems to share not only the same cable but also data, printers, and other resources.

In this chapter, you also look at integrating Windows NT's servers with Macintosh computer workstations and workstations running DOS or Windows 3.*x*.

Using LAN Manager Server Resources

As you might expect, integrating Windows NT with Microsoft's own LAN Manager isn't really all that difficult. In fact, NT Server was often called "LAN Manager for NT" in the early Windows NT marketing materials.

Integrating LAN Manager and Windows NT is simple because they have a similar architecture. Both LAN Manager and Windows NT use Microsoft's server message block (SMB) protocol with NetBEUI or TCP/IP transports, and LAN Manager 2.*x* has a domain-based administration system that is similar to NT Server's. In fact, if all you want is to give users at DOS workstations access to both LAN Manager and Windows NT or NT Server, you don't have to do anything. As you discover later in this chapter, DOS workstations use the same requester to access Windows NT and LAN Manager servers.

I recommend that any organization currently running LAN Manager, except possibly for those using LM/X, should plan to upgrade to NT Server. Microsoft is clearly putting their new development efforts behind NT Server. Getting support for obsolete products such as LAN Manager gets harder and harder as time passes because even the tech support staff at Microsoft isn't being trained on old products. After the old-timer tech support operators are promoted (or burn out), getting support becomes very hard. In fact, at some point upgrading is cheaper than staying put.

If your network is slow, if it's growing and needs more servers, or if you need some of NT Server's new features such as the Remote Access Service (RAS), a faster upgrade path is in your future.

LAN Manager Servers in NT Server Domains

Unless you choose to upgrade all your LAN Manager servers to NT Servers over a long weekend, you will, at least temporarily, be running a mixed network. When you're running LAN Manager and NT Servers on the same network, you can configure the network in one of two ways:

■ You can build separate domains so that some of your domains run Windows NT Server on all their file servers, and other domains are made up of LAN Manager servers.

■ You can include some LAN Manager servers in your NT Server domains.

LAN Manager 2.*x* servers (including LM/X LAN Manager for UNIX servers) can be servers or (in LAN Manager terms) backup domain controllers in NT Server domains. Because NT Server stores more information about users and other accounts in its domain database than does LAN Manager 2.*x*, the domain controller in a domain that has both NT Servers and LAN Manager 2.*x* servers must be running NT Server.

The LAN Manager servers in your domain store a copy of the domain database—at least for fields that LAN Manager supports. As backup domain controllers, they can validate logon requests for users at Windows for Workgroups, DOS, and OS/2 workstations. Because Windows NT workstations need some of the additional information found only in the NT Server domain database, a LAN Manager server can't validate user logon requests from Windows NT stations.

If you're going to be running a mixed domain (whether permanently or as an interim step as part of your upgrade), you should have at least two NT Servers to act as the domain controller and a backup. That way, if the domain controller goes down, or you take it down for preventive maintenance or an upgrade, you can promote the other NT Server to domain controller and keep on truckin'.

LAN Manager servers don't recognize a domain's local groups because LAN Manager has no local group feature. Therefore, you can't assign access permissions to resources on a LAN Manager server to a domain's local groups. In addition, because LAN Manager domains are completely independent of each other without trust relationships, LAN Manager servers don't recognize trust relationships. Therefore, you can't assign access permissions to resources on a LAN Manager server to users from a domain other than the domain the server is a member of, even if the server's domain trusts the user's domain so much that it's signed an irrevocable power of attorney.

If a user wants to access data on a LAN Manager server in a LAN Manager domain, he or she must log on using an account in that domain, or the LAN Manager domain must enable guest logons to access the resource. If a user from a LAN Manager domain wants to access data on an NT Server domain, you have to create a local account for that user. Local accounts act just like regular user accounts, except that they don't let a user log on from a workstation in this domain and aren't available for use in domains that trust this domain.

When users with Windows NT workstations browse for resources, they see only LAN Manager 2.*x* domains—that is, domains in which the domain controller is running LAN Manager 2.*x*—if a Windows for Workgroups or Windows NT workstation is a member of the domain, or if the domain controller is explicitly told to look for it.

To add a LAN Manager domain to your NT Server domain's browser list, open the Network applet in the domain controller's Control Panel, select Computer Browser, and click the Configure button. When you see the dialog box, you can add the names of LAN Manager domains to browse.

To make an NT Server domain available for users on DOS or OS/2 workstations using the LAN Manager 2.*x* client software, configure the server service and enable the Make Browser Broadcasts to LAN Manager 2.*x* Clients checkbox by clicking it.

Managing LAN Manager Servers

With some limitations, you can manage LAN Manager servers through the NT Server management tools. Server Manager, User Manager for Domains, and other NT Server management tools enable you to administer features that exist on LAN Manager servers. The following are some of the more significant differences:

- LAN Manager user accounts can't be renamed.
- Users can't be forced to change their passwords at their next logon.
- Local groups don't exist.
- LAN Manager doesn't support user profiles but does support logon scripts.
- User rights, audit polices, and trust relationships don't exist on LAN Manager servers.
- Server Manager can't manage LAN Manager replication.

LAN Manager 1.*x*

If you're still running LAN Manager 1.*x* (including OEM versions such as 3Com's 3Plus Open), you have a more difficult task. At one time, Microsoft had a LAN Manager 1.1 to 2.*x* upgrade utility that copied your user accounts and other information from 3Plus Open or some other LAN Manager 1.*x* server to a LAN Manager 2.*x* server or domain. When I contacted the Microsoft sales department for information on this tool, they didn't have any record of it in their files. Your best bet is to find a reseller who worked with LAN Manager 1.*x* and therefore probably has the tools on the shelf somewhere.

Realistically, your LAN Manager 1.*x* network is now at least three or four years old, and in the intervening years you've found at least a few things you want to change. You can take the opportunity to create new user accounts and groups while you install NT Server. You can still connect to both servers from a DOS or OS/2 workstation and copy your data files from the old LAN Manager server to your shiny new NT Server.

Supporting DOS Workstations

If your company is like most, you probably won't be installing Windows NT for all your users right away. In fact, even Bill Gates has been quoted as saying that 90 percent of the PC users in the field don't need the power of NT. Your comptroller and his divisions of bean counters probably aren't looking forward to upgrading all your users' machines to 16M 486s either.

Therefore, you're probably looking for a way to let your users with DOS workstations share the data and printers connected to your Windows NT workstations and NT Servers. Your best bet is to install Windows for Workgroups on those systems. Because Windows NT servers look just like Windows for Workgroups servers to Windows for Workgroups, you don't have to do anything special to enable your users with Windows for Workgroups to access your NT systems.

18

INTEGRATING
WINDOWS NT

In fact, Windows for Workgroups goes with Windows NT so well that in earlier chapters of this book I discuss Windows for Workgroups right along with Windows NT. Windows for Workgroups has three big advantages over the kind of DOS requester often used with LAN Manager.

The first advantage is that Windows for Workgroups gives your users more available conventional memory than other requesters. Windows for Workgroups 3.11 implements its network features as 32-bit virtual device drivers. In addition to providing faster performance, this architecture uses very little conventional memory for device drivers, leaving it for your users' applications.

The second advantage is that Windows for Workgroups allows your users to access not only the NT servers on your network, but also any NetWare or VINES servers. Doing so with conventional requesters leaves the user with little conventional memory because the requesters for both network operating systems the user is going to be accessing need to be loaded into memory simultaneously.

The third advantage is that Windows for Workgroups lets you share printers connected to your users' workstations. This capability makes it much easier to place convenient printers where your users actually work, but it also adds some problems as users turn off their machines or make similar mistakes that screw up other users' print jobs.

Sometimes, however, Windows for Workgroups just isn't the right answer. Users with old 1M ATs or even 4M 386 machines shouldn't use Windows for Workgroups. Other users might have applications, either commercial or developed in-house, that don't run with Windows for Workgroups or, like AutoCAD, that simply run better under plain old DOS because they can take full control of the machine. Some of these programs themselves provide network services—forwarding e-mail messages between locations, sending faxes for users, and providing other communications services.

The LAN Manager Client

When Microsoft first released Windows NT and Advanced Server, they announced that you could buy client software for DOS PCs in multiuser packs. Shortly thereafter, as part of their campaign to make NT Advanced Server an attractive alternative to Novell's NetWare, Microsoft decided that they would stop charging for each user's client software and distribute it free of charge.

If it wasn't included with your copy of Windows NT, you can now download the LAN Manager requester from the MSCLIENT forum on CompuServe, the Microsoft download server (MSDL), or Microsoft's FTP server (ftp.microsoft.com 131.107.1.11) on the Internet. The package is made up of five files, which correspond to the five disks in the commercial distribution set. You download the files, decompress them to a set of five disks, and then install the requester as if you had bought the disks at your local Egghead Software. The files you need to download are self-extracting archives corresponding to the disks in the commercial distribution of the client software, as shown in the following list:

3 1/2-Inch Disks	5 1/4-Inch Disks	Contents
DSK3-1.EXE	DSK5-1.EXE	Setup
DSK3-2.EXE	DSK5-2.EXE	Drivers (disk 1 of 2)
DSK3-3.EXE	DSK5-3.EXE	Drivers (disk 2 of 2)
DSK3-4.EXE	DSK5-4.EXE	RAS
DSK3-5.EXE	DSK5-5.EXE	NetWare support files

After you download the files, you can install the LAN Manager basic or enhanced client for DOS. The basic client uses less memory and provides file and print services to LAN Manager, Windows for Workgroups, or Windows NT servers. It provides a command-driven user interface but doesn't support multiple protocol support or a menu-driven interface.

The enhanced client adds the menu-driven user interface, support for multiple protocols, and named pipe support. This is the client of choice if your users are going to be accessing client/ server databases such as Microsoft's SQL Server. You'll also want the enhanced client if your computers have more than 2M of memory because it loads most of itself into extended memory, giving you more net conventional memory than the basic client—even though overall it's larger.

If you don't have a modem, if your company has a policy against downloaded software, or if you'd just rather buy disks with those neat-looking Microsoft labels, you can order the requester package from the Microsoft inside-sales line at (800) 426-9400. Ask for part number 2723850V100.

The download package includes a detailed readme file on how to install, but it doesn't include the full documentation for the client software. If you've used LAN Manager 2.1, you can use the manuals from that product; if not, you can muddle your way through or order the manual set separately from the same 800 number (give part number 272-055-040). You might have to explain that you want the manuals for the network client software on CompuServe or the Internet; Microsoft usually doesn't sell manuals separately.

If you have Windows NT Server, the client software is included in the \CLIENTS directory on your CD-ROM. It is essentially the same software I mentioned earlier, except that the LAN Manager client is version 2.2c and has been enhanced to use the DHCP and WINS services.

NetWare and Windows NT

Because Novell's NetWare operating system enjoys a 55 to 75 percent share of the PC LAN operating system market (depending on whose market research you read), you're probably reading this chapter to see how to get the Windows NT machine to print to a NetWare print queue or how to access a Windows NT application server from your DOS and Windows workstations that also access a NetWare file server.

When you buy Windows NT or NT Server, it comes with Microsoft's NWLink support for Novell's IPX (internetwork packet exchange) network layer and SPX (sequenced packet exchange) transport layer protocol. Because NWLink supports the NetBIOS API, you can use NWLink as transport protocol for Windows NT's SMB (server message block) protocol. The usual Windows NT networking functions, therefore, can run across a network carried by IPX rather than the usual NetBEUI protocol. Consequently, you can do peer-to-peer or NT Server networking across networks that can't or, for management purposes, won't carry NetBEUI traffic.

One of NetBEUI's limitations is that, because it uses a single-level naming system, it can't be sent from network to network through routers. If your company has a medium- to large-sized network running Novell's NetWare, Novell routers probably connect the network segments.

It's likely that you have Novell routers, because Novell includes a basic router program with NetWare (which you can use to make any AT class or better PC into a local router), and it builds even better routing software into NetWare file servers. If you have multiple LAN cards in a NetWare file server, it automatically routes IPX traffic between the segments. Because this routing function takes place at the network layer, you can even use a NetWare file server to link dissimilar networks by simply installing both Token Ring and Ethernet cards.

If you have a network in which a Token Ring network and an Ethernet network are linked by a NetWare file server, you can use NWLink on Windows NT workstations to enable stations on the Token Ring to share resources with servers on the Ethernet.

When you set up an IPX network, you need to assign each network segment—that is, each Ethernet or each Token Ring—a unique number. IPX then identifies each node on the network by the network number and the Ethernet or Token Ring card's MAC layer address. You can think of the network numbers as the name of the street and the node addresses as the house number.

NetWare routers exchange information about which networks they're connected to so that each NetWare router can build a table that shows how to get from its location to any other network number it's connected to.

NOTE

Every system connected to any given network segment must refer to that network by the same number. In addition, each network segment that is interconnected by routers must have a unique number that's different from those of all the other segments connected to it. Novell runs a network number registry, but most NetWare network administrators have come up with their own numbering systems.

Although you can use NWLink to connect Windows NT systems this way, it's really intended to let you access NetWare file servers or to allow NetWare workstations to access application servers such as Microsoft's own SQL Server for NT. If you load NWLink, you can use the IPX NetBIOS interface to send and receive messages from NetWare workstations running Novell's NetBIOS emulator for IPX.

Configuring NWLink

Because NWLink is part of the standard Windows NT distribution, you can install and configure it using standard Windows NT networking tools. To start using NWLink, follow these steps:

1. Fire up the Network applet in the Control Panel, and click the Protocol page tab.

2. Select the NWLink IPX/SPX Compatible Transport list box. The program prompts you for the path to the appropriate drivers and copies NWLink to your Windows NT system directories.

3. Click OK, and the system configures and binds—that is, establishes the relationships between the network protocols.

   In the Frame Type field, you can configure your Ethernet card to use one of a variety of slightly different MAC layer frame types. The Ethernet II frame is the oldest and is typically used for DEC and TCP/IP networks. Ethernet 802.3 is the IEEE 802.3 frame without an 802.2 header. Novell used 802.3 as their default frame type until NetWare 4.0. 802.2 is the full OSI-style frame and the default for NetWare 4.*x* and NetWare 3.12. SNAP is an extension of 802.2 used by Token Ring networks and networks with Macintosh computers.

4. Set the frame type and network number to match the other systems on your network, and click OK.

> **NOTE**
>
> You can find out what the current frame type and network address are for your network by typing **config** at the file server console.

5. Click the reboot button when NT prompts you to restart the system to start NWLink.

You can now install a network requester to access NetWare file servers or set up the application service, such as SQL Server, to use NWLink. An application service typically sends out Novell Service Advertising Protocol packets to let the client workstations on the network know that the server is available.

Novell's NetWare Client for Windows NT

Novell's NT requester seems to have been developed by a programming team that decided not to study the Windows NT architecture carefully and build a NetWare requester that would fit in comfortably, but instead to look over Windows NT and figure out how to take over as much of the networking as possible (because, presumably, they know networking better than anyone else).

In the first release, you had to replace the NDIS LAN driver from Windows NT with a Novell ODI driver (open data interface, a specification similar to NDIS but developed by Novell and Apple) that worked like Novell's NetWare and DOS LAN card drivers. If you wanted to use NetBEUI, TCP/IP, or some other NDIS protocol stack, you either had to have two LAN cards or use Novell's ODINSUP module, which lets NDIS drivers talk to ODI drivers.

The current release of the requester can be used with either Novell ODI drivers and Novell's IPX/SPX II drivers or with Microsoft's NWLink. Using Novell's drivers allows the requester to determine the right frame type automatically. It can be somewhat faster for some applications, but using NWLink retains Microsoft's networking architecture and the NDIS driver you're already sure works.

After you download the requester (from the NOVFILES download section on CompuServe or from Novell's FTP server `ftp.novell.com` on the Internet) and install it, you can access data and print queues on the NetWare file server, link to a NetWare directory, and so on. When you log onto your Windows NT workstation, it automatically attaches to your preferred server and to servers needed to reestablish any permanent connections you created.

Because the requester tries to log onto your NetWare file server using the same username you used to log onto the Windows NT workstation, synchronizing all your usernames is a good idea. If you don't, you have to use the Connect As option in File Manager to connect to NetWare directories.

Because NetWare print servers don't run Windows NT printer drivers, you have to load the printer drivers for any NetWare printers you want to access in all the Windows NT systems that will be printing to it.

The current requester isn't perfect. It has some bugs, particularly in the printing arena, and you can't run DOS or 16-bit Windows applications that take advantage of any NetWare-specific function calls or APIs. Therefore, you can't run SYSCON or any other NetWare management utilities under Windows NT. Windows NT workstations also ignore NetWare logon scripts.

> **NOTE**
>
> You can't install both the Novell and Microsoft requesters, or even both NWLink and Novell's ODI IPX/SPX II protocol stacks, at the same time. In fact, if you decide to change from one to the other, be sure to delete all the files that were installed. Both use the same names for some of their DLLs, which, of course, include different code and entry points.

Microsoft's Client Services for NetWare

Microsoft's Client Services for NetWare differs from the NetWare requester in a few simple ways. The most significant is that the Microsoft requester is a better NT citizen, acting more like the Microsoft Workstation service. You can, for example, use Microsoft's UNC names to refer to NetWare resources in profiles, logon scripts, and dialog boxes. If you want to link your E: drive to the SYS:LOGIN directory on the NetWare file server named Porthos, you could use the following command line in a logon script or batch file:

```
NET USE e: \\porthos\sys\LOGIN
```

Microsoft's requester uses NWLink and normal Windows NT NDIS drivers. You install it through the normal Control Panel Network applet procedures you would use to install any other network software into Windows NT.

NetWare's DOS APIs are supported better than in the current Novell requester. You can run some of the more sophisticated NetWare management utilities, but you get no guarantee that they will all run.

The other big difference is that you can use the Microsoft requester as a gateway. After connecting to a NetWare directory or print queue, you can then share that directory. This capability allows other users on Windows NT, Windows for Workgroups, or DOS workstations running the LAN Manager requester to access the NetWare server without having to load the NetWare requester themselves.

This pass-through feature really comes in handy because you can install just one requester or shell on your DOS and Windows workstations, allowing them to access both Windows NT and NetWare resources. It's the only way you can allow remote access users running Windows NT Remote Access Service (RAS) to dial into your network to have access to NetWare resources. The problem with this pass-through feature is that it creates a possible security problem. The user logged onto the system running Windows NT and the NetWare requester can give another Windows for Workgroups or RAS system user access to NetWare file server data that the NetWare administrator didn't want that user to be able to see.

You can install the Client Services for NetWare from the Control Panel's Network applet.

All in all, I prefer working with the Microsoft requester rather than the Novell requester. My opinion might change as both companies bring their products up to production levels.

Beame and Whiteside's MultiConnect Server

Beame and Whiteside's MultiConnect Server lets NetWare workstations access data and printer resources on Windows NT systems acting as servers. The program installs as a network service into Windows NT or NT Server and makes the system it's running on act like a NetWare 3.*x* file server on the network. The system running MultiConnect Server sends out Novell server advertising protocol messages, validates users against a bindery, and responds to NetWare Core Protocol requests like a NetWare file server.

Even if you plan to keep NetWare as your primary file server operating system and are looking at Windows NT primarily as a power user's client and application server, MultiConnect Server might be worth a look. If your NetWare server goes down, you can run MultiConnect Server on a Windows NT workstation to act as a backup server. It even comes with Beame and Whiteside's own version of NetWare's Login, Logout, MAP, and other utilities, so you can use it even where no NetWare servers exist.

If you're planning a transition from NetWare to Windows NT, Advanced Server MultiConnect Server can relieve you of the pressure to change every user's client software overnight. Users can use their NetWare client software until you get around to updating it.

You can buy MultiConnect Server from this vendor:

Beame and Whiteside Software
706 Hillsborough St.
Raleigh, NC 27603-1655
Phone: (919) 831-8989
Fax: (919) 831-8990

Banyan VINES and Windows NT

If you're currently using Banyan's VINES, which is probably the most sophisticated LAN operating system on the market for large networks, you'll be glad to hear that Banyan has made a requester for Windows NT available on their support bulletin board through their early availability program. Like both Novell's and Microsoft's NetWare requesters, the VINES requester is available to the general public.

The requester gives you full file and print services, including support for Banyan's VINES IP protocol (which is not quite the same as the TCP/IP IP protocol, even though they have the same name), VINES logon, and support for StreetTalk and StreetTalk directory assistance.

Currently missing is support for named pipes, OS/2 applications, NetBIOS applications on VINES IP, and support for Banyan's 3270 gateway.

You can download the requester package (currently NTEAP3.ZIP) from Banyan's support bulletin board at (508) 836-1834. You have to fill out a survey agreeing not to hold Banyan responsible if this beta test software makes your computer burst into flames. After you have the package, run the enclosed setup program to install the VINES support, answer a few questions about your VINES setup, and restart your machine.

The NetWare requester automatically logs you onto your NetWare server when you log onto Windows NT, but you aren't automatically logged onto your VINES network. To log onto the VINES network, run the logon program from the VINES group on your desktop.

Macintosh Services

One of Macintosh's advantages has long been the fact that every Macintosh includes a built-in network interface. Granted, LocalTalk interface runs at a snail's pace (just 230Kbps), but any network is better than no network. Just the fact that Apple included a network port on every Mac (and, therefore, networking software in every version of the Macintosh operating system) has resulted in Macs being networked to an even higher degree than Intel-based PCs.

If your organization is like most, a few Macintosh computers and their users are hidden away in the advertising, art, and publications departments. These users, convinced that their computers are the true personal computer, might start wanting their own file server so that they can share their files and printers. Over time, they'll find that they don't want to exchange files with only their clique of Mac users, but that they also need to see that Excel spreadsheet in the master budget and take advantage of corporate resources, such as e-mail.

NT Server can support Macintosh workstations through its Macintosh services option. Macintosh services allow an NT Server to support Apple's AppleTalk protocol stack on Ethernet (which Apple and Mac users call EtherTalk), Token Ring (TokenTalk), and FDDI, as well as LocalTalk networks. Because the server "speaks" to the AppleTalk protocol stack, Mac workstations don't need any special client software to access the NT Server. In fact, an NT Server looks just like an AppleShare file server to Macintosh users.

A single NT Server can support up to 255 Mac workstations, providing file and print services, and serve as an AppleTalk Phase 2 router, passing AppleTalk messages between multiple network segments.

Requirements

To support Macintosh workstations, you need 2M of additional memory in your file server (more is better, of course). Because Macintosh files and filenames are more complex than DOS files and filenames, Mac users can access directories only on NTFS disk volumes. Your Macs must be running System 6.0.7 or later; System 7 is fine. LocalTalk is fine for printer sharing and an occasional file transfer, but you need EtherTalk or TokenTalk cards in the Macs to get reasonable file-sharing performance.

How Macintosh Services Work

Providing file services for Macs and PCs on the same server presents a few challenges. Each Mac file is actually made up of two parts: the data fork contains the actual data for the file, and the resource fork contains descriptive information about the file (including which application created the file). In addition, Mac filenames can be up to 32 characters long. Some method must be used to shorten Mac filenames for users at DOS or Windows for Workgroups stations.

NT Server stores both the data and resource forks of Mac files in a single NTFS file through the use of multiple data streams. It also shortens Macintosh filenames that don't fit in the DOS 8.3 file convention to a six-character string followed by a tilde (~) and a number. Therefore, DOS users see a filename such as JonesLetterhead as JONESL~1. If the Mac user then creates a file called JonesLabels, DOS users see it as JONESL~2. Because NTFS filenames can be even longer than Mac filenames (up to 256 characters), a similar shortening function applies to NTFS files that are more than 32 characters long.

To make it easier for users on different platforms to share files, Mac services also does automatic translations between the DOS file extensions (used to identify which application created a file) and the Mac resource fork. Mac users automatically see .XLS files created by DOS users as Excel spreadsheets, .DOC files as Word documents, and so on.

> **TIP**
>
> You should recommend that your Mac users stick to valid DOS filenames and the extensions normally used by Windows applications for their file types when creating files that they expect to share with DOS or Windows users.

Macintosh users also can send data to printers connected to NT Servers, including printers such as HP LaserJets that don't include PostScript support (which is usually needed for a Macintosh to print). Macintosh print jobs are queued just like PC print jobs. Some Mac networks simply share printers, locking other users out when a user is printing. Spooling gives users back the use of their workstations faster.

Some Mac networks have a continuing problem, known as LaserPrep wars, which slows printing and forces the LaserWriter to print multiple startup pages. When a Macintosh tries to print to a LaserWriter or other PostScript printer, it asks the printer what version of the PostScript setup file (called a LaserPrep file) the printer is running. If the version doesn't match, it sends a new LaserPrep file and asks the printer to make it the resident file. The process of making a LaserPrep file resident takes some time for the printer to process and causes the printer to print a new startup page.

If users on the network have different versions of the Mac Chooser that use different LaserPrep files—a common occurrence—the printer will spend much of its time switching back and forth between LaserPrep files. NT Server solves this problem by sending a temporary LaserPrep file at the beginning of each print job. This file slows things down a little if you have just one version of Chooser, but it speeds things up a lot if your users are running different versions.

Security

Like any other users, Macintosh users need to log onto the domain before they can access resources on it. Because they aren't actually part of the domain, Mac workstations don't need accounts the way Windows NT workstations do.

If you use the standard Mac networking software that's built into the Mac system, your users on Mac workstations can send their passwords across your network in clear text. If someone connects a network protocol analyzer, such as a Network General Sniffer or a Novell LANalyzer, to your network, he or she can capture the logon packets and discover the other users' passwords. Microsoft has included a User Authentication Module for the Mac that, if installed on your Macs, encrypts passwords before they're sent over the wire.

Mac/AppleShare permissions are a little different from NT Server file permissions. On an AppleShare system, you can grant permissions to the owner of a folder, to a group that shares the folder, or to all the users on the network. Unlike with PC networks, you can't grant different permissions to different groups of users except for the owner, the group, and everyone. Mac administrators can grant the owner, the group, and everyone one of the four levels of access:

Level of Access	Description
See files	The user has read-only access to files and can't see folders in the current folder
See folders	The user has read-only access to files and folders in the current folder
Make changes	Full access
Cannot move, rename, or delete	Prohibits moving, renaming, or deleting folders or files in the folder

If you have applied more restrictive NT Server permissions, they apply to the Mac users as well.

18

INTEGRATING
WINDOWS NT

Setting Up Macintosh Services

In this section, you learn about the process of installing and configuring NT Server Macintosh services. The configuration process of designing an AppleTalk network, placing routers, choosing LocalTalk and/or EtherTalk, and configuring the AppleTalk network is beyond the scope of this book. If you don't already have a Mac network up and running and have no idea what a zone is or how to number your networks, you should read the Services for Macintosh manual that comes with NT Server, read a good AppleTalk networking book, or hire an experienced consultant. Note that an NT Server can act as a router, or seeding router, between two or more network segments, including acting as an Ethernet to LocalTalk router.

Macintosh Services installs on your NT Server just like any other network software. To install it, follow these steps:

1. Fire up the Network applet in the Control Panel, and click the Services tab.
2. Click the Add button and select Services for Macintosh from the resulting dialog box. Windows NT prompts you for the path to the required files.
3. Click OK and reboot your system to start the AppleShare servers for the first time.

As soon as you restart your system, you have to configure the AppleTalk protocol stack. Like any other protocol, it's configured through the Network applet in the Control Panel. To configure AppleTalk, follow these steps:

1. Start the Network applet in the Control Panel, select Services for Macintosh from the Services page, and click the Configure button.
2. From the Network list box, select which of the network adapters in your system you want to use as the default network for AppleTalk.

> **NOTE**
>
> A LocalTalk adapter can't be the default AppleTalk adapter. If you want to serve Macs on a LocalTalk network, configure an Ethernet card in addition to the LocalTalk card.

3. From the Zone list box, choose the zone in which you want this server's printers and volumes to appear.
4. If you want this server to also act as an AppleTalk router, turn on the Enable Routing checkbox by clicking and then click the Advanced button to configure the router.
5. From the resulting dialog box, you can select another network adapter, set the router to seed one or more network numbers, and configure AppleTalk zones.

> **TIP**
>
> If you want your users to send encrypted passwords from their Macs (PCs always send encrypted passwords), copy the Microsoft UAM from the AppleShare folder in the Microsoft UAM volume to the user's AppleShare folder in his or her System folder. Just in case the worst happens, copy the old UAM first.

Macintosh Printing

In addition to the print spooling that any Windows NT server provides to PC users, NT Servers offering Mac print services also allow PC users to print to network laser printers connected to an AppleTalk network (LocalTalk or EtherTalk) and convert PostScript print jobs to print on non-PostScript printers.

Because your NT Server can spool print jobs for your Mac users as well as your PC users, you probably want to capture—that is, lock—your printers to the NT Server, preventing other users from printing directly to the printer. Doing so maximizes printing performance and helps eliminate LaserPrep wars.

All the Mac users on your network will use a single user account to gain permission to the printers on your server. Create an account (I recommend that you name it MACPRINT or something similar) through User Manager for Domains, and grant it permissions to some or all of your printers through Print Manager, just as you would for other users on Windows NT workstations. You then need to tell the Mac print server process on your server to use that username for Mac print jobs, as follows:

1. Start the Services applet in the Control Panel, and select Print Server for Macintosh.
2. Click the Startup button.
3. Click the This Account button, and enter the account that Mac print jobs should use.

Macintosh-Accessible Volumes

For Mac users to access data on your NT Server, you need to create one or more Macintosh-accessible volumes. Although you usually use the term *volume* as the equivalent of a logical disk drive, in this context a volume is roughly the equivalent of a Windows NT *sharepoint*. The rules for defining Macintosh-accessible volumes are somewhat different from those for setting up standard sharepoints:

- A volume name can be no more than 27 characters long.
- You can't define one volume to have its root under another volume. (You also can't give one NTFS directory two different volume names, even though you can give it two different sharenames.)

■ All the volume names on a server must fit within a single AppleTalk buffer of 4,624 bytes. Note that 2 bytes are added to each name in the buffer.

To make a directory (and its descendants, of course) a Macintosh-accessible volume, follow these steps:

1. Start File Manager and select the directory you want your Macintosh users to be able to access.

NOTE

Remember that you can create Macintosh-accessible volumes only on NTFS or CDFS CD-ROM volumes. Mac users can't access data on FAT volumes.

2. Choose MacFile | Create Volume (which exists only on servers with Mac support loaded). The volume name defaults to the directory name.

3. To use a longer or clearer name, enter it in the Volume Name box. The path defaults to the directory selected earlier.

4. To assign a password to the volume, enter the same password into the Password and Confirm Password boxes. Users who want to access this data must enter the password you choose here before access will be granted. Note that assigning a password prevents users from connecting to the volume at startup.

5. If necessary, set the volume as read-only, prevent guest users from accessing the volume, and limit the number of users who can access this volume in this dialog box. Click OK to finish.

If you decide to change any of the properties of the Mac volume, choose MacFile | Properties.

You also can set Macintosh-style permissions for the volume through File Manager by choosing MacFile | Permissions. This way, you can set all the Mac-style permissions discussed earlier in this chapter. You can still set NT permissions in the usual way in addition to Mac-style permissions.

The MacFile menu, or at least some of its functions, is available through File Manager, Server Manager, and the MacFile applet in the Control Panel. Choose MacFile | View/Modify Volumes | Properties from Server Manager to access the dialog box.

Click the Permissions button to tighten your security. In the resulting dialog box, you can force users to use the Microsoft UAM (and therefore prevent them from sending clear text passwords across your network), prevent users who don't have a valid account from logging on as guest users, and prevent users from storing their passwords on their Macs.

> **NOTE**
>
> Allowing Mac users to store their passwords on their machines basically allows anyone who sits down at that Mac access to your server. If you want to run a secure system, you shouldn't allow workstations to store passwords.

In this Permissions dialog box, you also can set the logon message, displayed at logon time for users running Mac System 7.1, and limit the number of Mac users allowed to access the server at the same time.

The User, Files, and Volumes buttons do basically the same things that the User, Shares, and Files buttons in Server Manager normally do. They allow you to manage logged-on users and open files.

As you've seen, NT Services for Macintosh uses DOS and NTFS file extensions to tell Mac users which application to run when a user double-clicks the name of a file that doesn't have a resource fork. You can maintain the table of associations to add new extensions or change the application to use for some file types through the Associate option on File Manager's MacFile menu.

After you enter an extension or select an existing extension and click Edit, enter a creator and file type for the extension to allow Mac users to access these files.

> **NOTE**
>
> If you have data that will be used only by Mac users, you don't need to share the directory that is the Mac volume.

18

INTEGRATING
WINDOWS NT

Summary

You've covered a wide variety of material in this chapter, mainly dealing with adding non-Microsoft protocols and machines onto your Windows NT network. As NT matures and becomes even more popular, there are bound to be many new products introduced to the market to expand the interconnectivity options for system administrators. A good place to check for new information is the Microsoft home page, or conduct a search on a Web engine like AltaVista (http://www.altavista.digital.com) for your platform or protocol.

Optimizing Your Network

CHAPTER

19

Funny, isn't it, how the server that was fast enough last year when you had 20 users on the network now feels like someone stole your Pentium motherboard in the middle of the night and replaced it with the motherboard from someone's old XT?

Because there's no such thing as an infinitely fast processor, local area network, or disk drive, the art of network optimizing is a constant contest of finding the most troublesome bottleneck in your network and improving that component. If 200 users are accessing one file server that has one disk drive to get their applications, it's clear that adding another server, or maybe even another disk drive, to share the load will solve that bottleneck and improve performance. If, however, you have 20 file servers and 200 users on one Ethernet network, adding another server isn't likely to increase efficiency because the bottleneck is in the network cable, not the file server.

The sad truth is that even though you can upgrade your network and widen each bottleneck, you still don't solve your performance problems. You simply shift the bottleneck to the next narrowest point. As your users' demands for network services increase, that bottleneck will become too narrow, and you'll need to figure out where the new bottleneck is.

Figuring out where your network's bottlenecks are, and which one affects your users' performance the most, is more of an art than a science. Several tools are available to help you determine whether some parts of your network are overloaded. The Windows NT Performance Monitor, included with Windows NT Server, helps you find problems in NT file servers or workstations by letting you monitor how well Windows NT performs.

To find network bottlenecks, you can use the following tools:

- Performance Monitor with the Network Monitor Agent counters
- A network protocol analyzer
- A software network monitor program, such as Novell's LANalyzer for Windows or Triticom's Ethervision
- A hub management program, such as Synoptics' Optivity
- The tachometer display on your hub

What you're looking for is a display of what percentage of the available network bandwidth is in use.

Luckily, NT is basically self-tuning. You don't have to manually set server parameters, such as the maximum number of open files or the number of data packet receive buffers, to get reasonable performance, as you do with other LAN operating systems, including LAN Manager. NT can dynamically allocate processor resources and memory for different purposes, so you don't have to hand-tune it at installation time. That said, there are a few things you can do to speed data on its way.

Using Performance Monitor to Locate Bottlenecks

Performance Monitor is an application that lets you graph, report, log, and set alerts based on the values of literally hundreds of counters that can track everything from the percentage of processor time used by any thread on your Windows NT machine to the amount of disk space that's free on a disk drive.

Performance Monitor can track these counters for the computer it's running on and for other Windows NT systems. It can even track counters on several systems simultaneously, so it's easy to set up a Windows NT machine in your network control center that triggers an alert whenever a server is running slowly, running out of disk space, or otherwise misbehaving. Performance Monitor can even run other applications if an alert is triggered.

Performance Monitor can track counters for several Windows NT objects. An *object* is a functional subsystem in Windows NT, such as TCP/IP or the processor. Each object type, such as the physical disk, can have multiple occurrences. For example, each drive on your server is an occurrence of the physical disk object type. The object types you can monitor with Performance Monitor are listed in Table 19.1.

Table 19.1. The object types you can monitor with Performance Monitor.

Object Type	Description	Counters
Browser	Computer announcements	Announcement totals, number of browse requests
Cache	The disk cache	Write hit ratio, read hit ratio
Logical disk	Disk volumes	Disk queue length, percentage of time disk is busy
Memory	Virtual memory management	Page faults per second, available cache, cache size
NetBEUI	The NetBEUI protocol	Bytes sent, number of timeouts
NetBEUI resource	NetBEUI buffers	Number used
NWLink IPX	IPX protocol	Bytes transferred, window size
NWLink NetBIOS	IPX NetBIOS interface	Bytes transferred, window size
Objects	Windows NT multitasking	Events, threads
Paging file	Swap file	Percentage used
Physical disk	Physical disk drives	Time used, reads/writes per second

continues

19

OPTIMIZING YOUR
NETWORK

Table 19.1. continued

Object Type	Description	Counters
Process	Each process in system	Processor time, memory used
Processor	Each processor in system	Percentage time in user tasks, percentage time used
Redirector	File and print service I/O	Bytes sent/received
Server	Service process	Bytes sent/received, errors
System	All processors in system	Percentage time in user tasks, percentage time used
Thread	Each thread in system	Percentage processor time

NOTE

If you install optional components, such as RAS or an NFS server, you might find additional objects when you run Performance Monitor.

NOTE

To track physical or logical disk counters, you need to run the Diskperf program on each system where you want to track disk performance. Diskperf lets you collect disk performance data, effective at the next reboot. Collecting disk performance data is disabled by default because it has a small effect on system performance (about 1.5 percent on 386 machines—less on faster systems, more if you have several disk drives).

Within each of these object types, you'll find several different counters you can track to keep an eye on your system's performance. Some object types, such as threads, allow you to track several counters for each occurrence, or each thread, in the system. Other data can be followed at different levels of detail. The System object type, for example, describes the aggregate data for all the processors in your system, but the Processor object type has independent counters for each processor.

If you're like most system administrators, you'll find the hundreds of possible counters to track intimidating. I've found that the counters listed in Table 19.2 provide the best information for server performance monitoring. You might find that others, such as percentage of disk in use, are useful for managing or monitoring your network, but the ones in Table 19.2 seem to be the simplest to manage.

Table 19.2. The counters supplying the best information for server performance monitoring.

Object Type	Counter	Description
System	% Total Processor Time	The aggregate time for all processors in the system during which the processor is busy. Does not include time spent running the idle thread waiting for something to do.
Logical Disk	% Disk Time	Percentage of time the disk is busy.
Logical Disk	Avg sec/disk transfer	The average time it takes to process each disk transfer. Higher figures indicate that additional disk channels will help performance.
Logical Disk	Free Meg	Space remaining on the drive.
Logical Disk	Disk Queue Length	The number of requests waiting for the drive. A snapshot value, not the average over a time period. Higher figures indicate that additional disk channels will help performance.
Server	Context Block Queue Time	The time, in milliseconds, that requests wait for file service processes.
Memory	Pages/sec	The number of page faults that require reading or writing to the paging file. A high figure indicates that more memory will speed server performance.
Network Segment	% Network Utilization	Percentage of network bandwidth in use. A high figure indicates that splitting the network segment will improve performance.
Paging File	% Usage Peak	The peak percentage of the swap file that's in use. Increase paging file size if it's over 75 percent.

19

OPTIMIZING YOUR
NETWORK

continues

Table 19.2. continued

Object Type	Counter	Description
Redirector	Current Commands	The number of requests pending service. If the number of pending requests exceeds the number of network cards in your server by more than two, your server is overloaded.
Redirector	Network Errors/sec	The number of serious network errors per second. Any value other than 0 needs attention.

When you start Performance Monitor, you'll see the screen shown in Figure 19.1. This graph screen is just one of four different views of your data that Performance Monitor can give you.

FIGURE 19.1.

Performance Monitor's graph screen.

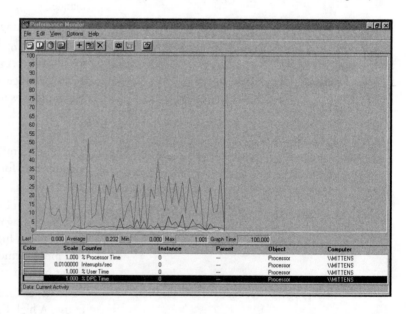

First, select the counters you want to graph. Click the Add button (the one with the plus sign) to select the counters you want to track. When you do, you'll see the Add to Chart dialog box shown in Figure 19.2.

Here you can select the computer, object type, counter, and instance that you want to track. You also can select the graph's scale, along with the color, width, and style for the line representing this value.

FIGURE 19.2.

Adding a counter to the graph.

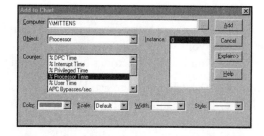

Choose Options | Chart from the main menu or click the Chart Options button (the one on the far right) to adjust how the data will be graphed on your screen. In the Chart dialog box, you can set the update interval, specify whether you want a line graph or a bar histogram, and choose other options that affect how the graph looks.

After you've selected the counters you want to chart, you can display the average, current, minimum, and maximum values for that counter by selecting it at the bottom of the screen. You can edit the settings for any counter by double-clicking on it, and you can remove a counter by selecting it and choosing Edit | Delete from the Chart window.

You can also save the set of counters you're tracking so you can use them later by choosing File | Save Chart Settings.

If you want to set alerts, choose View | Alerts or click the Alerts button (the one with the exclamation mark on it) on the button bar. Figure 19.3 shows where alerts are displayed when the counters you're tracking generate them.

FIGURE 19.3.

Checking the Alert Log.

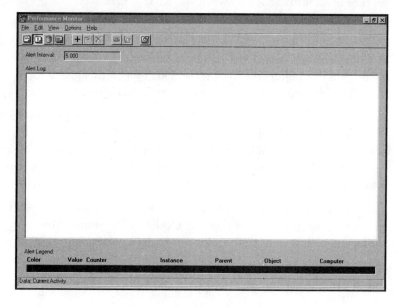

Notice that the counters you selected in the chart view aren't active in the Alerts window. Each of the four kinds of Performance Monitor windows has an independent set of counters that it tracks. When you save your settings, if you choose Save Workspace rather than Save Chart, Alert, Log, or Report, you'll save the settings for all four windows.

To add counters, click the Add button to get the dialog box shown in Figure 19.4. Here, as in the Add to Chart dialog box shown in Figure 19.2, you can select the counter you want to monitor. You also can set the counter's high or low limit and select an application to run when the limit is exceeded, such as WinBeep, which sends a message to your pager when a critical error occurs. You can choose to have the application run each time the limit is reached or just the first time.

FIGURE 19.4.

The Add to Alert dialog box lets you add another circumstance that generates alerts.

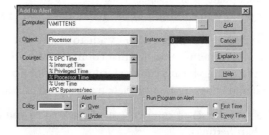

Choose Options | Alert from the main menu to set options for how Performance Monitor should respond to any alert. You can tell it to switch to the Alert window or send a message to another station on the network. You can also set the polling interval for how often the counters are checked or set it to check only when you tell it to manually.

If you want to collect data for later analysis, you can start a log file by clicking the Log button (the one with a cylinder). When you create a log, you can select which object types you want to log information from. (See Figure 19.5.) Performance Monitor then logs data for all the counters in that object type to your file. Don't go overboard and log everything, or your log file will rapidly become the monster that ate Philadelphia and devour all your disk space.

To select which object types you want to log, click the Add button in the Add to Chart dialog box. After selecting the object type, from the main menu choose Options | Log to set the name of the log file, set the polling interval, and start the log. If you select manual polling, the data will be entered into the log only when you click the Snapshot button (the one that has a camera on it).

Once you've created a log file, you can use it as input for the Chart, Alert, or Report windows by opening that window and choosing Options | Data From. You also can set bookmarks in the log file so you can recognize what other actions were going on in the network at that time.

If you'd rather see your data in numerical form, choose View | Report or click the Report button (the one with a little report) to open the Report window. (See Figure 19.6.)

FIGURE 19.5.
The Log File window shows the system's log file for you.

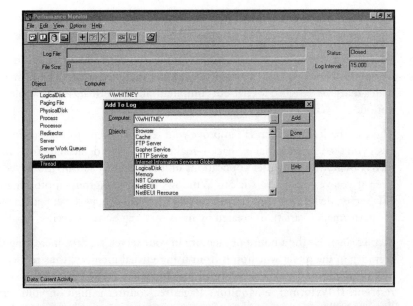

FIGURE 19.6.
The Report window lets you see data in a numerical format instead of graphically.

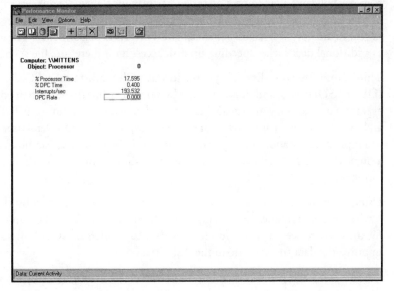

19

You can set the polling interval from this window when you choose Options | Report.

Optimizing Your Server

The key to optimizing server performance is to keep in mind what a file server's job is. A file server is responsible for responding to user requests for disk data by locating and retrieving data from its disks and sending it to the network or receiving data from the network and storing it on its disk drives. Your job is to balance the performance of the server's subsystems.

Your first step is to buy a basic system for your server that's designed to provide high-speed I/O performance. I'd much rather see a server designed for I/O performance and reliability than a machine designed for flat-out computational performance that would make a great workstation.

There are basically five ways to improve your server's I/O performance. First—and this option gives you the biggest initial payback—make your servers dedicated. You can dedicate your file servers by not running user applications on them and by setting the server's priority to high. Even if you've decided to stick to Windows NT's workgroup approach and not upgrade to NT Server, dedicating your file servers will speed up overall server performance and eliminate the performance variations created by users working on the server.

Second, increase the amount of memory in your server. At first, increasing the amount of real memory in the server will stop it from using virtual memory, thus reducing the load on the disk subsystem and making all the processes needed in the server faster because they're memory-resident. If Performance Monitor's Pages/sec counter is high on your server, adding more memory will have a big impact on server performance. Even if your server has enough memory to page only occasionally—to load a backup process from virtual memory, for example—adding more memory will have a beneficial effect on server performance. The extra memory is used as additional disk cache, speeding up disk access and, therefore, file service.

Third, optimize your disk subsystem. Just as with workstations, SCSI drives are better than IDE or ESDI drives, and 9ms drives are better than 12ms drives. When you're configuring the average workstation, you probably take a good guesstimate of how much disk space you'll need and then buy a single disk drive that size. Your server will need several times as much disk space as a typical workstation, probably more than a single disk drive can hold. Even if you can buy a single drive to hold all your server's data, you should consider breaking it up to improve performance.

Using multiple drives reduces the user's average access time to data by allowing each drive to service a different request simultaneously. The entire disk channel doesn't need to stop waiting for the drive to seek. If you add multiple disk controllers or SCSI host adapters, you also can improve the data transfer rate to the disk drives.

I recommend that you run your important server drives as mirrored pairs with each of the two drives on separate host adapters. In this duplexed configuration, the server can send write requests to both disk drives simultaneously. I also recommend that you have two drives per host adapter until you have four host adapters, or eight drives, total. In general, the more drives and the more host adapters (up to four), the merrier. If you use striping, you can significantly increase throughput. If your budget can handle it, a hardware RAID solution is a good idea, too.

Fourth, choose the right bus architecture. Using an ISA bus system as a server creates a serious bottleneck at the bus. Modern SCSI II disks and multiple Ethernet or Token Ring adapters can transfer data faster than an 8MHz 16-bit ISA bus can. A fast server needs a faster channel between its processor and peripherals.

> **NOTE**
>
> Remember that your servers aren't going to be running CAD or multimedia applications that require local bus video systems. In fact, a server with VL bus Ethernet and VL bus disk adapters will run faster with an ISA VGA than with a fancy VL bus video accelerator.

Intel's PCI bus is now widely used as a server platform. PCI bus, used primarily with Pentium and high-end 80486 systems, is 64 bits wide and has bus arbitration features that allow it to support multiple adapters.

Fifth, choose the right processor. In a workstation, the processor is probably the primary determinant of overall performance. In a server, the choice of processor plays a smaller, but still important, part in determining file server speed.

> **NOTE**
>
> Based on your NetWare experience, you might think that the processor isn't important in server performance, but that's not true for Windows NT or NT Server. Their performance is more sensitive to the server's processor than NetWare's is. In fact, NT Server requires more processor horsepower than NetWare to deliver similar performance.

If you're going to be using a processor-intensive application service, such as SQL Server or SNA Server, or if you're supporting many users, a RISC system or multiprocessor server is a good idea.

Now that you've built a system with multiple Pentium processors, 64M of memory, and a series of fast disk drives connected through the 128-bit miracle bus of tomorrow, you'll find that the bottleneck has moved to the network adapter. You just won't be able to move data in and out of the server fast enough through a single 10Mbps Ethernet or 16Mbps Token Ring card.

Reducing Network Bottlenecks

Network bottlenecks typically start to raise their ugly heads when you have 20 or more users and three or four file servers. A single file server is usually limited in how much data it can

19

OPTIMIZING YOUR
NETWORK

handle, so the disk channel or Ethernet card and bus is the bottleneck. As your network grows, the data capacity of the network cable itself becomes the limiting factor in your network's performance.

If you suspect that the network itself is becoming the worst bottleneck on your network, your first step should be to measure just how busy your network actually is. Several products are available that measure traffic on your Ethernet or Token Ring and report the percentage of the network's available bandwidth that's currently in use.

> **NOTE**
>
> Consider upgrading or subdividing your Ethernet when it shows an average of 20 percent or more bandwidth use and Token Rings when they hit 50 percent.

You can use a network protocol analyzer, such as a Network General Sniffer or HP Network Advisor. A protocol analyzer is built from a portable or laptop computer and carries a price tag of $3,000 to $10,000 or more. Buying a protocol analyzer just to monitor network traffic is the computer equivalent of buying a Range Rover for a 10-mile freeway commute. It does the job, but it's overkill. Protocol analyzers can capture all the packets rushing by on your network and decode them to tell you onscreen what each packet is doing. They're great tools for an expert to use when debugging a troubled network but aren't necessary for just load balancing.

What you really need is a network monitor or probe that doesn't store every packet for later decoding but just keeps statistics on how much data is going by. This is where the Network Monitor Agent counters and Performance Monitor can prove useful. If you need more information, you can buy standalone network probes, devices that you connect to your Ethernet or Token Ring and monitor from another computer, such as Novell's LANtern, for about $2,500. You can also find monitoring functions built into other network devices, such as bridges, routers, and intelligent hubs from Cabletron, David Systems, and Synoptics. Some lower-end hubs include a simple tachometer display that gives you a quick view of your network traffic.

For a small network, less than 300 nodes or so, your best bet might be to buy a software traffic monitor, such as Triticom's EtherVision or TokenVision. For just $400 to $500, they turn any computer on your network into a traffic monitor and can give you a "skyline" display showing network traffic levels over time.

For larger networks, you should put a monitor on each network segment so that you can set SNMP alerts. That way, when the traffic level on any of your networks exceeds an acceptable level, you'll get a message in your network command center.

The simplest way to speed up your network is to upgrade from Ethernet or Token Ring to a faster network, such as FDDI, if you're willing to replace all your current network hardware. Another solution to network bottlenecks is subdividing your networks into smaller pieces. If you divide your 100-user network into three subnetworks—for example, one each for users in the accounting, sales, and manufacturing departments—and give each network its own file servers, your users will notice better performance because each of the three networks needs to carry only one-third as much data.

The problem with just subdividing is that you take a corporate-wide resource and turn it into three islands of technology. If someone in sales needs a special quote from someone in manufacturing or a credit check from accounting, he or she must resort to Sneakernet—carrying the data on a floppy disk from one network to the other.

You can solve this problem by connecting each file server to all three networks through three Ethernet or Token Ring cards. Each user can then access all the data on any of the file servers, but the traffic on each network is still limited to the traffic generated by the users in one of the three departments. (See Figure 19.7.)

FIGURE 19.7.

Using multiple LAN cards in your server.

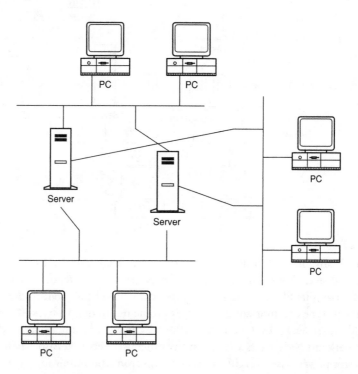

Once you set up more than two or three subnets, however, putting multiple LAN cards in each file server isn't such a good idea. First, there's a limit on the maximum number of network cards in a server, so you can't have more than five or six networks before you run out of slots for LAN cards in a typical server. Even more important, you'll now be limited to keeping all your workstations within the maximum cable length of the network you choose.

If you have more than two or three subnets, you should use bridges, or routers, to connect your networks. (See Figure 19.8.) Just as in a wide area network, the bridges or routers forward the data intended for other networks and keep communications between two stations on the same network on that network alone.

FIGURE 19.8.

Using bridges to build a large network.

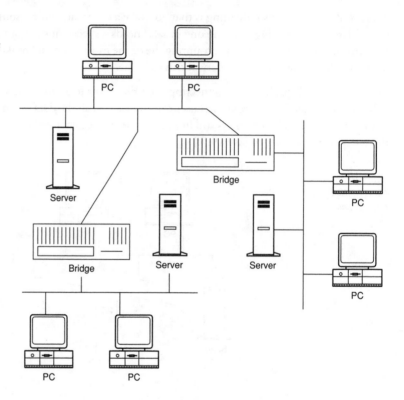

The disadvantage of bridges and routers is that it takes time for each packet to be received by the bridge, examined, and forwarded. Every bridge or router in the data path between a workstation and its file server reduces the performance of file service across that link by 10 to 40 percent. One common solution to this problem is to build a backbone network that connects all the user networks. (See Figure 19.9.) By using a backbone network, you keep each user network just two routers away from any other user network. Also, a failure of one user network doesn't prevent users on the other networks from communicating with each other.

As your network grows, you should seriously consider using TCP/IP rather than NetBEUI to carry your file and print service traffic. Although TCP/IP can be up to 15 percent slower on a single network than NetBEUI, it's more efficient when the delays of bridges or routers are added to the network.

FIGURE 19.9.
A backbone network.

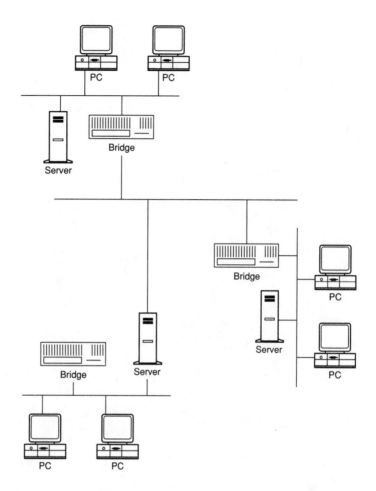

NetBIOS can't be routed (you must use bridges to connect NetBEUI networks) and uses many broadcast packets to run. As a result, a NetBIOS network with bridges has many overhead packets taking up valuable bandwidth. In a complex network, up to 40 percent of all the traffic can be overhead. TCP/IP, on the other hand, can be routed and has much lower overhead on complex nets.

Summary

In this chapter, you've looked at a few ways to optimize your system and network's performance. There are a number of diagnostic and reporting tools in Windows NT that help you detect where bottlenecks and problems are, and usually the solutions are evident when the problem is identified. Of course, buying faster equipment is always an option for bottlenecks, but usually not as practical as you might wish.

19

OPTIMIZING YOUR
NETWORK

Troubleshooting Your Network

CHAPTER 20

This chapter covers ways to keep your network up and running. In addition to traditional, reactive troubleshooting, you'll learn methods for testing and monitoring your network and its components so you can prevent problems from occurring in the first place.

The main thing you need to remember about troubleshooting is to stay calm. As it says on the cover of *Hitchhiker's Guide to the Galaxy:* "Don't panic!" I've seen too many people make a bad situation worse by reformatting a hard disk or replacing all their network cables when a much less drastic solution would have worked better.

Assessing the Problem

The key to successful troubleshooting is to take a careful look at the problem before doing anything. First, determine how severe the problem is. If a single modem in a modem pool or one of your 20 laser printers fails, that's obviously less severe than all your file servers being destroyed in an earthquake. You can classify the problem by the number of users affected and how severely they're affected. There are several kinds of problems:

- Problems that prevent a mission-critical application from running or that prevent a large group of users from accessing their normal applications and data. Example: A file server or Ethernet hub failure.

- Problems that prevent a small group of users from accessing their normal applications and data. Examples: A user who forgets his password, or a failed LAN card.

- Problems that inconvenience the majority of users. Example: A failed drive in a stripe set with parity.

- Problems that inconvenience a small group of users. Example: A printer or communications server failure when others are available.

Second, determine the risk to your data. Your data is probably the most valuable asset your company has. A study sponsored by the Firemen's Fund insurance companies several years ago showed that more than half the companies that suffered a catastrophic data loss had gone out of business or merged with a competitor within two years.

Protecting Your Data

If you're following a good backup plan, data loss should theoretically be limited to the single day's work since the last backup. However, if you don't pay careful attention to your backup process, you might have a substantially larger risk of data loss without even knowing it.

Network administrators make several common mistakes when it comes to backups. The most common is creating a batch file to back up the server and then just changing the tape in the tape drive every morning without looking at the backup program's output log or trying to restore any files.

One of my clients made their backups this way for more than a year before they discovered, after a hard-disk crash, that one of their main database files hadn't been backed up in 17 days. Most backup systems, including this client's, can back up only files that aren't open or locked by another user or task. Because their new comptroller never exited the accounting applications and never logged out of the network, the files he used were always open and, therefore, not backed up.

You might think the best solution would be to design a backup system that backed up files even while they were in use. However, if you tried to back up a database while it actually was in use, the backup program would probably back up the inventory table, for example. After a user entered a transaction that updated the inventory and sales order table, it would back up the sales order table. If you had to restore the data from that tape and use it to run your company, you'd find that the sales order table and the inventory table wouldn't be in synch.

The answer is either to make sure you have database applications with well-designed backup functions that can log transactions and keep the database in synch or to make sure your users aren't using valuable files during the backup process.

Another client checked his error logs, made sure he had all his files closed when his backup ran from 2 to 4 a.m., and securely transported copies of his tapes off-site every evening. However, he didn't know that his tape drive had a blown chip and that bit seven of every byte was always recorded on his tapes as a zero. If he had tried to restore any of his backup tapes, he would have found the problem before he needed one of the tapes. He actually found out when he was looking for an important file that a senior vice president had mistakenly deleted.

Even with a good backup plan, you might find yourself in a situation where you need to use all your skills—and the Norton Utilities for NT—to try to reconstruct some data on your server. Your primary goal should be to follow the Hippocratic oath: "First, do no harm." Never delete a file or reformat a disk that has data you might need to recover. Specialized firms like On-Track Data Recovery can work their magic only if you haven't wiped the slate clean.

Common Problems

The rest of this chapter is devoted to identifying and solving common networking problems. I'll start with the most common problem you're likely to find on any network: the well-known "My computer can't access network resources" phone call.

When a workstation can't communicate with the file servers on the network, one of these factors could be the cause:

- A bad network card
- A LAN card driver configuration that doesn't match the card setting
- A wrong protocol setup

- A bad cable
- Duplicate computer names

Determining exactly which problem or combination of problems is keeping your station from working is a process of elimination. Your detective work, like Sherlock Holmes's, consists of a series of deductions as you eliminate causes one by one.

Your first question should be, "When did this system last work properly?" If the answer is the day before yesterday, start looking for things that have changed since the day before yesterday. If a major earthquake or hurricane tore through town yesterday, you'd probably be safe in assuming that your system problems were caused by yesterday's events. However, usually it's less catastrophic events that cause the station to lose its connection to the server. A visit from telephone installers, for example, is a good clue that the problem is with a cable in the wiring closet. Or, the user might have installed a new network protocol or service, such as TCP/IP, an NFS client or server, or especially Novell's workstation requester. In that case, you should start by looking in the Control Panel's Network applet to see if something there was inadvertently changed.

After the user answers "Nothing" to the question "What happened yesterday?", walk to the back of his computer and make sure his cables are actually connected to the right jacks in the back of his computer and in the wall socket. More than once I've run to a user site to respond to a phone call implying the user was going to jump out of his 45th-floor window if his computer wasn't working in 10 minutes, only to find that, while redecorating his office, the user plugged his computer into the phone jack and vice versa.

Once you're plugged in, you should fire up the Event Viewer to see whether any errors there can help you find the source of the problem. Most problems related to LAN card configurations generate multiple entries in the system's Event Log that you can use to diagnose the problem. When the problem's cause is not obvious, you can use the Network Troubleshooter, which is part of the Windows NT 4 package. It can be started from the Help screens (use Network as the subject to find Help About) or from the Network Neighborhood's Help menu. Most of the suggestions Network Troubleshooter gives you are obvious, but sometimes it's the obvious that's overlooked.

Using the Event Viewer

At system start time, any service with difficulty starting places an entry in the system log. When an Administrator-class user tries to log into this computer, she gets a dialog box informing her that something went wrong at system start time. You'll find that the Event Log is at least as good as, if not better than, your users at identifying where the problem is.

If you have a typical Windows NT workstation or NT Server, when you open the Event Viewer after seeing that dialog box, you'll discover that errors tend to domino or cascade. Therefore, you'll have six to ten events in the Event Viewer from a single typical problem, such as a bad or misconfigured adapter.

Bad LAN Cards and Driver Configuration Problems

If your LAN card is configured to user I/O address 300 and IRQ3, but its driver is configured to use an I/O address of 200 and IRQ5, you'll start a chain reaction as the driver fails to load because it couldn't find the card. The LAN protocols, server service, and workstation service can't start because they depend on the LAN card driver in order to run.

When your LAN card driver fails to load because of an error on the card or in its configuration, you can get a list in the Event Log with many resulting errors. When I changed the address of the Ethernet card in one of my test servers, all but one of the 26 entries in this Event Log were caused by the first error from the SMC8000 driver, which couldn't find the card.

The first step is to locate the first error in the log from the current session. The upper-layer protocol errors are almost always there, because many other services and protocols rely on whatever service or driver failed first.

If that first error is from the LAN card driver, there could be a problem with either the driver's configuration or the LAN card itself. Your next step is probably to take the system down and run a diagnostic program for the LAN card. Most LAN card manufacturers have DOS-based diagnostics that can test their cards and identify most problems.

NOTE

Remember that a LAN card with a bad transceiver can be identified only by diagnostics that use a loop-back adapter or another workstation. If you're running a thin Ethernet network, you can try using a T connector with two terminators attached as a loop-back. If that works, try a two-workstation test.

If your card passes its diagnostics, you need to go back to the Control Panel's Network applet and check the driver's configuration. If the diagnostics fail, first check the card's configuration to make sure that a jumper or DIP switch isn't set wrong. If the card seems OK, try replacing it with a fresh one. It's usually better to just swap the card and figure out what was wrong with the old one back in the lab, because the user gets back to work faster.

Protocol Problems

If the errors in the log start with TCP/IP, NWLINK, or some other protocol, you'll need to configure the protocol through the Control Panel's Network applet. Not having a valid IP address or using a IPX or IP network or subnet address different from the other devices on the network might start the error log cascade.

Setting two computers on your network to use the same NetBIOS machine name is also a protocol problem because it prevents the NetBIOS interface you're using—NetBEUI, IPX, or NBT for TCP/IP—from properly identifying a system on the network. Luckily, Windows NT scans the network to detect other computers on the network using this computer's name during the Setup process or when changing a computer's name. Unfortunately, unless you're using NT Server and making all your systems members of the same domain, there isn't a central database of names so that you can name a second computer MARY if the existing MARY is down or otherwise unavailable when you set up the new MARY.

Bad Cable Problems

A Novell study done a few years ago indicated that as much as 75 percent of network downtime is caused by cable problems. Diagnosing cable problems can be relatively easy for star-wired architectures, such as 10Base-T Ethernet.

If you have a star-wired network, and a single workstation can't locate the server at installation time or later, you can rule out cable problems by simply connecting a workstation that's working at another location on the network to the cable that's plugged into the failed workstation. If the new workstation works properly, you can be pretty sure the problem isn't with the cables.

If that method doesn't work, try replacing the patch cable that runs from the workstation to the wall jack in the user's office. These patch cords are the most likely part of your cable system to fail because they're exposed to abuse from users. I've seen users roll over their patch cables with their chairs, rip the cable out of the connector and just jam it back in, and commit other innovative acts of patch-cable abuse.

While I'm talking about patch cables, I want to throw in my two cents' worth about making your own: Don't. I've found that even skilled network administrators with the best tools don't always make great patch cables. It's hard to get all eight wires in the right positions and still get the strain relief bar on the RJ-45 to close on the cable's jacket so that when the user pulls on the cable the actual electrical connections don't take the strain. Given that factory patch cables typically cost about $1 more than the cost of the components and that a good crimper costs more than $100, factory patch cables can be cheaper than the ones you make yourself, even before you figure in the cost of your own labor and the connectors you ruin by getting it right.

If changing the patch cable doesn't solve the problem, you should check the wiring closet and make sure no one accidentally disconnected this port from the hub or concentrator. After all, just plugging the cable back in might not show off your technical skills or your fancy tools and diagnostics, but it does get the problem solved, and that's what's important.

The next step is to check the cable end-to-end for conductivity. If you don't have a full toolbox, run down to Radio Shack and buy some alligator clip leads for connecting the two wires of a pair in your cable and a cheap volt-ohm meter. When you put the meter across the other ends of the wires, you should read well under 100 ohms.

Unfortunately, although this simple test can tell you that the problem is in the cables, it can't tell you that the problem *isn't* in the cables. High-speed digital signals, such as Ethernet and Token Ring, need more than just simple conductivity from a cable. They also need cables that meet certain specifications for signal loss, electrical noise, and length.

Remember that the quality of your installation is just as important as the quality of the parts you use. Running cables over fluorescent light fixtures, using telephone grade splices and punch-down blocks, and other installation errors can keep even the best cable from working properly.

Bus networks, on the other hand, can be quite difficult to figure out if you don't have the right tools and techniques. Because a problem in a bus network such as Thin Ethernet can cause the whole cable segment to go down, locating a cable break or other problem on a bus can be difficult.

Several manufacturers, including Microtest, Fluke, and DataComm Northwest, make hand-held cable testers designed specifically to test LAN cables to see whether they meet the appropriate specifications. These testers typically have a signal injector that connects to one end of the cable and a main tester that connects to the cable's other end and measures the noise and strength of the signal it receives. These cable testers also take advantage of the fact that a break, a short, a bad connector, or another impedance mismatch in a cable causes any high-speed signal in the cable to be reflected, just as light is reflected by a mirror. By sending a high-speed pulse into the cable and measuring how long it takes for the reflection to come back, a cable tester or time domain reflectometer (TDR) can determine how far down the cable the problem is.

On a bus network, a TDR is the easiest way to find the problem. Without one, you have to split your network in half, putting terminators on both of the new ends at the break and checking whether the stations on each half can "see" each other. If there's just one problem, the stations on one half of your network will be able to see the others, and the stations on the other half won't. You just have to continue the process of dividing the network until you find the segment or connector with the problem.

If you have a cable tester, it's a good idea to check and document all your cable runs. That way, when you have a problem, you can throw the tester on the line and find out in seconds whether the problem is at one of the connectors or in the walls, where it's basically impossible to fix.

Replacing a Failed Drive in a Mirrored or Stripe Set with Parity

The first, and most important, step in replacing a failed drive in a mirrored or stripe set with parity is to recognize that it needs doing. I had one client, now out of business, who ran their computers in difficult conditions, so they always built their servers with mirrored drives. What they forgot to do was check the status of their servers periodically. One day I got a panicked call after the second drive on one of their servers failed.

An examination of the error log from a backup tape showed that the server had run with a failed drive for three months. Had they swapped that drive—and had they not been indicted for mail fraud—they might still be in business today. If you want to avoid a similar fate, you should look at the error log for each of your NT Servers on a regular basis.

Once you know you have a drive you need to replace, the next step is to back up the volume in question. I always make a backup before doing anything to the disk subsystem on a server.

Fixing a Mirrored Set

When a drive in a mirrored set fails, the system automatically sends the data requests to the remaining drive, leaving the working drive as an orphan. You then need to go into Disk Administrator (from the Administrative Tools group under the Startup menu), select the mirrored set, and choose Fault Tolerance | Break Mirror, which makes the mirrored set two separate partitions. The working drive gets the drive letter formerly used by the set, and the failed drive gets the next available letter on your system.

Next, you need to bring the server down, turn it off, and replace the disk drive. Your best bet is to look in the server documentation (you did document everything in this server, didn't you?) and configure another drive of the same make and model to replace the failed drive.

Once the new drive is in place, run Disk Administrator again and mirror the good drive by selecting the partition and the unused space on the new drive and choosing Fault Tolerance | Establish Mirror. If you're using SCSI drives, and I hope you are, your best bet is to add the new drive to the same host adapter as the failed drive, but use a different SCSI address so that you can replace the drive and then run Disk Administrator once to break and make the mirrored set.

When you restart the computer, it automatically copies the data from the good drive to the new secondary drive in the background and places an entry in the error log when the copy is complete.

Fixing Stripe Sets with Parity

When a drive in a stripe set with parity fails, it's automatically ejected from the set and orphaned. To fix the stripe set, you just need to add the new drive and run Disk Administrator to add it to the stripe set.

When the Domain Controller Is Down

One of NT Server's strengths is that a user's logon request can be processed by any NT Server in a domain, not just at the domain controller. Because all servers in the domain have a copy of the domain database, they can continue to process logon requests for as long as the domain controller is down. In fact, the only thing you can't do when the domain controller is down is to update the domain database by adding users and changing group memberships and user rights.

The first decision to make when your domain controller is down is whether you're going to repair that server and bring it back up as the domain controller or take one of the other servers in the domain and make it the domain controller. If you're going to bring the domain controller down for an hour or so to add more memory or a new disk drive, promoting another server and then demoting it again when you bring the domain controller back up doesn't make a whole lot of sense. On the other hand, if a couple of wild-eyed terrorists machine-gun your domain controller into submission, you'll want to promote a server with less severe wounds.

To promote a server to domain controller, you need to use Server Manager from the Control Panel to select the server and then choose Computer | Promote to Domain Controller. If the domain controller is running at the time, it's automatically demoted.

You then have to decide whether you want to resynchronize the whole domain, which you should do if you think the domain controller had changes that hadn't yet been duplicated on all the file servers in the domain. Resynchronizing a large domain can create a huge amount of network traffic, so you might decide to postpone it until off-hours, when it won't affect user performance as much.

If any of the other NT Servers in your domain fails or loses its connection with the domain controller, you should resynchronize that server with the domain controller when you restore it to the network. Use the Server Manager, select the server, and choose Computer | Resynchronize Server.

Browser Errors

If, while scanning your system log, you run into an error that reads `The Browser has forced an election on network (some network name) because a Windows NT Server (or Domain Master) browser is started`, you have nothing to worry about. This message is simply telling you that your computer wanted to be the *master browser*—the computer that all the other computers ask when they want a list of computers in the domain—but that some other NT Server machine declared itself the master browser first. Your network will continue to work without incident.

Summary

In this chapter, you've looked at some of the standard procedures to follow when you encounter trouble with your network. Most of the steps are routine and quick to perform, and although they sometimes isolate the problem for you, more likely they help by eliminating the more obvious causes of trouble. By following these steps, and by using the Network Troubleshooter included with Windows NT 4, you should be able to overcome most network problems your machine might encounter.

20

TROUBLESHOOTING YOUR NETWORK

IV
PART

Setting Up a World Wide Web Site Using NT Workstation

Introduction to the Web, Web Sites, and Home Pages

CHAPTER 21

This chapter gives you an introduction to the World Wide Web (WWW), Web sites, and home pages on the Internet. If you are already familiar with these topics, feel free to skip to the next chapter, which starts with an overview of hardware platforms that can be used to host a Windows NT–based Web site. By reading the next chapter, you will learn basic material about the WWW that's needed to understand topics covered in later chapters.

Introduction to the WWW

Until the early 1980s, what's now called the Internet was a relatively small network called *ARPAnet*. This small network was mainly used as a research tool for about 15 years. After the Internet was created in the early 1980s, many universities and government organizations used it to exchange and distribute information. Later, commercial organizations realized the potential of the Internet and started using it as well. The recent increase in the WWW's size is a result of more and more commercial organizations establishing a presence on the Web.

Until the creation of the World Wide Web (WWW), almost all information distribution was done through e-mail, FTP, Archie, and Gopher. E-mail became widely used for exchanging information between groups of people as well as individuals. FTP was used to transfer files from one host to another, and Archie was used to find files on the Internet. Because of the Internet's nature, before long, information was scattered all over it. Therefore, unless you knew exactly where the information was, you had no way to search for it.

To help users search for information on the Internet, "Gopher" was invented at the University of Michigan. Gopher is a database of information that's organized with a hierarchical menu interface. Gopher was designed to take someone looking for information from the general to the specific by offering selections of topics from layers of menus. To extend the amount of information being provided, gophers were often connected to other gophers. Although this proved to be an efficient way of locating and distributing information, its capabilities were limited. Mainly, the information being distributed was limited to plain text, and access to information at different locations wasn't very well organized.

Because of Gopher's limitations, a new platform-independent method had to be invented to distribute information on the Internet. This issue was addressed at CERN in Switzerland when *Hypertext Markup Language* (*HTML*) was created. HTML was derived from a document formatting language called *Standard Generalized Markup Language* (*SGML*). HTML was designed to be a document markup language that's easy to learn, use, and transmit over the Internet, and it's simpler to use and easier to learn than SGML. To transmit HTML documents, a TCP/IP-based (Transport Control Protocol/Internet Protocol) protocol was invented that became known as *Hypertext Transport Protocol* (*HTTP*). Web servers speak HTTP to transmit HTML files, and Web browsers use HTTP to retrieve HTML files. Web browsers display objects, both static and interactive (such as text, images and Java applets), after retrieving them from Web servers.

With text and graphics unified, the WWW became an exciting medium of information interchange compared to Gopher. Someone looking for information could finally browse information sources and easily travel from one to another by following hyperlinks. With the help of special applications and browsers, the WWW quickly became a vehicle of text and multimedia distribution. Also, locating information on the Web has become much easier, thanks to many search engines and Web-site cataloging databases used on the Web.

The World Wide Web is perhaps the most influential vehicle of information distribution since the invention of the television, as the recent boom in the number of Web sites on the Internet attests. As more and more people gain access to the WWW through online services, or directly through a local Internet Service Provider (ISP), many organizations will focus on using the WWW to keep their customers informed of new products, carry out business transactions, and provide customer service.

Compared to other methods of distributing information, the WWW is a very attractive medium because the cost of publishing data and making it available to a global audience is relatively low. Furthermore, by registering a Web site with search engines and Web-site cataloging databases, you can potentially get your customers to come to you for information when they need it. This is different from traditional advertising, such as television or radio advertising, in which advertisers take the information directly to their customers.

Clearly, by setting up a Web site, you're catering to a different kind of audience. Usually, someone who is visiting your Web site is there because he or she needs access to some information. Therefore, when designing your Web site, you should keep in mind that your first priority is to make the information at your Web site as accessible as possible.

In the past few years, the Internet has grown by leaps and bounds. If you look at Figure 21.1, you can see that the Internet has been almost doubling each year since 1991. The WWW is responsible for most of this growth.

FIGURE 21.1.

The growth of the Internet.

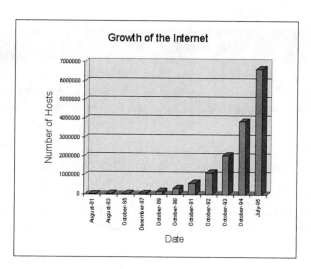

Introduction to Web Sites

Web sites can be thought of as TV broadcast stations. It's much less expensive, however, to set up and maintain a Web site. You can generally have your own Web site up and running in just a few weeks (in all likelihood, much sooner after reading this section!), unlike TV broadcast stations; also, Web sites broadcast information on a per-demand basis. When a client requests certain information from a Web server, it delivers the information to the client and then closes the connection. Refer to Figure 21.2 for a simple diagram of how Web sites and Web clients are connected to the WWW.

FIGURE 21.2.

A basic diagram of WWW connections.

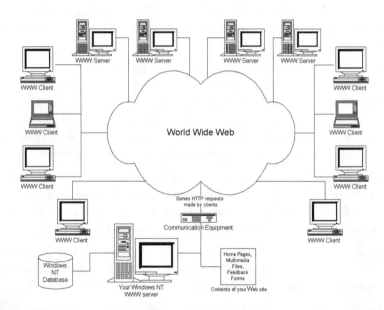

The WWW is a collection of servers on the Internet that speak HTTP, which is a "connectionless protocol." Web servers listen for incoming HTTP requests, and when one is received, the requested data is sent to the client. Figure 21.3 illustrates this interaction.

When someone accesses a page at your Web site, usually more than one HTTP connection is made. Generally, a new connection is made for each object, such as a graphics file or Java applet, that's embedded in the document. For example, if you type **netstat** at the command prompt when someone is accessing your Web site, you'll notice that usually more than one connection is made by the client accessing your Web site. Figure 21.4 shows that several connections are made by a Web browser accessing one page.

FIGURE 21.3.

How Web servers handle HTTP requests.

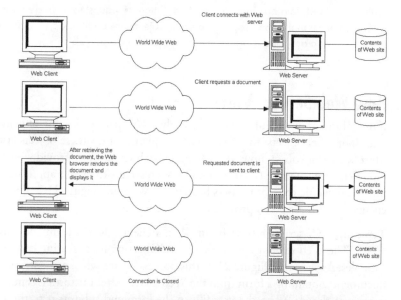

FIGURE 21.4.

Multiple HTTP connections for a Web page access.

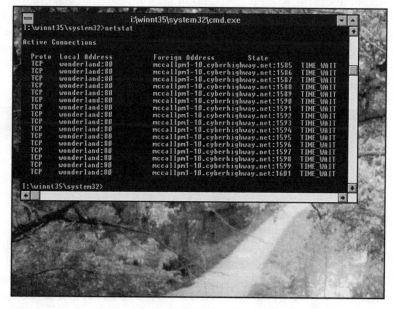

> **NOTE**
>
> A connectionless protocol doesn't need a persistent connection. When a Web server receives an HTTP request, the data is sent to the client. Then the connection is closed when the requested data has been transmitted. Often, a request for a page creates more than one connection if inline graphics or other objects are on the page. Each connection is good for retrieving only one graphic or other object from the Web server.

How Web Servers Work

If the information a client requests is simply a Web page consisting of plain text, a few images, sound, or other objects, the Web server simply transmits these objects at the client's request. More work is involved, however, when the Web server must provide dynamic content. Common Gateway Interface (CGI) is used by Web servers to invoke applications on your server to provide dynamic content to users browsing a Web site. Figure 21.5 illustrates how Web servers invoke CGI scripts to provide dynamic content.

Typically, CGI scripts receive input when a client fills in a form and submits it to the Web server. The Web server then invokes the CGI script after creating certain CGI environment variables. As shown in Figure 21.5, this process begins when a client first requests an HTML document containing a form from the Web server. After the form is sent to the client, the connection is closed. When the user fills in the form and submits it to the server, the server executes the CGI script with the information entered in the form. The CGI script then processes the data, possibly by accessing a database, and sends a message to the client who invoked the CGI script. This message typically contains the results of processing the information provided by the client and supplies a link to another page so that the user can continue to browse the Web site.

> **NOTE**
>
> Web servers usually listen on port 80 for incoming HTTP requests.

Introduction to Home Pages

Home pages are documents formatted in HTML that might contain inline graphics or other objects. HTML documents are in plain text (usually ASCII) format and can be created with any text editor. Chapter 23, "What Software Do You Need?" shows you programs that can be used to create HTML files and Windows NT Web servers that can be used to host Web sites. Just like the World Wide Web, HTML is evolving. More and more features are being added to HTML, which has been standardized by the WWW consortium, to accommodate users' needs. For more information about standard HTML and its proposed enhancements, you can visit this site:

`http://www.w3.org/hypertext/WWW/MarkUp/`

> **NOTE**
>
> Just because a Web browser like Netscape or Microsoft's Internet Explorer supports a "neat" HTML tag doesn't mean that it's valid HTML. When you're using HTML enhancements that are beyond standard HTML, remember that your pages might not be rendered properly when someone looks at your Web site with a browser that supports only standard HTML.

FIGURE 21.5.

How Web servers use CGI to provide dynamic content to Web browsers.

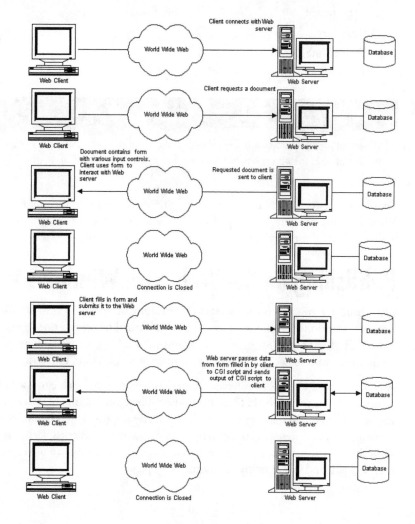

Home pages can contain inline graphics or other objects. Here are a few commonly used file formats found in Web pages:

File Type	Extension
AIFF sound	.AIFF
AU sound	.AU
GIF image	.GIF
HTML document	.HTML or .HTM
JPEG image	.JPG or .JPEG
MPEG movie	.MPEG or .MPG
PostScript file	.PS
TIFF image	.TIFF or .TIF
Plain text	.TXT
QuickTime movie	.MOV
XBM bitmap image	.XBM

NOTE

When you embed objects in file formats not commonly supported by Web browsers, you should always include a link to software that can be used to view the files.

Graphics formats like the ones mentioned previously and new technologies, such as Java and Virtual Reality Markup Language (VRML) home pages, can present information to a global audience in a completely new way.

Publishing on the Web with Windows NT

After you have your Web site all set up, publishing on the Web with Windows NT is easy to learn. As mentioned, content on the Web is published by using a document markup language called HTML. To publish on the Web, you need a basic understanding of HTML, but this requirement will change in the near future when WYSIWYG HTML editors become common.

After consulting some Web reference materials, you should be able to use HTML and publish information on the Web. HTML isn't a very powerful document markup language, so you might not be able to make everything look exactly the way you'd like it to. By using HTML, however, you can present your content in an organized manner to Web surfers browsing your Web site. As you gain more experience in Web publishing, you can use enhancements to standard HTML and create richly formatted Web pages.

What's Needed to Publish on the Web

Many Web authoring services can do all your Web authoring for a price. If you're setting up your own Web server, however, you might as well spend some time familiarizing yourself with Web publishing and do it yourself. Take advantage of Windows NT's user-friendly environment to publish on the Web; thanks to its many Web publishing applications, you can easily create an outstanding Web site, even with no previous Web publishing experience.

To learn how to publish on the Web, the single most important thing you need is time. By using the many resources available on the Internet, you can familiarize yourself with HTML and how to publish on the Web in just a few days. For more information on publishing on the Web by using HTML, you can visit Yahoo's World Wide Web authoring resources page at this site:

```
http://www.yahoo.com/Computers_and_Internet/Internet/World_Wide_Web/Authoring/
```

As more and more powerful Web publishing tools are invented, however, HTML knowledge won't be necessary. Very soon, what word processors like Microsoft Word did for document publishing will be done to Web publishing by Web publishing suites.

Web Publishing Tools

Although most Web publishing tools are simple HTML editors, a new breed of WYSIWYG Web publishing tools is on its way. With these powerful new tools, publishing on the Web will become easier and less time-consuming.

Although initial versions of Microsoft Internet Assistant for Microsoft Word were limited in functionality, recent versions have many added features to make Web publishing tasks easier to handle. For example, the current version of Internet Assistant handles inline images, document backgrounds, text colors, font attributes, tables, and many other document formatting attributes, which are accessible through an easy-to-use GUI. Other WYSIWYG HTML editors will be available by the time you read this book.

Several other companies, including Netscape and Vermeer Technologies, will be unveiling Web publishing suites. These tools will make setting up and maintaining a Web site easier by letting you concentrate on the contents of your Web site instead of worrying about how it should be formatted with HTML.

Database Publishing Tools

Because the main goal of setting up a Web site is to provide information, publishing databases on the Web is a good way to meet that goal. Database publishing applications for Windows NT are easy to install and offer a great deal of functionality. By using these applications, you can make databases on an NT server available to users browsing a Web site, and with CGI, you can set up database-interface applications to let users browsing a Web site update and query a database. There are a number of Windows NT–based database applications from companies like Lotus (IBM), Corel, Informix, Oracle, and others.

Why Not UNIX?

Until recently, if you wanted to establish a presence on the Web, you had very few options other than UNIX. For this reason, most Web servers are currently UNIX Web servers. These Web servers are quite capable of hosting a Web site and serving HTTP (Hypertext Transport Protocol) requests. However, the development environment UNIX offers for Web site developers leaves much to be desired. Web site developers on UNIX servers spend a fair amount of time worrying about operating system–imposed restrictions and inconveniences, which take time that could be better spent working on the Web site's content. The often cryptic user interfaces of UNIX tools makes the task even harder for UNIX Web site developers. On the other hand, Windows NT offers a user-friendly and robust environment for developing a Web site. If you already have a UNIX Web server acting as your primary Web server, you'll benefit from making the switch to Windows NT.

Web Publishing Issues

You should be concerned about several issues when publishing on the Web. Some of these issues might not apply to you, but you should pay particular attention to some issues, such as security.

Benefits of Publishing on the Web

Recently, many organizations have set up Web sites on the Internet. If you know a company's name, you can now almost guess its Web site address. Also, TV commercials and other product literature are mentioning HTTP addresses more often. When the Web becomes more widely used by the general public and an even more popular way to dsitribute information, customers will start visiting companies' Web sites for information. The cost savings of publishing on the Web will be huge when printing color brochures and mailing them to prospective customers isn't necessary anymore. By using the Web, organizations can publish pieces of product literature and allow customers to access this information. All this can be done at a fraction of the cost required to keep customers informed through traditional methods.

Furthermore, when information is added to a Web site, it's immediately available to millions of users. No other information distribution medium can distribute information to such a large audience at a relatively minor cost. Besides providing information quickly, by using the Web, you can also get customer feedback almost immediately. The cost savings and time savings are two of the biggest advantages of using the Web to distribute information. Also, by incorporating multimedia and new technologies, such as Java, into a Web site, you can make its content richly interactive, which makes the information more appealing to Web surfers.

Drawbacks of Publishing on the Web

Using the WWW to distribute information has some drawbacks. One of the biggest drawbacks is the lack of security standards for transmitting sensitive data on the Internet. Because the WWW was born in an academic environment, security wasn't initially an issue. With the increasing commercial use of the Web, however, security has become a major concern. Several companies, such as Microsoft and Netscape, have come up with data-encryption technologies that can be used to make the Internet a secure place to do business.

Another drawback of publishing on the Web is the lack of formatting control over content. Although standard HTML offers many document formatting attributes, its capabilities are somewhat limited. You can use Netscape or Microsoft enhancements to HTML, however, to improve formatting of content published on the Web. Unfortunately, not all Web browsers support these HTML enhancements. This is a major drawback because special HTML tags can make the content almost unintelligible for users without browsers that support those tags. For example, users of online services with technologically challenged Web browsers can't enjoy Web sites as much as those who use Netscape Navigator and Microsoft Internet Explorer.

How to Use the Web to Your Advantage

Although there are certain disadvantages to publishing on the Web, the advantages far outweigh them. By using the Web judiciously, you can not only supply content to your customers, but also do it in a timely and appealing manner to increase business and customer satisfaction. Also, the Web can be used as an efficient medium to communicate with customers and get their feedback, as well as other information. In Chapter 27, "Making Your Web Site Interactive," you will be shown how to set up a feedback form to get feedback from users browsing your Web site. Also, by using other Internet services like FTP, you can distribute software to those surfing your Web site. After reading the next few chapters, you should be able to set up a Web server and some CGI programs and unleash the Web's potential by using Windows NT.

Summary

This chapter has covered basic information about the WWW that's needed to understand topics covered in subsequent chapters. In this chapter, you have been introduced to the WWW, its architecture, and its evolution, and you have learned about Web servers, how they work, and how home pages on Web servers can be used to distribute information. You have also learned about some of the available Web publishing tools and how to use them to make Web publishing tasks easier to tackle. This chapter has also covered some common Web publishing issues and how you can use the Web to your advantage.

Before setting up a Web site, you need to select the proper hardware to host your Web server. The following chapter discusses the hardware platforms that are available to host a Windows NT–based Web server. Chapter 28, "Internet Information Server," discusses how you can set up an Internet server using the software supplied with Windows NT.

Choosing the Right Hardware for the Job

CHAPTER

22

The hardware you need for your Web site depends on the kinds of services you will be setting up on your Web server. When you're hosting a Web site, by far the most important performance factors are input/output performance and the amount of memory available apart from the bandwidth of your Internet connection.

This priority changes somewhat dramatically when you start getting 40 to 60 simultaneous users running Common Gateway Interface (CGI) applications. If these CGI programs query and update a database on your site, raw input/output performance and RAM aren't going to be enough. Although adding more memory will increase performance, you might need a powerful server to host your Web site. Therefore, when choosing your hardware, you need to think about the amount of traffic you expect your Web site to generate.

> **NOTE**
>
> Regardless of the hardware platform you use, make sure your Web server is on an NTFS partition. This enhances the performance of your Web server and provides better security. For security and performance reasons, you might want to set up your Web server on another hard disk (not just another partition on the same hard disk, but a different physical hard disk).

Platforms Suitable to Run NT

Although Windows NT runs on several hardware platforms, Intel is the most widely used hardware platform. Lately, however, Power PC–based and Digital Alpha–based servers have been gaining popularity because of their high performance. Tradeoffs are involved when you're choosing one platform over another. Depending on your current and anticipated needs, you need to choose the right server platform.

Choosing an Intel-Based Web Platform

Hosting your Web server on an Intel-based Web server might be the most practical solution for you. Intel-based servers are generally less expensive than Alpha-based or Power PC–based servers. If you don't need an extremely high-performance server, an Intel-based server will be fine for your needs. Often, the biggest bottleneck is the bandwidth of the line connecting you to the Internet. Therefore, unless you're thinking about burdening your Web server with other tasks that require a fair amount of processing time, an Intel-based server will be adequate. Another advantage to choosing an Intel-based Web server is that you can use the many applications written for Intel-based computers to develop your Web site.

> **TIP**
>
> If you'll be using an Intel-based Web server, it might be a good idea to buy one that supports Symmetric Multiprocessing (SMP). By investing in a server that supports SMP under Windows NT, if you outgrow your server, you can simply add another processor.
>
> Be sure to talk about Windows NT compatibility issues with your vendor when choosing an SMP server.

Choosing a Power PC–Based or DEC Alpha–Based Web Platform

Power PC and Alpha servers are clearly high-performance servers that can be used for other tasks in addition to hosting a Web site. If you're using your Web server for internal use (it's an easy way of distributing information), you do want a fast system. However, even if you're using it as a proxy server, you still want a fast system. A Web server on a Power PC–based or Alpha-based server will work well in the latter case.

On the downside, Power PC–based and Alpha-based servers generally require more RAM to run the same applications that run on an Intel-based server. Lack of software or delayed release of software is another drawback. Although this situation might change in the future, at the moment, most software vendors are focusing on Intel-based platforms.

> **NOTE**
>
> Although more and more applications are becoming available for non-Intel Windows NT platforms, support is still very limited. Make sure you're comfortable with the available software for the Windows NT platform you choose.

Hardware Requirements for Each Platform

Here are the minimum hardware requirements for a basic Windows NT–based Web server. Depending on whether you provide additional services, such as hosting a database or providing mail services, you might need more RAM or processing power.

Minimum Requirements for an Intel-Based Web Server

486 DX2/66 or better (Pentium recommended)

16M of RAM

Around 100M of free disk space on an NTFS partition

At least a 28.8 PPP (Point-to-Point Protocol) link to the Internet

UPS that supports Windows NT

CD-ROM drive

NOTE

With 16M of RAM, you can basically get by for a Web site. If, however, you're planning to run a few other applications or set up a database on your Web server, a RAM upgrade to 64M will make a tremendous difference.

TIP

You can boost the performance of your Web server by using more than one hard disk and by using a dual-channel Wide-SCSI card. By having Windows NT reside on one hard disk, your data files on another, and your applications on another, you can increase your server's performance. Also, when setting up swap file space, you can increase the performance of your server by splitting your swap files over two or more hard disks.

Minimum Hardware Requirements for an Alpha-Based or Power PC–Based Web Server

Any Alpha-based or Power PC–based server

32M of RAM

At least a 64/128Kbps ISDN link to the Internet

Around 100M of free disk space on an NTFS partition

CD-ROM drive

UPS that supports Windows NT

Price and Performance Issues

Although Power PC–based and Alpha-based Web servers are inherently more powerful than Intel-based servers, they tend to be more expensive. Unfortunately, most software vendors don't seem to port their NT software to non-Intel platforms. Therefore, the number of applications available for non-Intel platforms is limited. This lack of available software might be an issue if you'll be using the same machine to develop your Web site because tools for non-Intel platforms are limited. With the recent Microsoft-Digital alliance, however, and the development of an Intel emulator for the Alpha, the availability of software might change in the near future.

If you will be linking your Web site to a large database or are planing to use one server for other tasks, such as Microsoft Mail Server, a DHCP server, or a RAS server, in addition to hosting a Web server, then choosing a Power PC or an Alpha server makes sense. If not, your best bet would be an Intel-based server. Also, with the introduction of new Pentium Pro–based servers optimized for 32-bit operating systems, such as Windows NT, you can enjoy a higher level of performance from Intel-based servers.

NOTE

There's currently an Intel emulator for Alpha computers running Windows NT, but this emulator runs only Windows applications that don't require Windows to be run in 386-enhanced mode. In other words, the new 32-bit applications don't work with this emulator. In the near future, however, you can expect to see an Intel emulator that runs 32-bit Windows applications on an Alpha.

The Importance of a UPS

The importance of having an Uninterruptible Power Supply (UPS) can't be stressed enough when you're dealing with an operating system like Windows NT that will be serving up documents on the Web 24 hours a day. A sudden power failure in the middle of a disk read/write operation can be detrimental to your server's health. What's really bad about such an incident is that a file might get corrupted and you might never know about it until you need the file. Although NTFS has many safeguards to prevent such incidents from happening, you should never take a chance with your data. It's always wise to invest in a UPS that shuts down your server safely if there's an extended power outage. Depending on your hardware, you need to choose a UPS that's at least capable of providing power until Windows NT has enough time to shut down services and applications running on your server.

TIP

Be sure your UPS supports Windows NT. Although you can use the UPS applet that comes with Windows NT, many UPS vendors bundle software with added features that give you more control and flexibility.

Summary

This chapter has covered the hardware platforms that are suitable for hosting a Windows NT–based Web site. Although Alpha-based and Power PC–based platforms are high-performance server platforms, software for them is limited. Therefore, you might be more productive by choosing an Intel-based server to host your Web site.

The next chapter covers the software you need to host your Web site and shows you how to use available tools to simplify Web publishing.

What Software Do You Need?

IN THIS CHAPTER

CHAPTER 23

After you have chosen your hardware, it's time to select your Web server software and other tools to develop your Web site. Depending on the nature of the Web site you will be setting up, you need to first determine the features you need your Web server to support, and then you can select the Web server that best satisfies your needs.

Choosing Your Web Server

About two dozen Web servers are available for hosting a Windows NT–based Web site. Web servers support different features, and because their capabilities change frequently, this chapter doesn't cover their specific features. Instead, it gives you an overview of Web server features and which ones you should look for. This chapter also lists URLs of about two dozen Windows NT–based Web servers. You can get the most up-to-date features of available Web servers by visiting some of these URLs.

What to Look For in a Web Server

When choosing your Web server software, one of the most important considerations is how easy the Web server is to set up and administer. For example, the Netscape server uses forms to administer its aspects. By entering a user ID and a password, the Web site administrator can manage all aspects of the server from a remote location. This feature might be useful to you if you don't always have ready access to your Web server.

Another feature you should look for is the degree of security each server offers. The level of security you need depends on what you're using your server for. If your Web site isn't disclosing confidential information to those browsing your Web site, security isn't a major concern for you. When providing sensitive information over the Web, however, you should make sure it's encrypted by the Web server and then transmitted only through a secure medium. However, the server you choose should at least support restricting access to the part of your server with user names and passwords. With some Web servers, you can create user ID groups and assign permissions to users on a per-group basis. If you have a large user database, this feature will be very useful to you. Some Web servers can use the Windows NT user database to authenticate users who want to access certain areas of your Web site. This authentification feature is quite handy if you need to restrict access for particular parts of your Web site to users of your NT server. By restricting access based on the client's IP address, you can deny access to visitors browsing your Web site from other domains and countries, if you need to.

CAUTION

You should never judge your Web server's security based on the IP address of the Web client. There are ways to trick your Web server by misrepresenting the IP address from which the client is accessing your Web server. Before transmitting secure data, you should authenticate the user with a user ID and password by using a secure medium.

If you're using your Web server to distribute security-sensitive data, you should make sure it encrypts the data before transmitting it over the Web. This feature is especially important if you're transmitting or receiving valuable data like customer credit-card numbers. Your Web server should also give you control over *directory browsing*, which is the Web server's ability to list the contents of a directory when a URL is given without a filename, just a directory. If you want to make sure that Web surfers can get to certain pages only if they know a file's complete URL name, you should disable directory browsing. Otherwise, someone visiting your Web site can search your directory structure and get files you didn't intend anyone to have access to.

Support for CGI scripts is a definite must for a Web server. By using CGI scripts, you can interact with visitors browsing your Web site by providing dynamic content and immediately responding to user input. You should make sure your Web server offers CGI scripts with access to CGI environment variables and libraries. Some Web servers also give you an interface with Visual Basic programs. This feature could be useful if you're familiar with Visual Basic programming because you can use Visual Basic's power and simplicity to interact with those browsing your Web site.

NOTE

By using server-side includes, you can make information in your static HTML pages change based on variables. Server libraries and include files should not, however, be used often because they tax your Web server by making HTTP request processing take longer.

A few other features are standard for most Web servers, but you should make sure your Web server supports these features. After you host a Web site for a while, you'll notice that your Web server's log file keeps getting bigger and bigger. This file logs all your Web server accesses; it records who accessed what from your Web server and when they accessed it. Many different log file–analyzing programs are available. To use most of them, you should make sure your Web server generates logs in CERN/NCSA common log format. Having a way to automatically archive log files is another plus. This feature renames the current log file, creates a new log file, and then starts logging Web server accesses again to the new log file.

TIP

Depending on the number of hits your Web site gets, you should recycle your log file about once a week. Old log files should be archived for future reference.

Last, but not least, is the price of the Web server. Currently, about two dozen Web servers are available that will run on Windows NT. Some are free and, in most cases, will meet your needs. If, however, you're very concerned about security and performance, you might want to get a commercial Web server that will suit your needs better. Here's a summary of the features you should look for when choosing a Web server:

- The Web server generates logs in CERN/NCSA common log format.
- The server includes performance measurement logs and tools.
- The server can be configured to prohibit access by domain name and IP address.
- Access can be controlled by requiring a password based on user IDs and user groups.
- Access to data hierarchies can be configured based on the IP address of the client accessing the Web site.
- The server supports server-side includes.
- The server supports directory browsing.
- CGI scripts have access to all CGI environment variables.
- Easy setup and administration are available through a GUI.
- The server can be administered while it is running.
- The server can be administered remotely.
- The server can serve different directory roots based on the client's IP address.
- The server offers automatic archival of log files.

NOTE

The support provided by free Web servers is limited if you run into a problem. If quick, easy support is a must for you, consider using a commercial Web server.

Following is a list of Web servers for Windows NT. Because their features change so rapidly, they aren't covered in this chapter. Instead, by visiting the Web sites listed here, you can find the most up-to-date information.

WWW Server	For More Information
Alibaba	http://www.csm.co.at/csm/
Commerce Builder	http://www.aristosoft.com/ifact/inet.htm
Communications Builder	http://www.aristosoft.com/ifact/inet.htm
Folio Infobase	http://www.folio.com/
FolkWeb	http://www.ilar.com/folkweb.htm
HTTPS	http://emwac.ed.ac.uk/html/internet_toolchest/https/ ➡contents.htm
Internet Office Web Server	http://server.spry.com/
NaviServer	http://www.navisoft.com/products/server/server.htm
NetPublisher	http://netpub.notis.com/
Netscape Commerce	http://www.netscape.com/comprod/netscape_commerce.html
Netscape Communications	http://www.netscape.com/comprod/netscape_commun.html
PowerWeb	http://www.cyberpi.com
Purveyor	http://www.process.com/prod/purveyor.htp
SAIC	http://wwwserver.itl.saic.com/
SuperWeb Server	http://www.frontiertech.com
Web Commander	http://www.flicks.com./homepage.htm
WebBase	http://www.webbase.com/
WebNotes	http://webnotes.ostech.com/
WebSite	http://website.ora.com/

> **TIP**
>
> If you find any mailing lists that have been set up to discuss issues about the Web server you're using, you should add your name to them. By joining these mailing lists, you can learn more about hosting a Web site. Also, if you have a question, you can ask for help and get answers. Windows NT mailing lists are discussed in Chapter 29, "Windows NT Resources on the Internet."

Web Site Development Tools

The following sections list some tools you can use to simplify your Web publishing tasks.

LView Pro

LView Pro is a very handy graphics manipulation program. You can use it to handle virtually all your basic graphics manipulation tasks. You can get LView Pro from this site:

```
http://world.std.com/~mmedia/lviewp.html
```

Giftrans

Giftrans is a graphics file manipulation program that can be used to make backgrounds of .GIF files transparent and to save them as "interlaced" .GIF files. Visit this site to get Giftrans:

```
http://melmac.harris-atd.com/files/giftrans.exe
```

Map Edit

Map Edit is useful when you want to create an image map for one of your pages. An *image map* is a graphic with "hot spots." Image maps allow you to send different pages to a Web client, depending on where on the image the user clicks the mouse. You can get Map Edit from this site:

```
ftp://ftp.mcp.com/pub/software/Internet/mapedit.zip
```

Color Manipulation Device

Color Manipulation Device is a helpful utility for choosing background and text colors. By using this program, you can find out the HTML tag you need to get a certain background and text color. If you're confused about RGB color values, you can use this program to take the mystery out of things because you can just pick any color you want and assign it to a text element. You can get Color Manipulation Device from this site:

```
http://www.meat.com/software/cmd.html
```

Programmer's File Editor

This is a handy program that can be used for many tasks. You might find Programmer's File Editor useful when you're editing large files, and it's a great substitute for Windows Notepad. Programmer's File Editor can be downloaded from one of these sites:

```
Intel:        ftp://ftp.csusm.edu/pub/winworld/nt/pfe0602i.zip
Power PC:     ftp://ftp.csusm.edu/pub/winworld/nt/pfe0602p.zip
```

HTML Editors

Although it's possible to insert HTML tags manually, this method is too time-consuming for large projects. Listed next are a few HTML editors that will make inserting HTML tags easy. You might want to try a few and pick the one you like the best.

```
Arachnid          http://bcpub.com/software/arachnid.zip
HTML Easy         http://www.seed.net.tw/~milkylin/heasy13.zip
HTML Edit         http://www.ist.ca/~peterc/htmled12.zip
HTML Notepad      http://bcpub.com/software/htmln119.zip
Hypertext Master  ftp://ftp.tcp.co.uk/pub/ibmpc/windows/utils/htmled24.zip
Web Edit          http://wwwnt.thegroup.net/webedit/webedit.zip
```

Internet Assistant for Microsoft Word

Internet Assistant for Microsoft Word is a useful application when it comes to adding a large number of Microsoft Word files to your Web server. Although earlier versions of Internet Assistant lacked many features, the new versions have many added features that make Web publishing easier. For example, the current version supports document backgrounds, tables, inline images, and various font attributes. Visit this site to get Internet Assistant for Microsoft Word free of charge:

```
http://www.microsoft.com/word/fs_wd.htm
```

> **NOTE**
>
> Internet Assistant for Microsoft Word is ideal for editing files saved in standard HTML. However, it might not handle enhancements to HTML that well. Before loading a file containing HTML enhancements to Internet Assistant for Microsoft Word and saving your changes, you might want to make a backup copy of the file. If your HTML files contain standard HTML, you don't need to do this.

HoTMetaL Pro

HoTMetaL Pro is a feature-rich HTML editor with a built-in thesaurus and spell checker. When compared with other HTML editors, HoTMetaL Pro has one major difference—it makes sure that whatever you create with it conforms to standard HTML so your Web pages are rendered properly by all Web browsers. HoTMetaL Pro is an upgrade to a shareware version of the software called HoTMetaL, which is available on many online services, at Web sites, and from the vendor.

As you can see in Figure 23.1, HoTMetaL marks HTML tags with special tags so that they're clearly visible when you edit HTML files. On the downside, HoTMetaL Pro makes it hard to create files with HTML enhancements. A new version of HoTMetaL Pro will be released by the time you read this book. Therefore, you might want to visit the following URL for the most up-to-date information about HoTMetaL Pro:

```
http://www.sq.com/
```

FIGURE 23.1.

HoTMetaL marks HTML tags with special symbols when files are edited.

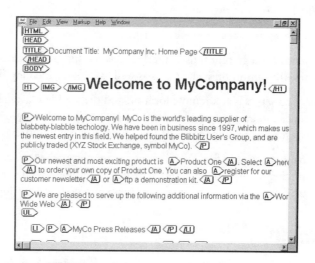

Log File-Analyzing Tools

To get statistics about your Web server, you need to analyze its log file. Although some Web servers come with utilities to analyze log files, you can get more information about Web server statistics by using different programs. Listed next are two Web server log-analyzing tools you can use. By using a spreadsheet application like Excel, you can create a table like the one shown in Figure 23.2 by using the output of one of these log-analyzing programs.

```
Analyze      http://www.net-shopper.co.uk/software/nt/analyse/index.htm
WebStat      http://www.huntana.com/webstat/index.html
```

FIGURE 23.2.

Using the output of a Web server log-analyzing program to generate Web server statistics with Excel.

For The Week Of	# New Hosts	# Repeat Visits	# Requests Served
07-Aug-95	8	12	445
14-Aug-95	189	248	5594
21-Aug-95	102	140	2995
28-Aug-95	109	152	3538
04-Sep-95	165	193	4534
11-Sep-95	301	356	8817
18-Sep-95	228	297	8196
25-Sep-95	276	321	7480
02-Oct-95	104	130	3670

WebTrends

Both log-analyzing programs listed in the preceding section have command-line user interfaces. If you'd rather use one program to analyze your Web server's log file, create graphs, and supply other statistics, you should give WebTrends a try. WebTrends can be used to analyze your log file and provide useful statistics about your Web site. If you have disabled DNS lookups on your server, WebTrends will also perform DNS lookups while analyzing the log file. You can get WebTrends from this site:

```
http://www.egsoftware.com/webtrend.htm
```

WebTrends has a graphical user interface. Using this GUI, you can specify several options to customize the output of WebTrends as well as define which log files to analyze.

If your Web server is at a remote location and the log file is available through HTTP or FTP, WebTrends can be configured to retrieve the log file and analyze its content. WebTrends also has a way for you to enter a user ID and password if you retrieve the log file by using FTP.

After analyzing the log file, WebTrends creates comprehensive tables and graphics charts. By analyzing them, you can get access statistics about your Web site. About a dozen graphs and tables are created after WebTrends analyzes your Web server's log file.

Summary

This chapter has covered Web servers that are available to host Windows NT–based Web sites and what features you should look for when selecting a Web server. After analyzing your needs, you should be able to list all the features you need when you shop for a Web server. This chapter has also covered some Windows NT tools you can use to create an outstanding Web site in the least amount of time possible. You have also learned how to analyze your Web server's access log file to create statistical tables and charts.

The next chapter covers ways of connecting your Web server to the Internet; it will help you analyze your needs and choose the right Internet connection for your Web site. If you can't afford a high-speed Internet link just yet, you will also learn how to use the services of a Web space provider and host your Web site by using a regular 28.8 POTS (Plain Old Telephone Service) link to the Internet.

Getting Your Lines Right: ISDN, POTS, and Service Providers

IN THIS CHAPTER

This chapter gives you an overview of Internet connection types and how to choose the best type based on your needs, as well as factors such as availability and affordability. By reading about connection types and how to get the most from a POTS link, you can make the best use of the Internet link you select.

Examining the Bandwidths of Connection Lines

Most likely, your Web server's biggest bottleneck is the limited bandwidth of your Internet connection. If possible, you should go with at least an *Integrated Services Digital Network* (ISDN) link to the Internet. As the chart in Figure 24.1 shows, even a basic, single B channel ISDN line is several times faster than a 28.8Kbps POTS (plain old telephone service) link.

FIGURE 24.1.

ISDN Internet links have a higher bandwidth than POTS Internet links.

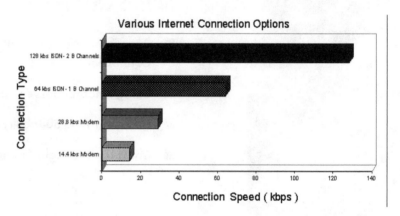

Another reason for using an ISDN link is that it doesn't need to be up all day for your Internet link; you use the line only when data is transferred, so you can disconnect when the line isn't in use. This is practical with ISDN lines because of their fast call setup and tear-down times—typically, about one second. On the other hand, as you can see in Figure 24.2, a POTS link usually takes more than 30 seconds to establish a call.

FIGURE 24.2.

ISDN connect/ disconnect speeds are faster than POTS connect/disconnect speeds.

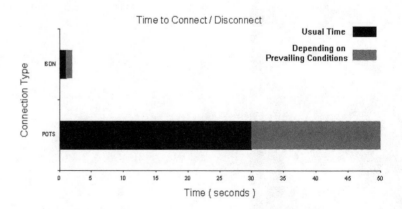

If you will be starting out with a 28.8Kbps POTS link to the Internet, you shouldn't get carried away with too many graphics. If you do have a few graphics and you start getting more and more hits, your Web surfers might become frustrated with the slow data-transfer rates of your Web server. You can solve this problem with a very low-cost solution: Simply find a Webspace provider with a fast link to the Internet (T1 or T3) who rents out space on a Web server. This service is inexpensive; it usually is less than $20 a month. Then, you just move all your graphics files to this Web server. In your page, you can call the graphics files on the other Web server instead of the graphics on your own server. This method can make a significant difference, because you will be providing only HTML files to clients who access your server. They will go to the other server for all your inline graphics and other objects. This method frees up your relatively limited Internet bandwidth for transmitting plain-text HTML files and processing and responding to user input that interacts with a database on your server. If you're looking for such a location to store your graphics files, you might want to check out this URL:

```
http://www.Four11.com
```

You might be able to find similar Webspace providers locally in your area.

Using Another Server

As you just learned, you can use another server to store all your graphics and other non-text objects if all you can afford right now is a POTS link to the Internet. Suppose that you have a local inline image called WindowsNT.GIF with this HTML tag:

```
<img src="/graphics/icons/WindowsNT.gif">
```

You can free up your bandwidth for this graphic by moving WindowsNT.GIF to another server (for example, www.server.com) and changing the HTML tag to this:

```
<img src="http://www.server.com/graphics/icons/WindowsNT.gif">
```

You can conserve your bandwidth by following the tip in the preceding section, because HTTP is a connectionless protocol. Therefore, after a connection is made for the Web page, the page is transmitted and the connection to your server is closed. Subsequently, for inline images and objects on the page, the Web browser goes to the other Web server.

24

GETTING YOUR LINES RIGHT

Evaluating the Suitability of Lines

Obviously, a POTS link is suitable only for limited Web traffic. By using another server to store your graphics files, you can get the maximum from your POTS link by using it only for transmitting HTML text files. As you get more hits and the data on your pages increases, however, a POTS link might not be enough. In this case, you might need to consider an alternative, such as ISDN.

Although ISDN has been around for a while, it's still not as widely used as it should be. ISDN technology has a lot of potential. At the time of this writing, maintaining a 24-hour link to the Internet with a single-channel ISDN link (64Kbps) can cost as much as $650 or as little as $50 for the ISDN line, depending on the telephone company. On top of the phone company's charges, you need to add in the *Internet Service Provider* (ISP) charges. You might want to call your local phone company and consider what its rates are and what you get in return before going with ISDN.

If ISDN and POTS aren't suitable for you, you have a third option for Internet access. You might be able to get a much better deal if your local cable company provides Internet services in your area. Because of the nature of the cable carrying your data, by choosing a cable-based Internet connection, you typically get a bandwidth of more than 4Mbps! A cable connection to the Internet gives you a bandwidth that is as much as 350 times faster than a 28.8Kbps dial-up modem connection. For more information about a cable-based Internet access provider, you might want to visit this URL:

```
http://www.tci.east-lansing.mi.us/metshome.htm
```

Choosing the Right Connection

Choosing the right Internet connection is an equation that depends on several variables, such as your bandwidth requirements, expected Web traffic, availability and cost of ISDN in your area, and, of course, your budget for the Internet link.

Recently, cable companies have been exploring the possibility of providing Internet service. If ISDN prices seem to be too high or unreasonable for you, you might want to check with your local cable company to see whether it offers Internet service or whether it plans to do so. The bandwidth your cable company can give you is much greater than what ISDN offers. If cable companies realize the potential of providing Internet services at a reasonable cost, everyone can afford high-speed Internet links, which will make the Internet a much nicer place to live!

Summary

In this chapter, you have learned about choosing an Internet link for your Web site. You now should be able to select the Internet link that best suits you—depending on your needs, budget, and the Internet links available in your area. This chapter has given you an introduction to Internet connection types and an outline of their capabilities and drawbacks. Because many companies can't afford a high-speed Internet link, you have also learned how to use a secondary Web server to get the most out of a POTS link. Finally, you have reviewed the Internet connection types, evaluated their suitability, and learned how you can choose the right Internet connection to meet your needs.

The next chapter reviews several Web-publishing tools. You can use many Windows NT Web-publishing tools to make publishing on the Web easier. By using the applications outlined in that chapter, you'll be able to create an outstanding Windows NT–based Web site.

24

GETTING YOUR
LINES RIGHT

Putting Your Pages Together: HTML Tools

IN THIS CHAPTER

This chapter gives you an overview of tools that can be used to design your Web site. You will be shown how to use these tools to add special effects to your graphics and convert them to different formats. Learning which graphics formats are suitable for different tasks helps you take advantage of the formats' features. If you use the tools and tips in this chapter, you will have an outstanding Web site that's optimized for distributing information on the Internet.

HTML tags, their syntaxes, and how they are used are topics beyond the scope of this chapter. Instead of discussing such details, this chapter supplies Web sites where you can find more information; you should also refer to Chapter 23, "What Software Do You Need?," to find out where you can locate the tools covered in this chapter.

HTML Resources on the Web

In case you aren't very familiar with HTML, here are a few Web sites containing information about HTML. By visiting them, you can familiarize yourself with HTML tags and how they can be used.

HTML Reference Manual:

http://www.sandia.gov/sci_compute/html_ref.html

The Bare Bones Guide to HTML:

http://werbach.com/barebones/

A Beginner's Guide to URLs:

http://www.ncsa.uiuc.edu/demoWeb/url-primer.html

A Beginner's Guide to HTML:

http://www.ncsa.uiuc.edu/General/Internet/WWW/HTMLPrimer.html

The Structure of HTML 3.0 Documents:

http://www.w3.org/pub/WWW/MarkUp/html3/overview.html

HTML Writers Guild List of HTML Resources:

http://Webwww.hwg.org/resources/html/

Web Publishing Issues

When publishing information on the Web, keep in mind that your audience often has a short attention span. For some people, browsing Web sites is like channel surfing for a good TV program—the only difference is that the remote control is replaced by the mouse. Even though large graphics might look nice when you view them locally, remember that not everyone has high-speed connections to the Internet. You should use the content of your Web site to captivate your audience; however, adding a few small graphics as "eye candy" won't hurt if they can be viewed easily by someone using a 14.4 modem.

You should also make it easy for users to give you feedback or comments. People visiting your Web site might get frustrated when they have questions or comments but no way of e-mailing this feedback to you. It's a good idea to have a button bar or a standard set of selections at the bottom or top of each page; one of them should be a link to a feedback page. You will be shown how to set up an e-mail feedback form in Chapter 27, "Making Your Web Site Interactive." This form allows users browsing your Web site to answer questions on your feedback form and e-mail their comments to you.

Not Everyone Uses Netscape...

Although *Netscapisms* (or "Netscape enhancements to HTML") might look nice, not everyone uses Netscape. Other browsers can make your pages look entirely different from the way they look with Netscape. However, by following proper HTML coding standards, you can make sure that no matter what browser is used, your page will look the way you intended it to.

If you use Netscape enhancements and discover that your pages look bad when viewed with another browser, but you really want to use Netscape enhancements, you can create two sets of pages—one for Netscape and one for other browsers. If you have just a few pages and are concerned about the appearance of your Web site, this might be practical; however, it's not practical for a large Web site. In Chapter 27, you will be shown how to use a simple CGI program to offer a customized Web page based on the browser used to access your Web site. Because this example provides the program's source code, you will also learn the basics of writing CGI programs.

Optimizing Graphics by Reducing the Number of Colors

Graphics saved in the .GIF format can have up to 256 colors. However, unless you have a photograph saved in .GIF format, you probably aren't using all 256 colors. Chances are you can use only a fraction of them and still have your graphic look remarkably similar to the original file. By reducing the number of colors used in a graphic, you can actually reduce the file size by as much as 40 percent, depending on the graphic. To reduce the number of colors, experiment with different amounts of colors until your graphic looks almost identical to the original. Reducing the number of colors to 24 or 32 yields a workable combination of a smaller file size and good graphic quality. By using LView Pro, you can reduce the number of colors in your .GIF files by choosing Retouch | Color depth; then select the options "Palette image" and "Custom number of colors," and enter a value like 24, as shown in Figure 25.1.

FIGURE 25.1.

Reducing the number of colors to make .GIF files smaller.

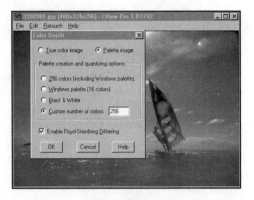

TIP

If the image doesn't look like the original after you enter a number, you can choose Edit | Undo and try again with a few more colors.

You might wonder why you should go to all this trouble to reduce your graphics files by just a few kilobytes. Although the reduction of each file might not be that much, the kilobytes add up when you have more than one graphic on a page and more than one person accessing your Web site at the same time. People with slow links to the Internet will appreciate the small graphics sizes.

Limiting Graphics File Sizes

Make sure the images on your Web site are as small as possible. If you have large graphics files, users with slow modem links might get frustrated and leave your Web site. After all the work you've put into setting up your Web site, you don't want that to happen. If you need to have large graphics files, you should let the user decide if he or she wants to see them. This could be done by just showing a "thumbnail" representation of the graphic file that the user can click on to see the full picture.

Keeping your graphics small makes them load faster. In particular, try to limit the graphic's height. Vertical space is "golden" on a Web page, quite apart from loading speed. When users look at your Web pages, they generally expect to see some information. It might look rather unappealing if most of their screen is taken up by a large graphics file that takes several seconds to load.

> **TIP**
>
> After you have designed your Web site, be sure to look at your pages on a monitor set to a resolution of 640 × 480 with 256 colors. If you designed your pages correctly, users should still be able to see all the information without using the horizontal scroll bar. Remember that not everyone has high-resolution super VGA monitors!

You can make your graphics files load faster by defining the graphic's dimensions in the HTML tag so that the browser can map around it and load the text before the image. For example, if you have an inline image called DEMO.GIF, you should find the dimensions of the image and include this data in the HTML tag as follows:

```
<IMG SRC="/graphics/icons/ WonderlandNewIcon.gif"
    height=125 width=325 border=0 ALT= "Demonstration Graphic" >
```

> **TIP**
>
> You should always use the ALT tag and give a short description of your image, so that if someone browsing your Web site has "turned off" automatic display of images, they will see a description of the graphics file instead of just an icon with a graphic. Your Lynx users will also appreciate letting them know what they are missing! (Lynx is a nongraphical, text-based Web browser.)

You can use almost any shareware or commercial graphics manipulation application to find out the dimensions of your graphics. A handy graphics manipulation utility called LView Pro is used for this example. If you load a graphic in LView Pro as shown in Figure 25.2, you can see the image's dimensions on the application's title bar. You can get the latest version of LView Pro from this site:

```
http://world.std.com/~mmedia/lviewp.html
```

> **TIP**
>
> Specifying the graphic's dimensions gives users the impression that pages at your Web site load faster because they can start reading the text before all the graphics are displayed. Specifying the dimensions also allows users to scroll a page before all the images are loaded.

FIGURE 25.2.

The graphic's dimensions are shown on LView Pro's title bar.

Using Graphics Formats

In addition to making graphics smaller, reducing the number of colors, and specifying dimensions of graphics in HTML tags, you can further optimize graphics at your Web site by using different file formats. Two of the most commonly used formats are .GIF and .JPEG. By knowing their strengths and weaknesses, you can use these two formats judiciously and optimize graphics at your Web site. The following sections explain how to enhance graphics at your Web site and when to use each format.

Using Interlacing

If you have photographs at your Web site stored in the .GIF format, it's a good idea to interlace them. What is *interlacing*? You might have noticed how some graphics on Web sites appear in bands. First the graphic looks out of focus, then gets clearer and more focused as more data about it is sent to the Web browser. Adding this effect to a .GIF file is called "interlacing."

To save .GIF files as interlaced files, first load the file into LView Pro, then choose File | Properties, select the ".gif" crosstab, and make sure that "save Interlaced" is checked. Next, when you save your file, be sure to save it as a "gif89a" file.

> **TIP**
>
> Interlacing photographs at your Web site lets someone who's not interested in the entire picture to go to another page, rather than wait for the whole picture to load. You can use the interlace feature only on graphics stored in the .GIF format.

NOTE

Be careful when using interlaced .GIF files. Even though interlacing makes your graphics look "neat," interlaced .GIF files are larger than non-interlaced ones and generally take longer to display, especially if the user's computer has a relatively slow processor. So don't get carried away with interlacing and interlace all the .GIF files at your Web site! Interlacing is a useful tool, but you should use it for the right job. Generally, interlacing should be used when displaying photographs because you can guess what the final photograph will look like from the interlaced file's early rendering. The same is not true for .GIF files that contain text.

Creating Invisible Backgrounds

You can give your Web site a professional look by making the backgrounds of .GIF files transparent. With this effect, when someone looks at your graphic with a browser, the graphic's background becomes the browser's background color. This gives the impression that the graphic is floating in the background, which adds a sophisticated touch to your graphic. You can make a particular background color of your .GIF files transparent by using a utility program called giftrans, along with LView Pro.

Although you can create a similar effect by changing the graphic's background color to the default background color of a browser like Netscape, as soon as someone changes the default color or looks at your Web site using a browser with a different background color, your image no longer seems to be floating in the background.

TIP

.GIF files of photographs aren't suitable for making a certain background color invisible unless the background color doesn't appear anywhere in the photograph. Photographs are usually very rich in colors and a .GIF file can have only 256 colors, so it's a good bet that the background color is used somewhere else in the photograph. Consequently, if you make that color "invisible," it's going to make the photograph look bad because parts of it will be invisible. If this happened in a photograph of a person, it could make him or her look like an alien! However, if a .GIF file's background color is distinctly different from other colors in the graphic, you will have more luck making the photograph's background transparent.

It's very simple to make a background color of a .GIF file invisible. As you can see in Figure 25.3, the graphic's background color is white, so it stands out against the Web browser's background color. If you make the white background of the image transparent, then all you'll see is the text "Having Fun With Windows NT!"

FIGURE 25.3.

The original graphic with white background when viewed with Netscape.

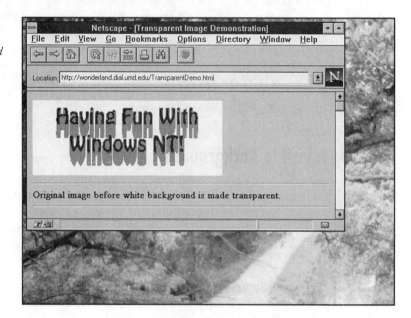

To make a color transparent, first load the .GIF file into LView Pro. Next, you need to determine the "index color" that's been used for the image's background. To do this, choose Options | Background Color. You then see a color chart, shown in Figure 25.4. Since you need to find the index color of the background, you have to mask out everything but the background color. Click the "Mask selection using" checkbox and select Black. Now when you click on a color in the color palette, every other color in the graphic is shaded in black. For example, there's no red in the graphic (it's a grayscale graphic), so if you click on red, the whole image is shaded in black. However, if you click on white in the color palette, everything but the background is shaded in black. As you can see in Figure 25.4, this color has an index value of 215. You need to remember this index value because you will be using it shortly.

After finding the index value of the background color, you can use giftrans to make the image's background color invisible. Although there are many command line switches for giftrans, this is the syntax to make a background color invisible:

```
giftrans -t <index value of background color> <original filename> > <new filename>
```

For example, since the background color's index value is 215, the original file is called `original.gif`, and the new file will be called `new.gif`, use the following command:

```
giftrans -t 215 original.gif > new.gif
```

FIGURE 25.4.

Determining the index value of the background color.

TIP

You can save time hunting for utility programs on your hard disk by creating a subdirectory called "utilities," adding this directory to your path, and storing all utility programs, like giftrans, in this directory. Then, whenever you need to use a utility program, you can just type its name without worrying about where you put the application.

As you can see in Figure 25.5, when you view the graphic with Netscape after making the background invisible, the graphic's background is the same color as the browser's background color.

Choosing the Best Graphic Format for Photographs

When displaying photographs at your Web site, you should convert your pictures to .JPEG (pronounced "jay-peg") format, which is a standardized image compression mechanism. *JPEG* stands for Joint Photographic Experts Group, the original name of the committee that wrote the standard. You can save a file in JPEG format by choosing File | Save As, then selecting ".jpg" as the file format in LView Pro.

25

FIGURE 25.5.

The original graphic with transparent background when viewed with Netscape.

TIP

Although most Web browsers can display .JPEG files, a few browsers can't. Therefore, you should make an identical file in the .GIF format available for viewing in case a Web browser doesn't support .JPEG format graphics. However, almost all Web browsers used today support the .JPEG format.

The .JPEG format can be used to compress color or grayscale images. .JPEG compression works best when the image being converted has "natural colors," so it works well on photographs, naturalistic artwork, and similar material. However, .JPEG is a poor choice for any graphic containing letters, cartoons, sharp edges, or line drawings. Since you typically gain a 4:1 compression ratio with .JPEG, as opposed to .GIF, your images are much smaller, which is a great advantage when they have to be transmitted over the Internet. Web surfers with slow Internet links appreciate the small file sizes.

NOTE

You should never convert a cartoon or line art image to .JPEG format because the resulting image is often much bigger than the original! The same is true for images containing letters because .JPEG has a hard time compressing graphics files that have sharp edges.

.JPEG image compression is *lossy*, which means that the resulting image isn't exactly the same as the original image. The human eye has some limitations, and .JPEG image compression is designed to take advantage of these limitations. Since the human eye perceives color differences less accurately than differences in brightness, .JPEG images exploits a limitation in how people perceive images.

> **TIP**
>
> By using .JPEG, your graphics can be in 24-bit color instead of the 8-bit color used in the .GIF format, which supports only 256 colors. On the other hand, .JPEG supports up to 16.7 million colors.

Choosing Colors with Color Manipulation Device

You can use Color Manipulation Device (CMD) to determine colors for the text elements of your Web pages. By using CMD, you can pick the colors you want and assign them to text elements, as shown in Figure 25.6. After picking your colors, you can simply copy them to the Clipboard and paste the HTML tag to a Web page.

FIGURE 25.6.

You can easily pick text element and background colors with the Color Manipulation Device.

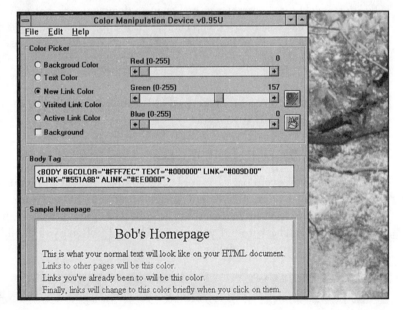

Finding Web Page Publishing Tools on the Web

Listed below are a few Web publishing tools found on the Web that might be helpful when you're setting up Web pages. You can add these tools to the bookmark file of your favorite Web browser for future reference. The tools listed in the following sections are available free of charge on the Web.

Checking for Correct HTML

If you want to make sure your Web pages conform to a certain HTML standard, such as HTML 2.0/3.0, use an HTML validating program to check your Web site, such as one of those listed here:

```
Weblint                              http://www.unipress.com/cgi-bin/WWWeblintWeb
A Kinder, Gentler HTML Validator     http://ugWeb.cs.ualberta.ca/~gerald/
validate.cgi
Doctor HTML                          http://imagiware.com/RxHTML.cgi
WebTechs HTML Validation Service     http://www.Webtechs.com/html-val-svc/
```

> **NOTE**
>
> Don't worry if you get a lot of error messages for one of your Web pages. The HTML validator might misinterpret something you were doing correctly because some validators (especially public domain ones) can't handle all usages. Also, if you have used Netscape or Internet Explorer enhancements that aren't part of standard HTML, they will be flagged by the HTML validator.

By checking your Web pages for correct HTML, you can increase the consistency and quality of the HTML documents at your site.

Online Web Page Color Selector

If you want to change your page's text or background colors, but are confused about what color is represented by a certain RGB (red, green, blue) value, Color Selector Page at `http://catless.ncl.ac.uk/Lindsay/colours.html` can be a useful tool. By using a form to select colors for your text and background, you can see which HTML tag you should use and what your combination of colors will look like.

> **TIP**
>
> If you find yourself using this tool frequently to find RGB color values for your HTML tags, you might want to get a copy of Color Manipulation Device, described in Chapter 23.

Summary

This chapter has covered Windows NT utilities and tools that can be used when designing your Web site. By using these tools, you can tackle virtually any Web publishing task. You can also give your Web site a professional touch by adding special effects to your graphics, such as interlacing them and making their backgrounds transparent. This chapter has also covered different graphics file formats and how they are used.

The next chapter covers Web site maintenance and legal issues you should be concerned about when providing information on the Internet.

Maintaining Your Web Site

CHAPTER 26

After setting up a Web site, you need to maintain it and keep it up-to-date. This chapter covers maintenance and legal issues you should know about when providing information on the Web. You will also be shown how to make your Web site visible for users doing Internet searches by registering your Web site with Internet search engines and Web site databases.

Web Site Maintenance Issues

Once you have your Web site up and running, you should take a few steps to make sure that people visiting your Web site return for more information. If you followed the guidelines and suggestions given in previous chapters, you should already have a user-friendly Web site. However, you can do other things to make your Web site outstanding.

Even though your Web site's contents are the most important factor, you need to pay some attention to the appearance of the information you're presenting to the viewer. It's always a good idea to look at your Web site with more than one browser to make sure your pages look the way you intended them to look. Sometimes a page that looks absolutely fabulous with the latest version of Netscape might look quite unattractive when viewed with another Web browser.

Think of your Web site as a channel in a large cable network. The cable network is, of course, the Web, and the remote control is simply replaced by the mouse. When users can't find the information they're looking for or get frustrated with large graphics that take forever to load with a slow modem link, they will just change the channel (or visit another Web site).

Keeping the Information Up-To-Date

By its very nature, information on the Web is expected to be as current as possible. In the past, information needed to be prepared and sent to a publisher before it could be distributed; this was often a lengthy process. However, on the Web, as soon as information is ready, it can be distributed to a large audience. You should take advantage of this by making sure the information at your Web site is up-to-date.

TIP

It's a good idea to maintain a log of additions and changes you make to your Web site so that visitors can find out when information was added, modified, and so forth.

Registering with Internet Search Engines and Databases

One of the best ways to advertise your new Web site is to register it with Internet databases and online search engines. By registering your Web site, those who are interested in its contents can find it easily. Registering services are usually free.

> **TIP**
>
> When registering your Web pages, be sure to register only pages or links that won't be changed in the future. If you have set up temporary links at your Web site, don't register them. Also, be sure to keep any URLs (Uniform Resource Locators) you register the same. By keeping the URL names constant, those who are interested in the contents of your Web site can find it by doing a search.

To add your Web site to WWW search engines, you need to register your URLs with some databases; several are listed below. It's always best to register your site with as many search engines as you can so that your Web site is visible to as many Web surfers as possible.

```
Yahoo!                     http://www.yahoo.com/bin/add
WebCrawler                 http://webcrawler.com/WebCrawler/SubmitURLS.html
Starting Point             http://www.stpt.com/util/submit.html
Infoseek                   http://www2.infoseek.com/doc/help/AddingSites.html
Galaxy                     http://galaxy.einet.net/cgi-bin/annotate?Other
Whole Internet Catalog     http://gnn.com/gnn/forms/comments.html
Apollo                     http://apollo.co.uk/
Pronet                     http://www.pronett.com/member/goldlink.htm
The Huge List              http://thehugelist.com/addurl.html
New Rider's WWW YP         http://www.mcp.com/newriders/wwwyp/submit.html
Nerd World Media           http://www.nerdworld.com/nwadd.html
```

If you want to submit URLs of your Web site to more than one WWW search database, you might want to visit "Submit It!" at `http://www.submit-it.com/`. "Submit It!" allows you to fill in some information about the URL you're submitting and use the same information to submit your URL to more than one search database.

Legalities: What You Should Know About Providing Information

When setting up a Web site, you should be aware of certain legalities. By following a few guidelines, you can avoid unnecessary legal problems. The first thing to remember is that normal copyright laws do indeed apply to the Web. Copyright laws don't change just because the method of information distribution changes. If you own a copyright on something, you can publish it on the Web, and if others misuse your work, you can take legal action—they're as guilty as though they'd done the same thing in a non-electronic medium.

You should be concerned about copyright laws when designing your Web site and making information available to the public. The goal of the WWW and the Internet is to make information readily available to those who need it. On the other hand, copyright law is designed to restrict access and use of information to a certain degree. Therefore, there's a conflict between the intentions of copyright law and the spirit of the Internet. However, copyright law is part of the law, and the spirit of the Internet isn't. Make sure your Web site complies with copyright law.

It's also a good idea to have a link to a disclaimer page at your Web site, which states that your company (or client) is not endorsing any product or other company; instead, the links are meant for informational purposes and to explore the Web. Therefore, if someone doesn't like what you've linked to (even though you're not responsible for the content at the other end of the link), he or she can't complain to you about it or take legal action against you.

You should also be careful about using graphics that are trademarks of organizations mentioned in your Web pages. If you want to use such a graphic, make sure you get permission first. You can get permission to use a graphic simply by asking the Webmaster of the site that has the graphics you want to use.

> **TIP**
>
> If you're concerned about your work, you can register it with the Copyright Office for a small fee. Furthermore, you should also include a copyright symbol © in your work. You can insert the copyright symbol by using © in your Web pages.

Downloading graphics from other sites and adding them to your own pages can also get you in legal trouble. If you'd like to use a graphic from another site, e-mail and ask for permission. If you can't get permission from that particular site, you can visit one of the public graphics archives or icon collections and get all the graphics you need.

Here are some icon collections available on the Internet:

- `http://www.infi.net/~rdralph/icons/`
- `http://www.meat.com/textures/`
- `http://www.cs.yale.edu/homes/sjl/clipart.html`
- `http://www.yahoo.com/Computers/World_Wide_Web/Programming/Icons`
- `http://www.sfsu.edu/~jtolson/textures/textures.htm`
- `http://www.stars.com/Vlib/Providers/Images_and_Icons.html`

26

> **TIP**
>
> Ask nicely! If you need to use some information or a graphic from another Web site, ask for permission to use it. As long as the information is not too proprietary, chances are you'll be given permission to use it.

Of course, you should also avoid issues that are illegal in the real world, such as slander, libel, or child pornography. Even though the electronic medium of the Web might seem different from the real world, keep in mind that some things are illegal no matter what medium you're using. For more information about copyright law, visit the following URL:

```
http://www.law.indiana.edu/law/lawindex.html
```

Summary

This chapter has covered issues that need to be addressed when providing information on the Internet, such as copyright laws and how they affect the information you provide on your Web site. By following the advice in this chapter, you can make sure your Web site is legally safe. This chapter has also covered maintenance issues for Web sites and explained how to register your Web site with search engines and cataloging databases on the Web.

The next chapter demonstrates how you can make your Web site interactive by introducing you to CGI and its capabilities. You will learn how CGI (Common Gateway Interface) can be used to provide dynamic content to users browsing your Web site, how to set up Perl scripts, and how to design and set up an e-mail feedback form.

Making Your Web Site Interactive

CHAPTER 27

After you set up your Web site and create some Web pages, it's time to think about making your site dynamic. You can do this by setting up a few CGI scripts on your server. You can fully exploit the capabilities of your Web site by creating customized feedback forms and database update/query forms. In this chapter, you'll learn about the basics of CGI and providing dynamic content to users browsing your Web site. You'll also see a few CGI programming examples, and you'll learn how to install Perl on your Web server. After you write a sample CGI script in Perl, you'll see how to execute Perl CGI scripts on your NT Web server by using a Web browser. You'll also take a look at using the C programming language to develop CGI scripts.

Understanding CGI

Common Gateway Interface (CGI) is a standard for linking applications to your Web server so that clients accessing your Web site can call these scripts to get and provide information. Plain-text HTML files retrieved by Web clients are static; the information in these files never changes unless you manually edit the files and make changes. On the other hand, by using CGI scripts, your Web pages can be created dynamically each time a client accesses your Web site. To clients, it looks as though the page was created especially for them based on the information they requested. Obviously, CGI is a very powerful tool for interacting with Web surfers.

Suppose you have a database that needs to be updated or queried. Depending on the information needed by browsers of your Web site and the information you need from them, you must set up a mechanism that allows updating and querying. Although you can use plain old e-mail to correspond with people and take care of the queries and updates manually, this option isn't very practical as you start getting more and more visitors. Eventually, you'll end up spending the whole day answering and responding to e-mail. (Maybe you do this already, but just imagine how much worse it will be!) By setting up a simple form, you can update your database by using a CGI script. You also can set up a CGI script to query your database so that your clients get the most up-to-date information when they need it.

CGI programs can be written in almost any programming language that lets you create an executable file or execute the program in real time with an interpreter (as in the case of awk and Perl). A few languages you can use to create CGI scripts under Windows NT follow:

- awk
- C/C++
- FORTRAN
- Pascal
- Perl
- Visual Basic

You should choose the language that best suits your needs, taking into account your expertise, available resources, and the type of CGI project. Generally, CGI scripts are stored in the CGI-BIN directory of your Web server's document root directory.

Looking at Some Applications of CGI

Many organizations and individuals use CGI for a variety of tasks, ranging from simple counters on Web pages to track the number of times pages are accessed, to CGI scripts that manage the entire front-ends of stores. Such CGI scripts also can allow users visiting a Web site to look at the merchandise being sold and even place orders. You can also use CGI to offer search capabilities for Web sites to make finding information easier.

You can use CGI to interact with browsers of your Web site, to get their feedback, and to provide them with dynamic content. Here's a few ways you can use CGI to enhance your Web site's capabilities:

- Setting up a guest book
- Creating a feedback form
- Adding a counter to a Web page
- Designing a database front-end for the Web
- Allowing Web surfers to visit Web pages via a pull-down list
- Letting users who browse your Web site e-mail you with their comments and feedback
- Providing customized Web pages based on the Web browsers used by clients
- Allowing your Web site's browsers to search your Web site

Before you move on to more advanced topics, you should take a brief look at the fundamentals of CGI.

Examining the Fundamentals of CGI

Generally, CGI scripts are used to provide dynamic content to the client who called the CGI script. CGI scripts communicate with Web browsers, as shown in Figure 27.1. If the CGI script is an interactive script, a form with input controls generally is sent to the Web client. After filling out the form, the client submits the form to the Web server. The Web server then uses CGI to call the CGI script with data from the Web client. The CGI script then processes the data, possibly accessing a database on the server, and sends a message to the client who made the request.

FIGURE 27.1.

A typical Web server with CGI scripts.

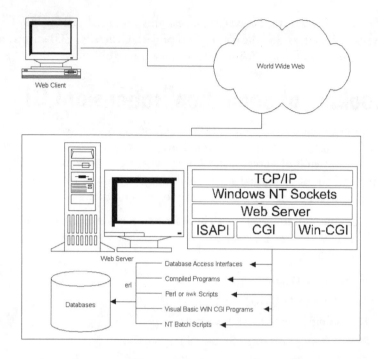

After a CGI script is called, the Web server examines the REQUEST_METHOD that called the script to determine how the Web client is sending data to the CGI script. (See Figure 27.2.) If the REQUEST_METHOD that called the CGI script is GET, any data supplied by the Web client for the CGI script immediately follows the URL of the CGI script. In such a case, this information is stored in the environment variable QUERY_STRING. If the REQUEST_METHOD used is POST or PUT, the size of input for the CGI script is stored in CONTENT_LENGTH, which contains the size of data supplied to the CGI script in bytes. The CGI script then can read from standard input the number of bytes returned by CONTENT_LENGTH to find the data given to the CGI script.

FIGURE 27.2.

The Web server executes the CGI script based on how the browser starts it.

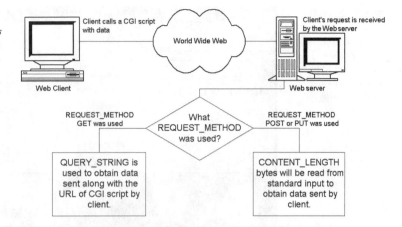

Using CGI with Your Web Site

CGI programs don't always need to be interactive. You can use non-interactive CGI scripts to provide dynamic information that doesn't need user input. To take advantage of features offered by Web browsers, such as Netscape Navigator and Microsoft Internet Explorer, you can write a CGI program to determine the browser being used by a client and to send a page specifically designed to take advantage of that browser's capabilities. This process is very easy. In fact, you'll write an easy CGI program with customized content based on the browser accessing your page later in this chapter, in the section "Creating Your First Perl CGI Script: Hello World!" In this case, the CGI script doesn't need to interact with the person browsing the Web site. By using a CGI program, you can supply dynamic content without any user intervention. If the default Web page of a Web site is welcome.html, for example, you can map the main Web page of the Web site to a CGI script. You can do this by creating a URL-CGI mapping, as shown in Figure 27.3. Such a script can determine the browser being used by the client and then display a page with dynamic content optimized for the client's browser. Refer to your Web server's documentation for more information on creating URL-CGI mappings.

If a CGI script doesn't take advantage of user input, what happens when a client accesses the page is very simple. First, the client connects to the Web server and requests a Web page. Because the document requested is linked to a CGI script, the Web server executes the CGI program to which the page is linked. Output of the CGI program is then sent to the client who requested the page. Next, the connection between the Web server and the Web client is closed. Figure 27.4 shows this interaction.

One of CGI's advantages is its ability to interact with your Web site's browsers. You can facilitate this interaction by asking a user to fill in and submit a form. The CGI script can then validate the user's input, ask the user to fill in any missing information, and process the user's input. Figure 27.5 shows how this process works.

FIGURE 27.3.

By mapping a Web page to a CGI script, you can provide dynamic content based on variables like the browser invoking the CGI script.

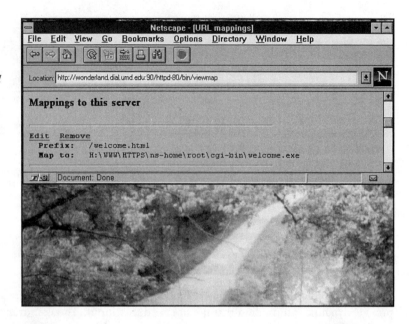

FIGURE 27.4.

Providing dynamic content with a non-interactive CGI script.

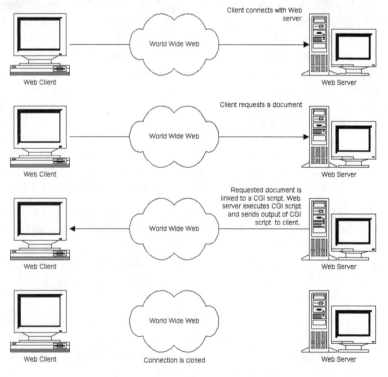

FIGURE 27.5.

Providing dynamic content with an interactive CGI script.

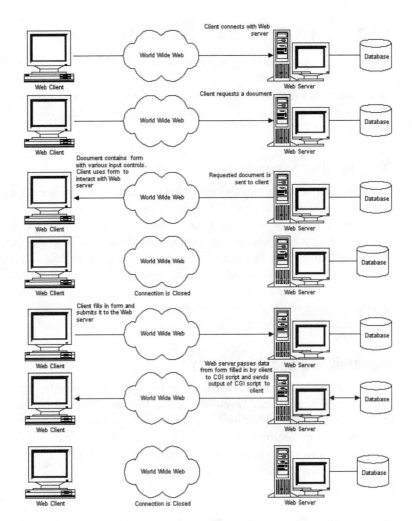

When a CGI script interacts with a Web client to display customized output, a Web page with input controls is sent to the Web browser. After the user fills in the form, it's submitted to the Web server to be processed. Depending on the method by which the client requests the script, the CGI script gets data sent from the client and then processes the data, displaying its output to standard output. Everything written to standard output by the CGI script is visible to the client who called the CGI script.

Considering Some CGI Issues

When setting up CGI scripts, you should consider a few points. Each time a CGI script is executed by someone surfing your Web site, you allow someone to execute a program on your server, which can lead to security breaches. Although that might sound a little perilous, it's actually not that bad, as long as you follow a few guidelines. CGI is very safe as long as you use it properly.

Maintaining Security

CGI is a powerful tool for making information available to users browsing your Web site. You should be aware of certain issues, however. The first issue you should look at is security. By allowing CGI scripts to be executed, you allow anyone browsing your Web site to execute CGI applications on your server. Be particularly careful about CGI scripts that take input from a Web client and use that data as a command-line argument without first checking. If you have sensitive data in sections of your Web site, you might want to disable directory browsing of your Web server. This ensures that, unless the people browsing your Web site know the URL of a certain page or are transferred to a page from one of your own pages, they can't snoop around your Web site by browsing directories and their contents.

Transmitting Sensitive Data

You should never set up CGI applications to distribute personal information that could be harmful in the wrong hands. If you're distributing valuable financial information, such as credit card numbers, you shouldn't use CGI unless you have configured your Web server to encrypt data before it's transmitted over the Internet. If you need to transmit sensitive data and your Web server doesn't encrypt data before transmitting, you should consider using a medium like *Pretty Good Privacy* (PGP) protected e-mail to transmit such data. PGP is a very safe medium for distributing sensitive data.

Controlling Processing Time

Another issue to consider is the time it takes for a CGI script to fulfill a client's request. If you're supplying data to users browsing your Web site in real time, you should make sure no one has to wait longer than 5–10 seconds. If it's going to take longer to process a request, you should get the e-mail address of the person requesting the information and then e-mail the information as soon as the data is processed. If it takes longer than 10 seconds to process a request, the user waiting at the other end might think there's a problem and just stop waiting.

NOTE

If you really need to provide data in real time, and the CGI scripts take longer than about 10 seconds to execute, you're probably outgrowing your server and need more processing power or RAM.

Controlling Access to the CGI Directory

You should be cautious about who has access to your Web server's CGI directory. It's dangerous to allow users who upload files to your Web site through FTP to have access to your CGI directory. It doesn't take too much programming knowledge for a user to write a malicious program, upload it to the CGI directory, and execute it with a Web browser. Therefore, you should control who has access to your CGI directory through FTP or by any other method.

Handling Simultaneous Use of Your Script

Because of the nature of HTTP, it's possible that two or more clients will call the same CGI script at the same time. If the CGI script locks files or databases when it's processing data, data loss can occur. CGI scripts should be able to handle such a situation without any problems.

Writing CGI Perl Scripts

Practical Extraction and Report Language (Perl) is a popular CGI programming language. By installing Perl on your Web server, you can use many Perl CGI scripts to perform a variety of tasks. This introduction to Perl shows you how to set up CGI Perl scripts on Windows NT Web servers.

With the growth of the Web, Perl is being used more often to write CGI programs. Most of the best features of C, sed, awk, and sh are incorporated in Perl. These features allow you to develop Perl scripts in the least amount of time possible because you don't have to reinvent the wheel for fundamental tasks, such as string manipulation. The expression syntax of Perl corresponds closely to the expression syntax of C programs, which makes Perl an easy language to learn for those already familiar with C.

Perl for Windows NT is provided free of charge on the Internet. You can get Perl for Windows NT at this site:

```
http://info.hip.com/ntperl/
```

27

MAKING YOUR
WEB SITE
INTERACTIVE

After you get Perl for NT, create a directory for Perl and copy the Perl distribution file to the directory. Then, decompress the distribution file, being sure to use the option for using stored directory names in the archive. If you don't use this option, all files will be extracted to the Perl directory you created, and you'll find yourself in a mess! After the archive is decompressed, run INSTALL.BAT to install Perl on your server. Then, you need to copy PERL.EXE to the root CGI directory of your Web server so your Web server can execute Perl CGI scripts.

TIP

When decompressing the .ZIP file, be sure to use a 32-bit unzipping program that supports long filenames. Otherwise, the distribution files might not install properly. WinZip is a fine file-decompressing program that supports long filenames and a variety of file-compression formats. You can get WinZip at this site:

```
http://www.winzip.com/WinZip/download.html
```

NOTE

After installing Perl, you need to reboot your server for the installation directory paths to become effective. Failure to do so causes Perl to greet you with an `Unable to locate DLL` message. (Yes, I was naive and tried it!) If you don't feel like rebooting your server, you can just copy all files in the Perl\bin directory to the CGI directory of your Web server.

For more information about Perl and sample CGI Perl scripts, you might want to give the following URLs a click:

```
Yahoo - Computers and Internet:
Internet:World Wide Web:Programming:Perl Scripts
http://www.yahoo.com/Computers_and_Internet/Internet/
➥World_Wide_Web/Programming/Perl_Scripts/

Yahoo - Computers and Internet:Languages:Perl
http://www.yahoo.com/Computers_and_Internet/Languages/Perl/
```

Creating Your First Perl CGI Script: Hello World!

This section gives you an example of a simple Perl CGI script, written by Sanjaya Hettihewa. You'll also learn how to set up a Perl script on a Windows NT Web server and how a Web client can invoke it. The script, which displays the text `Hello World!`, as well as information about the Web browser used to invoke the CGI script, is very simple to write in Perl. Listing 27.1 shows the code for this Perl script, and Figure 27.6 shows the output from this code.

Listing 27.1. The Hello World script.

```
*** Beginning of Program Listing: "HelloWorld.pl" ***

# Sanjaya Hettihewa, http://wonderland.dial.umd.edu/
# December 31, 1995
# "Hello World" CGI Script in Perl
# Display content type being outputted by CGI script
print "Content-type: text/html\n\n";

# Label title of contents being outputted
print "<TITLE>Perl CGI Script Demonstration</TITLE>\n";

# Display text
print "<H1>Hello World!</H1>\n";
print "<H3>Welcome to the fun filled world of<BR>\n";
print "Windows NT CGI programming with Perl!<BR><BR>\n";
print "The Web browser you are using is:";

# Display value of the environmental variable HTTP_USER_AGENT
print $ENV{"HTTP_USER_AGENT"} , "<BR>\n" ;
print "Arguments passed in: ";

# Display value of the environmental variable QUERY_STRING
print $ENV{"QUERY_STRING"} , "<BR>\n" ;

# Obtain date and time from the system
($sec, $min, $hour, $mday, $mon, $year, $wday, $yday, $isdst) = localtime(time);

# display time
print "\nThe current time is: ";
print  $hour, ":", $min, ":", $sec , "<BR>\n";

# display date
print "\nThe current date is: ";
print $mon + 1 , "/", $mday , "/", $year, "<BR>\n";
```

Pay particular attention to how the Perl CGI script is invoked by the Web browser. In this example, the URL used to invoke the CGI script is

```
http://wonderland.dial.umd.edu/cgi-bin/
➥perl.exe?PerlScripts/HelloWorld/HelloWorld.pl+Argument
```

When calling a Perl script on a Windows NT Web server, the general syntax of the URL is

```
http://A/B?C+D
```

Here, A is the hostname of the Web server (`wonderland.dial.umd.edu`, in this example), B is the relative path to PERL.EXE (`cgi-bin/perl.exe`, in this example), and C is the location of the Perl script (the path depends on the location of PERL.EXE). D contains any arguments passed to the Perl script. You can get these arguments by examining the contents of the CGI environment variable QUERY_STRING.

FIGURE 27.6.

Output of the Hello World CGI Perl script.

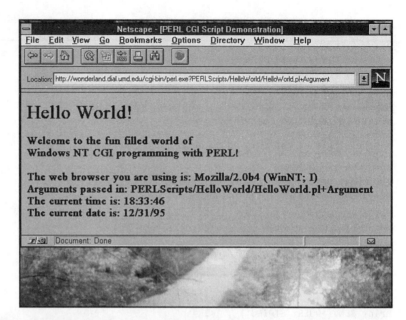

As you can see in Listing 27.1, when Perl scripts are called with arguments, URLs can become quite long. You can avoid this situation by creating aliases for Perl scripts on your Web server. For example, if an alias called "Hello" is created for

```
http://wonderland.dial.umd.edu/cgi-bin/
➥perl.exe?PerlScripts/HelloWorld/HelloWorld.pl
```

the URL to call the Perl CGI script is reduced to

```
http://wonderland.dial.umd.edu/Hello+Argument
```

See your Web server's documentation for more information on creating aliases for URLs.

Whenever you have a complex URL for a CGI script, you should create an alias for the script. By hiding gory details such as long and complicated URL paths, your Web site actually looks friendlier to someone browsing your site. This also saves you time when you refer to such a CGI script from one of your Web pages, because you do less typing. If you still aren't convinced, notice how much easier it is to remember this:

```
http://wonderland.dial.umd.edu/Hello+Argument
```

instead of this:

```
http://wonderland.dial.umd.edu/cgi-bin/
➥perl.exe?PerlScripts/HelloWorld/HelloWorld.pl+Argument
```

Providing Dynamic Content in Your Web

Approximately two dozen Web servers are available for Windows NT, and just as many Web browsers are available for browsing the Web. One of the most commonly used Web browsers is Netscape Navigator. Because Netscape Navigator supports additional HTML tags, you can provide rich formatting enhancements to your information by using Netscape enhancements to HTML. If the appearance of your Web site is very important to you, you might want to consider setting up a CGI script to provide a customized Web page depending on the browser being used. This obviously isn't practical for a very large Web site. By setting up a simple CGI script, though, you can find out which Web browser is being used by the person browsing your Web site. If the browser is Netscape Navigator or Microsoft's Internet Explorer, you can offer a richly formatted Web page with HTML enhancements, or you can provide a basic page with the same content. The CGI script in Listing 27.2 uses the CGI variable HTTP_USER_AGENT, as Figure 27.7 shows.

FIGURE 27.7.
Using the CGI variable HTTP_USER_AGENT *to display a customized Web page.*

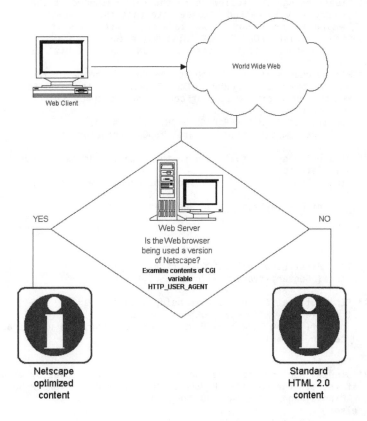

World Wide Web

Web Client

YES

NO

Web Server

Is the Web browser being used a version of Netscape?
Examine contents of CGI variable HTTP_USER_AGENT

Netscape optimized content

Standard HTML 2.0 content

Listing 27.2. A CGI C program to provide customized content.

```c
/* (C) 1995 Sanjaya Hettihewa http://wonderland.dial.umd.edu/
 * January 1, 1996
 * Program to output a customized Web page based on
   Web browser being used.
 */

/* Special function libraries being used by this program */
#include <stdio.h>
#include <stdlib.h>
#include <string.h>

/* Please note the use of double quotes. This is because a single quote is
   ➥used to quote the next character */

/* If you provide content specially formatted for a different browser, please
   ➥change the following */
#define  SPECIAL_BROWSER_SUB_STRING "Mozilla"

/* Please change the following to the full pathname of the HTML file that's
     ➥specially formatted. Please note that the following two lines should be a
     ➥single line of code. (Due to space limitations it's listed as two lines.) */
#define  SPECIAL_BROWSER_PAGE "H:\\www\\https\\
         ns-home\\root\\documents\\WSDGNT\\special.htm"

/* Please change the following to the full pathname of the HTML file that's
     ➥formatted using standard HTML. Please note that the following two lines
     ➥should be a single line of code. (Due to space limitations it's listed as two
     ➥lines.) */
    #define  OTHER_BROWSER_PAGE   "H:\\www\\https\\
         ns-home\\root\\documents\\WSDGNT\\regular.htm"

/* Please change the following to the e-mail address of your Website
     administrator */
#define  WEBMASTER              "mailto:webmaster@wonderland.dial.umd.edu"

static int DisplayPage ( char *pageName ) ;

main ( )
{

/* The "First Line" of all CGI scripts... */
  printf("Content-type: text/html%c%c",10,10) ;

/* Find out what Web browser is being used */
  if ( getenv ( "HTTP_USER_AGENT" ) == NULL ) {
    printf("FATAL ERROR: HTTP_USER_AGENT CGI variable undefined!\n") ;
    return   ( 0 ) ;
  }

/* Display appropriate page based on browser being used by client */
  if (strstr (getenv ("HTTP_USER_AGENT" ), SPECIAL_BROWSER_SUB_STRING)!=NULL)
    DisplayPage ( SPECIAL_BROWSER_PAGE ) ;
  else
    DisplayPage ( OTHER_BROWSER_PAGE ) ;
  return   ( 0 ) ;
```

```
}

/* Contents of file passed into this function will be displayed to standard
   ➥output. The Web server will transmit what's displayed to standard output
   ➥by this CGI script to the client that called the CGI script */
int DisplayPage ( char *pageName )
{

  FILE *inFile  ;
  char character ;

/* Check to ensure a valid filename is given */
  if ((inFile = fopen(pageName, "r")) == NULL) {
    printf ( "FATAL ERROR: Content file can't be opened! %s<BR>", pageName);
    printf ( "Please contact the  <A HREF=%s>Webmaster.</A><BR>",
             WEBMASTER );
     return ( 0 ) ;
  }

/* Displaying contents of file to standard output
   Please note that this can be done more efficiently by reading chunks of the
   ➥file at a time */
  fscanf ( inFile  , "%c" , &character ) ;
  while ( !feof(inFile) ) {
    printf ( "%c" , character ) ;
    fscanf ( inFile  , "%c" , &character ) ;
  }
  fclose(inFile);
  return ( 1 ) ;

}
```

The CGI script in Listing 27.2 gives you customized content by examining the environment variable HTTP_USER_AGENT. Depending on the value of this variable, a page with Netscape enhancements to HTML can be displayed if the browser used is Netscape. On the other hand, a page that contains only standard HTML 2.0 is displayed if the browser used to invoke the CGI script isn't Netscape. By modifying the script, you always can add more customized pages for other browsers. You can use such scripts for important pages, such as the main home page of your organization. By using CGI to supply dynamic content, you'll give a good impression to someone browsing your Web site.

> **TIP**
>
> You can make Listing 27.2 more efficient by reading chunks of the file at a time instead of reading and outputting the file character by character.

Listing 27.3 shows the standard HTML Web page:.

```
H:\\www\\https\\ns-home\\root\\documents\\WSDGNT\\regular.htm
```

The location of this file is defined in the C program so that its contents can be displayed for non-Netscape browsers. In the C program, the location of the file is defined in OTHER_BROWSER_PAGE.

Listing 27.3. A standard HTML page for non-Netscape browsers.

```
<TITLE>Standard HTML page</TITLE>
<BODY>
Welcome to the standard HTML page for technically challenged Web browsers.
<P>
Option One<BR>
Option Two<BR>
Option Three<BR>
</BODY>
```

Listing 27.4 shows the Netscape-enhanced HTML Web page designed for those browsing your Web site with Netscape. This HTML code displays the same three options displayed by the standard HTML page, but they are shown in a table with some Netscape enhancements. Because the C program needs to know the location of this file, for the purpose of this example, the page in Listing 27.4 is located here:

```
H:\\www\\https\\ns-home\\root\\documents\\WSDGNT\\special.htm
```

In the C program, the full pathname of this file is stored in SPECIAL_BROWSER_PAGE. The contents of this file are displayed by the CGI program whenever Netscape Navigator is used. You need to change this variable, depending on where you store the Netscape-enhanced Web page.

Listing 27.4. A Netscape-enhanced page for Netscape browsers.

```
<TITLE>Netscape Enhanced page</TITLE>
<BODY>
<CENTER>
<TABLE BORDER=15 CELLPADDING=10 CELLSPACING=10 >
<TR>
<TD >
Welcome to the
<FONT SIZE=4>Ne</FONT><FONT SIZE=5>ts</FONT>
<FONT SIZE=6>ca</FONT><FONT SIZE=7>pe</FONT>
<FONT SIZE=6>En</FONT><FONT SIZE=5>ha</FONT>
<FONT SIZE=4>nc</FONT><FONT SIZE=3>ed </FONT>
 Web page!
</TD>
<TD >Option One<BR></TD >
<TD >Option Two<BR></TD >
<TD >Option Three<BR></TD >
</TR>
</TABLE>
</CENTER>
</BODY>
```

After compiling this program and placing it in your Web server's CGI directory (depending on the browser used to call the CGI script), the appropriate page is displayed. When compiling the C program, be sure to change SPECIAL_BROWSER_PAGE, OTHER_BROWSER_PAGE, and WEBMASTER to the appropriate values. Figures 27.8 and 27.9 show the output of the CGI program for providing customized content. The Web browsers Netscape and Mosaic were used for these figures. Notice that the enhanced HTML page is displayed when accessing the script with Netscape, and the standard HTML page is displayed when using Mosaic.

FIGURE 27.8.
Output of the CGI program when invoked by Netscape.

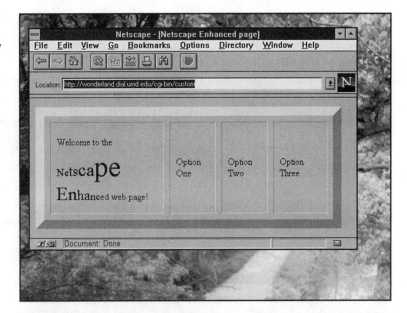

FIGURE 27.9.
Output of the CGI program when invoked by a non-Netscape browser (Mosaic, in this case).

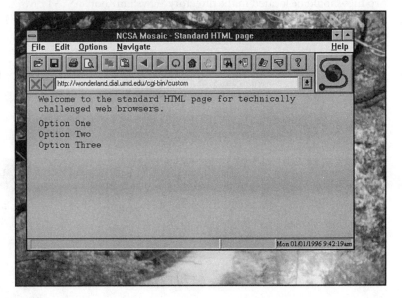

Setting Up a Feedback Form

One of the best features of CGI is that it lets you interact with the people browsing your Web site. What better way is there to interact with them than to ask for their feedback? By using the Windows NT command-line mail utility Blat and another utility program that e-mails the contents of a form, you can set up a feedback form at your Web site in just a few minutes.

First, you need to get a copy of Blat at this Web site:

```
http://gepasi.dbs.aber.ac.uk/softw/blat.html
```

Blat is a public domain Windows NT console utility that sends the contents of a file as an e-mail message by using the *Simple Mail Transfer Protocol* (SMTP). Blat is useful for creating scripts for automatically sending mail (CGI scripts, results of backups, and so on). To use Blat, you must have an SMTP mail server installed and configured properly.

> ### NOTE
>
> If you haven't set up a Windows NT SMTP mail server, you need to do so before installing Blat. You can download a free SMTP mail server for Windows NT from this site:
>
> ```
> http://www.emwac.ed.ac.uk/
> ```
>
> See the next chapter for instructions on installing the public domain EMWAC mail server for Windows NT.

After downloading Blat, you need to install it on your Web server. Blat is distributed with the source code. The only two files you really need are BLAT.EXE and GWINSOCK.DLL. These two files should be located in the directory %SystemRoot%\SYSTEM32. After unzipping the Blat distribution file, you need to copy BLAT.EXE and GWINSOCK.DLL to %SystemRoot%\SYSTEM32. Then, install Blat by typing the following:

```
Blat -install your_site_address your_userid@your_site_address
In my case,
your_site_address = wonderland.dial.umd.edu
your_userid@your_site_address = sanjaya@wonderland.dial.umd.edu
```

As long as you set up your SMTP server software properly, Blat installs and lets you know that the SMTP server was set up properly.

> ### TIP
>
> At this point, if you want to quickly e-mail a file, you can do so by typing this:
>
> ```
> Blat <filename> -t <recipient>
> ```

After you set up Blat, you need to set up a form to e-mail your feedback. First, however, you need to download a program, WWWMAIL.EXE, that will process the contents of the form after it's submitted. You can download it from this site:

```
http://www.esf.c-strasbourg.fr/misc/amsoft.exe?www
```

Next, copy the program to the CGI directory of your Web server. Then, you need to set up a form that lets the user type in and submit feedback. You also need to create a page that appears after users submit their feedback. This page should thank users for the feedback and let them choose another link to follow.

> **NOTE**
>
> For the program to work properly, you need to enable CGI on your Web server. Consult your Web server's manual to learn how to do this. Generally, the CGI directory is the CGI-BIN directory from the root directory of your Web server. After creating this directory, you might need to define it as your CGI directory before you can execute CGI scripts.

Now all that's left to do is to create a feedback form and a response page to display after the form is submitted. Listing 27.5 shows a sample feedback page.

Listing 27.5. A feedback form.

```
<HTML>
<HEAD>
<title>Feedback Form Demonstration</title>
</HEAD>

<BODY>
<FORM method=POST
       action="/cgi-bin/wwwmail.exe/cgi-bin/feedback.hfo">
<INPUT TYPE=hidden name="mailto"
       value="webmaster@wonderland.dial.umd.edu">
<INPUT TYPE=hidden name="WWWMail-Page" value="H:\www\netscape_commerce\ns-
home\root\documents\feedback\ThanksForFeedback.html">

<PRE>
<b>Subject:</b> <SELECT name="subject">
  <OPTION> I have some Feedback
  <OPTION> I have a comment...
  <OPTION> I have a suggestion...
<OPTION> I need assistance with...
  <OPTION> Other
</SELECT>
<B>Your E-mail address please:</B>    <INPUT name="sender" SIZE=30>
<b>Your name Please:</b>              <INPUT name="name" SIZE=30 >
<b>Your phone # (If you wish)</b>    <INPUT name="phoneno" SIZE=20 >
<b>Would you like a reply from me?</b> <SELECT name="Reply">
  <OPTION> If you wish
  <OPTION> Yes, please
```

continues

Listing 27.5. continued

```
  <OPTION> No thanks
</SELECT>
<b>Is this message urgent?</b>        <SELECT name="Urgency">
  <OPTION> Not particularly
  <OPTION> Yes, very urgent
  <OPTION> Not at all
</SELECT>
<b>And how are you doing today?</b> <SELECT name="Status">
  <OPTION> Oh, just fine, thanks
  <OPTION> Doing great, thanks!
  <OPTION> Don't even ask!
</SELECT>

<b>Please type your message and click the submit button:</b>
<TEXTAREA name="comments" cols=65 rows=3> </TEXTAREA>
<input type=submit value="Please click here to send message">
</FORM>
</PRE>
</BODY>
</HTML>
```

You can use a similar feedback page for your Web site. Just change the following values:

```
name="mailto"
     value="user_ID@your.site"
name="WWWMail-Page"
     value="<Full path of page to display after submitting the form">
action="<your CGI directory>/wwwmail.exe/cgi-bin/feedback.hfo">
```

Your feedback form now should look similar to the form shown in Figure 27.10.

FIGURE 27.10.

A feedback form.

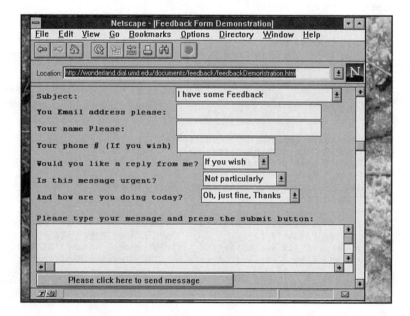

Looking at the Benefits of Using CGI on Your Web Site

The benefits of CGI are invaluable to any Web site. These benefits range from having a customized input form for feedback to allowing someone browsing your Web site to update and retrieve information from a database on your server. By using a customized e-mail feedback form, you can make sure that you get the information you need. You also can make sure your e-mail feedback form always works and doesn't depend on the setup of the client's Web browser (in case it isn't set up correctly for e-mail). Furthermore, if you need to set up a database that collects data from users browsing your Web site, you can easily set up a CGI script to update information to a database on your server without any intervention by you. ColdFusion (`http://www.allaire.com/cfusion/`) is a CGI application you can use to allow users browsing your Web site to update a database on your server. As you can see, the possibilities and applications of CGI are endless.

Summary

This chapter has introduced you to CGI and demonstrated how you can set up CGI scripts on a Windows NT-based Web server. You have also seen how to install Perl and run CGI Perl scripts on your Web server. You have looked at developing and setting up CGI scripts so that they aren't a threat to the security of your Web server, and then examined practical applications of CGI, along with the source code, so that you can modify these examples to enhance your Web site and experiment with CGI.

The next chapter tells you how you can extend the capabilities of your Web site. You'll see how to extend the capabilities of your Web server by setting up and configuring the Windows NT FTP server to distribute information on the Internet. You'll also see how to set up the EMWAC mail server so that you can send and retrieve Internet e-mail.

27

MAKING YOUR
WEB SITE
INTERACTIVE

Internet Information Server

CHAPTER 28

IN THIS CHAPTER

One of the major changes to Windows NT Server 4 is the addition of the Microsoft Internet Information Server (IIS) version 2.0 as part of the operating system. Previous versions of NT included no similar software, although components such as FTP servers could be configured. You had to buy IIS separately before this release. The version of IIS included with NT 4 is tightly integrated with the operating system, making it an attractive add-in for those looking to set up Web servers for an intranet or the Internet. IIS also includes standard TCP/IP servers for FTP and Gopher.

> **NOTE**
>
> As this book goes to print, Microsoft has released version 3 of IIS. The beta version of IIS v3 can be downloaded from the Microsoft home page. When the product emerges from beta, the updates should be freely available.

IIS is a rather complex package that has a simple purpose: It allows you to set up a Web server quickly and easily. It also allows for connections through other protocols such as FTP with a minimum of fuss and configuration. Because IIS is installed as part of the operating system, you don't have to take extra steps to install the software unless you particularly specified not to load IIS as part of the original server load.

The IIS is composed of a number of utilities, wizards, and templates that are designed to allow you to create Web pages more quickly and manage your site. Included in the IIS package is FrontPage, a wizard designed to help you create Web pages quickly without requiring knowledge of HTML.

In this chapter, you look at how to install and configure the IIS system, but I make no attempt to teach you how to set up Web home pages and directory structures. That's a topic for another book!

Examining IIS Installation and Requirements

You probably saw the option to install IIS when you loaded the operating system from CD-ROM. If you didn't load it at that point, you can load it at any time from the distribution disk. To install IIS, insert the Server 4.0 CD-ROM in the drive and click the IIS name on the window that appears. Alternatively, open the Networks applet in the Control Panel, select Services, and then select the Microsoft Internet Information Service from the list. Selecting this option activates the same installation procedure as running directly from the CD-ROM.

To run IIS, you need TCP/IP installed on the server. If your local network does not support TCP/IP, you still need TCP/IP to act as the connection to the Internet. You can install TCP/IP through the Network icon on the Control Panel.

To install and configure the basic IIS system, follow these steps (many of which are performed or information asked for while installing IIS):

1. Install IIS from the CD-ROM.
2. Configure TCP/IP through the Network icon on the Control Panel. TCP/IP must be present for IIS to work.
3. Configure the site's domain name and IP address.
4. Configure the name resolution system, such as WINS or DNS.

If you're upgrading or installing IIS on a machine that already has some TCP/IP services such as an FTP server of Gopher server, you must disable these services before installing IIS. If you have a third-party Web server (including those from Netscape, O'Reilly, or Luckman), you have to disable them, too.

During the installation process, you are asked which services you want to install. By default, all of them are selected. You should probably install them all and then disable the ones you don't want in the Manager window, unless you know for sure you do not need one of the services or components such as the ODBC drivers.

You can administer IIS from a machine running Windows NT 4 Workstation, but it must connect to a machine running NT Server. To use this approach, you must have already installed the Peer Web Services Internet Service Manager on the Workstation machine. It can then connect to the machine running the Server version of NT and hosting the IIS system through the network.

To run IIS, you need a minimum configuration for NT Server. As long as Server runs, IIS should be able to run. However, as a Web server can quickly become heavily used, a good chunk of RAM is recommended, as is a lot of available hard disk space for your Web pages and other content. A good working principle for an IIS connected to the Internet or an intranet that is expecting a reasonable amount of load is a minimum of 32M RAM, with 64M or even 128M better. As the number of users connected to your server increases, the memory available for tasks drops rapidly and swapping becomes a bottleneck.

The disk that contains the IIS content should have adequate space, of course. If you intend to support a lot of traffic, you might want to provide a dedicated disk or partition for the IIS content. I highly recommend that you format the IIS content disk with HPFS instead of the older compatible file system.

If you're using virtual domains (in which more than one domain name or IP address is handled by the single machine), you need to set up a TCP/IP entry for each virtual domain in the Networks window.

Starting the IIS Manager

You can open the main manager screen of IIS by choosing Programs from the Start button, selecting Microsoft Internet Server (Common) from the list, and then selecting Internet Service Manager from the submenu. The main window, shown in Figure 28.1, then appears. It shows you the services currently running on your system. In Figure 28.1, you can see that a Web server, a Gopher Server, and an FTP Server are all running.

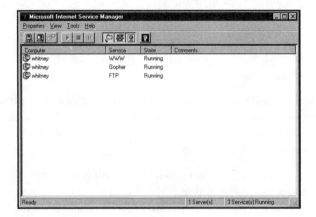

If you want to find out more about any of the services, you can either double-click the service name, or select it and then choose Properties | Service Properties. You look at each of the services in more detail later in this section, but for now you should know how to start and stop each service.

Starting and Stopping Services

You can start and stop any of the services on the IIS main window in two ways. One way is to select the service name and right-click to display a pop-up menu. Choosing Stop from this menu changes the status to Stopped on the main window and halts IIS from accepting any requests for that service. Alternatively, you can choose Properties | Stop Service. In either case, the main window changes to show the service is stopped. Figure 28.2 shows the main IIS window with both the WWW and Gopher services stopped.

You can pause a service, which stops it from accepting new requests but doesn't unload the drivers. A paused service is useful when you have to make quick changes to the service's content or properties. A paused service shows up as such on the IIS Manager window.

FIGURE 28.2.

You can stop a service from accepting requests with pull-down or pop-up menus.

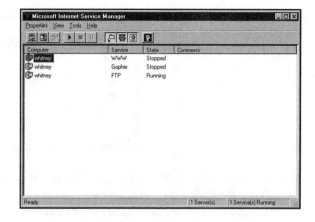

Changing the View

The default view the IIS Manager uses is to show the servers on the network that are running IIS services with the services on each sorted alphabetically. You can change the order of this display (which is usually necessary only when you have a lot of servers and services) by using the View menu.

By choosing View menu options, you can modify the displayed order to sort by Service name, by Server name, by State (running, stopped, or paused), or by Comment. Most Services don't have a comment by default, so this option allows you to tag particular services and servers with comments (such as "troublesome" or "main FTP server") for quick identification. To change the order of the display, select the option you want from the View menu, and the effect is immediate.

You can suppress the display of particular services if you want, using either hot buttons on the toolbar or options under the View menu. If you want to see only the FTP services, for example, you can turn off the Gopher and WWW services by selecting those names from the View menu or by using the icons on the toolbar representing a globe and a gopher head. The FTP icon is the folder with an arrow underneath. If you leave the cursor on any of the toolbar icons for a second or so, the identification tag is displayed.

Finally, you can also use the View menu to display only the server names, the services, or the normal view (which is called Report). To display just the server names, for example, choose View | Servers View. Figure 28.3 shows the Server view of a demonstration network provided with the IIS documentation.

Connecting to Other Servers

The IIS Manager can run any IIS servers on your network, not just the one on the local machine. If you're running more than one Web server to spread the load, for example, you can use IIS from any workstation or server to connect to those servers and manage their behavior.

FIGURE 28.3.

You can change the Manager view to just show servers on the network.

If you want to connect to another Web server, choose Properties | Connect to Server in the IIS Manager. A dialog box that lets you enter the name of the server to be connected to then appears. You can enter the machine's host name, its IP address, or its NetBIOS name.

An alternative method is to choose Properties | Find All Servers. This method searches the entire network (which might take a while) and displays a window with a list of all found Web servers (the server has to be active to be found, of course). Click the name of the server you want to manage on this list, and the Manager connects to it.

Configuring the Services

You can configure and manage each of the services supported by IIS separately through the IIS Manager. By double-clicking one of the service names, or selecting the service and choosing Properties | Service Properties, you can configure and control all aspects of the service. In this section, you look at the configuration of each of the three services supplied with IIS.

Configuring FTP

The FTP service allows other machines to connect to the server and transfer files. The Properties sheet for the FTP service is shown in Figure 28.4. It contains five different pages, each of which handles a particular aspect of the service. In many cases, the default settings are sufficient for servers, but you should know what the options are, anyway.

On the Service page, the first page to appear in the FTP Properties sheet, you can set the TCP port that is used by FTP. By convention, FTP uses TCP port 21, and you should change it only when you know exactly what port clients will be using. TCP ports have been assigned by convention for many years, and FTP uses ports 20 and 21. Changing this port means most FTP clients that are not set for the same port cannot connect to the service.

The Connection Time-out is the amount of time to allow with no activity before the client is logged out of the FTP server. The default represents 15 minutes, expressed in seconds. For most systems, this amount is enough. You might want to shorten the time on heavily used systems or for systems that have very tight security, or relax the amount of time if you expect clients connecting to transfer large files where the operator might be away from the workstation for a while. If you're unsure, leave the default value alone.

FIGURE 28.4.

The FTP Properties sheet showing the Service page.

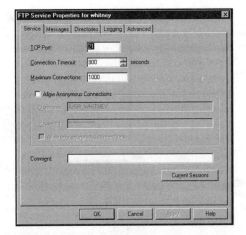

The Maximum Connections, as the name implies, limits the number of clients that can connect to the server at any one time. The default value of 1,000 is much higher than most systems can support with standard memory, so it should be sufficient. If you want to limit the amount of simultaneous use, you can cut the number down to a more reasonable value such as 25. Any users trying to connect when the number of connections is reached receive a message that the server is at its maximum limit. If you want to set a low limit for the number of connections allowed, you might want to set the connection time-out to a lower value to allow more people to use the server.

By default, FTP does not allow anonymous connections. Instead, it requires a valid logon and password from everyone trying to connect. If you want to allow anonymous connections, check the box in the center of the Service screen. You can specify a name for anyone connecting as anonymous for system reasons, if you want. The option at the bottom of the screen allows you to set FTP to accept only anonymous connections. You might need to set this option if you have a site that distributes information to customers at will, but does pose security breach problems. Anonymous FTP is a commonly used method of hacking into a system, so if you don't need to support anonymous FTP, disable it.

The Comment field at the bottom of this page shows the comment that will appear on the IIS Manager window. You can use the Comment field for any reason you want. To display the names of everyone currently using FTP on your system, you can click the Current Sessions button to display a window, shown in Figure 28.5, with all current users' names listed.

The Messages page, shown in Figure 28.6, is blank by default. On this page, you can enter the messages that connecting clients see when they connect, when they leave, and when the number of connections is exceeded. The page shown in Figure 28.6 has sample messages added, but you can make the message anything you want. If your settings are low, having a message for the Maximum Connection violation problem is a good idea. This message lets the users know the problem is with the server, not their software.

FIGURE 28.5.

You can display the list of current FTP users in this window from the Properties sheet for the service.

FIGURE 28.6.

On the Message page, you can specify what messages clients see when they use your FTP server.

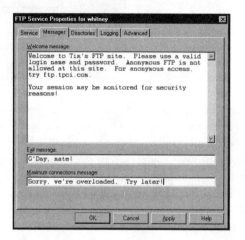

The Directories page, shown in Figure 28.7, shows you where the FTP material is stored. This information is specified during the installation and rarely needs changing. You can use the Add and Remove buttons to change the directory list, if you want to modify the list. The bottom of the screen indicates whether the FTP service should use UNIX or Windows naming schemes for directory displays. The best choice depends on the type of network and connections you use. If your network is mostly UNIX, and you expect connections from mainly UNIX users, change the directory style to make life a little easier for the clients.

The Logging page, shown in Figure 28.8, lets you log all the connection activity to a file or printer. This capability is useful for security purposes and to allow problem tracing. By default, FTP activity is enabled with output sent to a file. To disable logging, remove the checkmark in the Enable Logging checkbox. You can change the frequency with which the file is erased and start anew by selecting a different button on this page.

On the right side of the Logging page, you can alter the logging from a standard file to an ODBC database. You do so when you need to have tight audit trails that can be searched and retained for long periods of time. Be warned that this chews up a lot of system resources, so use it only when necessary.

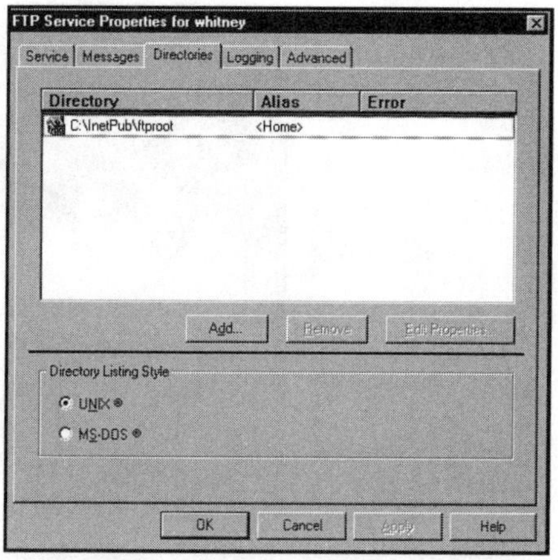

FIGURE 28.7.

On the Directories page, you can set the names of the directories and the naming conventions used by FTP.

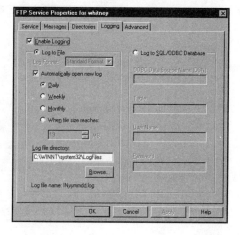

FIGURE 28.8.

On the Logging page, you can control how FTP transactions are recorded by the system.

The last page in the FTP Properties sheet is the Advanced page, shown in Figure 28.9. On this page, you can alter a few behaviors of the FTP server. For example, the default is to allow any computers to connect to the FTP server (although the user logons are controlled through the Service page). If you want to limit access to only certain workstations, click the Denied Access button and fill in the center list with the names or IP addresses of all the workstations that are to be granted access.

Configuring Gopher

The Gopher Properties sheet has four pages. The first, shown in Figure 28.10, is labeled Service and sets the basic handling of the Gopher system. The TCP port is by default set to 70, and as I discussed in the "Configuring FTP" section, changes can affect the way clients connect to your server. The maximum time-out and connection limits on this page are the same as on the FTP page.

FIGURE 28.9.

On the Advanced page, you can control machine access to the FTP server.

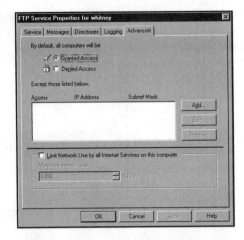

FIGURE 28.10.

On the Gopher Properties Service page, you can set basic behavior for the system.

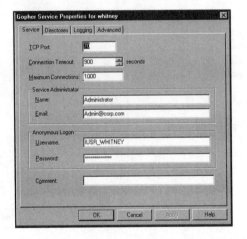

The administrator logon and e-mail address for the Gopher service are provided in the middle of the Service page. When a Gopher user wants to contact the Gopher site administrator, he or she uses this e-mail address. The lower part of the Service page is used to enable anonymous logon to the Gopher site, and specifies which NT system logon the anonymous user is assigned. Finally, the Comment field appears on the IIS Manager window.

On the Directories page, shown in Figure 28.11, you can specify the directories the Gopher system uses as home. The default directory is provided during installation but can be changed at any time. Use the Add and Remove buttons to modify the directory list to suit your requirements.

The Logging and Advanced pages for the Gopher Properties sheet, shown in Figure 28.12 and 28.13, respectively, behave the same as those you examined in the FTP Service. You can control the audit trail location and the names of authorized workstations through these two pages.

FIGURE 28.11.

On the Gopher Directories page, you can specify the Gopher home directory.

FIGURE 28.12.

On the Logging page, you can log all Gopher activity to a file or database.

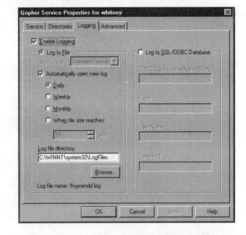

FIGURE 28.13.

On the Advanced page, you can set access to the Gopher service to just a limited number of workstations or open to anyone.

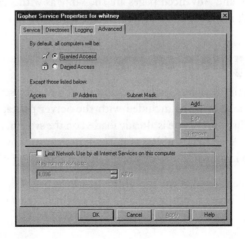

28

INTERNET
INFORMATION
SERVER

Configuring WWW

Not surprisingly, the WWW Properties sheet has much the same functionality as the FTP and Gopher sheets you just examined. The WWW Properties sheet has the same four pages as the Gopher service. On the first page, you can set the TCP port, which should not be modified if you're connecting to the Internet. For access to the Web server, you can choose one or more of three options: anonymous, basic, and Windows NT authentication. You can use any combination of these options that you need.

The Directories page, shown in Figure 28.14, shows the directories and purposes used by the Web server. You can see that the default configuration uses three directories—one for home, one for scripts, and one for administration. Depending on the size and content of your Web site, you might need to add more directories by using the Add and Remove buttons.

FIGURE 28.14.

The WWW Service has three directories used by default, but you can easily change the layout of your system to suit your needs.

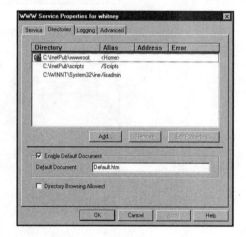

The Logging and Advanced pages are the same as with the FTP and Gopher services, so you should check those sections earlier in this chapter for more information.

Getting Help on IIS

The IIS system includes documentation in a Web browser-readable format only. No printed documentation for IIS is included with the Server package. To see the documentation, you need a Web browser (if one is already loaded on the system, it is used). Clicking the Help button launches the Web help and lets you use hypertext to move to the subject you want. The first page of help is shown in Figure 28.15, in this case using Netscape Navigator.

The index mentioned at the top of the first help page takes you to an alphabetical list of subjects, but the index is not complete. You might have to use intuition and luck to find some subjects.

FIGURE 28.15.

The IIS help is a hypertext document that requires a Web browser to access.

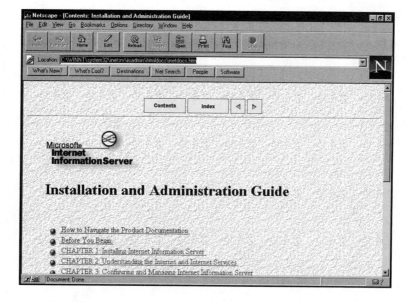

Summary

In this chapter, you've looked at how to set up and configure the Internet Information Service. This book isn't big enough to allow coverage of creating your directory structure and writing your Web pages, but you can find many useful books on the subject, as well as the IIS Help pages to give you a hand. This chapter has explained the configuration Properties sheets and how you can use them to manage the IIS services.

28

INTERNET
INFORMATION
SERVER

Windows NT Resources on the Internet

IN THIS CHAPTER

One of the best things about the Internet is that, generally, people are willing to help you in whatever way they can. If you have a question about almost anything, you usually can get an answer in about 24 hours if you know where to look for help. Many Windows NT resources are available on the Internet. Even though you can call Microsoft for questions about Windows NT, first, you might want to find out whether anyone has come across the same problem and learn what was done to solve the problem. This approach could save you some time and money. Another advantage of posting questions on the Internet is that they are read by a diverse group of people, so the responses you get are varied and include a wide range of experiences. You then can sift through the responses and select the best solution to suit your needs.

Where to Go When You Need Help

With a few exceptions, the Internet is a friendly place where people sometimes go out of their way to help you. If you're supporting Windows NT, consider joining one or more Windows NT Internet mailing lists (discussed in more detail in the following section). You also can visit Windows NT newsgroups and participate in discussions; these Internet options let you keep up-to-date with new information. You should also check out Microsoft's home page and the Windows NT information found there.

Windows NT Mailing Lists

A great way to learn how to do different things with Windows NT is to join one or more Windows NT mailing lists. Most people who subscribe to these mailing lists are people who use Windows NT every day, and they are quite helpful when someone has a problem. Before you join a mailing list, be aware that some of them generate quite a few e-mail messages each day. If you don't want to receive multiple e-mails throughout the day, it's better not to subscribe to a mailing list. In my opinion, however, the knowledge you can gain from being on one or more mailing lists is well worth the extra e-mail. By joining a mailing list, you not only get a chance to find solutions to your questions, but you can also discuss options with other NT users and learn innovative ways to accomplish your objectives. It's a safe bet that you will see me occasionally on some of the Windows NT mailing lists.

TIP

If your e-mail application supports rules (which let you specify what to do with incoming mail messages before you read them), use a rule to divert all e-mail from mailing lists to a folder. Then, the dozens of messages you might get from mailing lists won't distract you from your personal and business e-mail. It's generally a good idea to use a different folder for each mailing list so that when you have some free time, you can open a folder and read all the messages. An alternative would be to get a mailing list's digest, a single file summary of the relevant postings for a given period (usually weekly).

To join any of the Windows NT mailing lists in this chapter, simply send an e-mail message to the addresses listed. Be sure that your message body contains the text specified in each list. Usually, after a few hours, you will start receiving messages directed to the list.

TIP

After you subscribe to a mail list, you get a welcome message with information about the mailing list. Be sure to save this message; it also has information on how to unsubscribe from the mail list in case you change your mind. Some list members aren't very friendly when unsubscribe messages are sent to the main list!

A Few Windows NT Mailing Lists

There are quite a few Windows NT–related mailing lists you can subscribe to for information about NT in general, or particular aspects of the operating system and its configuration. Although it may be tempting to subscribe to them all, be careful because you will undoubtedly end up with more mail messages than you can easily handle. Try a few lists at a time and winnow out the ones that aren't useful to you. The list below shows some of the mailing lists that might be of interest to you.

For mailing lists related to Windows NT–based Web servers:

- Send e-mail to

    `webserver-nt-request@DELTA.PROCESS.COM`

    Include this in the body of your message:

    `subscribe webserver-nt`

- Send e-mail to

    `http_winnt@Emerald.NET`

    Include this in the body of your message:

    `subscribe` in the subject line; leave the body blank

For general discussions related to Windows NT:

- Send e-mail to

    `list@bhs.com`

    Include this in the body of your message:

    `join iwntug`

- Send e-mail to

    `listserv@eva.dc.lsoft.com`

    Include this in the body of your message:

    `subscribe winnt-l`

29

WINDOWS NT
RESOURCES ON
THE INTERNET

Windows NT Resources on the Web

Many resourceful Windows NT Web sites are available on the Internet. The following Web sites are devoted solely to Windows NT. You might want to add some of these sites to your favorite Web browser's bookmark list and visit them frequently to keep up-to-date with Windows NT developments and to find solutions to problems.

Microsoft Windows NT Hardware Compatibility List

You can visit this URL to find out whether a certain peripheral is compatible with Windows NT:

```
http://www.microsoft.com/isapi/hwtest/hsearchn4.idc
```

Microsoft Windows NT from a UNIX Point of View

The paper at the following site provides a technical overview of Windows NT for the information technology professional with a strong background in UNIX:

```
http://www.microsoft.com/BackOffice/reading/nt4unix.htm
```

It approaches the subject from the UNIX point of view and relates the concepts of Windows NT to corresponding UNIX concepts. The paper begins with a technical comparison of the two operating systems and moves on to cover how the two can coexist in a heterogeneous environment. It finishes with a brief section describing some of the tools available to help developers create applications for both platforms.

FAQs for Porting from UNIX to Windows NT

If you're interested in learning about NT versions of UNIX and TCP/IP utilities, you should visit this list of *frequently asked questions* (FAQs):

```
http://www.shore.net/~wihl/unix2nt.html
```

You might find these utilities quite useful. This site also has a list of FAQs about porting UNIX applications to Microsoft's Windows NT. This list should be read by anyone who intends to port UNIX applications or is actively porting UNIX applications; it's updated with new information about once a month.

Windows NT on the Internet

This site offers many resources for using Windows NT to host a Web site:

```
http://www.neystadt.org/winnt
```

European Microsoft Windows NT Academic Center (EMWAC)

EMWAC acts as a focus for activities and events that support the use of Windows NT. The following Web site is very useful for finding Internet tools and services for Windows NT:

```
http://www.emwac.ed.ac.uk/
```

Be sure to browse the Internet Tool Chest for NT at this site for Internet services such as finger, Gopher, HTTP Server, Internet Mail, WAIS, and WAIS Toolkit.

Digital's Windows NT Home Page

This URL leads you to the Windows NT resources page at Digital and has many Windows NT information resources:

```
http://www.windowsnt.digital.com/
```

If you are hosting your Web server on a DEC Alpha-based server, you will find this Web site particularly useful.

Beverly Hills Software Windows NT Resource Center

This site is a useful source for Windows NT resources and information:

```
http://www.bhs.com
```

Beverly Hills Software is a complete Internet consulting and presence firm specializing in the design, installation, and implementation of Microsoft Windows NT–based Internet Servers. It's also the home of The Windows NT Resource Center—a highly regarded Web site for Windows NT information and resources.

Microsoft NT Server Web Site

This site contains many Windows NT server resources, as well as information about creating Web sites by using Windows NT:

```
http://www.microsoft.com/ntserver/default.asp
```

Self-Reported Windows NT Links

This site has hundreds of Windows NT resources reported by users:

```
http://COBA.SHSU.edu/messages/nt-list.htm
```

The goal of this page is to create a dynamic source of information on Windows NT and to announce this information in a timely manner.

29

WINDOWS NT
RESOURCES ON
THE INTERNET

San Diego Windows NT User Group (SDWNTUG)

SDWNTUG encourages the use of Windows NT Server and Workstation and offers a free exchange of information and discussion of NT-related issues. You can get information about SDWNTUG at this site:

```
http://www.fbsolutions.com/sdwntug
```

NT Web Server Security Issues

This site tells you how to make your NT Web server more secure:

```
http://www.telemark.net/~randallg/ntsecure.htm
```

NT Web Server Resource Guide

This site provides a comprehensive list of Windows NT software and resources to host a Windows NT–based Web site:

```
http://mfginfo.com/htm/website.htm
```

Rick's Windows NT Information Center

Windows NT links about NT download sites, user groups and associations, newsgroups, mailing lists, and so on are provided at this site:

```
http://infotech.kumc.edu/winnt/
```

Sanjaya's Windows NT Resource Center

This resource center contains Windows NT information resources and is maintained by a Windows NT user:

```
http://Wonderland.dial.umd.edu/~NT
```

It contains information about hosting a Windows NT–based Web site, and it looks at issues you must deal with when using Windows NT.

Windows NT Software on the Web

Many Web sites distribute Windows NT software. You can accomplish tasks more efficiently by using the utilities and applications in the following Web sites. In addition, you will find applications that give you solutions to limitations of Windows NT, such as a lack of disk quota management and disk defragmenting.

Internet Shopper

Internet Shopper, found at the following site, is a company that promotes Windows NT on all platforms:

```
http://www.net-shopper.co.uk/
```

This site contains a number of Internet services for Windows NT for mail, hosting a list server, NNTP news server, Domain Name Service (DNS), and more.

California State University Windows NT Shareware Archive

This site offers an extensive collection of Windows NT shareware applications, as well as Windows NT drivers and Windows NT ports of useful UNIX utilities:

```
http://coyote.csusm.edu/cwis/winworld/nt.html
```

NT Perl Distribution Site

You can get the latest version of NT Perl from this FTP site at no fee:

```
ftp://ntperl.hip.com/ntperl/
```

Perl is a very powerful programming language commonly used to develop Web CGI programs.

NT DNS

You will find this site very useful if you're setting up a Windows NT Internet server and need DNS:

```
http://www.telemark.net/~randallg/ntdns.htm
```

This link gives you a free Windows NT port of UNIX Bind.

Pragma Systems Telnet Server

Pragma Systems has a Telnet server for Windows NT that you can use to connect to a Windows NT Internet server via Telnet. You can download an evaluation version of its Telnet service from this Web page:

```
http://www.ccsi.com:80/pragma/
```

Sunbelt International

This site offers many Windows NT disk-management utilities, such as a utility to check your disk fragmentation:

```
http://www.ntsoftdist.com/ntsoftdist/
```

29

WINDOWS NT
RESOURCES ON
THE INTERNET

Carmel Anti-Virus for Windows NT

Carmel Anti-Virus is a Windows NT virus detection and eradication utility, available at this site:

```
http://www.fbsolutions.com/ntav
```

Windows NT/Web Authoring Newsgroups

A few Internet newsgroups that discuss issues on Web site development follow. To keep up-to-date with new technologies and to learn procedures, it's a good idea to visit these newsgroups every now and then:

```
comp.infosystems.www.servers.ms-windows
comp.infosystems.www.servers.misc
comp.infosystems.www.browsers.ms-windows
comp.infosystems.www.authoring.cgi
comp.infosystems.www.authoring.misc
```

Many newsgroups have been set up on the Internet for discussions about Windows NT. To take part in these discussions, you might want to check out some of these newsgroups:

```
comp.os.ms-windows.nt.pre-release
comp.os.ms-windows.nt.misc
comp.os.ms-windows.nt.setup.misc
comp.os.ms-windows.nt.setup.hardware
comp.os.ms-windows.nt.admin.networking
comp.os.ms-windows.nt.admin.misc
comp.os.ms-windows.nt.software.backoffice
```

The Future of Windows NT and the Web

As the Web evolves, many people will discover how they can use it to effectively distribute information to a global audience and conduct business. Thanks to newly evolving technologies, such as Java and VRML, the Web's capabilities will be expanded further. By using Windows NT, anyone can establish a Web presence in very little time and take advantage of the Web's benefits.

As the popularity of the Web continues to grow, higher bandwidths will soon be available to home users. Although Internet connections to homes are usually established by using 14.4Kbps or 28.8Kbps modems, this trend will change soon when ISDN becomes more widely available. When cable companies realize the potential of offering Internet access through cable lines and start offering customers high-speed Internet access by cable, most home users will be able to connect to the Internet at higher speeds and use emerging Internet technologies, such as MBone, which supports real-time video multicasting on the Internet.

As these new technologies fuse with the Web, you might actually notice the television and the Web merging into one device. Currently, the only thing holding back video-on-demand on the Internet is low bandwidth communications lines. By using high-speed, fiber-optic lines and multicast routers, more efficient ways of distributing information will evolve. The first Internet TV broadcast station might not be that far away after all.

All these technologies need robust operating systems that are easy to set up and manage. Windows NT is an ideal operating system for such a task. Although UNIX servers traditionally have been used to handle such tasks, they often are more expensive to set up and administer than Windows NT–based servers. By going with Windows NT, many organizations can become part of the Web and contribute something meaningful to the Internet community.

Summary

This chapter has given you an overview of Windows NT resources available on the Internet. These resources include Windows NT mailing lists, Web sites, FTP sites, and newsgroups. By using these resources, you can find help whenever you have a problem or a question, and you can keep up-to-date with new Windows NT developments.

29

WINDOWS NT
RESOURCES ON
THE INTERNET

V

PART

Appendixes

New Features in
Windows NT Server 4

APPENDIX A

Windows NT Server 4 has many new features added since the last version, NT 3.51. This appendix divides these features into general categories to make them easier to digest.

Ease of Use

Windows 95 user interface   The Windows 95 user interface is integrated into Windows NT Server 4, enhancing ease of use and providing consistency with Windows 95 and Windows NT Workstation 4.

Administrative wizards   These wizards group the common server-management tools into a single place and walk you through the steps required for each task. Windows NT Server 4 includes the following wizards:

> **Add User Accounts Wizard**   Adds new users to a Windows NT Server network.
>
> **Group Management Wizard**   Creates and manages groups of users.
>
> **Managing File and Folder Access Wizard**   Shares drives and folders for Macintosh, Microsoft, and Novell network clients in one step, and specifies security settings.
>
> **Add Printer Wizard**   Sets up printers connected to your computer or on a network and shares them. Installs printer drivers on the server for point-and-print installation on clients.
>
> **Add/Remove Programs Wizard**   Installs or removes programs from your computer.
>
> **Install New Modem Wizard**   Sets up and detects modems connected to your computer.
>
> **Network Client Administrator Wizard**   Installs or updates network client workstations.
>
> **License Wizard**   Makes it easy for administrators to keep track of the software licenses they use for servers and clients.

Network Monitor   This powerful network diagnostic tool allows you to examine network traffic to and from the server at the packet level. You can capture network traffic for later analysis, making it easier to troubleshoot your network problems.

System policy and user profiles   These features allow system administrators to consistently manage and maintain users' desktops. System policies standardize desktop configurations, enforce behavior, and control users' work environments and actions. User profiles contain all user-definable settings for the work environment of a computer running Windows NT. Both policies and profiles can be stored on a network server, so as users log onto different computers, they always get the same desktop.

Task Manager   Task Manager is an integrated tool for monitoring applications, tasks, and key performance measurements of a Windows NT Server–based system. Task Manager gives you detailed information on each application and process running on the workstation, as well as memory and CPU use. It allows you to easily terminate applications and processes that aren't responding, thereby improving system reliability.

Printing enhancements   Printing performance is improved through the server-based rendering of print jobs, resulting in quicker return-to-application times and quicker return of control to users after print jobs are initiated. Printer drivers for shared printers are located on the server for point-and-print automatic client driver installation. Remote Printer folders allow you to easily browse shared printers.

Improved Windows NT diagnostics tool   Windows NT Server 4 includes an improved Windows NT diagnostics program that allows for easy examination of the system. The new version contains information on device drivers; network use; and system resources, such as IRQ, DMA, and I/O addresses. This information is presented in a easy-to-view graphical tool that can also run on a remote Windows NT system.

Performance Improvements

Higher network throughput   Higher file server throughput offers up to 66 percent improved performance on Fast Ethernet (100Mbps) LANs. (Test results from National Software Testing Laboratories [NSTL].)

Improved scalability   Improvements in Windows NT Server 4 deliver better performance scalability on multiprocessor systems—especially those with more than four processors. New APIs for server application developers and better server performance deliver up to 33 percent better throughput and scalability for server applications, such as Microsoft SQL Server.

Faster Internet server   The combination of Windows NT Server 4 and Microsoft Internet Information Server (IIS) 2.0 delivers up to 40 percent better Web server performance (Microsoft test results).

Internet and Intranet Access

This section lists IIS 2.0 improvements.

Complete Integration with Windows NT Server 4

- Installation integrated into Windows NT 4 setup, allowing installation of IIS while installing Windows NT Server
- Integrated with Windows NT Server security and directory service
- Fastest Web server available for Windows NT Server—more than 40 percent faster than IIS 1.0, with better scaling on multiprocessor systems

Comprehensive Web Server Solution

- The Index Server allows for content indexing and search capabilities of HTML and Office documents

- Server administration of IIS from any Web browser or Internet Service Manager tool

- Supports logging server traffic to NCSA Common Log File format, as well as any ODBC database

- Easier migration from UNIX systems; supports NCSA- and CERN-style map files

- Easier to set up *Secure Socket Layer* (SSL) security by using the new Key Manager tool

- Supports HTTP byte range, allowing browsers to begin receiving data from any part of a file for enhanced performance

- Real-time performance monitoring with the Windows NT Performance Monitor

Easy Platform for Building Internet Applications

- Improved programmability using *Internet Server API* (ISAPI)—for example, several server variables now are exposed, and nested IF statements are supported, offering greater programming capabilities

- Improved database programmability with the *Internet Database Connector* (IDC); multiple database queries can be grouped for improved performance

- Integration with BackOffice and thousands of other Win32-based applications

- Supports CGI, WinCGI, Visual Basic, and Perl scripting technologies

Microsoft Index Server

Microsoft Index Server automatically indexes the full text and properties of files (including HTML) on your server—whether it's an intranet, an Internet, or simply a file-and-print server. The Index Server offers these capabilities:

Indexes all documents Index Server allows you to query indexes and entire documents on Internet or intranet sites that are stored on an IIS server. The search engine has a unique ability to find documents in a wide variety of formats, such as text in a Word document, statistics on a Microsoft Excel spreadsheet, or the contents of an HTML page.

Customizable query form The Index Server allows the network administrator to create a customized query form, letting end-users choose parameters for their search. This form modification allows a user to search by contents or other document properties, such as author and subject.

Automatic maintenance The Index Server is designed for a zero-maintenance environment in which a server must be running 24 hours a day, seven days a week. After Index Server is set up, all the operations are automatic, including updates, index creation and optimization, and crash recovery in case of power failure.

Administrative tools   A number of built-in tools help administrators optimize their query service. The performance-monitoring capability gives administrators key information to gauge site performance—including the number of queries processed and the response time.

Multiple Languages   Index Server provides built-in language support, allowing end-users to query documents in seven languages. Documents written in Dutch, English (U.S. and International), French, German, Italian, Spanish, and Swedish can be searched.

Microsoft FrontPage

Microsoft FrontPage is designed for non-programmers, yet it's robust enough even for experienced Web site developers. Microsoft FrontPage 1.1 is the fast, easy way to create and manage professional-quality Web sites. With features such as WYSIWYG editing and wizards to step you through creating your Web site, it has never been easier to publish on the Web. Microsoft FrontPage also makes it easy for large teams to work together to create and manage sites. Its combination of flexible client/server architecture, passwords, user authentication, and other security features lets contributors in different locations securely update different pages simultaneously on the same site.

Internet Explorer 2.0

Microsoft's easy-to-use Internet browser embraces existing HTML standards, such as tables, while advancing HTML with new improvements, such as online video, backgrounds, and SSL support.

Communications Features

RAS multilink channel aggregation   With PPP-compliant channel aggregation, *Remote Access Service* (RAS) allows clients dialing into Windows NT Server 4 to combine all available dial-up lines to get higher transfer speeds. Users can combine two or more ISDN B channels to get speeds of 128K or greater or to combine two or more standard modem lines, for example. This feature provides overall increased bandwidth and even allows users to combine ISDN lines with analog modem lines for increased performance.

Point-to-Point Tunneling Protocol **(PPTP)**   Provides a way to use public data networks, such as the Internet, to create a virtual private network connecting client PCs with servers. PPTP offers protocol encapsulation to support multiple protocols through TCP/IP connections and encryption of data for privacy, making it safer to send information over non-secure networks. This technology extends the capacity of RAS to allow remote access and securely extend private networks across the Internet without the need to change client software.

Restartable file copy   This feature automatically begins transferring a file again after reconnection whenever your RAS connection has been lost. Nearly anyone who has used a modem can remember times when he or she has nearly completed a file transfer across a modem only to have the remote connection disabled before the transmission was finished. Re-establishing the connection and starting the file-transfer process all over again can be frustrating, time-consuming, and expensive. Restartable file copy addresses this problem by remembering the status of your file transmission and continuing the transfer from that point after you reconnect.

Idle disconnect   This new feature automatically terminates your RAS connection after a certain period of time if no activity has occurred over the remote dial-up communications link. The user or administrator can specify the amount of time before this feature is activated. Idle disconnect reduces the cost of remote access carrier service and can even allow a company to reduce the capacity of its dial-in communications links, all based on reducing wasted remote connect time.

Autodial and logon dial   Windows now can map and maintain an associate between a Dial-Up Networking entry and a network address to seamlessly integrate Dial-Up Networking with files and applications. This means that if you double-click an icon to open a file and that file is accessible only over a dial-up connection, Dial-Up Networking automatically initiates to give you quick and easy access to the information you need.

Client and server API enhancements   A number of new APIs are now available to extend RAS capabilities on Windows NT Server 4 and Dial-Up Networking with Windows NT Workstation 4. These APIs allow third-party developers to add value to RAS and Dial-Up Networking, making an already great platform for remote access and communications even better. For a complete list and detailed descriptions of how to use the new RAS APIs in Windows NT 4, see The Microsoft Developer Network.

Multiprotocol router (MPR)   This service allows small and medium-size sites to use Windows NT Server as a low-cost LAN-to-LAN routing solution, eliminating the need for a dedicated router. MPR provides LAN-to-LAN routing for IPX/SPX, TCP/IP, and AppleTalk.

Telephony API 2.0   Windows NT Server offers built-in, comprehensive telephony support with *Telephony API* (TAPI) 2.0. TAPI allows you to develop integrated computer-telephony applications. This makes telephony application support on industry standard hardware platforms and integration with legacy phone systems much easier and less expensive.

Cryptography APIs   This set of encryption APIs allows developers to develop applications that will work securely over non-secure networks, such as the Internet.

Network Integration Services

***Distributed Component Object Model* (DCOM)**   The COM allows software developers to create component applications. Windows NT Server and Windows NT Workstation 4 include Distributed COM, which extends COM to allow components to communicate across networks. An example of a DCOM application is a stock quote server object running on Windows NT Server, distributing quotes to multiple Windows NT Workstation clients. DCOM supplies the infrastructure for connecting the objects on the two workstations and supports communication between the objects so that users can get the stock quotes. DCOM uses the same tools and technologies as COM, thus preserving investments in training and software.

DNS Server   This is a completely new version of DNS service. Features include a graphical administration utility and integration with *Windows Internet Name Service* (WINS) for dynamic updates of hostnames and addresses. Through the WINS/DNS integration, an end-user can use DNS compound names to access a network resource. By using Windows NT Explorer, for example, you can access a share through a DNS name, such as `\\srv1.myco.com\public`.

Updated Novell NetWare interoperability services   Client and gateway services for NetWare are extended to support *NetWare Directory Services* (NDS). Added functionality includes browsing NDS resources, NDS authentication, and NDS printing. These services provide support for authentication to multiple NDS trees and processing logon scripts.

Windows 95 *Remote Initial Program Load* (RIPL)   Allows diskless Windows 95 clients to be booted from a Windows NT Server.

Windows NT Features

The following tables give you a summary of the new features in Windows NT 4 and some of the different aspects of the operating system that you might need to refer to. These tables compare Windows NT Server 4 to the last two releases of NetWare, usually considered Windows NT's closest competitor. As you can see, Windows NT offers many more features than the latest version of NetWare.

Table A.1. New features in Windows NT Server 4.

	Windows NT Server 4	NetWare 3.12	NetWare 4.1
Ease of Use and Management			
Easy graphical user interface—consistent with desktop operating systems	✓		
Administrative Wizards	✓		
Task Manager for process and memory monitoring	✓		
Network Monitor (network traffic analyzer)	✓		
Graphical system diagnostics tool	✓		

continues

Table A.1. continued

	Windows NT Server 4	NetWare 3.12	NetWare 4.1
Ease of Use and Management			
System policy editor and user profiles	✓		
Internet and Communications Services			
Built-in Internet (Web, FTP, Gopher) server	✓		
HTML and document content indexing and search engine	✓		
Web site content creation and management application	✓		
DCOM	✓		
Multilink channel aggregation	✓		
PPTP	✓		
Network Integration			
DNS Server with graphical administration and WINS integration	✓		
MPR	✓	✓	✓
Windows 95 *Remote Program Load* (RPL)	✓	✓	✓
Cryptography APIs	✓		

Table A.2. Key features.

	Windows NT Server 4	NetWare 3.12	NetWare 4.1
Architecture			
Preemptive multitasking	✓		
Processors—Intel	✓	✓	✓
Processors—RISC	✓ (MIPS, DEC Alpha, PowerPC)		
Symmetric multiprocessing (separate product)	✓ 32 processors		
Virtual memory	✓		
Microkernal architecture	✓		
Memory protection for applications (for debugging only) and subsystems	✓		
Transports			
Protocols included	NetBEUI, IPX, TCP/IP (native)	IPX	CP/IP (tunneling)
Multilink channel aggregation	✓		
PPTP	✓		
MPR	✓	✓	✓
Internet Features			
Web server	✓		
FTP server	✓		
Gopher server	✓		
Web database connectivity and publishing	✓		
Remote Web server administration	✓		

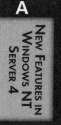

continues

Table A.2. continued

	Windows NT Server 4	NetWare 3.12	NetWare 4.1
Internet Features			
CGI and native programming interfaces	✓		
Supports standard administration tools; now includes support for *Systems Management Server* (SMS) and SNMP administration tools	✓		
Supports NCSA-style map files, as well as CERN-style map files, facilitating porting from UNIX systems	✓		
Easy to set up SSL security via Key Manager Tool	✓		
DCOM for easily distributed applications	✓		
File System			
Efficient sub-block allocation	✓ 512 bytes	✓ 16K	✓ 16K
File compression	✓		✓
High-performance asynchronous I/O	✓		
Performance Optimizations			
Dynamic cache	✓ 1GB per process		(static cache)

	Windows NT Server 4	NetWare 3.12	NetWare 4.1
Security			
Designed to meet C2 security	✓		✓ (requires special hardware)
Single logon compatibility for client/server applications	✓		✓
Centralized security event auditing	✓		
Network Management			
Administrative wizards	✓		
Graphical system diagnostics tool	✓		
System policy editor and user profiles	✓		
GUI utilities	✓		✓
Remote administration, performance, and event monitoring	✓		
DHCP support for TCP/IP	✓		✓
WINS support for TCP/IP	✓		
DNS server with WINS integration	✓		
Network protocol analyzer	✓		
Directory Service			
Automatic replication	✓		✓
Single network logon	✓		✓
Applications can be integrated into directory service	✓		✓

continues

Table A.2. continued

	Windows NT Server 4	NetWare 3.12	NetWare 4.1
Performance Monitoring			
Graphical remote performance monitoring	✓		
Fault Tolerance			
File System Recovery Log	✓		

Table A.3. Feature comparisons.

	Windows NT Server 4	NetWare 3.12	NetWare 4.1
Architecture			
Multiuser operating system	✓	✓	✓
Preemptive multitasking	✓		
Processors—Intel	✓	✓	✓
Processors—RISC	✓ (MIPS, DEC Alpha, PowerPC)		
Symmetric multiprocessing	✓ up to 32 processors		(separate product)
Asymmetric multiprocessing clustering		✓	
Minimum memory RAM	16M	4M	6M
Maximum memory RAM	4G	4G	4G
Paged virtual memory	✓		
Dynamic memory cache	✓		
Maximum number of user connections	unlimited	250	1000
32-bit operating system	✓	✓	✓
Dynamic loading of services	✓	✓	✓

	Windows NT Server 4	NetWare 3.12	NetWare 4.1
Architecture			
Memory protection of applications	✓		
Audit alerts	✓	✓ Audit Y, Alerts N	✓
Structured exception handling	✓		
Microkernel-based architecture	✓		
Protected subsystems	✓		
Hardware abstraction layer	✓		
Unicode support	✓		
Installable file systems	✓	✓	✓
NIC Support: Client			
16-bit, Ethernet support	✓	✓	✓
32-bit, Ethernet support	✓	✓	✓
16-bit, token-ring support	✓	✓	✓
32-bit, token-ring support	✓	✓	✓
NDIS support	✓		✓
ODI support	✓	✓	✓
Third-party driver support	✓	✓	✓
NIC Support: Server			
16-bit, Ethernet support	✓	✓	✓
32-bit, Ethernet support	✓	✓	✓
16-bit, token-ring support	✓	✓	✓
32-bit, token-ring support	✓	✓	✓
NDIS support	✓		
ODI support	✓ Novell requester only	✓	✓

continues

A

NEW FEATURES IN
WINDOWS NT
SERVER 4

Table A.3. continued

	Windows NT Server 4	NetWare 3.12	NetWare 4.1
NIC Support: Server			
Third-party driver support	✓	✓	✓
Multiple network adapters	✓	✓	✓
Other Hardware Support			
CD-ROM	✓	✓	✓
SCSI adapters	✓	✓	✓
Plotters	✓	✓	✓
Scanners	✓		
Transports			
IPX	✓	✓	✓
IPX dial-in	✓	✓	✓
Packet burst	✓	✓	✓
LIP	✓	✓	✓
AppleTalk	✓	✓(extra cost)	✓(extra cost)
NetBEUI	✓		
TCP/IP (tunneling)	✓	✓	✓
TCP/IP (native)	✓		
PPP	✓(IPX, NetBEUI, TCP/IP)		
OSI	✓(in SDK)		
DECNet	✓(DEC)		
DLC	✓	✓	✓
Internal routing	✓	✓	✓

	Windows NT Server 4	NetWare 3.12	NetWare 4.1
IPCs			
Named pipes (client side)	✓	✓	✓
Named pipes (server side)	✓		
Sockets	✓	✓	✓
Transport Library Interface	✓		
DCE-compatible RPC	✓		
LU 6.2, LU1, LU0, LU2, LU3	✓(SNA Server)	✓ (NetWare SAA)	✓ (NetWare SAA)
HLLAPI	✓(third party)	✓(third party)	✓(third party)
Local procedure call (LPC)	✓		
Semaphores	✓		✓
Mutexes	✓		✓
Timers	✓		
Asynchronous procedure calls	✓		
File System			
Maximum number of file locks	Unlimited	100K	100K
Maximum number of file opens	Unlimited	100K	100K
Maximum file size	17 billion G	4G	4G
Efficient sub-block allocation	✓512 bytes	✓	✓16K
File compression	✓		✓
Transaction-based file system	✓		✓
Support for MS-DOS files	✓	✓	✓
Support for Macintosh files	✓	✓	✓
Support for OS/2 files	✓	✓	✓
Support for NFS	✓(third party)	✓(extra cost)	✓(extra cost)
Volumes/files span drives	✓	✓	✓
Total disk storage	408 million T	32T	32T

continues

A

NEW FEATURES IN
WINDOWS NT
SERVER 4

Table A.3. continued

	Windows NT Server 4	NetWare 3.12	NetWare 4.1
File System			
Maximum volumes/server	25	64	64
Maximum physical drives/server	limit of hardware	1024	1024
Maximum partition size	17,000T	drive size	drive size
Maximum volume size	17,000T	32T	32T
Disk quotas	✓(third party)	✓	✓
High-performance asynchronous I/O	✓		
Memory-mapped file I/O	✓		
Maximum length of filename	255	255	255
Long filenames made visible to clients	✓	✓(only with OS/2 namespace)	✓(only with OS/2 namespace)
Performance Optimizations			
Dynamic cache	✓(1G per process)		(static cache)
Elevator seeking	✓	✓	✓
Read-ahead caching	✓	✓	✓
Background writes	✓	✓	✓
Overlapped seeks	✓	✓	✓
Split seeks	✓	✓	✓
Directory hashing	✓	✓	✓
Directory caching	✓	✓	✓
File caching	✓	✓	✓
Virtual memory	✓		
Returnable memory	✓	✓	✓
Data scattering		✓	✓

	Windows NT Server 4	NetWare 3.12	NetWare 4.1
Security			
Designed to meet C2 security	✓Redbook	✓Orangebook	✓(requires special hardware)
Designed to meet B2 security	✓(third party)		
Single logon to network	✓		✓
Single, secure logon	✓	✓	✓
Minimum password length restriction	✓	✓	✓
Passwords encrypted	✓	✓	✓
Packet signing (secure authentication)	✓	✓	✓
Password aging	✓	✓	✓
Password history	✓	✓	✓
Minimum time until password can be changed	✓	✓	✓
Account lockout	✓	✓	✓
Restrict logon to specific workstation	✓	✓	✓
Replaceable client logon	✓		✓
Limit concurrent connections for single user	✓		✓
Restrict logon by time and day	✓	✓	✓
Set account expiration date	✓	✓	✓
Disconnect when access time expires	✓	✓	✓
Re-key password verify	✓	✓	✓
Configurable administrative rights	✓	✓	✓
Centralized security event auditing	✓		

continues

Table A.3. continued

	Windows NT Server 4	NetWare 3.12	NetWare 4.1
Security			
Security event alerts	✓		
File system auditing	✓	✓	✓
Directory and File Rights			
Read	✓	✓	✓
Write	✓	✓	✓
Execute	✓	✓	✓
Delete	✓	✓	✓
Change permissions (grant)	✓	✓	✓
Take ownership	✓	✓	✓
List directory	✓	✓	✓
Create files in directory	✓	✓	✓
User Rights			
Access workstation from network	✓		
Log on locally	✓		
Back up files and directories	✓	✓	✓
Restore files and directories	✓	✓	✓
Change the system time	✓		
Shut down system locally	✓	✓ (rconsole)	✓ (rconsole)
Force system shutdown remotely	✓	✓ (rconsole)	✓ (rconsole)
Load and unload device drivers	✓	✓ (rconsole)	✓ (rconsole)
Manage audit and security logs	✓		
Take ownership of files or other objects	✓	✓ (yes, with supervisor rights)	✓ (yes, with supervisor rights)

	Windows NT Server 4	NetWare 3.12	NetWare 4.1
Security Auditing			
Audit user security transactions	✓	✓	✓
Audit user file transactions	✓	✓	✓
Audit administrator transactions	✓	✓	✓
Audit file-creation statistics	✓	✓	✓
Audit volume statistics	✓	✓	✓
Filter audit logs	✓	✓	✓
Audit security policy changes	✓		
Audit restart or shutdown of system	✓		✓
Non-dedicated server	✓		✓ (with OS/2 add-in product)
Remote printer port on workstation	✓	✓	✓
Peer print services	✓		
Assign priorities to print queue	✓	✓	✓
Multiple queues to a single printer	✓	✓	✓
Multiple queues on multiple printers	✓	✓	✓
Multiple printers on one queue	✓	✓	✓
PostScript supported	✓	✓	✓
Maximum shared printers per server	unlimited	16	255
Cross-platform printing (OS/2)	✓	✓	✓
Cross-platform printing (UNIX)	✓	✓ (extra cost)	✓ (extra cost)

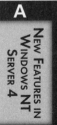

A

NEW FEATURES IN
WINDOWS NT
SERVER 4

continues

Table A.3. continued

	Windows NT Server 4	NetWare 3.12	NetWare 4.1
Security Auditing			
Cross-platform printing (NetWare)	✓	✓	✓
Cross-platform printing (SNA)	✓	✓	✓
Remote queue management	✓	✓	✓
Support for multiple forms		✓	✓
Network attached printer support	✓	✓	✓
User notification of job completion	✓	✓	✓
Operator notification of print problem	✓	✓	✓
Printer Alerts			
Out of paper	✓	✓	✓
Print request deleted	✓	✓	✓
Print request completed	✓	✓	✓
Printer offline	✓	✓	✓
Paper jam	✓	✓	✓
Needs specific form		✓	✓
Configure error reporting to specific users		✓	✓
Network Management			
Command-line utilities	✓	✓	✓
GUI utilities	✓		✓
Remote administration, performance, and event monitoring	✓	✓	✓

	Windows NT Server 4	NetWare 3.12	NetWare 4.1
Network Management			
Asynchronous remote administration	✓	✓	✓
Remote installation	✓	✓	✓
Remote upgrade	✓	✓	✓
Remote corrective service	✓	✓	✓
Remote session security	✓	✓	✓
Remote modem callback	✓	✓ (extra cost)	✓ (extra cost)
DHCP support for TCP/IP	✓		✓
WINS support for TCP/IP	✓		
Performance Monitoring			
View total percentage CPU use	✓	✓	✓
View total privileged CPU use	✓		
View total user CPU use	✓		
View logical disk use	✓	✓	✓
View physical disk use	✓	✓	✓
View cache utilization	✓	✓	✓
View packets/bytes sent	✓	✓	✓
View page/faults per second	✓		
View number of active processes	✓	✓	✓
View number of active threads	✓		
View processor time by process	✓		
View processor time by thread	✓		
Log performance statistics	✓		

continues

A

NEW FEATURES IN
WINDOWS NT
SERVER 4

Table A.3. continued

	Windows NT Server 4	NetWare 3.12	NetWare 4.1
Delegating Administrative Responsibility			
Account operators	✓	✓	✓
Backup operators	✓	✓	✓
Directory administrator	✓	✓	✓
Enterprise administrator	✓	✓	✓
Print operator	✓	✓	✓
Replication operator	✓		
Server operator	✓	✓	✓
Alert Messages			
Volume is getting full	✓	✓	✓
Volume is full	✓	✓	✓
Error log is full	✓	✓	✓
Connection slots depleted	✓	✓	✓
Memory for resource allocation depleted alert	✓ (low virtual memory)	✓	✓
Disk utilization above threshold	✓	✓	✓
Fault Tolerance			
File system recovery log	✓		
Redundant directory structures	✓	✓	✓
Directory verification during powerup	✓	✓	✓
Read-after-write verification	✓	✓	✓
Hot fix	✓	✓	✓
Salvage/undelete	✓ (FAT only)	✓	✓

	Windows NT Server 4	NetWare 3.12	NetWare 4.1
Fault Tolerance			
UPS support	✓	✓	✓
Disk duplexing	✓	✓	✓
Disk mirroring	✓	✓	✓
Software RAID 5	✓		
Server mirroring	✓ (third party)	✓	
Dynamic volume sets	✓		
Backup			
Backup/restore of server disk w/security	✓	✓	✓
Online backup of account files	✓	✓	
Backup utility included	✓		
Workstation backup (Windows for Workgroups, Windows NT Workstation)	✓	✓ (TSR)	✓ (TSR)
Automatic file replication service	✓		
Server job scheduling	✓		

IIS 2.0 Summary Tables

This section covers the features of IIS and what it's capable of. In most cases, I compare IIS 2.0 to the last release, which was an add-on with Windows NT 3.51. Now that IIS 2.0 is included with Windows NT 4, you can set up a powerful and feature-rich server environment without spending any extra money.

A

NEW FEATURES IN WINDOWS NT SERVER 4

Table A.4. New features of IIS 2.0.

Feature	Description
Fully Integrated with Windows NT Server 4	
Installation integrated into Windows NT Server 4 installation	Installation integrated into Windows NT 4 setup; allows you to easily install IIS while installing Windows NT Server
Integrated with Windows NT Server 4 directory and security services	Fully integrated with security and directory services
High-performance Web server	More than 40 percent faster than IIS 1.0
Comprehensive Web Server Solution	
Microsoft Index Server	Provides content indexing and search capabilities of HTML and Microsoft Office documents (free downloadable component)
Microsoft FrontPage	Now included free of charge
FrontPage extensions	Facilitate remote content authoring on your Web server without the need for file shares
HTML-based administration	Server administration of IIS from any Web browser in addition to the Internet Service Manager
Internet Service Manager enhancements	Internet Service Manager now also runs on Windows 95; the TCP/IP port that IIS listens for incoming connections on can now be configured
Key Manager tool	Easier to set up SSL security
Configurable TCP/IP port	The Internet Service Manager allows specification of the port on which the server operates
Supports standard administration tools	IIS now includes support for SNMP administration tools, as well as Systems Management Server
Easy Platform for Building Internet Applications	
Improved programmability using the ISAPI	Several additional server variables now are exposed and nested; IF statements are supported, providing greater programming capabilities; ISAPI filters now can receive notification when a request is denied

Feature	Description
Easy Platform for Building Internet Applications	
Improved database programmability with the *Internet Database Connector* (IDC)	IDC now supports multiple queries from a single HTML page and associated result sets; also, all server variables now are exposed to IDC scripts
HTTP read byte range	Allows clients to resume reading a file from where they left off if the network connection is lost
Image map file enhancements	Support for both NCSA- and CERN-style image map files facilitates porting from UNIX systems; IIS 2.0 always sends redirects on image map lookup

Table A.5. Windows NT Server 4/IIS 2.0 versus Netscape Enterprise Server.

	Microsoft Windows NT Server 4	Netscape Enterprise Server
Installation		
Installs with operating system—No additional setup required	✓	
Automatic upgrading from previous version	✓	✓
Security		
Integrated with operating system security	✓	
User and groups available for a single server	✓	✓
User and groups available to all servers on network	✓	
Uses existing file access control lists for internal Webs	✓	

continues

A

Table A.5. continued

	Microsoft Windows NT Server 4	*Netscape Enterprise Server*
Security		
Restrict access by user and group	✓	✓
Restrict access by directory and file	✓	✓
Restrict access by IP address	✓	✓
Restrict access by hostname	✓	✓
Basic HTTP user authorization with clear-text passwords	✓	✓
Secure Windows NT user authorization with encrypted passwords	✓	
Cross-platform access control	✓	✓
SSL 2 security	✓	✓
SSL 3 security		✓(only for clients that support it)
Server key management	✓	✓
Client authorization using certificates		✓(requires server to grant certificates and clients that support it)
Support for secure private intranets over public Internet	✓(only for clients that support it)	
Performance and Reliability		
Based on open standards and protocols	✓	✓
HTTP byte range	✓	✓
HTTP keep alives	✓	✓
Serves Web sites with millions of hits per day	✓	✓

	Microsoft Windows NT Server 4	Netscape Enterprise Server
Server Administration/Management		
Administer a server from any Web browser	✓	✓
Administer from any Web client anywhere	✓	✓
Manage multiple host machines simultaneously	✓	
Secure management through user authentication	✓	✓
Default administrative control by server administrator group	✓	
SNMP support	✓	✓
Limit network bandwidth used	✓	
Custom logging	✓	✓
Log to text file	✓	✓
Log with common log format	✓	✓
Log to any ODBC data source	✓	
Built-in log file analysis		✓
Hardware virtual servers	✓	✓
Software virtual servers		✓ (only for clients that support it)
Server configuration rollback		✓
Content Creation and Management (Microsoft FrontPage)		
Graphical Web page creation	✓	✓ (requires Navigator Gold)
HTML page and site wizards and templates	✓	✓ (available only on the Internet)
Image and document conversion support	✓	✓ (requires Netscape LiveWire)

continues

Table A.5. continued

	Microsoft Windows NT Server 4	*Netscape Enterprise Server*
Content Creation and Management (Microsoft FrontPage)		
Graphical file and directory management	✓	✓ (requires Netscape LiveWire)
Graphical site map	✓	
Automatic link validation	✓	✓ (requires Netscape LiveWire)
Automatic link recalculation	✓	✓ (requires Netscape LiveWire)
One-button publishing	✓	✓ (requires Netscape LiveWire)
Document revision control	✓ (requires Microsoft SourceSafe)	✓
Content Indexing (Microsoft Index Server)		
Integrated HTML and text search	✓	✓
Integrated Microsoft Office document search	✓	
Query HTML document property meta tags	✓	
Query Microsoft Office and OLE document properties	✓	
Rich set of query operators	✓	
Multilingual indexing and querying	✓ (seven languages)	✓ (English only)
Linguistic stemming for fuzzy searches	✓	
Result set customizable with any document property	✓	
Catalog HTML document property meta tags		✓
Display only documents that user has permission to view	✓	

	Microsoft Windows NT Server 4	Netscape Enterprise Server
Content Indexing (Microsoft Index Server)		
Automatic corruption detection and repair	✓	
Web-based administration	✓	✓
Development Environment		
CGI and WinCGI support	✓	✓
Support for standard languages such as Perl and Visual Basic	✓	✓
ISAPI support	✓	
NSAPI support		✓
Cross-platform ODBC database connector	✓	✓ (requires Netscape LiveWire)
Server-side JavaScript		✓ (requires Netscape LiveWire)
Server-side Java applets		✓
Cost Effectiveness		
Included in operating system	✓	
Integrates with existing network infrastructure	✓	
Add-on product		✓
Requires separate duplicate network infrastructure		✓
Includes FTP server	✓	
Includes Gopher server	✓	

Some information in this appendix courtesy of Microsoft Corporation

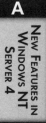

APPENDIX B

Windows NT Workstation 4 Versus Windows NT Server 4

IN THIS APPENDIX

Microsoft's plethora of products can lead users to wonder whether they're seeing double at times. With all the flavors of its products (16-bit, 32-bit, and different version numbers and packaging schemes), who can blame potential customers for being confused? When Windows for Workgroups first came out, that was simple. It was Windows with some built-in networking capabilities. But then there was Windows 3.11, then Win95, and then…the variations of Windows NT. At first, there was simply Windows NT. You *could,* if the spirit moved you, buy a special variation of NT called Advanced Server, but it wasn't pitched very heavily. Since NT 3.5, the two products (Workstation and Server) have been marketed to different audiences. In an effort to keep you clear on what's what, I've put together a few sections listing the distinguishing characteristics of the Windows family members. This appendix covers the following topics:

- Differences between Windows NT Workstation 4 and Windows NT Server 4
- New features of NT Workstation 4
- NT Workstation 4 versus Windows 95
- New features of NT Server 4

This appendix details some of the differences between the NT Workstation and Server products.

Windows NT Server 4 Versus Windows NT Workstation 4

Table B.1 summarizes some of the technical differences between Windows NT Workstation 4 and Windows NT Server 4.

Table B.1. Windows NT Workstation 4 versus Windows NT Server 4.

Functionality	*Windows NT Workstation 4*	*Windows NT Server 4*
Pricing/licensing	$319: Maximum of 10 computers connected; includes sharing, such as file and print and peer Web services (see license for details)	$809: 5-client access licenses $1,129: 10-client access licenses (see license for details)
System design goals	Keep workstation responsive to the local user with minimum memory footprint	Network performance is the priority; use all available memory and CPU to provide fastest network file access

Windows NT Workstation 4 Versus Windows NT Server 4

APPENDIX B

747

B

NT WORKSTA-
TION 4 VERSUS
NT SERVER 4

Functionality	Windows NT Workstation 4	Windows NT Server 4
Windows 95 user interface	Yes	Yes
Win32 API	Yes	Yes
Memory	Minimum 12M RAM Recommended 16M+ RAM	Minimum 16M RAM Recommended 32M+ RAM
Hard drive	Minimum 110M	Minimum 160M
Number of processors supported	2	32
Fault tolerance	None	Mirroring, duplexing, RAID 5
Number of inbound, dial-in connections	1	256
File and print serving	Peer (limited—see license)	Yes (requires client-access licenses)
HTTP, Gopher, FTP serving	Peer (limited—see license)	Yes (IIS)
DNS server	No	Yes
DHCP server	No	Yes
WINS server	No	Yes
Index server	No	Yes (available free on Internet)
Web authoring	No	Yes (Microsoft FrontPage included)
Services for Macintosh	No	Yes
File and Print Services for NetWare	No	Yes (add-on product)
Directory Services Manager for NetWare	No	Yes (add-on product)
Runs Microsoft BackOffice and BackOffice Server Logo applications	No	Yes

continues

Table B.1. continued

Functionality	Windows NT Workstation 4	Windows NT Server 4
Administrative control	Local administrative control and restricted remote administration	Centralized administrative control across all desktops and servers
Performance tuning	User's foreground application maintains highest priority; applications granted minimum memory at startup; Scheduler uses short timeslices for maximum user response	Network services retain highest system priority; file cache is preserved above all other services; applications granted maximum requested memory at startup; Scheduler uses long timeslices to respond to network requests

Windows NT Performance Optimizations

Windows NT Workstation, as its name suggests, is optimized to give the best performance to a single user stationed at the computer's screen and keyboard. Graphics, user input, and task switching are given high priorities. Windows NT Server, on the other hand, prioritizes incoming requests for file and printer sharing, processor resources, and Web-page access. These differences are outlined here.

Task scheduling   Tasks in Windows NT Server are given longer timeslices, which allows NT Server to process network requests with less interruption. *Symmetric multiprocessing* (SMP) benefits from this in particular, because longer timeslices allow better processor and cache synchronization. Windows NT Workstation gives tasks shorter timeslices, allowing quicker response to user input. The system feels more responsive.

Memory allocation   Windows NT Server grants applications the maximum amount of memory they need, if available. Servers generally have more memory than workstations, and tasks are not loaded and unloaded as often. Windows NT Workstation grants the application the minimum amount of memory needed to run.

I/O throughput   A critical distinction of Windows NT Server's architecture is that access to key system resources is dynamically and equally parceled out. A few worker tasks or threads service the queue of incoming user requests with dynamic load balancing across CPUs and high-performance access to protected virtual memory space and network I/O. Windows NT Workstation doesn't have the same number of dedicated resources to support a heavy file server load and funnels any incoming network requests through a single queue.

File cache   Windows NT Server gives the highest memory priority to the file cache, which boosts network performance. NT Workstation offers maximum responsiveness to the user by giving priority to the user's foreground process.

Peer Web Service Versus IIS

Peer Web Service (PWS) allows NT Workstation users to publish Web pages and produce Web applications. *Internet Information Server* (IIS) is a full-fledged Web server with a complete set of tools. It uses NT Server's security information and can connect to all of Microsoft's BackOffice applications. Table B.2 lists the differences between PWS and IIS.

Table B.2. PWS versus IIS.

Feature	PWS	IIS
Operating system	Windows NT Workstation 4	Windows NT Server 4
Purpose	For peer publishing on a non-dedicated workstation in the corporate intranet; similar to peer-level file services	High-performance Web server for powerful publishing on the Internet or corporate intranet
Services	WWW, FTP, and Gopher	WWW, FTP, and Gopher
Control access via IP address	No	Yes
Virtual servers	No	Yes
Log to ODBC database	No	Yes
Limit network bandwidth	No	Yes
Internet Database Connector	Included	Included
SSL support	40-bit keys	40-bit and 128-bit keys (128-bit support is available in U.S. and Canadian versions only)
HTML-based administration	Yes	Yes
HTTP version string	Microsoft-IIS-W/2.0	Microsoft-IIS-S/2.0
TransmitFile()	Restricted to two concurrent TransmitFile() operations	Yes

continues

Table B.2. continued

Feature	PWS	IIS
Concurrent connect limit	10 (by license)	No limit
Completion ports used	Yes	Yes
Remote IIS server discovery	No	Yes
Filehandle caching	No	Yes
CPU scaling for threads	No	Yes
Socket listen backlog	5	None

Information in this appendix courtesy of Microsoft Corporation

New Features in Windows NT Workstation 4

IN THIS APPENDIX

This appendix presents a summary of additions to NT Workstation 4 since the last version, NT Workstation 3.51. It starts with a general outline of features and then summarizes the additions. Features not available and features that will become available are presented next. Finally, Windows 95 and Windows NT Workstation 4 are compared side-by-side, which will be helpful if you're trying to decide which product best suits your needs.

General Technical Features

Application support   Offers native application support for all applications based on Windows 95, Win32, 16-bit Windows, 16-bit MS-DOS, 16-bit OS/2, and POSIX 1003.1. Includes separate memory spaces for 16-bit applications (multiple virtual MS-DOS machines). Provides preemptive multitasking for 16-bit and 32-bit applications. The 486 emulator allows 386-enhanced, 16-bit applications to run on RISC machines. OLE support among all 16-bit and 32-bit Windows-based applications is provided. Provides asynchronous I/O queue for improved responsiveness. Offers structured exception handling for easy troubleshooting.

Graphics and multimedia   Includes significant performance gains for graphic-intensive applications. Includes OpenGL APIs for high-performance, three-dimensional color graphics. Also offers 16-bit and 32-bit API support for the Video for Windows 1.1 feature set.

Hardware   Includes multiple hardware configuration. Users can specify a hardware profile at start time, including services, devices, and video resolutions. Includes Intel, Alpha AXPTM, MIPS, and PowerPC platforms, as well as *symmetric multiprocessing* (SMP) support.

Interface   Contains the Windows 95 interface and features such as the Start button, task bar, Explorer, Network Neighborhood, Briefcase, and more.

Messaging capabilities   Offers the Windows Messaging Subsystem (the Microsoft Exchange Client) technologies, The Microsoft Network online service (MSNTM), and Internet Explorer. Microsoft Exchange and Microsoft Schedule+ are included.

Networking   Provides NetWare client and logon script support, *enhanced metafile* (EMF) spooling for improved over-the-network printing speed, support for 15 network protocols, peer-to-peer and FTP server capabilities, and client software for Telnet and FTP services.

Remote Access Service (RAS)   Supplies Internet access to Windows NT Server and *Domain Name Service* (DNS) names for resource connections. Includes dial-out capability to remote servers, including Internet services, and remote dial-in capability to any workstation. Provides full network functionality over remote links by using NetBEUI, IPX-SPX, and TCP/IP protocols. Offers dial-in capability to remote NetWare servers using RAS and multilink capability for channel aggregation of multiple modem connections.

Remote management   Includes remote management utilities, such as Event Viewer, Performance Monitor, Service Controller, and Registry Editor. Also offers dial-out capability to remote servers and remote dial-in capability.

Security Offers per-file and per-directory security with the *NT file system* (NTFS). Includes local desktop security; user ID and password are required for access. Account lockout capabilities prevent unlimited logon attempts. Provides network security with single network logon using challenge/response protocol. Includes Government C2–level certifiable security.

Utilities Provides file compression with NTFS. User Manager offers configuration and security. Disk Administrator supports graphical disk configuration. Includes a diagnostics utility that reports basic system information. Performance Monitor allows you to perform local and remote troubleshooting. Includes a tape backup Event Viewer and logging utility for local and remote troubleshooting. Supports long filenames on FAT and NTFS. Configuration details are managed in the Registry database.

New Features

Windows NT Workstation 4 has many new features since version 3.51. This section divides these features into general categories to make it easier to digest them.

Ease of Use

Windows 95 user interface This new interface combines the ease of use of Windows 95 with the reliability and security of Windows NT. It allows you to work more easily and efficiently and means you can enjoy the same user interface for all your Windows 32-bit desktops and servers. The Windows 95 interface includes some of the following features:

> My Computer
> Network Neighborhood
> Recycle Bin
> shortcuts
> Start button
> task bar

Windows NT Explorer This is a powerful, flexible, efficient, and extensible tool for browsing and managing files, drives, and network connections. Its displays your computer's contents as a hierarchy, or tree, so that you easily can see the contents of each drive and folder on your computer, as well as any network drives to which your computer is connected. Windows NT Explorer replaces File Manager, which was used in previous Microsoft Windows operating systems.

Simplified installation The new installation process simplifies the setup procedure when upgrading to Windows NT Workstation. Enhancements include a new, easy-to-use interface; improved hardware detection; installation wizards; and a series of tools that make it much easier for corporate customers to use Windows NT Workstation on multiple systems.

C

NEW FEATURES IN
WINDOWS NT
WORKSTATION 4

Task Manager   The new Task Manager is an integrated tool for managing applications and tasks, as well as providing key performance measurements of the Windows NT system. Task Manager maintains detailed information on each application and process running on the desktop. It also gives you a simple way to terminate applications and processes that aren't responding, making the overall system more reliable.

Accessibility options   Many accessibility options are now installed by default, making the system easier to use for people with disabilities or certain preferences. These features include the following:

- Special key functions and support for alternative input devices emulate the keyboard and mouse for users with limited dexterity.

- Scalable user interface elements, audible prompts during setup, and high-contrast color schemes help users with impaired vision.

- SoundSentry and ShowSounds functions translate audible cues to visual cues for the hearing-impaired.

These new features are the result of working with users who have disabilities, organizations that represent people with disabilities, and software developers who create products for this market.

New accessories   A number of additional applications and utilities (many of which first appeared in Windows 95) are now included so that users can take advantage of new areas of the operating system, such as these:

HyperTerminal   A new, 32-bit communications application that provides asynchronous connectivity to host computers such as online services. HyperTerminal is configured to allow easy access to AT&T Mail, CompuServe, MCI Mail, and other systems.

WordPad   A 32-bit editor that allows users to create simple documents and memos.

Paint   A 32-bit graphics application that allows users to read PCX and BMP file formats.

Quick Viewers   Lets users view files in the most popular file formats without opening the application used to create the file.

Internet and Intranet Access

Microsoft Internet Explorer   Microsoft Internet Explorer 2.0 is Microsoft's easy-to-use Internet browser. Internet Explorer 2.0 embraces existing HTML standards, such as tables, while advancing HTML with new improvements, such as inline sound and video, background *Secure Socket Layer* (SSL) support, and support for Internet shopping applications. It also features performance enhancements that make it one of the fastest browsers available on even the most complex Web pages. Microsoft continues to update Internet Explorer. You can find the latest updates at this site:

```
http://www.microsoft.com/ie
```

Peer Web Service   Microsoft *Peer Web Service* (PWS) makes it easy to publish personal Web pages. PWS makes it easy for users to share information on their corporate intranets. It's ideal for developing, testing, and staging Web applications, as well as peer-to-peer publishing. As with Microsoft *Internet Information Server* (IIS), PWS supports all ISAPI extensions and filters. PWS is optimized for interactive workstation use and doesn't have the system requirements (memory requirements, server processes, and footprint) of a full Web server like IIS.

Client support for PPTP   The *Point-to-Point Tunneling Protocol* (PPTP) offers a way to use public data networks, such as the Internet, to create virtual private networks connecting client PCs with servers. PPTP offers protocol encapsulation to support multiple protocols through TCP/IP connections and data encryption for privacy, making it safer to send information over non-secure networks. This technology extends the Dial-Up Networking capability by allowing remote access and securely extending private networks across the Internet without requiring a change of client software.

WINS and DNS integration   Windows NT Workstation 4 now takes advantage of the integration between two Windows NT Server services, *Windows Internet Name Service* (WINS) and DNS, to provide a form of dynamic DNS that exploits the best features of both services. With WINS and DNS integration, users can enter DNS fully qualified domain names, making it easier to connect to network resources. By using the Windows NT Explorer, for example, a user can gain access to a share by using a DNS name, such as \\srv1.myco.com\public.

Improved Network Integration

Improved Network Control Panel   The Network Control Panel is improved to provide a single access point where all network settings—such as identification, services, protocols, adapters, and bindings—can be easily installed and configured. This new design simplifies system administration and reduces the overall management cost.

Client support for NDS   An improved version of client services for NetWare is included that supports Novell *NetWare Directory Services* (NDS). Users of Windows NT Workstation 4 now can log onto Novell NetWare 4.*x* servers running NDS to access files and print resources. This service is integrated into Windows NT Workstation and offers the key features Novell users need, such as these:

- ■ NDS authentication, including authentication to multiple NDS trees
- ■ The ability to browse NDS resources
- ■ The ability to print to NDS print queues
- ■ Full support for processing NetWare logon scripts, NDS property pages, and NDS passwords

Dial-Up Networking multilink channel aggregation   This updated version of Dial-Up Networking now provides channel aggregation that allows users to combine all available dial-up lines to get higher transfer speeds. You can combine two or more *Point-to-Point Protocol* (PPP) compliant ISDN B channels, for example, to get speeds of up to 128K, or to combine two or more standard modem lines. This feature provides increased bandwidth and allows you to combine ISDN lines with analog modem lines for higher performance.

Windows Messaging Client   Windows Messaging Client is a universal e-mail inbox you can use with many e-mail systems. Windows NT Workstation 4 includes drivers for Internet Mail and Microsoft Mail. You can use Internet Mail to communicate on the Internet or on any network with *Simple Mail Transfer Protocol* (SMTP) or *Post Office Protocol 3* (POP3) services. The Windows Messaging Client includes full *Messaging API* (MAPI) 1.0 support. You can send, receive, organize, and store e-mail and file system objects. You also can store e-mail addresses for any e-mail system with a MAPI driver. When Microsoft Exchange Server is installed, the Windows Messaging Client allows you to take full advantage of Microsoft Exchange Server's advanced messaging and groupware functionality.

Improved Management Features

System policies and user profiles   These allow system administrators to consistently manage and maintain their users' desktops. System policies standardize desktop configurations, enforce behavior, and control users' work environments. User profiles contain all user-defined settings for the work environment of a computer running Windows NT Workstation 4. Profiles can be stored on a Windows NT Server so that users always see the same desktop, regardless of their location.

Setup Manager   This is a new utility that helps system administrators create installation scripts, which reduces the time and effort of using Windows NT Workstation 4. The new Setup Manager offers an easy-to-use graphical interface for creating hands-free installation scripts that allow system administrators to automate installation for end-users. These hands-free scripts eliminate the need for users to answer questions during the installation process, which helps them avoid mistakes that can happen during system software upgrades.

System Difference utility   The System Difference utility, sysdiff, is an easy way to preinstall additional applications simultaneously with the operating system. The sysdiff utility allows system administrators to create packages that can be applied to a system during installation. These packages can also be applied during Windows NT Workstation 4 setup. These features make the System Difference utility an exceptional tool for application deployment.

Improved Windows NT diagnostics program   This updated and improved Windows NT diagnostics program simplifies troubleshooting. The new version has information such as build number, device drivers, network usage data, and system resources (such as IRQ, DMA, and I/O address). You view the diagnostics information in an easy-to-use graphical tool that you can also run remotely on Windows NT.

Easier printer management   Printer management is simplified by allowing printers to be managed remotely with the Remote Printers folder on the local machine. Additionally, printer drivers for shared printers can be located on the server for point-and-print automatic client driver installation. Printing performance is also improved through server-based rendering (spooling) of non-PostScript print jobs. This results in rapid return-to-application times, which means that control returns to users more quickly after print jobs are initiated.

Easier Mobile Computing

Dial-Up Networking   The functionality offered by Dial-Up Networking is extended, and users can automatically dial a connection when required. With automatic dialing, Dial-Up Networking is smoothly integrated into the new Windows NT interface. Whether users are connecting to the Internet, running client/server applications, accessing remote databases, or accessing shared files, mobile network access is as easy as network access in the office. Establishing a remote connection works the same as establishing a local connection: simply double-click the network object you want. By using the new automatic dialing feature, for example, you can establish a remote connection to the Internet just by clicking the Internet Explorer icon.

Hardware profiles   Hardware profiles allow you to create hardware-configuration lists to meet specific computer needs. At system startup, you can select from these hardware profiles to establish a specific hardware setup. This allows for different computer settings, depending on the environment in which a computer is being used, making it easier to use computers in different configurations. If you have a portable computer, for example, you probably use a different hardware configuration, depending on whether the computer is docked or undocked.

Briefcase   Briefcase allows portable PC users to escape the hassle of managing document versions by tracking relationships between different file versions on different computers. You specify which files and directories you want to track simply by dragging-and-dropping them into the Briefcase.

Multimedia and Graphics Improvements

Multimedia APIs   Windows NT Workstation 4 now supports the multimedia APIs first introduced in Windows 95: DirectDraw, DirectInput, DirectPlay, and DirectSound. Supporting these APIs allows developers to create games and other applications simultaneously for Windows 95 and Windows NT Workstation 4 platforms.

Imaging for Windows NT   The Microsoft imaging software for Microsoft Windows 95 now is available on Windows NT. This imaging software provides powerful imaging services that enable users to access and control information directly at their desktops.

CDFS Enhancements   The Auto-Run and CD-XA formats now are supported as part of the *Compact Disc File System* (CDFS) enhancements. Auto-Run allows the operating system to recognize that a compact disc has been inserted into the drive and to start the application immediately. CD-XA is an extended format for video compact discs that have MPEG movies.

Improved driver support   Many new video drivers improve screen quality and are especially useful when using multimedia features. Some of the newly supported drivers are WD ThinkPad, Matrox Millennium, Trident, Number 9 Imagine, C&T, and Cirrus.

New APIs and Additional Features

Telephony API (TAPI)   TAPI integrates advanced telephone features with the powerful capabilities of PCs. It provides a level of abstraction for developing applications that aren't bound to specific telephone hardware by supplying the means for applications to set up and control telephone calls. Through the TAPI interface, communications applications can ask for access to the modem or telephone device, allowing the communications subsystem in Windows NT Workstation 4 to arbitrate device contention and negotiate with applications to share the communications device in a cooperative manner. *Universal Modem Driver* (Unimodem) provides TAPI services for data/fax modems and voice so that users and application developers don't have to learn or maintain difficult modem AT commands to dial, answer, and configure modems. Some of the new Windows NT 4 applets that take advantage of TAPI/Unimodem support are Dial-Up Networking, HyperTerminal, and Phone Dialer.

Cryptography APIs   This set of encryption APIs allows developers to easily create applications that work securely over non-secure networks, such as the Internet.

Distributed COM   The *Component Object Model* (COM) allows software developers to create component applications. Now, *Distributed COM* (DCOM) in Windows NT Workstation 4 and Windows NT Server 4 provides the infrastructure that allows DCOM applications (the technology formally known as Network OLE) to communicate across networks without requiring you to re-develop applications. An example of a DCOM application is a stock quote server object running on Windows NT Server that distributes quotes to multiple Windows NT Workstation clients. DCOM supplies the infrastructure for connecting and providing uniform communication between client/server objects; it uses the same tools and technologies as COM, thus preserving investments in training and software.

486 emulator   The 486 emulator allows 386-enhanced, 16-bit applications to run on RISC machines.

Windows 95 Features Not Available in Windows NT Workstation 4

This section lists features that are available in Windows 95 but not offered in Windows NT Workstation 4.

Plug-and-Play   Plug-and-Play is both a design philosophy and a set of PC architecture specifications. Microsoft's goal for Plug-and-Play is to make the PC, add-in hardware devices, drivers, and operating system work together without user intervention. To reach this goal, all the components need to be Plug-and-Play–compatible.

Power management   The bane of a portable computer users' existence is battery life. Although true innovation in battery life depends on physics and hardware engineering, operating systems need to provide power-management features that help manage and reduce power consummation from the battery.

Fax   Windows 95 introduced Microsoft Fax, which offers an integrated set of tools that allow users to send and receive fax messages through the Windows Messaging inbox and can communicate with other Windows 95 applications.

Direct3D   Direct3D delivers the next generation of real-time, interactive, 3-D technology for mainstream PC users on the desktop and the Internet. It's supported by more than 80 leading software developers, hardware vendors, and PC manufacturers.

Infrared   *Infrared* (IR) communications, based on technology similar to remote controls, offers a convenient, inexpensive, and reliable way to connect computers and peripheral devices without cables. A set of standards for IR communications has been agreed on by the *Infrared Data Association* (IrDA) to provide infrared communications for PCs.

Features That Will Become Available for Windows 95 and Windows NT Workstation 4

Windows Driver Model (WDM)   In the same way that Microsoft Win32 offers a common API for Windows-based applications, the Win32 Driver Model provides a common set of I/O services and binary-compatible device drivers for Microsoft Windows NT and future Windows operating systems.

Universal Serial Bus (USB) and IEEE 1394   USB and IEEE 1394 enable high-performance multimedia connections; control of business and consumer electronic devices; and traditional PC devices, such as hard drives, CD-ROM drives, printers, scanners, and docking stations for portable computers.

Windows 95 Versus NT Workstation: Which Is Better for You?

This section presents a brief summary of the differences between Windows NT 4 and Windows 95. Since many users will be trying to decide between loading Windows NT Workstation and Windows 95 on their memory-laden fast Pentiums, it's interesting to see what you give up and gain by going from Windows 95 to Windows NT.

Table C.1. Windows NT Workstation 4 versus Windows 95.

Feature	Windows 95	Windows NT Workstation
System and Peripheral Requirements and Support		
Runs MS-DOS device drivers	Yes	No
Runs Win16 device drivers	Yes	No
Recommended RAM for running multiple applications	8M+	16M+
Typical disk space requirement	40M	120M
Runs on PowerPC, MIPS R4x00, and DEC Alpha AXP-based RISC systems	No	Yes
Supports multiprocessor configurations for scalable performance without changing operating system or applications	No	Yes
Application Support		
Win32 API for application development and OLE for linking data across applications	Yes	Yes
Preemptive multitasking of Win32 applications	Yes	Yes
Runs Win16 applications	Yes	Yes
Multimedia APIs (DibEngine, DirectDraw, DirectSound, DirectInput, Reality Lab 3D	Yes	DirectDraw and DirectSound; others: 1997
DCOM	No (in future release)	Yes
OpenGL graphics libraries for 3-D graphics	Yes (Service Pack 1)	Yes
System resources capacity	Greatly expanded	Unlimited
Runs MS-DOS applications	Yes	Most

Feature	Windows 95	Windows NT Workstation
Runs IBM Presentation Manager (through 1.3) and POSIX 1003.1 applications	No	Yes

Application and Data Protection

Feature	Windows 95	Windows NT Workstation
Preemptive multitasking for Win16 applications	No	Yes
System completely protected from errant Win16 and Win32 applications	No	Yes
NTFS provides complete protection of files on a standalone system (files, folders, and applications can be made invisible to specific users)	No	Yes
Automatic recovery from system failure	No	Yes

Ease of Use

Feature	Windows 95	Windows NT Workstation
Next-generation Windows user interface	Yes	Yes
Plug-and-Play technology that lets you automatically add hardware and dynamically reconfigure the system	Yes	No

Connectivity

Feature	Windows 95	Windows NT Workstation
LAN connectivity and peer-to-peer networking, with all popular protocols, including TCP/IP, IPX/SPX, DLC, and NetBEUI	Yes	Yes
Open networking architecture provides choice of clients, transports, drivers, and extensibility for support of third-party networking applications	Yes	Yes

C

NEW FEATURES IN
WINDOWS NT
WORKSTATION 4

Table C.1. continued

Feature	Windows 95	Windows NT Workstation
Built-in Remote Access Services	Yes	Yes
Built-in Windows Messaging Client providing e-mail and fax	Yes	Fax support Delivered separately (in future release)
Built-in Microsoft Network (MSN) client software	Yes	Delivered separately (in future release)

Manageability

Feature	Windows 95	Windows NT Workstation
Open system management provides infrastructure for third-party system-management solutions	Yes	Yes
Supports existing and emerging system-management standards (SNMP, DMI)	Yes	Yes
System policies to provide centralized control over desktop configuration	Yes	Yes
User profiles to provide consistent configuration for roving users or different users sharing a single system	Yes	Yes
Remote monitoring of system performance	Yes	Yes

System and Peripheral Support

Feature	Windows 95	Windows NT Workstation
Fully exploits 386DX, 486, and Pentium platforms	Yes	486 and Pentium (no support for 386)

Information in this appendix courtesy of Microsoft Corporation

APPENDIX D

An NT Command-Prompt Reference

As has been discussed throughout this book, the Windows NT command prompt is functionally a superset of the DOS prompt you're familiar with. In other words, it's a character-based interface in which you enter commands from the keyboard. However, this interface is much more capable than the DOS command-line interpreter.

The most striking difference is that NT doesn't issue an error message when you try to run Windows 3.1, Windows NT, POSIX, or OS/2 character-based applications from the prompt. Instead, NT detects the type of program you're running, creates an instance of the appropriate environment subsystem, and launches the application in the environment.

In addition, the NT command prompt supplies many commands not found in DOS, such as those for working with NTFS and HPFS partitions, for piping and redirection between subsystems, and for command-line editing. It also supports many LAN Manager commands for administering networks, and it even allows you to cut and paste material between dissimilar subsystems.

> **NOTE**
>
> The basics of running the command prompt are covered in Chapter 3, "Working with Windows NT." Configuring the command-prompt window is covered in Chapter 8, "Using the Control Panel to Configure Windows NT."

This appendix lists the commands and functions available from the command prompt and offers some additional notes. Several categories of command-prompt commands are listed:

- Native commands
- Configuration commands
- Subsystem commands
- TCP/IP commands
- Network commands
- Other utility commands

Native Commands

This section lists NT's *native commands*, which are built around the 32-bit NT Command Interpreter. Some of these commands run external programs, such as FORMAT.COM; others are built into the Command Interpreter, so the Interpreter must be running for them to execute.

You can determine whether a command is internal or external by using the `dir` command from the \SYSTEM32 directory. For example, typing `dir format.*` results in the onscreen listing of

FORMAT.COM. Therefore, you know that dir is an external command. External commands can be called directly from a shortcut icon, or the Start/Run box. You could, for instance, set up a shortcut to run the Tree program to display the directory tree.

The assoc Command

The assoc command displays or modifies file extension associations.

Syntax:

```
assoc [.ext[=[filetype]]]
```

Parameters:

.ext	Specifies the file extension to associate with the file type.
filetype	Specifies the file type to associate with the file extension.

- Type assoc without options to display the current file associations.
- Type assoc .ext to display the current association for a file extension.
- Type assoc .ext= to delete the association for a file extension.

The at Command

The at command schedules commands and programs to run on a computer at a specified time and date. You must be running the Schedule service to use the at command.

Syntax:

```
at [\\computername] [[id] [/delete [/yes]]
at [\\computername] time [/interactive] [/every:date
➥[,...] ¦ /next:date[,...]] "command"
```

Parameters:

none	Used without parameters, at lists scheduled commands.
\\computername	Specifies a remote computer. If this parameter is omitted, the commands are scheduled on the local computer.
id	This parameter is an identification number assigned to a scheduled command.
/delete	Cancels a scheduled command. If id is omitted, all the scheduled commands on the computer are canceled.
/yes	Forces a yes answer to all queries from the system when deleting scheduled events.
time	Specifies the time when command is to run. Time is expressed in hours:minutes in 24-hour notation (00:00 [midnight] through 23:59).

continues

Parameters:

/interactive	Allows the job to interact with the desktop of the user who's logged on at the time the job runs.
/every:*date*[,...]	Runs the command on every specified day(s) of the week or month (for example, every Thursday, or the third day of every month). Specify date as one or more days of the week (M, T, W, Th, F, S, Su) or one or more days of the month (using numbers 1 through 31). Separate multiple date entries with commas. If date is omitted, the current day of the month is used.
/next:*date*[,...]	Runs the specified command on the next occurrence of the day (for example, next Thursday). Specify date as one or more days of the week (M, T, W, Th, F, S, Su) or one or more days of the month (using numbers 1 through 31). Separate multiple date entries with commas. If date is omitted, the current day of the month is used.
"command"	This parameter specifies the Windows NT command, program (.EXE or .COM file) or batch program (.BAT or .CMD file) to be run. When the command requires a path as an argument, use the absolute path (the entire pathname beginning with the drive letter). If command is on a remote computer, specify the server and sharename, rather than a remote drive letter. You can use quotation marks around the command, whether you are using at in the command line or in a batch file. If the command includes switches used by both the command and at, you *must* enclose command in quotation marks. If the command is not an executable (.EXE) file, you must precede the command with cmd /c (for example, cmd /c dir > c:\test.out).

The attrib Command

The attrib command displays, sets, or removes the read-only, archive, system, and hidden attributes assigned to files or directories.

Syntax:

```
attrib [+r¦-r] [+a¦-a] [+s¦-s] [+h¦-h][[drive:][path] filename] [/s]
```

Parameters:

`[[`*`drive:`*`][`*`path`*`]` *`filename`*`]`	Specifies the location and name of the directory, file, or set of files you want to process.
`+r`	Sets the read-only file attribute.
`-r`	Clears the read-only file attribute.
`+a`	Sets the archive file attribute.
`-a`	Clears the archive file attribute.
`+s`	Sets the file as a system file.
`-s`	Clears the system file attribute.
`+h`	Sets the file as a hidden file.
`-h`	Clears the hidden file attribute.
`/s`	Processes files in the current directory and all its subdirectories.

The `cacls` Command

The `cacls` command displays or modifies access control lists (ACLs) of files. You can specify more than one file or user in a command.

Syntax:

```
cacls filename [/t] [/e] [/c] [/g user:perm] [/r user [...]] [/p user:perm
➡[...]] [/d user [...]]
```

Parameters:

`filename`	Displays ACLs of specified file or files.
`/t`	Changes ACLs of specified files in the current directory and all subdirectories.
`/e`	Edits ACL instead of replacing it.
`/c`	Continues changing ACLs, ignoring errors.
`/g` *`user:perm`*	Grants access rights to a specified user. The `perm` parameter can be `r` (read), `c` (change [write]), or `f` (full control).
`/r` *`user`*	Revokes a specified user's access rights.
`/p` *`user:perm`*	Replaces a specified user's access rights. The `perm` parameter can be `n` (none), `r` (read), `c` (change [write]), or `f` (full control).
`/d` *`user`*	Denies access to a specified user.

D

NT COMMAND-
PROMPT
REFERENCE

The call Command

The call command calls one batch program from another without causing the parent batch program to stop.

Syntax:

```
call [drive:][path] filename [batch-parameters]
```

Parameters:

[*drive:*][*path*] *filename*	Specifies the location and name of the batch program you want to call. The filename must have a .BAT or .CMD extension.
batch-parameters	Specifies any command-line information required by the batch program.

The chcp Command

The chcp command displays the number of the active console code page or changes the active console code page that Windows NT should use for the console.

> **NOTE**
>
> Only the OEM code page installed with Windows NT displays correctly in a command prompt window that's using Raster fonts. Other code pages display correctly in full-screen mode or command prompt windows that are using TrueType fonts.

Syntax:

```
chcp [nnn]
```

Parameters:

none	Used without parameters, the chcp command displays the number of the active console code page.
nnn	Specifies the code page. The following list shows each code page that Windows NT supports and its country or language:
437	United States
850	Multilingual (Latin I)
852	Slavic (Latin II)
855	Cyrillic (Russian)
857	Turkish

Parameters:

860	Portuguese
861	Icelandic
863	Canadian-French
865	Nordic
866	Russian
869	Modern Greek

The chdir (cd) Command

The chdir or cd command displays the name of the current directory or changes the current directory.

Syntax:

```
chdir [/d] [drive:][path] [..]
or
cd [/d] [drive:][path] [..]
```

Parameters:

none	Used without parameters, chdir displays the names of the current drive and directory.
[/d]	Changes the current drive in addition to changing the current directory for a drive.
[drive:][path]	Specifies the drive (if other than the current drive) and directory you want to change to.
[..]	Specifies that you want to change to the parent directory.

The chkdsk Command

The chkdsk command creates and displays a status report for a disk based on the file system used; it also lists and corrects errors on the disk. If chkdsk can't lock the drive, it offers to check it the next time the computer reboots.

You must be a member of the Administrators group to issue the chkdsk command on a fixed disk.

Syntax:

```
chkdsk [drive:][[path] filename] [/f] [/v] [/r]
```

continues

D

Parameters:

none	Used without parameters, chkdsk displays the status of the disk in the current drive.
drive:	Specifies the drive containing the disk you want chkdsk to check.
[*path*] *filename*	Specifies the location and name of a file or set of files you want chkdsk to check for fragmentation. You can use wildcards (* and ?) to specify multiple files.
/f	Fixes errors on the disk, which must be locked. If chkdsk can't lock the drive, it offers to check it the next time the computer reboots.
/v	Displays the name of each file in all the directories as the disk is checked.
/r	Locates bad sectors and recovers readable information. The disk must be locked.

The cls Command

The cls command clears the screen, leaving only the command prompt and cursor.

The cmd Command

The cmd command starts a new instance of the Windows NT command interpreter, CMD.EXE. A *command interpreter* is a program that displays the command prompt at which you type commands. Use the exit command to stop the new command interpreter and return control to the old one.

Syntax:

```
cmd [/x ¦ /y] [/a ¦ /u] [/q] [/t:fg] [ [/c ¦ /k] string]
```

Parameters:

/c	Carries out the command specified by the string parameter and then stops.
/k	Carries out the command specified by string and continues.
/q	Turns the echo off.
/a	Creates ANSI output.
/u	Creates Unicode output.
/t:*fg*	Sets the foreground and background colors. (For more information, see the color command.)

/x	Allows you to add extensions to the Windows NT version of CMD.EXE, to provide a richer shell programming environment. The following commands use the extensions: del (erase), color, cd (chdir), md (mdir), prompt, pushd, popd, set, setlocal, endlocal, if, for, call, shift, goto, start, assoc, and ftype. For details, see Help for each command.
/y	Disables extensions to the Windows NT version of CMD.EXE, for backward compatibility reasons. The extensions are enabled by default.
string	Specifies the command you want to carry out.

The color Command

The color command sets the default console foreground and background colors.

Syntax:

```
color bf
```

Parameters:

bf	Specifies color attributes of console output. b is a hex digit that specifies the background color; f specifies the foreground. Hex digits have the following values:
0	Black
1	Blue
2	Green
3	Aqua
4	Red
5	Purple
6	Yellow
7	White
8	Gray
9	Light blue
A	Light green
B	Light aqua
C	Light red
D	Light purple
E	Light yellow
F	Bright white

For example, `color fc` produces light red on a bright white background.

If no argument is given, this command restores the color to what it was when CMD.EXE started. If the foreground and background values are the same, `color` returns ERRORLEVEL 1.

The comp Command

The `comp` command compares the contents of two files or sets of files byte by byte. It can compare files on the same drive or on different drives, and in the same directory or in different directories. As `comp` compares the files, it displays their locations and filenames.

Syntax:

```
comp [data1] [data2] [/d] [/a] [/l] [/n=number] [/c]
```

Parameters:

`data1`	Specifies the location and name of the first file or set of files you want to compare. You can use wildcards (* and ?) to specify multiple files.
`data2`	Specifies the location and name of the second file or set of files you want to compare. You can use wildcards to specify multiple files.
`/d`	Displays differences in decimal format. (The default format is hexadecimal.)
`/a`	Displays differences as characters.
`/l`	Displays the number of the line on which a difference occurs, instead of displaying the byte offset.
`/n=number`	Compares the first number of lines of both files, even if the files are different sizes.
`/c`	Performs a comparison that's not case-sensitive.

The compact Command

The `compact` command displays and alters the compression of files or directories.

Syntax:

```
compact [/c] [/u] [/s] [/i] [/f] [/l] filename
```

Parameters:

none	Used without parameters, `compact` displays the compression state of the current directory.
`/c`	Compresses the specified directory or file.
`/u`	Uncompresses the specified directory or file.

Parameters:

`/s:directory`	Specifies that the requested action (compress or uncompress) be applied to all subdirectories of the specified directory, or of the current directory if none is specified.
`/i`	Ignores errors.
`/f`	Forces compression or uncompression of the specified directory or file. This parameter is used in the case of a file that was partly compressed when the operation was interrupted by a system crash. Use the `/c` and `/f` parameters and specify the partially compressed file to force the file to be compressed in its entirety.
`filename`	Specifies the file or directory. You can use multiple filenames and wildcards.

The convert Command

The convert command converts FAT volumes to NTFS. You can't convert the current drive. If convert can't lock the drive, it offers to convert it the next time the computer reboots.

Syntax:

```
convert [drive:] /fs:ntfs [/v] [/nametable:filename]
```

Parameters:

`drive`	Specifies the drive to convert to NTFS.
`/fs:ntfs`	Specifies converting the volume to NTFS.
`/v`	Specifies *verbose mode*, which means all messages are displayed during conversion.
`/nametable:filename`	Creates a name-translation table, using the specified filename, in the root directory of the converted volume. Use this switch if you have difficulty converting files with unusual filenames.

The copy Command

The copy command copies one or more files to another location; it can also be used to combine files. When more than one file is copied, Windows NT displays each filename as the file is copied.

Syntax:

```
copy [/a¦/b] source [/a¦/b] [+ source [/a¦/b] [+ ...]] [destination [/a¦/b]
➥ [/v] [/n] [/z]
```

continues

D

NT COMMAND-
PROMPT
REFERENCE

Parameters:

source	Specifies the location and name of a file or set of files from which you want to copy. The *source* parameter can consist of a drive letter and colon, a directory name, a filename, or a combination.
destination	Specifies the location and name of a file or set of files to which you want to copy. The *destination* parameter can consist of a drive letter and colon, a directory name, a filename, or a combination.
/a	Indicates an ASCII text file. When the /a switch precedes the list of filenames on the command line, it applies to all files whose names follow the /a switch, until copy encounters a /b switch, in which case the /b switch applies to the file whose name precedes the /b switch.
	When the /a switch follows a filename, it applies to the file whose name precedes the /a switch and to all files whose names follow the /a switch, until copy encounters a /b switch, in which case the /b switch applies to the file whose name precedes the /b switch. An ASCII text file can use an end-of-file character (Ctrl+Z) to indicate the end of the file. When combining files, copy treats files as ASCII text files by default.
/b	Indicates a binary file. When the /b switch precedes the list of filenames on the command line, it applies to all files whose names follow the /b switch, until copy encounters an /a switch, in which case the /a switch applies to the file whose name precedes the /a switch.
	When the /b switch follows a filename, it applies to the file whose name precedes the /b switch and to all files whose names follow the /b switch, until copy encounters an /a switch, in which case the /a switch applies to the file whose name precedes the /a switch.
	The /b switch specifies that the command interpreter is to read the number of bytes specified by the file size in the directory. The /b switch is the default value for copy unless copy is combining files.
/v	Verifies that new files are written correctly.
/n	Uses a short filename, if available, when copying a file with a non-8dot3 name.
/z	Copies over a network in restartable mode.

The date Command

The date command displays the date or allows you to change the date from your terminal or from a batch program.

Syntax:

```
date [mm-dd-yy]
```

Parameter:

`mm-dd-yy`	Sets the date you specify. Values for day, month, and year must be separated by periods, hyphens, or slash marks. The `mm` parameter can be 1 through 12; `dd` can be 1 through 31; and `yy` can be 80 through 99 or 1980 through 2099.

The del (erase) Command

The `del` and `erase` commands delete specified files.

Syntax:

```
del [drive:][path] filename [; ...] [/p] [/f] [/s] [/q] [/a[:attributes]]
erase [drive:][path] filename [; ...] [/p] [/f] [/s] [/q] [/a[:attributes]]
```

Parameters:

`[drive:][path] filename`	Specifies the location and name of the file or set of files you want to delete. Multiple filenames can be used. Filenames can be separated by spaces, commas, or semicolons.
`/p`	Prompts you for confirmation before deleting the specified file.
`/f`	Forces deletion of read-only files.
`/s`	Deletes specified files from the current directory and all subdirectories.
`/q`	Quiet mode; does not prompt for delete confirmation.
`/a`	Deletes files based on specifed attributes.
`attributes`	Can be any of the following file attributes:
r Read-only	
h Hidden	
s System	
a Archive	
-	Prefix meaning *not*

D

NT COMMAND-
PROMPT
REFERENCE

The dir Command

The dir command displays a list of a directory's files and subdirectories.

Syntax:

```
dir [drive:][path][filename] [; ...] [/p] [/w] [/d] [/a[[:]
➥attributes]][/o[[:]sortorder]] [/t[[:]timefield]] [/s] [/b] [/l] [/n] [/x]
```

Parameters:

none	Used without parameters or switches, dir displays the disk's volume label and serial number; one directory or filename per line, including the filename extension, the file size in bytes, and the date and time the file was last modified; and the total number of files listed, their cumulative size, and the free space (in bytes) remaining on the disk.
[drive:][path]	Specifies the drive and directory for which you want to see a listing.
[filename]	Specifies a particular file or group of files for which you want to see a listing. Multiple filenames can be used. Filenames can be separated by spaces, commas, or semicolons.
/p	Displays one screen of the listing at a time. To see the next screen, press any key.
/w	Displays the listing in wide format, with as many as five filenames or directory names on each line.
/d	Same as wide but files are sorted by column.
/a[[:] attributes]	Displays only the names of those directories and files with the attributes you specify. If you omit this switch, dir displays the names of all files except hidden and system files. If you use this switch without specifying attributes, dir displays the names of all files, including hidden and system files. The following list describes each of the values you can use for attributes. The colon is optional. Use any combination of these values, and do not separate the values with spaces:
h	Hidden files
s	System files
d	Directories
a	Files ready for archiving (backup)
r	Read-only files

Parameters:

-h	Files that are not hidden
-s	Files other than system files
-d	Files only (not directories)
-a	Files that haven't changed since the last backup
-r	Files that aren't read-only
/o[[:] *sortorder*]	Controls the order in which dir sorts and displays directory names and filenames. If you omit this switch, dir displays the names in the order in which they occur in the directory. If you use this switch without specifying sortorder, dir displays the names of the directories, sorted in alphabetic order, and then displays the names of files, sorted in alphabetic order. The colon is optional. The following list describes each of the values you can use for sortorder. Use any combination of the values, and do not separate these values with spaces.
n	In alphabetic order by name
e	In alphabetic order by extension
d	By date and time, earliest first
s	By size, smallest first
g	With directories grouped before files
-n	In reverse alphabetic order by name (Z through A)
-e	In reverse alphabetic order by extension (Z through A)
-d	By date and time, latest first
-s	By size, largest first
-g	With directories grouped after files
/t[[:] *timefield*]	The following list describes each of the values you can use for timefield. Controls which time field is displayed or used for sorting.
c	Creation
a	Last access
w	Last written
/s	Lists every occurrence, in the specified directory and all subdirectories, of the specified filename.

continues

Parameters:

/b	Lists each directory name or filename, one per line (including the filename extension). This switch displays no heading information and no summary. The /b switch overrides the /w switch.
/l	Displays unsorted directory names and filenames in lowercase. This switch does not convert extended characters to lowercase.
/n	Displays long list format with filenames on far right.
/x	Displays the short names generated for files on NTFS and FAT volumes. The display is the same as with the /n switch, but short names are displayed after the long names.

The diskcomp Command

The diskcomp command compares the contents of two floppy disks.

Syntax:

```
diskcomp [drive1: [drive2:]]
```

Parameters:

drive1	Specifies the drive containing one of the floppy disks.
drive2	Specifies the drive containing the other floppy disk.

The diskcopy Command

The diskcopy command copies the contents of the floppy disk in the source drive to a formatted or unformatted floppy disk in the destination drive.

Syntax:

```
diskcopy [drive1: [drive2:]] [/v]
```

Parameters:

drive1	Specifies the drive containing the source disk.
drive2	Specifies the drive containing the destination disk.
/v	Verifies that the information is copied correctly. Using this switch slows the copying process.

The doskey Command

The doskey command calls the Doskey program, which recalls Windows NT commands, edits command lines, and creates macros.

Syntax:

```
doskey [/reinstall] [/listsize=size] [/macros:[all ¦ exename] [/history]
➥[/insert¦/overstrike] [/exename=exename] [/macrofile=filename]
➥[macroname=[text]]
```

Parameters:

/reinstall	Clears the command history buffer.
/listsize=size	Specifies the maximum number of commands in the history buffer.
/macros	Displays a list of all Doskey macros. You can use a redirection symbol (>) with the /macros switch (which can be abbreviated as /m) to redirect the list to a file.
all	Displays Doskey macros for all executables.
exename	Displays Doskey macros for the specified executable.
/history	Displays all commands stored in memory. You can use a redirection symbol (>) with the /history switch (which can be abbreviated as /h) to redirect the list to a file.
/insert ¦ /overstrike	Specifies whether new text you type replaces old text. If you use the /insert switch, the new text you type on a line is inserted into old text (as though you had pressed the Insert key). If you use the /overstrike switch, new text replaces old text. The default setting is /overstrike.
/exename=exename	Specifies the program (executable) in which the Doskey macro will run.
/macrofile=filename	Specifies a file containing macros to install.
macroname=[text]	Creates a macro that carries out the commands specified by text. Macroname specifies the name you want to assign to the macro, and text specifies the commands you want to record. If text is left blank, macroname is cleared of any assigned commands.

D

NT COMMAND-
PROMPT
REFERENCE

The echo Command

The echo command turns the command-echoing feature on or off or displays a message.

Syntax:

```
echo [on ¦ off] [message]
```

Parameters:

on ¦ off	Specifies whether to turn the command-echoing feature on or off. To display the current echo setting, use the echo command without a parameter.
message	Specifies text you want Windows NT to display onscreen.

The endlocal Command

The endlocal command ends localization of environment changes in a batch file. Each setlocal command must have an endlocal command to restore environment variables.

Syntax:

```
endlocal
```

The HDExit Command

The HDExit command quits the CMD.EXE program (the command interpreter) and returns to the program that started CMD.EXE, if one exists, or to the Program Manager.

The fc Command

Compares two files and displays the differences between them.

Syntax:

```
fc [/a] [/b] [/c] [/l] [/lbn] [/n] [/t] [/u] [/w] [/nnnn]
➥[drive1:][path1]filename1
➥[drive2:][path2]filename2
```

Parameters:

/a	Abbreviates the output of an ASCII comparison. Instead of displaying all the lines that are different, fc displays only the first and last line for each set of differences.
/b	Compares the files in binary mode. The fc command compares the two files byte by byte, but doesn't try to resynchronize the files after finding a mismatch. This is the default mode for comparing files that have extensions of .EXE, .COM, .SYS, .OBJ, .LIB, or .BIN.

Parameters:

/c	Ignores the case of letters.
/l	Compares the files in ASCII mode. The fc command compares the two files line by line and attempts to resynchronize the files after finding a mismatch. This is the default mode for comparing files that don't have extensions of .EXE, .COM, .SYS, .OBJ, .LIB, or .BIN.
/lbn	Sets the number of lines for the internal line buffer. The default length of the line buffer is 100 lines. If the files being compared have more than this number of consecutive differing lines, fc cancels the comparison.
/n	Displays the line numbers during an ASCII comparison.
/t	Doesn't expand tabs to spaces. The default behavior is to treat tabs as spaces, with stops at each eighth character position.
/u	Compares files as Unicode text files.
/w	Compresses white space (tabs and spaces) during the comparison. If a line contains many consecutive spaces or tabs, the /w switch treats these characters as a single space. When used with the /w switch, fc ignores (and doesn't compare) white space at the beginning and end of a line.
/nnnn	Specifies the number of consecutive lines that must match before fc considers the files to be resynchronized. If the number of matching lines in the files is less than this number, fc displays the matching lines as differences. The default value is 2.
[drive1:][path1]filename1	Specifies the location and name of the first file you want to compare.
[drive2:][path2]filename2	Specifies the location and name of the second file you want to compare.

D

**NT COMMAND-
PROMPT
REFERENCE**

The find Command

The find command searches for a specific string of text in a file or files. After searching the specified files, find displays any lines of text containing the specified string.

Syntax:

```
find [/v] [/c] [/n] [/i] "string" [[drive:][path]filename[...]]
```

continues

Parameters:

`"string"`	Specifies the group of characters you want to search for. You must enclose the text for string in quotation marks.
`[drive:][path] filename`	Specifies the location and name of the file in which to search for the specified string.
`/v`	Displays all lines not containing the specified string.
`/c`	Displays only a count of the lines containing the specified string.
`/n`	Precedes each line with the file's line number.
`/i`	Specifies that the search isn't case-sensitive.

The `findstr` Command

The `findstr` command searches for strings in files using literal text or regular expressions.

Syntax:

```
findstr [/b] [/e] [/l] [/c:string] [/r] [/s] [/i] [/x] [/v] [/n] [/m] [/o]
➥[/g:file] [/f:file] strings files
```

Parameters:

`/b`	Matches pattern if it's at the beginning of a line.
`/e`	Matches pattern if it's at the end of a line.
`/l`	Uses search strings literally.
`/c`	Uses specified text as a literal search string.
`/r`	Uses search strings as regular expressions. This switch is not required; `findstr` interprets all metacharacters as regular expressions unless the `/l` switch is used.
`/s`	Searches for matching files in the current directory and all subdirectories.
`/i`	Specifies that the search isn't case-sensitive.
`/x`	Prints lines that match exactly.
`/v`	Prints only lines that don't have a match.
`/n`	Prints the line number before each line that matches.
`/m`	Prints only the filename if a file contains a match.
`/o`	Prints seek offset before each matching line.
`/g`	Gets search strings from the specified file.
`/f`	Reads file list from the specified file.
`strings`	Text to be searched for.
`files`	Files to be searched.

Use spaces to separate multiple search strings unless the argument is prefixed with /e. In that case, the expression is treated a literal regardless of the use of /c. For example, the following command searches for "hello" or "there" in file x.y:

```
findstr "hello there" x.y
```

On the other hand, this command searches for "hello there" in file x.y:

```
findstr /c:"hello there" x.y
```

The for Command

The for command runs a specified command for each file in a set of files. You can use the for command in a batch program or directly from the command prompt.

Syntax in a batch program:

```
for %%variable in (set) do command [command-parameters]
```

Syntax from the command prompt:

```
for %variable in (set) do command [command-parameters]
```

Parameters:

%%variable or %variable	Represents a replaceable variable. The for command replaces %%variable (or %variable) with each text string in the specified set until the command (specified in the command parameter) processes all the files. Use %%variable to carry out the for command in a batch program, and %variable for use from the command prompt.
(set)	Specifies one or more files or text strings that you want to process with the specified command. The parentheses are required.
command	Specifies the command you want to carry out on each file included in the specified set.
command-parameters	Specifies any parameters or switches you want to use with the specified command (if it uses any).

The format Command

The format command formats the disk in the specified drive to accept Windows NT files. You must be a member of the Administrators group to format a hard drive.

Syntax:

```
format drive: [/fs:file-system] [/v[:label]] [/a:unitsize] [/q] [/f:size]
➥[/t:tracks /n:sectors] [/1] [/4] [/8]
```

continues

Parameters:

`drive:`	Specifies the drive containing the disk you want to format. If you don't specify any of the following switches, `format` uses the drive type to determine the default format for the disk.
`/fs:file-system`	Specifies the file system to use, FAT or NTFS. Floppy disks can use only the FAT file system.
`/v:label`	Specifies the volume label. If you omit the `/v` switch, or use it without specifying a volume label, Windows NT prompts you for the volume label after the formatting is done. Use `/v:` to prevent the prompt for a volume label. If you use a single `format` command on more than one disk, all the disks are given the same volume label. The `/v` switch isn't compatible with the `/8` switch. For more information about disk volume labels, see the `dir`, `label`, and `vol` commands.
`/a:unitsize`	Specifies the allocation unit size to use on NTFS disks. Use one of the following values for `unitsize`. If `unitsize` isn't specified, it's chosen based on disk size.
`512`	Creates 512 bytes per cluster, 1024 bytes per file record; the default if disk is less than 512M.
`1024`	Creates 1024 bytes per cluster, 1024 bytes per file record; the default if disk is 512M to 1G.
`2048`	Creates 2048 bytes per cluster, 2048 bytes per file record; the default if disk is 1G to 2G.
`4096`	Creates 4096 bytes per cluster, 4096 bytes per file record; the default if disk is over 2G.
`/q`	Deletes the file table and the root directory of a previously formatted disk, but doesn't scan the disk for bad areas. You should use the `/q` switch to format only previously formatted disks you know are in good condition.
`/f:size`	Specifies the size of the floppy disk to format. When possible, use this switch instead of the `/t` and `/n` switches. Use one of the following values for size:

160 or 160k or 160kb or 160K, single-sided, double-density, 5.25-inch disk

180 or 180k or 180kb 180K, single-sided, double-density, 5.25-inch disk

320 or 320k or 320kb 320K, double-sided, double-density, 5.25-inch disk

360 or 360k or 360kb or 360K, double-sided, double-density, 5.25-inch disk

Parameters:

720 or 720k or 720kb 720K, double-sided, double-density, 3.5-inch disk

1200 or 1200k or 1200kb or 1.2 or 1.2m or 1.2mb or 1.2MB, double-sided, quadruple-density, 5.25-inch disk

1440 or 1440k or 1440kb or 1.44 or 1.44m or 1.44mb or 1.44MB, double-sided, quadruple-density, 3.5-inch disk

2880 or 2880k or 2880kb or 2.88 or 2.88m or 2.88mb or 2.88MB, double-sided, 3.5-inch disk

20.8 or 20.8m or 20.8mb or 20.8MB, 3.5-inch floptical disk

/t:*tracks*	Specifies the number of tracks on the disk. When possible, use the /f switch instead of this switch. If you use the /t switch, you must also use the /n switch. These two switches give you another way to specify the size of the disk being formatted. You can't use the /f switch with the /t switch.
/n:*sectors*	Specifies the number of sectors per track. When possible, use the /f switch instead of this switch. If you use the /n switch, you must also use the /t switch. You can't use the /f switch with the /n switch.
/1	Formats a single side of a floppy disk.
/4	Formats a 5.25-inch, 360K, double-sided, double-density floppy disk on a 1.2M disk drive. Some 360K drives can't reliably read disks formatted with this switch. When used with the /1 switch, this switch formats a 5.25-inch, 180K, single-sided floppy disk.
/8	Formats a 5.25-inch disk with 8 sectors per track. This switch formats a floppy disk to be compatible with MS-DOS versions before 2.0.

The ftype Command

The ftype command displays or modifies file types used in file extension associations.

Syntax:

```
ftype [filetype[=[command]]]
```

Parameters:

filetype	Specifies the file type you want to display or change.
command	Specifies the open command to use when launching files of this type.

D

- Type ftype without options to display the current file types that have open command strings defined.
- Type ftype *filetype* to display the current open command string for this file type.
- Type ftype *filetype=* to delete the open command string for the file type.

Within an open command string, ftype substitutes the following variables:

- %0 or %1 are substituted with the filename being launched.
- %* is substituted with all the parameters
- %3 is substituted with the first parameter, %4 with the second, and so on.

The goto Command

The goto command directs Windows NT to a line in a batch program marked by a label you specify. When Windows NT finds the label, it processes the commands beginning on the next line.

Syntax:

```
goto label
```

Parameter:

label   Specifies the line in a batch program that Windows NT should go to.

The graftabl Command

The graftabl command allows Windows NT to display the extended characters of a specified code page in full-screen mode. Extended characters don't display in window mode.

Syntax:

```
graftabl [xxx] [/status]
```

Parameters:

xxx   Specifies the code page for which you want Windows NT to define the appearance of extended characters in graphics mode. The following list shows each valid code-page identification number and its country or language:

437   United States

850   Multilingual (Latin I)

852   Slavic (Latin II)

855   Cyrillic (Russian)

857   Turkish

Parameters:

860	Portuguese
861	Icelandic
863	Canadian-French
865	Nordic
866	Russian
869	Modern Greek
/status	Identifies the code page selected for use by graftabl.

The help Command

The help command provides online information about Windows NT commands (non-network).

Syntax:

```
help [command]
```

Parameter:

command	Specifies the name of the command you want information about. If you don't specify a command name, the help command lists and briefly describes every Windows NT system command.

NOTE

There are two ways to get online Help for a command. You can specify the name of the command on the help command line, or you can type the name of the command and the /? switch at the command prompt. For example, you can type either of the following commands to get information about the xcopy command:

```
help xcopy
xcopy /?
```

The second command is slightly faster. See the section on net help for information about help with network commands.

The if Command

The if command is used in batch files for conditional processing (branching). If the condition specified in an if command is true, Windows NT carries out the command that follows the condition. If the condition is false, Windows NT ignores the command.

D

NT COMMAND-
PROMPT
REFERENCE

Syntax:

```
if [not] errorlevel number command
if [not] string1==string2 command
if [not] exist filename command
```

Parameters:

not	Specifies that Windows NT should carry out the command only if the condition is false.
errorlevel number	Specifies a true condition only if the previous program run by CMD.EXE returned an exit code equal to or greater than the number.
command	Specifies the command that Windows NT should carry out if the preceding condition is met.
string1==string2	Specifies a true condition only if *string1* and *string2* are the same. These values can be literal strings or batch variables (%1, for example). Literal strings don't need quotation marks.
exist filename	Specifies a true condition if *filename* exists.

The keyb Command

Starts the keyb program, which configures a keyboard for a specific language. Use keyb to configure a keyboard for a language other than United States English.

Syntax:

```
keyb [xx[,[yyy][,[drive:][path] filename]]] [/e] [/id:nnn]
```

Syntax for your CONFIG.NT file:

```
install=[[drive:]path]keyb.com [xx[,[yyy][,[drive:][path] filename]]] [/e]
➥[/id:nnn]
```

Parameters:

xx	Specifies the keyboard code. See the list of valid values for this parameter at the end of this section.
yyy	Windows NT and the MS-DOS subsystem don't use this parameter. It's accepted only for compatibility with MS-DOS files.
[drive:][path] filename	Windows NT and the MS-DOS subsystem don't use this parameter. It's accepted only for compatibility with MS-DOS files.
[drive:]path	Windows NT and the MS-DOS subsystem don't use this parameter. It's accepted only for compatibility with MS-DOS files.

Parameters:

/e	Windows NT and the MS-DOS subsystem don't use this parameter. It's accepted only for compatibility with MS-DOS files.
/id:*nnn*	Windows NT and the MS-DOS subsystem don't use this parameter. It's accepted only for compatibility with MS-DOS files.

The following list shows the valid values (keyboard codes) for *xx* for each country or language:

Values for xx:

Belgium	be
Brazil	br
Canadian-French	cf
Czech	cz
Slovak	sl
Denmark	dk
Finland	su
France	fr
Germany	gr
Hungary	hu
Italy	it
Latin America	la
Netherlands	nl
Norway	no
Poland	pl
Portugal	po
Spain	sp
Sweden	sv
Switzerland (French)	sf
Switzerland (German)	sg
United Kingdom	uk
United States	us
Serbo-Croatian	yu

D

NT COMMAND-
PROMPT
REFERENCE

The label Command

The label command creates, changes, or deletes a disk's volume label (name). Windows NT displays the volume label as part of the directory listing. If a volume serial number exists, Windows NT displays this number, too.

Syntax:

label [*drive:*][*label*]

Parameters:

none	Type **label** without parameters to change the current volume label or delete the existing label.
drive:	Specifies the location of the disk you want to name.
label	Specifies the new volume label. You must include a colon between drive and label.

The mkdir (md) Command

The mkdir (or md) command creates a directory or subdirectory.

Syntax:

mkdir [*drive:*]*path*

or

md [*drive:*]*path*

Parameters:

drive:	Specifies the drive on which you want to create the new directory.
path	Specifies the name and location of the new directory. The maximum length of any single path is determined by the file system.

The mode Command

The mode command configures system devices and performs many different tasks, such as displaying system status, changing system settings, or reconfiguring ports or devices. Because the mode command can perform many different tasks, the syntax for each task is different, too. Here's a list of tasks for which you can use the mode command:

- Reconfiguring a printer attached to a parallel port (PRN, LPT1, LPT2, or LPT3) for printing at 80 or 132 characters per line, 6 or 8 lines per inch, or both (if the printer supports these features)
- Configuring the baud rate, parity, and number of data bits and stop bits of a serial communications port (COM1, COM2, COM3, and COM4) for use with a specific printer, modem, or other serial device

- Displaying the status of all devices or of a single device
- Redirecting printer output from a parallel port to a serial port so that the serial port becomes the system's default printer port
- Changing the size of the command prompt window
- Setting the keyboard's repeating-key speed

The more Command

The more command displays one screen of output at a time and is commonly used to view long files. Enabling extended features activates commands that control display.

Syntax:

```
command name ¦ more [/e] [/c] [/p] [/s] [/tn] [+n]
more [/e] [/c] [/p] [/s] [/tn] [+n] < [drive:] [path] filename
more [/e] [/c] [/p] [/s] [/t n] [+n] files
```

Parameters:

command name	Specifies a command whose output will be displayed.
[drive:] [path] filename	Specifies the file to display.
/e	Enables extended features.
/c	Clears the screen before displaying the page.
/p	Expands form-feed characters.
/s	Changes multiple blank lines to one blank line.
/t n	Changes tabs to n spaces.
+n	Displays the first file beginning at the line specified by n.
files	Specifies a list of files to display. Separate filenames with a space.

If extended features are enabled, the following commands are accepted at the More prompt:

Key	Action
space	Display next page
Enter	Display next line
F	Display next file
q	Quit
?	Show available commands
=	Show line number
P n	Display next n lines
S n	Skip next n lines

The move Command

Moves one or more files from one directory to the specified directory.

Syntax:

```
move [source] [target]
```

Parameters:

source	Specifies the path and name of the file or files to move.
target	Specifies the path and name to move files to.

The path Command

The path command sets a search path for executable files. Windows NT uses the path command to search for executable files in the directories you specify. By default, the search path is the current directory only.

Syntax:

```
path [[drive:]path[;...]] [%path%]
```

Parameters:

none	Used without parameters, path displays the current search path.
[drive:]path	Specifies a drive, directory, and any subdirectories to search.
;	When used as the only parameter, clears all search-path settings and specifies that Windows NT is to search only the current directory.
%path%	Appends current path to the new setting.

The pause Command

The pause command suspends processing of a batch program and displays a message prompting the user to press any key to continue.

Syntax:

```
pause
```

The popd Command

The popd command changes to the directory stored by the pushd command. Popd can be used only once to change directories; the buffer is cleared after the first use.

Syntax:

```
popd
```

The print Command

The print command prints a text file while you're using other Windows NT commands. This command can print in the background if you have an output device connected to one of your system's serial or parallel ports.

Syntax:

```
print [/d:device] [drive:][path] filename[ ...]
```

Parameters:

none	Use print without parameters to display the contents of the print queue.
/d:device	Specifies the name of the print device. Valid values for parallel ports are LPT1, LPT2, and LPT3; for serial ports, they're COM1, COM2, COM3, and COM4. You can also specify a network printer by its sharename (\\servername\print_share). The default value is PRN. The values PRN and LPT1 refer to the same parallel port.
[drive:][path] filename	Specifies the location and name of a file or set of files you want to print. You can include multiple files on one command line.

The prompt Command

The prompt command changes the Windows NT command prompt. You can customize the command prompt to display any text you want, including information such as the name of the current directory, the time and date, and the Windows NT version number.

Syntax:

```
prompt [text]
```

Parameters:

text	Specifies any text and information you want included in your system prompt. The following list shows the character combinations you can include instead of, or in addition to, any character string(s) in the text parameter. The list includes a brief description of the text or information that each character combination adds to your command prompt.

Characters	*Displays*
$q	= (equal sign)
$$	$ (dollar sign)

continues

D

NT COMMAND-
PROMPT
REFERENCE

Characters	Displays
$t	Current time
$d	Current date
$p	Current drive and path
$v	Windows NT version number
$n	Current drive
$g	> (greater-than sign)
$1	< (less-than sign)
$b		(pipestem)
$_	ENTER-LINEFEED
$e	ANSI escape code (code 27)
$h	Backspace (to delete a character that has been written to the prompt command line)
$a	& (ampersand)
$c	((left parenthesis)
$f	) (right parenthesis)
$s	space

The pushd Command

The pushd command stores the current directory for use by the popd command, then changes to the specified directory.

Syntax:

```
pushd [path ¦ ..]
```

Parameter:

path   Specifies the directory to make the current directory.

The recover Command

The recover command recovers readable information from a bad or defective disk. The recover command reads a file sector by sector and recovers data from the good sectors; data in bad sectors is lost.

Syntax:

```
recover [drive:][path] filename
```

Parameter:

`[drive:][path] filename`	Specifies the location and name of the file you want to recover.

The redirection Command

Redirection characters change where a command gets information from or sends information to. Unless you specify otherwise, Windows NT receives input from your keyboard and sends output to your screen. Sometimes it's useful to redirect the input or output to a file or a printer. For example, you might want to redirect a directory listing from the screen to a file.

To redirect the input or output of a command, use one of the following redirection characters:

- The greater-than sign (>) sends the output of a command to a file or a device, such as a printer.
- The less-than sign (<) takes the input needed for a command from a file, rather than from the keyboard.
- The double greater-than sign (>>) adds output from a command to the end of a file without deleting the information already in the file.

Almost all commands send output to your screen. Even commands that send output to a drive or printer also display messages and prompts on your screen. To redirect the output from the screen to a file or printer, use the greater-than sign. You can use the greater-than sign with most Windows NT commands. For example, in the following command, the directory listing produced by the `dir` command is redirected to the DIRLIST.TXT file:

```
dir > dirlist.txt
```

If the DIRLIST.TXT file doesn't exist, Windows NT creates it. If DIRLIST.TXT exists, Windows NT replaces the information in the file with the output from the `dir` command.

To add the output from a command to the end of a file without losing any of the information already in the file, use a double greater-than sign. For example, in the following command, the directory listing produced by the `dir` command is appended to the DIRLIST.TXT file:

```
dir >> dirlist.txt
```

NOTE

Some command output, such as error messages, might not be redirected when using the greater-than sign.

D

NT COMMAND-
PROMPT
REFERENCE

Just as you can send the output of a command to a file or printer rather than to your screen, you can take the input for a command from a file, rather than from the keyboard. To take input from a file, use the less-than sign. For example, the following command takes the input for the sort command from the LIST.TXT file:

```
sort < list.txt
```

Windows NT alphabetizes the lines of the LIST.TXT file and displays the result on your screen.

The rem Command

The rem command allows you to include comments (remarks) in a batch file or in your configuration files.

Syntax:

```
rem [comment]
```

Parameter:

comment   Specifies any string of characters you want to include as a comment.

The rename (ren) Command

The rename (or ren) command changes the name of a file or files. You can rename all files matching the specified filename. However, you can't use the rename command to rename files across drives or to move files to a different directory location.

Syntax:

```
rename [drive:][path] filename1 filename2
```

or

```
ren [drive:][path] filename1 filename2
```

Parameters:

[drive:][path] filename1	Specifies the location and name of the file or set of files you want to rename.
filename2	Specifies the new name for the file or, if you use wildcards, the new names for the files. (You can't specify a new drive or path.)

The replace Command

The replace command replaces files in the destination directory with files in the source directory that have the same name. You can also use replace to add unique filenames to the destination directory.

Syntax:

```
replace [drive1:][path1] filename [drive2:][path2] [/a] [/p] [/r] [/w]

replace [drive1:][path1] filename [drive2:][path2] [/p] [/r] [/s] [/w] [/u]
```

Parameters:

`[drive1:][path1] filename`	Specifies the location and name of the source file or set of files.
`[drive2:][path2]`	Specifies the location of the destination file. You can't specify a filename for files you replace. If you specify neither a drive nor a directory, `replace` uses the current drive and directory as the destination.
`/a`	Adds new files to the destination directory instead of replacing existing files. You can't use this switch with the `/s` or `/u` switch.
`/p`	Prompts you for confirmation before replacing a destination file or adding a source file.
`/r`	Replaces read-only files as well as unprotected files. If you don't specify this switch but try to replace a read-only file, an error results and stops the replacement operation.
`/s`	Searches all subdirectories of the destination directory and replaces matching files. You can't use the `/s` switch with the `/a` switch. The `replace` command doesn't search subdirectories specified in `path1`.
`/w`	Waits for you to insert a disk before `replace` begins to search for source files. If you don't specify `/w`, `replace` begins replacing or adding files immediately after you press Enter.
`/u`	Replaces (updates) only those files on the destination directory that are older than those in the source directory. You can't use the `/u` switch with the `/a` switch.

D

NT COMMAND-
PROMPT
REFERENCE

The `rmdir` (`rd`) Command

The `rmdir` (or `rd`) command deletes (removes) a directory.

Syntax:

```
rmdir [drive:]path [/s]
```

or

```
rd [drive:]path [/s]
```

continues

Parameters:

`[drive:]path`	Specifies the location and name of the directory you want to delete.
`/s`	Removes the specified directory and all subdirectories, including any files. Used to remove a directory tree.

The set Command

The `set` command displays, sets, or removes Windows NT environment variables. You use environment variables to control the behavior of some batch files and programs and to control the way Windows NT and the MS-DOS subsystem look and work. The `set` command is often used in the AUTOEXEC.NT file to set environment variables.

Syntax:

```
set [variable=[string]]
```

Parameters:

none	Used without parameters, `set` displays the current environment settings.
`variable`	Specifies the variable you want to set or modify.
`string`	Specifies the string you want to associate with the specified variable.

The setlocal Command

The `setlocal` command begins localization of environment variables in a batch file. Each `setlocal` command must have an `endlocal` command to restore environment variables.

Syntax:

```
setlocal
```

The shift Command

The `shift` command shifts the position of replaceable parameters in batch files.

Syntax:

```
shift
```

The sort Command

The `sort` command reads input, sorts data, and writes the results to the screen, to a file, or to another device.

Syntax:

```
sort [/r] [/+n] [<] [drive1:][path1] filename1 [> [drive2:][path2] filename2]
➥[command ¦] sort [/r] [/+n] [> [drive2:][path2] filename2]
```

Parameters:

`[drive1:][path1] filename1`	Specifies the location and name of the file whose data you want to sort.
`[drive2:][path2] filename2`	Specifies the location and name of a file in which the sorted output is to be stored.
`command`	Specifies a command whose output is the data you want to sort.
`/r`	Reverses the order of the sorting operation; that is, sorts from Z to A, and then from 9 to 0.
`/+n`	Sorts the file according to the character in column *n*. If you do not use this switch, the `sort` command sorts data according to the characters in column 1.

The start Command

The `start` command opens a separate window to run a specified program or command.

Syntax:

```
start ["title"] [/d path] [/i] [/min] [/max] [/separate] [/low] [/normal]
➥[/high] [/realtime] [/wait] [/b] [filename] [parameters]
```

Parameters:

none	Used without parameters, `start` opens a second command prompt window.
`"title"`	Specifies the title to display in the window's title bar.
`/d path`	Specifies the startup directory.
`/i`	Passes the CMD.EXE startup environment to the new window.
`/min`	Starts the new window as minimized.
`/max`	Starts the new window as maximized.
`/separate`	Starts 16-bit Windows programs in a separate memory space.
`/low`	Starts an application in the idle priority class.
`/normal`	Starts an application in the normal priority class.
`/high`	Starts an application in the high priority class.
`/realtime`	Starts an application in the realtime priority class.

D

continues

Parameters:

/wait	Starts an application and waits for it to terminate.
/b	Does not create a new window. Ctrl+C handling is ignored unless the application allows Ctrl+C processing. Use Ctrl+Break to interrupt the application.
filename	Specifies the command or program to start.
parameters	Specifies parameters to pass to the command or program.

The subst Command

The subst command associates a path with a drive letter.

Syntax:

```
subst [drive1: [drive2:]path]
subst drive1: /d
```

Parameters:

none	Used without parameters, subst displays the names of the virtual drives in effect.
drive1:	Specifies the virtual drive you want to assign a path to.
drive2:	Specifies the physical drive that contains the specified path (if different from the current drive).
path	Specifies the path that you want to assign to a virtual drive.
/d	Deletes a virtual drive.

The time Command

The time command displays the system time or sets your computer's internal clock.

Syntax:

```
time [hours:[minutes[:seconds[.hundredths]]]][A¦P]
```

Parameters:

none	Used without parameters, time displays the computer's clock time and prompts for the new time. Press Enter to leave the time unchanged or type the new time by using the syntax shown.
hours	Specifies the hour. Valid values are from 0–23.
minutes	Specifies the minutes. Valid values are from 0–59.

Parameters:

seconds	Specifies the seconds. Valid values are from 0–59.
hundredths	Specifies hundredths of a second. Valid values are from 0–99.
A¦P	Specifies A.M or P.M. for the 12-hour time format. If you enter a valid 12-hour time, but don't type A or P, the time command uses A (for A.M.).

The title Command

The title command sets the title for the command prompt window.

Syntax:

```
title [string]
```

Parameter:

string	Specifies the title for the command prompt window.

The tree Command

The tree command graphically displays the directory structure of a path or of the disk in a drive.

Syntax:

```
tree [drive:][path] [/f] [/a]
```

Parameters:

drive:	Specifies the drive that contains the disk you're displaying the directory structure for.
path	Specifies the directory you're displaying the directory structure for.
/f	Displays the names of the files in each directory.
/a	Specifies that the tree command will use text characters instead of graphic characters to show the lines linking subdirectories.

The type Command

The type command displays the contents of a text file. Use the type command to view a text file without modifying it.

Syntax:

```
type [drive:][path] filename [...]
```

D

NT COMMAND-
PROMPT
REFERENCE

continues

Parameter:

`[drive:][path] filename`	Specifies the location and name of the file or files you want to view. Separate multilple filenames with spaces. If you're using an NTFS or HPFS drive, and the filename contains spaces, you must enclose the filename with quotation marks.

The ver Command

The `ver` command displays the Windows NT version number.

The verify Command

Windows NT doesn't use this command. It's accepted only for compatibility with MS-DOS files.

The vol Command

The `vol` command displays the disk volume label and serial number, if they exist. A serial number is displayed for a disk formatted with MS-DOS version 4.0 or later.

Syntax:

`vol [drive:]`

Parameter:

`drive:`	Specifies the drive that contains the disk for which you're displaying the volume label and serial number.

The winnt32 Command

The `winnt32` command performs an installation or upgrade of Windows NT 3.51.

Syntax:

`winnt32 [/s:sourcepath] [/i:inf_file] [/t:drive_letter] [/x] [/b] [/o[x]]`

Parameters:

`/s:sourcepath`	Specifies the location of the Windows NT files.
`/i:inf_file`	Specifies the filename (no path) of the setup information file. The default is DOSNET.INF.
`/t:drive_letter`	Forces Setup to place temporary files on the specified drive.

Parameters:

/x	Prevents Setup from creating setup boot floppies. Use this when you already have setup boot floppies (from your administrator, for example).
/b	Causes the boot files to be loaded on the system's hard drive rather than on floppy disks, so that floppy disks don't need to be loaded or removed by the user.
/o	Specifies that Setup only create boot floppy disks.
/ox	Specifies that Setup create boot floppy disks for CD-ROM or floppy-based installation.

The xcopy Command

The xcopy command copies files and directories, including subdirectories.

Syntax:

```
xcopy source [destination] [/w] [/p] [/c] [/v] [/q] [/f] [/l] [/d[:date]]
➥[/u] [/i] [/s [/e]] [/t] [/k] [/r] [/h] [/a¦/m] [/n] [/exclude:filename]
➥[/z]
```

Parameters:

source	Specifies the location and names of the files you want to copy. The source parameter must include either a drive or a path.
destination	Specifies the destination of the files you want to copy. The destination parameter can include a drive letter and colon, a directory name, a filename, or a combination.
/w	Displays the following message and waits for your response before starting to copy files: Press any key to begin copying file(s).
/p	Prompts you to confirm whether you want to create each destination file.
/c	Ignores errors.
/v	Verifies each file as it's written to the destination file to make sure that the destination files are identical to the source files. This switch is ignored because the functionality is inherent to the Windows NT operating system. The switch is accepted only for compatibility with previous versions of MS-DOS.
/q	Suppresses display of xcopy messages.
/f	Displays source and destination filenames while copying.

continues

Parameters:

/l	Doesn't copy files, only displays (lists) files that would be copied.
/d[:*date*]	Copies only source files changed on or after the specified date. If the date value is missing, xcopy copies all source files that are newer than the time of existing destination files. This option allows you to update only files that have changed. If you specify a date, use a - as the separator rather than a /, so that the date isn't interpreted as another parameter.
/u	Copies (updates) only files from source that exists on destination.
/i	If source is a directory or contains wildcards, and destination doesn't exist, xcopy assumes destination specifies a directory name and creates a new directory, then copies all specified files into the new directory. By default, xcopy prompts you to specify whether destination is a file or directory.
/s	Copies directories and subdirectories, unless they are empty. If you omit this switch, xcopy works within a single directory.
/e	Copies all subdirectories, even if they are empty; used with the /s and /t switches.
/t	Copies only subdirectory structure (tree), not files. To copy empty directories, you must include the /e switch.
/k	Copies files and keeps the read-only attribute on destination files, if present on the source files. By default, the read-only attribute is removed.
/r	Copies over read-only files.
/h	Copies files with the hidden and system file attributes. The xcopy command doesn't copy hidden or system files by default.
/a	Copies only source files that have their archive file attributes set. This switch doesn't modify the source file's archive file attribute. For information about how to set the archive file attribute, see the attrib command.
/m	Copies source files that have their archive file attributes set. Unlike the /a switch, the /m switch turns off archive file attributes in the files specified in source. For information about how to set the archive file attribute, see the attrib command.
/n	Copies files using NTFS short file or directory names. This switch is required when copying files or directories from an NTFS volume to a FAT volume or when the FAT file system naming convention (8.3) is required on the destination volume. The destination file system may be FAT, HPFS, or NTFS.

Parameters:

/exclude:*filename*	Excludes the files listed in the specified file from the copy operation. The exclusion file can have a list of exclusion patterns (one per line; no wildcard characters are supported). If any exclusion pattern in the file matches any part of the path of a subject file, that file isn't copied.
/z	Copies over a network in restartable mode.

Configuration Commands

The configuration commands are used to customize the MS-DOS environment. As in 16-bit MS-DOS, these commands are used from within CONFIG.NT, the file that's analogous to the MS-DOS CONFIG.SYS file. CONFIG.NT goes into effect when NT runs the MS-DOS subsystem.

> **NOTE**
>
> Several of these commands are useful only for the OS/2 subsystem. See Chapter 8, "Using the Control Panel to Configure Windows NT," for details on modifying the OS/2 subsystem.

The buffers Command

Windows NT and the MS-DOS subsystem don't use this command. It's accepted only for compatibility with files from MS-DOS.

The codepage Command

The codepage command selects the code pages the system uses for the MS OS/2 subsystem. To use this command, place it in your OS/2 C:\CONFIG.SYS file.

Syntax:

codepage=*xxx*[,*yyy*]

Parameters:

xxx	Specifies the first code page; it must be a three-digit number from this list:
437	United States
850	Multilingual (Latin I)
852	Slavic (Latin II)

continues

Parameters:

855	Cyrillic (Russian)
857	Turkish
860	Portuguese
861	Icelandic
863	Canadian-French
865	Nordic
866	Russian
866	Modern Greek
yyy	This parameter isn't used by the OS/2 subsystem. It's accepted only for compatibility with files from MS OS/2 version 1.3 or earlier.

The country Command

The country command allows the MS-DOS subsystem to use international time, dates, currency, case conversions, and decimal separators. It configures the MS-DOS subsystem to recognize the character set and punctuation conventions observed when using one of the supported languages.

Syntax:

```
country=xxx[,[yyy][,[drive:][path] filename]]
```

Parameters:

xxx	Specifies the country code.
yyy	Specifies the code page for the country.
[drive:][path] filename	Specifies the location and name of the file containing country information.

The device Command

The device command loads into memory the device driver you specify. Use the systemroot%\SYSTEM32\CONFIG.NT file, or the equivalent startup file specified in a program's PIF (program information file), to load device drivers for the MS-DOS subsystem.

Syntax:

```
device=[drive:][path] filename [dd-parameters]
```

Parameters:

`[drive:][path] filename`	Specifies the location and name of the device driver you want to load.
`[dd-parameters]`	Specifies any command-line information required by the device driver.

The devicehigh Command

The `devicehigh` command loads device drivers into the upper memory area. Loading a device driver into the upper memory area frees more bytes of conventional memory for other programs.

Syntax:

```
devicehigh=[drive:][path] filename [dd-parameters]
```

To specify the minimum amount of memory that must be available before `devicehigh` tries to load a device driver into the upper memory area, use the following syntax:

Syntax:

```
devicehigh size=hexsize [drive:][path] filename [dd-parameters]
```

Parameters:

`[drive:][path] filename`	Specifies the location and name of the device driver you want to load into the upper memory area.
`dd-parameters`	Specifies any command-line information required by the device driver.
`hexsize`	Specifies the minimum amount of memory (the number of bytes, in hexadecimal format) that must be available before `devicehigh` tries to load a device driver into the upper memory area. You must use both `size` and `hexsize`, as shown in the second syntax line.

The devinfo Command

The `devinfo` command prepares a device to use code pages. To use this command, place it in your OS/2 C:\CONFIG.SYS file.

Syntax:

```
devinfo=devtype,subtype,[drive:][path]filename [,ROM= [[(]xxx[,yyy)]][,...]]
```

continues

Parameters:

`devtype`	Specifies the type of device: keyboard, monitor, or parallel printer. See the following list for possible values.
`subtype`	Specifies the style or model of the device. For a keyboard, this argument would specify the keyboard layout. See the following list for possible values.
`filename`	Specifies the file containing information about the code pages for that device. See the following list for possible values.
`ROM=`	This parameter isn't used by the OS/2 subsystem. It's accepted only for compatibility with files from MS OS/2 version 1.3 or earlier.
`xxx`	This parameter isn't used by the OS/2 subsystem. It's accepted only for compatibility with files from MS OS/2 version 1.3 or earlier.
`yyy`	This parameter isn't used by the OS/2 subsystem. It's accepted only for compatibility with files from MS OS/2 version 1.3 or earlier.

Possible values for keyboard configuration:

`devtype`	`kbd`
`subtype`	Keyboard code, such as uk (see the keyb command)
`filename`	`keyboard.dcp`

Example:

```
devinfo=kybd,uk,c:\os2\keyboard.dcp
```

Possible values for monitor configuration:

`devtype`	`scr`
`subtype`	`ega` or `vga`
`filename`	`viotbl.dcp`

Example:

```
devinfo=scr,vga,c:\os2\viotbl.dcp
```

The dos Command

The dos command specifies that the MS-DOS subsystem is to maintain a link to the upper memory area or is to load part of itself into the high memory area (HMA).

Syntax:

```
dos=[high,¦low,]umb¦noumb
```

Parameters:

high¦low	Specifies whether the MS-DOS subsystem should try to load part of itself into the HMA. Use the high parameter to allow the MS-DOS subsystem to load itself into the HMA; use the low parameter to keep all the MS-DOS subsystem in conventional memory. The default setting is low.
umb¦noumb	Specifies whether the MS-DOS subsystem should maintain a link between conventional memory and the upper memory area. The umb parameter provides this link, and the noumb parameter—the default setting—disconnects this link.

The dosonly Command

The dosonly command prevents starting applications, other than MS-DOS–based ones, from the COMMAND.COM prompt.

The driveparm Command

Windows NT and the MS-DOS subsystem don't take action for the driveparm command. It's accepted only for compatibility with MS-DOS files.

The echoconfig Command

The echoconfig command displays messages while processing the MS-DOS subsystem's CONFIG.NT and AUTOEXEC.NT when the MS-DOS subsystem is invoked. If this command isn't present, messages aren't displayed. This command must be in the MS-DOS subsystem CONFIG.NT file.

The fcbs Command

The fcbs command specifies the number of file control blocks (FCBs) that the MS-DOS subsystem can have open at the same time. A *file control block* is a data structure that stores information about a file.

Syntax:

fcbs=x

Parameter:

x	Specifies the number of file control blocks that the MS-DOS subsystem can have open at one time. Valid values for x are from 1–255; the default value is 4.

The files Command

The files command sets the number of files that the MS-DOS subsystem can access at one time.

Syntax:

```
files=x
```

Parameter:

x   Specifies the number of files that the MS-DOS subsystem can access at one time. Valid values for x are from 8–255; the default value is 8.

The install Command

The install command loads a memory-resident program into memory.

Syntax:

```
install=[drive:][path] filename [command-parameters]
```

Parameters:

[drive:][path] filename   Specifies the location and name of the memory-resident program you want to run.

command-parameters   Specifies parameters for the program you specify for filename.

The lastdrive Command

Windows NT and the MS-DOS subsystem don't take action for the lastdrive command. It's accepted only for compatibility with MS-DOS.

The libpath Command

The libpath command specifies which directories the OS/2 subsystem searches for dynamic link libraries. To use this command, use an OS/2 editor to edit the C:\CONFIG.SYS file.

Syntax:

```
libpath=[drive:]path[;[drive:]path][...]
```

Parameters:

drive: Specifies the drive where dynamic link libraries are located. If you don't specify a drive, the OS/2 subsystem searches the disk in the current drive.

path   Specifies the directory to search for dynamic link libraries. You can specify more than one directory, separating the names with semicolons.

The ntcmdprompt Command

The ntcmdprompt command runs the Windows NT command interpreter, CMD.EXE, rather than COMMAND.COM after running a TSR or after starting the command prompt from within an MS-DOS application.

Syntax:

```
ntcmdprompt
```

The protshell Command

Windows NT and the OS/2 subsystem don't use the protshell command. It's accepted only for compatibility with files from Microsoft OS/2 version 1.3 or earlier.

The shell Command

The shell command specifies the name and location of another command interpreter you want Windows NT to use for the MS-DOS subsystem.

Syntax:

```
shell=[[drive:]path] filename [parameters]
```

Parameters:

[[drive:]path] filename	Specifies the location and name of the command interpreter you want Windows NT to use.
parameters	Specifies any command-line parameters or switches that can be used with the specified command interpreter.

The stacks Command

The stacks command supports the dynamic use of data stacks to handle hardware interrupts.

Syntax:

```
stacks=n,s
```

Parameters:

n	Specifies the number of stacks. Valid values for n are 0 and numbers from 8–64.
s	Specifies the size (in bytes) of each stack. Valid values for s are 0 and numbers from 32–512.

D

**NT COMMAND-
PROMPT
REFERENCE**

The switches Command

The switches command forces an enhanced keyboard to behave like a conventional keyboard. Use this command in your CONFIG.NT file.

Syntax:

```
switches=/k
```

Subsystem Commands

The subsystem commands are, for the most part, throwbacks to the 16-bit MS-DOS world. They're not built in as NT native commands, either because they're no longer useful or because their functionality has been incorporated into NT in another form.

The append Command

The append command allows programs to open data files in specified directories as though these files were in the current directory. The specified directories are called *appended directories* because, for the sake of opening data files, they can be found as though they were appended to the current directory.

Syntax:

```
append [;] [[drive:]path[;...]] [/x:{on | off}][/path:{on | off}] [/e]
```

Parameters:

;	Cancels the list of appended directories.
[drive:]path	Specifies the drive (if other than the current drive) and directory you want to append to the current directory. You can specify multiple entries of [drive:]path, separating the entries with semicolons. When used by itself, append cancels the existing list of appended directories.
/x:{on | off}	Specifies whether the MS-DOS subsystem searches appended directories when executing programs. If you use the /x:on switch, the program searches appended directories; if you use the /x:off switch, however, it doesn't. You can abbreviate /x:on to /x. If you want to specify /x:on, you must do it the first time you use append after starting your system. After that, you can switch between /x:on and /x:off.
/path:{on | off}	Specifies whether a program searches appended directories for a data file when a path is already included with the name of the file the program is looking for. The default setting is /path:on.

Parameters:

/e	Assigns the list of appended directories to an environment variable named append. This switch can be used only the first time you use append after starting your system. If you use /e, you can use the set command to display the list of appended directories. For information about environment variables, see the set command.

The backup Command

The backup command backs up one or more files from one disk onto another. You can back up files onto either a hard disk or floppy disk(s). Files can also be backed up from one floppy disk onto another, even if the disks have different numbers of sides or sectors. Windows NT displays the name of each file it backs up.

Syntax:

```
backup source destination-drive: [/s] [/m] [/a][/f[:size]] [/d:date
➥[/t:time]][/l[:[drive:][path]logfile]]
```

Parameters:

source	Specifies the location of files you want to back up. The source parameter can consist of a drive letter and colon, a directory name, a filename, or a combination.
destination-drive:	Specifies the drive containing the disk on which you want to store any backup files. The backup files are stored in the BACKUP.*nnn* and CONTROL.*nnn* files. That is, backup assigns the names BACKUP.001 and CONTROL.001 to the files it creates on the first backup disk you use, BACKUP.002 and CONTROL.002 to the files it creates on the second backup disk, and so on.
/s	Backs up the contents of all subdirectories.
/m	Backs up only files that have changed since the last backup, and turns off the archive attribute of the original files.
/a	Adds backup files to an existing backup disk without deleting existing files. (The /a switch is ignored if the existing backup disk contains backup files created by using the backup command from MS-DOS version 3.2 or earlier.)

D

NT COMMAND-
PROMPT
REFERENCE

continues

Parameters:

/f[:*size*]	Formats the backup disk to the size you specify. (The format command must be present in the current path.) With this switch, you direct backup to format floppy disks that don't match the drive's default size. The backup command formats an unformatted destination disk, even if you don't specify the /f switch. When backup finishes formatting, it begins backing up files onto the last disk it formatted. The *size* parameter specifies the size in kilobytes of the disk to be formatted. If you don't specify *size*, the /f switch uses the drive's default size. The following list shows the valid values for *size* and a brief description of each size:

Values	Description
160 or 160k or 160kb	160K, single-sided, double-density, 5.25-inch disk
180 or 180k or 180kb	180K, single-sided, double-density, 5.25-inch disk
320 or 320k or 320kb	320K, double-sided, double-density, 5.25-inch disk
360 or 360k or 360kb	360K, double-sided, double-density, 5.25-inch disk
720 or 720k or 720kb	720K, double-sided, double-density, 3.5-inch disk
1200 or 1200k or 1200kb or 1.2 or 1.2m or 1.2mb	1.2-MB, double-sided, quadruple-density, 5.25-inch disk
1440 or 1440k or 1440kb or 1.44 or 1.44m or 1.44mb	1.44-MB, double-sided, quadruple-density, 3.5-inch disk
2880 or 2880k or 2880kb or 2.88 or 2.88m or 2.88mb	2.88-MB, double-sided, 3.5-inch disk

/d:*date*	Backs up only files modified on or after the specified date. The date format depends on the setting you're using for the country command.
/t:*time*	Backs up only files modified at or after the specified time. The time format depends on the setting you're using for the country command.
/l[:[*drive*:][*path*]*logfile*]	Creates a log file and adds an entry to that file to record the backup operation. If you don't specify a location for the log file, backup puts the file in the root directory of the source drive. If you don't specify *logfile*, backup names the file BACKUP.LOG. You shouldn't specify a removable drive (such as a floppy disk drive) for this parameter; however, once the backup is done, you can copy the log file to a floppy disk.

The break Command

Windows NT does not use the break command. It's accepted only for compatibility with files from MS-DOS.

The debug Command

The debug command starts Debug, a program that allows you to test and debug MS-DOS executable files.

Syntax:

```
debug [[drive:][path] filename [testfile-parameters]]
```

Parameters:

[drive:][path] filename	Specifies the location and name of the executable file you want to test.
testfile-parameters	Specifies any command-line information required by the executable file you want to test.

The edit Command

The edit command starts MS-DOS Editor, which creates and changes ASCII text files.

Syntax:

```
edit [[drive:][path] filename] [/b] [/g] [/h] [/nohi]
```

Parameters:

[drive:][path] filename	Specifies the location and name of an ASCII text file. If the file doesn't exist, MS-DOS Editor creates it. If the file exists, MS-DOS Editor opens it and displays its contents onscreen.
/b	Displays MS-DOS Editor in black and white. You use this option if MS-DOS Editor isn't displayed correctly on a monochrome monitor.
/g	Uses the fastest screen updating possible for a CGA monitor.
/h	Displays the maximum number of lines possible for the monitor you're using.
/nohi	Allows you to use 8-color monitors with MS-DOS Editor. (Usually, Windows NT uses 16 colors.)

D

NT COMMAND-
PROMPT
REFERENCE

CAUTION

MS-DOS Editor doesn't work if the file QBASIC.EXE isn't in the current directory, in the search path, or in the same directory as the file EDIT.COM. If you delete QBASIC.EXE to save space on your hard disk, you can't use MS-DOS Editor.

NOTE

Some monitors might not support displaying shortcut keys by default. If your monitor doesn't display shortcut keys, use the /b switch (for CGA monitors) and the /nohi switch (for systems that don't support bold characters).

The edlin Command

The edlin command starts Edlin, a line-oriented text editor you can use to create and change ASCII files.

Edlin numbers each line of the text file that's located in memory. You can use Edlin to insert, modify, copy, move, and delete lines of the file. If you want to use a full-screen editor, use the edit command.

Syntax:

```
edlin [drive:][path] filename [/b]
```

Parameters:

[drive:][path] filename	Specifies the location and name of an ASCII file on a disk. If the file exists, Edlin opens it. If the file doesn't exist, Edlin creates a file in memory and uses the specified location and filename to create the file on a disk when you use the Edlin e command.
/b	Tells Edlin to ignore the end-of-file character (Ctrl+Z).

The exe2bin Command

The exe2bin command converts .EXE (executable) files to binary format. Exe2bin is included with Windows NT as a courtesy to software developers. It's not that useful for general users.

Syntax:

```
exe2bin [drive1:][path1]input-file [[drive2:][path2]output-file]
```

Parameters:

`[drive1:][path1]input-file`	Specifies the location and name of the input file.
`[drive2:][path2]output-file`	Specifies the location and name of the output file.

The expand Command

The expand command expands one or more compressed files. It's used to retrieve compressed files from distribution disks.

Syntax:

```
expand [-r] source [destination]
```

Parameters:

`-r`	Renames expanded files.
`source`	Specifies the files to expand. The `source` parameter can consist of a drive letter and colon, a directory name, a filename, or a combination. Wildcards may be used.
`destination`	Specifies where files are to be expanded. If `source` is multiple files and `-r` is not specified, `destination` must be a directory. It can consist of a drive letter and colon, a directory name, a filename, or a combination.

The fastopen Command

Windows NT and the MS-DOS subsystem don't use the `fastopen` command. It's accepted only for compatibility with MS-DOS files.

The forcedos Command

The `forcedos` command starts the specified program in the MS-DOS subsystem. It's necessary only for those MS-DOS programs not recognized as such by Windows NT.

Syntax:

```
forcedos [/d directory] filename [parameters]
```

Parameters:

`/d directory`	Specifies the current directory for the specified program to use.
`filename`	Specifies the program to start. If not in the current directory or Windows NT path, you must specify the drive letter or directories to the program.
`parameters`	Specifies parameters to pass to the program.

The graphics Command

The graphics command loads a program into memory that allows Windows NT to print the displayed contents of the screen when you're using a color or graphics adapter.

Syntax:

```
graphics [type] [[drive:][path] filename] [/r] [/b] [/lcd]
➡[/printbox:std ¦ /printbox:lcd]
```

Parameters:

type — Specifies the type of printer. The following list shows each valid value for this parameter and a brief description of its meaning:

Value	Description
color1	An IBM Personal Computer Color Printer with black ribbon
color4	An IBM Personal Computer Color Printer with RGB (red, green, blue, and black) ribbon
color8	An IBM Personal Computer Color Printer with CMY (cyan, magenta, yellow, and black) ribbon
hpdefault	Any Hewlett-Packard PCL printer
deskjet	A Hewlett-Packard DeskJet printer
graphics	An IBM Personal Graphics Printer, IBM Proprinter, or IBM Quietwriter printer
graphicswide	An IBM Personal Graphics Printer with an 11-inch-wide carriage
laserjet	A Hewlett-Packard LaserJet printer
laserjetii	A Hewlett-Packard LaserJet II printer
paintjet	A Hewlett-Packard PaintJet printer
quietjet	A Hewlett-Packard QuietJet printer
quietjetplu	A Hewlett-Packard QuietJet Plus printer
ruggedwriter	A Hewlett-Packard RuggedWriter printer
ruggedwriterwide	A Hewlett-Packard RuggedWriterwide printer
thermal	An IBM PC-convertible Thermal Printer
thinkjet	A Hewlett-Packard ThinkJet printer

[drive:][path] filename — Specifies the location and name of the printer profile that contains information about all supported printers. If this parameter is omitted, Windows NT looks for a file called GRAPHICS.PRO in the current directory and in the directory containing the GRAPHICS.COM file.

Parameters:

/r	Prints the image as it appears onscreen (white characters on a black background) rather than reversed (black characters on a white background). The latter occurs by default.
/b	Prints the background in color. This switch is valid for color4 and color8 printers.
/lcd	Prints an image by using the liquid crystal display (LCD) aspect ratio instead of the CGA aspect ratio. The effect of this switch is the same as that of /printbox:lcd.
/printbox:std ¦ /printbox:lcd	Selects the print-box size. You can abbreviate printbox as pb. You should check the first operand of the printbox statement in your GRAPHICS.PRO file and specify the /printbox:std switch if that operand is std or the /printbox:lcd switch if it's lcd.

The loadfix Command

The loadfix command makes sure a program is loaded above the first 64K of conventional memory and runs the program.

Syntax:

```
loadfix [drive:][path] filename [program-parameters]
```

Parameters:

[drive:][path]	Specifies the drive and directory of the program.
filename	Specifies the name of the program.
program-parameters	Specifies any of the program's parameters that you want to use.

The loadhigh (lh) Command

The loadhigh (or lh) command loads a program into the upper memory area, which leaves more room in conventional memory for other programs.

Syntax:

```
loadhigh [drive:][path] filename [parameters]
lh [drive:][path] filename [parameters]
```

continues

D

NT COMMAND-
PROMPT
REFERENCE

Parameters:

[*drive:*][*path*] *filename*	Specifies the location and name of the program you want to load.
parameters	Specifies any command-line information required by the program.

The mem Command

The mem command displays information about allocated memory areas, free memory areas, and programs currently loaded into memory in the MS-DOS subsystem.

Syntax:

```
mem [/program¦/debug¦/classify]
```

Parameters:

none	Use mem without parameters to display the status of the MS-DOS subsystem's used and free memory.
/program	Displays the status of programs currently loaded into memory. You can't use the /program switch with the /debug switch or the /classify switch. You can abbreviate /program as /p.
/debug	Displays the status of currently loaded programs and of internal drivers and displays other programming information. You can't use the /debug switch with the /program switch or the /classify switch. You can abbreviate /debug as /d.
/classify	Displays the status of programs loaded into conventional memory and the upper memory area. This switch lists the size of each program in decimal and hexadecimal notation, provides a summary of memory use, and lists the largest memory blocks available. You can't use the /classify switch with the /program switch or the /debug switch. You can abbreviate /classify as /c.

The nlsfunc Command

Windows NT and the MS-DOS subsystem don't use the nlsfunc command. It's accepted only for compatibility with MS-DOS files.

The qbasic Command

The qbasic command starts Windows NT QBasic, a program that reads instructions written in the Basic computer language and interprets them into executable computer code.

Syntax:

```
qbasic [/b] [/editor] [/g] [/h] [/mbf] [/nohi] [[/run][drive:][path]
➥filename]
```

Parameters:

`[drive:][path] filename`	Specifies the location and name of the file to load when QBasic starts.
`/b`	Displays QBasic in black and white if you have a color monitor.
`/editor`	Invokes MS-DOS Editor, a full-screen text editor.
`/g`	Provides the fastest update of a CGA monitor.
`/h`	Displays the maximum number of display lines possible on your screen.
`/mbf`	Converts the built-in functions MKS\$, MKD\$, CVS, and CVD to MKSMBF\$, MKDMBF\$, CVSMBF, and CVDMBF, respectively.
`/nohi`	Allows the use of a monitor that doesn't support high-intensity video. Don't use this switch with COMPAQ laptop computers.
`/run`	Runs the specified Basic program before displaying it. You must specify a filename.

D

NT COMMAND-
PROMPT
REFERENCE

The restore Command

The `restore` command restores files that were backed up by using the MS-DOS `backup` command.

Syntax:

```
restore drive1: drive2:[path[filename]] [/s] [/p] [/b:date] [/a:date]
➥[/e:time] [/l:time] [/m] [/n] [/d]
```

Parameters:

`drive1:`	Specifies the drive on which the backed up files are stored.
`drive2:`	Specifies the drive to which the backed up files will be restored.
`path`	Specifies the directory to which the backed up files will be restored. You must specify the same directory from which the files were backed up.
`filename`	Specifies the names of the backed up files you want to restore.
`/s`	Restores all subdirectories.

continues

Parameters:

/p	Prompts you for permission to restore files that are read-only (that have the read-only attribute set) or that have changed since the last backup (that have the archive attribute set).
/b:*date*	Restores only those files last modified on or before the specified date. For information about specifying date, see the date command.
/a:*date*	Restores only those files last modified on or after the specified date. For information about specifying date, see the date command.
/e:*time*	Restores only those files last modified at or earlier than the specified time. For information about specifying time, see the time command.
/l:*time*	Restores only those files last modified at or later than the specified time. For information about specifying time, see the time command.
/m	Restores only those files modified since the last backup.
/n	Restores only those files that no longer exist on the destination disk.
/d	Displays a list of the files on the backup disk that match the names specified in filename without restoring any files. Even though no files are being restored, you must specify drive2 when you use /d.

The setver Command

The setver command sets the MS-DOS version number that the MS-DOS subsystem reports to a program.

Syntax:

```
setver [drive:path] [filename n.nn]

setver [drive:path] [filename [/delete [/quiet]]
```

To display the current version table, use the following syntax:

```
setver [drive:path]
```

Parameters:

[*drive:path*]	Specifies the location of the setver.EXE file.
filename	Specifies the name of the program file (.EXE or .COM) that you want to add to the version table. You can't use a wildcard (* or ?).
n.nn	Specifies the MS-DOS version (for example, 3.3 or 4.01) that the MS-DOS subsystem reports to the specified program file.
/delete	Deletes the version-table entry for the specified program file. You can abbreviate this switch as /d.
/quiet	Hides the message typically displayed during deletion of an entry from the version table.

The share Command

Windows NT and the MS-DOS subsystem don't use the share command. It's accepted only for compatibility with MS-DOS files.

TCP/IP Commands

The utility commands listed in this section are useful when you connect to systems like UNIX that use TCP/IP protocol. Note that many of these commands won't work unless you've installed the TCP/IP network protocol.

The arp Command

The arp command displays and modifies the IP-to-Ethernet or Token Ring physical address translation tables used by address resolution protocol (ARP). This command is available only if the TCP/IP protocol has been installed.

Syntax:

```
arp -a [inet_addr] [-N [if_addr]]
arp -d in_addr [if_addr]
arp -s in_addr ether_addr [if_addr]
```

Parameters:

-a	Displays current ARP entries by querying TCP/IP. If inet_addr is specified, only the IP and physical addresses for the specified computer are displayed.
-g	Identical to -a.
inet_addr	Specifies an IP address in dotted decimal notation.
-N	Displays the ARP entries for the network interface specified by if_addr.
if_addr	Specifies, if present, the IP address of the interface whose address translation table should be modified. If not present, the first applicable interface will be used.
-d	Deletes the entry specified by inet_addr.
-s	Adds an entry in the ARP cache to associate the IP address inet_addr with the physical address ether_addr. The physical address is given as 6 hexadecimal bytes separated by hyphens. The IP address is specified by using dotted decimal notation. The entry is permanent, that is, it isn't automatically removed from the cache after the timeout expires.
ether_addr	Specifies a physical address.

D

**NT COMMAND-
PROMPT
REFERENCE**

The finger Command

The finger command displays information about a user on a specified system running the Finger service. Output varies based on the remote system. This command is available only if the TCP/IP protocol has been installed.

Syntax:

```
finger [-l] [user]@computer [...]
```

Parameters:

-l	Displays information in long list format.
user	Specifies the user you want information about. Omit the user parameter to display information about all users on the specifed computer.
@computer	Specifies the server on the remote system whose users you want information about.

The ftp Command

The ftp command transfers files to and from a computer running an FTP server service (sometimes called a *daemon*). The ftp command can be used interactively. This command is available only if the TCP/IP protocol has been installed.

Syntax:

```
ftp [-v] [-d] [-i] [-n] [-g] [-s:filename] [-a] [-w:windowsize] [computer]
```

Parameters:

-v	Suppresses display of remote server responses.
-n	Suppresses auto-login upon initial connection.
-i	Turns off interactive prompting during multiple file transfers.
-d	Allows debugging, displaying all ftp commands passed between the client and server.
-g	Disables filename globbing, which permits the use of wildcard characters in local file and path names. (See the glob command in the online Command Reference.)
-s:filename	Specifies a text file containing ftp commands; the commands automatically run after ftp starts. No spaces are allowed in this parameter. Use this switch instead of redirection (>).
-a	Uses any local interface when binding data connection.

Parameters:

-w:*windowsize*	Overrides the default transfer buffer size of 4,096 bytes.
computer	Specifies the computer name or IP address of the remote computer to connect to. The computer, if specified, must be the last parameter on the line.

The hostname Command

The hostname command prints the name of the current host. This command is available only if the TCP/IP protocol has been installed.

Syntax:

```
hostname
```

The ipconfig Command

This diagnostic command displays all current TCP/IP network configuration values. It's particularly useful on systems running DHCP, allowing users to determine which TCP/IP configuration values have been configured by DHCP. With no parameters, the ipconfig utility presents all the current TCP/IP configuration values to the user, including IP address and subnet mask.

Syntax:

```
ipconfig [/all ¦ /renew [adapter] ¦ /release [adapter]]
```

Parameters:

all	Produces a full display. Without this switch, ipconfig displays only the IP address, subnet mask, and default gateway values for each network card.
renew [*adapter*]	Renews DHCP configuration parameters. This option is available only on systems running the DHCP Client service. To specify an adapter name, type the adapter name that appears when you use ipconfig without parameters.
release [*adapter*]	Releases the current DHCP configuration. This option disables TCP/IP on the local system and is available only on DHCP clients. To specify an adapter name, type the adapter name that appears when you use ipconfig without parameters.

D

NT COMMAND-
PROMPT
REFERENCE

The lpq Command

This diagnostic utility is used to get the status of a print queue on a computer running the LPD server.

Syntax:

```
lpq -S Server -P Printer [-l]
```

Parameters:

-S *Server*	Specifies the name of the computer that has the printer attached to it.
-P *Printer*	Specifies the name of the printer for the desired queue.
-l	Specifies that a detailed status should be given.

The lpr Command

This connectivity utility is used to print a file to a computer running an LPD server.

Syntax:

```
lpr -S Server -P Printer [-C Class] [-J Jobname] [-O option] filename
```

Parameters:

-S *Server*	Specifies the name of the computer that has the printer attached to it.
-P *Printer*	Specifies the name of the printer for the desired queue.
-C *Class*	Specifies the content of the banner page for the class.
-J *Jobname*	Specifies the name of this job.
-O option	Indicates the type of file. The default is a text file. Use -ol (lowercase *L*) for a binary file (for example, PostScript).
filename	The name of the file to be printed.

The nbtstat Command

This diagnostic command displays protocol statistics and current TCP/IP connections using NBT (NetBIOS over TCP/IP). This command is available only if the TCP/IP protocol has been installed.

Syntax:

```
nbtstat [-a remotename] [-A IP address] [-c] [-n] [-R] [-r] [-S] [-s]
➡[interval]
```

Parameters:

`-a remotename`	Lists the remote computer's name table using its name.
`-A IP address`	Lists the remote computer's name table using its IP address.
`-c`	Lists the contents of the NetBIOS name cache giving the IP address of each name.
`-n`	Lists local NetBIOS names. Registered indicates that the name is registered by broadcast (Bnode) or WINS (other node types).
`-R`	Reloads the LMHOSTS file after purging all names from the NetBIOS name cache.
`-r`	Lists name resolution statistics for Windows networking name resolution. On a Windows NT computer configured to use WINS, this option returns the number of names resolved and registered by broadcast or WINS.
`-S`	Displays both client and server sessions, listing the remote computers by IP address only.
`-s`	Displays both client and server sessions. It tries to convert the remote computer IP address to a name using the HOSTS file.
`interval`	Redisplays selected statistics, pausing the number of seconds specified in `interval` between each display. Press Ctrl+C to stop redisplaying statistics. If this parameter is omitted, `nbstat` prints the current configuration information once.

The `net start dhcp client` Command

The `net start dhcp client` command starts the DHCP Client service. This command is available only if the TCP/IP protocol has been installed.

Syntax:

```
net start "dhcp client"
```

The `net start ftp publishing service` Command

The `net start ftp publishing service` command starts the FTP publishing service. This command is available only if Internet Information Server has been installed.

Syntax:

```
net start "ftp publishing service"
```

The net start lpdsvc Command

The net start lpdsvc command starts the Lpdsvc service. This command is available only if the TCP/IP protocol has been installed.

Syntax:

```
net start lpdsvc
```

The net start microsoft dhcp server Command

The net start microsoft dhcp server command starts the Microsoft DHCP Server service. This command is available only on computers running Windows NT Server and those on which the TCP/IP protocol and DHCP server have been installed.

Syntax:

```
net start "microsoft dhcp server"
```

The net start simple tcp/ip services Command

The net start simple tcp/ip services command starts the Simple TCP/IP Services service. This command is available only if TCP/IP and the Simple TCP/IP Services have been installed.

Syntax:

```
net start "simple tcp/ip services"
```

The net start snmp Command

The net start snmp command starts the SNMP service. The SNMP service allows a server to report its current status to an SNMP management system on a TCP/IP network. This command is available only if TCP/IP and SNMP have been installed.

Syntax:

```
net start snmp
```

The net start tcp/ip netbios helper Command

The net start tcp/ip netbios helper command enables the Netbios over TCP service. This command is available only if TCP/IP has been installed.

Syntax:

```
net start "tcp/ip netbios helper"
```

The net start windows internet name service Command

The `net start windows internet name service` command starts the Windows Internet Name Service. This command is available only on Windows NT Servers if TCP/IP and the Windows Internet Name Service have been installed.

Syntax:

```
net start "windows internet name service"
```

The netstat Command

The `netstat` command displays protocol statistics and current TCP/IP network connections. This command is available only if the TCP/IP protocol has been installed.

Syntax:

```
netstat [-a] [-e] [-n] [-s] [-p protocol] [-r] [interval]
```

Parameters:

`-a`	Displays all connections and listening ports; server connections are normally not shown.
`-e`	Displays Ethernet statistics; it can be combined with the `-s` option.
`-n`	Displays addresses and port numbers in numerical form (rather than attempting name look-ups).
`-s`	Displays per-protocol statistics. By default, statistics are shown for TCP, UDP, ICMP, and IP; the `-p` option can be used to specify a subset of the default.
`-p protocol`	Shows connections for the protocol specified by `proto`; `proto` may be `tcp` or `udp`. If used with the `-s` option to display per-protocol statistics, `proto` can be `tcp`, `udp`, `icmp`, or `ip`.
`-r`	Displays the contents of the routing table.
`interval`	Redisplays selected statistics, pausing the number of seconds specified in `interval` between each display. Press Ctrl+C to stop redisplaying statistics. If this parameter is omitted, `netstat` prints the current configuration information once.

The nslookup Command

This diagnostic tool displays information from Domain Naming System (DNS) name servers. Before using this tool, you should be familiar with how DNS works. `Nslookup` is available only if the TCP/IP protocol has been installed.

Nslookup has two modes: interactive and non-interactive. If you need to look up only a single piece of data, use non-interactive mode. For the first argument, type the name or IP address of the computer to be looked up. For the second argument, type the name or IP address of a DNS name server. If you omit the second argument, the default DNS name server will be used.

If you need to look up more than one piece of data, you can use interactive mode. Type a hyphen for the first argument and the name or IP address of a DNS name server for the second argument. If you omit both arguments, the default DNS name server is used.

Syntax:

nslookup [-*option* ...] [*computer-to-find* ¦ - [*server*]]

Parameters:

-*option* ...	Specifies one or more nslookup commands as a command-line option. For a list of commands, see Nslookup Commands. Each option consists of a hyphen followed immediately by the command name and, in some cases, an equal sign and then a value. The command line length must be less than 256 characters. For example, to change the default query type to host (computer) information and the initial timeout to 10 seconds, you would enter:

nslookup -querytype=hinfo -timeout=10

computer-to-find	Look up information for *computer-to-find* by using the current default server or using server if specified. If *computer-to-find* is an IP address and the query type is A or PTR, the name of the computer is returned. If *computer-to-find* is a name and doesn't have a trailing period, the default DNS domain name is appended to the name. (This behavior depends on the state of the set options: domains, srchlist, defname, and search.) To look up a computer not in the current DNS domain, append a period to the name.
	If you type a hyphen instead of *computer-to-find*, the command prompt changes to nslookup interactive mode.
server	Use this server as the DNS name server. If you omit server, the default DNS name server is used.

The ping Command

The ping command verifies connections to a remote computer or computers. This command is available only if the TCP/IP protocol has been installed.

Syntax:

```
ping [-t] [-a] [-n count] [-l length] [-f] [-i ttl] [-v tos] [-r count]
➥[-s count] [[-j computer-list] ¦ [-k computer-list]] [-w timeout]
➥destination-list
```

Parameters:

-t	Pings the specified computer until interrupted.
-a	Resolves addresses to computer names.
-n *count*	Sends the number of ECHO packets specified by count; the default is 4.
-l *length*	Sends ECHO packets containing the amount of data specified by length; the default is 64 bytes, and the maximum is 8192.
-f	Sends a Do Not Fragment flag in the packet. The packet won't be fragmented by gateways on the route.
-i *ttl*	Sets the Time To Live field to the value specifed by ttl.
-v *tos*	Sets the Type Of Service field to the value specifed by tos.
-r *count*	Records the route of the outgoing packet and the returning packet in the Record Route field. A minimum of 1 and a maximum of 9 computers may be specified by count.
-s *count*	Specifies the timestamp for the number of hops specified by count.
-j *computer-list*	Routes packets through the list of computers specified by computer-list. Consecutive computers may be separated by intermediate gateways (loose source routed). The maximum number allowed by IP is 9.
-k *computer-list*	Routes packets through the list of computers specified by computer-list. Consecutive computers may not be separated by intermediate gateways (strict source routed). The maximum number allowed by IP is 9.
-w *timeout*	Specifies a timeout interval in milliseconds.
destination-list	Specifies the remote computers to ping.

D

NT COMMAND-
PROMPT
REFERENCE

The rcp Command

This connectivity command copies files between a Windows NT computer and a system running rshd, the remote shell daemon. The rcp command can also be used for a third-party transfer to copy files between two computers running rshd when the command is issued from a Windows NT computer. The rshd daemon is available on UNIX computers, but not on Windows NT, so the Windows NT computer can participate only as the system from which the commands are issued. The remote computer must also provide the rcp utility by running rshd.

Syntax:

```
rcp [-a ¦ -b] [-h] [-r] source1 source2 ... sourceN destination
```

Parameters:

-a	Specifies ASCII transfer mode. This mode converts the carriage return/linefeed characters to carriage returns on outgoing files and linefeed characters to carriage return/linefeeds for incoming files. This is the default transfer mode.
-b	Specifies binary image transfer mode. No carriage return/linefeed conversion is performed.
-h	Transfers source files marked with the hidden attribute on the Windows NT computer. Without this option, specifying a hidden file on the rcp command line has the same effect as though the file didn't exist.
-r	Recursively copies the contents of all subdirectories of the source to the destination. Both the source and destination must be directories, although using -r works even if the source is not a directory; there just isn't any recursion.
source and *destination*	Must be of the form [computer[.user]:]filename. If the [computer[.user]:] portion is omitted, the computer is assumed to be the local computer. If the user portion is omitted, the currently logged on Windows NT username is used. If a fully qualified computer name is used, which contains the period separators, then the [.user] must be included. Otherwise, the last part of the computer name is interpreted as the username. If multiple source files are specified, the destination must be a directory.
	If the filename doesn't begin with a forward slash for UNIX or a backward slash for Windows NT systems,

Parameters:

it's assumed to relate to the current working directory. On Windows NT, this is the directory from which the command is issued. On the remote system, it's the logon directory for the remote user. A period means the current directory. Use the escape characters (\ , ", or ') in remote paths to use wildcard characters on the remote computer.

The rexec Command

The rexec command runs commands on remote computers running the Rexec service. Rexec authenticates the user name on the remote computer before executing the specified command. This command is available only if the TCP/IP protocol has been installed.

Syntax:

```
rexec computer [-l username] [-n] command
```

Parameters:

computer	Specifies the remote computer on which to run command.
-l username	Specifies the user name on the remote computer.
-n	Redirects the input of rexec to NULL.
command	Specifies the command to run.

The route Command

The route command manipulates network routing tables. This command is available only if the TCP/IP protocol has been installed.

Syntax:

```
route [-f] [-p] [command [destination] [mask subnetmask] [gateway]
➡[metric costmetric]]
```

Parameters:

-f	Clears the routing tables of all gateway entries. If -f is used with one of the commands, the tables are cleared before running the command.
-p	When used with the add command, -p makes a route persistent across boots of the system. By default, routes aren't preserved when the system is restarted. When used with the print command, it displays the list of registered persistent routes.

continues

D

NT COMMAND-
PROMPT
REFERENCE

Parameters:

	Ignored for all other commands, which always affect the appropriate persistent routes.
command	Specifies one of four commands:

Command	Purpose
print	Prints a route.
add	Adds a route.
delete	Deletes a route.
change	Modifies an existing route.
destination	Specifies the computer to send the command to.
mask subnetmask	Specifies a subnet mask to be associated with this route entry. If not specified, 255.255.255.255 is used.
gateway	Specifies the gateway.
metric costmetric	Assigns an integer cost metric (ranging from 1 to 9999) used in calculating the fastest, most reliable, or least expensive routes.

NOTE

All symbolic names used for destination or gateway are looked up in the network and computer name database files NETWORKS and HOSTS, respectively. If the command is print or delete, wildcards can be used for the destination and gateway, or the gateway argument may be omitted.

The rsh Command

The rsh command runs commands on remote computers running the RSH service. This command is available only if the TCP/IP protocol has been installed.

Syntax:

```
rsh computer [-l username] [-n] command
```

Parameters:

computer	Specifies the remote computer on which to run command.
-l username	Specifies the username to use on the remote computer. If omitted, the logged on username is used.
-n	Redirects the input of rsh to NULL.
command	Specifies the command to run.

The `telnet` Command

The `telnet` command starts terminal emulation. The Windows Terminal program is started, the Telnet port is opened, and the Telnet prompt is displayed. This command is available only if the TCP/IP protocol has been installed.

The `tftp` Command

The `tftp` command transfers files to and from a remote computer running the TFTP service. This command is available only if the TCP/IP protocol has been installed.

Syntax:

```
tftp [-i] computer [get ¦ put] source [destination]
```

Parameters:

`-i`	Specifies binary image transfer mode (also called *octet*), which moves the file literally byte by byte. Use this mode when transferring binary files. If `-i` is omitted, the file is transferred in ASCII mode, the default transfer mode. ASCII mode converts the EOL characters to a carriage return for UNIX and a carriage return/line feed for personal computers. This mode should be used when transferring text files. If a file transfer is successful, the data transfer rate is displayed.
`computer`	Specifies the local or remote computer.
`put`	Transfers the file destination on the local computer to the file source on the remote computer.
`get`	Transfers the file destination on the remote computer to the file source on the local computer.

D

NOTE

Use put if you're transferring File-B on the local computer to File-A on remote computer; use get if you're transferring File-B on the remote computer to File-A on the remote computer.

If the local file is -, the remote file is printed out on `stdout` (if using get) or is read from `stdin` (if using put). If file-B is omitted, it's assumed to have the same name as file-A.

Since the `tftp` protocol doesn't support user authentication, the user must be logged on and must be able to write the files on the remote computer.

`source`	Specifies the file to transfer.
`destination`	Specifies where to transfer the file.

The tracert Command

This diagnostic utility determines the route taken to a destination by sending Internet Control Message Protocol (ICMP) echo packets with varying Time-To-Live (TTL) values to the destination. Each router along the path must decrement the TTL on a packet by at least 1 before forwarding it, so the TTL is effectively a *hop count.* When the TTL on a packet reaches 0, the router is supposed to send back an ICMP Time Exceeded message to the source system. The tracert command determines the route by sending the first echo packet with a TTL of 1 and incrementing the TTL by 1 on each subsequent transmission until the target responds or the maximum TTL is reached. The route is determined by examining the ICMP Time Exceeded messages sent back by intermediate routers. Notice that some routers silently drop packets with expired time-to-live (TTLs) and are invisible to tracert.

Syntax:

```
tracert [-d] [-h maximum_hops] [-j computer-list] [-w timeout] target_name
```

Parameters:

-d	Specifies not resolving addresses to computer names.
-h maximum_hops	Specifies maximum number of hops to search for target.
-j computer-list	Specifies loose source route along computer-list.
-w timeout	Waits the number of milliseconds specified by timeout for each reply.
target_name	Name of the target computer.

Network Commands

The commands listed in this section are used from the command prompt to initiate network-related activities. Some of them depend on specific network services or protocols. Service names of two or more words, such as Net Logon or Computer Browser, must be enclosed in quotation marks.

The net accounts Command

The net accounts command updates the user accounts database and modifies password and logon requirements for all accounts. The Net Logon service must be running on the computer you're changing account parameters for.

Syntax:

```
net accounts [/forcelogoff:{minutes | no}] [/minpwlen:length]
➡[/maxpwage:{days | unlimited}] [/minpwage:days]
➡[/uniquepw:number] [/domain]

net accounts [/sync] [/domain]
```

Parameters:

none	Use net accounts without parameters to display the current settings for password, logon limitations, and domain information.
/forcelogoff:{*minutes* ¦ no}	Sets the number of minutes to wait before ending a user's session with a server when the user account or valid logon time expires. The no option, which is the default, prevents forced logoff.
	When the /forcelogoff:*minutes* option is specified, Windows NT sends a warning (the number of minutes specified by *minutes*) before it forces the user off the network. If any files are open, Windows NT warns the user. If *minutes* is less than 2, Windows NT warns the user to log off the network immediately.
/minpwlen:*length*	Sets the minimum number of characters for a user-account password. The range is 0–14 characters; the default is 6 characters.
/maxpwage:{*days* ¦ unlimited}	Sets the maximum number of days that a user account's password is valid. A value of unlimited sets no maximum time. The /maxpwage option must be greater than /minpwage. The range is 0-49,710 days (unlimited); the default is 90 days.
/minpwage:*days*	Sets the minimum number of days before a user can change a new password. A value of 0 sets no minimum time. The range is 0-49,710 days; the default is 0 days.
/uniquepw:*number*	Requires that a user not repeat the same password for the number of password changes. The range is 0–8 password changes; the default is 5 password changes.
/domain	Performs the operation on the primary domain controller of the current domain. Otherwise, the operation is performed on the local computer. This parameter applies only to Windows NT Workstation computers that are members of a Windows NT Server domain. By default, Windows NT Server computers perform operations on the primary domain controller.

D

NT COMMAND-
PROMPT
REFERENCE

continues

Parameters:

/sync	When used on the primary domain controller, it causes all backup domain controllers in the domain to synchronize. When used on a backup domain controller, it causes that backup domain controller only to synchronize with the primary domain controller. This command applies only to computers that are members of a Windows NT Server domain.

The net computer Command

The net computer command adds or deletes computers from a domain database. This command is available only on computers running Windows NT Server.

Syntax:

```
net computer \\computername {/add ¦ /del}
```

Parameters:

\\computername	Specifies the computer to add or delete from the domain.
/add	Adds the specified computer to the domain.
/del	Removes the specified computer from the domain.

The net config Command

The net config command displays the configurable services that are running, or displays and changes settings for a service.

Syntax:

```
net config [service [options]]
```

Parameters:

none	Use net config without parameters to display a list of configurable services.
service	Is a service (server or workstation) that can be configured with the net config command.
options	Are specific to the service. See net config server or net config workstation for the complete syntax.

The `net config server` Command

The `net config server` command displays or changes settings for the Server service while the service is running.

Syntax:

```
net config server [/autodisconnect:time] [/srvcomment:"text "] [/hidden:{yes
➥¦ no}]
```

Parameters:

none	Use `net config server` without parameters to display the current configuration for the Server service.
/autodisconnect:*time*	Sets the maximum number of minutes a user's session can be inactive before it's disconnected. You can specify -1 to never disconnect. The range is -1–65535 minutes; the default is 15.
/srvcomment:"*text*"	Adds a comment for the server that's displayed in Windows NT screens and with the `net view` command. The comment can have as many as 48 characters. Enclose the text in quotation marks.
/hidden:{yes ¦ no}	Specifies whether the server's computername appears on display listings of servers. Note that hiding a server doesn't alter the permissions on that server. The default is no.

The `net config workstation` Command

The `net config workstation` command displays or changes settings for the Workstation service while the service is running.

Syntax:

```
net config workstation [/charcount:bytes] [/chartime:msec] [/charwait:sec]
```

Parameters:

none	Use `net config workstation` without parameters to display the current configuration for the local computer.
/charcount:*bytes*	Specifies the amount of data Windows NT collects before sending the data to a communication device. If `/chartime:`*msec* is also set, Windows NT acts on whichever option is satisfied first. The range is 0–65535 bytes; the default is 16 bytes.

continues

D

NT COMMAND-
PROMPT
REFERENCE

Parameters:

/chartime:*msec*	Sets the number of milliseconds Windows NT collects data before sending the data to a communication device. If /charcount:*bytes* is also set, Windows NT acts on whichever option is satisfied first. The range is 0–65535000 milliseconds; the default is 250 milliseconds.
/charwait:*sec*	Sets the number of seconds Windows NT waits for a communication device to become available. The range is 0–65535 seconds; the default is 3600 seconds.

The net continue Command

The net continue command reactivates suspended services.

Syntax:

net continue *service*

Parameters:

service	Services that can be continued are file server for macintosh (Windows NT Server only), ftp publishing service, lpdsvc, net logon, network dde, network dde dsdm, nt lm security support provider, remoteboot (Windows NT Server only), remote access server, schedule, server, simple tcp/ip services, and workstation.

The net file Command

The net file command displays the names of all open shared files on a server and the number of file locks, if any, on each file. This command also closes individual shared files and removes file locks.

Syntax:

net file [*id* [/close]]

Parameters:

none	Use net file without parameters to get a list of the open files on a server.
id	Is the identification number of the file.
/close	Closes an open file and releases locked records. Type this command from the server where the file is shared.

The net group Command

The net group command adds, displays, or modifies global groups on Windows NT Server domains. This command is available for use only on Windows NT Server domains.

Syntax:

```
net group [groupname [/comment:"text"]] [/domain]

net group groupname {/add [/comment:"text"] ¦ /delete} [/domain]

net group groupname username[ ...] {/add ¦ /delete} [/domain]
```

Parameters:

none	Use net group without parameters to display the name of a server and the names of groups on the server.
groupname	Is the name of the group to add, expand, or delete. Supply only a groupname to view a list of users in a group.
/comment:"text"	Adds a comment for a new or existing group. The comment can have as many as 48 characters. Enclose the text in quotation marks.
/domain	Performs the operation on the primary domain controller of the current domain. Otherwise, the operation is performed on the local computer. This parameter applies only to Windows NT Workstation computers that are members of a Windows NT Server domain. By default, Windows NT Server computers perform operations on the primary domain controller.
username[...]	Lists one or more usernames to add to or remove from a group. Separate multiple username entries with a space.
/add	Adds a group, or adds a username to a group. An account must be established for users added to a group with this command.
/delete	Removes a group, or removes a username from a group.

The net help Command

The net help command lists network commands and topics you can get help with or offers help with a specific command or topic. The available net commands are also listed in the "Network Commands" section of this appendix.

Syntax:

```
net help [command]

net command {/help ¦ /?}
```

continues

Parameters:

none	Use net help without parameters to display a list of commands and topics for which you can get help.
command	Is the command you need help with. Don't type net as part of command.
/help	Gives you another way to display the help text.
/?	Displays the correct syntax for the command.

The net helpmsg Command

The net helpmsg command provides help with a Windows NT error message.

Syntax:

net helpmsg *message#*

Parameters:

message#	Is the four-digit number of the Windows NT message you need help with. NT displays this number along with error messages.

The net localgroup Command

The net localgroup command adds, displays, or modifies local groups.

Syntax:

net localgroup [*groupname* [/comment:"*text*"]] [/domain]

net localgroup *groupname* {/add [/comment:"*text*"] ¦ /delete} [/domain]

net localgroup *groupname* *name* [...] {/add ¦ /delete} [/domain]

Parameters:

none	Use net localgroup without parameters to display the name of the server and the names of local groups on the computer.
groupname	Is the name of the local group to add, expand, or delete. Supply only a groupname to view a list of users or global groups in a local group.
/comment:"*text*"	Adds a comment for a new or existing group. The comment can have as many as 48 characters. Enclose the text in quotation marks.
/domain	Performs the operation on the primary domain controller of the current domain. Otherwise, the operation is performed on the local computer. This parameter applies only to Windows NT

Parameters:

	Workstation computers that are members of a Windows NT Server domain. By default, Windows NT Server computers perform operations on the primary domain controller.
`name [ ...]`	Lists one or more usernames or groupnames to add to or remove from a local group. Separate multiple entries with a space. Names can be local users, users on other domains, or global groups, but not other local groups. If a user is from another domain, preface the username with the domain name (for example, `SALES\RALPHR`).
`/add`	Adds a global groupname or username to a local group. An account must first be established for users or global groups before it's added to a local group with this command.
`/delete`	Removes a groupname or username from a local group.

The net name Command

The `net name` command adds or deletes a messaging name (sometimes called an *alias*), or displays the list of names the computer will accept messages for. The Messenger service must be running to use `net name`.

Syntax:

```
net name [name [/add ¦ /delete]]
```

Parameters:

none	Use `net name` without parameters to display a list of names currently in use.
name	Specifies the name to receive messages; it can have as many as 15 characters.
/add	Adds a name to a computer. Using `/add` is optional; typing `net name` *name* works the same as typing `net name` *name* `/add`.
/delete	Removes a name from a computer.

The net pause Command

The `net pause` command pauses running services.

Syntax:

```
net pause service
```

continues

Parameter:

service	Is `file server for macintosh` (Windows NT Server only), `ftp publishing service`, `lpdsvc`, `net logon`, `network dde`, `network dde dsdm`, `nt lm security support provider`, `remoteboot` (Windows NT Server only), `remote access server`, `schedule`, `server`, `simple tcp/ip services`, or `workstation`.

The `net print` Command

The `net print` command displays or controls print jobs and printer queues.

Syntax:

```
net print \\computername\sharename
net print [\\computername] job# [/hold ¦ /release ¦ /delete]
```

Parameters:

computername	Is the name of the computer sharing the printer queue(s).
sharename	Is the name of the printer queue. When including the sharename with the computername, use a backslash to separate the names.
job#	Is the identification number assigned to a print job in a printer queue. A computer with one or more printer queues assigns each print job a unique number. If a job number is being used in one printer queue shared by a computer, that number isn't assigned to any other job on that computer, not even to jobs in other printer queues on that computer.
/hold	When used with job#, holds a print job waiting in the printer queue. The print job stays in the printer queue, and other print jobs bypass it until it's released.
/release	Releases a print job that has been held.
/delete	Removes a print job from a printer queue.

The `net send` Command

The `net send` command sends messages to other users, computers, or messaging names on the network. The Messenger service must be running to receive messages.

Syntax:

```
net send {name ¦ * ¦ /domain[:name] ¦ /users} message
```

Parameters:

`name`	Is the username, computername, or messaging name to send the message to. If `name` is a computername that contains blank characters, enclose the alias in quotation marks.
`*`	Sends the message to all the names in your group.
`/domain[:name]`	Sends the message to all the names in the computer's domain. If `name` is specified, the message is sent to all the names in the specified domain or workgroup.
`/users`	Sends the message to all users connected to the server.
`message`	Is the text to be sent as a message.

The net session Command

The net session command lists or disconnects the sessions between a local computer and the clients connected to it.

Syntax:

```
net session [\\computername] [/delete]
```

Parameters:

none	Use net session without parameters to display information about all sessions with the local computer.
`\\computername`	Identifies the computer for which to list or disconnect sessions.
`/delete`	Ends the computer's session with `\\computername` and closes all open files on the computer for the session. If `\\computername` is omitted, all sessions on the local computer are canceled.

The net share Command

The net share command creates, deletes, or displays shared resources.

Syntax:

```
net share sharename
net share sharename=drive:path [/users:number ¦ /unlimited] [/remark:"text"]
net share sharename [/users:number ¦ unlimited] [/remark:"text"]
net share {sharename ¦ drive:path} /delete
```

continues

Parameters:

none	Use net share without parameters to display information about all resources being shared on the local computer.
sharename	Is the network name of the shared resource. Use net share with a sharename only to display information about that share.
drive:path	Specifies the absolute path of the directory to be shared.
/users:number	Sets the maximum number of users who can simultaneously access the shared resource.
/unlimited	Specifies an unlimited number of users who can simultaneously access the shared resource.
/remark:"*text*"	Adds a descriptive comment about the resource. Enclose the text in quotation marks.
/delete	Stops sharing the resource.

The net start Command

The net start command starts a service, or displays a list of started services. Service names of two or more words, such as Net Logon or Computer Browser, must be enclosed in quotation marks.

Syntax:

```
net start [service]
```

Parameters:

none	Use net start without parameters to display a list of running services.
service	Includes the following services:
	alerter
	client service for netware
	clipbook server
	computer browser
	dhcp client
	directory replicator
	eventlog
	ftp publishing service

Parameters:

lpdsvc

messenger

net logon

network dde

network dde dsdm

network monitor agent

nt lm security support provider

ole

remote access connection manager

remote access isnsap service

remote access server

remote procedure call (rpc) locator

remote procedure call (rpc) service

schedule

server

simple tcp/ip services

snmp

spooler

tcp/ip netbios helper

ups

workstation

These services are available only on Windows NT Server: file
server for macintosh, gateway service for netware, microsoft
dhcp server, print server for macintosh, remoteboot, and
windows internet name service.

D

NT COMMAND-
PROMPT
REFERENCE

The net start alerter Command

Starts the Alerter service, which sends alert messages.

Syntax:

net start alerter

The net start client service for netware Command

Starts the Client Service for NetWare service. This command is available only on Windows NT Workstation if Client Service for NetWare has been installed.

Syntax:

```
net start "client service for netware"
```

The net start clipbook server Command

Starts the ClipBook Server service. Service names with two words, such as ClipBook Server, must be enclosed in quotation marks.

Syntax:

```
net start "clipbook server"
```

The net start computer browser Command

Starts the Computer Browser service.

Syntax:

```
net start "computer browser"
```

The net start directory replicator Command

Starts the Directory Replicator service. The Directory Replicator service copies designated files to specified servers. This service can also be started with the command net start replicator.

Syntax:

```
net start "directory replicator"
```

The net start eventlog Command

Starts the event logging service, which logs events on the local computer. This service must be started before you use the Event Viewer to view the logged events.

Syntax:

```
net start eventlog
```

The net start file server for macintosh **Command**

Starts the File Server for Macintosh service, permitting the sharing of files with Macintosh computers. This command is available only on NT Servers.

Syntax:

```
net start "file server for macintosh"
```

The net start gateway service for netware **Command**

Starts the Gateway Service for NetWare service. This command is available only on Windows NT Server if Gateway Service for NetWare has been installed.

Syntax:

```
net start "gateway service for netware"
```

The net start messenger **Command**

Starts the Messenger service, which allows a computer to receive messages.

Syntax:

```
net start messenger
```

The net start net logon **Command**

Starts the Net Logon service. The Net Logon service verifies logon requests and controls replication of the user accounts database domainwide. This service can also be started with the command net start netlogon.

Syntax:

```
net start "net logon"
```

The net start network dde **Command**

Starts the Network DDE service.

Syntax:

```
net start "network dde"
```

The net start network dde dsdm Command

Starts the Network DDE server service.

Syntax:

```
net start "network dde dsdm"
```

The start network monitor agent Command

Starts the Network Monitor Agent service. This command is available only if the Network Monitor Agent has been installed.

Syntax:

```
net start "network monitor agent"
```

The net start nt lm security support provider Command

Starts the NT LM Security Support Provider service. This command is available only if the NT LM Security Support Provider has been installed.

Syntax:

```
net start "nt lm security support provider"
```

The net start print server for macintosh Command

Starts the Print Server for Macintosh service, permitting printing from Macintosh computers. This command is available only on computers running Windows NT Server.

Syntax:

```
net start "print server for macintosh"
```

The net start remoteboot Command

Starts the Remoteboot service, permitting computers on the network to load the operating system from the computer. This command is available only on computers running Windows NT Server.

Syntax:

```
net start remoteboot
```

The net start remote access connection manager Command

Starts the Remote Access Connection Manager service. This command is available only if the Remote Access Service has been installed.

Syntax:

```
net start "remote access connection manager"
```

The net start remote access isnsap service Command

Starts the Remote Access ISNSAP Service service. This command is available only if the Remote Access Service has been installed.

Syntax:

```
net start "remote access isnsap service"
```

The net start remote access server Command

Starts the Remote Access Server service. This command is available only if the Remote Access Service has been installed.

Syntax:

```
net start "remote access server"
```

The net start remote procedure call (rpc) locator Command

Starts the RPC Locator service. The Locator service is the RPC name service for Microsoft Windows NT.

Syntax:

```
net start "remote procedure call (RPC) locator"
```

The net start remote procedure call (rpc) service Command

Starts the Remote Procedure Call (RPC) Service service. The Remote Procedure Call (RPC) Service service is the RPC subsystem for Microsoft Windows NT. The RPC subsystem includes the endpoint mapper and other miscellaneous RPC services.

Syntax:

```
net start "remote procedure call (rpc) service"
```

The net start schedule Command

Starts the Schedule service, which allows a computer to start programs at a specified time with the at command.

Syntax:

```
net start schedule
```

The net start server Command

Starts the Server service, which allows a computer to share resources on the network.

Syntax:

```
net start server
```

The net start snmp Command

Starts the SNMP service, which allows a server to report its current status to an SNMP management system on a TCP/IP network. This command is available only if TCP/IP and SNMP have been installed.

Syntax:

```
net start snmp
```

The net start spooler Command

Starts the Spooler service.

Syntax:

```
net start spooler
```

The net start ups Command

Starts the Uninterruptible Power Supply service.

Syntax:

```
net start ups
```

The net start workstation Command

Starts the Workstation service, which allows a computer to connect to and use network resources.

Syntax:

```
net start workstation
```

The net statistics Command

The net statistics command displays the statistics log for the local Workstation or Server service.

Syntax:

```
net statistics [workstation | server]
```

Parameters:

none	Use net statistics without parameters to list the running services for which statistics are available.
workstation	Displays statistics for the local Workstation service.
server	Displays statistics for the local Server service.

The net stop Command

The net stop command stops a Windows NT network service.

Syntax:

```
net stop service
```

Parameters:

service	Includes the following services:
	alerter
	client service for netware
	clipbook server
	computer browser
	dhcp client
	directory replicator
	eventlog
	ftp publishing service

continues

D

NT COMMAND-
PROMPT
REFERENCE

Parameters:

lpdsvc

messenger

net logon

network dde

network dde dsdm

network monitor agent

nt lm security support provider

ole

remote access connection manager

remote access isnsap service

remote access server

remote procedure call (rpc) locator

remote procedure call (rpc) service

schedule

server

simple tcp/ip services

snmp

spooler

tcp/ip netbios helper

ups

workstation

These services are available only on Windows NT Server: file server for macintosh, gateway service for netware, microsoft dhcp server, print server for macintosh, and windows internet name service.

The net time Command

The net time command synchronizes the computer's clock with that of another computer or domain. Used without the /set option, it displays the time for another computer or domain.

Syntax:

```
net time [\\computername ¦ /domain[:name]] [/set]
```

Parameters:

computername	Is the name of a server you want to check or synchronize with.
/*domain*[:*name*]	Specifies the domain with which to synchronize time.
/*set*	Synchronizes the computer's clock with the time on the specified computer or domain.

The net use Command

The net use command connects a computer to or disconnects a computer from a shared resource, or displays information about computer connections. The command also controls persistent net connections.

Syntax:

```
net use [devicename ¦ *] [\\computername\sharename[\volume]] [password ¦ *]]
[/user:[domainname\]username] [[/delete] ¦ [/persistent:{yes ¦ no}]]

net use devicename [/home[password ¦ *]] [/delete:{yes ¦ no}]

net use [/persistent:{yes ¦ no}]
```

Parameters:

none	Enter net use without parameters to get a list of network connections.
devicename	Assigns a name to connect to the resource or specifies the device to be disconnected. There are two kinds of devicenames: disk drives (D: through Z:) and printers (LPT1: through LPT3). Type an asterisk instead of a specific devicename to assign the next available devicename.
*computername**sharename*	Is the name of the server and the shared resource. If the computername contains blank characters, enclose the double backslash and the computername in quotation marks. The computername may be from 1 to 15 characters long.
volume	Specifies a NetWare volume on the server. You must have Client Service for NetWare (Windows NT Workstation) or Gateway Service for NetWare (Windows NT Server) installed and running to connect to NetWare servers.
password	Is the password needed to access the shared resource.

continues

D

**NT COMMAND-
PROMPT
REFERENCE**

Parameters:

*	Produces a prompt for the password. The password isn't displayed when you type it at the password prompt.
/user	Specifies a different username with which the connection is made.
domainname	Specifies another domain. For example, `net use d: \\server\share /user:admin\mariel` connects the user `mariel` as though the connection were made from the admin domain. If `domain` is omitted, the current logged on domain is used.
username	Specifies the username with which to log on.
/home	Connects a user to their home directory.
/delete	Cancels the specified network connection. If the user specifies the connection with an asterisk, all network connections are cancelled.
/persistent	Controls the use of persistent network connections. The default is the setting used last. Deviceless connections are not persistent.
yes	Saves all connections as they are made, and restores them at next logon.
no	Doesn't save the connection being made or subsequent connections; existing connections are restored at next logon. Use the `/delete` switch to remove persistent connections.

The ntbooks Command

The ntbooks command accesses online Windows NT manuals.

Syntax:

```
ntbooks [/s] [/w] [/n:path]
```

Parameters:

/s	Used from a Windows NT workstation to access Windows NT server documentation.
/w	Used from a Windows NT server to access Windows NT workstation documentation.
/n	Specifies the path to the online books. Normally, the last used path is remembered and used.

Parameters:

>The ntbooks command searches for Windows NT manuals at the last used location, but doesn't display the path to the location. If the location was a CD-ROM drive and the CD-ROM with the books isn't in the drive, you're prompted to insert the CD-ROM.

The pax Command

The pax command starts the Portable Archive Interchange (Pax) utility.

Syntax:

```
pax [-cimopuvy] [-f archive] [-s replstr] [-t device] [pattern...]

pax -r [-cimnopuvy] [-f archive] [-s replstr] [-t device] [pattern...]

pax -w [-adimuvy] [-b blocking] [-f archive] [-s replstr] [-t device] [-x
format] [pathname...]

pax -rw [-ilmopuvy] [-s replstr] [pathname...] directory
```

Pax is a POSIX program, and pathnames used as arguments must be specified in POSIX format. Use //C/USERS/DEFAULT instead of C:\USERS\DEFAULT.

Combinations of the -r and -w command line arguments specify whether pax will read, write, or list the contents of the specified archive or move the specified files to another directory.

Parameters:

-r
: Reads an archive file from the standard input. Only files with names that match any of the pattern operands are selected for extraction. The selected files are conditionally created and copied in relation to the current directory tree, subject to the options described below. By default, the owner and group of selected files will be that of the invoking process, and the permissions and modification times will be the same as those in the archive. The supported archive formats are automatically detected on input. The default output format is ustar, but may be overridden by the -x format option described below.

-w
: Writes the files and directories specified by the pathname operands to the standard output together with the pathname and status information prescribed by the archive format used. A directory pathname operand refers to the files and (recursively) subdirectories of that directory. If no pathname operands are given, then the standard input is read to get a list of pathnames to copy, one pathname per line. In this case, only those pathnames appearing on the standard input are copied.

continues

Parameters:

-rw	Reads the files and directories named in the pathname operands and copies them to the destination directory. A directory pathname operand refers to the files and (recursively) subdirectories of that directory. If no pathname operands are given, the standard input is read to get a list of pathnames to copy, one pathname per line. In this case, only those pathnames appearing on the standard input are copied. The directory named by the directory operand must exist and have the proper permissions before the copy can occur.
-a	The files specified by pathname are appended to the specified archive.
-b blocking	Block the output at blocking bytes per write to the archive file. A k suffix multiplies blocking by 1024, a b suffix multiplies blocking by 512, and an m suffix multiplies blocking by 1048576 (1 megabyte). If not specified, blocking is automatically determined on input and is ignored for -rw.
-c	Complements the match sense of the pattern operands.
-d	Intermediate directories not explicitly listed in the archive aren't created. This option is ignored unless the -r option is specified.
-f archive	The archive option specifies the pathname of the input or output archive, overriding the default of standard input for -r or standard output for -w.
-i	Interactively rename files. Substitutions specified by -s options (described below) are performed before requesting the new filename from the user. A file is skipped if an empty line is entered and pax exits with an exit status of 0 if end-of-file is encountered.
-l	Files are linked rather than copied when possible.
-m	File modification times aren't retained.
-n	When -r is specified, but -w is not, the pattern arguments are treated as ordinary filenames. Only the first occurrence of each of these files in the input archive is read. Pax exits with a 0 exit status after all files in the list have been read. If one or more files in the list is not found, pax writes a diagnostic to standard error for each of the files and exits with a non-zero exit status. The filenames are compared before any of the -i, -s, or -y options are applied.
-o	Restore file ownership as specified in the archive. The invoking process must have appropriate privileges to do this.
-p	Preserve the access time of the input files after they have been copied.

Parameters:

-s replstr	Filenames are modified according to the substitution expression, using the syntax of ed(1), as shown:

-s /old/new/Π

Any non-null character can be used as a delimiter (a / is used here as an example). You can specify multiple -s expressions; the expressions are applied in the order specified terminating with the first successful substitution. The optional trailing *p* causes successful mappings to be listed on standard error. The optional trailing *g* causes the old expression to be replaced each time it occurs in the source string. Files that substitute to an empty string are ignored both on input and output.

-t device	The device option argument is an implementation-defined identifier that names the input or output archive device, overriding the default of standard input for -r and standard output for -w.
-u	Copy each file only if it's newer than a pre-existing file with the same name. This implies -a.
-v	List filenames as they are encountered. Produces a verbose table of contents listing on the standard output when both -r and -w are omitted, otherwise the filenames are printed to standard error as they are encountered in the archive.
-x format	Specifies the output archive format. The input format, which must be one of the following, is automatically determined when the -r option is used. These are the supported formats:
cpio	The extended CPIO interchange format specified in Extended CPIO Format in IEEE Std. 1003.1-1988.
Ustar	The extended TAR interchange format specified in Extended TAR Format in IEEE Std. 1003.1-1988. This is the default archive format.
-y	Prompt for the disposition of each file. Substitutions specified by -s options (described above) are performed before prompting the user for disposition. EOF or an input line starting with the character *q* caused pax to exit. Otherwise, an input line starting with anything other than *y* causes the file to be ignored. This option can't be used with the -i option. Only the last of multiple -f or -t options take effect.
directory	The destination directory pathname for copies when both the –r and -w options are specified. The directory must exist and be writable before the copy, or an error results.

continues

Parameters:

`pathname`	A file whose contents are used instead of the files named on the standard input. When a directory is named, all its files and subdirectories are copied as well.
`pattern`	A pattern is given using wildcards. The default is all files.

The pentnt Command

The `pentnt` command detects floating-point division error, when present, in the Pentium chip, disables floating-point hardware, and turns on floating-point emulation.

Syntax:

```
pentnt [-c] [-f] [-o] [-?¦-h]
```

Parameters:

`-c`	Enables conditional emulation. Floating-point emulation is forced on if, and only if, the system detects the Pentium processor floating-point division error at start time. If you select this parameter, you must restart the computer for the changes to take effect.
`-f`	Enables forced emulation. Floating-point hardware is disabled and floating-point emulation is always forced on, regardless of whether the system exhibits the Pentium processor floating-point division error. This parameter is useful for testing software emulators and for working around floating-point hardware defects known to the operating system. If you select this parameter, you must restart the computer for the changes to take effect.
`-o`	Disables forced emulation and re-enables floating-point hardware if it's present. If you select this parameter, you must restart the computer for the changes to take effect.
`-?¦-h`	Displays Help for the command.

The net user Command

The `net user` command adds or modifies user accounts or displays user-account information.

Syntax:

```
net user [username [password ¦ *] [options]] [/domain]

net user username {password ¦ *} /add [options] [/domain]

net user username [/delete] [/domain]
```

Parameters:

none	Use net user without parameters to view a list of the user accounts on the computer.
username	Is the name of the user account to add, delete, modify, or view. The name of the user account can have as many as 20 characters.
password	Assigns or changes a password for the user's account. A password must satisfy the minimum length set with the /minpwlen option of the net accounts command. It can have as many as 14 characters.
*	Produces a prompt for the password. The password isn't displayed when you type it at a password prompt.
/domain	Performs the operation on the primary domain controller of the computer's primary domain. This parameter applies only to Windows NT Workstation computers that are members of a Windows NT Server domain. By default, Windows NT Server computers perform operations on the primary domain controller.

NOTE

This action is taken on the primary domain controller of the computer's primary domain, which might not be the logged on domain.

/add	Adds a user account to the user accounts database.
/delete	Removes a user account from the user accounts database.

The choices for the *options* parameter are as follows:

/active:{no ¦ yes}	Enables or disables the user account. If the user account isn't active, the user can't access resources on the computer. The default is yes (active).
/comment:"*text*"	Provides a descriptive comment about the user's account that can have as many as 48 characters. Enclose the text in quotation marks.
/countrycode:*nnn*	Uses the operating-system country codes to implement the specified language files for a user's help and error messages. A value of 0 means the default country code.

continues

D

Parameters:

/expires:{*date* ¦ never}	Causes the user account to expire if *date* is set; never sets no time limit on the user account. Expiration dates can be in mm/dd/yy, dd/mm/yy, or mmm,dd,yy format, depending on the /countrycode. Note that the account expires at the beginning of the date specified. Months can be indicated by a number, spelled out, or abbreviated with three letters. Years can be two or four numbers. Use commas or slashes to separate parts of the date (no spaces). If yy is omitted, the next occurrence of the date (according to your computer's date and time) is assumed. For example, the following date entries are equivalent if entered between January 10, 1994, and January 8, 1995: jan,9 1/9/95 january,9,1995 1/9
/fullname:"*name*"	Specifies a user's full name rather than a username. Enclose the name in quotation marks.
/homedir:*path*	Sets the path for the user's home directory. The path must exist.
/homedirreq:{yes ¦ no}	Sets whether a home directory is required.
/passwordchg:{yes ¦ no}	Specifies whether users can change their own password. The default is yes.
/passwordreq:{yes ¦ no}	Specifies whether a user account must have a password. The default is yes.
/profilepath:[*path*]	Sets a path for the user's logon profile. This pathname points to a registry profile.
/scriptpath:*path*	Sets a path for the user's logon script. Path cannot be an absolute path; it's relative to %systemroot: %\SYSTEM32\REPL\IMPORT\SCRIPTS
/times:{*times* ¦ all}	Specifies the times the user is allowed to use the computer. The times value is expressed as day[-day][,day [-day]] ,time[-time][,time[-time]], limited to one-hour time increments. Days can be spelled out or abbreviated (M, T, W, Th, F, Sa, Su). Hours can be 12-hour or 24-hour notation. For 12-hour notation, use AM and PM or A.M. and P.M. The value all means a user can always log on. A null value (blank) means a user can never log on. Separate day and time with commas, and units of day and time with semicolons (for example, M,4AM-5PM;T,1PM-3PM). Do not use spaces when designating /times.

Parameters:

/usercomment:"*text*"	Lets an administrator add or change the "user comment" for the account. Enclose the text in quotation marks.
/workstations: ➥{*computername*[,...] ¦ *}	Lists as many as eight workstations from which a user can log onto the network. Separate multiple entries in the list with commas. If /workstations has no list, or if the list is *, the user can log on from any computer.

The net view Command

The net view command displays a list of domains, a list of computers, or the resources being shared by the specified computer.

Syntax:

```
net view [\\computername ¦ /domain[:domainname]]
net view /network:nw [\\computername]
```

Parameters:

none	Use net view without parameters to display a list of computers in your current domain.
computername	Specifies the computer whose shared resources you want to view.
/domain[:*domainname*]	Specifies the domain for which you want to view the available computers. If *domainname* is omitted, it displays all domains in the network.
/network:nw	Displays all available servers on a NetWare network. If a computer name is specified, the resources available on that computer in the NetWare network are displayed. Other networks added to the system can also be specified with this switch.

Other Utility Commands

This section covers several miscellaneous utilities that don't fall into the other command categories.

The `aclconv` Command

The `aclconv` command converts OS/2 HPFS386 file and directory permissions to NTFS volumes.

Syntax:

```
aclconv /data:datafile /log:logfile [/newdrive:drive] [/domain:domain]
↪[/codepage:n]

aclconv /list /log:logfile /codepage:n
```

Parameters:

`/data:datafile`	Specifies the LAN Manager for OS/2 backacc data file.
`/log:logfile`	Specifies the file where `aclconv` should log information about failed conversions.
`/newdrive:drive`	Specifies the drive on which to restore permissions. This parameter is necessary only if the permissions were backed up from a different drive letter.
`/domain:domain`	Searches only the specified domain for account names.
`/codepage:n`	Specifies the Code Page associated with the backacc data file.
`/list`	Lists the contents of the specified log file.

The `diskperf` Command

The `diskperf` command starts and stops system disk performance counters.

Syntax:

```
diskperf [-y¦-n] [\\computername]
```

Parameters:

none	Used without the `-y` or `-n` switches, `diskperf` reports whether disk performance counters are enabled on the local or specified computer.
`-y`	Sets the system to start disk performance counters when the system is rebooted.
`-n`	Sets the system to not use disk performance counters when the system is rebooted.
`computername`	Is the name of the computer on which you want to see or set disk performance counter use.

The `ipxroute` Command

The `ipxroute` command displays and modifies information about the routing tables used by the IPX protocol. The command has different options for IPX routing and for source routing. Separate all options with spaces.

IPX Routing Options

Syntax:

```
ipxroute servers [/type=x]
ipxroute stats [/show] [/clear]
ipxroute table
```

Parameters:

`servers [/type=x]`	Displays the SAP table for the specified server type; *x* is an integer. For example, `/type=4` displays all file servers. If no `/type` is specified, then servers of all types are shown. The list is sorted by server name.
`stats [/show] [/clear]`	Displays or clears IPX router interface statistics. `/show` is the default; `/clear` clears the statistics.
`table`	Displays the IPX routing table, sorted by network number.

Source Routing Options

Syntax:

```
ipxroute board=n [clear] [def] [gbr] [mbr] [remove=xxxxx]
ipxroute config
```

Parameters:

`board=n`	Specifies the network adapter card for which to query or set parameters.
`clear`	Clears the source routing table.
`def`	Sends packets to the ALL ROUTES broadcast. If a packet is transmitted to a unique mac address that's not in the source routing table, the default is to send the packet to the SINGLE ROUTES broadcast.
`gbr`	Sends packets to the ALL ROUTES broadcast. If a packet is transmitted to the broadcast address (FFFFFFFFFFFF), the default is to send the packet to the SINGLE ROUTES broadcast.

continues

D

NT COMMAND-
PROMPT
REFERENCE

Parameters:

`mbr`	Sends packets to the ALL ROUTES broadcast. If a packet is transmitted to a multicast address (C000xxxxxxxx), the default is to send the packet to the SINGLE ROUTES broadcast.
`remove=xxxxx`	Removes the given node address from the source routing table.
`config`	Displays information on all the bindings for which IPX is configured.

The portuas Command

The portuas command merges a LAN Manager 2.*x* user accounts database into an existing Windows NT user accounts database.

Syntax:

```
portuas -f filename [-u username] [-v] [/codepage codepage] [/log filename]
```

Parameters:

`-f filename`	Specifies the LAN Manager 2.*x* NET.ACC file.
`-u username`	Specifies a single user or group to restore.
`-v`	Displays all messages (verbose).
`/codepage codepage`	Specifies the OEM codepage the LAN Manager 2.*x* NET.ACC file is in.
`/log filename`	Specifies a file to log results.

What's on the CD-ROM?

The CD-ROM included with this book has several hundred megabytes of software on it. You will find graphics and graphics tools, CGI scripts, productivity shareware, and more. Here's a quick rundown of the directories on the CD-ROM, and what they contain:

\3rdparty

\Graphics

\MainActor   A modular animation processing and editing package that you can use to load, edit, play, save, and convert many animation, picture, and sound formats.

\Breeze   Breeze Designer is a 32-bit, 3-D modeling and design tool for Windows NT, Windows 95, and Win32s.

\RocketShop   An animated and static .GIF library.

\Java

\Widget   An Applet Widget Kit that allows nonprogrammers to make some inventive Java applets without having to do any coding.

\JDK   Sun Microsystems Java Developer's Kit, version 1.0.2.

\Jamba   Aimtech's object-oriented, visual authoring tool for creating interactive, media-rich Java applets.

\Misc

\Gplains   ScreenCAM presentation of Great Plains Software's Dynamic C/S+.

\Netinsta   Analyst/Probe is a network protocol analyzer for NT.

\Neinsto   Observer is a network monitor and protocol analyzer for NT.

\Ntcert   Sample guides from Transcender for Microsoft Certification Exams.

\Camellia   A complete batch-job management environment for Windows NT that includes Batch Job Server and Batch Job Administrator demos.

\Tools

\Ashwin   A job scheduling package (evaluation version) from Seagate.

\Wilson   Includes shareware versions of WinBatch (system utility language), WinEdit (a programmer's editor), and WebBatch (a Windows CGI scripting language).

\Utils

\NetAlert   Monitors the status of a TCP/IP network port by checking whether the port is listening; then sends either an e-mail alert, or pages you, or both.

\Portscan   Checks system ports.

\FaxMail   Adds a Fax button to your Windows programs, giving you access to all the fax/modems and fax/machines, making them become your printers.

\Command   A shareware product similar to Norton Commander.

\Qcolor   Provides a more logical and convenient approach to making use of NT 4's feature of monitor refresh rate settings, resolution changes, and color depth on-the-fly.

\NetSpy   Monitors the availability of IP nodes, supports sound alerts and task bar notification, and includes topographical representation of distributed sites.

\MiniNote   Not just another Windows Notepad replacement, but a feature-rich program with a selection of original productivity tools.

\WinZip   A 32-bit file compression tool from Nico Mak Computing.

\Opalis   Lets you automate many tasks in the Windows NT environment.

\Somarsoft   Includes DumpEVT, DumpREG, DumpACL, and ACTS.

\Diskeeper   A disk-defragmentation program from executive software.

\FileEat   A trash can utility for Windows NT.

\Snagit   A Windows screen-capture utility for the 32-bit environment.

\Pcany   An evaluation copy of PCANYWHERE32, the remote and mobile access utility from Symantec.

\ZetaFax   A set of programs that allows users on a network to send and receive faxes.

\NoteTab   Super NoteTab is the "big brother" version of MiniNote.

\Web

\DomainAdmin   Allows you to track your IP addresses and more.

\Purveyor   A Web server for Windows NT.

\cgikit   Includes a small CGI kit for the EMWAC HTTPs.

\WebData   The WebData Daemon by Adageus, Inc., offers Web users database access, regardless of platform type.

\HTML IMg   Produces Web pages showing .GIF or .JPG pictures from the directory you select.

\Web Des   A WYSIWYG Web design program by Frontier Technologies.

\Servers   Includes several different Web servers:

  \Ali   Alibaba's Windows 95/NT Web server.

  \BindNT   A DNS server maintained by the Internet Software Consortium and ported to NT by Larry Kahn, Viraj Bais and Greg Shueman.

  \EMWAC   Windows NT freeware servers for Gopher and HTTP, both from the University of Edinburgh.

  \Folkweb   A shareware HTTP Web server from ILAR.

  \PostOff   An Internet messaging server software from Software.com.

  \ZB Serve   A full-featured Internet/intranet server package for NT that includes HTTP, Gopher, FTP, and chat services.

E

WHAT'S ON THE CD-ROM?

\Ebooks

\NTWebDev   The HTML version of *Windows NT Web Development.*

\LLWW   The HTML version of *Laura Lemay's Web Workshop: ActiveX and VB Script.*

Most of the utilities and programs mentioned in this book are included on the CD-ROM. If they aren't, a reference to a Web site or FTP location is usually given in the text. If a reference is missing, you can almost always get up-to-date information from one of the Windows NT Web sites (refer to Chapter 29, "Windows NT Resources on the Internet").

The Windows NT Boot Sequence

IN THIS APPENDIX

The Windows NT boot process is a relatively complex operation. Many things can go wrong during this process. For example, configuration, driver, and Registry errors can cause a system boot failure. An understanding of what happens during this critical time in the life of a computer can help you troubleshoot problems that might otherwise leave you looking at NT's "Blue Screen of Death" and scratching your head.

This appendix covers BOOT.INI, the file that controls the the boot process. You learn about the items you can insert into this file to help with troubleshooting. This appendix also outlines the steps in the boot process for Intel and non-Intel computer systems.

The ARC Pathname

Before you can understand the boot sequence, you need to understand the syntax used to describe partitions in hard disks attached to controllers. This syntax is very germane to the process that determines which partition is used to start the computer. This syntax is called *ARC* (Advanced RISC Computing). Its generalized specifications were developed to allow Windows NT to run on a variety of computer platforms.

An ARC pathname points to a specific directory in a computer system, starting from the controller and working down to the hard disk, the partition, and, finally, the directory. This full ARC pathname is necessary to specify a particular directory unambiguously.

The Controller and Hard Disk

From the perspective of the NT boot process, there are two basic types of hard disk controllers: those that rely on the system's BIOS to access the disks and those that rely on NTBOOTDD.SYS, the NT device driver. In general, when defining boot partitions in a system, *scsi* refers to a disk controller that uses NTBOOTDD.SYS, and *multi* refers to a controller that relies on the system BIOS. Therefore, there are two forms of the ARC pathname: one for multi devices and one for SCSI devices. The following are two examples of ARC pathnames for multi devices:

multi(0)disk(0)rdisk(0) specifies the first hard disk on the first multi controller. (All numbering starts with 0.)

multi(1)disk(0)rdisk(2) specifies the third hard disk on the second multi controller.

Note that for multi controllers, the disk() parameter is always 0. In contrast, scsi controllers use the disk() parameter to specify the disk's SCSI ID. The rdisk() parameter is used for the LUN (Logical Unit Number) in the ID. However, because most systems have only one LUN per SCSI ID, this parameter is almost always 0. The following is a typical pathname for a SCSI device:

scsi(0)disk(8)rdisk(0) specifies the hard disk set to LUN 0 (as most are) and SCSI ID 8 on the first SCSI controller.

The Partition

Once the hard disk is identified, the partition on the disk needs to be specified. Unlike controllers and disks, however, partitions are numbered from 1 as follows:

- All primary partitions are numbered first, corresponding to their physical location on the drive.
- Extended partitions in logical drives are numbered next, in order of their logical drives and their order within the logical drive.
- EISA configuration partitions, DOS extended partitions, and any unused partitions are not assigned numbers.

As mentioned above, partition numbering starts at 1. The number 0 refers to the entire physical disk and should not be used.

The Directory

The last part of the ARC pathname is the directory in the partition in which the operating system was installed. For NT, this directory is usually called WINNT and is typically located off the root directory. Therefore, \WINNT completes the pathname.

Putting It All Together

The full ARC pathname combines all the elements described in the preceding sections. For example, `scsi(0)disk(8)rdisk(0)partition(1)\WINNT` specifies the WINNT directory in the first partition of the first Logical Unit Number of SCSI ID 8 on the first controller in the system. Now that youhave an understanding of ARC paths, you can proceed to the boot sequence and BOOT.INI file.

The NT Boot Sequence

Every process has to start somewhere. The boot sequence starts when the computer is turned on or reset. After performing various systems checks and procedures, the BIOS reads the first physical sector of the disk into memory and executes it. In DOS-based systems, this boot sector looks for the DOS system files, IO.SYS and MSDOS.SYS.

The Windows NT installation process replaces this boot sector program with one that runs NTLDR, the Windows NT loader. The old boot sector is saved as BOOT-SECT.DOS. A file called BOOT.INI is created or modified if it already exists. This file determines what operating systems are presented in the boot selection menu and what the ARC paths are for each.

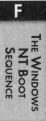

Once the Windows NT Setup program has configured the boot sector and BOOT.INI file, the boot sequence for Intel-based machines is as follows:

1. When the computer is turned on or reset, the BIOS loads the Master Boot Record from the Master Boot Sector and executes it.

2. The NT Loader program, NTLDR, is loaded.

3. NTLDR switches the processor to 32-bit protected mode.

4. NTLDR reads BOOT.INI and presents a menu of the specified operating systems.

5. The user selects an operating system or waits for the default timer to count down to 0 (usually from 30 seconds). Because this is a Windows NT boot sequence, Windows NT is selected as the boot option.

6. NTLDR starts the hardware recognizer (NTDETECT.COM). This program sleuths out the computer's hardware configuration and reports its findings back to NTLDR.

7. NTLDR loads the NT kernel (NTOSKRNL.EXE), Hardware Abstraction Layer (HAL), and HKEY_LOCAL_MACHINE\SYSTEM subtree from the Registry into memory.

8. NTLDR reads the information it just loaded from the Registry and loads appropriate boot device drivers before passing control to the NT kernel. At this point, the computer screen turns blue and goes into 50-line mode. This is a familiar sight to anyone who is a regular user of Windows NT.

9. The kernel initializes the boot device drivers and loads system device drivers.

10. The kernel initializes the Registry control sets in the HKEY_LOCAL_MACHINE\ HARDWARE key.

11. The kernel starts the Session Manager (SMSS.EXE), which now takes over the boot sequence.

12. The Session Manager starts the disk checking utility AUTOCHK.EXE. This utility makes sure the disk system is logically healthy.

13. The Session Manager sets up the NT paging files and runs the Win32 Subsystem (CSRSS.EXE).

14. The Win32 Subsystem runs Winlogon.

15. Winlogon starts the Service Controller (SERVICES.EXE), the Local Security Authority (LSASS.EXE), and the Print Spooler (SPOOLSS.EXE).

16. The system loads automatic device drivers.

17. The Begin Logon dialog box appears, and the system is ready for use.

The RISC Boot Sequence

RISC NT systems differ from Intel systems in that they have ARC firmware that stores the hardware configuration and boot selection menu. Therefore, NTDETECT.COM is not needed. The following sequence replaces steps 1 through 6 in the Intel boot process:

1. When the power is turned on or the system is reset, the RISC computer runs a self-test that gathers details of its hardware configuration and updates the ARC firmware.
2. The ARC firmware determines which drive to boot from and loads the Master Boot Record (MBR) into memory.
3. The MBR loads OSLOADER.EXE.
4. OSLOADER.EXE looks at the ARC firmware for hardware configuration information.
5. The ARC firmware displays the boot choice menu.
6. The user selects an operating system from the menu.

The BOOT.INI File

The Control Panel has a System applet that allows you to change the default operating system and the default menu time-out period (usually 30 seconds). However, if you need to add or remove operating systems or insert troubleshooting command switches, you must edit the BOOT.INI file directly with a text editor.

The Structure of the BOOT.INI File

The following is a sample BOOT.INI file:

```
[boot loader]
timeout=30
default= multi(0)disk(0)rdisk(0)partition(1)\WINNT
[operating systems]
C:\="Microsoft Windows"
multi(0)disk(0)rdisk(0)partition(1)\WINNT="Windows NT Workstation Version 4.00_
multi(0)disk(0)rdisk(0)partition(1)\WINNT="Windows NT Workstation Version 4.00_
➥[VGA mode]" /basevideo /sos
```

Note that this file has two sections. The first, `[boot loader]`, contains the time-out count in seconds and the default operating system. If the time-out count is set to 0, the menu will not appear at all and the default operating system will be booted.

The second section, `[operating systems]`, contains one line per operating system. Each line has the full ARC pathname to the operating system's home directory and the text, in quotes, that the menu displays for that entry. Non-NT entries do not have an ARC pathname. They usually have a simple logical drive path entry, C:\ in the above example.

Only the first 10 operating system choices are displayed in the boot menu. This number should be more than enough, even for the most hard-core computer users out there. Keep in mind, though, that Windows NT adds two lines to the menu every time it is installed. If you don't manually edit this file, multiple installation attempts can quickly push you over the 10-line limit.

Also, note that you should keep both entries that the installation process adds to the menu. The [VGA mode] entry is there for good reason. It gives you a way to get around faulty display drivers, display cards that can't work in higher resolution anymore, and other possible display problems. This display escape hatch is provided because seeing what is going on is so important to troubleshooting. You can't fly blind when trying to fix a problem.

Editing the BOOT.INI File

The BOOT.INI file is a read-only system file, and as such, it is not directly editable. In order to edit the file, you must first use the attrib command to change these attributes. BOOT.INI is located in the root directory of the boot partition. Assuming your boot partition is C:\, the following commands will bring up BOOT.INI in the DOS text editor, EDIT (you may substitute any text editor you want for EDIT):

```
c:
cd\
attrib -r -s boot.ini
edit boot.ini
```

After you have finished editing BOOT.INI, you must reset the read-only and system attributes. If you don't, Windows NT will not recognize the file. To reset these attributes, use the following command:

```
attrib +r +s boot.ini
```

If you plan to edit the BOOT.INI file often, you may want to combine all of these commands into a batch file as follows:

```
c:
cd\
attrib -r -s boot.ini
edit boot.ini
attrib +r +s boot.ini
```

Simply run this batch file whenever you want to edit the BOOT.INI file.

UPS Problems

Some uninterruptible power supplies (UPSs) connect to the serial port so they can supply power status to the computer and so the computer has a means of controlling them. Unfortunately, as NT chats with devices during the boot process to figure out what they are, some of these devices shut down the computer—not an auspicious start to the boot process.

To solve this problem, NT has a command-line switch that you can put at the end of the menu line:

```
/NoSerialMice=COMx
```

In this line, *x* is the UPS's COM port. This switch stops NT from querying that serial port and keeps the UPS from making the boot process self-terminating.

Driver Watch

Many drivers are loaded during the boot process. Any one of them, if damaged or simply wrong, can cause the boot process to fail. If you are having trouble booting an NT system, and you suspect it might be a driver problem, you can easily find out which driver it is by adding the switch /SOS to the end of the menu line in BOOT.INI.

If you use this switch, Windows NT will display driver names as they are loaded. When the system crashes, the last driver listed is probably the culprit, giving you a starting place in solving the problem.

No Memory at 1M

Sometimes a computer doesn't seem to have memory in the critical bottom 1M address space. Windows NT must load the kernel in this area. The following error will result:

```
OS LOADER: Image can't be relocated, no fixup information.
The system did not load because it cannot find the following file:
<winnt root>\system32\ntoskrnl.exe
Please re-install a copy of the above file.
Boot failed
```

This error message can be misleading. If this missing memory is the problem, you must change your EISA or BIOS configuration to make the memory at this location visible instead of reloading anything. Consult your system's instruction manual for details.

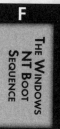

Mouseless Survival Guide: Keyboard Commands

IN THIS APPENDIX

You can use Windows NT without a mouse or other pointing device. Why would you want to do this? Suppose your mouse dies, falls off your laptop computer and gets lost, or one of your colleagues suddenly needs to borrow a mouse to get some work done. You're not dead in the water, though, if you follow the instructions presented in this appendix.

NT has two keyboard features that, when used together, give you a relatively efficient means of controlling mouse functions. The first feature is MouseKey, a keyboard substitute for moving the pointer, clicking, double-clicking, dragging, and so on. The second feature is the regular keyboard shortcuts, many of which you may already be using. If you use Alt+Tab to switch between tasks or Alt+F and then S to save a file, you are already familiar with keyboard shortcuts. It's generally easier to use a shortcut for a particular operation, if one is available, than to use the MouseKey pointing keys.

MouseKey Operation

You must activate MouseKey through the Control Panel before you can use it. If you're reading this section, you probably don't have a pointing device available. Therefore, the following instructions are keyboard-based. They will be more awkward than other keyboard procedures because MouseKey isn't yet available. You have to use shortcuts exclusively.

For simplicity's sake, I'll assume that you're beginning with a freshly started NT system with no applications open. Follow these steps:

1. Press Ctrl+Esc to open the Start menu.
2. Press the up arrow until the Setting option is highlighted. Press Enter to select it.
3. Control Panel should be highlighted. If it isn't, use the up-arrow and down-arrow keys to select it. Press Enter to open the Control Panel.
4. Press the spacebar to select the first item in the Control Panel. It should be Accessibility Options. If it isn't, use the arrow keys to select this item. Press Enter to open the Accessibility Options settings. A tabbed property sheet will open.
5. Press Ctrl+Tab to move to the Mouse tab.
6. Press Alt+M to activate the checkbox for the Use MouseKeys option.

At this time, you may want to adjust the MouseKey settings. Remember that you can readjust these settings at any time. Press Alt+S to access the MouseKey Settings dialog box. The first option is the Use shortcut option. Because MouseKey usurps the normal function of the numeric keypad, this option is provided to enable you to turn MouseKey on and off at any time. Press Alt+U to activate the checkbox; press Alt+U again to deactivate the checkbox.

There are two pointer speed settings. These settings combine to allow fine control of the pointer for accurate positioning and the speed necessary to travel across today's high resolution screens. The "Top speed" option sets how fast the pointer can travel at its maximum. The Acceleration option controls how quickly the pointer attains this speed. If you find you can't do the detail work you need to do before the pointer skitters away, slow down the Acceleration option. Likewise, if it takes forever for the pointer to get where it's going, speed up the "Acceleration" option. Press Alt+A to adjust the Acceleration option; then use the left-arrow and right-arrow keys to either slow it down or speed it up. Press Alt+T to adjust the "Top speed" option by using the left-arrow and right-arrow keys. Set this option so the pointer has a comfortable pace that your eye can follow onscreen. Some experimentation is probably necessary here.

Most numeric keypads have a dual function: cursor control and numeric input. Set the "Use MouseKeys when NumLock is off" option according to which function is most important. If number entry is most important, turn off this option by pressing Alt+F. Press Alt+N to turn on the Use MouseKeys when NumLock is off" option.

When you're finished with the settings, press Enter to accept the changes, or press Esc to cancel. Next, use the Tab key to highlight the OK button on the Mouse tab of the Accessibility Properties dialog box. Press Enter to close the dialog box.

Next, NT asks you whether you want to save the current settings as the default for new users and the login prompt. Answer Yes by pressing Enter to accept the highlighted button. Now you can use the numeric keypad to control your pointer. The following sections summarize the key functions. All keys are on the numeric keypad only.

Movement Keys

The following keys move the mouse pointer:

Key	Function
↑	Move pointer up
↓	Move pointer down
←	Move pointer left
→	Move pointer right
Home	Move pointer diagonally to the upper-left
PgUp	Move pointer diagonally to the upper-right
End	Move pointer diagonally to the lower-left
PgDn	Move pointer diagonally to the lower-right

Selection Keys

The selection keys require some further explanation. The - and / keys control whether the 5 and + keys represent the left or right mouse buttons. The default is for the left button to be active. If - is pressed, the 5 and + keys act like single-right and double-right clicks, respectively. This mode lasts until the / key is pressed to activate the left button.

Key	Function
5	Single click
+	Double-click
-	Enable right-button functionality
/	Enable left-button functionality
Ins	Start dragging
Del	Stop dragging

Keyboard Shortcuts

Moving the pointer using MouseKey is obviously not as efficient as using a pointing device. Generally, it is better to use keyboard shortcuts whenever possible. For example, rather than moving the cursor to a button using the arrow keys and then clicking the button with the 5 key, you can simply use the Alt key combination that activates the button instead. For this reason, you should know and use all the shortcuts that are available. (See Appendix H, "Keyboard Shortcuts," for more information.)

Alt Key Combinations

You can access any item that has a letter of its name underlined by pressing the Alt key in conjunction with the underlined letter. If you activated MouseKey in the previous section, you have already used this type of shortcut. These shortcuts are used extensively in menus. For example, almost every word processor uses Alt+F and then S to save a file. Note that the File menu advertises its Alt key shortcut by showing the *F* underlined.

Ctrl Key Combinations

Ctrl key combinations are usually even shorter shortcuts than the Alt key combinations. They usually activate a specific pad of a drop-down menu without even having to display the menu. For example, Ctrl+S usually saves a file in a one-step process. These shortcuts are advertised on the menu selection pads. You can find the Ctrl+S shortcut on the Save pad of the File menu. Because these shortcuts are generally hidden in a menu system, you must memorize them or jot them down to use them.

Selection Shortcuts

Usually, at any given time, there are many items that can be selected. This is what gives Windows its "event-driven" interface. You are able to select what you want when you want. With a pointing device, selecting is easy. It is a bit more difficult with keyboard shortcuts, although it's still possible in most cases. Some operations, however, just can't be done without moving the pointer. One example is activating the task bar when you are in Microsoft Word. In these cases, MouseKey solves the problem.

Selecting Tasks

You don't have to try to use the task bar to switch from one open task to another. Alt+Tab is a very quick way to move among running windows. This shortcut is often used even when a pointing device is available.

Working in Windows

When working in a window, use the arrow keys to select items. The window will scroll with the selection if necessary. Pressing Enter opens the selected item. Pressing Alt+F4 closes the window.

To minimize, maximize, resize, or move the window, use the Window menu. You can access this menu by pressing Alt+Space. Once you have chosen the command you want from the menu, use the arrow keys to perform the operation, and then press Enter. For example, to move a window to the left, press Alt+Space, select Move, and press the left-arrow key until the window is in the position you want. Then press Enter.

Working with Dialog Boxes

Dialog boxes usually have several objects: data-entry fields, checkboxes, buttons, and so on. Only one of these items can be active at a time. The active item accepts input, which is indicated by some sort of outline. Active checkboxes, sliders, data-entry fields, and so on have a dotted line box around them. Active buttons have a darker border shadow than their inactive counterparts. To select an active item, press the Enter key. The Tab key advances the active indicator from one field to the next. Shift+Tab moves the indicator in the reverse direction. Some dialog boxes have tabs. The Accessibility Options dialog box used in the MouseKeys section is an example of this type of dialog box. Press Ctrl+Tab to select different tabs.

APPENDIX H

Keyboard Shortcuts

IN THIS APPENDIX

This appendix lists keystrokes you can use in lieu of or in addition to the mouse when you're running Windows and some of the supplied applications. You might want to use this list for reference if you're using a laptop computer on the road without a mouse or if you want to speed up your work by keeping your hands on the keyboard. Touch typists in particular often find keystroke commands preferable to mouse procedures.

Of course, keystrokes for Windows applications that you purchase aren't listed here. With so many available programs, each with its own keystroke commands, this kind of listing isn't possible. However, lots of applications have keyboard commands similar to the ones listed here for common operations such as editing, cutting, copying, pasting, saving and opening files, and exiting.

Help Shortcut Keys

All Windows applications use the same Windows Help engine. The keys below pertain to any application that has Help available:

Key	Action
F1	Display Help for the currently active application; may or may not be context-sensitive Help
Shift+F1	Change pointer to question mark so you can click on a command or region to get Help on it (only in some applications)
Tab	Jump clockwise through hot spots in the Help window
Shift+Tab	Jump counterclockwise through hot spots in the Help window
Enter	Jump to Help or pop-up explanation on the selected hot spot
Ctrl+Tab	Move forward through tabs in a tabbed Help window
Shift+Ctrl+Tab	Move backward through tabs in a tabbed Help window
Ctrl+Ins	Copy all or a selected portion of a Help topic to the Clipboard
Shift+Ins	Paste contents of the Clipboard into an annotation box

General Keys

The following keys are ones that work throughout Windows. They apply to general Windows procedures:

Key	Action
Shift+F10	View the context-sensitive menu for the selected item
F1	Display a Help screen if the application offers it
Ctrl+Esc	Activate the Start button
Ctrl+Esc, Esc	Move the focus to the task bar so you can use Shift+F10 for the context menu, or use Tab and the arrow key to change tasks, or use Tab to go to the desktop
Alt+M	When the focus is on the task bar or desktop, minimize all windows and move the focus to the desktop
Alt+Tab	Switch to the application you last used
Alt+Tab	Switch to the next running application in forward order (release Alt when correct name shows)
Alt+Shift+Tab	Switch to next running application in reverse order (release Alt when correct name shows)
Alt+Esc	Cancel the Alt+Tab switching process and stay with the current application
PrtScr	Place an image of the entire screen on the Clipboard (DOS applications must be in text mode; may require Shift key)
Alt+PrtScr	Place an image of the active window on the Clipboard (may require Shift key)
Alt+Spacebar	Open an application window's Control menu
Alt+Hyphen (-)	Open a document window's Control menu
Alt+F4	Quit a running application or close a window
Ctrl+F6	Cycle through child windows within a parent window
Ctrl+F4	Close the active document window
Alt+Enter	Switch a non-Windows application between windowed and full-screen mode

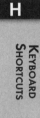

Hold Shift while inserting a CD-ROM	Bypass AutoPlay when inserting a CD-ROM
Open Control menu and choose Move, then press ↑, ↓, ←, or →, followed by Enter	Move a window without the mouse
Open Control menu and choose Size, then press ↑, ↓, ←, or →, followed by Enter	Size a window without the mouse

Menu Keys

These commands affect the displaying and choosing of commands from menus:

Key	Action
Alt or F10	Activate the menu bar
Single letter	Choose the menu or command with that letter underlined or highlighted (case doesn't matter)
← or →	Move between menus
↑ or ↓	Move between commands
Enter	Choose the highlighted menu name or command
Esc or Alt	Cancel the highlighted menu or deactivate the menu bar

Dialog Box Keys

These commands control what you select in a dialog box:

Key	Action
Tab	Move between sections and options
Shift+Tab	Move in reverse order bewteen options and sections
Ctrl+Esc	Move between tabs in a tabbed dialog box
Alt+underlined letter	Quickly jump to a section or choose an option
↑, ↓, ←, or →	Move the selection cursor between options within a section

Alt+↓	Open a drop-down list box
↑ or ↓	Move the cursor up or down within a list box
End	Move to the last item a list box
Home	Move to the first item in a list box
PgUp or PgDn	Quickly scroll up or down in a list, one screen at a time
Spacebar	Select or cancel an option or item in a list box
Spacebar	Select or clear a check box
Ctrl+/	Select all the items in a list box
Ctrl+\	Cancel all except the current item in a list box
Shift+→ or Shift+←	Extend or contract the selection in a text box
Shift+End	Extend or contract the selection to the last letter in a text box
Shift+Home	Extend or contract the selection to the first letter in a text box
Esc	Close a dialog box without putting changes into effect

H
KEYBOARD
SHORTCUTS

Keys for Moving the Cursor Around

These keys quickly move the text cursor within text boxes or within text-based applications:

Key	Action
↑	Move cursor up a line
↓	Move cursor down a line
→	Move cursor right one character
←	Move cursor left one character
Ctrl+→	Move cursor right one word
Ctrl+←	Move cursor left one word
Home	Move cursor to the beginning of the line
End	Move cursor to the end of the line
PgUp	Move cursor up one screen
PgDn	Move cursor down one screen
Ctrl+Home	Move cursor to the beginning of the document
Ctrl+End	Move cursor to the end of the document

Text-Selecting Keys

The keys in this list select text within Windows applications. First place the insertion point (I-beam) at the beginning of the text you want to select. Then use the keys to extend the selection in the direction you desire. If text is already selected, it may be be cancelled or it may be extended further or possibly contracted when you use these keys. What happens depends on where the insertion point is relative to the anchor point (the point from which you began the selection process). Experimentation is the best way to learn how selecting, extending, and contracting work.

Key	Action
Shift+←	Select one character left
Shift+→	Select one character right
Shift+↑	Select one line of text up
Shift+↓	Select one line of text down
Ctrl+Shift+←	Select previous word
Ctrl+Shift+→	Select next word
Shift+PgUp	Select preceding full screen of text
Shift+PgDn	Select next full screen of text
Shift+Home	Select text to beginning of the line
Shift+End	Select text to end of the line
Ctrl+Shift+Home	Select text to beginning of document
Ctrl+Shift+End	Select text to end of document

Text-Editing Keys

Use these keys when editing text. Note that not all of these keys will work with all applications. Some applications use other keys, particularly for cut, copy, and paste operations:

Key	Action
Del	Delete a character to the right of the I-beam
Backspace	Delete a character to the left of the I-beam
Del or Backspace	Delete selected text
Shift+Del or Ctrl+X	Cut all selected text and put it on the Clipboard
Ctrl+Ins or Ctrl+C	Copy all selected text to the Clipboard
Shift+Ins or Ctrl+V	Paste text from the Clipboard into the active window
Ctrl+Z or Alt+Backspace	Undo the last editing action

The Desktop

Use these keys for actions on the desktop.

Key	Action
F2	Rename an item
F3	Find a folder or file
Shift+Del	Delete an item without placing it in the Recycle Bin
Alt+Enter	View item properties

My Computer

Use these keys in the My Computer windows:

Key	Action
Ctrl+A	Select all
F5	Refresh view
Backspace	View folder one level up
F2	Rename an item
F3	Find a folder or file
Shift+Del	Delete item without placing it in the Recycle Bin
Alt+Enter	View item properties

Explorer

The following lists summarize the keyboard shortcuts available in Windows Explorer. The first list applies to all parts of Explorer:

Key	Action
Tab, F6	Move between the drive, tree, and file areas
Ctrl+G	Go to a specific folder
Asterisk (*) on the numeric keypad	Expand all subfolders under the selected folder
Plus (+) on the numeric keypad	Expand the selected folder
Minus (-) on the numeric keypad	Collapse the selected folder
→	Expand the current selection if it's collapsed; otherwise, select the first subfolder

Key	Action
←	Collapse the current selection if it's expanded; otherwise, select the parent folder
F2	Rename an item
F3	Find a folder or file
Shift+Del	Delete an item without placing it in the Recycle Bin
Alt+Enter	View item properties

Folder Pane Keys

Use these keys in the folder pane of Windows Explorer:

Key	Action
↓	Select the next folder in the tree
↑	Select the preceding folder in the tree
Ctrl+↑	Scroll folder pane one line up without changing the selected folder
Ctrl+↓	Scroll folder pane one line down without changing the selected folder
PgUp	Scroll up one screen
PgDn	Scroll down one screen
Ctrl+PgUp	Scroll up one screen without changing the selected folder
Ctrl+PgDn	Scroll down one screen without changing the selected folder
Home	Jump to the desktop
End	Jump to the last directory in the list
letter or number	Jump to the next directory beginning with a particular letter or number

File Pane Keys

These keys are used in the file pane of Windows Explorer. The word *file* in the following list also applies to directories if they are displayed:

Key	Action
PgUp	Scroll up a screen
PgDn	Scroll down a screen
↑	Move up a file
↓	Move down a file
Home	Jump to the first file in the list
End	Jump to the last file in the list
letter or number	Jump to the next file beginning with a particular letter or number
Shift+arrow key	Select multiple consecutive files
Enter	Open a directory, a document, or an application

Clipboard Shortcut Keys

These keys are useful in the Clipboard:

Key	Action
Ctrl+X or Shift+Del	In an application, cut the selected item to the Clipboard
Ctrl+C or Ctrl+Ins	In an application, copy the selected item to the Clipboard
Ctrl+V or Shift+Ins	In an application, paste an item from the Clipboard to the target document
Del	In the Clipboard Viewer, delete whatever is on the Clipboard
Shift+PrtScr	Copy the entire screen image to the Clipboard (works for non-Windows applications only if they are running in text mode)
Alt+PrtScr	Copy the active window's image to the Clipboard

Wordpad Shortcut Keys

In addition to some of the text-selection keys described earlier, you can use the following keys in Wordpad:

Key	Action
Ctrl+X or Shift+Del	Cut the selection to the Clipboard
Ctrl+C or Ctrl+Ins	Copy the selection to the Clipboard
Ctrl+V or Shift+Ins	Paste from the Clipboard
Ctrl+Enter	Insert a manual page break
Ctrl+Z or Alt+Backspace	Undo last typing or editing
Alt+F6	Jump between the document and the Find or Replace dialog box

Sound Recorder Shortcut Keys

Use these keys for the Sound Recorder:

Key	Action
Tab or Shift+Tab	Move between buttons and the scrollbar
Spacebar	Choose a button or the scrollbar
Select scrollbar, then ← or →	Move forward or backward in the scrollbar
PgUp	Jump back one second with the scrollbar selected
PgDn	Jump forward one second with the scrollbar selected
Home	Jump to the beginning of the sound with the scrollbar selected
End	Jump to the end of the sound with the scrollbar selected

Volume Control Shortcut Keys

Use these keys for the Volume Control:

Key	Action
Tab or Shift+Tab	Move between controls
↑, ←	Move the vertical slider up slowly
↓, →	Move the vertical slider down slowly
PgUp	Move the vertical slider up quickly
PgDn	Move the vertical slider down quickly
Home	Move the vertical slider all the way to the top
End	Move the vertical slider all the way to the bottom
→, ↓	Move the horizontal slider to the right slowly
←, ↑	Move the horizontal slider to the left slowly
Home	Move the horizontal slider all the way to the left
End	Move thehorizontal slider all the way to the right
Spacebar	Toggle the Mute checkbox

Calculator Shortcut Keys

The following keys use their keyboard equivalents in the Calculator:

%

(

)

*

+

-

/

.

0–9

A–F

The following is a table of additional keyboard equivalents:

Button	Key
+/−	F9
1/x	r
=	Enter
And	&
Ave	Ctrl+A
Back	Backspace
Bin	F8
Byte	F4
C	Esc
Ce	Del
cos	o
Dat	Ins
Dec	F6
Deg	F2
dms	m
Dword	F2
Exp	x
F−E	v
Grad	F4
Hex	F5
Hyp	h
In	n
Int	;
Inv	I
Log	l
Lsh	<
M+	Ctrl+P
MC	Ctrl+L
Mod	%
MR	Ctrl+R
MS	Ctrl+M

n!	!
Not	~
Oct	F7
Or	|
Pi	P
Rad	F3
S	Ctrl+D
Sin	s
Sqrt	@
Sta	Ctrl+S
Sum	Ctrl+T
Tan	t
Word	F3
Xor	^
x^2	@
x^3	#

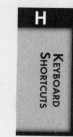

Keyboard Shortcuts for the Microsoft Natural Keyboard

The following shortcuts work with the Microsoft Natural keyboard or compatible:

Key	Action
WIN+R	Display the Run dialog box
WIN+M	Minimize all windows currently open
WIN+ Shift+M	Undo command to minimize all windows
WIN+F1	Start Help
WIN+E	Start Explorer
WIN+F	Open the Find Files/Folders dialog box
Ctrl+WIN+F	Open the Find Computer dialog box
WIN+Tab	Cycle through task bar buttons
WIN+Break	Display the Systems Properties panel

The Windows NT Registry

IN THIS APPENDIX

APPENDIX

The material in this appendix augments the discussion of the Registry in Chapter 11, "Maintenance and Troubleshooting." For those of you who are familiar with Windows 3.*x*, the Registry replaces the .INI configuration files, AUTOEXEC.BAT, and CONFIG.SYS with a hierarchical object. The .INI files used in Windows 3.*x* are plain text files. In these files, settings are usually organized into groups of related settings. Some application programs create individual .INI files to store their own settings. (To maintain compatibility with older programs that still use .INI files to record their configuration information, Windows NT automatically updates the Registry with changes made to any existing .INI files.) The result is many configuration files scattered around your disk, each organized as a text file. Administering these files becomes difficult as a system grows.

The Registry imposes order on the Windows configuration. The Registry has a tree structure similar to the file system that must be adhered to by all programs that run under Windows. Not all programs do this, but more and more programs are being written to interact with the Registry. Some simpler programs just don't need to involve the Registry, and older ones designed for Windows 3.*x* predate the Registry. Notice the folders in the left pane. These are *keys*. Each folder in the Registry Editor represents a key in the Registry that contains other keys or data. The Registry uses this structure to store system settings, application state information, user information, and interapplication information. Applications and Windows itself can add, update, and remove configuration information in the Registry.

It's generally much safer and preferable to work with the Registry through dialog boxes in Windows Explorer, the Control Panel, and other shell applications. However, some things just can't be done without getting directly into the Registry. If you're interested in learning how to directly edit the Registry and have complete permission to do anything to your computer (in other words, don't try this at work), the "The Emergency Repair Disk" section guides you through performing some Registry changes.

Registry Structure

Start the Registry Editor by clicking the Start button. Choose Run and type `regedt32`. (Note that there is no *i* in *regedt32*. Mistyping this command is an easy mistake to make, especially if you are used to using Windows 95's regedit.) Click OK to run the Editor. The Registry Editor is shown in Figure I.1.

FIGURE I.1.

*The initial Registry
Editor screen.*

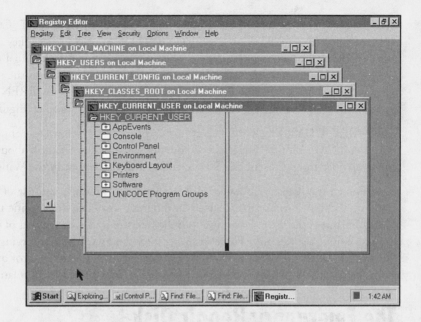

Notice that the Windows NT Registry has five main keys: HKEY_CLASSES_ROOT, HKEY_CURRENT_USER, HKEY_LOCAL_MACHINE, HKEY_USERS, and HKEY_CURRENT_CONFIG. Each key has its own child window. A key can contain values or other keys. The ability to contain other keys supplies the organizational structure to manage the values. Containing values is the reason the Registry exists.

There are, in fact, only two real main keys in the Registry. One key, HKEY_LOCAL_MACHINE, contains all machine information including hardware, applications, and services. The other, HKEY_USERS, contains all user information. The other three keys are merely pointers to the structures of these two. This is where the similarity between the Registry structure and the file structure differs. The file system does not allow a directory to point to a branch of another directory's tree. However, the pointer keys are how the Registry keeps track of which single user from all the possible users is the current one. The HKEY_CURRENT_USER key points to a particular user's profile in the HKEY_USERS tree to reference which user is currently logged onto the system.

To see this system in action, click the HKEY_USERS key's child window. There should be a .DEFAULT entry and at least one entry similar to S-1-5-21-89866128-325127250-.... This long entry is a Security ID (SID) for a user. Double-click the SID's folder and its contents are displayed. Now go back to the HKEY_CURRENT_USER pane and see the similarity. It is, in fact, more than similar—it's the same portion of the Registry.

The same is true of the machine configuration key, HKEY_CURRENT_CONFIG. All possible configurations are stored under the HKEY_LOCAL_MACHINE key. These configurations might include a configuration for when the machine is attached to a network, another one for when the machine is standalone, one for a portable that is on the road, and one for when the portable is plugged into its docking station. The HKEY_CURRENT_CONFIG key points into this tree at the appropriate level for the current physical configuration.

The HKEY_CLASSES_ROOT is another pointer key that references a part of the HKEY_LOCAL_MACHINE key that contains essential information about OLE and drag-and-drop operations, file extension association, and core aspects of the Windows 95 GUI.

Even though the Registry contains only two keys, the structure and use of these keys is still complex. Applications use the Registry in different ways that are specific to their function. Therefore, one approach to learning about the Registry is to use examples of what can be done through editing the Registry. This approach avoids the complex task of trying to present all the functions of the Registry for all cases. These examples will answer a lot of questions and give you a good understanding of the Registry's function and how to manipulate the Registry.

The Emergency Repair Disk

You must have a current Emergency Repair Disk on hand before you try to make any changes to the Registry. What you intend to do may cause the system to crash or not boot. You might also make mistakes while editing the Registry. Registry editing utilities give you no safeguards against mistakes. You have free reign over all Registry contents, so tread thoughtfully and carefully and take the precaution of making a current Emergency Repair Disk.

To create an Emergency Repair Disk, start the Repair Disk utility (RDISK.EXE) by performing these steps:

1. Click the Start menu button.
2. Click Run on the pop-up menu.
3. Type **rdisk** in the Open text box.
4. Click OK. The Repair Disk Utility appears, as shown in Figure I.2.

FIGURE I.2.
*The Repair Disk
utility.*

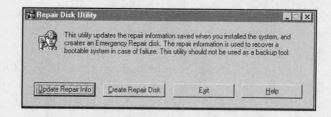

5. Click the Update Repair Info button so the disk reflects the most current settings.

6. Click the Create Repair Disk button and follow the prompts.

In addition to the Emergency Repair Disk, Windows NT has a built-in procedure to restore the last working set of Registry files. During the boot process, pressing the spacebar in response to the `Press the spacebar to invoke the Hardware Profile/Last Known Good menu to re-store your Registry to a stable state` message returns your Registry to the last working state. This feature makes editing Windows NT's Registry much safer than editing Windows 95's, but you should still play it safe by making the Emergency Repair Disk. Now, armed with an Emergency Repair Disk and the Hardware Profile/Last Known Good menu, you can proceed on your Registry adventure with relative safety, but be careful out there!

Automatic Logon: The First Journey into the Registry

In using this step-by-step teaching example, I'm assuming that you have complete authority over all aspects of the machine you are using, including security issues. If this isn't true, then you should certainly not be experimenting with the Registry! In this example, you will completely eliminate the logon sequence from the start of Windows NT by changing one Registry entry, adding another, and checking a few more.

You can make Windows NT automatically log on as a predetermined user, password included. Use this feature carefully—it can completely undermine the security of Windows NT. Define the reason this automatic logon feature is needed, and set up the account to be used with only those privileges necessary for its function. You can bypass autologon by pressing the Shift key during startup. This procedure describes in detail how to find, edit, and add Registry values to configure the autologon feature:

1. Run the Registry Editor by first clicking the Start menu button. Then, select Run from the pop-up menu and type **regedt32** into the Open text box. Finally, click OK to open the Registry Editor.

2. Navigate to the following path by starting in the HKEY_LOCAL_MACHINE pane. Double-click the + box in the left half of the pane for each name in the path, starting with the pane of the leftmost name (in this case, HKEY_LOCAL_MACHINE) and continuing down. As in the file system, names are separated by a \.

   `HKEY_LOCAL_MACHINE\SOFTWARE\Microsoft\Windows NT\CurrentVersion\Winlogon`

   When you have arrived at Winlogon, your screen should look like Figure I.3.

FIGURE I.3.

Displaying the Winlogon data.

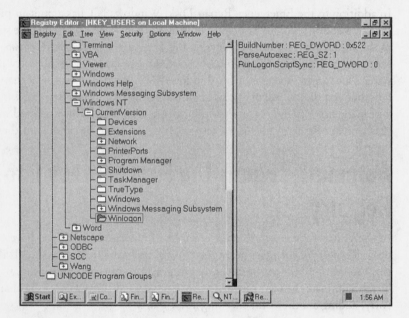

3. Check the right part of the pane for an entry called AutoAdminLogon. This entry is the value name. If it's there, go to Step 8. If it's not there, select the Edit menu.

4. Choose Add Value from the Edit menu.

5. Enter **AutoAdminLogon** for the value name.

6. Leave REG_SZ as the data type and click OK. (Refer to Chapter 12, "An Overview of Windows NT Networking," for a full description of data types.) The String Editor will appear.

7. Enter 1 to enable AutoAdminLogon; enter 0 to disable it.

8. Click OK.

In this example, you need to change the following set of parameters in the Registry:

Parameter	*Value*
Path	The location of the key in the Registry where the value resides
Value Name	The name of the value, AutoAdminLogon, for example
Data Type	The data type of the value, such as REG_SZ or REG_DWORD
Data Value	The actual data stored in the Registry

For example, if you choose to have the password automatically supplied in the previous scenario, you must change the following parameters in the Registry:

Parameter	*Value*
Path:	HKEY_LOCAL_MACHINE\SOFTWARE\Microsoft\ Windows NT\CurrentVersion\Winlogon
Value Name:	DefaultPassword
Data Type:	REG_SZ
Data Value:	The account's password

If you want the password to be automatically supplied, follow Steps 2 through 8 outlined previously, substituting these parameters for the Autologon ones. Note that the account's password is case-sensitive! In addition, you must make sure that DefaultUserName has the value for the account you want to automatically log onto and DefaultDomainName reflects where you want to log onto—the domain or the workstation.

When everything is set up the way you want it, test the new settings:

1. Close the Registry Editor.
2. Click the Start button and choose Shut Down.
3. Click the "Restart the computer" radio button in the Shut Down Windows dialog box.
4. Click the Yes button. When the computer restarts, it should log on automatically.

If this procedure presents a security risk, be sure to go back and use the Registry Editor to reset values as follows:

1. Remove DefaultPassword from the following:

   ```
   HKEY_LOCAL_MACHINE\SOFTWARE\Microsoft\Windows NT\CurrentVersion\Winlogon
   ```

2. Change the AutoAdminLogon data value in the same path to 0.
3. Close the Registry Editor and restart the computer again. It should ask you for your password this time.

Congratulations! You have successfully completed your first adventure in the Registry. The following sections assume you have completed and understand this procedure.

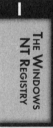

MS Mail Tricks

You can also set up an automatic logon for MS Mail. As with the Windows NT automatic logon, you should think through the security implications before implementing this feature. Follow these steps:

1. Be sure that the proper username is filled in by making sure the following key exists and has the proper value:

Path:	HKEY_CURRENT_USER\Software\Microsoft\Mail\Microsoft Mail
Value Name:	Login
Data Type:	REG_SZ
Data Value:	Your username

2. Set up the automatic password by adding the following key. It probably does not yet exist in your system.

Path:	HKEY_CURRENT_USER\Software\Microsoft\Mail\Microsoft Mail
Value Name:	Password
Data Type:	REG_SZ
Data Value:	Your password

3. You can configure MS Mail to require a password when it's restored after being minimized. To secure your mail when it's minimized, enable the password by adding or modifying the following key:

Path:	HKEY_CURRENT_USER\Software\Microsoft\Mail\Microsoft Mail
Value Name:	Security
Data Type:	REG_SZ
Data Value:	1

4. You can also specify the character that precedes each line of a quoted message in a reply (this character is often >) by modifying the following key. Replace the > character with anything you want.

Path.	HKEY_CURRENT_USER\Software\Microsoft\Mail\Microsoft Mail
Value Name:	ReplyPrefix
Data Type:	REG_SZ
Data Value:	>

LOGIN Notice

You can make Windows NT display a banner when the user presses Ctrl+Alt+Del to log on. The user must acknowledge the banner before proceeding with the logon. This banner is especially useful for vertical market turnkey applications. To set up this notice, edit or add the following keys:

Path:	HKEY_LOCAL_MACHINE\SOFTWARE\ Microsoft\WindowsNT\CurrentVersion\Winlogon
Value Name:	LegalNoticeCaption
Data Type:	REG_SZ
Data Value:	Whatever you want to appear in the caption
Path:	HKEY_LOCAL_MACHINE\SOFTWARE\ Microsoft\Windows NT\CurrentVersion\Winlogon
Value Name:	LegalNoticeText
Data Type:	REG_SZ
Data Value:	Whatever you want to appear as the notice

Change the My Computer Default Icon

You can also use the Registry to change the default icon for My Computer. The following key controls which icon represents My Computer:

Path:	HKEY_LOCAL_MACHINE\SOFTWARE\Classes\ CLSID\{20D04FE0-3AEA-1069-A2D8- 08002B30309D}\DefaultIcon
Value Name:	(default)
Data Type:	REG_SZ
Data Value:	Any file, number of icon in file

There are two new items to note in this key. One is the long identifier in the key path. Windows components, including applications and files, are represented by these identifiers. The following is a partial table of these codes:

Component	Code
Control Panel	{21EC2020-3AEA-1069-A2DD-08002B30309D}
Printers	{2227A280-3AEA-1069-A2DE-08002B30309D}
Recycle Bin	{645FF040-5081-101B-9F08-00AA002F954E}
My Computer	{20D04FE0-3AEA-1069-A2D8-08002B30309D}

I

THE WINDOWS
NT REGISTRY

Dial-Up Networking	{A4D92740-67CD-11CF-96F2-00AA00A11DD9}
Network Neighborhood	{208D2C60-3AEA-1069-A2D7-08002B30309D}
Inbox	{00020D75-0000-0000-C000-000000000046}
Desktop	{00021400-0000-0000-C000-000000000046}
Shortcut	{00021401-0000-0000-C000-000000000046}

The second is the *Any file, number of icon in file* line in the data value. Icons are stored in files; many times, there's more than one to a file. *Any file* is the name of the file containing the icons, and the *number* is an index that specifies which icon to use. Explorer.exe, 1 asks for the second icon stored in the Explorer.exe file. (Icon counts start with 0.)

Rename My Computer

The easy way to rename My Computer is to click the name of the icon, in this case My Computer. The name is highlighted, showing that it will be replaced by anything you type. Type in the new name and press Enter. You're done, but you really haven't learned anything.

Now try doing it in the Registry by editing the following key:

Path:	HKEY_LOCAL_MACHINE\SOFTWARE\Classes\CLSID\{20D04FE0-3AEA-1069-A2D8-08002B30309D}
Value Name:	(default)
Data Type:	REG_SZ
Data Value:	The name you want to replace My Computer

Change the Desktop's Default Folder Icon

Yet another item you can change through the Registry is the default folder icon. If you're tired of looking at that boring old folder icon everywhere you go, you can change it by editing the following key:

Path:	HKEY_CLASSES_ROOT\Folder\DefaultIcon
Value Name:	(default)
Data Type:	REG_EXPAND_SZ
Data Value:	Any file, number of icon in file

The default data value is %SystemRoot%\System32\shell32.dll,2. Remember that the icon numbering starts from 0, so the third icon from shell32.dll is being used. Also note that `%SystemRoot%` is a method of using environment variables in the file specification. Windows NT sets up environment variables for use by any program that needs the information. An enumeration of these variables and the data they contain is beyond the scope of this section, but you should know that `SystemRoot` is assigned the full Windows NT directory pathname. This example uses this variable to find the shell32.dll file.

Application Event Sounds

There's a standard set of events for all applications that can have sounds assigned to them. Defaults sounds can be applied to all applications through the following key:

`HKEY_CURRENT_USER\AppEvents\Schemes\Apps\.Default`

Each of the following events have an entry under this key:

> Close
>
> Open
>
> G.P. Fault
>
> RestoreDown
>
> Maximize
>
> RestoreUp
>
> MenuCommand
>
> SystemAsterisk
>
> MenuPopup
>
> SystemExclamation
>
> Minimize
>
> SystemQuestion

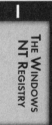

In addition to default sounds, each application can have its own sounds. To set up these additional sounds, create a subkey under HKEY_CURRENT_USER\AppEvents\Schemes\Apps for each application and then create subkeys for each event under each application. After that's done, you can assign different sounds to each event for each application. However, it's much easier to use the Control Panel and desktop schemes to control sounds. Editing the Registry is appropriate only for tweaking a few sounds.

Registry Utilities

Working with the Registry can be a daunting task. There are third-party tools available that make the job easier. The following sections point you to the companies that make these tools and describe what some of the available tools do.

OPALIS

OPALIS is the company that makes Grep_Reg (for Windows NT/95). Grep_Reg recursively searches for a string in the Registry; it's a command-line tool that you can use to search on values and keys. You can reach OPALIS at the following addresses:

```
E-mail: support@opalis.com
Web:    http://www.opalis.com
```

Somarsoft, Inc.

Somarsoft, Inc. makes Somar DumpReg and Somar RegEdit, two helpful Registry utilities. Somar DumpReg dumps the Windows NT or Windows 95 Registry, making it easy to find keys and values matching a string. In Windows NT, you can sort dumped entries can be sorted by reverse order of last modified time, making it easy to see changes made by recently installed software. Somar DumpReg is a must-have product for Windows NT system administrators.

Somar RegEdit is a DLL-callable (by 32-bit Visual Basic) utility that can be used to view and modify user Registry profiles. For example, a 10-line VBA for Excel program can change the mail server path in the Registry profiles of all users at once. RegEdit is a great tool for Windows NT system administrators who can program in Basic. V1.4 adds new API functions.

You can contact Somarsoft, Inc. at the following addresses:

```
E-mail: 72202.2574@compuserve.com
Web:    http://www.somarsoft.com
```

Steven J. Hoek Software Development

The Registry can grow to many hundreds of lines in complex systems that support many programs, users and activities. Managing the Registry can get to be a daunting task. The Registry Search and Replace Utility, available from Steven J. Hoek Software Development, is a good alternative to RegEdit's limited search ability. It's shareware and well worth the current $20 registration fee if you're going to be working with the Registry often. Its features include the following:

- Easy-to-use tabbed interface
- New search profiles that let you save, restore, and automatically start search sets
- Integration with the Windows 95 and Windows NT 4.0 Start Menu -> Find
- Ability to search registries on remote machines

- Ability to search for Registry values in addition to data
- Prompted or specified replacement
- Improved Registry search criteria
- Enhanced performance and thoroughness

You can find it at the following address:

```
http://ourworld.compuserve.com/homepages/shoek/REGSRCH.HTM
```

Windows NT Technical Information Sources

IN THIS APPENDIX

APPENDIX

J

When you're stuck with tedious or infuriating technical questions or other NT problems, who ya gonna call? Ghostbusters? NOT. Like most folks, you thumb through the indexes in the books on your shelf, check the NT Help files, and then maybe ask the folks in the cubicle next to you. But what if they can't help you? Or what if you want to save a few bucks and not call some expensive tech support service? This section offers you some valuable tips for NT trouble-shooting when you're really up against the wall.

Use Existing Technical Support...But When?

Although it's often the most expensive option, official technical support from the companies whose products you're working with can be the most efficient route to solutions. The people you're dealing with usually know the products in question and have the answers for many common problems. Having worked in technical support for a major computer manufacturer myself, I know that a well-organized technical support service can resolve the bulk of customer complaints quickly.

Some companies charge you by the hour, others by the number of calls or "incidents." In either case, the costs can escalate beyond your budgetary means, so you do have to be careful of the temptation to call at the first sign of a problem. In my opinion, official technical support should be considered only after you've exhausted other sources of help, such as the Web, user groups on CompuServe, and the like. I often do a search on the Web, look for a user group on the Net, check CompuServe for an SIG (Special Interest Group) or, if the problem I'm having involves pieces of software or hardware from several companies, I phone the one with free technical support *first!*

> **TIP**
>
> When calling technical support, keep a log of who you talk to, the date and time of your call, and the "incident" ID number they may assign to your case. This information can be a time-saver when and if you call back for additional service or have to refer to the problem again. That way you needn't repeat yourself (at your own expense) next time, which is especially useful if you get a different person on the phone next time.

Some vendors offer "fax-back" services that you make a standard phone call to and request specific documents. This reduces your telephone time and is often free. It saves companies big bucks to send you a fax by computer rather than hire someone to talk to you on the phone. Another resource from the company can be a dial-up BBS service. So first try calling a company and asking for information about their BBS, Web site, and fax-back services.

Microsoft has a "Fast Tips" fax-back service you might want to take advantage of. They'll either fax or snail-mail solutions to you. You can order information 24 hours a day, seven days a week. Here are the numbers to call (order the Fast Tips catalog first):

Personal OS (DOS, Windows, Windows 95)	800-936-4200
Business Systems (NT BackOffice)	800-936-4000
Desktop Applications (Office)	800-936-4100
Development Tools	800-936-4300

Each Windows NT package comes with technical support and registration materials, so you can check them for additional phone numbers.

NOTE

World Wide Web NT resources are covered later in this appendix.

Windows NT Resource Kit

Since the days of Windows 3.0, Microsoft has been offering a sizable collection of how-to material for both developers and users of Windows. NT has its own version of this kit, the Windows NT Resource Kit. It includes several volumes of printed material and a CD-ROM. The material is updated by Microsoft about twice a year. As you might expect, it offers a huge amount of information. There are two kits, one for Server and one for Workstation. Each costs approximately $150 and is published by Microsoft Press. You can find information about them at this site:

`www.microsoft.com/mspress/Books`

The Microsoft Windows NT Server 4.0 Resource Kit includes three volumes:

- Microsoft Windows NT Server Resource Guide
- Microsoft Windows NT Server Networking Guide
- Microsoft Windows NT Server Internet Guide

It comes with a companion CD-ROM that has several useful tools, including the following:

- Third-party developers' utilities
- Utilities useful in solving typical support issues
- Add-on utilities developed by Microsoft to enhance NT
- The complete text of both the Microsoft Windows NT Workstation 4.0 Resource Guide and all three volumes in the Server 4.0 Resource Kit

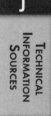

J

TECHNICAL INFORMATION SOURCES

> **NOTE**
>
> Although the CD-ROM has lots of useful utilities on it, they're not supported by Microsoft directly, but at least they've been tested. They even end up in the supported product sometimes because Microsoft has a tendency to buy up companies that produce such utilities and then incorporate them into Windows NT.

The resource kits are indispensable if you have to support NT at your work place.

The NT Workstation Resource Kit is similar to the one for Server. It contains a technical guide and a CD-ROM with utilities and accessory programs. Topics cover reference information on installing, configuring, and troubleshooting Windows NT Workstation version 4.0. It includes the following items:

- A discussion of the NT Workstation architecture
- An optimization guide, including coverage of the optimization programs on the CD-ROM
- In-depth coverage of the Windows NT Registry
- A guide to file system options, boot sequence, and using multiple file and operating systems on one computer
- Lots of network coverage, including Windows NT and the TCP/IP transport details
- A troubleshooting section
- Deployment information for administrator types
- A CD-ROM with lots of utilities and accessory programs

Official Training and Certification Programs

Both Microsoft and third-party outfits now offer officially endorsed NT training programs. Microsoft's program is fairly pricey, but then again, nobody ever lost his or her job for buying Microsoft. It'll cost you about $2000 for a five-day course. Or, you can go with one of the many outfits that are offering their own training programs, possibly at a lower cost. Some vendors' mail-order training programs aren't all they promise to be, so make sure Microsoft has endorsed the program. The vendor should display the official Microsoft logo reading "Approved Study Guide."

Microsoft Developer Network

Are you in the business of developing programs that are written in, run with, or run on other Microsoft products? If so, you'll find scads of indispensable material in a package called the Microsoft Developer Network (MSDN). You get all the operating systems, developer kits (excluding major languages, such as Visual C++ or VBA, however), a knowledge base with development information, online product documentation, and some periodicals on applications development. The idea is to give software developers Microsoft programs to play with, help debug, and help ensure compatibility with third-party vendors' programs.

There are four levels of membership, ranging in price from $250 to $2400 dollars per year. At the top level, you get just about everything Microsoft has to offer, including beta versions of upcoming software.

As of this writing, joining MSDN at the top level gives you close to 100 CD-ROMs per year and a nice binder to keep them in. You get some weird stuff, such as every foreign-language version of Windows NT, but they can be useful if you're developing programs for other countries. You'll rarely be stuck without that latest Service Release or other application or programming language update.

TIP

Check with Microsoft for a special subscription program for C++ and other languages.

The four levels of subscription to the MSDN program are dubbed Library, Professional, Enterprise, and Universal. Table J.1 explains what's included in each and their respective prices.

Table J.1. Comparing the four subscription levels of the MSDN program.

Included Goodies	Level 1 "Library"	Level 2 "Professional"	Level 3 "Enterprise"	Level 4 "Universal"
Quarterly Development Library CD-ROM	✓	✓	✓	✓
Bimonthly MSDN newsletter	✓	✓	✓	✓
Two free product-support telephone incidents	✓	✓	✓	✓
Full access to CompuServe member forums	✓	✓	✓	✓
Quarterly Development Platform CD-ROMs (operating systems, including NT Workstation, SDKs, DDKs)		✓	✓	✓

J

TECHNICAL
INFORMATION
SOURCES

continues

Table J.1. continued

Included Goodies	Level 1 "Library"	Level 2 "Professional"	Level 3 "Enterprise"	Level 4 "Universal"
Interim CD-ROMs containing new tools and operating system beta releases			✓	✓
Quarterly BackOffice CD-ROMs containing products for development and testing purposes (including NT Server)			✓	✓
Interim CD-ROMs containing new BackOffice tools and product beta releases			✓	✓
Two additional free product-support telephone "incidents" (problems)			✓	✓
Multiple-user licenses	available	not available	included	included
Microsoft Visual Basic Enterprise Edition				✓
Visual C++ Enterprise Edition				✓
Visual FoxPro Professional Edition				✓
Microsoft Visual J++				✓
Microsoft Access Developer's Toolkit				✓
Microsoft Office products, including a development and test license for the latest versions of Microsoft Word, Microsoft Excel,				✓

Included Goodies	Level 1 "Library"	Level 2 "Professional"	Level 3 "Enterprise"	Level 4 "Universal"
Microsoft Access, and Microsoft Project				
Upcoming development tools, including select ActiveX development tools				✓
Annual subscription cost	$199	$499	$1499	$2499

For more information about MSDN, check this site:

```
http://www.microsoft.com/msdn/subscribe/
```

> **TIP**
>
> Educational Pricing for MSDN is available if you're among the impoverished student population. For more information, you can try calling (800) 426-9400 or visit the following URL:
>
> ```
> http://www.microsoft.com/referral
> ```

Online Groups

Although Microsoft has conducted its beta programs and user groups on CompuServe for more than 10 years, it's slowly moving onto the Internet. You'll find your NT cronies out there in NG (newsgroup) land if you look around. As is always the case with newsgroups, group names and addresses come and go quickly. Microsoft lists many on their Web pages, so you can always go to www.microsoft.com and drill down to find them, or you can start with these addresses:

```
comp.os.ms-windows.nt.admin.misc
comp.os.ms-windows.nt.admin.networking
comp.os.ms-windows.nt.misc
comp.os.ms-windows.nt.setup.misc
comp.os.ms-windows.nt.setup.hardware
comp.os.ms-windows.nt.software.backoffice
comp.os.ms-windows.nt.pre-release
```

J

TECHNICAL INFORMATION SOURCES

Windows NT is a whole world unto itself. Software, setup, administration, security, and networking issues are large, sometimes mystifying, subjects. An NT administrator has to deal with them all, but you're not alone in this. If you visit newsgroups, you'll find people out there who want what knowledge you have to offer and want to help you when you run into a problem or need advice.

Web Authoring Newsgroups

Assembling a Web page can be a daunting task. There are so many options available when it comes to tools, utilities, and type of content. Once these options are decided on, many issues come up with implementation. All these products have bugs, workarounds, tricks and secrets. In addition, there are design, page layout, and site content decisions to be made. Other people are grappling with the same decisions and problems you are, but many have more experience. Take advantage of that resource and visit related newsgroups often.

```
comp.infosystems.www.servers.ms-windows

comp.infosystems.www.servers.misc

comp.infosystems.www.browsers.ms-windows

comp.infosystems.www.authoring.cgi

comp.infosystems.www.authoring.misc
```

> **NOTE**
>
> Microsoft used to host a number of Windows NT forums on the CompuServe Information Service (CIS). It no longer does. All support and information about Windows has been moved and can now be found only on the Microsoft Web sites and on Microsoft's own information service, MSN. Check those locations instead.

Windows NT Mailing Lists from the Internet

A great way to learn all the different things you can do with Windows NT is to join one or more Windows NT mailing lists. Most people who subscribe to these mailing lists are people who use Windows NT every day and are quite helpful when someone has a problem. Before you join a mailing list, however, be aware that some of them generate quite a few e-mail messages each day. If you don't want to get a lot of e-mails throughout the day, it's better not to subscribe to a mailing list. In my opinion, however, the knowledge that can be gained from being on one or more mailing lists is well worth the extra e-mail. You not only get a chance to find solutions to your questions, but you can also discuss options with other NT users and learn innovative ways to accomplish your objectives. It's a safe bet that you will see me occasionally on some of the Windows NT mailing lists.

Although I subscribe to several of the lists, I typically ferret them away in the NT Newsletter folder in my Netscape mail reader for a rainy day, but they have been useful on more than one occasion.

> **TIP**
>
> If your e-mail application supports "rules," use a rule to divert all e-mail from mailing lists to a folder. Then the dozens of messages you get from different mailing lists won't distract you from your personal and business e-mail. It's a good idea to use a different folder for each mailing list so that when you have some free time, you can open a folder and read all the messages.

To join any of the following Windows NT mailing lists, simply send an e-mail message to the addresses listed. Make sure the body of your message contains the appropriate text listed in Table J.2. Usually after a few hours, you start getting messages from the mailing list.

> **TIP**
>
> When you subscribe to a mailing list, you get a welcome message with information about the mailing list. Be sure to save this message because it also has information about how to unsubscribe from the mailing list in case you change your mind. Some list members aren't very pleased when unsubscribe messages are sent to the main list.

These mailing lists will get you started, but before subscribing to one of these newsletters, make sure you're logging in through the correct account (or adjust the settings in your mail reader) so the newsletters are sent to the right destination. Also, you'll probably want to subscribe to the "digest" form of the list. Otherwise, you'll be inundated with hundreds of mail messages every day from people on the list. The digest form lumps all the mail into one large message that you can easily identify, so you'll then get one or two messages a day rather than tens or hundreds.

Table J.2. Online NT newsletters.

Newsletter	Description/Subscription Information
WINNEWS	This is Microsoft's newsletter for all Windows products. Send e-mail with a blank subject line and only the words `subscribe winnews` in the message body to this address: `admin@winnews.microsoft.com`.

continues

Table J.2. continued

Newsletter	Description/Subscription Information
WINNTNEWS	Microsoft and Beverly Hill software teamed up to bring you this newsletter exclusive to NT topics. Subscribe by sending e-mail with just `subscribe winntnews` as the first line of the message to `winntnews-admin@microsoft.bhs.com`.
BACKOFFICENEWS	Microsoft and Beverly Hill software teamed up to bring you this newsletter on BackOffice topics. Subscribe by sending e-mail with just the words `subscribe backofficenews` in the body of the message to `backofficenews-admin@microsoft.bhs.com`.
Win NTools News	This is a biweekly newsletter designed for administrators using NT in a software production environment. Send e-mail to `listproc@intnet.net` and include as the first line `subscribe NT-list <your first name> <your last name>`.
WEBSERVER-NT	For discussions on Windows NT–based Web servers, send e-mail to `webserver-nt-equest@DELTA.PROCESS.COM`. Include this in the body of the message: `subscribe webserver-NT`.
International Windows NT Users Group	For general discussions on Windows NT, send e-mail to `list@bhs.com`. Include this in the body of the message: `join iwntug`.
Windows NT Discussion List	Send e-mail to `listserv@eva.dc.1soft.com`, and include this in the body of the message: `subscribe winnt-1`.

Windows NT Resources on the Web

The Web is a worldwide resource, bringing together thousands of people with common interests and expertise, so it's a valuable resource. You are bound to find at least one person out there who has done what you're trying to do, has had the same problem, or has had to overcome the same obstacle. Usually, you get more responses than you can use, so you can look for the one that fits your situation the best. Quite often, what starts as a simple question and answer takes on the form of an ongoing dialogue. Take advantage of this pool of knowledge. Once you have Internet access, the rest is free, so there's no reason not to make good use of it.

Using Windows NT Web Sites

There are many helpful Windows NT Web sites on the Internet. The sites listed in this section are devoted solely to Windows NT or have some NT content. You might want to add some of these sites to your favorite Web browser's bookmark list and visit them often to keep up with Windows NT developments and find solutions to problems.

A recent set of searches one of my co-authors did on Windows NT–related topics with Yahoo!'s default search engine (`http://www.yahoo.com`) yielded 424 pages mentioning Windows NT, 77 pages mentioning Windows NT Server, and 27 pages that touch on BackOffice. By now, there are probably more than a few additions to this list. Conduct searches regularly, using different search engines (Megellan, Alta Vista, and so forth) to keep up with the more useful NT Web sites.

Want to keep up to date on the world as seen from Microsoft's perspective? Check their home page at `http://www.microsoft.com`. From this site, you have lots of options: You can get to online support, gather new data about all their products (of course), and even download free software updates.

For a focus on NT Server and BackOffice, check out this site:

```
http://www.microsoft.com/BackOffice
```

This page links to all sorts of useful information about current and future trends, case studies, and so on.

> **TIP**
>
> Before buying or installing new hardware, make sure it's compatible with NT. However, the NT compatibility supplied with your CD-ROM doesn't always include all the latest gear. You can find an up-to-date Windows NT Server Hardware Compatibility List (HCL) by visiting `http://www.microsoft.com/BackOffice/ntserver/hcl`. I highly recommend checking it.

Digital Equipment Corporation (DEC) hosts a Windows NT resources page at `http://www.windowsnt.digital.com`. This page includes lots of links to useful information. As you might expect, it leans a bit toward information about NT on the Alpha RISC platform.

Windows NT from a UNIX Point of View

The paper *Microsoft Windows NT from a UNIX Point of View* gives you a technical overview of Windows NT for the information technology professional with a strong background in UNIX. It looks at the subject from the UNIX point of view and correlates Windows NT concepts to those in UNIX. The paper begins with a technical comparison of the two operating systems and moves on to cover how the two can co-exist in a heterogeneous environment. It ends by describing some of the tools available to help developers create applications for both platforms. You can find the paper at this site:

```
http://www.microsoft.com/BackOffice/reading/nt4unix.htm
```

J

TECHNICAL
INFORMATION
SOURCES

Windows NT on the Internet

This site explains how to create an Internet presence using only Windows NT. It's one long document that you can get to through an outline of hot links. The outline lets you jump directly to the area you're interested in. Topics include DHCP, DNS, RAS, WWW, e-mail, FTP, NNTP, and WINS servers, as well as connection to the Internet and security issues. You can find this site at the following address:

http://www.neystadt.org/winnt

European Microsoft Windows NT Academic Center (EMWAC)

EMWAC is a focus for Windows NT activities, events, and use in the academic community. A mirror of Microsoft's knowledge base is available, as well as useful Internet tools and utilities. EMWAC's tool chest includes Finger, Gopher, HTTP, Mail, and WAIS servers. Visit this site at the following address:

http://www.emwac.ed.ac.uk/

Digital's Windows NT Home Page

This is the definitive site for users of Digital's Alpha technology. Digital is a large company with lots of resources, and this site shows it. It has a clean, professional look and is a well-organized collection of events calendars, press releases, news, product descriptions, white papers on subjects from architecture to security issues, and links to other helpful sites. You can find it at this URL:

http://www.windowsnt.digital.com/

Beverly Hills Software (BHS) Windows NT Resource Center

BHS provides downloads for CGI programming, drivers, HTML, mail, Internet Information Server, security, and virus protection utilities, among others. The download screen is very accessible for browsing; it keeps the list of categories on the left while you review the actual files on the right. Some interesting downloads include Internet telephone programs, video conferencing software, URL grabbers, proxy server, and so on.

BHS also provides a Windows NT 4–only section in their technical center. You can find BHS at this address:

http://www.bhs.com

San Diego Windows NT User Group (SDWNTUG)

SDWNTUG supplies links to downloadable files, including drivers, utilities, programming tools, demos, and so forth. This site also includes a decent magazine with articles on new software, hardware, security issues, and book reviews. SDWNTUG is at this site:

http://www.fbsolutions.com/sdwntug

Frank Condron's World O' Windows

This site is a clean, well-organized one that doesn't overwhelm you with information:

```
http://www.conitech.com/windows/winnt.html
```

It has just the basics: news, drivers, comprehensive vendor updates, and tips and tricks. One section covers connecting to the Internet with Windows NT Dial-Up Networking. You can get to it directly at this address:

```
http://www.conitech.com/windows/ntdun/ntdun.html
```

This site also has an industry news section with brief "What's Up" articles that keep you abreast of current releases and updates.

Internet Nexus

Internet Nexus is a basic site. One page reorganizes the Microsoft Web site's offerings for Windows NT. Simple layout and organization make Mircosoft's resources more accessible. Another page presents the best of other sites in the same clear format. If the Web makes your head swim, this is a refreshing change. Visit Internet Nexus at this address:

```
http://www.netwrx.net/thurrott/winnt.html
```

Justin Weber's Computing Center

Justin Weber maintains a fairly active bulletin board system with many NT-related threads. The Links section gives you access to Microsoft's Knowledge Base, online magazines, and software archives. You can visit this site at the following address:

```
http://computing.net/
```

CMP's NT Solution Center

The Solution Center offers many resources, all of which you can get to from a well-organized home page. It features many articles on NT from *Windows Magazine, Information Week, Communications Week, Network Computing*, and others. They're organized under headings such as "Is NT For You?," "NT Products," "Using NT," and "Industry Overview." The "Features & Opinions" section has an in-depth discussion and analysis of current events. The Solution Center is at this site:

```
http://techweb.cmp.com/ntsolutions/main/default.shtml
```

NT Advantage

This site has some links, but it mostly has news and editorial articles about NT events. It's informative (and sometimes humorous), and the articles keep you connected to the pulse of the industry. You can find NT Advantage at this address:

```
http://www.ntadvantage.com/default.asp
```

J

TECHNICAL INFORMATION SOURCES

Microsoft Windows NT Server Support Online

This site is the definitive knowledge base for Windows NT support. You can find it at this address:

```
http://www.microsoft.com/ntserversupport/
```

Windows-NT

The most valuable part of this site is its "Tip & Info" section. It offers good coverage of hardware and communication issues and gives you handy bits of information. Look for it at this address:

```
http://www.windows-nt.com/
```

InterGreat

InterGreat is a collection of Internet-specific software packages that includes Internet servers, clients, programming tools, and links to other useful sites. You can find it at this address:

```
http://www.intergreat.com/winnt/winnt.htm
```

Jim Buyens - Windows NT Resource Site

Jim maintains a huge number of links for everything you could need. The site is organized into three levels. The first has sections such as "Windows NT Web Server Tools," "Windows NT Tips," and "Web Browser Add-Ins." The second level groups the products by type. For example, in the "Browser Add-Ins" section, there are headings for ActiveX Controls, Audio, Document Readers, Video, and Virtual Reality, among others. Each heading lists products and links to their home page for further information. This format makes it easy to quickly see what's available. You can find Jim Buyens's site at this address:

```
http://www.primenet.com/~buyensj/index.html
```

Inside the Windows 95 and NT Registry

You can learn how the Registry works and what it does at this site. Two useful programs, RegMon and NTRegMon, are available here. They log communication between the Registry and programs on your system under Windows 95 and Windows NT, respectively. By reviewing these logs, you can see how programs use the Registry, what information they store in it, and when it's accessed or changed. You can find this site at the following address:

```
ftp://ftp.ora.com/pub/examples/windows/win95.update/registry.html#ntregmon
```

Windows NT Magazine

A very active Windows NT section is available in this magazine's "Forum" section. Topics include installation, security, resource kits, network issues, and many others. The "Update" section has short summaries of current happenings, and the "Resource" section has well-organized links to other sites and press releases. A search engine completes the site. You can visit it at this address:

```
http://www.winntmag.com/
```

Rocky Mountain Windows NT User Group

This user group is on the most link pages of any I have seen, and with good reason. This site has news, technical help, newsgroups, software archives, white papers, and links of its own. You can find it at this address:

```
http://budman.cmdl.noaa.gov/rmwntug/rmwntug.htm
```

The Windows NT Resource Center

This site is an attractive, well-organized, Windows NT 4–only technical center. You can visit it at this address:

```
http://www.bhs.com/default.asp
```

WindowsNT-Plus

This contents of this site are organized in a tabbed window that looks much like the Windows NT desktop. Behind this effective interface are many resources, including news, editorials, software, drivers, and links to other sites. Visit it at this address:

```
http://www.windowsnt-plus.com/
```

Microsoft Windows NT-Platform Tools

This Microsoft-maintained site has well-organized, usable links. Good product descriptions make browsing for the tool you need much easier. Main categories include Developer, Client, Server, Utilities, and Other. These categories are further broken down into types. For example, the Utilities category is further divided into Graphics, Maintenance, HTML, and Documents Management. You can find this site at the following address:

```
http://www.microsoft.com/ntserver/tools/tools.htm
```

Windows Magazine Online

Windows Magazine offers provides a good selection of shareware and freeware. You can also find utilities featured in past issues, FAQs, news, and an NT-specific area. Visit this site at this address:

```
http://www.winmag.com/
```

Windows NT 4.0 Hardware Compatibility List

This site contains the definitive list of hardware that's compatible with NT from the definitive source, Microsoft. You should always check this site before installing NT on a machine or before buying or installing new hardware on an NT system. You can find it at this address:

```
http://www.microsoft.com/isapi/hwtest/hsearchn4.idc
```

NT Security Suggestions

At this site, you'll find many suggestions to secure an NT server for Web server use. The document covers routers, bindings, account setup, FTP, RAS, and the C2 Configuration Manager. You can visit this site at the following address:

```
http://www.telemark.net/~randallg/ntsecure.htm
```

Windows NT Links

This atractive, well-organized site has many links for Windows NT. Categories include Internet Servers, Internet Programming, Internet Security, Helpful Hints, Telephony, Server Applications, Client Applications, and Utilities. There's also a book and magazine review section and a bulletin board system. Visit this site at this address:

```
http://www.datawide.com/nt/
```

Finding Windows NT Software on the Web

Many Web sites provide Windows NT software. Packages can enhance existing Windows NT features, such as added security systems, and add functions such as disk defragmentation. There are different levels of cost. *Freeware* (try and never buy) is just that: free. It's in the public domain and can generally be used with no restrictions. *Shareware* (try before you buy) allows unlimited downloads and use for a limited time; it then asks for payment to the publisher based on the honor system. If you like the product and use it, then pay for it. *Commercial packages* (buy before you try) require payment before you get the software. However, there's usually some sort of return or exchange policy if it turns out to be unsatisfactory.

Some of the preceding section's sites offer software and links to software sites. Some of these sites, such as Jim Buyens's site of links, gather disparate resources on the Web into one well-organized, easy-to-use site. The following sites are oriented more toward actually providing the software:

- Internet Shopper (nothing about NT 4)

  http://www.net-shopper.co.uk/

  The Internet Shopper mainly covers communications products. They have mail servers, fax servers, domain name servers, and NNTP servers, and they host a list server. They also have some support for DEC's Alpha processor.

- NT PERL Distribution Site

  http://www.perl.hip.com/

  You can get free access to Perl at this site. Perl is a programming language used with CGI for creating interactive Web sites.

- Sunbelt International

  http://www.ntsoftdist.com/ntsoftdist/

  At the Sunbelt International Web site you can find many Windows NT system management utilities, such as a utility to check your disk fragmentation, remote access software, security software, performance monitors, and others. This is a commercial site with very little in the way of free software.

- Carmel Anti-Virus for Windows NT

  http://www.fbsolutions.com/ntav

  Carmel Anti-Virus is a Windows NT virus detection and eradication utility. If you decide to use the product, virus signature updates are available by download so you can keep on top of new threats to your system's health. The site also lets you download a demo.

- Sharware's Top NT Files

  http://www.shareware.com/top/MS-WindowsNT-table.html

  Many useful items for system administration and development are available here. Past entries (still available in the archives) have included the following:

msie301mnt.exe	Internet Explorer for NT 4
navntscn.exe	Norton Anti-Virus for NT 4
0nav96.exe	Definition update for Norton Anti-Virus
wnti25e.zip	McAfee ViruScan for WinNT v2.5
vjtrialb3.exe	Visual J++ beta
domadmin.zip	Domain Administrator utility

Glossary

10Base2   Thin coaxial cable running at 10Mbps, as defined in the IEEE 802.3 standard. Segment length is limited to 185 meters, typically in a bus topology.

10Base5   Thick coaxial cable running at 10Mbps, as defined in the IEEE 802.3 standard. Segment length is limited to 500 meters, typically in a bus topology.

10Base-T   Unshielded twisted pair running at 10Mbps, as defined in the IEEE 802.3 standard. Segment length is limited to 100 meters, typically in a bus topology. See also **twisted pair**.

16-bit   A memory model limited to 16-bit addressing. To access more than 64K of memory, segment addressing schemes must be used, in which base and offset addresses are added together. DOS and Windows 3.1 use the 16-bit memory model.

32-bit   A memory model that uses 32-bit addressing. This model provides access to 4.3G of memory without needing segment addressing. Most of Windows 95 and all of Windows NT use this model.

access method   The method used by a service provider (such as a file server) to allow (usually) secure access to its contents.

account   See **user account**.

account policy   Determines how passwords are to be used by users on a workstation or on an entire domain.

ACE (Access Control Entry)   An element of an ACL that maps a user account to specific access permissions.

ACK   Acknowledgment.

ACL (Access Control List)   A list of ACEs.

active hub   See **hub**.

active monitor   The processor responsible for monitoring token traffic on Token Ring networks. Detects lost tokens, among other things.

active partition   The system partition the computer boots from when first started. Managed by the Disk Administrator utility.

active window   The window that's "in front" of all others or whose title bar is in a different color or intensity from the others.

address   The location in memory or on disk of a specified instruction or piece of data. Could also refer to the location of a workstation on the network.

administrative alerts   Messages sent to specified groups of users, typically administrators, announcing system security problems, impending power loss, printer contention problems, and so forth.

Alerter service   The internal NT service required for administrative alerts. The Messenger service must be running for the Alerter to work.

Alpha AXP   A RISC CPU designed and manufactured by DEC. Versions of Windows NT 3.*x* and later are available for machines based on this CPU.

AMP   Asymmetric multiprocessing.

ANSI (American National Standards Institute)   An ISO member group that coordinates voluntary standards groups.

API (Application Programming Interface)   A collection of low-level software routines that programmers can use to send requests to the operating system.

applet   A small utility program. The Clipboard, Notepad, Calculator, and Paint are all considered applets.

AppleTalk   Apple's network protocol. Used for network communications by Macintosh computers.

application   A computer program, such as Microsoft Word for Windows.

application layer   The highest layer of the seven-layer OSI reference model. It provides high-level network services to applications.

application window   The window an application is running in, as opposed to a document (or *child*) window, which runs inside an application window.

ARC (Advanced RISC Computing)   A design specification that establishes hardware and firmware interface standards for RISC computers running Windows NT.

archive attribute   This is usually a single bit used as an archive flag, which is set when a file is modified. A full backup processes all files regardless of the archive flag setting and resets all archive flags; an incremental backup processes all files with their archive flag set and then resets the flag; and a differential backup is the same as an incremental backup, but doesn't reset the archive flag.

archive bit   A single bit stored in a disk directory to indicate whether a file has been changed since it was last backed up. Backup programs clear a file's archive when they back up the program. Modifying the program sets the bit again so that a backup program knows to make a backup the next time you do one.

arcname   The ARC pathname that specifies a device on the computer. Arcnames are used on both RISC and Intel architectures.

ARCnet (Attached Resource Computer Network)   A simple, low-cost, token-passing network technology introduced by Datapoint Corporation in 1968, using 2.5MHz coaxial media.

K

GLOSSARY

ASCII (American Standard Code for Information Interchange) file   A simple text file with no formatting.

associate   The process of informing Windows which program to run when you double-click on a document file (not an executable file). For example, .WRI files run Windows Write and open the document because the two are associated. This association is managed through the View|Options|FileType menu in My Computer.

asymmetric multiprocessing   A multiprocessing scheme in which one CPU is dedicated to running the operating system and others are used for running applications, as opposed to symmetric multiprocessing.

asynchronous I/O   Input/output operations are performed without holding up the CPU for other tasks. The requesting process is allowed to continue, if it can, while the request is processed by another agent. The requesting process is notified when the operation is complete. This way, relatively slow I/O operations don't keep the system from performing other useful work. See also **synchronous I/O**.

ATM (Asynchronous Transfer Mode)   A high-speed networking technology, providing speeds from 1Mbps to 1Gbps.

attenuation   The loss of signal strength, usually over distance, caused by internal cable resistance and external EMI interference.

attributes   In FAT systems, settings for each file that indicate whether the file is used by the operating system, has read-only status, has its archive bit set, or is a hidden file.

audit policy   Determines whether and which types of events are written to an audit log. Set audit policy with the User Manager program.

auditing   A process NT uses to keep track of certain security-related activities of users on the system, such as who logs on and who copies files. Audits are stored in audit logs, which can be examined through the Event Viewer application.

AUI (Attachment Unit Interface)   A device used to connect a node to a thick Ethernet network transceiver. See also **DIX**.

authentication   The process NT uses at logon time to determine whether a user is legitimate. If the user is interacting with computers on a trusted domain, authentication for the user is vouched for by one computer, and the others respect (trust) this authentication. Note that domain authentication is performed based on the domain controller, rather than on the local security database.

autoplay   A feature of Windows NT and Windows 95 that automatically starts a CD-ROM disc inserted into the computer's drive. What actually happens in the autoplay sequence is determined by autoplay files on the CD-ROM. Usually, a greeting screen is displayed with several options, such as a tour, installation instructions, and browsing options.

autorun   See **autoplay**.

AVIO (Advanced Video I/O)   An OS/2 graphical interface. Only OS/2 1.*x* AVIO applications can be run on NT and only if the Windows NT Add-on Subsystem for Presentation Manager is available.

backbone network   A high-speed network that connects other networks to each other.

back-end   See **server**.

BackOffice   A Microsoft marketing name for its server products, including Windows NT Server, SQL Server, Systems Management Server, SNA Server, Mail Server, Exchange Server, and Internet Information Server.

backup browser   A computer that maintains a backup copy of servers and resources used in browsing the network. Backup browsers request database updates from the master browser at predetermined intervals, usually every 15 minutes.

backup domain controller (BDC)   A member computer of an NT domain that shares the load of user security. This machine has to run Windows NT Server and maintains a copy of the SAM (Security Accounts Manager) database. The database is updated by the primary controller when changes are made.

base-level synthesizer   The lowest standard for the sound-effects section of Windows multimedia systems. A base-level synthesizer can play a minimum of six notes on three different instruments and three notes on three percussive instruments simultaneously.

basic rate interface (BRI)   An ISDN interface that provides voice, data, and video communication through two B channels and one D channel.

batch program   A text file that instructs NT to perform one or more tasks sequentially. Used for automating the loading or execution of programs. Batch files have a .BAT or .CMD extension.

bcc   Blind carbon copy.

BDC   See **backup domain controller**.

beta   A version of software released to select members of the user community for testing and debugging purposes before it's commercially available.

binary   A numbering system with only two values, 0 and 1.

binary-file transfer   A data transfer process in which files aren't converted at all. Typically used with a modem to send programs or complex documents from computer to computer.

bindery   The NetWare equivalent to NT's SAM database. The bindery keeps track of users and their privileges. Bindery information can be converted to SAM information by using the Migration Tool for NetWare utility.

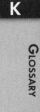

K

GLOSSARY

binding   A connection between layers of network components. Binding creates paths between the hardware layer, transport protocols, and higher level network application components (like the server and redirector). Network bindings are created with the Network application in the Control Panel.

binding path   The chain of connections binding the top-level network component to the bottom.

bit   A single binary digit having a value of either 1 or 0.

bits per second (bps)   A measurement of data transmission speed, usually over a serial data link; roughly equivalent to baud rate. A single character requires approximately 10 bits, so a transfer rate of 9600 baud results in about 960 characters per second (cps) being transferred.

Blue Screen of Death   The affectionate nickname for the screen that appears when the Windows NT operating system halts because of a critical error. This screen displays information about the failure. Depending on the type of failure, NT might perform a memory dump and/or automatic restart.

boot loader   The most basic information NT needs to start loading when the computer is powered up or rebooted. The boot loader points to the system files so that NT can continue loading.

boot partition   The hard-disk partition that contains the NT operating system. The boot partition is actually the active primary partition, and it doesn't have to include the NT OS files.

bps   See **bits per second**.

BRI   See **basic rate interface**.

bridge   Not quite as intelligent as a router, this device passes all network data between two segments of a network.

broadcast   A message sent to all nodes on a network.

broadcast address   An address reserved for referring to all nodes on a network.

broadcast storm   If many broadcasts are sent at one time, the network can be overloaded, resulting in slow connections and time-out conditions.

browse   To search through or examine a directory tree of files, directories, disks, workstations, workgroups, or domains. Often done by using a browse button in a dialog box.

browse master   See **master browser**.

buffer   A temporary holding area for data, such as in a disk controller or printer.

bus mastering   A bus mastering adapter can take over the system bus to perform its own communication with RAM or other devices. This frees the system CPU to continue on with other tasks. Adapters with this intelligence boost overall system performance.

bus topology A network topology in which all workstations are connected to the same cable, or *bus*.

byte A binary "word" consisting of 8 bits. A byte can represent a number from 0 to 255 or -127 to +128 depending on the coding used. A byte can also represent a character, an instruction, or part of an instruction. A byte is the basic unit of computing.

C2-level security A computer security specification set by the U.S. Government's National Computer Security Council, a department of the U.S. National Security Agency. Windows NT meets C2-level security because it requires password logon and authentication, and it supplies audit trails for operations affecting security.

carrier sensing Part of the traffic control used on some networks; a node that wants to send data listens for other nodes using the network and sends data when no other carrier is "sensed," that is, when the network is available. Carrier sensing is part of Ethernet's CSMA/CD access method.

cell The standard package of data sent on an ATM network.

Cheapernet See **10Base2**.

checkbox A square option box in many dialog boxes. Clicking on it adds or removes an × from the box, indicating whether the setting is on (checked) or off (unchecked).

checksum See **CRC**.

Chicago Windows 95's code name while in development.

choose A term used in many instructions in this book and in Windows books and manuals. It usually means opening a menu and clicking on a command, and can also refer to dialog box items, as in "Choose LPT1 from the drop-down list."

CISC (Complex Instruction Set Computer) A computer based on more complex instruction sets. Because the instructions are more complex, they also tend to be more specialized, which generally means more instructions. This complexity has given rise to a new and different approach to processor design The Intel i86 series of CPUs, for example, are CISC machines. See also **RISC (Reduced Instruction Set Computer)**.

clear Typically refers to turning off the × in an option or checkbox.

click To click the left mouse button (unless a left-handed user has switched the functions of the left and right buttons).

client As opposed to a server, a client is a workstation that connects to another computer's resources. A client can also include RPC (that is, client/server) and doesn't necessarily have to be another workstation. Basically, a client is just another application, workstation, or whatever that uses resources from another process.

client application In OLE context, a program that uses an object (such as a graphic) supplied by another application (the server application). See also **client**.

K

GLOSSARY

client/server networking   As opposed to peer-to-peer networking, an arrangement in which central computers, called *servers*, supply data and peripherals for use by client computers (*workstations*). Typically, a server has a large hard disk that supplies not only data but programs; it can even execute programs. A server might also supply printers and modems for network clients to use. In another sense of the term, client/server refers to an architecture for distributed processing in which subtasks can be distributed between services, CPUs, or even networked computers for more efficient execution.

Clipboard   An internal temporary storage area in all versions of Windows used for sharing data of various types (for example, text, graphics, sound, video) between applications. In NT, Clipboard works with the ClipBook. The Clipboard is a local storage area only; it's not available to networked machines.

ClipBook   An extension of the Clipboard that allows network users to share the contents of their Clipboards with other workstations.

ClipBook page   As opposed to the Clipboard, a user's ClipBook can store any number of items, not just one. Each item, even of a dissimilar type, is stored on a ClipBook page. Pages are then individually "shared" for use by other network workstations. Like Windows for Workgroups, NT has a 127-page limit.

ClipBook service   The internal NT service that allows you to share ClipBook pages over the network.

cluster   A logical unit of disk allocation. Space is allocated to files in clusters. *Cluster* can also refer to a set of computers connected to provide fault-tolerant operation. When part of a cluster fails, redundant members fill the gap and the cluster continues to operate.

CMD.EXE   This 32-bit Windows NT command interpreter provides a DOS-like character-based interface. Included are most DOS features and commands, including batch files and intrinsic commands.

coaxial cable (coax)   A cable with an inner wire conductor surrounded by a hollow outer cylindrical conductor. This configuration provides very good resistance to outside interference.

collision   When two nodes on a CSMA/CD network, such as Ethernet, try to communicate at the same time, a collision occurs. A CSMA/CD network supplies logic to arbitrate in this situation. This arbitration can be as simple as a random amount of time passing before they try again.

collision detection   The part of CSMA/CD network logic that listens to the messages on the network and detects when a collision has occurred and who the offenders are.

color scheme   A selection of colors that Windows uses for screen display of applications, dialog boxes, and so forth, set from the Control Panel.

command   Usually an option from an application's menus. Also refers to commands typed in from a command-prompt session or from the Run dialog box of the Windows Start menu. In essence, a way of telling an application or NT to perform a major chore, such as running an application or utility program.

command interpreter   The program that processes keyboard input in a DOS window or in DOS itself. Intrinsic DOS commands, as well as capabilities for running batch files, are built into the command interpreter.

command prompt   The symbols that the command interpreter uses to signal that it's ready for input. These symbols can be set by using the PROMPT environment variable. C:\> is a common prompt.

common groups   As opposed to local groups, NT's Program Manager lets you set up groups of application and document icons that all users on the workstation will have access to in addition to their personal (local) groups.

compound device   A multimedia device that plays files stored in the computer. For example, a synthesizer board is a compound device, as opposed to a simple device like a CD-ROM drive that contains its own data (files on the CD-ROM disc).

compound document   A document that uses OLE to combine different document types into one. A compound document might contain word processing, spreadsheet, and graphics files, for example. With OLE 2.0, the user can easily see how to edit the parts of a compound document.

computer account   An entry in the SAM database that describes a particular computer in a Windows NT domain. Each computer has its own entry.

Computer Browser Service   An internal NT service that keeps an up-to-date list of which computers are on the network. When an application supplies a dialog box that lets you choose a network computer, the information about workstations and servers in that box is supplied by the Browser service. If you terminate the service by using the Control Panel's Services applet, that application can't provide the list.

computer name   Each computer on the network must have a unique name of up to 15 uppercase characters. It can't be the name of another computer or domain. Names must be unique only within a workgroup or domain.

concentrator   See **hub**.

Configuration Registry   A database of configuration information central to NT's operations. Similar to WIN.INI and SYSTEM.INI in Windows 3.1, it also has settings similar to CONFIG.SYS and AUTOEXEC.BAT. Applications designed for Windows NT also store their own .INI settings in the Registry. The overall effect is to centralize all NT settings and provide security and control over system, security, and user account settings.

K

GLOSSARY

connect   To tie into a shared resource on the network and give it a name, drive letter, or other assignment that allows your local computer to use the device.

context switch   The shift of a CPU's attention away from its current task to a new task. The shift can be from one thread to another, from on process to another, from any operation to an interrupt handler, an so on. The CPU's current state must be saved and the state of the new process restored before processing can continue in the new context. This is the basic operation of a multitasking operating system.

Control menu   The menu you open by clicking on the control box in the upper-left corner of any window.

Control Panel   Windows's primary configuration program for options users can set, such as screen colors, fonts, and printers.

controller   See **domain controller**.

control set   The part of the NT registry containing boot information and the last known good configuration. This information is stored under the HKEY_LOCAL_MACHINE\SYSTEM key.

conventional memory   System RAM from 0–640K.

cooperative multitasking   This approach relies on applications cooperating with each other to manage their multitasking. It's up to each of them to relinquish the CPU after a reasonable amount of time. One ill-behaved application can dominate the system to the detriment of all others. See also **preemptive multitasking**.

copy backup   A type of backup in which the archive attribute flag is not reset on files included in the backup.

CPU (Central Processing Unit)   The main computing device in a PC system. Usually an i86 series device or compatible processor in a DOS/Windows-based system.

CRC (cyclic redundancy code or cyclic redundancy check)   An error-checking protocol used in data transmission in which the sender calculates a value (CRC) based on the data in the dataset and includes this CRC value in the header of the data block. The receiver knows the rules the sender used to calculate the value, so it can re-calculate it using the received data and compare it to the CRC from the sent data in the header. If they aren't the same, there has been a data-transmission error.

Cryptography API (CAPI)   Data encryption and decryption functions made available to applications by Windows NT 4.

CSD (Customer Service Disk)   See **service pack**.

CSMA/CD (Carrier Sense Multiple Access/Collision Detection)   The collision detection protocol used by Ethernet network technology, among others.

current directory   The directory that would be active if you logged onto the drive at the command prompt by typing the drive letter and pressing Enter. When you switch drives, the operating system remembers the directory that was current when you switched away. It will still be the active or current directory when you switch back, and it becomes the default directory where applications store or look for files if they're not specifically told which directory to use.

cyclic redundancy check   See **CRC**.

cyclic redundancy code   See **CRC**.

daily backup   Only files created or modified on a specific date are included in the backup.

Data Link Control (DLC)   A low-level network protocol at the data link layer of the OSI model. DLC is required by HP JetDirect network-connected printers.

data link layer   The second layer of the OSI model. This layer packages data in frames for transmission and detects errors in them.

DCOM   See **Distributed Component Object Model**.

DDE (dynamic data exchange)   Implemented in Microsoft Windows products, a means by which running applications can exchange information, as opposed to OLE (object linking and embedding), which has become more favored over time—especially OLE version 2. DDE is more often used by cooperating applications or tasks in the background, and OLE is used by people who want to link documents to create compound documents.

dedicated server   A computer that doesn't host any users directly. It supplies file, printer, communication, and application services to other computers on a network. Dedicated servers are usually locked away in a closet for security and reliability.

dedicated server network   A network designed around one or more dedicated servers.

default button   In almost every dialog box, one button has a darker border around it. Pressing Enter has the same effect as clicking this button.

default gateway   The node in a TCP/IP network that knows how to route data to other networks.

default printer   The printer, set in the Printer applet of the Control Panel, that documents are sent to if the user doesn't specify another printer.

default profile   When a new user is added to a workstation, the default profile sets up the user's account with a basic set of rights, privileges, and auditing setups. Can be altered through the User Manager.

dependent service   Interlocking NT internal services. The Alerter service is dependent on the Messenger service, for example.

K

GLOSSARY

descendent key The Configuration Registry consists of a number of keys. Like subdirectories in Explorer, a descendent key is a subordinate key.

destination document The document into which a linked or embedded document is placed.

device contention A problem that occurs when two or more processes try to use the same physical hardware at the same time. For example, two communications programs could simultaneously try to use a modem hooked to a COM port.

device driver Software that allows NT to use a piece of hardware attached to the computer, such as a printer, modem, sound card, screen, or mouse.

DHCP See **Dynamic Host Configuration Protocol service**.

DHCP scope A range of IP addresses that a DHCP server can use to assign addresses to other machines in the network. Permanently assigned addresses can be excluded from the range.

differential backup Like the incremental backup, this backup type includes all files with the archive flag set. Unlike the incremental type, however, it doesn't reset the archive flag.

differential SCSI A SCSI wiring scheme that allows longer, more reliable cable runs though the use of balanced lines. Each signal is carried on two lines: the signal and its inverse or opposite. Because interference affects both lines in the same direction, this interference can be canceled out at the end of the run without losing the signal.

DIMM Dual Inline Memory Module.

directory An object in a file system that can contain other objects (files or directories).

directory replication A process that easily copies and maintains a specific set of directories and files from a master computer to a number of remote computers. The Replicator service maintains (synchronizes) all the remote files so that they're updated whenever the master files or directories are modified.

Directory Replicator service An internal NT service responsible for performing and updating directory replication.

disabled user account A user account that has temporarily been disabled through User Manager. It can be enabled again, but prevents logging on until it is.

discretionary access The owner of a resource can give access to any individual or group at his or her discretion. Required for C2 certification.

disk configuration information Information stored in the Registry that tells NT how your hard disks are partitioned and what drive letters are assigned to the partitions. Also included is information about stripe, volume, and mirrored sets. The disk configuration information should be backed up onto floppy disks whenever you make changes to the disk settings through the Disk Administrator.

disk duplexing   Using a second hard drive as an exact replica of the first as a data security measure. The second drive has its own disk controller.

disk mirroring   Using a second disk or partition to contain a complete copy of a disk or partition. This is a data redundancy technique that provides fault-tolerance for disk systems.

disk striping   Writing data across multiple disks to increase efficiency.

Distributed Component Object Model (DCOM)   The next step in the evolution of OLE. Provides support for RPC, object caching, and other techniques to add reliable network functionality to OLE. Currently supported by Windows NT, DCOM will be supported on Windows 95 and the Macintosh in the future.

DIX (Digital-Intel-Xerox)   A connector sometimes used to connect a node to a thick Ethernet network transceiver. See also **AUI**.

DLC   See **Data Link Control**.

DLL   Dynamic Link Library.

DMA (direct memory access)   An architecture that allows peripheral devices to access the computer's main RAM directly. This structure frees the computer's CPU to perform other tasks while relatively slow I/O is processing. ISA adapters are limited to accessing the first 16M of RAM without performance penalties. EISA, VLB, and PCI do not have this limitation.

DNS   See **Domain Naming System**.

document   As opposed to an application, a document is a file, such as a business letter, that stores data created by using an application.

domain   In Windows NT Server, a group of computers that have the same domain database. The domain maintains security on the system and allows workstations to interact by setting up trust relationships between them and the server(s).

domain controller   In each domain, one computer holds the domain database responsible for security and authentication of logons, which is called the *primary domain controller*. In addition, there can be normal domain controllers that have copies of the domain database. These copies are kept synchronized by the primary domain controller. This is an NT Server function only.

domain database   The security and logon authentication database stored in the domain controller.

domain extension   The three-letter extension for domain names in a TCP/IP network. This extension shows the domain's type of organization, such as .COM for commercial, .EDU for educational, .GOV for government, and so forth.

K

GLOSSARY

domain model   A way to represent a group of one or more Windows NT Server domains and the trust relationships set between them. Domain models include single domain, single master domain, and multiple master domain.

domain name   Each domain must have a name, just as a workgroup or user must. This name appears in the Browser as users scan the network for workgroups, workstations, and domains.

Domain Naming System (DNS)   A distributed database of host names and their corresponding IP addresses. Each machine involved in the database, whether it's a host or router, has its information updated on a need-to-know basis. Windows NT Server has a DNS Server.

domain synchronization   The domain controller is responsible for keeping an updated copy of the domain database on all other domain controllers in a multiple-domain network. Synchronization is the process of making sure all the databases are identical and up-to-date.

dotted-decimal notation   The notation used to express IP addresses. A dot is placed between each byte in the 32-bit IP address (for example, 129.37.15.6).

double-attached nodes   Nodes with connections to both FDDI rings. This arrangement provides maximum network fault-tolerance in case of FDDI ring failure. See also **single-attached nodes**.

DoubleSpace   A disk compression product for DOS and Windows 3.*x*. Windows NT does not support DoubleSpace compression.

downloaded fonts   Fonts sent to the printer from the computer before printing and stored in the printer's internal RAM. Downloaded fonts are lost when the printer's power is turned off.

DRAM   Dynamic Random Access Memory.

dual-boot   An option that allows one computer to use two or more operating systems or different versions of the same operating systems. You can use the System applet in the Control Panel to configure this feature—choices, default, and time-out option, among others.

duplexing   See **disk duplexing**.

DWORD   A 4-byte hexadecimal data structure.

dynamic data exchange   See **DDE**.

Dynamic Host Configuration Protocol (DHCP) service   An optional TCP/IP services component that automates assigning client TCP/IP addresses.

ECC   See **error-correcting code**.

EDO RAM   Extended Data Out RAM.

EIDE   Enhanced Integrated Drive Electronics.

EISA (Extended Industry Standard Architecture)   When IBM introduced MCA (Micro Channel Architecture), many PC vendors banded together to introduce a competing 32-bit interface bus. Unlike IBM's MCA, EISA was designed to be backward-compatible with ISA.

embedded object   Data stored in a document that was created by another application. As opposed to a linked object, this type of object doesn't have its own file on disk. However, it runs its source application for editing when you double-click on it. For example, a Paintbrush drawing can be an embedded object in a Write document.

EMI   Electromagnetic interference.

EMS (Expanded Memory Specification)   An industry standard for allowing 8088/8086 and above Intel CPUs to access more than 640K of RAM, using a RAM banking method. Developed jointly by Intel, Lotus, and Microsoft, EMS was used by a number of programs, such as Lotus 1-2-3, until it fell out of favor as Windows became popular and XMS (Extended Memory Specification) came into widespread use.

Encapsulated PostScript (EPS)   A file format for storing PostScript-style images that allows a PostScript printer or program capable of importing such files to print a file in the highest possible resolution for your printer.

environment subsystem   A system that provides program interface support for applications written for different operating systems. Windows NT includes environment subsystems for DOS, Win32, OS/2, and POSIX.

environment variable   Set from the System applet in the Control Panel, NT's environment variables are similar to those used in DOS to control operating system internals, such as search paths, aliases, system prompts, and so on.

error-correcting code (ECC)   A code created through calculations based on the contents of a dataset. In addition to detecting all errors, the code usually has enough information to correct some errors.

error-detecting code (EDC)   A code created through calculations based on the contents of a dataset. The code usually has enough information to detect all errors.

Ethernet   A LAN architecture devised by Xerox Corporation and later adopted by the IEEE; also called the 802.3 standard.

EtherTalk   The combination of AppleTalk protocols running on an Ethernet network.

event   A significant NT happening worthy of user notification or a log entry. A user logging on or off the system, or attempting to use a protected service or file, for example, are events.

Event Log service   An internal NT service responsible for logging important events.

Exchange Server   A multi-use communications server that provides back-end support for e-mail, group scheduling, messaging, and fax management.

expanded memory   Also called EMS, expanded memory is a memory specification developed by Intel, Lotus, and Microsoft. Allows for up to 32M of memory to be accessible even by computers based on 8088/8086 chips from Intel. Not widely used at this point. See also **extended memory** and **XMS**.

export path   Related to directory replication. A network path informing the replication server (export server) where to send files it's responsible for replicating. Typically, the path leads to another workstation (import computer). This is an NT Server–only feature.

export server   See **export path**.

extended memory   Memory over 1M in 80286 machines and above. See also **XMS**.

extended-level synthesizer   A multimedia definition set by the multimedia PC council; more advanced than a basic-level synthesizer. Must be able to play 16 notes on nine instruments and 16 notes on eight percussion instruments simultaneously.

extended partition   One of four partitions on a physical disk that can be made into an extended partition, which can be subdivided into zero or more logical drives.

extension   The last three letters of a filename after the period.

external command   As opposed to an internal command, a command that requires a separate file to run. The format command, for example, runs the executable file FORMAT.COM.

family set   A collection of backup tapes made during the same backup session.

FAT   See **file allocation table**.

fault tolerance   A device that can continue uninterrupted operation in the face of catastrophic failure is said to be fault-tolerant. Many levels of fault tolerance are available, from simple uninterruptible power supplies for power failures, to component duplication for hard disk and controller failures, to whole computer system duplication for any catastrophic failure of an entire computer system.

FDDI (Fiber Distributed Data Interface)   A fiber-optic, dual ring, 100Mbps, token-passing physical data transport method, typically used for high-speed networks or network backbones.

fiber   A lightweight thread that's used by an application. Fibers ease porting of applications that schedule their own threads. See also **multithreading**.

fiber-optic cable   The thin, flexible optical cable used by FDDI. Modulated light carries the data instead of electricity, making for theoretically zero susceptibility to EMI. This cable costs more and has higher data rates than electrical cable.

file allocation table (FAT)   The table used by a native DOS file system to store information about the sizes, locations, and properties of files stored on a disk.

filename   The name that a file system or operating system gives to a file when it's stored on disk. Filenames in the NT File System (NTFS) can be 256 characters long. NT differentiates between uppercase and lowercase letters in filenames when displaying them, such as in Explorer. However, it isn't case-sensitive when accessing such files.

file system   The means an operating system uses to store files on a disk.

folder   An object in the Windows 95 and Windows NT 4 interface that can contain other objects, such as files and other folders; the same thing as a directory.

FQDN   Fully qualified domain name.

frame   A packet of data with a header containing error detection and correction information. Used at the data link layer of the OSI network model.

Frame Relay   A faster replacement for X.25 protocol. Used to communicate between servers, routers, and switching nodes.

free space   Physical disk space that has yet to be assigned to a logical partition, or a region within a partition that has yet to be assigned to a logical drive.

FTP (File Transfer Protocol)   A protocol designed to move files from one node to another over a TCP/IP network.

full backup   See **normal backup**.

full name   When you establish an account in User Manager, the full name is typically a person's whole name: last name, first name, and middle initial. It's used for identification purposes in User Manager, but it doesn't show up on the network and it isn't required at logon.

gateway   A computer that acts as a router between two network types, a translator between two different network protocols, or a translator between data formats of incompatible network applications.

Gateway Services for NetWare (GSNW)   A gateway that provides transparent access to network resources on a NetWare server. Provided with Windows NT Server, GSNW translates between the Windows NT SMB and the NetWare NCP protocols.

GDI (Graphics Device Interface)   The component of Windows NT (specifically the kernel mode portion of the Win32 subsystem) that manages low-level graphical elements on a display or other output device. Moved from user mode to kernel mode in Windows NT 4 to improve performance.

General MIDI   An industry specification governing the format of MIDI files. This is an evolving standard, but Windows adheres fairly well to it. Hardware and software you buy for a Windows system should be General MIDI–compatible.

global account   A typical user account on an NTFS trusted domain is global in nature, as opposed to local. When an account is set to global status, the domain allows the user access to resources on the domain.

global group   In an NT Server domain, a global group is a convenient means for setting up several users in a group, all of whom can be granted access to all the local domain resources as well as to resources in trusted domains. Can contain only accounts from its own domain.

group   A collection of user accounts organized in User Manager to expedite the assignment of rights and privileges. Each person in the group is called a *group member*.

group name   The name given to a group of users created in User Manager. See also **group**.

GSNW   See **Gateway Services for NetWare**.

HAL   See **hardware abstraction layer**.

handle   A data structure that describes an object's attributes and location.

hardware abstraction layer (HAL)   The most basic level of the NT operating system, which forms a bridge between the operating system and the computer's physical hardware.

header information   Data sent to the printer to define aspects of the printout and prepare the printer before printing. PostScript documents include headers.

headless server   A server that requires no attached video monitor. Most aspects of NetWare, for example, can be managed from network nodes with remote console programs. Windows NT doesn't support the use of headless servers.

heterogeneous network   A network that includes more than one type of protocol, cable type, operating system, hardware platform type, or any other dissimilar technology as it relates to networking.

hexadecimal   A base-16 numbering system with values ranging from 0 to 9, a to f, and A to F. Used in many programming languages; not particularly relevant to users.

high memory area   Also called the HMA, this is actually the first 64K (minus 16 bytes) above the 1M boundary. Therefore, it's actually the RAM address area 1024 to 1088 and is accessed by enabling the A20 line in real mode. Originally reserved for memory-mapped hardware, such as video cards, it's often used by memory manager programs to relocate portions of DOS and used by device drivers to provide more conventional memory for applications.

high-performance file system (HPFS)   The file system used by OS/2.

hive   A portion of the Registry that's recorded on disk as a separate file. Hives can be copied, but you need the Registry Editor to edit them.

home directory   A default directory declared by an administrator (through User Manager) for a user that's the default directory for storing applications and documents. Using a home directory makes backing up a user's files easier because most document files for the user end up there.

homogeneous network   A network that includes no more than one type of protocol, cable, operating system, hardware platform, or any other dissimilar technology as it relates to networking.

hop   The transmission of a datagram through one level of a network on its way to its destination—a router, for example.

hop count   The number of hops between a source and a destination. Used as a measure of virtual distance on the Internet.

host   A TCP/IP node that needs a TCP/IP address. Hosts include clients, servers, and network-connected printers. A node with more than one network adapter is considered a multiple host.

host name   The name of the host computer assigned by the DNS server. See **Domain Naming Service**.

HPFS   See **high-performance file system**.

hub   The device at the center of a star topology network. All network cables radiate out from the hub to the servers and nodes. A passive hub simply distributes the incoming signal to all outgoing lines with no conditioning or amplification. An active hub supports longer cable lengths by amplifying the signal before re-transmission.

IDE   Integrated Drive Electronics.

idle thread   The special thread assigned to a CPU when there are no other tasks to complete.

IEEE (Institute of Electrical and Electronic Engineers)   A professional organization that establishes electrical and electronic standards, including network standards.

import   An OLE term. In Object Packager, you can import a file into a package for later embedding into a destination document.

import computer   Relates to directory replication; the computer that receives replicated directories or files.

import path   The path over which an import computer receives the copies of the master set of replicated directories from an export computer.

in-place editing   A feature that allows all objects of a complex document (one consisting of multiple file types) to be edited without leaving the host application (Word, for example). As the cursor is placed on different objects in the document, the menu bar and other options change to reflect the type of object being edited. All applications must be OLE 2.*x* compliant. In-place editing allows the user to focus on the document at hand, rather than the programs required to edit it.

K

GLOSSARY

in-place file system conversion   When using in-place file system conversion, it's not necessary to remove files from a file system to change the file system type. A FAT partition may be converted to a HPFS without removing and restoring the partition's contents. However, it's still *highly* recommended that a verified backup of the partition be made before proceeding.

incremental backup   A backup that includes all files whose archive flags are set. All archive flags are reset for files included in the backup.

input queue   The central repository that gathers all input events, such as mouse movements, mouse clicks, and keystrokes. From here, these events are sent to the appropriate application for processing.

internal command   A command embedded in CMD.EXE, the command interpreter for NT DOS, or in COMMAND.COM, the MS-DOS equivalent. Internal commands, such as DIR, don't require additional support files. See also **external command**.

internal fragmentation   Disk space wasted by storing many files that are smaller than the smallest unit of disk allocation (cluster). Each file requires at least one cluster. If the file isn't large enough to fill the cluster, internal fragmentation results.

Internet   The world's largest internetwork, connecting over 20,000 networks in 132 countries, with nearly 35 million users worldwide. See also **internetwork**.

Internet Information Server (IIS)   Microsoft's Internet application platform. IIS includes a Web server, an application development environment, multimedia streaming, full-text search ability, and site management extensions. It's tightly integrated with Windows NT Server.

Internet Protocol (IP)   See **TCP/IP**.

internetwork   A collection of networks, designed to operate as a single, larger network by using intelligent routers. The Internet is just one example of this type of network.

InterNIC (Internet Network Information Center)   This is the organization that assigns and tracks domain names and Internet addresses.

interoperability   The ability of network nodes, perhaps of dissimilar protocols and technologies, to communicate with each other over a network by using translating routers and gateways.

interrupt request line (IRQ)   A line (conductor) on the internal bus of the computer (typically on the motherboard) over which a device such as a port, disk controller, or modem can get the attention of the CPU to process some data.

intranet   An internal internet, usually put in place by a company for its own use. It's a TCP/IP network that can make use of all programs and technologies available to the Internet. Intranets can span the globe, connecting a company's worldwide offices.

I/O (input/output) address   Many I/O devices, such as COM ports, network cards, printer ports, and modem cards, are mapped into an I/O address. This address allows the computer and operating system to locate the device, and thus send and receive data. I/O addresses don't tie up system memory RAM space, either. However, there are a limited number of them. You can access an I/O port in one of two ways: Either map it into the 64K I/O address space, or map it as a memory-mapped device in the system's RAM space. Memory-mapped devices are easier to work with, because they can use any memory-related CPU command instead of an in/out I/O port command.

I/O request packet (IRP)   An operating system data structure used to communicate information about an I/O request between I/O drivers.

IP (Internet Protocol)   See **TCP/IP**.

IP address   A 32-bit address assigned to every host on a TCP/IP network. See also **dotted-decimal notation**.

IPX/SPX (Internetwork Packet Exchange/Sequenced Packet Exchange)   The names Novell uses for its proprietary network layer and transport layer.

IRP   See **I/O request packet**.

IRQ   See **interrupt request line**.

ISA   Industry Standard Architecture.

ISDN (Integrated Services Digital Network)   A set of communication protocols that permit telephone networks to carry voice, data, and video into businesses and homes.

ISO   International Standards Organization.

ISO/OSI reference model   See **OSI reference model**.

ITG (Information Technology Group)   The internal MIS organization at Microsoft Corporation.

Kermit   A communications program popular on PCs. Kermit has a communications protocol to prevent data loss or corruption when files are transmitted between computers. Because of its popularity, many communications programs now support the Kermit protocol. It's not the fastest communications protocol around, but it's popular. See also **Xmodem/CRC**, **Ymodem**, and **Zmodem**.

kernel   The core of an operating system, usually responsible for basic I/O and process execution.

kernel driver   A driver that has direct access to hardware; a hardware driver.

kernel mode   The highest privilege mode on a CPU; no restrictions are placed on access to memory or hardware. Used by device drivers and file systems. See also **user mode**.

key   In Registry Editor, analogous to a folder in Explorer or My Computer. Keys are displayed in the left pane of the Editor window.

keyboard buffer   Memory set aside to store keystrokes as they're entered from the keyboard. Once it's stored, the keystroke data waits for the CPU to pick up the data and respond accordingly.

key map   In MIDI terminology, a remapping of MIDI signals to appropriate key numbers (each key on a synthesizer has a number). Nonstandard keyboards might not comply with General MIDI specifications, so they play the wrong sounds when sent a MIDI file for sound effects if a key map isn't set up to correct the mismapping.

LAN   See **local area network**.

LAN Manager   A network operating system product from Microsoft, developed for OS/2. LAN Manager can interface with NT Server without problems as a backup domain controller, but it can't be a primary domain controller. NT offers much of LAN Manager's functionality.

LAN Server   An OS/2 version of LAN Manager offered by IBM.

Last Known Good configuration   NT tracks the last configuration that booted successfully on the computer. When booting, it offers this configuration as an option.

least recently used (LRU)   A method used to determine which memory pages should be discarded to make room for new data. This method assumes that pages that have gone the longest without reference are the most likely candidates for discarding.

linked object   In OLE terminology, an icon stored in the destination file, representing the file that has been embedded.

LLC   See **logical link control**.

local account   An account type that's not necessary when trust exists between domains. If trust doesn't exist, a local account is set up for a user.

local area network (LAN)   A collection of computers connected to one another over high-speed cable for sharing data and resources. LANs tend not to use telephone or other leased lines from another source. Typically, computers on a LAN are in the same building, as opposed to those on a WAN, or wide area network, which might be in different buildings, states, or countries.

local group   A group of users that can be set up and given privileges and rights. These settings apply only to the single workstation on which the group was created. By setting up a local group, you can easily give a whole group of workers on the network access to your resources without risking giving those rights to everyone on the network or bothering with assigning rights individually.

local printer   A printer connected directly to your computer.

local procedure call (LPC) Similar to RPC (remote procedure call), but used within a single system to pass data and commands between subsystems of NT.

Local Security Authority (LSA) Part of the NT security system that provides user authentication services to other operating system components on the local computer.

LocalTalk The most common network hardware used by Apple Macintosh computers. Macintosh computers usually run AppleTalk protocols on LocalTalk. See also **EtherTalk** and **TokenTalk**.

local user profile A user profile that resides on one machine. If the user moves to another machine, the profile does not follow.

logical drive A drive that isn't a physical drive, such as floppy drive A or B. Instead, a logical drive is created on a subpartition of an extended partition and given an arbitrary letter such as C, D, or E.

logical link control (LLC) Manages node-to-node data flow; it's part of the data link layer of the OSI model.

logical printer See **print queue**.

logical topology See **topology**.

logon hours Hours during which a user is permitted to log onto the system.

logon process Accepts logon requests, displays dialog boxes, communicates with other security subsystem components, and accepts or rejects the request.

logon script A batch file or other executable program that executes immediately when the user logs onto the system. The script is declared in User Manager.

logon script path The location of the logon script.

logon workstations In NT Server, the only stations the user is allowed to log onto.

long-haul network See **wide area network**.

LPC See **local procedure call**.

LRU See **least recently used**.

LUN (logical unit number) The logical address of a SCSI device on a single device ID. The LUN is typically zero. It's possible, however, for more than one device to be assigned to a SCSI ID. In this case, each device has its own LUN.

Mach A kernel intended for use on PCs and relatively small computers. Based on the University of California's BSD 4.3 UNIX-derived operating system, Mach was developed at Carnegie-Mellon University and is the model after which NT was designed.

K

GLOSSARY

machine account   See **computer account**.

MAC (media access control) sublayer   The part of the data link layer responsible for managing the network's access method.

Mailslot File System (MSFS)   The Windows NT file system that provides mailslot functionality and connections.

mailslots   Allows broadcast of many-to-one and one-to-many interprocess messages. Implemented in Windows NT through the Mailslots File System.

MAN (metropolitan area network)   A network too small to be a WAN, but too big to be a LAN. Typically, MANs are referred to as WANs.

mandatory user profile   In NT Server, a profile of rights and privileges assigned to a user that can't be altered by that user.

master account domain   The one domain in a multidomain network that's used for maintenance and security. This master domain is trusted by other domains that offer access to network resources.

master browser   A computer that maintains a master list of available servers and resources used in browsing the network. It designates one or more other computers as backup browsers, which are updated with changes to the browse list every 15 minutes.

MAU   See **multistation access unit**.

maximum password age   The maximum time a password can be in effect until the user must change it.

MCA (Micro Channel Architecture)   IBM's 32-bit computer bus architecture introduced in its PS/2 models.

MCI   See **Media Control Interface**.

media access control (MAC)   See **MAC sublayer**.

Media Control Interface (MCI)   A standard interface for all multimedia devices, devised by the MPC council, that allows multimedia applications to control any number of MPC-compliant devices, from sound cards to MIDI-based lighting controllers.

medium   See **network medium**.

message queue   See **input queue**.

Messages database   A database supplied on the CD-ROM with NT that lists all the error and information messages that NT is likely to produce.

Messenger service   A Windows NT service that allows alert messages to be sent between computers. Required to send and receive alert messages between computers when those messages originate from administrators or the Alerter service. See also **Alerter service**.

MIB (Management Information Base) variables   A database of information on objects that can be accessed and managed by using network management protocols like SNMP.

microkernel   The center of a kernel, containing the primitives of the operating system. Using a microkernel allows developers to easily extend the operating system's capabilities by adding alterable outer "layers" to it that perform additional functions, such as running programs of different types. See also **kernel**.

MIDI (Musical Instrument Digital Interface)   Originally a means of connecting electronic instruments (synthesizers) and letting them communicate with one another. Computers then came into the MIDI landscape and were used to control the synthesizers. MIDI has been adapted for many purposes, and both Windows and Windows NT can play MIDI files.

MIDI setup   To play MIDI files, NT needs to know the type of MIDI device you have and the port or other relevant settings.

minimum password age   The minimum amount of time that must pass before a user is allowed to change his or her password.

minimum password length   The shortest possible password that the user is allowed.

MIPS RX000   A CPU developed through the joint venture of MIPS and Silicon Graphics. This RISC CPU can run Windows NT 3.*x* and later versions.

mirrored disk set   Several hard disks working together as a redundant fault-tolerant system, preventing loss of data in case one of the drives fails. See also **fault tolerance**.

mission-critical application   An application considered indispensable to the operation of a business, government, or other organization. Often these applications are transaction-based, such as for point-of-sale, reservations, or real-time stock, security, or money trading.

MLID   See **Multiple Link Interface Driver**.

MMTA   Multitasking Message Transfer Agent.

MPR   Multi-Protocol Routing.

MPR   Multiple Provider Router.

MSAU   See **multistation access unit**.

MS-DOS–based application   An application that normally runs on a DOS machine and doesn't require NT.

MSFS   See **Mailslot File System**.

MTA   Message Transfer Agent.

MTBF (Mean Time Between Failure)   The average expected time between failure for hardware components. The higher the number, the more reliable the component.

MTF (Microsoft Tape Format)   The tape format used by Windows NT's backup program when writing to a tape device. Some third-party backup providers support this format.

multihomed computer   A computer containing more than one active network adapter. This computer has multiple network homes.

multiple access   A network method in which a single cable is shared by multiple computers. Ethernet is one such network.

Multiple Link Interface Driver (MLID)   The NetWare standard for network drivers; corresponds to NDIS on NT.

multiprocessor system   A computer containing more than a single CPU.

multistation access unit (MAU or MSAU)   A device that connects a node to a star topology network.

multitasking   A process that allows a computer or operating system to concurrently run multiple applications or tasks by dividing the CPU's time between them so rapidly that it isn't noticed or isn't a problem for the user.

multithreading   A process that allows a multitasking operating system to, in essence, multitask subportions (threads) of an application smoothly. Applications must be written to take advantage of multithreading, which is supported by Windows NT.

named pipe   A vehicle that allows processes to communicate with one another without having to know where the sender and receiver processes are located. The name acts like an alias, connecting the two processes regardless of whether they're on the same computer or across connected domains.

Named Pipe File System (NPFS)   The part of the Windows NT file system that provides named pipe access and connections.

name resolution   The activity of looking up the IP address for a particular computer name, usually performed by WINS on Windows NT.

NBF   See **NetBEUI Frame**.

NBT   NetBIOS over TCP/IP.

NCP   See **NetWare Core Protocol**.

NCSC   National Computer Security Center.

NDIS   See **Network Driver Interface Specification**.

NDIS wrapper   A standard function library available to NDIS device driver developers to make drivers more independent of operating system specifics.

Net Logon service   In NT Server, an internal NT service that authenticates logons and synchronizes the user database among computers on the domain.

NetBEUI (NetBIOS Extended User Interface)   The network transport protocol used by all Microsoft's networking systems as well as IBM's LAN Server–based networks.

NetBEUI Frame (NBF)   The name of the implementation of the NetBEUI transport protocol on Windows NT.

NetBIOS (Network Basic Input/Output System)   A network API (application programming interface), as opposed to the transport protocol, NetBEUI. NetBIOS allows networked computers to send, receive, and process input and output requests from each other over the network. NetBIOS is the standard API for all Microsoft's networking systems, as well as for IBM's LAN Server–based networks and most other PC-based networking systems.

NetWare   Novell's network operating system. This system offers fast and robust file and print sharing, but didn't support application sharing easily when Windows NT 4 was released. It's the current market share leader in dedicated file and print server applications.

NetWare Core Protocol (NCP)   A high-level network protocol that's similar in function to Microsoft's SMB. It handles communication between requester and server components.

NetWare Link (NWLink)   Microsoft's implementation of Novell's IPX/SPX protocol, allowing interoperation with Novell NetWare networks.

network   A hardware and software link between at least two computers, allowing them to share information and, possibly, resources.

network adapter   The hardware device that allows a computer to connect to a network.

network analyzer   A tool—also called a *sniffer*—that can capture and analyze data packets on a network. These devices can help tremendously with network problem diagnosis and resolution. The Network Monitor utility included with Windows NT Server performs limited sniffing functionality.

Network DDE DSDM service   The Network DDE share database manager. Required by the network DDE service to function.

Network DDE service   Supporting DDE over the network.

network device driver   A software driver required to interface the network interface card (NIC) with the computer and operating system.

network directory   A shared directory.

Network Driver Interface Specification (NDIS)   A low-level device driver interface that provides a virtual network device for developers to write to. It decouples the transport protocols in the upper layers from network adapter–specific functions. Windows NT network programs are written to the NDIS 3.0 interface. See also **Open Datalink Interface**.

network interface card (NIC)   The network card that plugs into the computer and allows physical connection to the network.

network layer   The third layer of the OSI model; it routes data between network nodes and packages the data into network packets.

network medium   The physical medium that carries the data packets. This can be copper wire as in Ethernet, optical cable, or radio waves, for example.

Network OLE   See **Distributed Component Object Model**.

network operating system (NOS)   The software system that manages file and resource sharing between multiple users, implements security features, and provides administrative functions for managing users and resources. This software can be added to an existing operating system, as with LANtastic, be included in an operating system, as with Windows NT, or be its own, complete, special-purpose operating system, as with NetWare.

network topology   The physical topology refers to the cabling layout between nodes and servers. The most common are star and bus. The logical topology refers to the logical programming path taken by data traveling in the network.

NeXTSTEP   A UNIX-based operating system from NeXT Computer, Inc. Recently ported from NeXT machines to run on x86-based PCs.

NIC   See **network interface card**.

NMI (Non-Maskable Interrupt)   A very high-level hardware interrupt, indicating something has happened that can't be ignored. A memory parity error will generate an NMI. Windows NT usually halts in response to an NMI.

node   Any network-aware device connected to a network, including computers, servers, network printers, and routers.

node address   A unique number assigned to a network node to differentiate it from all other network nodes.

nondedicated server   A server that can perform other functions while running the server program. The most common use of a nondedicated server is as a client workstation. Used in smaller networks, it's generally not a good idea, as the client software can crash the whole computer, bringing the server down.

non-Windows NT application   Any application other than one specifically written to run under NT's 32-bit operating system, including Windows 3.1 applications.

normal backup   A backup that copies all the files, and then clears the archive flag to signal that the files have been archived.

NOS   See **network operating system**.

NPFS   See **Named Pipe File System**.

NT (New Technology)   Refers to Windows NT, including both Windows NT Server and Windows NT Workstation products.

NTAS (Windows NT Advanced Server) version 3.1   The product was later called Windows NT Server.

NT Executive   The bulk of NT's operating system kernel. This portion is fully protected from user-mode applications and from the subsystems.

NTFS (NT File System)   The advanced file system supplied with NT that features numerous security features over competing FAT and HPFS file systems.

NTLDR   The Windows NT operating system loader for the Intel platform.

NT native services   APIs that provide an interface between user-mode and kernel-mode programs.

NT Server   A robust, platform-independent, multiprocessing, fault-tolerant network file and print server sharing a common user database. Often used as an object or resource server in a client/server environment, such as an SQL Server database.

NWLink   See **NetWare Link**.

object   Any item that is or can be linked into another Windows application, such as a sound, graphic, piece of text, or portion of a spreadsheet. Must be from an application that supports OLE.

object linking and embedding   See **OLE**.

octet   Archaic term for byte.

ODI   See **Open Datalink Interface**.

OLE (object linking and embedding)   A data-sharing scheme that allows dissimilar applications to create single complex documents through a cooperative scheme. The documents can consist of material that a single application couldn't have created on its own.

OLE client   A program that can display a foreign object in its document. Microsoft Word is an OLE client when it displays an embedded Excel worksheet in a Word document.

OLE server   A program that allows its files to be edited as an object from within another document.

Open Datalink Interface (ODI)   A NetWare standard that separates protocols from network adaptor drivers; similar to NDIS on Windows NT.

orphan   One partition in a mirrored or stripe set that has crashed or failed beyond the point of return. With any luck, NT detects the problem and continues operating by redirecting reads and writes to another disk. In a mirrored set, continued operation is possible because the second partition can likely pick up where the original left off. With a striped set, the set will fail unless striping with parity is used.

OS   Operating system.

OS/2   IBM's entry into the new generation of operating systems. Released to complement IBM's PS/2 line of computers, it was originally developed by Microsoft and IBM in a joint venture. It's now the exclusive property of IBM, and Microsoft has gone on with its own "Windows" products. Earlier versions (1.*x*) were 16-bit systems; versions 2.*x* and Warp are 32-bit systems. All support multitasking and multithreading.

OS/2 subsystem   A set of APIs provided by Windows NT that offers compatibility with 16-bit OS/2 1.*x* applications.

OSI (Open Systems Interconnect)   The international standardization program that developed the OSI seven-layer reference model. OSI was created to set network standards to promote interoperability between network vendors' products.

OSI reference model   A seven-layer model for network communication developed by the OSI standardization program. It's used for designing networks and studying existing network designs.

package   In OLE, an icon representing an embedded object that, when clicked on, opens, plays a sound, or becomes active in some other way.

packet   A piece of data including header and data sections. The header usually has information such as version, source, destination, and error detection codes. The data section contains the actual information transmitted by the packet.

page   A block of memory used in virtual memory systems. A page may be in RAM or in the virtual memory swap file on disk. The Virtual Memory Manager tracks each page's location, whether it's on disk or in memory.

page fault   If a process accesses a page that's not in RAM, the memory manager halts the process with a page fault and retrieves the requested page from the swap file. Once the page is loaded into RAM, the process can continue.

paging file   A virtual memory file stored on a physical hard disk. It's used to effectively extend the amount of physical RAM in the computer by shuffling data into and out of the RAM.

parity   An additional portion of data added to each byte of stored or transmitted data. Used to make sure the data isn't lost or corrupted. In NT Server, parity striping uses this principle to guard against loss of data in case one of the striped disks crashes. The parity information is created by "exclusive ORing" the data being written to the stripe set before it's striped across the set. If one disk goes out, the Boolean reverse of this process can be used to figure out what was on the crashed disk and to reconstruct the stripe that was lost. Using this technique, any disk in the stripe set can fail. The parity information, along with the other disks' data, is adequate for restoring the lost stripe. However, if two disks go down at once, there is no hope. Parity is also used on every RAM chip in IBM PCs and compatibles to determine whether RAM errors have occurred. Parity is also used with communications programs to determine whether data has been lost or corrupted in transmission.

partition   A portion of a hard disk that behaves as a separate disk, even though it isn't.

passive hub   See **hub**.

patch map   In MIDI setups, similar to a key map but applicable to MIDI "patches," which are sound presets (marimba, piano, and so on). Nonstandard synthesizers might need patch maps to behave appropriately when playing MIDI files, multimedia CD-ROMs, or games in Windows.

path   The location of a file or a computer in the directory tree or on the network.

PC Card   A standard bus and form factor for peripheral cards used in laptop computers. There are adapters that allow you to use PC Cards in desktop systems and laptops. Windows NT does support PC Cards, but not their Plug-and-Play feature. Windows NT must be re-booted to recognize the status change generated by a newly inserted or removed PC Card.

PCI (Peripheral Computer Interface)   A 64-bit wide, high-speed bus architecture.

PCMCIA (People Can't Memorize Computer Industry Acronyms)   Later simplified to PC Card. See **PC Card**.

PDC   See **primary domain controller**.

peer NOS (Network Operating System)   Software that allows each node on the network to act as a client, a server, or both. See also **peer-to-peer network**.

peer-to-peer   A type of networking in which no workstation has more control over the network than another. Each station may share its resources, but no station is the sole resource sharer or file server. Typically less expensive than client/server networks, peer-to-peer networks are also more difficult to administer and less secure because there's no central repository of data.

peer-to-peer network   A network in which any node can be a client and a server. Usually reserved for small informal networks where performance, security, and reliability are not as high a priority as cost.

pel   Picture element; the smallest controllable dot in a screen or printer image. Sometimes called a pixel, but it's not actually the same. A pixel can be composed of several pels.

permission   A property assigned to an object that controls who can have access to it. As opposed to a right, which is given to you or other users by an administrator.

personal user profile   In NT Server, this profile allows the user to change some settings, as opposed to mandatory user profile. Applies to only a single user.

physical layer   The lowest layer of the OSI model. The physical aspects of data links are specified by this layer, including cable type, signal voltage, mechanical connections, and distances.

physical-layer-service-data-unit   See **frame**.

physical topology   See **topology**.

K

GLOSSARY

PIF   See **program information file**.

PIO (programmed I/O)   Unlike DMA I/O or bus mastering I/O, PIO relies on the system's CPU to perform I/O operations. Generally, systems using PIO are less expensive and offer less performance than systems that offload I/O duties to more intelligent I/O controllers.

PM   See **Presentation Manager**.

Point-to-Point Protocol (PPP)   Standard protocols to establish and maintain a remote node connection. Windows NT RAS clients can dial into any PPP host, Windows NT or not. The converse is also true—any client running non-Windows PPP can dial into a Windows NT RAS Server. PPP handles any combination of TCP/IP, IPX/SPX, and NetBEUI on PPP clients. See also **SLIP**.

Point-to-Point Tunneling Protocol (PPTP)   A protocol provided by Windows NT Server 4 that lets you create virtual private networks (VPNs) over the Internet. The Tunneling protocol packages any other protocol's packets in its own and transmits them over the Internet. At the receiving side, the Tunneling protocol's packaging is removed and the native protocol's packet is released on the receiving LAN or host.

port   A connection or socket for connecting devices to a computer. See **I/O address**.

POSIX   A UNIX implementation that ensures source-code compatibility of UNIX applications that comply with the standard. NT complies with character-based POSIX application requirements.

POSIX subsystem   The environment subsystem in Windows NT that supplies an API to 32-bit POSIX-compliant character-based applications.

Postoffice   The central e-mail repository for Microsoft Mail.

PowerPC   The result of a joint venture between Motorola, IBM, and Apple to create a RISC CPU to run Windows NT 3.51 and later versions.

PPC   See **PowerPC**.

PPP   See **Point-to-Point Protocol**.

PPTP   See **Point-to-Point Tunneling Protocol**.

preemptive multitasking   A multitasking scheme that empowers the operating system to override an application that's hogging the CPU, as opposed to cooperative multitasking, in which the applications are responsible for relinquishing the CPU on a regular basis.

presentation layer   The sixth layer of the OSI reference model. This layer prepares data for use in different environments. Encryption, compression, and translation of data between applications are performed by this layer.

Presentation Manager (PM)   The user interface used by IBM's OS/2 operating system. Windows NT can support this interface for OS/2 1.*x* PM applications if the Windows NT add-on subsystem for Presentation Manager is installed.

PRI (Primary Rate Interface)   An ISDN interface that provides voice and data communication via two B channels and one D channel.

primary domain controller (PDC)   A single-member computer of an NT domain that's running Windows NT Server. This computer maintains the SAM database for the domain, authenticates users as they log on, and informs the backup domain controllers of changes to the SAM database. See also **backup domain controller**.

primary member   A member of a mirrored hard disk set. This disk contains the working data for the system. The shadow disk is also updated immediately with changes and can take over instantly should the primary disk fail. See also **disk mirroring**.

primary partition   A portion of the hard disk that can be used by the operating system and can't be subpartitioned as an extended partition can. Each disk can have up to four primary partitions, unless there's an extended partition on the disk, in which case only three primary partitions are allowed. Only primary partitions are bootable.

print queue   A list of print jobs waiting to be serviced. Windows NT maintains this list in a print spooler. Jobs are serviced on a first-come, first-served basis within a given priority level. Newly arriving jobs are inserted in the queue ahead of all jobs with a lower priority. Jobs may be rearranged and deleted by the queue's administrator.

print spooler   See **spooler**.

printer driver   A software driver required to send documents to the printer. Translates the document into the codes necessary for actual printing.

printer fonts   Fonts stored in the printer's ROM.

printer pool   A single print queue that has access to many physical printers. Printer pools are assigned to high-volume print queues to maximize efficiency. Print jobs are dispatched to the first available printer.

privilege   See **right**.

process   A program running in its own address space. An application usually consists of one process with optionally multiple threads. An application can also have multiple processes.

processor   The main CPU of a computer system. Windows NT provides support for systems with multiple processors. See also **symmetric multiprocessing**.

program file   A program that runs an application directly (not through an association) when you click on it. In NT, such files have the extensions .BAT, .COM, .EXE, or .CMD.

program information file (PIF)   A specialized file stored on disk. It contains settings that affect how the DOS environment in a VDM is constructed by NT before running a specified DOS application, such as requesting expanded memory or reserving shortcut keys for the application's use.

protected mode   A memory-addressing mode of Intel processors that allows direct "flat-memory" addressing (linear addressing), rather than the awkward "segmented" scheme required by real mode, which was pioneered on the Intel 8088 and 8086 processors. Protected mode derives its name from the fact that sections of memory owned by a particular process can be physically protected from rogue programs that try to access those addresses. Windows NT uses protected mode at all times after bootup.

protected subsystem   A major portion of the NT operating system that allows applications access to NT's core functions. For example, MS-DOS applications run in a protected subsystem that emulates the DOS environment and passes application calls (DOS API calls) to the NT operating system for handling.

protocol   A standard set of communication conventions used by computer devices to reliably pass data to each other.

provider   An add-on client network component that establishes Windows NT as a client of a remote server. The NT redirector is a provider, as is Novell's client requester for NT.

provider interface   A DLL that implements a standard set of the WNet APIs for a specific provider (for example, the NT redirector, or the NetWare requester for NT).

queue   Documents lined up and waiting to be printed, or commands lined up and waiting to be serviced. In printing, each printer on a local machine or shared on the network has a queue. Use Print Manager to view and manage the print queue.

quick format   A quick way to format a floppy disk, quick format doesn't actually wipe the whole disk, nor does it test the media for bad sectors. It just erases the FAT.

RAID   See **redundant array of inexpensive disks**.

RAM (Random Access Memory)   Physical memory chips located in the computer. Typical NT machines have 16 million bytes (16M) of RAM.

RAS   See **Remote Access Service**.

real mode   As opposed to protected mode, a mode in which Intel x86 processors can run. Memory addressing in real mode is nonlinear, requiring a program to stipulate a segment and memory offset address to access a location in memory. Originally appeared on the Intel 8086 CPU and has been the bane of PC programmers ever since. Although subsequent CPU chips supported protected-mode linear addressing, backward-compatibility with the thousands of real-mode applications has slowed the evolution of operating systems. All Intel CPUs boot in real mode and require specific software support to switch into protected mode.

redirector   A networking software module that traps requests for networked resources from the local computer and directs them to the correct supplier of that resource on the network. For example, a call for a printer, file, or named pipe on the network would be trapped by the redirector.

redundant array of inexpensive disks (RAID)   A set of hard disks and controllers configured to increase performance and reliability by spreading data across the disk set. Different levels of RAID offer different levels of performance and reliability. Almost all levels can survive the failure of one hard disk.

registration database   See **Configuration Registry**.

Registry   See **Configuration Registry**.

remote access   Logging onto computer services from offsite locations; usually refers to either remote control of a computer or remote file access. Windows NT Server supplies remote access through its RAS (Remote Access Services) options.

Remote Access Service (RAS)   A communication server that provides communication services to remote nodes, connecting them to the local area network. Each remote computer has full access, as though it were directly attached to the network. This method requires transmitting files to and from the remote node, but not much intelligence at the server side.

remote administration   Connecting to, altering settings on, making backups from, or otherwise managing a computer not at your desk, but from the computer at your desk.

remote control   A remote computer takes over the operation of a local computer connected to the local area network. This method is faster than RAS because no files need to be transmitted; only screen, keyboard, and mouse data are needed. The downside is that it requires the use of an entire computer or its equivalent at the server end.

remote node   Remote access is provided by giving the appearance that a node is part of the network, usually connected over phone lines. The RAS hosts the connection at the network side.

remote procedure call (RPC)   A programming term referring to a means that one program can use to ask another computer on the network to perform a task for it.

Remote Procedure Call service   A service that must be running on both NT machines before an RPC can be initiated and properly responded to.

repeater   A device that regenerates and amplifies an incoming signal and retransmits it. Repeaters substantially increase possible data cable lengths and data reliability. See also **hub**.

replication   See **directory replication**.

requester   The Novell client-side software, equivalent to the Windows NT redirector.

Request for Comments (RFC)   An online publication, maintained by InterNIC, that offers a forum for working documents on Internet ideas and research. All items are encouraged, from casual ideas to detailed specifications, from expressions of operational concern to whimsical fantasy.

resource   A physical aspect of a computer that a process, application, or user might need access to, such as a disk, memory, a screen, or a sound card. In network terminology, *resource* typically refers to shared resources, such as printers, directories, and modems.

resource domain   A domain in a multidomain model that performs no user authentication. Instead, it trusts the master domain to perform security operations. A resource domain contains only resources to be shared among users: files, applications, printers, and so forth.

retensioning   An operation usually performed on tape backup media to make sure the media isn't wrapped too tightly on its reels. Usually, the tape is fast-forwarded to the end and the rewound to the beginning.

RFC   See **Request For Comments**.

right   As opposed to a permission, a right is given to a user by an administrator, and, in general, it affects what the user can do on the network. For example, backing up files is a right. See also **permission**.

Ring   Privilege levels on the Intel i86 series of processors. Ring 0 is the least secure ring, usually reserved for operating system kernel operations. Ring 3 is the most secure level, mostly used by user applications.

ring topology   A logical network topology in which the network looks like a ring with all the nodes attached to it. The physical topology of such a network is usually a star. Token-passing networks, such as IBM's Token Ring network, use this topology. See also **topology**.

RIPL (Remote Initial Program Load)   This process uses a boot PROM on the network adapter to access a set of shared network files to boot the operating system, instead of booting directly from a floppy or hard disk.

RISC (Reduced Instruction Set Computer)   A computer based on a CPU that has few instructions built into its internal microcode. Therefore, more instructions are needed to execute a particular task on a RISC chip than are required by a CISC (Complex Instruction Set Computer) for the same task. RISC theory postulates that simple instructions execute faster than more complex ones, so although more instructions are required per task, the actual computational efficiency is enhanced by using RISC chips. CISC chips, by comparison, perform many preprogrammed complex internal operations in response to a single request; less programming code is required to get results from a CISC processor. The DEC Alpha, MIPS 4000, Hewlett-Packard HP-PA, and Sun SPARC processors are examples of modern RISC chips. Note that the 80486 and higher use a combination of RISC/CISC architecture, even though they're called CISC CPUs.

roaming user profile   A user profile that's available to the user wherever he or she goes in a domain. The user profile is downloaded to the client machine from the server as part of the logon process. See also **local user profile** and **mandatory user profile**.

ROM (Read-Only Memory)   A type of chip capable of permanently storing data without the aid of an electric current source to maintain it, as in RAM. The data in ROM chips is sometimes called *firmware*. ROM is found in many types of computer add-on boards, as well as on motherboards. CPUs often have an internal section of ROM, as well.

router   A device that forwards data packets from one network to another, often between two different network technologies. Routers maintain routing tables on an as-needed basis that store information about their neighbors and distances to them (cost information). Tables are updated as the router becomes aware of new destinations and new neighbors. Routers are responsible for using this information to determine the best route for a packet to take to its destination. See also **gateway**.

roving profile   See **roaming user profile**.

RPC   See **remote procedure call**.

RPC Locator service   The service that keeps track of which networked machines are available to perform tasks for a distributed-server application (one that can spread its tasks across the network for faster processing).

SAM   A protected subsystem that operates and maintains the Security Accounts Manager (SAM) database.

SAM database   The database that contains the user account, password, and other settings for each user.

Schedule service   An NT internal service required to allow a workstation to perform a service at a predetermined time by using the AT command—for example, for scheduled automatic backups during off-hours.

screen buffer   Reserved memory space that stores the screen image when you switch between full-screen command-prompt sessions and the Windows screen display. The amount of memory required varies with the resolution and the number of colors in the display.

screen fonts   Font files used to show type styles on the screen; they're different from the files used by Windows to print the fonts. The two must match for accurate screen portrayal of the final output.

SCSI   See **Small Computer Systems Interface**.

secure attention sequence   A keyboard combination that can't be remotely transmitted to a system. Windows NT uses Ctrl+Alt+Del to initiate the logon process. Because this combination can be entered only from the keyboard, a program couldn't automate the process of trying different logon ID's and passwords until it got in.

security access token   An internal data structure generated by the LSA whenever a user logs on, used to validate access to computer and network resources.

Security Accounts Manager   See **SAM**.

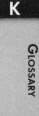

security database   See **SAM database**.

security ID   Each user or group of users is given an SID (security ID) used to identify the user or group when they log on. Even when a user account is deleted and re-created using the same information, such as name and password, the SID won't be identical because each SID is unique and is never reused. Therefore, after an account is deleted, it can't be restored.

security identifier   See **security ID**.

security log   A log file that keeps track of events in NT that have affected security, such as password changes, changes to user account management, and who has logged onto the system. The log can be viewed with the Event Viewer.

security policies   Administrator-set rules that affect how security is maintained on an NT or NT Server network, or even on a given workstation. On an NT system, these rules consist of accounts, user rights, and audit policies; on an NT Server system, they include trust relationships. Use the User Manager or the User Manager for Domains to manage these settings.

security reference monitor (SRM)   A Windows NT kernel-mode program that makes sure each request to access an object has valid security before allowing access. This program can also produce an audit trail of an object's access..

security subsystem   A user-mode component of Windows NT that includes the local security authority (LSA), security account manager (SAM), and the logon process.

segment addressing   A memory-addressing scheme in which an offset address is added to a base segment address to form an address space larger than either of the individual addresses could achieve.

Sequenced Packet Exchange (SPX)   See **IPX/SPX**.

server   A machine on the network that has something to serve—that is, it contains a shared resource, such as a directory or a printer. In NT Server language, *server* refers to any machine that qualifies as a domain controller. See **domain controller**.

server application   In OLE terminology, an application that supplies an object, such as a drawing, to a client application, such as a word processing program, for inclusion in a complex document.

Server Manager   An NT Server application for managing domains, workgroups, and stations; similar to User Manager in NT.

Server Message Block (SMB)   A communication protocol between redirector and server for Windows NT, LAN Manager, LAN Server, Windows for Workgroups, Windows 95, MS-NET, and PC-LAN.

Server service   The internal NT service required to share any local resource for network use.

service   An internal software routine that can supply a particular function to an application; similar to an API. All NT services are RPC-capable, so they can be used by other computers on the network if needed. However, the application on the remote computer must be designed around NT's RPC functionality.

service pack   A generic update for a computer program that includes any bug fixes to date. Microsoft releases service packs for Windows NT on a quarterly basis.

Services for Macintosh (SFM)   A Windows NT feature that allows integration of AppleTalk networks. The services include printer and file sharing, security, and administration features.

session layer   The fifth layer of the OSI model. Connections between processes on different nodes are established, maintained, and terminated by the session layer.

SFM   See **Services for Macintosh**.

shadow member   A member of a mirrored hard disk set that contains the backup data for the system. This shadow disk is updated immediately with changes and can take over instantly should the primary disk fail. See also **disk mirroring**.

shared pages   ClipBook pages shared for network use.

shared resource   See **resource**.

sharename   When you share a resource, it must be given an identifying name, such as Joe's HP printer or Lotus directory. The sharename appears in dialog boxes when network users are browsing the network.

sharepoint   A directory or device that other network users can connect to, typically expressed as a UNC name consisting of the server name and the sharename.

shell   An operating system's user interface

Shell Update Release (SUR)   The name given to the Windows NT 4 release because of its new Windows 95–like shell.

shortcut   An icon that contains a pointer to a program or file anywhere on the available domain. The shortcut can be located almost anywhere: on the desktop, in a directory, on a network, and so forth. Many shortcuts can point to the same resource.

shortcut key   A key or key combination (such as F12 or Ctrl+F12) that performs a prescribed action, such as jumping to or launching an application. DOS session and DOS application property sheets let you reserve shortcut keys for DOS applications rather than for Windows use. A shortcut icon's property sheet lets you specify a shortcut key for executing a Windows program.

SID   See **security ID**.

SIMM   Single Inline Memory Module.

K

GLOSSARY

simple device In multimedia, a self-contained mechanism that can function without Windows sending it a file. A CD player and a video disc player are examples of simple devices.

single-attached nodes Nodes with connections to one FDDI ring. This arrangement means less network fault tolerance in case of FDDI ring failure. See also **double-attached nodes**.

single-ended SCSI The most common SCSI wiring scheme; a single wire is used for each signal. Although not as reliable as differential SCSI, because of the short cable runs inside a computer box, reliability is excellent.

single network logon A user can log onto a domain once and get permission to use all assigned resources on all servers in the domain without having to log onto the individual servers.

SLIP (Serial Line Internet Protocol) A protocol that runs the IP protocol over serial communication lines. See also **Point-to-Point Protocol**.

Small Computer Systems Interface (SCSI) Pronounced "scuzzy"; an interface standard used to connect hard disks, CD-ROM drives, tape drives, printers, scanners, and other devices to computers. A SCSI host adapter is used to control and connect SCSI devices. Although other interfaces are closing the performance gap, SCSI is still considered the interface of choice for performance, reliability, and versatility.

SMB See **Server Message Block**.

SMP See **symmetric multiprocessing**.

SMS See **Systems Management Server**.

SMTP (Simple Mail Transfer Protocol) A TCP/IP protocol used to transmit electronic mail.

SNA Systems Network Architecture.

sniffer See **network analyzer**.

SNMP (Simple Network Management Protocol) A member of the TCP/IP protocol suite used for monitoring and setting network parameters. Required for gathering TCP/IP counters when using the Performance Monitor utility.

source document In OLE, the document that contains the information you want to link into (to appear in) another document (the destination document).

special group A group of users in Windows NT who have some common attribute. Special groups offer a convenient way to manage sets of users who might change over time. The Everyone group always includes all domain users and is automatically updated as user accounts are added and deleted.

special identity See **special group**.

spooler An operating system component that manages and services jobs stored in a print queue. The bulk of the Windows NT 4 print spooler now runs in kernel mode.

SPX (Sequenced Packet Exchange)   See **IPX/SPX**.

SQL   Structured Query Language.

SQL Server   An SQL database server; such a server is included in the BackOffice suite of server applications.

standard permissions   Permission sets that define a common type of user. For example, a guest can look at certain unrestricted areas and perhaps create files in a specific guest area, but little else.

star topology   A physical topology in which each node is wired directly back to a central hub. This physical topology is typically used for a logical ring topology, although it can accommodate a logical bus also, and has better fault tolerance than a physical bus topology. If one segment is lost, only the node associated with that segment is down. See also **topology**.

static object   As opposed to OLE, in which objects have a "hot" link to their original application, static objects are pasted into a destination document by using the Clipboard—the simple pasting that most Windows users are familiar with.

sticky drive lettering   Drive lettering that remains in effect through system restarts.

STP   Shielded twisted pair.

stripe set   A data-storage scheme that uses multiple hard disks. Data can be quickly written across several disks at a time, instead of waiting for a sequential read from, or write to, a single disk. If striping with parity is used, data can be recovered even if a single drive in the set fails, which isn't possible if parity is not used. Windows NT Server supports both forms of striping.

stripe set with parity   See **disk striping**.

stub function   A function that doesn't perform any operation other than handing off the request. Its presence is required so that programs expecting a function with its name will run without error. When a stub function is called, it passes the request to another function somewhere else for processing; then it gets the result and passes it back to the calling program. This approach is used by LPCs and RPCs.

subkey   A key in the Windows NT Registry that's stored within another key. Subkeys can have their own subkeys. Typically, the root of a subtree is called a *key*, and the nodes below it are called *subkeys*.

subnet   A subset of a LAN defined as a logical network for purposes of IP addressing. See also **subnet mask**.

subnet layers   The network, transport, and session (3, 4, and 5) layers of the OSI model. Complete network protocols can be implemented by using only these three layers.

subnet mask   This mask looks like an IP address, but is used to determine what part of the address is the network address and what part is the host address. The portion of the mask with bits set to 1 indicate the network portion of the address.

K

GLOSSARY

subtree   A portion of the NT Registry tree. Subtrees can be nested within other subtrees.

SUR   See **Shell Update Release**.

swap file   See **paging file**.

switching hub   See **hub**.

symmetric multiprocessing (SMP)   A computer architecture in which each CPU has equal access to system resources, including memory and I/O devices. SMP computers with multiple CPUs are supported by Windows NT.

synchronize   To keep two or more copies of a file stored on different computers identical. The Replicator service, for example, keeps directories of files synchronized on several machines by updating files on all import machines when any of the marked files on the export machine are altered.

synchronous I/O   A process requesting an I/O operation is blocked from further execution until the operation is finished. See also **asynchronous I/O**.

system default profile   See **default profile**.

system disk   The disk that contains the operating system, or at least enough of it to start the system so you can then look on another disk for the support files.

system partition   A disk partition containing the hardware driver files NT needs to interact with the computer: screen, mouse, printer, SCSI, and other drivers.

Systems Management Server (SMS)   Part of BackOffice that allows remote inventorying of hardware and software components on a network. It also provides automatic software upgrading.

T-1   A leased digital line that gives you a guaranteed transmission rate of 1.5Mbps through the telephone network. The monthly cost is approximately $1,500 to $2,000.

T-3   A leased digital line that gives you a guaranteed transmission rate of 45Mbps. The monthly cost is approximately $65,000 to $85,000.

tape retensioning   See **retensioning**.

TAPI (Telephony API)   A set of functions provided by an operating system or OS extension that supports applications for computer-integrated use of the telephone. Describes how the phone should be dialed (tone or pulse), dialing prefixes and suffixes, detection of dial tone, and so forth. See also **Telephony API**.

Task List   Pressing Ctrl+Esc brings up the Task List, which lists the running applications so the user can easily switch between them.

TCP/IP (Transport Control Protocol/Internet Protocol)   UNIX systems' most popular transport protocol, used in both local and wide area networking. Although Windows NT's preferred transport protocol is NetBEUI, TCP/IP capability is supplied with the product and can be easily installed, allowing interoperability with UNIX-based systems.

TDI   See **Transport Driver Interface**.

Telephony API (TAPI)   The Novell NetWare equivalent is TSAPI. See also **TAPI**.

Telnet   A TCP/IP program that performs terminal emulation.

terminator   A resistor pack installed at the end of a data transmission cable to prevent the signal from being reflected down the cable and generating errors. Ethernet and SCSI cables require terminators.

thread   See **multithreading**.

Thinnet   See **10Base2**.

timeout   A period of time after which a device or driver might signal the operating system and stop trying to perform. If a printer, for example, is turned off when you try to print, the driver waits for a predetermined period of time, then issues an error message. In computer terminology, the driver has *timed out*.

timeslice   A small amount of CPU time given to each simultaneously running application, one after another. Sometimes *multitasking* is called timeslicing. See also **multitasking**.

token   A special data packet used to pass control of a network from one node to the next. In a Token Ring network, only the node in possession of the token may transmit data. See also **token passing** and **Token Ring**.

token passing   A network access method that avoids data collision by allowing only one node to transmit data at a time. A single token is passed from node to node and determines which node may transmit data. See also **token** and **Token Ring**.

Token Ring   A networking strategy that relies on a single software token to determine which computer has the momentary right to use the network cabling for transmitting data. The token is passed from computer to computer in rapid succession along with the data, much the way a multitasking operating system assigns CPU time to a task or thread. Nontoken schemes typically try to transmit on the network, and if a data collision is detected, they simply delay for a random amount of time and try again. This method can cause additional noise and traffic on the system. On the other hand, Token Ring systems can come to a stop if the token is lost. IBM pioneered Token Ring networking.

TokenTalk   AppleTalk protocols running on Token Ring network technology.

topology   The physical topology refers to the cabling layout between nodes and servers. The most common physical topologies are star and bus. The logical topology refers to the programming path taken by data traveling in the network.

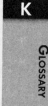

K

GLOSSARY

transceiver   See **multistation access unit (MAU or MSAU)**.

Transmission Control Protocol (TCP)   See **TCP/IP**.

Transport Driver Interface (TDI)   A standard interface between transport protocol drivers and the OSI session layer components (redirector and server) above them. Windows NT transport protocols present the TDI interface, and session layer components make calls into the TDI interface.

transport layer   This fourth layer of the OSI reference model ensures reliable data transmission from the source node to the destination node.

TrueType fonts   Developed by Microsoft in response to Adobe's success in the scalable font business, TrueType fonts greatly simplify using fonts on a Windows computer. They give all Windows applications a wide selection of fonts for screen and printer output. The same fonts can be used on Windows 3.1, Windows NT, and other Windows products, such as Windows 95 and Windows for Workgroups. Consisting of two files (one for screen and one for printer), hundreds of TrueType fonts are now available. Depending on your printer, the TrueType font manager internal to Windows, along with the printer driver, generates either bitmapped or downloadable soft fonts.

trust   A relationship between domains that allows users or groups of users to cross domain boundaries without having to log on and be authenticated each time. The source domain machine sends a message to other domain servers on the network that have a trust relationship with it, indicating who might be coming online. It says, in essence, "These people are allowed into the party. Don't card them at the door."

trusted domain   The domain that hosts the SAM database. This master domain usually handles logon authentication.

trusting domain   A domain that relies on another domain to authenticate users and privilege levels.

twisted pair   A network cable made of individual insulated wires twisted together. They can be either shielded (STP) or unshielded (UTP). This cable is generally more flexible and easier to route than coaxial cable; it's often used in physical star topologies.

UAM   See **User Authentication Module**.

UNC   Uniform Naming Convention.

Unicode   A 16-bit computer encoding format that can represent all world languages currently involved in computing.

Unimodem   A virtual modem supplied by Windows NT that supports the standard Hayes AT command set.

uninterruptible power supply (UPS)   A device containing a large battery that can keep a computer going for at least a few minutes in case of a power outage. A well-equipped UPS can be hooked up to a COM port on a server to signal when a power outage is detected. NT can then begin a power-down, alerting connected users to save their work and log off before the server actually dies. Of course, if the power has already gone out for all other connected users, they're out of luck. They've probably already lost some work unless they, too, have UPSs. In either case, however, data loss on the server is minimized. If the server is set up as an application server, if each user stores his or her data on the server, and if automatic saving is set up (as can be done in Microsoft Word, for example), users' data loss can be minimized by using a UPS.

UNIX   A multithreaded, multitasking operating system developed at Bell Labs and given to many institutions, particularly universities in the U.S. Many versions of UNIX now exist. However, it's large, complex, and, compared to Windows, relatively nonstandard. Applications written for one version of UNIX won't necessarily run on another version.

UPS   See **uninterruptible power supply**.

UPS service   An internal NT service that must be running for NT to respond to a message from a UPS that a power outage has occurred.

User   The user interface component of Windows that manages windows and other user interface components. Moved from user mode to kernel mode in Windows NT 4 to improve performance.

user account   A listing of rights, privileges, passwords, group memberships, NT interface settings, and so forth that compose a user's existence on an NT machine or NT Server system. Managed with User Manager or User Manager for Domains (in NT Server).

user account database   The database that stores the information about all user accounts on the workstation. See also **SAM database**.

User Authentication Module (UAM)   A component of Windows NT that provides password encryption across the network and the use of passwords up to 14 characters long.

user default profile   See **default profile**.

User Manager   An application in the Administrators group (seen only if you log on as an administrator) for managing user accounts.

User Manager for Domains   An application in the Administrators group (seen only if you log on as an administrator) for managing user accounts on a domain in NT Server.

user mode   This mode runs at the Ring 3 security level on Intel CPU's. Ring 3 is the most restricted security level, so programs running in user mode must rely on operating system services to give them access to shared or critical resources. User-mode programs are allowed to access only their own virtual space.

K

GLOSSARY

user profile   The personal settings a user has made to his or her NT environment, such as screen colors, desktop settings, network connections, printer connections, mouse settings, and more. Each user on an NT machine has a user profile that goes into effect when he or she logs on. See **default profile**.

User Profile Editor   In NT Server, a program used to edit a user's profile.

UTP   Unshielded twisted pair.

value entry   The string of characters on the right side of the Registry editor screen, showing the setting for the key selected in the left pane.

vampire tap   A connector that pushes metal prongs through a network cable's insulation to tap into the signals running through the conductor inside.

VDM (virtual DOS machine)   When you run a DOS or Windows 3.1 application in NT, a VDM is created that fools the application into thinking it's the only application running on a DOS-based IBM PC.

VESA Local Bus (VLB)   One of the first high-speed bus systems for i86 computers designed to provide a high-performance connection to video cards. It was general enough that its use grew into a general purpose bus, supporting disk controllers and other I/O devices.

VFAT   An extension to the DOS FAT files system that provides better performance and long filenames. VFAT was introduced in Windows 95 and is supported by Windows NT.

VGA (Video Graphics Array)   An IBM standard PC video adapter, first introduced in 1987, having a display resolution of 640 × 480.

VINES (VIrtual NEtwork System)   Banyan's entry into the network operating system market.

virtual DOS machine   See **VDM**.

virtual memory   A scheme that allows hard-disk space to emulate physical RAM, allowing large applications to run in less physical RAM than they would normally require. When RAM runs low, the operating system uses a Virtual Memory Manager program to temporarily store data on the hard disk (in a paging or swap file) as though it were in RAM, freeing up RAM for data manipulation. When needed, the data is read back from the disk and loaded into RAM again.

Virtual Memory Manager (VMM)   A kernel component of Windows NT that manages paging, memory allocation, the virtual swap file, and other virtual memory functions.

virtual printer memory   In PostScript printers, the portion of memory reserved for downloaded fonts; it exists on a hard drive internal to the printer. The other portion of memory, called *banded memory*, is reserved for formatting the printed page and processing graphics.

VLB   See **VESA Local Bus**.

VM   See **virtual memory**.

VMM   See **Virtual Memory Manager**.

volatile key   A key in the NT Registry that's reconstructed every time the machine is started.

volume   Disk partition(s) formatted and available for use by the operating system.

volume set   A logical drive can span physical hard disks to create a larger single logical drive. These sets can be FAT or NTFS partitions. Existing NTFS volumes and volume sets can be extended in this manner, but FAT volumes can't be extended.

volume spanning   See **volume set**.

WAN   See **wide area network**.

WFW   See **Windows for Workgroups**.

wide area network (WAN)   A network larger than a LAN that can span a building, campus of buildings, city, or even a country.

wildcard   A symbol that represents any character; used in searching for or listing items, such as files. In Windows and many other operating systems and applications, * represents any number of characters, and ? represents any one character.

Win16 application   A program designed to run on 16-bit versions of Windows, including Windows 3.*x* and Windows for Workgroups. Almost all of these programs run under Windows NT.

Win32 application   A program designed to run on 32-bit versions of Windows, including Windows NT, Windows 95, Win32s on Windows 3.1, or some combination of these.

Win32s application   A 32-bit Windows program that uses a subset of the Win32 API, which allows it to run on Windows 3.1, using Win32s in addition to Windows NT, and Windows 95.

Win32 subsystem   The part of Windows NT that provides the Win32 APIs, allowing 32-bit applications to run.

Windows 95   An operating system released by Microsoft in 1995. It offers a substantially different user interface from Windows 3.*x*, adds Plug-and-Play support, and includes several architectural features from Windows NT. Windows 95 uses a combination of 32-bit and 16-bit code. One of the main upgrades in Windows NT 4 is the use of the new interface from Windows 95.

Windows for Workgroups   Windows 3.*x* with built-in peer-to-peer networking, improved performance, and some groupware features.

Windows Internet Name Service (WINS)   An optional TCP/IP services component that automates the assignment of NetBIOS names to IP addresses.

K

GLOSSARY

Windows Messaging   Microsoft's communication and groupware technology.

Windows NT   Short for *Windows New Technology*, this moniker refers to both NT Server and NT Workstation products. Before version 3.5, Windows NT Server and Windows NT Workstation were referred to as Windows NT Advanced Server and Windows NT, respectively.

Windows NT Advanced Server   See **Windows NT**.

Windows NT Server   See **Windows NT**.

Windows NT Workstation   See **Windows NT**.

Windows on Win32   See **WOW**.

Windows Sockets   More commonly called WinSock, Windows Sockets provides an API for Windows-based programs to access TCP/IP networks.

WINS   See **Windows Internet Name Service**.

WinSock   See **Windows Sockets**.

wiring closet   A secured room providing a place to mount hubs, routers, servers, PBXs, and so on, and route wiring to them.

workgroup   A collection of networked PCs (optionally including Macintoshes) grouped to facilitate work that users of those computers tend to do together; however, the machines aren't necessarily in the same room or office. Windows for Workgroups and Windows NT machines can both be part of a workgroup setup. Windows NT recognizes existing Windows for Workgroup groups. Domains are different from workgroups and are more sophisticated. See also **domain**.

workstation   A single computer on an NT network; it runs NT, not NT Server. Machines running NT Server are called *servers* in Windows NT nomenclature.

workstation operating system (WOS)   A term for a network operating system running on a workstation computer.

Workstation service   An internal NT service that must be running for network connections and sharing to work.

WOS   See **workstation operating system**.

WOSA   Windows Open Services Architecture.

WOW (Windows on Win32)   The protected subsystem that allows any number of Windows 3.1 applications to run in NT. All Windows 3.1 applications run in a single VDM, unlike DOS applications, each of which gets its own VDM. Therefore, if one Windows 3.1 application crashes, it's possible they all will. However, NT has the same robustness feature that Windows 3.1 incorporates, so if one application crashes, it won't necessarily crash the whole WOW. Often, you can kill just the offending program.

WOW VDM   A single VDM that runs all 16-bit Windows 3.*x* programs by emulating the 16-bit Windows 3.*x* operating system environment. See also **VDM**.

WWW   World Wide Web.

WYSIWYG   What you see is what you get.

X.25   A communication standard for data transfers over a public network. See also **Frame Relay**.

Xenix   A version of UNIX developed by Microsoft. It was later marketed by the Santa Cruz Operation (SCO).

XModem/CRC   An error-correction protocol used by the DOS application XMODEM and many other communications programs. CRC stands for *cyclical redundancy check,* a means of detecting errors in transmission between modems or across wired serial links.

XMS (Extended Memory Specification)   An industry standard for allowing Intel 80286 and higher processors to access memory above 1M, as opposed to EMS (expanded memory specification). Not to be confused with actual extended memory, which is simply any physical memory mapped above 1M. Windows 3.1 and NT both require extended memory but don't require XMS memory.

YModem   Another form of XModem that allows batch transfers of files.

ZModem   Yet another version of XModem.

zone   A logical group of network devices in an AppleTalk network.

I

INDEX

X-Z

MACMILLAN COMPUTER PUBLISHING USA

A VIACOM COMPANY

Technical

---- Support:

If you need assistance with the information in this book or with a CD/Disk accompanying the book, please access the Knowledge Base on our Web site at **http://www.superlibrary.com/general/support**. Our most Frequently Asked Questions are answered there. If you do not find the answer to your questions on our Web site, you may contact Macmillan Technical Support **(317) 581-3833** or e-mail us at **support@mcp.com**.

Installing the CD-ROM

The companion CD-ROM contains software developed by the authors, plus an assortment of third-party tools and product demos. Using Windows Explorer, you can view information on products and companies and install programs with a single click of the mouse. To install the **Cowart** program group, follow these steps:

Windows 95/NT Installation Instructions

1. Insert the CD-ROM disc into your CD-ROM drive.
2. With Windows 95/NT installed on your computer and the AutoPlay feature enabled, a Program Group for this book is automatically created whenever you insert the disc into your CD-ROM drive.

   If Autoplay is not enabled, using Windows Explorer, choose Setup.Exe from the root of the CD-Rom to create the Program Group for this book.
4. Double-click on the "Browse the CD-ROM" icon in the newly created Program Group to access the installation programs of the software included on this CD-ROM.

   To review the latest information about this CD-ROM, double-click on the icon "About this CD-ROM."

·NOTE

For best results, set your monitor to display between 256 and 64,000 colors. A screen resolution of 640 × 480 pixels is also recommended. If necessary, adjust your monitor settings before using the CD-ROM.